THE PROPHETIC EVENTS OF YOUR LIFE

BEYOND YOUR HORIZON

THE PROPHETIC EVENTS OF YOUR LIFE

BEYOND YOUR HORIZON

"When the Spirit of truth comes, he will guide you into all truth. . .
He will tell you about the future."
John 16:13

KATHRYN GARLAND

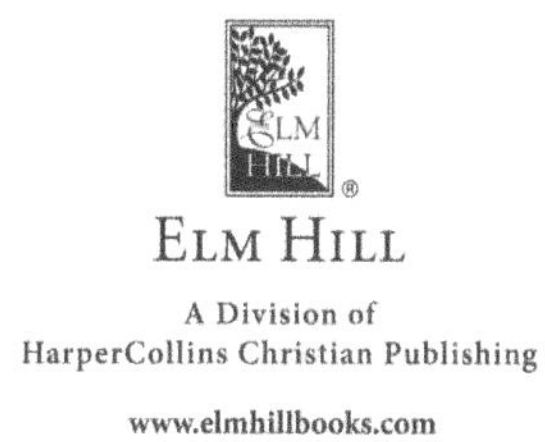

ELM HILL

A Division of
HarperCollins Christian Publishing

www.elmhillbooks.com

The Prophetic Events of Your Life
Beyond Your Horizon

Published in Nashville, Tennessee, by Elm Hill, an imprint of Thomas Nelson. Elm Hill and Thomas Nelson are registered trademarks of HarperCollins Christian Publishing, Inc.

Interior Design: Scott Garland

Elm Hill titles may be purchased in bulk for educational, business, fund-raising, or sales promotional use. For information, please e-mail SpecialMarkets@ThomasNelson.com.

Library of Congress Cataloging-in-Publication Data

Library of Congress Control Number: 2018939115

ISBN 978-1-595558015 (Paperback)
ISBN 978-1-595557506 (Hardbound)
ISBN 978-1-595557438 (eBook)

CONTENTS

PART TWO

ABOUT THE AUTHOR

Kathryn Garland received her B.S. in Missions from St. Paul Bible College (now Crown College, St. Bonifacius, Minn.).

Kathryn's. . .
Childhood was in Shenandoah, Iowa.
Teens in Omaha, Nebraska.
College years in St. Paul, Minnesota.
Adult life with Beefhide Gospel Mission, Kentucky, Colombia and Venezuela, South America with the Christian and Missionary Alliance.
Old-age in Missouri and Minnesota.

Kathryn's life purpose statement. . .
I bind myself to God's authority, acknowledging His supremacy, and devoting myself to His glory and service alone.

"The Lord is my strength and my song, and He has become my salvation."
Exodus 15:2

Retired from missionary service in 2001

Kathryn received the Lord Jesus as her personal Savior at the age of eighteen. The night after this life changing event, God called her to serve Him as a missionary to South America. She and her husband Herb, are grateful to their Lord for the opportunity to serve Him from 1958 – 2001 as Christ's ambassadors in home missions and overseas.

From the moment Kathryn found God's pathway for her life, a love for Jesus and a knowledge of God's Word has been her daily aspiration. She has been privileged to teach in pastoral and leadership preparation as well as lay training in both Colombia and Venezuela. Bible prophecy seems to be the area of Christian education in which the Lord has consistently enabled her. Kathryn has taught many courses of study that have greatly enhanced her gifting to teach Prophetic Events, such as, Prophecy, Hermeneutics, Bible, Church History, and Teaching Methods.

Herb and Kathryn had a joyful and adventurous family life with five "missionary" boys on the mission field. Their boy's contribution to God's work was invaluable. Their sons today are godly men, who love King Jesus and walk in His chosen pathway to do the works that God has prepared for them to do. Herb and Kathryn have five delightful daughters-in-law, seventeen grandchildren and sixteen great-grandchildren.

INTRODUCTION

JESUS CHRIST WORD OF GOD
John 1:1

"This is my dearly loved Son, who brings me great joy. Listen to him." (Matthew 17:5)

LET THE WORD SPEAK!

When I was a teenager I had the opportunity to ride horseback through the beautiful, but never-ending, grass covered sand hills of northern Nebraska. As we were riding, I kept begging our leader to "go to the top of just one more hill to see what lay beyond." Patiently he would lead the way up another hill then turn in his saddle and with a smile look at me. Result. . . another hill. I didn't want to give up because I just knew there must be something more than just another sand hill beyond our obstructed view.

I invite you, my friend, to join me on a ride that will take us beyond the next sand hill. I can guarantee that each "new sand hill" (which I will call an Event) will be a significant adventure. Our journey into biblical prophecy will go well beyond the rim of your present horizon.

THE PROPHETIC EVENTS OF YOUR LIFE

First of all, what relevance does "Beyond Your Horizon" have for you? This study book concerns The Prophetic Events of Your Life. To understand its importance, let's look at what this implies.

Events

The term "Event" found in this book refers to a progression of occurrences or happenings. Each Event has its own particular circumstances that bear significance within the larger picture. Knowing about God's future plans for this world will cause you to live differently from those who live with little or no thought of God.

Prophetic

The term "Prophetic" indicates that the described Events are specific, pre-determined occurrences which will take place in the future. The Prophetic Events discussed in this book are unconditional Events, meaning, nothing can be done to stop them from taking place. The term "Prophetic" also indicates that the Bible is the only authoritative source of knowledge in regard to these Events. Only God can reveal the future.

Your Life

This phrase "Your Life" indicates that you will be directly involved in these God-planned Events. Your relationship with God will be a significant factor in the meaning each Event will have for you.

"It is dangerous not to know what the world has determined to be in its rebellion against God. And it is equally dangerous not to know what the Church is destined to be in the plan of God."[1]

ARRANGEMENT OF THIS STUDY BOOK

PART ONE

Lessons
Each lesson follows in chronological order the Prophetic Events of your life starting with your birth and progressing all the way to the last Event of the book of Revelation. This study book is written in chronological order and must be studied in that order. You will accumulate knowledge that will help you interpret the next Event. Part One must be studied before Part Two. This will give you the necessary back drop for the study of Part Two. Because of the length of the lessons and for your convenience, I have divided some into lesson A and lesson B.

Timelines
The lessons will constantly refer you to the Timelines at the end of Part One which will help you visualize when the Prophetic Events take place and their relationship to one another.

Your Personal Opportunities
One of the greatest joys a Believer can experience is discovering meaning in Scripture. Quite often in this study you will be asked questions in order to increase your participation in this grand adventure of interpretation. The answers to the questions normally will be found in the commentary. This will help us to keep in step along our journey. If you have a difference of opinion, make sure that you have a viable Scriptural backing for your view. I would love to dialogue with you about our discoveries.

Also you will have the opportunity to make your own observations and ask questions of the Scripture text. Let the Holy Spirit bring you truth down the paths of your questions. This activity, along with the author's commentary, will be a learning opportunity for you to become a Bible interpreter— a pursuer of Scriptural meaning. One of the goals of this study book is to help you learn to interpret and discover prophetic truths.

This is a heart to heart Bible study where you and I will make our contributions through our thoughts. Mine are in the text. Alongside the text a margin is provided for you to journal your reflections in order for you to personalize or interact with my commentary.

PART TWO

In five lessons you will study <u>The Mystery of the System of the Antichrist</u>. These Bible studies will guard you against deception and will enable you to look in the right direction so that you can identify the Antichrist at his appearing. The last lesson focuses on the exaltation and crowning of the Believer.

APPENDIX

<u>A Chronological Order of the Book of Revelation</u> will serve as a key to open the door of your understanding on how to read and study the book of Revelation.

Definitions of the Prophetic Events of Your Life. These definitions, along with the three Timelines and the knowledge gained from the study of this book, will serve as tools to enable you to explain the Prophetic Events to others.

METHOD OF INTERPRETATION

The method used to interpret the Bible in this study book is the Literal-Grammatical, Historical Method.

Literal-Grammatical

All interpreters pay very close attention to the words of the text in order to arrive at its meaning. This means that the interpreter deals with words in their common ordinary, normally acknowledged meaning in its particular context. The golden rule of this method is "when the plain sense of Scripture makes common sense, seek no other sense."

"Repress the appetite to be wise above what is written. But make great efforts to be wise to the full extent of God's revelation in the Scriptures." [2]

Figurative language is commonly used in prophetic writings and is normally easily identified. Every figure of speech or symbol, such as, beasts, crowns, seven heads, ten horns, and white robes, illustrates a literal meaning. All Prophetic Events will be literally fulfilled.

Historical

History means a chronological record of events. Every Prophetic Event needs a historical setting, which means that it must be placed into God's timeline. The attempt to explain an Event without placing it in a timeline can weaken the interpretation or even lead to misinterpretation. Their historical order will enhance the understanding of the particulars of the Event because it will provide essential context to its meaning. End-time Events cannot be defined by looking at them as disconnected or isolated Events. They are caused by developing situations, therefore, each Event unfolds from former Events which in turn evolves into the next Events. For a sound interpretation their connection cannot be ignored. They become a series, a chain of Events progressing to the final Event.

A word of explanation is appropriate in regard to the term "The Seven-Year Tribulation" used in practically all of today's end-time prophetic teaching. It has been thought that the Tribulation period taught by Jesus in Matthew 24 is a seven-year period. There is no biblical evidence that this Tribulation period has a stipulated limitation to seven years. Once released from this seven-year limitation, the interpreter will be released from the need to attempt to accommodate certain end-time Events to a seven-year period. This book is written in terms of a Tribulation period that covers many, many years. You will see the chronology of certain prophetic Events unfold, and flow, in a natural manner not bound to having to conform to a seven-year period of time.

No Contradictions

God's Word is without error and it is understandable. The Bible never contradicts itself; therefore, there is total harmony among all the Scriptures. Scripture has only one meaning. This fact has become my North Star to guide me in the interpretation of God's Word. If I find a biblical contradiction to my conclusions, I realize that I am on the wrong track. This method is one of the most important to determine accuracy and verification of one's interpretation.

Hermeneutics
The art of applying interpretative principles called hermeneutics is essential to accomplish Bible interpretation. These principles compel the interpreter to choose to either be very honest or to pursue one's particular view disregarding biblical contradictions. I choose to be very honest.

WORK ETHICS

First of all, I recognized that I could not discover spiritual truths by my own endeavors. I looked to my Teacher, the Holy Spirit. *"When the Spirit of truth comes, he will guide you into all truth."* (John 16:13)

I adapted a method from one of my mentors. . .to place the Bible before me to ascertain, in the first place, what meaning it would present to a mind, humbly and honestly directing itself to the pursuit of truth. This truth, is compared and examined in the light of every source available to me. I would then "bend the knee" of my mind and heart in submission to the Scriptures.

I did a new study each time I taught Prophetic Events which gave me accumulated knowledge. I became a checker-outer by seeking two or three other sources to verify teachings from Bible scholars.
I resolved to be consistently scriptural.

The Word of God is the final authority. Truth is precious and must be held to. Nothing can be gained by false premises. The Spirit of truth, our Divine Teacher, will guide us into all truth. (John 16:13)

EXPLANATIONS

Capitalizations
Believer and Unbeliever are capitalized in order to emphasize the identification of these two individuals in their relationship to Jesus Christ. Who they are by definition will be clearly explained in Lesson 1.

All Events are capitalized in order to set them apart as major prophetic events. Specific times, such as "Present Age," and specific people, such as, "Ten Kings" will also be capitalized in order to stress them as part of major prophetic events.

Hebrew and Greek
The Old Testament was written for the most part in Hebrew and the New Testament in the Greek language. You will constantly be lead to these original languages in order to study words in their specific meaning.

Underlining or bold print of words or phrases and the inclusion of explanatory brackets in both Bible verses and quotations for emphasis or clarity have been added by the author.

Code for Hebrew, Greek, and English words
Word definitions from lexicons and dictionaries are used so often that it will facilitate the End Notes by using the following code:

(D) *The American Heritage Dictionary of the English Language*
(KW) *Hebrew-Greek Key Word Study Bible* (Spiros Zodhiates)
(M) *Mounce's Complete Expository Dictionary of Old & New Testament Words*
(S) *Strong's Exhaustive Concordance of the Bible with brief Dictionaries of the Hebrew and Greek Words of the Original with References to the English Words*
(V) *An Expository Dictionary of New Testament Words* (W.E. Vine)

You will find this same code at the beginning of the End Notes at the end of this study book.

PURPOSE

Every generation has to refocus on the hope that is within us and to convey this truth to the next generation. Future Events are just one aspect of the body of truths presented in the Bible, but their importance cannot be over stated. Our lives will reflect our long-range perspective when we understand God's activities beyond our horizon.

To pass on the results of years of study of end-time prophecy is the burden that God has laid on my heart when He called me to write this book. The burden expressed... Titus 1:1-2 (RSV) *"to further the faith. . .and their knowledge of the truth with which I have been entrusted."*

This book is personal. It is written to you.

My expectations for you. . .
- You will have moments of grace when the Holy Spirit illuminates your mind to grasp a precious truth.
- You will have new truths from God's Word to store in your personal belief system.
- You will find many "seed thoughts" on which to ponder and to expand.
- You will so fall in love with Jesus that you will be willing to bear all things for His sake, with joy.
- You will recognize and be prepared for each Prophetic Event.
- Your life here will count ever so much for eternity.
- You will have such an open mind that you will let the Word speak to your intellect and to your heart.
- You will have opportunities to share what you have learned.

For decades God's people have studied prophecy concerning the end times. We have day after day, year after year, moved inevitably toward those times and now have finally moved into them. That which was future has become our reality. We must understand these times in which we live. We must believe God's Word about them. We must commit our souls into His loving care. That is the safe place. (Psalm 91)

God bless you my fellow Believer, and all those who will be joining us in the "Way."

JESUS CHRIST WORD OF GOD

John 1:1

THE PROPHETIC EVENTS OF YOUR LIFE
BEYOND YOUR HORIZON

PART ONE

LESSON 1

JESUS CHRIST AUTHOR OF LIFE
John 1:3-4

Why do I exist? Why does anything exist? Why isn't there just. . .nothing? Because Jesus created all things, life is in Him. You are. . . for His glory.

YOUR LIFE BEGINS

> It is difficult for me to see why anything I am or do is meaningful unless I begin to understand my connectedness to others, to the past, and to the future. That connectedness is primarily the connectedness of story—of lives interwoven over time in a purposeful plot. Understanding my life in this way gives me better reasons than I otherwise have to live life with optimism and courage.
>
> DANIEL TAYLOR [1]

Sometimes ideas and thoughts are referred to as *seeds* because they grow and develop in your mind as you think about and ponder them. Write one seed-thought from this quotation that you can plant in the fertile soil of your mind.

____

____

____

Two thoughts came to my mind after reading Daniel Taylor's concept. First, when I "*begin to understand my connectedness to others, to the past*," I think of all the Christians who have preserved, preached, and portrayed the Gospel throughout history at tremendous cost. Someone once said, "We are the bus in which our ancestors ride." Who we are today is a direct result of characteristics and traits that we have inherited from our ancestors. This also applies to us who belong to Christ's Kingdom. When we step into God's story, we immediately inherit spiritual ancestors. We become the bus these spiritual ancestors ride in as well. What a legacy! What a heritage! I am connected to others. . .to the past.

Secondly, when I consider the phrase—"*and to the future.*" I see I am also connected to individuals who have not yet been born. Consequently, I am a vital link between those who lived in the past and those who will live in the future. This brings new questions, such as, what spiritual legacy will I leave? How will I impact Christ's church? What am I doing for the Lord right now, in my moment in history?

Richard Paul Evans made the following statement. Not only does it apply to each and every one of us, but it is also very motivating.

"Believe you have been sent from God as an arrow pulled from His own bow." [3]

John Baillie,
A Diary of
Private Prayer

O Thou who wast, and art, and art to come, I thank Thee that this Christian way whereon I walk is no untried or uncharted road, but a road beaten hard by the footsteps of saints, apostles, prophets, and martyrs. I thank Thee for the finger-posts and danger-signals with which it is marked at every turning and which may be known to me through the study of the Bible, and of all history. [2]

Isaiah 49:2
"I am like a sharp arrow in His quiver."

Max Lucado
"You weren't an accident. You weren't mass produced. You aren't an assembly-line product. You were deliberately planned, specifically gifted, and lovingly positioned on the earth by the Master Craftsman."

Ephesians 2:10
"For we are God's masterpiece. He has created us anew in Christ Jesus, so we can do the good things he planned for us long ago."

Think about how you are depicted in that statement. This is a poetic way of saying that you have been purposefully shot like an arrow from God into this particular moment in time.

Your personal story has already begun, and you are currently living your moment in history. If you have at a specific moment in your life been introduced to the gospel story of Jesus, and have chosen by faith to believe Jesus' story and to follow Him, you have stepped into the pages of God's story. You now have your very own chapter in His book, and you play an essential role in His purposeful plot. Your chapter will be filled with significance, direction, and purpose. It will be all about the role you play in building Christ's Eternal Kingdom.

Not only are you allowing God to direct your life's story, your name has been entered into a special book called the Lamb's (Jesus') book of life. This book is undoubtedly the most important book of all time because it is the register of all who have been saved by faith in Jesus' redeeming work on the cross. Only those whose names are written in the Lamb's book of life will live forever in God's Kingdom. (Revelation 21:27; 3:5; 20:15)

But perhaps you don't have a specific moment in your life where you've made this decision. Your story is independent from God's story. Tragically, you will not write the end of your story. Rather, God will be the one to write the final words in the last chapter of your life story.

Revelation 20:11-15 (NIV)

> *"Then I saw a great white throne and Him who was seated upon it. . .I saw the dead great* [you may be great] *and small* [you may be small], *standing before the throne, and books were opened* [your book included.] *Another book was opened which is the book of life. The dead were judged according to what they* [you] *had done as recorded in the books* [your own book]. *. .If anyone's name was not found written in the book of life, he was thrown into the lake of fire."*

Think about the significance of these verses. If your name is not registered in this book, it is urgent that you do something about it.

So, what exactly is your purpose? What part do you play in God's great plot? Perhaps, after completing this study, you will see that you have been placed into, what I consider, the most unique of all moments in history—the end times—the last chapter of this Present Age.

THE PROPHETIC EVENTS OF YOUR LIFE

The Prophetic Events discussed in this book are "unconditional" Events. In other words, nothing can be done to stop or prevent these Prophetic Events from taking place.

Unlike the unconditional Events described in this book, many of the prophecies found in the Old Testament were conditional. In other words, the people directly involved with or affected by these conditional prophecies could do specific things that dictated whether or not God would carry out certain judgments. For example, Exodus 7–12 records the story of God telling Pharaoh that the Egyptian people would endure ten plagues if Pharaoh did not release the

Hebrew people from slavery. The condition was: don't let them go—plagues; let them go—no plagues. It was Pharaoh's choice. However, this is not the case with the Prophetic Events of end-time prophecy.

The Prophetic Events of Your Life**. . .**this phrase *Your Life* indicates that you will be directly involved in these God-planned Events. This book is about God, you, and your place in end-time history.

Now that you have a better understanding of the title "The Prophetic Events of Your Life," we can begin this study and discover each of the pre-planned Events that you will encounter in your lifetime.

In this lesson we will study:

Event 1: Birth
Event 2: New Birth Experienced
New Birth Not Experienced

EVENT 1: BIRTH

YOUR BIRTH

This is your beginning**.** Although your birth is not specifically mentioned in the Bible. Psalm 139:13-18 expresses the truth that God knew you and formed you even before your birth. This is the first Event that God planned for your life**.**

Look at **Timeline One** (located at the end of Part One of this book). Above the timeline, **write:** Event 1, the year you were born, and **draw** an arrow pointing to the appropriate place on the timeline. You will find an example of how to do this at the end of this lesson.

Sinful Nature
All people are born with a disposition centered in one's self and lacking perfect goodness. Self is the boss and governs the mind, will, and emotions.

The Bible reveals many significant truths that specifically pertain to you. Consider the following two truths:

- **You were born under the power of sin**

This means that you were born a sinner and have a sinful nature. When you were born, you were born under the power of sin and spiritual darkness. The Bible says you are a member of the fallen human race.

Sinner
One who cannot stand before God in the condition of his sinful nature. (Luke 18:13)

Romans 5:12

"When Adam sinned, sin entered the world. Adam's sin brought death, so death spread to everyone, for everyone sinned."

Psalm 51:5

"I was born a sinner—yes, from the moment my mother conceived me."

- **You were born during the World System of the Antichrist**

The Present Age in which we are currently living is a period of history known as the World System of the Antichrist. This System can be described as being evil, and it will be further addressed within this book.

EVENT 2: NEW BIRTH

A Believer: One who believes and lives the Gospel of Christ. A disciple or follower of Jesus Christ.

The New Birth is the second God-planned Event for all people. The scope of God's love is all-inclusive, *"not wanting anyone to perish, but everyone to come to repentance."* (2 Peter 3:9 NIV)

NEW BIRTH EXPERIENCED

By His sovereignty and authoritative power, God created you to carry out a unique purpose in history. (Ephesians 1:4) Having been born a sinner, you needed to receive Jesus Christ as your Savior. You did this by repenting of your sins, and believing that Jesus died to take the penalty for your sin. By doing this, you have been born-again through faith. You have experienced personally the second Event—the New Birth. This Event has placed you in a relationship with God so that you may fulfil His purpose for your life.

In the following verse **underline** the part that the Bible states regarding how you were saved and how you were not saved. **Circle** the word "not."

Ephesians 2:8-9 (NASB)

> *"For by grace you have been saved through faith; and that not of yourselves, it is the gift of God; not as a result of works, that no one should boast."*

On **Timeline One** (located at the end of Part One of this book) write Event 2, and the year you were born again. Then, draw a cross at the appropriate place. You will find an example of how to do this at the end of this lesson.

I once was a sinner, now I am a child of God!

This visually marks the date when you were born-again into the Eternal Kingdom of God. Even though you still live in the world, where the kingdom of spiritual darkness reigns, you belong to God and have everlasting life. As a result, you will never come under judgment for sin. You have passed from death into life. God's divine purpose for your life as His child is to love Him with all your heart, and as His servant to willingly obey Him in joyful submission.

YOUR DEATH

As a Believer, you may not physically die before the return of Jesus at the Rapture, but if you do, both your soul and spirit will ascend to heaven to join Jesus and all Believers who have died before you. Your earthly body will return to dust. It is stated in 2 Corinthians 5:8 that to be absent from your body is to be present with the Lord. See Heaven on Timeline One (located at the end of Part One of this book).

After you die, your body will lie in the grave until the First Resurrection of God's children. Then, your new, glorified body will be reunited with your soul and spirit to enjoy eternal life in the presence of God.

Time wise, the First Resurrection will take place when Jesus comes at the Rapture. Most of us will likely be alive at that time. The Rapture will be discussed in much more detail further along in our study.

John 5:28-29 (NKJV)

> "*Do not marvel at this; for the hour is coming in which all who are in the graves will hear His voice and come forth—those who have done good, to the resurrection of life* [First Resurrection], *and those who have done evil, to the resurrection of condemnation* [Second Resurrection]."

Participants in the Resurrection of Life—the First Resurrection

- **Jesus Christ** was the first to rise from the dead. This resurrection occurred on the third day after His crucifixion. It should be mentioned here that Jesus' resurrection made it possible for Believers to also be resurrected from the dead. (1 Corinthians 15:20, 20-23; Acts 26:23)

- **All Believers**, Old and New Testament ages and the Present Age, who have died before the time of the Rapture. This resurrection occurs during the Rapture process. You will be included in this group on the condition that you are a Believer. (1 Thessalonians 4:13-18; 1 Corinthians 15:23)

- **The Two Christian-Jewish Witnesses** mentioned in Revelation 11. This resurrection occurs after the Rapture.

- **The Christian-Jewish Martyrs** who die for their faith after the Rapture and during the 3 ½ year period of the Wrath of God. This resurrection will take place at the Second Coming of Christ. (Revelation 20:4-5)

I Corinthians 15:22-23
"Just as everyone dies because we all belong to Adam, everyone who belongs to Christ will be given new life. But there is an order to this resurrection: Christ was raised as the first of the harvest; then all who belong to Christ will be raised when he comes back."

Even though all of these individuals are not resurrected simultaneously; they all belong to the First Resurrection. Let me explain. The Greek word *proton*, meaning "foremost" (ahead of all others) in time and place, or first as opposed to last, was a Greek term used to describe the First Resurrection. In other words, the First Resurrection is first in the sense of *before*. It does not mean only. Consequently, all Believers will be resurrected before the Second Resurrection occurs. The Second Resurrection is the resurrection of the wicked and will take place at the time of the Great White Throne judgment. This will be discussed later on in our studies.

A simple illustration will help you better understand the meaning of the word first in reference to the First Resurrection. Imagine a large group of people flying out of an airport. As they arrive at the terminal, they are divided into two groups: group one and group two. Now imagine that group one is to leave first. However, the people in group one are scheduled to leave at different times on different planes. Not everyone in group one will leave at exactly the same time. It could take hours for everyone in group one to finally depart. Moreover, no one from group two is permitted to leave until everyone in group one has departed.

YOUR GOD-ORDAINED LIFE

Psalm 139:16

> *"You saw me before I was born. Every day of my life was recorded in your book. Every moment was laid out before a single day had passed."*

Job 14:5

> *"You have decided the length of our lives. You know how many months we will live and we are not given a minute longer."*

These are two of the most remarkable truths found in Scripture. God has a plan for your life, and He is so interested in you that He actually records every minute detail of your life. God desires to walk down life's path with you, hand in hand, as you make decisions and face circumstances, stormy or joyful. Can you think of a better way to live your life?

The following quote from Kyle M. Yeats is not meant to discourage you. Rather, it should encourage you to embrace the wonderful experience of living the reality of God's Word as stated above in Psalm 139:16 and Job 14:5.

> "He knows the weak places in your being, and the aims and purposes that you have had. He knows how hard you have tried and how heavy the burdens are that you have been forced to carry. He understands the handicaps that have kept you from reaching the goals you set for yourself. He also knows how miserably you have failed to live up to His standard for your life.
>
> He can sense the barrenness, the ignorance, the lost opportunities, the wasted years. He can count up the lost souls who will spend eternity in hell because you failed to tell them the story of saving grace. He knows, too, the many deeds of kindness and thoughtfulness that you have taken time out to do in His holy name.
>
> He can put your own little puny life up against His blueprint of your life and record all the differences.
>
> Yes, dear friend, He knows it all. He is able to use His own divine fluoroscope and look through all the veneer, the tinsel, the make-up, and the genuine. It hurts to know that our God is like this—and yet it helps, too, since we will be spurred to live bigger, richer, sweeter, nobler, more Christ-like lives because of it. We will be encouraged to know that an all-wise and an all-knowing God will take account of some of the hidden riches and qualities that otherwise would be unnoticed and unrewarded. Thank God for the knowledge that He knows me!" [4]

If God has marvelously planned out my life, shouldn't my greatest passion, pursuit, and purpose be to live the life that God has planned for me? With God, it is never too late to start!

NEW BIRTH NOT EXPERIENCED

If you have not entered into a personal relationship with Jesus Christ, you have not experienced Event 2. God wants you to experience the new birth, and He has even planned for you to do so. Because you have been born with a sinful nature, you commit sins. As a sinner, you cannot enter heaven. Therefore, your condition or status as a sinner must be changed, and your sins must be forgiven. Jesus says in John 3:3 (NKJV), "*unless one is born again, he cannot see the 'Kingdom of God.'*" Again, in Mark 1:15 (NKJV), Jesus says, "*repent and believe in the gospel.*"

You see. . .to be born-again is to be born from above, or from God. This means you are supernaturally regenerated by God, the Holy Spirit, enabling you to enter the Kingdom of God and empowering you to live a holy life. To belong to God's Forever-Kingdom, you must be born into it. Your natural birth into this world came by the will of your natural parents, so your spiritual birth into God's Kingdom comes by a spiritual means—God's will. (John 1:12-13)

God, in His unfailing love, draws you to Himself. Can you recall a time or incident when you felt that God was leading you to enter into the life of a Bible-believing faith? If you are anything like me, you didn't even know that God was prompting you to put your trust in Him. However, as I look back on my life before I knew Jesus, I now realize that seemingly unrelated events and occurrences were leading me to the truth. They guided me toward Him. He was drawing me to Himself.

John 6:44
"For no one can come to me [Jesus] unless the Father who sent me draws them to me…"

By surrendering your life to Jesus, and placing your trust in Him, He becomes your very own personal Savior. Read the following verses, bearing in mind that they were written for you.

James 4:8, 10 (NKJV)
"Draw near to God, and He will draw near to you…Humble yourselves in the sight of the Lord, and He will lift you up."

John 3:16

> "*For God loved the world so much that he gave his one and only Son* [Jesus], *so that everyone who believes in him will not perish but have eternal life.*"

Write your name in the spaces below to see how much God loves you.

For God loved __________________________ so much that He gave His one and only Son, so that ______________________________ who believes in Him will not perish but have eternal life.

John 1:12 (RSV)

> "*But to all who received him, who believed in his name, he gave power to become children of God. . .*"

If you believe that Jesus died for your sin, repent and confess your sin to Him. By doing so, you will receive His forgiveness. With all sincerity, write your name in the spaces provided below, and you will experience God's will for your life.

But as ________________________________ receives Him, and believes in His name, to ___________________________________ He gives power to become a child of God.

God gives, I receive. I give, God receives.

Colossians 2:6-7

> *"And now, just as you accepted Christ Jesus as your Lord, you must continue to follow him. Let your roots grow down into him, and let your lives be built on him. Then your faith will grow strong in the truth you were taught, and you will overflow with thankfulness."*

These verses mean that when you become a Believer, you not only *receive* God's forgiveness and His gift of eternal life through the death of Jesus on the cross, but you also *give* your life to God. This means that you give God the right to lead you in all aspects of your life and to use you for His will and good pleasure.

YOUR DEATH

As an Unbeliever, it is highly probable that your death will take place during the Prophetic Events that we are going to study. Please consider the consequences of dying without becoming a child of God. If you die without entering into a personal relationship with Jesus Christ, your soul and spirit will abide in the torments of the bottomless pit. This is the place of the dead, referred to as the abyss and the bottomless pit. (Psalm 9:17; Matthew 7:13-14; Luke 16:23)

Revelation 9:1, 11 (NIV) "The fifth angel sounded his trumpet, and I saw a star that had fallen from the sky to earth. The star was given the key to the shaft of the Abyss... They had a king over them the angel of the Abyss, whose name in Hebrew is Abaddon and in Greek, Apollyon [that is, Destroyer]."

See the abyss on Timeline One (located at the end of Part One of this book).

The abyss is depicted as an immeasurable depth. It is:

- the abode of Unbelievers who have died until the Great White Throne judgment (Revelation 20:11-15)
- a prison for certain demons (Revelation 9:1-2, 11)
- the place from which the Antichrist will ascend (Revelation 11:7; 17:8) [5]

Did you know that there is a demon king of the bottomless pit or abyss? Read Revelation 9:1, 11. Write his name in Hebrew ____________________ (destruction) and in Greek __________________ (destroyer).

Let me share with you some thoughts on this subject by F.C. Jennings.

> "There is a continuance of existence after death. Man's ignorance of the place and condition of that continuance cries out with agony for light. Of one thing man is sure, death is, for *him, not the end.* The grave takes the body; but the body is not the whole of man. There is something that the grave does not take. His reason, apart from any divine revelation, rebels against the thought of there being no radical distinction between himself and his dog. But where, then, does that immaterial, that responsible part of himself that survives the dissolution of his body go? Where? To the underworld, the region of the unclothed spirits of the departed." [6]

If you die as an Unbeliever, both your soul and spirit will continue their existence in the abyss. However, your body will return to dust until the Second Resurrection, also known as the Resurrection of Condemnation, when it will be reunited with your soul and spirit for judgment at the Great White Throne. The Great White Throne will be the final time of judgment for all sinners or Unbelievers. If you are an Unbeliever, your ultimate destiny will be eternal death in everlasting fire. (Matthew 25:41; Revelation 20:11–15)

It should be noted that from here on out, the content of this study will be primarily directed toward Believers. Assuming that you are a Believer, you have already learned about two Events that God pre-planned for your life—Event 1 is your Birth and Event 2 is your New Birth.

REFLECTIVE QUESTIONS

If you are a born-again Believer, how does the sad truth regarding the tragic destiny of Unbelievers after death affect your zeal to bring lost souls to a saving knowledge of Jesus Christ? In what way are you actively engaged in doing your part of our God appointed mission to give every person in our generation an opportunity to receive the Lord Jesus Christ as their personal Savior?

____

____

____

Job describes the place of the dead as: "…the land of darkness and utter gloom. It is a land as dark as midnight, a land of gloom and confusion, where even the light is dark as midnight." (Job 10:21-22)

I became a Believer when I was 18 years old. The pastor of the church where I began to attend at that time was a man by the name of Joe Dahl. He gave me some advice regarding my new life in Christ. He said, "Kathy, as you think of your future as a missionary overseas, you must always be ready to preach, pray, or die at a moment's notice." Scary, but, oh, so true!

Right then and there, I accepted the fact that serving Christ wasn't meant to be a life of ease or dull, self-serving passivity. Looking back, I can say that my life's moment in history has been a worthwhile and fulfilling adventure. I have strived to walk with Jesus wherever He desired that I should go. . . together with Him. My life has truly been a story of surrender, trust, and purpose. The greatest joy a soul could ever know.

Timeline covered in Lesson 1

Please **write** the following two Events on **Timeline One** (located at the end of Part One of this book). The following serves as an example to show you how it should look.

1. EVENT 1. . .**Write** Event 1 and the year you were born in approximation to year 2016. I wrote my birth date and my arrow as an example.

2. EVENT 2. . .**Write** Event 2, the year you were born-again and a cross. My born-again date is 1954.

SYSTEM OF THE ANTICHRIST

JESUS CHRIST AUTHOR OF LIFE

John 1:3-4

LESSON 2

JESUS CHRIST CAPTAIN OF OUR SALVATION
Hebrew 2:10 (NKJV

The Captain goes before us. "If we don't know where we're going, we know with whom we go."
Charles Spurgeon

THE THREE PLOTS

THE THREE PLOTS

Have you ever read a novel that has several plots going on at the same time? The plots do not seem to move toward each other, but ultimately they come together at the end of the book. After reading this type of novel you often times find yourself wondering how you didn't see what was coming. This is precisely what will happen at the end of this Present Age.

During the end times there will be three separate plots which will ultimately come together. At that time, one of the plots, an evil one, will dominate over the other two. As a result, the other two plots will suffer. However, in the end a reversal will take place, and the two plots that suffered will gain the victory. The seemingly dominate evil plot will be totally defeated. At the moment, this may sound to you like a brainteaser, but hang in there!

All human beings belong to one of the following three plots. Throughout this study we will refer to these three plots as:

Plot 1 – The World System of the Antichrist
Plot 2 – The Believers
Plot 3 – The Nation Israel

It is very important for you to understand the significance of these end-time plots, because you are currently a part of one of them and are affected by the other two. Here is some background information that will serve as an introduction to the upcoming lessons involving the three plots.

PLOT 1: THE WORLD SYSTEM OF THE ANTICHRIST

Characters. . .The Antichrist, world leaders, and the earth people who join the World System of the Antichrist

Setting. . .If you will look at **Timeline One and Two** (located at the end of Part One of this book) you will see a period of years labeled the World System of the Antichrist. As you can see, this system has already begun. It has taken many, many years to develop and has not reached its final stage. The timeline shows that the World System of the Antichrist will last all the way through the time of the Rapture, and through a 3 ½ year period known as the Wrath of God. It will abruptly end when Jesus comes back to earth at His Second Coming. At that time,

King Jesus will destroy the World System of the Antichrist and will establish His Kingdom on the earth.

During the end times, the nations will choose to turn their back on God and follow Satan. Consequently, God will turn the nations over, by their own choice, to the reign of Satan. This evil reign will soon be carried out by Satan's servant, the Antichrist. In Part Two of this study book we will analyze Scriptures that specifically address the person of the Antichrist. This will enable you to recognize the Antichrist when he appears.

The Appearance of the World System of the Antichrist

In the book of Revelation, the apostle John, figuratively describes the commanding appearance of a rider on a horse. The rider represents the World System of the Antichrist which will eventually be led by a person known as the Antichrist. The next four horsemen of this vision symbolize the events of this distressing period of time.

When Jesus was crucified, "The soldiers wove a crown [stephanos] of thorns and put it on his head..." (John 19:2) Intending to mock Jesus, they actually crowned Him the victor... the winner!

Revelation 6:1-2 (NIV)

> [1] *"I watched as the Lamb opened the first of the seven seals. Then I heard one of the four living creatures say in a voice like thunder, 'Come!'* [2] *I looked, and there before me was a white horse! Its rider held a bow, and he was given a crown, and he rode out as a conqueror bent on conquest."*

World conflict and spiritual warfare are two defining characteristics that effectively describe the dramatic events that will unfold during the last days of this Present Age. The System of the Antichrist will ride out as a ________________________ bent on ________________________ (v. 2). The *bow* is a weapon of force and the *crown* given to the rider is the Greek word *stephanos* meaning a victor's crown, a symbol of triumph. This represents victory for the World System of the Antichrist in its conquest of the world.

The person of the Antichrist will be born and rise to power toward the end of the long era of this system. It is interesting that the line of *kings*, (Revelation 17:9-11) from which the Antichrist will come, wear *crowns* (Revelation 12:3) which is a different Greek word, *diadema*. "*Diadema* is never used as *stephanos* is; it is always the symbol of kingly or imperial dignity." [V] So we see that The World System of the Antichrist has been given a *stephanos* which indicates triumph, and the Antichrist will wear a *diadema* indicating that he will reign over the earth.

"People are only vulnerable to being deceived when they want what is being offered to them." [1]

Regrettably, the Antichrist will be mistakenly regarded as a holy man. The miraculous circumstances surrounding this man will deceive much of mankind, causing people to proclaim him savior. He will promise to bring unity to the nations, peace from the terrible ongoing wars, and prosperity in times of world-wide economic chaos and poverty.

Presently, the moral condition of our world is rapidly deteriorating, and it will continue to do so. God will allow Unbelievers to make their own poor choices which will lead them into great wickedness and in pursuit of lustful pleasures without restrictions imposed by a holy God. The world does not want and will not want God's rule. It will become increasingly evident that the key characteristics of these evil times are deceit, war, death, lawlessness, earthquakes, starvation, disease, and. . . persecution for both Believers and the people of Israel after their conversion to Christ.

The Day They See Jesus!

During the rule of the Antichrist, on a pre-determined day, the earth will begin to tremble, stars will fall and the sun and moon will be darkened. All the inhabitants of the earth will look in shocked disbelief as total chaos transpires in the heavens. At that moment, all of mankind will **see** Jesus as He magnificently appears in the clouds of the sky. Scripture tells us that earth people will be so terrified at Jesus' sudden appearance that they will literally cry out for the mountains to fall upon them. Unbelievers will actually prefer for the mountains to fall upon them, than to look at the face of God sitting on His throne. (Revelation 6:14-17) There will be dreadful consequences for all who belong to this World System during a time period called the Wrath of God .

PLOT 2: THE BELIEVERS

Characters. . .All Believers who belong to the Kingdom of God

During the World System of the Antichrist, the distinctions between Believers and Unbelievers will become very obvious. But, how do we define a Believer? The following definition is lengthy, but certainly something to think about.

The Believer

"According to Lewis Sperry Chafer, no less than 33 simultaneous and instantaneous divine undertakings and transformations, which collectively constitute the salvation of a soul, take place the moment one exercises faith in Christ and is saved.

Among these is that a believer in Christ has the guilt of his sins removed. Secondly, He is taken out of Adam, the sphere of condemnation, and placed in Christ, the sphere of righteousness and justification. Thirdly, he is given a new standing by virtue of his being placed in Christ by the Holy Spirit's baptizing work and made acceptable. (1 Corinthians 12:13; Romans 6:3-4; Ephesians 1:6 NKJV). [2]

The new Believer "has given up his spirit of disobedience. He has yielded his mind to the influence of truth. God's will has been accepted by him. He has laid aside his rebellion, and become an obedient subject of Christ." [3]

During the course of my life, I have met Believers from all over the world, and I marvel at my response to them. I joyfully reflect on the fact that these are my brethren, my family, who have experienced the very same personal encounter with Jesus just as I have experienced, only under different circumstances. It is a beautiful and awesome emotion.

What Believers do

Jesus gave a command to His disciples: "*Go into all the world and preach the Good News to everyone.*" (Mark 16:15) This is the message of the Good News: Jesus Christ is our Savior, Jesus Christ is our Sanctifier, Jesus Christ is our Healer and Jesus Christ is our Coming King. Down through the ages all Believers have been involved, in some measure, in going, giving, and praying to carry this life changing message to the far corners of the earth. The task is nearly done. King Jesus is coming soon.

Setting. . .All the inhabitants of the earth will be in accord with the World System of the Antichrist, with the exception of the true followers of Jesus Christ—the Believers. If you are a Believer, you are living in this world system but you are not a part of it. You must never under any circumstances become a part of it.

In the end times, under the crushing hand of the Antichrist, Believers will suffer for their faith. Sadly, many followers of Christ will even turn away from their Savior, but not all of them. It is my personal conviction that most Believers around the world are not prepared for this impending and final persecution. That is precisely why I am attempting to lay out a simple explanation of the dark days that are upon us, and other end-time Events that are just beyond our horizon.

How well do you think that you are prepared for the end-time Events on a scale of 1 to 10? ________

1 - not at all prepared
5 - I am still a little vague about end times, but I think I will be true to my Savior
10 - very well prepared

Throughout history, Christians all around the world have suffered the hardships of persecution. However, every Believer in every country of the world will face persecution under the reign of the Antichrist. This is a fact. A harsh, true, and real fact. Believers need to face this coming fiery trial with the full grace of God filling their souls. Keep in mind that even though Believers will be separated by time zones and location, they will be bound together as one community in suffering for Jesus' sake.

The Day They See Jesus!
One day, in the midst of this great tribulation, the sky will split apart and all Believers will **see** "*the blessed hope and glorious appearing of our great God and Savior Jesus Christ.*" (Titus 2:13 NKJV) This will be a moment of unspeakable magnitude! Immediately, Jesus will snatch suffering Believers out of the distress and persecution that they will be enduring on the earth. Jesus will literally transport every Believer to their heavenly home.

PLOT 3: THE NATION ISRAEL

Characters. . .The Jewish people

The Nation Israel is the only one of its kind. It is different from all of the other nations of this world because God has a special plan for Israel. The first Jew was a Gentile (non-Jew) named Abraham who was chosen and called by God to be the father of the Hebrew people. God's resolute purpose was to be their personal God. This exclusiveness distinguishes the Jewish race from all other nations. It should be noted that the terms "*Israel, Israelites*, and *Israelis*" along with the term "*Hebrews*" are all terms or names used in referring to the Jewish people.

Setting. . .God made the following promise to Abraham: "*All the families on earth will be blessed through you.*" (Genesis 12:3) Reading these words cause us to look at God with wonder. Really Lord, you intend to use just one man to bless all people? What a great nation of people these are going to be! The scope of God's purpose for the Jewish people is amazing. What did God propose to do to accomplish this marvelous feat?

Deuteronomy 7:6 "For you are a holy people, who belong to the LORD your God. Of all the people on earth, the Lord your God has chosen you to be his own special treasure."

- First of all, Abraham was chosen to belong to God to the exclusion of all other gods. Likewise, all of Abraham's descendants were also chosen to belong to God. God was, and is, their personal God—the God of Israel.
- The Jews were chosen to walk in God's ways, to love Him, and to serve Him with all their heart and all their soul. (Deuteronomy 10:12-13)
- The Jews were chosen to be spokespeople to the world on God's behalf. God's moral standards (in the form of instruction and guidance) as a way of life were to be written and preserved by His chosen people. We still have their words with us today—the Bible, the Word of God. All the writers of the Scriptures were Jews with the possible exception of Luke.
- Abraham was chosen so that God could live at the very center of his life. In other words, God's attributes and powerful acts were to be revealed to the world through His relationship with the Jewish people.
- The Jews were chosen to bring salvation to the world. Jesus said, ". . .*salvation comes through the Jews.*" (John 4:22) God chose to send His Son, Jesus, to be born of this nation. A direct line can be drawn from Abraham to Jesus. (Matthew 1:1-16) The incarnate Jesus was a Jew, and He was and is the Savior of the world.
- The Jews were chosen to spread the gospel of salvation throughout the entire world. They were to convert the gentiles to Christ by the preaching of redemption through the blood of Jesus shed on the cross. By doing this the Jews would fulfill God's plan: "*All the families on earth will be blessed through you.*"
- The Jews were chosen to be "spiritual statesmen" in the kingdom of Christ when He comes to rule the world during the Thousand-Year Reign of Christ and beyond into eternity. (Exodus 19:5-6; Luke 1:32-33)

As previously stated, the incarnate Jesus was a Jew. However, Jesus died for the sin of all mankind. That is, He also died for non-Jews, and He considers non-Jewish Believers as part of His *special treasure*. According to God's plan, both the Jews as a nation and the non-Jews were to form one body of Believers. Initially, many Jews did believe in Jesus. In fact, Jesus' first disciples were Jews who formed the first community of Believers referred to as the church. These believing Jews received the Holy Spirit and God's full blessing was upon them. At this point, opportunities were limitless. God's chosen people could now reach the entire world with the message of what Christ did on the cross.

Ephesians 3:6 calls this inclusion of the Gentile Believers (non-Jews) into the church a *mystery*, meaning that this truth had not been divinely revealed until that moment. **Read** the following verse and **underline** the word "together." Then fill in the following blanks.

Ephesians 3:6 (NIV)

> *"This mystery is that through the gospel the Gentiles are heirs together with Israel, members together of one body, and sharers together in the promise in Christ Jesus."*

Gentile believers are ________________ together with Jewish believers—co-inheritors of the Kingdom.

Gentile believers are ________________________ together in one body with Jewish believers—a corporate relationship.

Gentile believers are _______________________ together in the promise in Christ Jesus—partners in all the promises and benefits of the Gospel.

Believing Jews from the nation of Israel along with believing Gentiles make up one single unified body, the church of Christ.

Tragedy!

Thousands of believing Jews formed the church after the resurrection and ascension of the Lord Jesus. However, during the following forty years covered in the book of Acts, Israel rejected Jesus Christ as their Messiah. By their decision to reject God's Son, Jesus, they were unwittingly deciding that they no longer wanted to be God's chosen people. Tragically, Israel is still waiting for their redemption.

The Jewish community remained in their Old Testament practices of a religion based on works and merit. They became one of all the many religious groups that follow a man-made, worldly religion.

Home-landless

Because Israel rejected Jesus as their Messiah, God uprooted them from their homeland and scattered them throughout the nations. Consequently, the Jews have wandered from country to country as a persecuted people for almost 2,000 years. After all this time, God in His mercy has brought the Jewish people back to their original homeland because He plans to pour out

His salvation on them and to prepare them for their service to Jesus as their future King upon His return to earth.

The Day They See Jesus!

During the World System of the Antichrist the Jews will make a seven year treaty with the Antichrist. It is during this period of time that the Jews will actually **see** their Messiah! At a specific moment, every human being on the entire earth, Believers, Unbelievers and Jews alike, will look up and **see** Jesus in the clouds of the sky, in all His glory. The Jews will recognize Jesus as their Messiah. The people of Israel will be inconsolably grieved by their former unbelief, and will repent of their sin. Jesus will remove their sin in loving forgiveness and each believing Jew will be born-again, born of God, and will be filled with the Holy Spirit. They will have knowingly chosen to again be God's Chosen People.

Immediately, the Antichrist will seek to annihilate the Jews. If he can't take the place of God in their lives, he will attempt to slay them.

A VERY IMPORTANT QUESTION

There are three end-time plots. **Write** their names on the following blanks.

1. Plot 1 ____________________
2. Plot 2 ____________________
3. Plot 3 ____________________

Which plot do you belong to? The following test will help you decide which plot you are a part of.

A. I am not a Jew ______
I am a Believer ______
I belong to Plot ______

B. I am a Jew ______
I am not a Believer ______
I belong to Plot ______

C. I am not a Jew ______
I am not a Believer ______
I belong to Plot ______

D. I am a Jew ______
I am a Believer ______
I belong to Plot ______

THE PLOTS COLLIDE

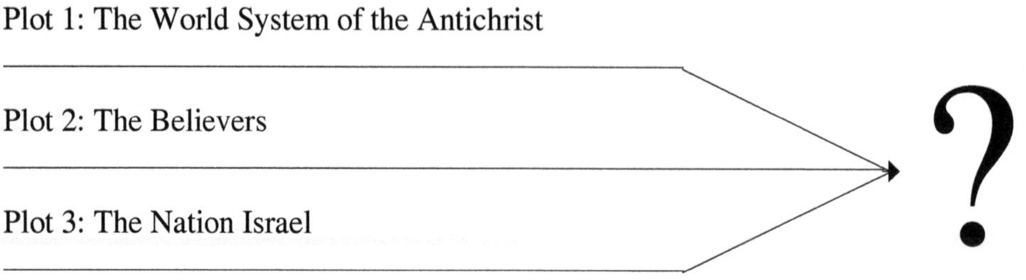

Plot 1: The World System of the Antichrist

Plot 2: The Believers

Plot 3: The Nation Israel

?

The three plots will suddenly come together during the most colossal Event in human history. The Event is represented by the question mark in the diagram. This Event will encompass both heaven and earth. Likewise, its effects will drastically impact all who are living at the time it takes place, whether a Believer, a Jew, or a worshiper of the Antichrist. This is the day that I have referred to as "the day they **see** Jesus." All people everywhere will see Jesus! Can you guess what this Event is called? **Write** what you think it might be in the following blank. ____

____

If you wrote the Rapture in the blank above, you are absolutely correct! The impact of the Rapture will have tremendous effects on each of the Three Plots, and leaving each one in a different situation. You and I live in one of the Three Plots. After the Rapture we will find ourselves in an altered situation.

The apostle John expresses the invitation to see the prophetic visions of the book of Revelation in the following words: *"Then as I looked, I saw a door standing open in heaven, and the same voice* [Jesus' voice] *I had heard before spoke to me like a trumpet blast. The voice said, 'Come up here, and I will show you what <u>must happen</u> after this.' And instantly I was in the Spirit, and I saw. . ."* (Revelation 4:1-2)

My desire for you is that the lessons of this book will serve as the open door to our, yours and my, personal investigation of the revelation of God concerning the things that *"must happen"* to all of us—His Prophetic Events. Together, as we step through this open door. . .we are beyond our horizon.

JESUS CHRIST CAPTAIN OF OUR SALVATION

Hebrews 2:10 (NKJV)

LESSON 3A

JESUS CHRIST THE ROCK
Daniel 2:35

The Rock became a huge mountain and filled the whole earth—the final Kingdom.

EVENT 3

PLOT 1: THE WORLD SYSTEM OF THE ANTICHRIST

THE SYSTEM

Write Plot 1 and the title of this lesson on the line below.

____ → **RAPTURE**

Review Plot 1 in Lesson 2.

If God said it, it will happen
All the Events mentioned in this study book are biblical, prophetic declarations. Each of them as divine declarations must and will take place. Due to their precise nature, their fulfillment is recognizable. For example, in the Gospel of Matthew, Matthew identifies twelve Old Testament prophecies that were fulfilled by Jesus. The religious leaders, at that time failed, or refused, to recognize that Jesus explicitly fulfilled all of the prophecies that spoke of His first advent. We must not make this same mistake when it comes to our understanding of the fulfillment of prophecies concerning the Lord's appearance at the Rapture and His Second Coming. You and I will examine the prophetic Events concerning the end times so we will be better equipped to recognize their fulfillment. It is amazing how clearly the Bible speaks on these important Events.

THE WORLD SYSTEM OF THE ANTICHRIST—YOUR EVENT

The World System of the Antichrist has been in the process of forming for a very long time. This study book focuses on the latter years of the World System of the Antichrist. To avoid confusion in the chronological order of end-time prophetic Events, we will consider the World System of the Antichrist to be your next prophetic Event. Please remember that it actually began before you were born.

For the Born-Again Believer this is Event 3
For you, prophetic Event 1 was your ______________. (If you don't remember go back to Lesson 1.) Event 2 was when you were ________________________________. At this time, you are living during Event 3, The World System of the Antichrist. Be aware that a moment will come when a line will be drawn in the sand. You will be forced to make a choice to either belong to this satanic system or to remain firm in your faith and stand on God's side. You will refuse to be a participant in this system. Not participating will ultimately cause you

much suffering for Jesus' sake, but it will result in your exaltation and glorification in the Kingdom of God.

For the Unbeliever (Not Born-Again) this is Event 2
For you, prophetic Event 1 was your ________________. You have not yet received God's gracious and loving gift of eternal life through a spiritual new birth. At this time, you are living during your Event 2, the World System of the Antichrist. You also will be compelled to make the choice of belonging or refusing to belong to the World System of the Antichrist. Whether you join this system willingly, or not-so-willing, this participation will bring you under the condemnation of God and will result in a great deal of suffering for you during your next prophetic Event known as the Wrath of God. Ultimately, you will receive eternal condemnation and punishment at the hand of the true and just God.

THE WORLD SYSTEM OF THE ANTICHRIST—A SYSTEM AND A PERSON.

THE SYSTEM

Christian Bible scholars refer to the World System of the Antichrist as a *system* and because it will be dominated by a *person*, therefore, the name—the System of the Antichrist. As previously stated, the system itself has existed for a very long time, but the person has not yet been revealed. You might also recognize today's political term for this system, the New World Order. In other words, the World System of the Antichrist and the New World Order are two interchangeable terms used to describe the same system. The term used for this system may change but its characteristics will not.

Lesson 3A is a study of the *System.* Consider the following definition of the word system.

> A *system* is "a group of interacting, interrelated or interdependent elements forming a collective entity [unit]." [D] This definition clearly describes the *System* of the Antichrist.

In this lesson we will study:

- The World System of the Antichrist Revealed in the Scriptures
  - Daniel's Interpretation of Nebuchadnezzar's dream – The Statue
  - Daniel's Interpretation of Nebuchadnezzar's dream – The Time
- The Developing World System of the Antichrist
  - The Ten Regions

THE WORLD SYSTEM OF THE ANTICHRIST REVEALED IN THE SCRIPTURES

God revealed this end-time system in the Old Testament book of Daniel. While Daniel the prophet was held captive in the country of Babylonia, the Lord gave Nebuchadnezzar, the king of Babylonia, a prophetic dream that Daniel interpreted. (Daniel 2) Later, the Lord gave the same prophetic dream to Daniel but with different and more detailed imagery. (Daniel 7) An understanding of Daniel's prophecy is essential to our comprehension of end-time Events.

Let's take a look at the interpretation of Nebuchadnezzar's dream found in Daniel chapter 2. God has purposefully given us this Scripture with some of the key elements of the World System of the Antichrist to help us recognize them when they take place. We will review this same prophecy in Part Two of this book.

DANIEL'S INTERPRETATION OF NEBUCHADNEZZAR'S DREAM – THE STATUE

Observe the parts of the statue and the action that takes place on the part of the rock. Please read all of chapter 2 in your Bible. One of the goals of this study book is to help you interpret and discover prophetic truths. A part of this process is that you read and observe what the Scriptures say. Make five observations from the following Scripture.

Daniel 2:32-35

> [32]*"The head of the statue was made of fine gold. Its chest and arms were silver, its belly and thighs were bronze,* [33]*its legs were iron, and its feet were a combination of iron and baked clay.* [34]*As you watched, a rock was cut from a mountain, but not by human hands. It struck the feet of iron and clay, smashing them to bits.* [35]*The whole statue was crushed into small pieces of iron, clay, bronze, silver, and gold. Then the wind blew them away without a trace, like chaff on a threshing floor. But the rock that knocked the statue down became a great mountain that covered the whole earth."*

Your observations

1. ____________________
2. ____________________
3. ____________________
4. ____________________
5. ____________________

How I would love to read your observations as you examine this dream statue.

Daniel gives an interpretation of what this statue represents. He stresses that this will take place in the latter days, apparently meaning the end times. The following verses will give you the basic essentials of Daniel's interpretation. **Underline** what the symbolic parts and metals of the statue represent in the following verses.

Daniel 2:28

Daniel 2: 37-39, 41-42 (RSV)

> *"You, O king. . .are the head of gold. After you shall arise another kingdom inferior to you, and yet a third kingdom of bronze. . .And there shall be a fourth kingdom, strong as iron. And you saw the feet and toes. . .it shall be a divided kingdom. . .as the toes of the feet were partly iron and partly clay."*

The following is a diagram of the interpretation of the dream as seen in Daniel 2:36-45. According to this interpretation each part of the statue was made of a different metal and represented four successive governments or kingdoms starting with the head of the statue. History tells us the names of these world empires which are listed in the chart below.

1. head............................ gold:	Babylonian Kingdom	606 B.C. – 539 B.C.
2. chest and arms........... silver:	Medo-Persian Kingdom	539 B.C. – 331 B.C.
3. belly and thighs .... bronze:	Greek Kingdom	331 B.C. – 146 B.C.
4. feet................................ iron:	Roman Kingdom	146 B.C. – A.D. 476
4. feet... part iron and part clay:	Roman Kingdom / Ten Kingdoms	(no date)
5. .... a rock:	The Divine Kingdom of King Jesus	

Did you notice that there are two "4's" in the chart describing Nebuchadnezzar's dream? This is not a typo. Try to capture the meaning of the statue. The vision began with the head of the statue and continued downward ending with the toes. God revealed to Daniel that throughout history there will be four successive human world empires beginning with Babylonia. How many human empires are listed above? __________

In the vision, the iron legs flowed right into the feet. Iron is the symbol of the ____________ Empire. Let's try to picture in our minds the feet with their ten toes. The feet are a combination of iron and clay. Each part of the statue made of different metals represents a kingdom, or empire, and, of course, its ruler. We know that the iron in the feet symbolizes Rome. Since all the elements of the statue represent kingdoms, it is reasonable to assume that clay also represents a kingdom. The emphasis on the *ten* toes would indicate *ten* kingdoms.

From this Scripture, we can draw the conclusion that at the time of Jesus' Second Coming, the world will be governed by Ten Kings under the strong leadership of a Roman Empire representative. As this study progresses we will see that the latter is the Antichrist; he is called *"the beast"* in the book of Revelation. The Ten Rulers will give their allegiance to the Antichrist, the supreme ruler.

Revelation 17:12-13

> *"The ten horns of the beast* [system] *are ten kings who have not yet risen to power. They will be appointed to their kingdoms for one brief moment to reign with the beast* [person]. *They will all agree to give him their power and authority."*

The Roman Kingdom was a *city based* kingdom meaning that it begin in the city of Rome with a single authority and from there extended its power. The Roman Empire, represented by the legs of the statue, was in power during the time of Christ but collapsed in the year A.D. 476. The collapse of the ancient Roman Empire was not due to the Second Coming of Jesus, the Rock, but due to the invasion of the Vandals, Visigoths, and other tribes of Europe.

If the Roman Empire ended in A.D. 476, what does the prophecy mean when it says that Jesus will come to establish His Kingdom during the time of the Roman Empire and destroy all human empires? Bear in mind that Daniel 2 is not talking about Jesus establishing His spiritual Kingdom. Daniel is referring to King Jesus' Thousand-Year Reign on the earth. Obviously, history tells us that this did not take place at Jesus' First Coming. God's Word never contradicts itself. What do you think Daniel's prophecy implies?________________________________

It implies a time gap between the expired Roman Empire and the end-time Roman Empire. According to the vision of the statue, in the end times a government will again rise out of Rome and will rule the world along with Ten Kings represented by the clay toes.

The prophecy with an interval of time looks like this:

1. head............................gold:	Babylonian Kingdom	606 B.C. – 539 B.C.
2. chest and arms............ silver:	Medo-Persian Kingdom	539 B.C. – 331 B.C.
3. belly and thighs......... bronze:	Greek Kingdom	331 B.C. – 146 B.C.
4. legs.............................. iron:	Roman Kingdom	146 B.C. – A.D. 476

TIME GAP lasting until the end times

4. feet..................... iron and clay:	Roman Kingdom / Ten Regions ruled by Ten Kings
5. .... a rock:	The Divine Kingdom of King Jesus

The fact that each empire historically occurred gives us the basis to categorically affirm that the future Roman Kingdom and its activities will take place. Even though there have been many attempts, there has not been a world empire since the fall of the ancient Roman Empire. . .that is, until the New World Order began to develop.

DANIEL'S INTERPRETATION OF NEBUCHADNEZZAR'S DREAM – THE TIME

Daniel 2:34, 44-45 gives us the time, or when, Jesus' future Kingdom will arrive and what will happen to this final world empire.

Daniel 2:34

> *"As you watched, a rock was cut from a mountain, but not by human hands. It struck the feet of iron and clay, smashing them to bits."*

Daniel 2:44-45

> [44] *"During the reign of those kings, the God of heaven will set up a kingdom that will never be destroyed or conquered. It will crush all these kingdoms into nothingness, and it will stand forever.* [45] *That is the meaning of the rock cut from the mountain, though not by human hands, that crushed to pieces the statue of iron, bronze, clay, silver, and gold. The great God was showing the king* [Nebuchadnezzar] *what will happen in the future. The dream is true, and its meaning is certain."*

1. According to verse 44, what will God do? ________________________________
and it will never be ________________________________.

2. **Circle** the words that tell us the *time* or *when* God will establish His Eternal Kingdom. According to this verse, what will be taking place on earth when this happens?

____

____

3. Who does the rock symbolize? ______________________ On what part of the statue did the rock fall? ______________________. This is significant. What will happen to the world system of government when Christ returns to establish His eternal Kingdom? ____________

____

Revelation 11:15 "The world has now become the Kingdom of our Lord and of his Christ, and he will reign forever and ever."

Your answer to the first question may be something like: God will establish His Kingdom which will never be destroyed or conquered; it will endure forever.

You may have answered the second question with something like this: God's Eternal Kingdom will be established during the time when the world is ruled by Ten Kings. Ten Kings have never before ruled the world.

Your third answer might look something like this: The rock symbolizes Jesus. The rock, will fall on the fourth kingdom destroying the Roman kingdom and the Ten Kings. As a result, all human kingdoms, will be totally crushed, never to rise again. Jesus' Divine Empire will literally cover the whole earth. This will take place at Jesus' Second Coming.

Other Scriptures agree that Jesus' Second Coming will terminate the World System of the Antichrist. (Revelation 19:11-21) Christ will then reign on the earth for one thousand years. (Revelation 20)

THE DEVELOPING WORLD SYSTEM OF THE ANTICHRIST

The Thousand-Year Reign of Christ on the earth, is mentioned six times in Revelation 20.

Watch the development of Ten Regions governed by Ten Rulers. This will result in the formation of a new world order through the process of *globalization.* A Roman Empire representative will become the supreme ruler of this new world order. (Daniel 2 and 7; Revelation 17:12)

This prophecy is NOW BEING FULFILLED. This is where we are at the present time.

The term *globalization* refers to the process by which the world unites under one collective entity which will rule over every area of life, such as: finance, politics, military, social, judicial, and law enforcement. This process has already begun; the world is becoming an integrated global society. All of the earth's inhabitants will become world citizens. But how will such a diverse world be ruled? It must be divided into manageable portions. As we have seen, God revealed to the prophet Daniel what these manageable portions would be: a one world government divided into ten regions. Many people today welcome this unity as the solution to the world's stressful complexities, but what seems a good thing will place the world into the hands of its arch enemy—Satan.

Watch for these things:

- The loss of national sovereignty, independence and self-government as the nations of the world rapidly become a part of the global community.
- The tightly woven, interdependence of world economies. How financial matters of countries around the globe, even small countries, directly impact other nations.
- The promotion of immigration and movement of people to other nations, resulting in conflicting heterogeneous societies which eventually become more and more homogeneous. This is a key component of the globalization process.
- An attempt to decrease or erode the sense of patriotism: the love, loyalty, support and defense of one's country.
- The acceptance of a need for reform or revision of the United States of America's Constitution, supported by the argument that it is outdated or inadequate in light of the modern world. This adjustment would occur in all nations.
- A demand for the redistribution of the world's wealth. A one world system cannot have wealthy countries and poor countries. Consider that statement. What must be done to the economy of wealthy countries? Good question.
- Demands by world leaders for a world political authority to manage the global economy.
- Appeals made by world leaders for a new world order.

Can you think of any other factors that are currently contributing to a one world community?_____

____

THE TEN REGIONS

Our world is already divided into ten regions, and each of the regions is currently working toward the formation of a regional government.

Generally speaking, most movements begin with small, baby-step changes that are taken in small, baby-size shoes. Initially, progress seems slow, and change is almost imperceptible. However, the baby shoes quickly become big, heavy boots that take giant steps leading to a point of no return.

An illustration of this is when the formation of the Ten Regions began after World War II ended in 1945. In 1946 British Prime Minister Winston Churchill called for a United States of Europe. What do we have today? We have the European Union, the first of the Ten Regions.

It was not feasible for the Ten Regions to be formed through military conquest or by political means. Doing so would have caused endless conflict. Rather, the Ten Regions were formed based on economic procedures, later to become political unions. Consequently, the economies of all nations around the world have become interdependent and completely intertwined. The European Union formation has had a measure of success and is the model being followed.

When President George Bush, Sr.'s State of the Union Address was televised on January 29, 1991, my husband and I were watching from Venezuela, South America. Just days before, an

American-led joint air strike was made against Iraqi forces occupying Kuwait. This marked the beginning of the Persian Gulf War, also known as the first Iraq War.

As we listened to this speech, we couldn't help but notice President Bush's appeal for a "new world order." The following are some of his remarks.

- At the beginning of his speech:
  "What is at stake is more than one small country, it is a big idea—*a new world order*, where diverse nations are drawn together in common cause to achieve the universal aspirations of mankind: peace and security, freedom, and the rule of law. Such is a world worthy of our struggle, and worthy of our children's future."

- During the speech:
  The term, *the world now stands as one*, was used, and the terms *world community*, and *the community of nations* were used at various times.

- At the end of his speech, he gave his appeal:
  "The world can therefore seize this opportunity to fulfill the long-held promise of a *new world order*—where brutality will go unrewarded, and aggression will meet collective resistance."

President Bush, Sr. was not specifically stating that the New World Order was established in 1991, but remarkably, he gave credence to its existence. The New World Order was recognizable, and it was embraced as a reality.

The Reverse Side of the Great Seal of the United States "The upper motto [above the pyramid], Annuit coeptis, means He has favored our undertakings. The lower motto [below the pyramid], novus ordo seclorum, means the new order of the ages that began in 1776, the date on the base of the pyramid." [1]

Look at **Timeline One** (located at the end of Part One of this book) and find the year 1776 located to the far left. This date marks the recognized initial formation of a New World Order spoken of by the prophet Daniel. You may verify this date by finding it at the bottom of the pyramid on the dollar bill along with the motto, *Novus ordo seclorum*, meaning the *New Order of the Ages*. This is the reverse side of the *Great Seal of the United States* which is located to the right. For this reason, in Lesson 1, it was mentioned that you were born during the World System of the Antichrist. I highly recommend Gary H. Kah's book En Route to Global Occupation (ISBN 0-910311-97-8) which gives complete coverage of this topic.

If you are a Believer, **write** on **Timeline One** Event 3 beside the date 1776 on the line by the asterisk (*_3_). If you are an Unbeliever or an unbelieving Jew, write Event 2 on that same line (*_2_).

Look at the map "Ten Regions of the World" located at the end of this Lesson. The information pertaining to this map, with a slight update, is taken from Gary H. Kah's book.[2] By conducting internet research using the names of each region listed on this map, you can easily discover information and the status of each region as they continue to develop.

The Ten Regions of the world are referred to as *supranational governments.* In short, this means that they are *above* or *over* national governments. Each nation must surrender a part of their sovereignty to the regional authorities.

The United States of America belongs to a region currently called *Security and Prosperity Partnership of North America* which will eventually be called *The North American Union.* This region includes the U.S.A., Canada, and Mexico. The treaty, establishing this region, took place on March 23, 2005 in Waco, Texas and was signed by President George Bush, Jr., Prime Minister Paul Martin of Canada, and Mexican President Vicente Fox.

According to the map, the United States of America is a member of Region number _____. What other countries belong to this Region? _________________________ and _________________________.

I have personally followed the development of these regions for some time now, especially that of South America, and I recommend that you conduct your own internet research on these regions. You will find information such as date of establishment, flag, emblem, administrative centers, government, members, etc.

It is a fact—our world is divided into ten, specific regions and each region is currently in the process of becoming fully organized with a parliament, monetary system, armed forces, and judicial system. Some regions have advanced more rapidly in their development than others. Once these elements are in position, what steps or actions must take place on a regional level to facilitate the formation of a central world government? Let's brainstorm a bit. The following is a hypothesis to get us thinking along these lines.

Steps to a central world government

- The next step might be that each of the regions elect a representative—regional president, or "king."

- It would follow that each of the elected representatives, or kings, form an organization that includes all Ten Regions. Currently, The United Nations has a representative membership from almost every nation in the world. However, the world is still fragmented and made up of many nations trying to work out world problems. Eventually, The United Nations will be replaced by a more manageable and efficient system made up of just Ten Regions with Ten Representatives.

- The next logical step—the election of a world leader, or king, who will preside over the Federation of Ten Regions. Who do you think this person will be? Yes, he will ultimately be the Antichrist.

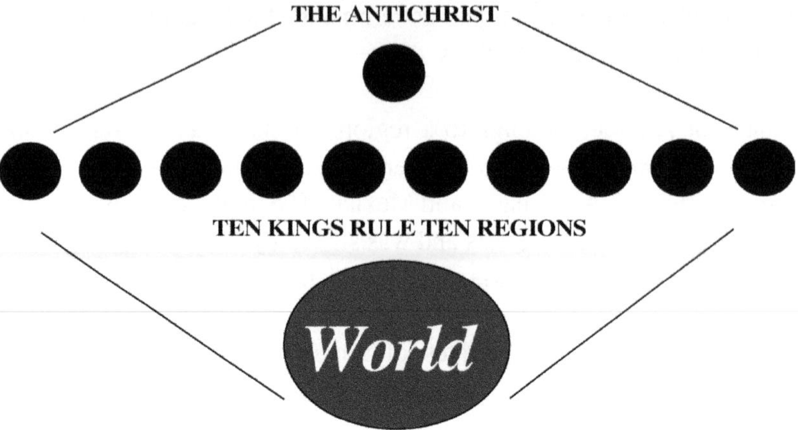

FEDERATION— "a union of states that recognize the sovereignty of a central authority while retaining certain lesser powers of government"

A closing thought.

God tells us in His word those things that will take place in the far distant future. For God, His prophecies are like a timetable, His schedule, listing the times at which certain events will take place. For generations people have opened their Bibles and read the prophecies of Daniel 2 just as we have done. They close their Bible and lay it on the end table to ponder and ask themselves, "When will this all happen? Probably not for a very long time," answering their own question.

Ecclesiastes 3:1 (NASB) "There is an appointed time for everything. And there is a time for every event under heaven."

We have just completed a study of Daniel 2, albeit a very brief study. We too ponder and ask questions. But our questions and ponderings are different. We close our Bibles and our study book and look up to our heavenly Father and exclaim, "Lord, the time is now! The future has arrived!" We waiver a little bit by adding, "Am I really living this prophecy? Father, give me discerning eyes to see and a vigilant spirit to understand. As conditions in the world shift, help me to live appropriately as your faithful servant."

JESUS CHRIST THE ROCK

Daniel 2:35

THE TEN REGIONS OF THE WORLD

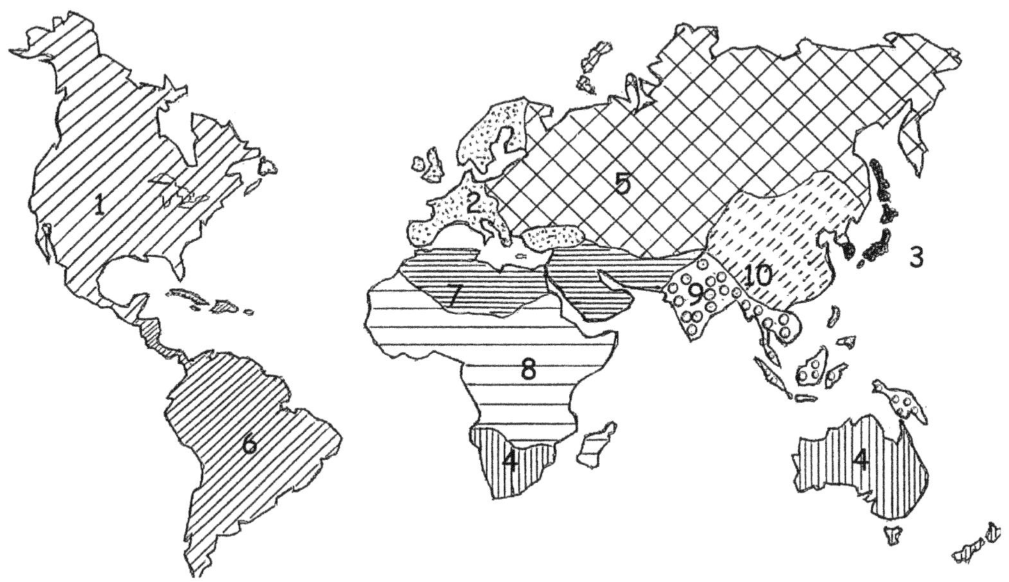

Map of Ten Regions of the World

1. Security & Prosperity Partnership of North America (Canada, U.S.A., Mexico / Mar. 23, 2005 Waco, Texas)

2. European Union (1993 – 27 nations)

3. Japan and South Korea

4. APEC: Asia-Pacific Economic Cooperation (2003 – 21 nations)

5. Commonwealth of Independent States (1991 – 10 nations)

6. Union of South American Nations (2008 – all 12 nations except French Guyana)

7. Organization of the Islamic Cooperation (2012 – 57 nations)

8. African Union - 1963 in Addis Ababa, Ethiopia (2002 – 54 nations)

9. Association of Southeast Asian Nations (includes the Indian sub-continent plus many of the southeast Asian countries and island nations). (1967 – 10 nations: 600 million people – Motto "One Vision—One Identity—One Community)

10. China

(Date of information: 2012)

LESSON **3B**

JESUS CHRIST THE BLESSED AND ONLY RULER
1 Timothy 6:15

In a world so obsessed with power, let us loudly proclaim the real Ruler of this world

EVENT 3

PLOT 1: THE WORLD SYSTEM OF THE ANTICHRIST

THE PERSON

World empires are usually built by powerful, charismatic individuals who inspire followers to accompany them in military conquest. However, this is not the case with The World System of the Antichrist. In this case, people are indoctrinated with a one-world ideology, and institutions are formed to create an integrated, interdependent, and united world. Then comes the Ruler.

In this lesson we will study:

The Person
Forewarnings: Seven Biblical Clues to Recognize the Antichrist
Characteristics of the World System of the Antichrist

THE PERSON

HIS POWER

In the end times, if the ten toes of the statue in Daniel chapter 2 symbolize Ten Kings of Ten Kingdoms, what or who will represent the iron—the Roman Empire? We know for a fact that the Antichrist, also known as the Beast, will rule the world in the end times along with Ten Kings. (Revelation 17:12) Does the Antichrist represent the iron of the Roman Empire? The Bible indicates that the Antichrist will be a known, powerful world figure with influence in three areas: *religion, government*, and *finance.*

Circle the correct area of power held by the Antichrist, as revealed in the following verses.

1. Revelation 13:7 *"He* [the Antichrist] *was given authority over every tribe, people, language, and nation."*
   religion government finance

2. Revelation 13:4 *"Men worshiped the dragon* [Satan] *because he had given authority to the beast* [the Antichrist], *and they also worshiped the beast. . ."*
   religion government finance

3. Revelation 13:17 *". . .no one could buy or sell unless he had the mark, which is the name of the beast* [the Antichrist] *or the number of his name."*
   religion government finance

The Antichrist is the masterpiece of Satan, and Satan will empower this imposter to work with astonishing deception. *"This man* [Antichrist] *will come to do the work of Satan with counterfeit power* [operative power] *and signs and miracles."* (2 Thessalonians 2:9) "He will be working in the power of Satan as Christ was of God, and he will perform miracles of various kinds as did the Lord. The *work* (*energeia*) means more than power; it is power in action. *The lawless one* then will embody the power of Satan." [1]

HIS NAME

Names in our culture are basically used to distinguish one person from another. In the Bible a name represented the attributes or characteristics of the person, as a result, names were chosen with care. It was believed the name revealed the person's nature, his identity, or, who he truly was. Keep this in mind as you study the following information.

The term Antichrist is a popular name for this ruler and is only found in 1 John 2:18, 22; 4:3; and 2 John 7. His very name is one of the clues that can be used to discover his identity. Antichrist, in Greek, is *antichristos*. Unlike the English definition for *anti*, which only means *to oppose*, the Greek definition means both *against* and *in the place of.* "The prefix 'anti' before 'Christ' denotes either someone who is '*against'* Christ or someone who claims to be a messiah '*instead of*' Christ; both of these essentially mean the same thing." [M] In other words, *antichristos* can mean either *against Christ*, or *in the place of Christ*, "or perhaps, combining the two, '*one who, assuming the guise* [the role] *of Christ, opposes Christ*'" [V] Therefore, *antichrist* has both the meaning "to take the place of Christ" and "against Christ, an enemy of Christ."

Isn't it interesting that the leader of a particular organization has retained the title Vicar of Christ for centuries? *Vicar of Christ* means "Jesus' representative on earth or in the place of Christ." Ironically, this is the exact meaning of the word *antichristos*. Other biblical names that have been given to the Antichrist are:

- the Beast (throughout the book of Revelation)
- son of perdition or destruction (2 Thessalonians 2:3)
- the man of lawlessness or sin (2 Thessalonians 2:3, 8, 9)
- the [Roman] prince or ruler, who is to come, literally: the one coming (Daniel 9:26, 27 RSV)
- the Abomination of Desolation (Matthew 24:15)
- the Little Horn (Daniel 7:8)

2 Thessalonians 2:8 "Then the man of lawlessness will be revealed, but the Lord Jesus will kill him with the breath of his mouth and destroy him by the splendor of his coming."

HIS END

When iniquity comes to full expression under the rule of the Antichrist, the True Ruler of the world, Jesus Christ, will come to destroy him. (2 Thessalonians 2:8) The satanic operations of the World System of the Antichrist, along with its horrific conditions, will be terminated. At that moment, righteousness will reign through Jesus Christ. . .forever. (Revelation 19:19-21)

This prophecy is not yet fulfilled.

FOREWARNINGS: SEVEN BIBLICAL CLUES TO RECOGNIZE THE ANTICHRIST

HOW TO RECOGNIZE THE ANTICHRIST
ONE. . .clues from 2 Thessalonians 2:1-8

First of all, let's look at some clues that indicate when the Antichrist will appear. The following Scripture tells us that we must watch for three things to happen *before* the Rapture at which time Jesus will take His followers to heaven (our gathering together to Him). If God indicates that certain things must take place before the Rapture occurs, can we look for the Rapture to take place before these things happen? That is a very interesting question.

Read the verses printed below and do the following exercise:

1. **Underline** all the words that refer to the Rapture in verse 1.
2. How many times can you find the word *revealed* in verses 1-8?
3. **Draw** a box around the words that refer to the *timing* of Jesus' coming in verse 3.
4. **Circle** the things, in verse 3 (two things) and verse 7 (one thing), that take place prior to the coming of Jesus at the Rapture.

2 Thessalonians 2:1–8 (NASB)

> [1] *"Now we request you, brethren, with regard to the coming of our Lord Jesus Christ and our gathering together to Him,* [2] *that you not be quickly shaken from your composure or be disturbed either by a spirit or a message or a letter as if from us* [Apostle Paul speaking], *to the effect that the day of the Lord has come.*
>
> [3] *Let no one in any way deceive you, for it will not come* [the Rapture] *unless the apostasy comes first, and the man of lawlessness is revealed, the son of destruction,* [4] *who opposes and exalts himself above every so-called god or object of worship, so that he takes his seat in the temple of God, displaying himself as being God.* [5] *Do you not remember that while I was still with you, I was telling you these things?*
>
> [6] *And you know what restrains him* [the man of lawlessness] *now, so that in his time he will be revealed.* [7] *For the mystery of lawlessness is already at work; only He who now restrains will do so until He is taken out of the way.* [8] *Then that lawless one will be revealed whom the Lord will slay with the breath of His mouth and bring to an end by the appearance of His coming."*

1. In verse 1, the phrases that should be underlined are: *the coming of the Lord* and *our gathering together to Him* which refer to the Rapture.

2. You should have found the word *revealed* three times: verse ________, verse, ________ and verse ________.

The word *reveal* in the Greek language is *apokalupto* which means: "literally, to remove a veil or covering exposing to open view what was before hidden. . .to make manifest or reveal a thing previously secret or unknown." [KW]

With regard to *the man of lawlessness* (the Antichrist) the word *revealed* "points to his existence *before* his manifestation. . .his beginning does not coincide with his manifestation." [2] What does this tell us? It tells us that the Antichrist will be known by the people of the world *before* he is openly revealed as the Antichrist.

3. You put a box around the specific words found in verse 3 that refer to the actual *timing* of Jesus' coming: "*it will not come unless*" and "*comes first.*"

4. This one may have been more difficult, but if you got it right, congratulations! The incidents that should be circled which take place *before* the Rapture occurs are as follows:

1) The apostasy, (the falling away), verse 3
2) The appearance of the man of lawlessness, the son of destruction (the Antichrist), verse 3
3) He (the Holy Spirit) who now restrains is taken out of the way, the Restrainer's withdrawal, verse 7

Let's examine the three things that you circled. However, our main focus in this lesson will be on the Antichrist.

- **Watch For: The Apostasy, The Falling Away**

2 Thessalonians 2:3 (NASB)

"*unless the apostasy comes first*" This will happen *before* Jesus comes at the Rapture.

1 Timothy 4:1-2

"Now the Holy Spirit tells us clearly that in the last times some will turn away from the true faith; they will follow deceptive spirits and teachings that come from demons. These people are hypocrites and liars, and their consciences are dead."

Matthew 24:10 (NIV)

"At that time many will turn away from the faith and will betray and hate each other."

According to these last two Scriptures, what are people turning away from? ______________

Some Bible scholars believe that apostasy is referring to a general rebellion against God by mankind as a whole. However, man has been rebelling against God since chapter 3 of the book of Genesis. Apostasy does indeed mean rebellion, and total rebellion against God will certainly characterize mankind before and after the Rapture during the reign of the Antichrist. But in these verses this particular rebellion or apostasy is referring to the many *followers of Jesus* who will turn away from the faith before the Rapture occurs. This interpretation holds true to other Scriptures referring to the end times. *The faith* means all the doctrinal truths expressed in Scripture pertaining to the Christian faith.

Definition of apostasy
Fall away or *turn away* is derived from the Greek word *apostasia* which is our word *apostasy* in English. This word means "stand away from, abandon, defect, deny, forsake, to revolt against." "In 2 Thessalonians 2:3 *'the falling away'* signifies apostasy from the faith." [V]

The use of the article the in "*the apostasy*" in 2 Thessalonians 2:3 indicates that Paul is speaking of a specific apostasy at a particular time in history. "The language indicates a specific event, not general apostasy which exists now and always will. Rather, this is an event that is clearly and specifically identifiable and unique, the consummate act of rebellion, and an event of final magnitude." [3]

Individual and Personal Apostasy
One must belong to Christ in order to commit the sin of apostasy against Him. This is a willful abandonment of the Christian faith, opposition to and denial of the truths of God's Word, and ceasing to be a follower of Jesus Christ. The reign of the Antichrist will necessitate the choosing of sides, joining the ranks of the Antichrist or remaining faithful to Jesus. The faith of many Believers will deteriorate as Christ's coming approaches. How inexpressibly sad!

Denominational Apostasy
The effects of the Reformation, when the Word of God was again seen as the final authority for the church in all matters of faith and practice, still exerts influence over every God-loving, Bible-teaching church (assembly) today. Any organization or denomination that calls itself *Christian* must adhere to all the doctrines of God's Word. Any deviation from, denial of, distortion of, or adding to the truths of the Holy Scripture is an act of apostasy in the sense of forsaking the divinely inspired Word of God. The result will lead the apostate denomination to spiritual ruin. Every authentic Christian denomination "*correctly handles* [teaches] *the word of truth*" as absolute truth, as God's very words. (2 Timothy 2:15 NIV)

The Reformation 14th - 16th centuries: This refers to a period of years when reformers of the Roman Church tried to "right the ship." The reasons for reform were manifold, among them the immorality of church leaders, false doctrines, and practices. The core principle of the Reformation was the recognition of the absolute supremacy of the Bible as the norm of life and doctrine.

Let me give you an example of this. When I was a little girl, I asked my Sunday school teacher how I could go to heaven when I died. Her reply was, "Just do good things and you will go to heaven when you die." I wasn't sure that was the correct answer, but I took her advice and tried very, very hard to do good things. Within a month or so I was discouraged and a little frightened, because I just couldn't keep doing good all the time on a day to day basis. I wasn't even sure how good I needed to be. I approached my teacher again, voice trembling and on the verge of tears. "Teacher, what if I try to do good things but I do bad things too?" She looked a little frustrated and replied sharply, "Well, just do more good things than bad things!" You see, she was telling me a means by which I could get to heaven that the Bible absolutely does not teach. Sad to say, the teacher was adhering to the modern day belief of that denomination.

Denomination A Christian group with a religious identity based on their understanding of the Bible, their convictions, values, and preferences.

As a young woman, the same *Christian* denomination taught me that there are no such things as miracles. I was told that all of Jesus miracles were just stories with a good moral teaching. For example, I was taught that Jesus did not perform a miracle when He fed 5,000 people with just

Ephesians 2:8-9 "God saved you by his grace when you believed. And you can't take credit for this; it is a gift from God. Salvation is not a reward for the good things we have done, so none of us can boast about it."

Inerrancy "The quality of freedom from error which is possessed by the Bible." [5] The Scriptures are without error and have authority over all people. It is the "word of truth." (2 Timothy 3:16; James 1:18)

Errancy The belief that the Bible makes assertions which deviate from what is correct, right, or true.

Luke 18:8 "But when the Son of Man [Jesus] returns, how many will he find on the earth who have faith?"

five loaves and two fish that a boy gave to Him. Rather, I was told that the multitude probably pulled out their lunch bags and starting sharing with each other when they saw the generosity of the boy. That is definitely not what John 6:1-14 says. This was definitely a miracle and is so stated in verse 14, *"When the people saw Him do this miraculous sign* (*semeion* Greek), (*miracle* English)."

Presently, this same denomination denies that the Bible is the divinely inspired Word of God. Harold Lindsell speaks to this issue in this way:

> ". . .once biblical infallibility is surrendered it leads to the most undesirable consequences. It will end in apostasy at last. . . Errancy and inerrancy constitute the two principles (belief, standard), and which one a person chooses determines where he will end up. I will contend that embracing a doctrine of errant Scripture will lead to disaster down the road. It will result in the loss of missionary outreach; it will quench missionary passion; it will lull congregations to sleep and undermine their belief in the full-orbed truth of the Bible; it will produce spiritual sloth and decay; and it will finally lead to apostasy." [4]

With reference to Bible teachers, the Bible clearly states in 1 Peter 4:11 (NIV): *"If anyone speaks, he should do it as one speaking the very words of God."* "The very words of God" are utterances from God's mouth. So what one says must be as God says it." [6] (1 Thessalonians 2:13)

Therefore, knowing that apostasy will be prevalent during the end times, all born-again Believers must be alert to any changes that occur to the Bible's fundamental doctrines or Bible-based, moral practices that may be embraced by particular religious organizations. Sadly, this happens all too often within many denominations, even among denominations that have their spiritual roots in the Reformation revival. How this must grieve the Holy Spirit! Furthermore, Bible-believing, Christian denominations must not enter into alliances, partnerships, or "team up" with secular or religious organizations that would compromise the teachings of the Word of God. (2 Corinthians 6:14-18; Galatians 1:6-10))

- **Watch For: The Man Of Sin (Lawlessness), The Antichrist**

Definition of *the man of sin* or *the lawless one*

The Antichrist is referred to as *the man of sin* or *the lawless one* because he will embody satanic lawlessness and will receive his power, his rule, and great authority from Satan. (Revelation 13:2) He will use all his evil power against God and all born-again Believers. The use of the article *the* in "the *man of sin*" means "a man of eminent wickedness; one distinguished for depravity." [7] (see Proverbs 6:12-15)

2 Thessalonians 2:1-3 (NKJV)

> *"Now, brethren, concerning the coming of our Lord Jesus Christ and our gathering together to Him. . .Let no one deceive you by any means; for that Day will not come unless the falling away comes first, and the man of sin* [the Antichrist] *is revealed, the son of perdition* [the Antichrist]."

In these verses we see that the Antichrist is revealed before the Rapture. During the Rapture, Jesus will not destroy the World System of the Antichrist and the Ten Kings, rather He will snatch the Believers out of the World System of the Antichrist.

The Antichrist will rule over the nations as if he were the only object worthy of the world's loyalty and worship. Immediately after the Rapture, the Antichrist will declare himself to be God, and he will continue to deceive mankind through his amazing counterfeit miracles, signs, and wonders. However, 2 Thessalonians 2:8 tells us that the Antichrist will be destroyed, along with the Ten Kings, when Jesus comes to establish His Kingdom on earth.

Look at **Timeline Two** (located at the end of Part One of this book.) Notice that The World System of the Antichrist continues to rule the world during the "Wrath of God" until the Second Coming of Christ and Armageddon.

- **Watch For: The Restrainer's Withdrawal**

2 Thessalonians 2:7, 8 (NKJV)

> *"For the mystery of lawlessness is already at work; only He who now restrains will do so until He is taken out of the way. And then that lawless one will be revealed. . ."*

Who do you think restrains or restricts evil? ________________________________

"*He who now restrains*" can best be interpreted as the Holy Spirit. That is, the Holy Spirit will remove His restraining power over lawlessness. When this happens, the lawless one, or the Antichrist, will appear.

Let's look at another version of these verses.

2 Thessalonians 2:6-8 (NIV)

> 6 *"And now you know what is holding him* [the Antichrist] *back, so that he may be revealed at the proper time.* 7 *For the secret power of lawlessness is already at work; but the one who now holds it back will continue to do so till he is taken out of the way.*
> 8 *And then the lawless one will be revealed, whom the Lord Jesus will overthrow with the breath of His mouth and destroy by the splendor of His coming. "*

Definition of the *Mystery or Secret Power of Lawlessness*

This is the supernatural activity of Satan creating a mindset in the soul of man to repel the rightful claims of God's will and law; as a result, leads man into spiritual anarchy.

The "*secret power of lawlessness,*" made known in 2 Thessalonians 2:6-7, is speaking of a climactic spirit of lawlessness in the world. Since the fall of man, the Holy Spirit has restrained mankind from unbridled and uninhibited immorality. He has set limitations to man's depravity and has exercised restraints over him. When the Holy Spirit stops holding back wickedness, Satan's influence on mankind will cause the world to quickly degenerate into a state of unspeakable evil. At this God-appointed time, the Antichrist will appear.

Some would argue that the Holy Spirit will completely withdraw from the earth when Believers are taken up to heaven at the time of the Rapture, as the Holy Spirit indwells Believers. However, the Holy Spirit is omnipresent. This means that He is present everywhere, and He cannot be confined to the bodies of Believers. This Scripture means that He will discontinue His restraint of evil, which is only one of His many gracious ministries. The Holy Spirit will have plenty of work to do on earth in the lives of the Christian Jews during a 3 ½ year period known as the Wrath of God.

Can you imagine what it will be like when the Holy Spirit does not restrain evil? How thankful we should be for the Holy Spirit, the Divine Deterrent! As the Holy Spirit's work of restraining recedes, we will see an increase in wickedness. Do you think that this is currently happening based on the way morality is already disintegrating in today's world?

We need to be alert and on the lookout for the appearance of the Antichrist in the midst of an increasing indifference to and intolerance of the Christian faith and the overwhelming wickedness in the world.

HOW TO RECOGNIZE THE ANTICHRIST
TWO. . .he will receive a fatal wound

The second thing that will clearly identify the Beast is that he will receive a *fatal wound.* Scripture indicates that this man's life will be beyond recovery due to a fatal wound. However, the fatal wound will be healed. The term *fatal* refers to circumstances that are cause for death. This incident should help us to identify the Beast. Consider the following statements taken from Revelation 13; all three refer to the Beast/Antichrist.

> Revelation 13:3 *"one of the heads of the beast seemed wounded beyond recovery-but the—but the fatal wound was healed!"*
>
> Revelation 13:12 *". . .whose fatal wound had been healed."*
>
> Revelation 13:*14* *". . .who was fatally wounded and then came back to life."*

Fatal
Fatal is the Greek word thanatos meaning "death" and comes from another Greek word thnesko meaning to die; be dead. [s]

HOW TO RECOGNIZE THE ANTICHRIST
THREE. . . he will die and come back to life

The Antichrist, also known as the Beast, is a man who will die and come back to life in God's timing and by God's resurrection power (not Satan's). Read these two Scriptures and write down the place from where the Beast will come.

Revelation 11:7 (NIV)
> *"Now when they have finished their testimony, the beast* [Antichrist] *that comes up from the Abyss will attack them, and overpower and kill them."*

Revelation 17:8

> *"The beast* [the Antichrist] *you saw was once alive but isn't now. And yet he will soon come up out of the bottomless pit* [Abyss] *and go to eternal destruction."*

Revelation 11:7: that comes ______________________________

Revelation 17:8: will soon come ______________________________

Do you remember what we learned about the abyss in Lesson 1? The abyss describes an immeasurable depth. It is. . .

- "the abode of the dead [Unbelievers] until the Great White Throne judgment (Revelation 20:11-15)
- a prison for certain demons (Revelation 9:1-2, 11)
- the place from which the Antichrist will ascend (Revelation 11:7; 17:8)" [8]

Revelation 13:2

> *". . .the dragon* [Satan] *gave the beast his own power and throne and great authority."*

Returning from the dead, the Antichrist will come back to earth and will be given great power. What is the source of his supernatural power? ____________________ What does the *dragon* give to his proxy, the Antichrist? ______________________________

Remember that Jesus is omnipotent, has all power: "*All authority* [power] *has been given to Me in heaven and on earth.*" (Matthew 28:8 NKJV) The power and authority that Satan gives to the Antichrist has initially been delegated to Satan by Almighty God. In himself, Satan has nothing.

Suffice it to say, anyone who becomes a part of the World System of the Antichrist, is in league with Satan himself.

His resurrection from the dead will be the most conclusive means by which we can identify the Antichrist, the Beast. The enormity of this well-known man rising from the dead will be the greatest cause of apostasy among the followers of Jesus. Many followers will abandon and deny their faith in Jesus to follow and to worship the Antichrist. Such will be the deplorable results of the depths of deception at that time.

HOW TO RECOGNIZE THE ANTICHRIST
FOUR. . . he will rule over the Ten Kings

Matthew 24:10 (NIV) "At that time many will turn away from the faith and will betray and hate each other."

The Ten Rulers, or Kings, of the Ten Regions of the world will give their power and authority to the Beast/Antichrist as the supreme ruler.

Revelation 17:12-13 (NIV)

> *"The ten horns you saw are* ten kings *who have not yet received a kingdom, but who for one hour will receive authority as kings along with the beast. They have one purpose and will give their power and authority to the beast."*

HOW TO RECOGNIZE THE ANTICHRIST
FIVE. . .he will be worshiped by all earth people

All unbelieving humans, those who have never been born-again spiritually, will worship and give their allegiance to the Antichrist. (Revelation 13:3-4, 8, 12, 14-15) Remember, all things considered, you will probably be alive when these events take place.

Circle the word "worship" along with the "object of the worship" in the following verses. **Underline** the word or phrase that states who is doing the worshipping.

Revelation 13:4, 8 (NIV)

> [4] *"Men worshipped the dragon* [Satan] *because he had given authority to the beast, and they also worshipped the beast and asked, "Who is like the beast? Who can make war against him?"* [8] *"All inhabitants of the earth will worship the beast—all whose names have not been written in the book of life belonging to the Lamb* [Jesus] *that was slain from the creation of the world."*

HOW TO RECOGNIZE THE ANTICHRIST
SIX. . .he persecutes those who oppose him

The Antichrist will persecute all who will not join his system and worship him.

Revelation 13:7, 15 (NIV)

> [7] *"He* [the Beast] *was given power to make war against the saints* [followers of Christ] *and to conquer them. And he was given authority over every tribe, people, language and nation.* [15] *He* [the False Prophet] *was given power to give breath to the image of the first beast, so that it could speak and cause all who refused to worship the image to be killed."*

According to the following verses, what will a person need in order to buy and sell during this time? ____

Victorious Believers in heaven "I saw before me what seemed to be a glass sea mixed with fire. And on it stood all the people who had been victorious over the beast and his statue and the number representing his name." Revelation 15:2

Revelation 13:16, 17

> *"He required everyone—small and great, rich and poor, free and slaves—to be given a mark on the right hand or on the forehead. And no one could buy or sell anything without that mark, which was either the name of the beast or the number representing his name."*

Believers must not receive the mark of the Beast! What consequences will Believers face if they do not receive this mark? What will happen to them? Think about it.

In 2 Thessalonians 2:1-12, the apostle Paul encourages Believers to stand firm in the faith and not be deceived by the Antichrist who will come back to life, and display *"counterfeit power"* and *"signs and miracles."*

Can you imagine the impact it will make when this well-known, world figure actually comes back from the dead? How will it affect you? The intention of this lesson is to help prevent you from being deceived!

As followers of Jesus Christ, we will face many difficult and terrible hardships when the Antichrist appears. We need to be mentally and spiritually prepared for this event. Believers will be the direct target of this formidable enemy. Some of us will die. However, we know that Christ will ultimately be victorious, and we will reign with Him forever.

HOW TO RECOGNIZE THE ANTICHRIST
SEVEN. . .he will declare himself to be "God"

The Antichrist will declare himself to be God. The Scriptures tell us that the Antichrist will be involved in a pact with the Jews, and other necessary parties, that will apparently allow the temple of the Jews to be built. Everything will seem to be going according to the Antichrist's evil strategy because he has a plan regarding the temple of the Jews.

2 Thessalonians 2:4

> "*He will even sit in the Temple of God, claiming that he himself is God.*"

CHARACTERISTICS OF THE WORLD SYSTEM OF THE ANTICHRIST

Complete Moral Degradation.
When He comes at the time of the Rapture, Jesus described the conditions on earth to be like the days of Noah and Lot.

Luke 17:26, 28

> "*When the Son of Man returns, it will be like it was in Noah's day. . .And the world will be as it was in the days of Lot.*"

The remainder of this passage in Luke 17 tells us that the world, in the latter days, will be oblivious to the fact that they are on the brink of impending judgment.

By referring to the times in which Noah and Lot lived, the Lord is calling our attention to conditions of total moral decay! Both of these comparisons given by Jesus describe the world as practicing extreme sexual immorality. **Underline** the words indicating the extent of immorality in Noah's day in the following verses. Notice God's watchfulness concerning human wickedness.

Genesis 6:5, 11-12

> [5] "*The Lord observed the extent of human wickedness on the earth, and he saw that everything they thought or imagined was consistently and totally evil.*" [11] "*Now God saw that the earth had become corrupt and was filled with violence.*" [12] "*God observed all this corruption in the world, for everyone on earth was corrupt.*"

The horrific degree of sin and wickedness committed by the people of Sodom, where Lot lived, became a Biblical standard used to measure the wickedness of other cities and nations. (See Isaiah 1:9; Jeremiah 23:14; Amos 4:11; Zephaniah 2:9; Luke 10:12; 2 Peter 2:6; Jude 7; Revelation 11:8)

"Sin grows from weakness to willfulness. 'The first makes a man contemptible; the second, abominable' (Daille). Our dignity is our likeness to God. What shame and degradation there is when we do not bear His image." 9

How do you think the world today stacks up against Sodom's standard of evil? Make your own list of moral evils currently occurring in our generation.

Think about modern day moral conditions in the light of these statistics from 2011 concerning just one of the many evils existing in our world today, sex trafficking.

- "A child is trafficked every 30 seconds." (UNICEF)
- "The average age of entry into sex slavery in the United States is 13 years old." (United States Department of Justice)
- "Human Trafficking occurs in 161 out of 192 countries." (The United Nations)
- "Human Trafficking is a 32 billion dollar per year industry." (The United Nations)
- "Pornography is a 96 billion dollar per year industry." (The Internet Filter Review)

On a scale of 1 to 10 (one: doesn't fit and ten: fits perfectly) how well do you think the following passage of Scripture characterizes the world that we are currently living in? Score ________

2 Timothy 3:1-5

> *". . .<u>in the last days</u> there will be very difficult times. For people will love only themselves and their money. They will be boastful and proud, scoffing at God, disobedient to their parents, and ungrateful. They will consider nothing sacred. They will be unloving and unforgiving; they will slander others and have no self-control. They will be cruel and hate what is good. They will betray their friends, be reckless, be puffed up with pride, and love pleasure rather than God. They will act religious, but they will reject the power that could make them godly. Stay away from people like that!"*

Moral degradation has many manifestations in the world, for example, the dreadful practice of spirit worship of pagan religions resulting in demonic influence in daily life. In developed countries, technology has brought immorality into the home where one can indulge in life-altering activities in private. Multiple forms of abuse abound in today's world.

What is a predictable outcome of unchecked indulgence? 1 Timothy 4:2 (NASB) gives the answer from God's standpoint. People become "*seared in their own conscience as with a branding iron. . .*" The conscience becomes non-functional and insensitive to evil. The conscience screams its warning, but it has no access to the mind that has closed and locked the door.

"Crime runs rampant as evil fills the void and desperation becomes the only moral guide many people recognize." 10

Bill Easum

> "North America is caught in the crack between what was and what is emerging. This crack began opening in 1960 and will close sometime around the year 2014. Trusted values held for centuries are falling into this crack, never to be seen again. Ideas and methodologies that once worked no longer achieve the desired results. This crack in our history is so enormous that it is causing a metamorphosis in every area of life.

> [The current years] are often called 'the hinge of history' or the transforming boundary between one age and another, between a scheme of things that has disintegrated and another that is taking shape." [11]

Men Scoff and Mock at the Thought of the Lord's Return
2 Peter 3:3-4

> *"Most importantly, I want to remind you that in the last days scoffers will come, mocking the truth and following their own desires. They will say, 'What happened to the promise that Jesus is coming again? From before the times of our ancestors, everything has remained the same since the world was first created.'"*

Corrie ten Boom
"Look within and be depressed. Look without and be distressed. Look at Jesus and be at rest."

Both my mother and I received Christ as our personal Savior about the same time. Soon after this life changing moment, we attended a family gathering where we excitedly shared our joy at having just learned that the Scriptures state that Jesus is coming again. Prior to this moment, neither my mom nor I had ever heard this before. My elderly, and dearly revered great-uncle, and minister at that time, was also present. My mom and I eagerly turned to her uncle to get his wisdom and insight. He coldly looked at us, and in no uncertain terms, insulted our pastor for such a "ridiculous" belief. We were shocked and shaken at this unexpected response. But even though his scorn was searing, we unwaveringly believed that if the Bible said it, then it was true.

Warren W. Wiersbe

> "The Word of God is still 'a light shining in a dark [squalid] place' (2 Peter 1:19). We can trust it. No matter what the scoffers may claim; God's Day of Judgment will come on the world, and Jesus Christ shall return to establish His glorious kingdom." [12]

You are living in the developing stages of this evil empire. Jesus said, "*I have told you all this so that you may have peace in me. Here on earth you will have many trials and sorrows. But take heart, because I have overcome the world.*" (John 16:33) Look to Jesus!

REFLECTIVE QUESTIONS

How would believing that these Prophetic Events will take place in an indefinite and vague future affect the way you live today? ____________________

____

How does your perspective change when you realize that these things are currently happening and developing at a rapid rate? What are your thoughts?

____

____

In light of the times in which we are living, what do you think the Lord wants you to do so that your life, heart, and priorities will be ready to "*stand firm and keep a strong grip on the teaching*" of God's Word? (2 Thessalonians 2:15) ____________________

____

JESUS CHRIST THE BLESSED AND ONLY RULER

1 Timothy 6:15

LESSON **4A** | # EVENT 3

JESUS CHRIST THE CONSUMMATE RULER OF HISTORY
Revelation 1:8

Jesus will bring to completion, perfection, and fulfillment all things. He will bring world history to its ultimate end.

PLOT 2: BELIEVERS AND THE WORLD SYSTEM OF THE ANTICHRIST

Write Plot 2 and the title of this lesson on the second line below.

Plot 1: The World System of the Antichrist

______________________________ →
______________________________ → **RAPTURE**

Review Plot 2 in Lesson 2.

Throughout my life, I have found that I can more effectively face trials and gain victory over difficult circumstances when I have been forewarned about them. This is what a study of prophetic Scripture does for you. The knowledge of what lies beyond your horizon will enable you to prepare for these Events. You will gain an awareness of the need to deepen your relationship with Jesus and His Word. This knowledge will help you to become "*rooted and built up in Him* [Jesus], *strengthened in the faith*," (Colossians 2:7 NIV) and it will help you to develop a calm, trusting spirit with a clear understanding, discernment, and mental alertness of what is to come.

This lesson will give you an understanding of what life will be like for Believers during the System of the Antichrist. We will study the topics:

The Great Tribulation
Matthew 24 and Revelation 6
Signs and Seals
The Great Tribulation - Four Signs and Seals

In Lesson 3 we learned that all who oppose the Antichrist will be persecuted, this will include all faithful Believers. Jesus gave the closing years of the World System of the Antichrist a special name—The Great Tribulation. It covers an indefinite period of years. However, at the peak of the Antichrist's power, suffering for the Believer will be intensified.

Timeline
First of all, let's look at **Timeline One and Two** at the end of Part One of this book in order to gain a basic understanding of each Event that falls into the time period of the World System of the Antichrist. These Events are the Great Tribulation, the Rapture, the Wrath of God, and the Second Coming of King Jesus and Armageddon. Look for each Event on the Timeline Charts

and observe the chronological order of the Events. Appendix B, at the end of this book, will give you a brief definition of each of these Events.

Tribulation "Then they will deliver you to tribulation..." Matthew 24:9 (NASB)

"for then there will be a great tribulation..." Matthew 24:21 (NASB)

"But immediately after the tribulation of those days..." Matthew 24:29 (NASB)

"These are the ones who come out of the great tribulation..." Revelation 7:14 (NASB)

THE GREAT TRIBULATION

Definition

God ends the Present Age, characterized by spiritual rebellion and wickedness, with two devastating judgments. Judgments in this case refers to calamities used of God by way of punishment when mankind rebels against His will. The first judgment is the Great Tribulation, and the second is the Wrath of God. The Great Tribulation marks the beginning of the end so to speak.

The term tribulation used by Jesus in Matthew 24 and Revelation 7:14 is a term used by the Christian church to identify a specific end-time judgment known as The Great Tribulation. The word tribulation in the Greek language is *thlipsis* taken from *thlibo* meaning "to crush, press, compress, and squeeze" and symbolically means "grievous affliction or distress." [KW] These Greek words indicate, in their context, a specific time of anguish, persecution, and trouble.

The Great Tribulation is a prolonged period in which God causes world-wide disasters to occur during the World System of the Antichrist. These disasters are self-inflicted involving all the nations of the world. Self-inflicted means that mankind's moral depravity has placed him in a state of enmity against God. Faithful followers of Christ face added suffering due to great persecution during this time at the hand of the Antichrist because of his hatred of God and God's people.

Look at **Timeline One** (located at the end of Part One of this book) and locate the Great Tribulation which takes place during the period of years that are labeled the World System of the Antichrist.

The People of the World and the Great Tribulation

The Antichrist will turn all worldly people away from God by deception, and consequently, man will give his loyalty and worship to the Antichrist, the evil underling of Satan. (Revelation 13:4) As the people of the world sink into a state of excessive unbelief, rejection, and unreceptiveness to God, God will remove His beneficial restraints. As a result, unrestrained mankind will freely express the inherent violence, wickedness, and corruption of his nature. When man turns his back on God, he suffers the consequences. God will not share His prize creation with an impostor.

Romans 1:28 "Since they thought it foolish to acknowledge God, he abandoned them to their foolish [distorted] thinking and let them do things that should never be done."

Believers and The Great Tribulation

To bear the name of Christ, Christ-ian, is to be an enemy of the fallen world system, and bearing His name will result in both suffering and reproach. This, however, is normal. Throughout church history God has actually brought about "special periods" of trial or judgment upon His followers. This is because the church has a tendency to break loose from its center—Jesus Christ. Consequently, when this happens, the church moves increasingly away from its biblical doctrines and values and is distracted from its mission to evangelize the world. Often times, "fiery trials" are used to discipline, purify and strengthen Christ's church to ultimately bring it back to its spiritual center in Jesus. This way, Jesus will be able to present those approved by trial to Himself as *"a glorious church without a spot or wrinkle or any other blemish. Instead, she will be holy and without fault."* (Ephesians 5:27)

James 4:4
"Don't you realize that friendship with the world makes you the enemy of God? I say it again: If you want to be a friend of the world, you make yourself an enemy of God."

MATTHEW 24 and REVELATION 6

Matthew 24 and Revelation 6 are the most important prophetic Scriptures with regard to the description of The Great Tribulation. Try to see in your mind the circumstances that gave birth to these two prophecies.

The story of Matthew 24

Jesus entered Jerusalem on what we now call Palm Sunday to affirm that He was the King of Israel and the expected Messiah. He was greatly acclaimed. Jesus then continued to speak to the people and religious leaders during the following week in the temple. The day of His crucifixion was fast approaching and yet no one but His precious disciples believed Him to be God in human flesh, Deliverer of mankind. For the last time, He left this great temple never to return. As Jesus departed from Jerusalem, He turned and cried out in anguish:

> *"O Jerusalem, Jerusalem, the one who kills the prophets, and stones those who are sent to her! How often I wanted to gather your children together, as a hen gathers her chicks under her wings, but you were not willing!*
>
> *See! Your house* [the temple] *is left to you desolate; for I say to you, you shall see Me no more till you say, 'Blessed is He who comes in the name of the Lord!'"* (Matthew 23:37-39 NKJV)

James 1:12 (NIV)
"Blessed is the man who perseveres under trial, because when he has stood the test, he will receive the crown of life that God has promised to those who love Him."

As Jesus and His disciples made their way up the side of Mt. Olivet, the disciples did not capture the turmoil Jesus was going through. They called Jesus' attention to the grandeur of the magnificent temple buildings, to which Jesus sadly replied that the whole structure would be completely destroyed.

We can thank the shocked and puzzled disciples for their persistent questions because they led to the revelation of the times in which we are now living. They asked Jesus when the temple would be destroyed, and then earnestly added two more questions of great significance, *"What will be the sign of Your coming, and of the end of the age?"* (Matthew 24:3 NKJV) What indications were to be given to alert Believers that Jesus' coming and the end of the Present Age is drawing near?

Jesus' sad countenance changed to joy because His disciples were asking insightful questions, the right questions. Jesus eagerly turned to them; He wanted them to understand these very things and to later record them in the Scriptures. Jesus looked into the distant future and gave the disciples, and us, a description of The World System of the Antichrist, The Great Tribulation, and all that will take place during that time. His words as recorded in Matthew 24 are *signs* that point to His coming at the Rapture at the end of the Present Age.

The story of Revelation 6

Jesus' disciple, John, was an old man. Nevertheless, he continued to preach the Word of God and witnessed for His beloved Jesus. While doing this, a persecution broke out during the reign of the Roman Emperor Domitian, approximately in the year A.D. 95. John was arrested and banished to a small, rocky island about ten miles off the coast of modern Turkey. The Romans used this island, named Patmos, to punish criminals by making them work in mines and quarries.

You will find the following conversation based on Revelation 1:9-12 and chapters 4 and 5.

Let's imagine that you and I decide to ask John personally about his 18 month ordeal. With deep respect we approach this aged apostle.

In a quivering voice, but ardent spirit, he replies to our questions, "First of all I was lashed with a whip; that was the custom of the Roman soldiers. All prisoners were forced to wear shackles; we had little clothing and never enough food. We slept on the bare ground in a dark prison and worked under the lash of military overseers." [1]

"It was hard, and I was very old, but let me tell you of the most wonderful encounter that a person could ever experience," John excitedly hurries on as if to say he wanted to waste no time on his sufferings. "*It was the Lord's Day, and I was worshiping in the Spirit. Suddenly, I heard behind me a loud voice like a trumpet blast. It said, 'Write in a book everything you see. . .' I turned to see who was speaking to me*, it was my Lord Jesus. Oh what a vision!"

"I wrote His message to seven churches (in modern day Turkey). *Then I looked, I saw a door standing open to heaven, and the same voice I had heard before spoke to me like a trumpet blast. The voice said, 'Come up here, and I will show you what must happen after this.' Instantly I was in the Spirit, and I saw a throne in heaven. . .the one sitting on the throne was as brilliant. . .*" he continues his story as we sit spellbound.

"*I saw a scroll in the right hand of the one who was sitting on the throne. There was writing on the inside and the outside of the scroll, and it was sealed with seven seals. And I saw a strong angel, who shouted with a loud voice: 'Who is worthy to break the seals on this scroll and open it?'* I wept because no one was found worthy to open the scroll and read it."

"How terrible!" you interrupt, 'the unopened scroll would mean that the closing scene of history could not begin; thus, evil would continue unabated on the earth, and there would be no future for God's people!' [2]

"But, wait!" John cuts off your outcry, "There *was* one worthy, the *only* one—the Lord Jesus, the Lamb of God. Jesus stepped forward and took the scroll from the hand of His Father. All heaven broke loose with praises, I did too," he humbly added, "but my feeble voice was lost among the thousands and millions who sang a mighty chorus."

Then, the old apostle looks at us and declares, "God's plan will never be prevented! Remember this!"

Matthew 24 and Revelation 6: Parallel Scriptures

I would like to mention at this point that John in his old age received from Jesus the very same teaching in Revelation 6 that he had received in his youth along with the other disciples in Matthew 24.

By carefully comparing Jesus' *signs* in Matthew 24 to the *seals* of Revelation 6, we can easily see that these verses are referring to the same events. It should be noted that each of the passages use slightly different terminology, but this is a common occurrence when prophecy is repeated throughout the Bible. One "subject may be only incidentally noticed in one place [or chapter] but treated with extensive fullness in another." [3] We should familiarize ourselves with these passages of Scripture, and thus, prepare ourselves for these events.

We observe that Jesus' teaching to His disciples used literal terminology in Matthew 24, but Jesus uses symbolic language in His account to John in Revelation 6. No doubt John was fascinated when he received in his advanced years the very same teaching in a different format. Another element John would have noticed was that Revelation 6 describes Jesus setting in motion the prophecy that He foretold in Matthew 24; the seals of Revelation 6 are the actual fulfilling of Jesus prophecy.

SIGNS AND SEALS

It is very important for you to understand the significance of Matthew 24 and Revelation 6. Jesus told His disciples that He would give *signs* or *indicators* that would point with precision to His coming at the Rapture, and, in due course, the end of this Present Age.

The purpose of Lessons 4A and 4B is to highlight Jesus' signs or indicators.

Diagram of the Seven Seals

- The Matthew 24 narrative stretches from the beginning of the Great Tribulation all the way to the Rapture. The Revelation 6 account covering the same time period seems to bring a sense of urgency as the judgments appear to intensify greatly as the Rapture draws near.

- The First Seal of the scroll corresponds to the appearance of "a conqueror." (Revelation 6:1-2) This "conqueror" is the World *System* of the Antichrist and, ultimately, the *person* of the Antichrist. The Great Tribulation takes place between the First Seal and the Sixth Seal. The Sixth Seal is the Rapture. (Revelation 6:12-17)

- The Seventh Seal is the Wrath of God and consists of seven judgments called the Trumpet/Bowl Judgments and lasts for a period of 3 ½ years. (Revelation 8-9; 15-16) The Seventh Trumpet/Bowl Judgment is the Second Coming of Jesus Christ. (Revelation 11:15-19; 19:11-17) We will study the Seventh Seal Judgment in another lesson.

- The Rapture and the Second Coming of Jesus are separated by the 3 ½ year period of the Wrath of God.

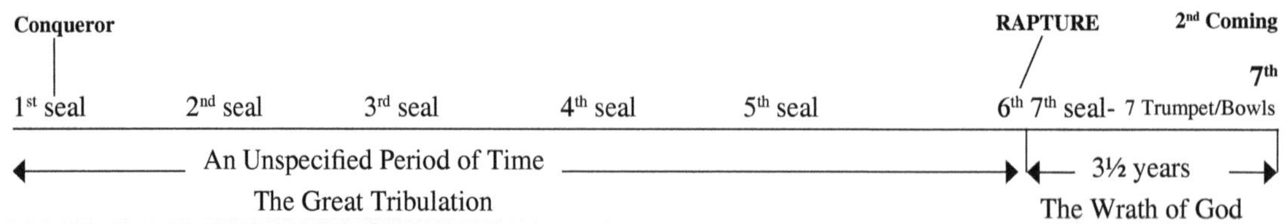

Deceive (Matthew 24:4-5, 24) To hoodwink by trickery; evil intentions to mislead; to victimize persons by devious and dishonest means. In these Scriptures it also has the sense of seducing: deceit by means of allurement, to entice with something fascinating.

The time has arrived, Jesus has taken the scroll that is sealed with seven seals from His Father's hand. (Revelation 5-6) This scroll, or book, contains the events that you and I will experience until King Jesus' Second Coming.

Unbeliever, when you see the signs taking place believe the truth of God's Word and place your faith and trust in Jesus for your salvation. Believer, *"Now when these things begin to happen, look up and lift up your heads, because your redemption draws near!"* (Luke 21:28 NKJV)

Write down your thoughts and observations as you continue to study the key components of the World System of the Antichrist. This will serve to confirm and validate what the Lord has revealed to you regarding the times in which we are currently living. Wouldn't it be great if we could all meet together somewhere to compile our findings and knowledge!

THE GREAT TRIBULATION - FOUR SIGNS AND SEALS

THE FIRST SIGN/SEAL: FALSE CHRISTS, THE ANTICHRIST

Sign: Matthew 24:4-5 (NIV)
"Watch out that no one deceives you. For many will come in my name, claiming, 'I am the Christ,' and will deceive many."

First Seal: Revelation 6:1-2 (NIV)
"I watched as the Lamb opened the first of the seven seals. Then I heard one of the four living creatures say in a voice like thunder, 'Come!' I looked, and there before me was a white horse! Its rider held a bow, and he was given a crown, and he rode out as a conqueror bent on conquest."

"False Christs" are impersonators of the Lord Jesus who pretend to speak with the authority of Christ. The greatest impersonator of all is the Antichrist. The globalization of the world, the System of the Antichrist, dominates the scene into which the Antichrist, the person, enters. He will actually portray himself to be in the place of Christ to his followers. He will be "*bent on conquest*" which indicates that he will not stop short of ruling the world and declaring himself to be God. The Antichrist will literally compel the whole world to worship him.

The major characteristic used to describe the reign of the Antichrist is *deception*. "*He* [the False Prophet] *deceives those who dwell on the earth because of the signs which it was given him to perform in the presence of the beast* [Anitchrist]. . ." (Revelation 13:14 (NASB)

Read 2 Thessalonians 2:9-12 (NASB) and take note of the world's reaction to the deception of the evil one. **Circle** the words: false, deception, and truth.

> [9] "*. . . the one* [the Antichrist] *whose coming is in accord with the activity of Satan, with all power and signs and false wonders,* [10] *and with all the deception of wickedness for those who perish* [Unbelievers], *because they did not receive the love of the truth so as to be saved.*
>
> [11] *And for this reason God will send upon them a deluding influence so that they will believe what is false,* [12] *in order that they all may be judged who did not believe the truth, but took pleasure in wickedness."*

Why will God's judgment be brought upon the people living during this time in history?

____

Satan's main concern is the Word of God. He will try to cast doubt on it, twist it, dilute it, pollute it, replace it, destroy it… "but the Word of our God stands forever." (Isaiah 40:8)

Notice the choice that is presented in this passage. Those living at this time will either choose to believe the ________________ of wickedness, or to believe the __________ of God. Think about the eternal consequences of this choice. It seems as though these Unbelievers will deliberately choose death. In what do they take *pleasure* instead of loving and believing the truth? ______________________________

Colossians 3:16 (NKJV) says: "*Let the word of Christ dwell in you richly. . .*" This means that we are to lovingly welcome Christ's truth to indwell us, to live in us abundantly, to feel at home in us, to fill every part of us. "*They did not receive the love of the truth*" implies that followers of the Antichrist do not welcome the love of the truth as one would receive a guest into one's home. Have you "*received the love of the truth*" in accordance with its biblical meaning?

____

In view of the fact that we are living in the end times, do you think that 2 Thessalonians 2:11 is a principle that God is applying to evil, depraved people of today? ________ Read in your Bible Romans 1:18-32.

George Mueller "The vigor of our spiritual life will be in exact proportion to the place held by the Bible in our life and thoughts."

In the light of what you just read how prepared do you think you are to be able to identify the Antichrist? What place does God's truth have in your life? Keep in mind that this sign should stabilize your life and focus your thoughts on Jesus' coming.

THE SECOND SIGN/SEAL: WAR

Sign: Matthew 24:6-8

6 *"You will hear of wars and threats of wars, but don't panic. Yes, these things must take place, but the end won't follow immediately.*
7 *Nation will go to war against nation and kingdom against kingdom. There will be famines and earthquakes in many parts of the world.*
8 *But all this is only the first of the birth pains, with more to come.*

Second Seal: Revelation 6:3-4

"When the Lamb broke the second seal, I heard the second living being say, 'Come!' Then another horse appeared, a red one. Its rider was given a mighty sword and the authority to take peace from the earth. And there was war and slaughter everywhere."

Wars According to Matthew 24

Do you think the statements "*Yes, these things must take place, but the end won't follow immediately*" and "*but all this is only the first of the birth pains, with more to come*" signify a brief few years or a long duration of time? ______________________________

____

The statements in verses 7 and 8 about wars, famine, and earthquakes indicate that all these things will take place over an extended period of time, and like a mother when the first birth pain hits, knows that there are a lot more to follow.

By recalling the devastation that has resulted from past world wars, we can better understand and prepare our hearts for the upsurge in war activities and our involvement in them. In World War I (1914-1918) there were approximately 15 million deaths (six million of them were civilians who died, mostly of famine) ". . .in the first three months of World War I, more than 1.5 million men fell on the western front alone." World War II [1939-1945] had even more loss. It "left 50 million to 60 million people dead, an equal number of refugees without homes, and probably the most tragic legacy in human history." [4]

As I was reading about World War I and II, I jotted down some of the words used to describe these wars. Don't read through this list too quickly. Envision the extent of human suffering represented in each word: death, starvation, hatred, slaughter, fear, degradation, destruction, disease, homelessness, exposure, collapse, genocide, mutilation, poverty, debt, futility, disillusionment, guilt, insanity, grief, hopelessness, tragedy, and loss.

How many wars, and how many deaths has the world and our country endured since these world wars occurred so long ago?

Fact: According to a United Nations statistic, there were 134 wars just in the year 2011 alone. Actually, there are hundreds of militia-guerillas, separatist groups, anarchic groups, terrorists, and drug cartels involved in constant conflict. The United Nations' definition of *war* states that: war must involve struggle by at least one province against another; it must be formally declared; and it has existed for at least six months.[5]

War According to Revelation 6

The sword given to the rider in Revelation 6:4 represents conditions of war. To take peace from the earth literally means "to submerge the world in a state of war," or "peace will be exiled from the earth." Barclay puts it this way:

> "The vision of the end was a vision of a time when all human relationships would be destroyed and the world a seething cauldron of embittered hate." [6]

The first seal brings forth a system of demonic power that seeks to subjugate the world and on its heels comes the second seal, war. This would indicate that most wars at this present time are basically fought to bring into line rogue nations or uncooperative government leaders with the goal of bringing about a one world empire. As the individual nations of the world form the regions of the global federation, many may not easily give up their sovereignty. Will ours? This could be a cause for serious conflict.

Wars are created by ideologies, greed, and lust for power. The atrocities of war embitter the soul of man to the point of hating or disbelieving in God. . .and this spills over onto God's people. How do you think Jesus felt as He looked through the centuries of time, and revealed the unimaginable tragedies of the last days to His disciples?

____

Oh, the unfathomable price man will pay for choosing to live independently from God, who paid so great a price to bring him perfect peace.

SIGN—EARTHQUAKES

Matthew 24:7 ". . .*and earthquakes in many parts* of the world"

Earthquakes rank high on the most feared of natural disasters. From personal experience in Central and South America I can say that earthquakes are terrifying as there is no escape from them. The earth moves below one's feet; everything is shaking. There is absolutely nothing stable to hold; you can't climb or be pulled out of it. I smile today remembering a man who in panic climbed a tree.

Tsunamis are a horrifying result of earthquakes. Think back to March 11, 2011 when a 9.0 earthquake resulted in a twenty-three foot tsunami that killed approximately 24,000 souls in Japan. None of us will ever forget the appalling images of the devastation that came about as a result of this natural disaster.

Fact: Over a 50 year span, between 1897 and 1946, only two to three earthquakes of a magnitude of 6 or above occurred every ten years. In the year 2010, the U.S. Geological Survey National Earthquake Information Center charted a staggering 2,156 earthquakes of a magnitude of 5 or above.

Consequently, it goes without saying that the occurrence of earthquakes is definitely on the rise. According to Jesus this is another observable *sign* that we are presently living in the Great Tribulation period during the System of the Antichrist. When you experience or hear of earthquakes in different places in the world you know that this is a sign of Jesus Coming.

THE THIRD SIGN/SEAL: FAMINES

Sign: Matthew 24:7
"There will be famines. . ."

Third Seal: Revelation 6:5-6
"When the Lamb broke the third seal, I heard the third living being say, 'Come!' I looked up and saw a black horse, and its rider was holding a pair of scales in his hand. And I heard a voice from among the four living beings say, 'A loaf of wheat bread or three loaves of barley will cost a day's pay. And don't waste the olive oil and wine!'"

King Jesus breaks the third seal and the domino effect continues. First, the evil system that aspires to conqueror the world is followed by wars, which leads to poverty and famine. These are natural result of wars.

The rider on the black horse is holding a pair of scales for weighing food which represents both famine conditions and scarcity of food resulting in times of extremely high prices. The symbolic use of a scale in the Bible reveals economic conditions. (2 Kings 6:25; 7:1, 16, 18) Try to picture in your mind having worked a full day and going to the grocery store to spend your daily wage on one single loaf of wheat bread, or if you have children, you will spend it on barley bread, a cheaper grain, so that you can get a little more for your money. The sheer cost of food will leave very little to no money to pay for other necessities of life. This is a picture of poverty.

In 1989, while we were living in Venezuela, South America, there was an attempted military coup. As a result, all the banks, stores, and offices closed. Virtually every business came to an abrupt stand still. Transportation of merchandise stopped, which included the most important of all, food! Panic gripped the general population. People violently forced their way into grocery stores and looted whatever they could find. The looting soon spread into other businesses, and homes were ransacked for both valuables and food. Owners of stores resorted to the use of guns to force people back, and many people were killed. The army stationed two military tanks outside of the small shopping mall near our home. Soldiers stood guard outside the mall entrance, only allowing two people at a time inside the super market to buy groceries.

We observed that a psychological change came over the population and in ourselves to a certain extent. We had the Lord to look to for help, while the majority didn't consider God an option. The frightful situation seemed to bring out survival instincts. There was a feeling that terrible violence, country-wide was seething just below the surface. Each family shrank into itself. All efforts were expended and focused on "me and mine" to gain and protect the bare essentials of life. A disturbing sense of insecurity was in the very air we breathed. Questions of uncertainty haunted our minds. What if we didn't have a means to buy food? What if it became an ongoing, prolonged condition?

Imagine what famine and scarcity of essential goods will be like on a world-wide scale. Famine can bring mankind to a state of desperation and madness.

Fact: According to the United Nations Food and Agriculture Organization, during 2010-2012 there were nearly 870 million people chronically undernourished of the 7.1 billion people in the world, meaning that 1 in every 8 go to bed hungry every night.[7]

The three main causes of hunger are war, poverty, and weather (drought, flooding, etc.); the very conditions that exist and worsen as the Great Tribulation advances. Do not despair. King Jesus is coming.

Habakkuk 3:17-19 "Even though the fig trees have no blossoms, and there are no grapes on the vines; even though the olive crop fails, and the fields lie empty and barren; even though the flocks die in the fields, and the cattle barns are empty, yet I will rejoice in the Lord! I will be joyful in the God of my Salvation! The Sovereign Lord is my strength!

THE FOURTH SIGN/SEAL: DISEASES, DEATH

Sign: Matthew 24:7 (NKJV)

"There will be famines, pestilences [epidemic disease]. . ."

Fourth Seal: Revelation 6:7-8

"When the Lamb broke the fourth seal, I heard the fourth living being say, 'Come!' I looked up and saw a horse whose color was pale green. Its rider was named Death, and his companion was the Grave [Hades]. *These two were given authority over one-fourth of the earth, to kill with the sword and famine and* [disease] *and wild animals."*

How many people world-wide die according to this prophecy? ______________________
How do they die? By the ____________________ (representing conditions of war), _____________, ______________________ and __________________________. It appears as though the wild beasts will also suffer from drought and famine. According to this passage, wild beasts will actually consume defenseless human beings.

The color of this horse is striking in that it is pale green, the color of a corpse. Authority from God is given to these two riders giving the impression that Death reigns over the earth. The Greek word for *Death* is *thanatos* which in this verse means death "by plague or pestilence and is joined to the Greek word *limos* which refers to destitution from a scarcity of food and therefore, death by famine." [KW] Hades, the abode of the dead, swallows multitudes of souls—one-fourth of the earth!

John 8:51 (NKJV) "Most assuredly, I say to you, if anyone keeps My word he shall never see [and experience] death." He will never see Death or experience Hades. He passes from life to life.

The resurrected Jesus tells us He has "*the keys of Death and Hades* [the abyss]. " (Revelation 1:18) This means that Jesus has power over life and death. On September 6, 1998, biblically speaking, I came to this door representing life on the one side and death on the other. I knew the first thing I would see when the door opened would be the face of my dear Savior. I stood so close to the door I could touch it, only a breath away. It did not open. I was healed on the spot, instantly. This is not the experience of the Unbeliever. When the door swings open, he looks directly into the face of Death and is immediately transported to Hades, the abyss.

Fact: We are all very aware of the many different deadly diseases that exist in the world today. The World Health Organization reports that there are 12,420 distinguishable disease categories in the world as of 2007.

Revelation 6:8 speaks of death caused by disease; it is possible that this may be referring to some sort of a pandemic. A *pandemic* can be defined as an epidemic that encompasses a wide geographic area, and it is often caused by war and famine. This coincides exactly with this prophecy.

One-fourth of earth's population will die as a result of the first four Signs/Seals.

Think about it:
In 2011, the world's population reached 7 billion. One-fourth of 7 billion is approximately 1,750,000,000. This represents the number of people who would die given the current population of the world. Let's try to get our minds around this huge figure. One-fourth of the world's population would be equal to all the people of North America (from Canada to Panama), all the people of South America, all the people of Europe (includes Russia), and just about all the people of Japan. How devastating to the world!

By all indications, the events of the seals will occur sequentially, and they will continue simultaneously. That is to say, once the events of each of the different seals occur, they will be ongoing. This truth has been revealed to us in God's Word, and it should awaken us to the realization of how severe conditions will become during the World System of the Antichrist and the Great Tribulation.

JESUS CHRIST THE CONSUMMATE RULER OF HISTORY

Revelation 1:8

LESSON 4B

JESUS CHRIST EVER-PRESENT HELP
Psalm 46:1

"My soul clings to you; your right hand upholds me." Psalm 63:8

"Is it God who holds me, and so keeps me safe? Or is it I who hold God and so am safe?" [1]

EVENT 3

PLOT 2: BELIEVERS AND THE WORLD SYSTEM OF THE ANTICHRIST

Before going into the specifics, I would like to underline the fact that during this time of great hardship and suffering, Believers will not only experience the same afflictions that Nonbelievers will be experiencing, but Believers will also face additional difficulties as a direct result of their faith in Jesus Christ. By having a clear understanding of what will increasingly become more difficult, you can prepare to meet it head on in victorious dependence on God.

The last signs of Matthew 24 will occur shortly before the Rapture and point to Jesus' coming deliverance of the Believer.

In this lesson we will study:

- Events Affecting Believers during the Great Tribulation
  - The Last Fiery Trial
  - Sign: Persecution
  - Sign: Apostasy and Betrayal
  - Sign: False Teachers
  - Sign: Wickedness, Lawlessness
  - Sign: Overcomers, Martyrs for the Faith
- Believers Preach the Gospel
- The Rapture

EVENTS AFFECTING BELIEVERS DURING THE GREAT TRIBULATION

THE LAST FIERY TRIAL

The New Testament book 1 Peter was written to forewarn Believers of the world's persecution of the church and how to live victoriously under the pressure this brings. Not long after the apostle Peter wrote this book, he was sentenced to death and died a martyr (about A.D. 65) in Rome during the Emperor Nero's terrible persecution of Christians. We are informed in 1 Peter that Believers will face an extraordinary, purifying trial before the Rapture occurs which will impact the church on a world-wide scale. This trial described in 1 Peter is probably the one designated by Jesus as the Great Tribulation and will be the last judgment that the church must endure.

Revelation 2:10
"But if you remain faithful even when facing death, I will give you the crown of life."

1 Peter 4:17

> *"For the time has come for judgment, and it must begin with God's household. And if judgment begins with us, what terrible fate awaits those who have never obeyed God's Good News?"*

The word *time* in this verse refers to a "fixed or definite period," [V] "when certain foreordained events take place." [KW] "These sufferings are to be viewed as an actual beginning of the judgment coming upon the world at the return of Christ; the 'fiery trial' was a herald of coming deliverance." [2]

According to 1 Peter 4:17, where will the judgment of mankind begin? ________________ ________________________ (the church). If God's judgment will begin with His own, what will His judgment be like for those who have never obeyed God's Word? God's last judgment of Believers living at the time of the Great Tribulation will be of great magnitude. Then, after testing the Believers, God will move on to the dreadful, unequaled judgment of those who have never obeyed God's Word. This judgment of Non-believers is known as the Wrath of God.

Believers who are living at the time of the Great Tribulation can expect to face great persecution. The *signs*, as difficult as they may be, are reason for the Believer to rejoice because as they take place with precision, they point with equal accuracy to the coming of King Jesus at the Rapture. The Rapture will be the harvest and separation of the wheat, the true follower of Christ and the tares, those who claim to know Jesus but have not been born-again into the family of God. (Revelation 14:14-16; Matthew 13:24-30)

SIGN: PERSECUTION

Milner
"Persecution often does in this life, what the last great day will do completely, separate the wheat from the tares." [3]
(Matthew 13:24-30)

I would like to give you the opportunity to analysis the following Scripture. **Read** and **write** below your observations of what each verse tells us will take place during the Great Tribulation.

Matthew 24:9-14

> *9 "Then you will be arrested, persecuted, and killed. You will be hated all over the*
> *world because you are my followers. 10 And many will turn away from me and betray*
> *and hate each other. 11 And many false prophets will appear and will deceive many*
> *people. 12 Sin will be rampant everywhere, and the love of many will grow cold. 13 But*
> *the one who endures to the end will be saved. 14 And the Good News about the Kingdom*
> *will be preached throughout the whole world, so that all nations will hear it; and then*
> *the end will come."*

Your Observations:

v.9 ____

v.10 ____

v.11 ____

v.12 ____

v.13 ____

v.14 ____

Think about it
During this time, when the people of the world become the enemies of God, persecution will be a natural result for God's followers. What else could we expect? "There is a battle involved and thus it may often happen that one of God's perfect and upright servants suffers." [4]

As the Rapture approaches, conditions will become increasingly hostile toward those of us who follow Christ Jesus. In fact, Believers won't even be allowed to buy or sell anything during this time, because they will refuse to bear the mark of the Beast.

Revelation 13:16-17

> [16] *"He* [the False Prophet] *required everyone—small and great, rich and poor, free and slave—to be given a mark on the right hand or on the forehead.* [17] And no one could buy or sell anything without that mark, which was either the name of the beast or the number representing his name."

Revelation 14:9-13

> [9] *"Then a third angel followed them, shouting, 'Anyone who worships the beast and his statue or who accepts his mark on the forehead or on the hand* [10] *must drink the wine of God's anger. It has been poured full strength into God's cup of wrath. And they will be tormented with fire and burning sulfur in the presence of the holy angels and the Lamb.* [11] *The smoke of their torment will rise for ever and ever, and they will have no relief day or night, for they worshiped the beast and his statue and have accepted the mark of his name.'*
>
> [12] *This means that God's holy people must endure persecution patiently, obeying his commands and maintaining their faith in Jesus.*
>
> [13] *And I heard a voice from heaven saying, 'Write this down: Blessed are those who die in the Lord from now on. Yes, says the Spirit, they are blessed indeed, for they will rest from their hard work; for their good deeds follow them.'"*

What are two things Believers will refuse to do regarding the commands of the Antichrist and his cohort the False Prophet? 14:9 ____

____

What are two temporary consequences for this decision mentioned in 13:17 and 14:12? _____

____

What eternal consequence will Unbelievers suffer? 14:10-11 ______________________

____

Think about the meaning in 14:13. Notice the contrast between *"those who die in the Lord from now on"* compared to the death of those who worship the Antichrist in 14:10-11. God's ____________________ or God's ________________________.

For the Believer, *"Weeping may last through the night, but joy comes with the morning."* (Psalm 30:5) Satan instigated cruelty for a night, but at daybreak joy beyond expression!

C.S. Lewis "God, who foresaw your tribulation, has specially armed you to go through it, not without pain but without stain."

Isaiah 41:10 (NKJV) "Fear not, for I am with you; be not dismayed, for I am your God. I will strengthen you, yes, I will help you, I will uphold you with My righteous right hand."

SIGN: APOSTASY, BETRAYAL

Matthew 24:10 (NIV)

> *"At that time many will turn away from the faith and will betray* [hand over] *and hate each other."*

Believer, when you see your brothers and sisters in Christ turning from the true and only God to the imposter, the Antichrist, remember this is a sign Jesus told us about that points to His soon coming.

> "The Scriptures speak of widespread apostasy as being one of the earmarks of the period immediately preceding Christ's return. Apostasy is nothing new. There have been cases of 'falling away' from the faith throughout the history of the church. The apostasy of the final days, however, will be qualitatively different from, and more terrible than anything previously experienced. Paul calls it '*the apostasy*' of the end times. (2 Thessalonians 2:3)." [5]

Take a moment to consider the extreme pressures and difficulties that Believers will face during this time.

- A prominent leader of the world will come back from the dead, perform many miracles, signs and wonders and he will be worshiped by everyone (with the exception of you and your fellow Believers.)

  You will be considered an enemy for not worshiping this (supposedly) "great one."

- The mark of the beast will be the only means of belonging to the New World Order. Survival will literally depend upon this mark, and your refusal to receive the mark of the beast will set you at odds with the one world social and economic structure established at this time.

  You are considered an enemy to society.

- There will be wars and rumors of war, food shortages, hospitals will be overflowing with the sick, and you will insist that the only way to remedy the world situation is through Jesus Christ. As a result, you will be handed over to the authorities because you are a Believer, a follower of Jesus. Anyone who is not a part of the system will be considered an adversary.

  Jesus-lovers will not be tolerated!

Look at Mark 13:12-13 in the margin and take note of how extreme the betrayals will be. "*Brother will betray his brother ____________________, a father will betray his own child, and children will rebel against their parents and cause them to be ____________________.*

And everyone will hate you because you are ____________________________. But the one who endures _____________________________ will be ___________________.”

These tragic verses reveal to Christian parents the urgent need to teach their children such a great love for Jesus that they will never deny Him. May God help each parent to show their children how to live in the Spirit and set their minds on the things of the Spirit which are eternal and greater than this life. (Romans 8:5)

Mark 13:12-13 “Brother will betray his brother to death, a father will betray his own child, and children will rebel against their parents and cause them to be killed. And everyone will hate you because you are my followers. But the one who endures to the end will be saved.”

Does the last sentence in Mark 13:13 suggest that there will be survivors? ____________

Does the wording from the following “Rapture” passage in 1 Thessalonians 4:16-17, tell us that there will be survivors? ____________

> *“For the Lord himself will come down from heaven with a commanding shout, with the voice of the archangel, and with the trumpet call of God. First, the Christians who have died will rise from their graves. Then, together with them, we who are still alive and remain on the earth will be caught up in the clouds to meet the Lord in the air.”*

Yes, indeed. If it is God’s divine will, it is possible that you and I will be one of those who will live through this tribulation to be caught up together at the Rapture!

SIGN: FALSE TEACHERS

Matthew 24:11
“and many false prophets will appear and will deceive many people.”

Matthew 24:23-25 (NIV)
“At that time if anyone says to you, ‘Look, here is the Christ!’ or, ‘There he is!’ do not believe it. For false Christs and false prophets will appear and perform great signs and miracles to deceive even the elect—if that were possible. See I have told you ahead of time.”

False Christs and False Prophets

“Empty-headed credulity [gullibility] is as great an enemy of true faith as chronic skepticism. Christian faith involves the sober responsibility of neither believing lies nor trusting impostors. As false Christs and false prophets proliferate, so will their heralds. Jesus’ disciples must not be deceived, even by spectacular signs and miracles. The impostor is perennial [appearing again and again].

‘*If that were possible*’ refers to the intent of the deceivers: they intend to deceive, if possible, even the elect [true Believers]—though Jesus makes no comment on how ultimately successful such attacks will be. That Jesus tells these things in advance not only warns and strengthens His followers (see John 16:4) but also authenticates Him [as God]. (see Deuteronomy 13:1-4; John 14:29).” [6]

The plural will become singular in the fulfillment of Jesus' prophecy in Matthew 24. False Christs will culminate in *the* Antichrist and false prophets in *the* False Prophet. (Revelation 13) This powerful False Prophet will appear to be enlightened and will elevate the Antichrist, the False Christ, before the public to be worshiped as God.

End-time Deception

1 Timothy 4:1

> *"Now the Holy Spirit tells us clearly that in the last times some will turn away from the true faith; they will follow deceptive spirits and teachings that come from demons."*

By whom and how is this warning given? ______________________________
What will happen to some Believers? ______________________________
What will cause this? ______________________________
When does the Holy Spirit say this will happen? ______________________________

The influence of demons always causes immoral behavior and the worship of other things in the place of worshiping the one true God. The Lord Jesus warns us that this will be shamelessly increased during the end times; therefore, it is of utmost importance for us to heed this warning.

Throughout history, there have been false prophets who have deceived people with their teachings. Some have formed large churches, while others have formed religious sects or cults. Many followers of Jesus have mistakenly acknowledged false prophets as part of the body of Christ ignoring the fact that their doctrines differ from the Scriptures. These false teachers will grow in number both outside and within the body of Christ, ranging from teachers in a local church setting to very well known, influential leaders with huge followings. Beware of anyone with a new slant or new views, over-done emphasis, and interpretations of the Bible that confuse the Believer and contradict the Scriptures. The greatest of all false teachers will be *the* deceiver, the Antichrist.

Gary Inrig, in his commentary on the book of Judges, has done an excellent job of defining a number of these new views. These new views have had a devastating effect on both Unbelievers and Believers alike. After examining each one, ask yourself, "Have I been misled by any one of these and, therefore, weakened my faith?"

> "***Pluralism*** calls us to respect and accept all religious claims as equally valid. The most that can be said of Christianity is that it stands alongside other options and alternatives. In fact, the claim that Jesus, as God the Son, is the only way of salvation is viewed as bigoted and hateful.
>
> ***Relativism*** denies the validity of all absolute moral, spiritual, or philosophical truth claims and celebrates the beauty of diversity and the validity of virtually all life-style choices.

> ***Syncretism*** is an attempt to unify different forms of belief and practice. [Many people in the countries where we served as missionaries practiced their traditional Christian religion along with superstitions and witchcraft. This was considered to be acceptable.]
>
> ***Consumerism*** defines the individual as the center of the universe, with a commitment that lasts only as long as my needs are being met.
>
> These various forces combine to produce a cultural tsunami that moves with enormous power, carrying away old moral and spiritual landmarks." [7]

Man does not have the authority to decide what and how he chooses to believe in things pertaining to God. Any concept of God has to begin and end with God's own revelation of Himself to us through His Word, the Bible. Jesus wants us to be very aware of these false promoters of human words.

Think about it:
Jude 3 (NIV) tells us to "*contend for the faith that was once for all entrusted to the saints* [Believers]." *Contend* in the Greek language is *epagonizesthai* and means "to agonize earnestly", like a wrestler expending intense effort. We must take a stand *for* the truth and fight *against* false teaching that will challenge the faith of Believers during these end times when they are most vulnerable.

Jude 3 (NLT)
> ". . .defend the faith that God has entrusted once for all time to his holy people."

"*The faith*" mentioned in this verse refers to the body of truths contained in the Scriptures. God warns that no one can add to His Word by introducing additional doctrines, nor take away from it by taking liberties to exclude any of its truths. No one can make the Bible say what they want it to say. It is what it is! (Revelation 22:18-19; Deuteronomy 4:2; 12:32; Proverbs 30:5-6)

SIGN: WICKEDNESS, LAWLESSNESS

Matthew 24:12-13 (NASB)
> "*Because lawlessness is increased, most people's love will grow cold. But the one who endures to the end will be saved.*"

Deuteronomy 12:32
"So be careful to obey all the commands I give you. You must not add anything to them or subtract anything from them."

The Greek word used in this passage for the word *increase* is *plethuno. Plethuno* means "to multiply." That is to say, during these evil days, wickedness will drastically increase or radically "multiply." In our everyday understanding of the word, does *most* mean many or the majority? ____________________

> "Although end time lawlessness will certainly include the disregard for human laws, it will be manifested most vehemently in increased disregard for God's law. Evil will multiply so rapidly and unashamedly that many people who are initially drawn to the gospel will turn away from it because of the multiplied enticements of sin.

> The lawlessness will be diabolically aggressive and unabashed. Rather than trying to hide their sins, people will flaunt them, and such gross evil will draw many people, including some professed Believers, away from whatever interest in the things of God they may once have had." [8]

We can easily become discouraged by all the crime, violence, adultery, and crudeness that we are exposed to via television and other forms of social media, but as Believers, we should take heart. Jesus told us this is a sign; it's going to happen. Don't give up! We won't be here much longer!

THE FIFTH SIGN/SEAL OVERCOMERS, MARTYRS FOR THE FAITH

Sign: Matthew 24:9

"Then you will be arrested, persecuted, and killed. You will be hated all over the world because you are my followers."

Fifth Seal—Revelation 6:9-11

9 "When the Lamb broke the fifth seal, I saw under the altar the souls of all who had been martyred for the word of God and for being faithful in their testimony. 10 They shouted to the Lord and said, 'O Sovereign Lord, holy and true, how long before you judge the people who belong to this world and avenge our blood for what they have done to us?' 11 Then a white robe was given to each of them. And they were told to rest a little longer until the full number of their brothers and sisters—their fellow servants of Jesus who were to be martyred—had joined them."

It is very difficult to obtain exact numbers, but the following facts will give you a better picture of the suffering that God's people are facing in our world today. Notice the trend.

Edward Mote "My hope is built on nothing less than Jesus' blood and righteousness; I dare not trust the sweetest frame, but wholly lean on Jesus' name."

Fact: ". . .105,000 Christian martyrs in 2011, between 287 and 288 martyrs per day, twelve per hour, or one every five minutes." [9]

> "According to the World Evangelical Alliance, over 200 million Christians in at least 60 countries are denied fundamental human rights solely because of their faith. David B. Barrett, Todd M. Johnson, and Peter F. Crossing in their 2009 report in the International Bulletin of Missionary Research (Vol. 33, No. 1: 32), estimate that approximately 176,000 Christians were martyred from mid-2008 to mid-2009. If current trends continue, Barrett, Johnson and Crossing estimate that by 2025, an average of 210,000 Christians will be martyred annually." [10]

The martyrs in heaven referred to in the Fifth Seal, will be slain at the time of the Great Tribulation during the reign of the Antichrist. We can assume this because the Lamb, Jesus Christ, will open the seals referred to in Revelation 6 one by one in a deliberate, sequential manner. This is the fifth seal.

Why were they killed? (Matthew 24:9 and Revelation 6:9) ______________________________
and ____.

Why was the apostle John exiled as a prisoner to the island of Patmos? **Underline** the reason,and then write it on the lines below. See Revelation 1:9 in the margin.

____

and

____

Victorious Overcomers

In the Fifth Seal, we see that the martyrs were slain *"for the word of God and for being faithful in their testimony."* Revelation 12:11 reveals three significant ways in which the martyrs stay true to Jesus as victorious overcomers during this time of great persecution. Highlight the words of the following verse in your Bible, commit them to memory, and incorporate them into your "life belief system."

Revelation 12:11

- "They have defeated him [Satan] by the blood of the Lamb. . ."
  They identified themselves with Jesus and stood with Him in the power and victory of His blood shed upon the cross. Satan is conquered, they were victorious.

- . . .and by their testimony.
  They believed and experienced the transforming message of the cross, and for their love of Jesus they proclaimed their salvation with all boldness. Even though Satan rose up in fury against them, he could not prevail against their victorious spirit. Satan is the loser. The martyrs are the ultimate winners.

- And they did not love their lives so much that they were afraid to die."
  "They would give up anything but Christ. They cared more for His honor and truth than for all their possessions, or all their status before men—even their own lives! It was apparent by their actions that nothing was worth more to them than Christ's presence in their lives. They would rather die than deliberately bring shame to His name. That is the way to overcome Satan. It means that you have not only exercised faith in the blood of the cross, and love towards others who are bound by Satan's lies, but you are also laying hold of the hope of a Christian—the fact that death is rendered meaningless because you have been promised an inheritance beyond." (–Ray Stedman, *Authentic Christianity*) [11]

The threat of death is a tool that Satan uses to render the Believer helpless. It instills a fear of being put to death. However, when Jesus died and rose again, the devil's work was completely destroyed. (1 John 3:8) The grave cannot hold Believers captive. They will rise again. By acknowledging the reality of the resurrection, the ultimate sacrifice of death becomes insignificant to Believers. A Believer's only goal is to know Christ and to make Him known. Satan stands defeated before those who are *"more than conquerors."* (Romans 8:37)

Revelation 1:9
"I, John, am your brother and your partner in suffering and in God's Kingdom and in the patient endurance to which Jesus calls us. I was exiled to the island of Patmos for preaching the word of God and for my testimony about Jesus."

1 John 3:8
"But the Son of God came to destroy the works of the devil."

Romans 8:35 (NKJV)
"Who shall separate us from the love of Christ? Shall tribulation, or distress, or persecution, or famine, or nakedness. or peril, or sword...or things to come?"

BELIEVERS STILL PREACH THE GOSPEL!

Matthew 24:14

"*And the Good News about the Kingdom will be preached throughout the whole world, so that all nations will hear it; then the end will come.*"

The church of Jesus Christ is very close to accomplishing this. Under great duress God's people are still reaching out to the lost by preaching His Word. What will happen when this is accomplished? ____________________

Think about it:
Jesus tied His Great Commission command to the end times. "*make disciples of all the nations. . .and lo, I am with you always, even to the end of the age.*" (Matthew 28:19-20 NKJV)

How long can Jesus' followers count on His presence as they obediently preach the Word of God and maintain their testimony? ____________________ (even during the Great Tribulation.)

As Believers, we must unflinchingly hold on to the grace of God with such deep conviction that our souls will remain untouched by the pollution of the spirit of the age that presses upon it. Our Savior perfectly demonstrated this for us, and we are to follow His example: "*Now it came to pass, when the time had come for Him* [Jesus] *to be received up* [depart for heaven], *that He steadfastly set His face to go to Jerusalem". . .*to His crucifixion. (Luke 9:51 NKJV) We too must be characterized by an unwavering dedication to be used as a witness of Christ's Word and of His Kingdom.

There will be Believers who die during the Great Tribulation, but they will be victorious in their death. They will have marched through the battlefield on earth, and will have gained their triumphant entrance into heaven. Then, from heaven's shores, they will cheer you on as you desperately, but resolutely maintain your testimony. The multitudes in heaven shout to you, "Hang in there!". . . "Be faithful!". . ."He is coming!"

And then the last Sign
As Believers, we will be a light shining in great spiritual darkness. We will be witnesses for our Lord Jesus despite hardship and very difficult conditions. But when that last person hears, believes, and receives Christ as his Savior, His Body, the church, will be completed! At that moment, the Rapture will take place! Jesus will remove His people from the earth! It reminds me of Noah and the ark. After the eight obedient people had safely entered the ark, "*Then the Lord closed the door behind them*" and the flood of judgment came upon the earth. (Genesis 7:16)

Immediately After The Tribulation Of Those Days...... The Lamb Broke The Sixth Seal

The world shakes violently. . .earthquake!
Look the sun has turned black!
The moon! It is red like blood!

The sky is splitting apart!
THERE HE IS!. . .IN THE SKY!

The followers of the Antichrist raise their eyes to heaven. . .they see the face of Him who sits on the throne. . . and begin to mourn. . .the Wrath of God and of the Lamb has come. . .who can escape His fury!

You see Jesus coming on the clouds
with Power and Great Glory!
Magnificent! Overwhelming! Blessed is He that comes in the Name of the LORD!

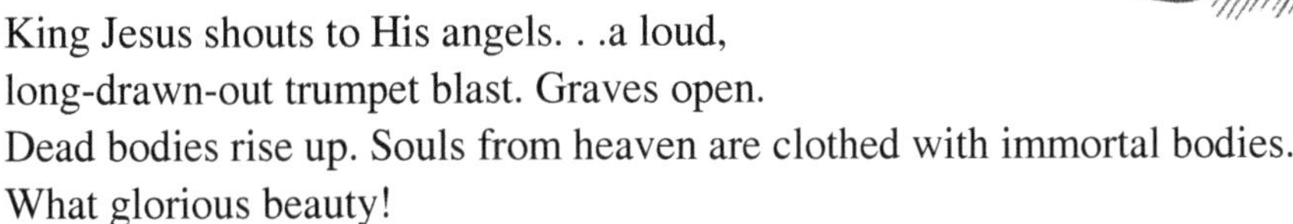

King Jesus shouts to His angels. . .a loud, long-drawn-out trumpet blast. Graves open.
Dead bodies rise up. Souls from heaven are clothed with immortal bodies.
What glorious beauty!

Myriads of angels harvest the earth. The great gathering together of Jesus' chosen people. . .from the four winds, from the farthest part of earth to the farthest part of heaven.
Suddenly your body is transformed! You begin to rise!

Isaiah 35:10 (NIV) "They will enter Zion with singing; everlasting joy will crown their heads. Gladness and joy will overtake them, and sorrow and sighing will flee away."

This is the RAPTURE. . .long awaited. . . KING JESUS has come!

The Sixth Seal—Revelation 6:12-17; Matthew 24:29-31; Mark 13:27 (NKJV)

Look on **Timeline One** (located at the end of Part One of this book) to see where the Rapture will occur and write EVENT **4** on the line by the asterisk (*_4_). Remember, only Believers will participate in this Event.

JESUS CHRIST EVER-PRESENT HELP

Psalm 46:1

LESSON **5A**

JESUS CHRIST THE GLORY OF ISRAEL
Luke 2:32

"Ichabod" your Shekinah glory has departed but in triumph, "chabod," your glory will return.
I Samuel 4:21 and Ezekiel 43:4

EVENT 3

PLOT 3: ISRAEL AND THE WORLD SYSTEM OF THE ANTICHRIST

Write Plot 3 and the title of this lesson on the 3rd line below:

Plot 1: The World System of the Antichrist

——————————————————————→

Plot 2: The Believers

——————————————————————→

——————————————————————→

RAPTURE

Review Plot 3 in Lesson 2.

After returning to the U.S.A. from the mission field and entering into retirement, our alarm clock died. We found a new one that met our specifications, so we bought it. Returning home, we read the information booklet that came with the clock which referred to it as an atomic clock. Puzzled, we looked at each other and wondered what in the world we had bought? As we continued reading, we learned that this little atomic clock was controlled by "something somewhere" in another part of the country, and it would automatically reset itself for daylight savings. A bit "out-of-touch" as a result of living overseas for so long we were intrigued by this idea, especially with daylight savings only a few days away. When the night of daylight savings arrived, I sat fascinated and waiting to see the thing change at two o'clock in the morning. It didn't change right on the hour so about 2:10 I sleepily glanced away, and yes, you guessed it! When I looked back at it, sure enough, our atomic clock had adjusted itself for daylight savings. Oh well. It struck us as quite remarkable, and a little eerie, knowing that "something out there" was controlling our little alarm clock.

Many consider the prophecies found throughout Scripture concerning Israel to be "God's prophecy-clock." In other words, we will know we are in the last days when certain biblical prophecies concerning Israel begin to take place, and when they do, we know all end-time prophecies will be set into motion. At the precise moment, much like our atomic clock, the "something out there" will activate the "prophecy-clock." Israel will be "reset" and each of the end-time prophecies will occur at their divinely appointed time.

To this day, Herb and I set all of our clocks and watches to our little atomic clock because it keeps the exact time. In the same way, it is imperative for you to set your "clock" to God's "prophecy-clock," so you and God are in sync as you begin to deal with end-time events. Every time Herb and I see something disturbing in the news, we remember one verse in particular that helps us keep our "clocks" set to God's "clock."

Luke 21:28 (NKJV)

> "*Now when these things begin to happen, look up and lift up your heads, because your redemption draws near.*"

End-Time Events Are Beginning To Happen

Prophecies concerning the Jews are presently being fulfilled. Also, prophecies concerning the World System of the Antichrist are currently being fulfilled. A new world order (globalization) is currently forming, and the world as we know it is rapidly moving toward a one world system of government. This system is paving the way for the Antichrist to rule the world.

In this lesson we will study:

- Israel—The Focus of Bible Prophecy
- Israel's Lost Opportunity
- The Most Tragic Day in History
- The Wandering Jew
- Men and Women Sent From God—The Righteous Among the Nations

ISRAEL—THE FOCUS OF BIBLE PROPHECY

Israel is crucial to end-time Events because Bible prophecy is centered on the Jewish people. Ultimately, Jesus will give Israel a very prominent place in His Thousand-Year Kingdom. God's plan is for the twelve apostles to rule Israel under the kingship of Christ during His earthly kingdom. (Matthew 19:28; Luke 22:28-30) However, the Jews rejected Jesus as their divine King at His First Coming, and sad to say, the Jews still do not recognize Jesus as their Messiah today. So, how will God's plan be accomplished?

Isaiah 43:14-15 (NKJV) "Thus says the Lord, your Redeemer, The Holy One of Israel…I am the Lord, your Holy One, The Creator of Israel, your King."

To understand the relationship between God and His chosen people, the Jews, we must look back into Israel's tragic history, and follow this relationship to the present time.

It would be impossible to effectively depict the whole spectrum of the suffering that Israel has experienced throughout history in the few pages of this lesson. The Jewish people were given a place of great privilege, but "greater privilege brings greater responsibility, and, in the case of failure, greater judgment." [1] However, we take great pleasure in the fact that the Jewish people that are living today are very close to the time of their redemption. A time that once seemed to be a nearly invisible pin-point of light at the end of a very long, dark tunnel of time.

Hebrews 10:31(NKJV) "It is a fearful thing to fall into the hands of the living God."

As God's chosen people and special treasure, the Lord's desire was to bless and prosper the Jewish nation so that they would manifest His glory to all nations. In the Old Testament, just before entering the promised land of Israel, God gave the Jewish people some significant instructions on obedience. They were told to go to the center of the land to a beautiful valley between Mount Ebal and Mount Gerizim. This was where Abraham, the father of the Hebrew nation, had built his first altar to the Lord 600 years earlier. Half of the people were to stand before Mount Gerizim to proclaim God's blessings upon them for their expected obedience, and the other half were to stand before Mount Ebal to proclaim God's curses upon them for their possible disobedience. The priests, along with the ark of the covenant, which represented God's presence, were to stand in the middle of the valley.

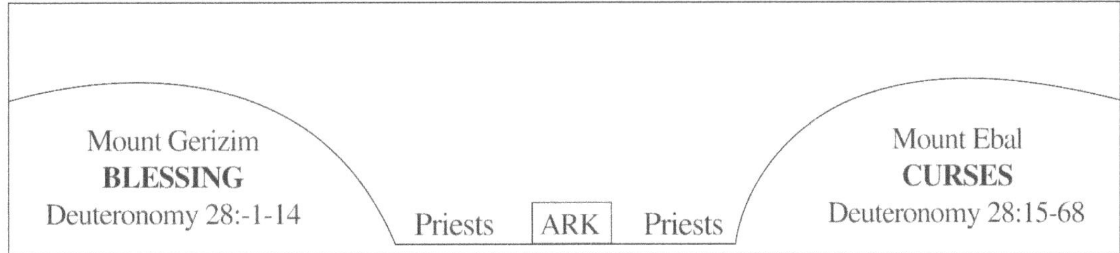

Deuteronomy 26:17-19

> *"You have declared today that the LORD is your God. And you have promised to walk in his ways, and to obey his decrees, commands, and regulations, and to do everything he tells you.*
>
> *The LORD has declared today that you are his people, his own special treasure, just as he promised, and that you must obey all his commands. And if you do, he will set you high above all the other nations he has made. Then you will receive praise, honor, and renown. You will be a nation that is holy to the Lord your God, just as he promised."*

Read Joshua 8:30-35 and Deuteronomy 27 and 28. These Scriptures describe this dramatic event. Deuteronomy 28 is a soul stirring chapter. Will Israel choose blessings or curses? Unfortunately, as Halley's Handbook points out, "the whole future history of the Hebrew Nation is outlined" in the curses because every curse was fulfilled in the Jews' distant future. How did this come to be?

ISRAEL'S LOST OPPORTUNITY

A question. In the New Testament, Jesus presents Himself as the Messiah and their divine King to the Jewish nation by His words and miracles. What opportunity is offered to them?

The great opportunity presented to the Jewish nation was to believe and receive Jesus as their Redeemer and King. The religious leaders of the time should have been able to have recognized the fulfillment of Old Testament prophecies in the person of Jesus. Furthermore, Jesus appeared as the Promised One at the precise time specified by the prophet Daniel. (Daniel 9:24-26)

A question. Having read the obedience-blessings and the disobedience-curses in Deuteronomy 27 and 28, how do you think God should have immediately responded toward His people, the Jews, at the specific moment they rejected and crucified Jesus His Son? ________________

My initial response to this question would read something like this: God should have responded to the Jews' denial of Christ by immediately pouring out His wrath upon them. Nevertheless, the depth of God's grace, patience, and mercy cannot be fathomed or measured. The heavy hand of the living God is checked, in reality, delayed! Why was God's wrath halted?

THE MOST TRAGIC DAY IN HISTORY

Let's imagine that you and I are a part of each of the following scenes. Place yourself with me in these moments of history.

The year is A.D. 30. We enter Pilate's courtroom. The Jewish leaders, the priests and the elders have brought Jesus to trial. As we hurry in a little late, we sense deep animosity and burning rage among those that form the crowd.

Pilate is saying, "*What shall I do, then, with Jesus who is called the Christ?*"

They all answered, "*Crucify Him!*"

"*Why? What crime has He committed?*"

They shout all the louder, "*Crucify Him!*"

Pilate is getting nowhere, and we see he is losing control of the crowd. In a gesture to absolve himself, Pilate turns to one side and washes his hands in a basin of water for everyone to see. Then, above all of the shouting, Pilate proclaims, "I am innocent of this man's blood. It is your responsibility!"

Angrily the people respond, "*Let His blood be on us and on our children!*" (Matthew 27:25 NIV) We can't help but notice that these men are involving a whole generation!

We hold our breath waiting for the curses of Deuteronomy 28 to immediately fall upon the crowd. What greater crime or act of disobedience could they commit? But, as we wait, nothing happens and things proceed to get worse.

Luke 17:25 "But first He must suffer terribly and be rejected by this generation."

We stand near the cross. It is nearly unbearable to listen to the jeers, mocking, and insults hurled at Jesus as He agonizes on the cross. The religious leaders scornfully shout for all to hear, "He saved others, but He can't save Himself! Let this Christ, this King of Israel, come down now from the cross, that we may see and believe." We hear even those who are being crucified on either side of Jesus heap insults on Him. (Matthew 27:44) The Roman soldiers also draw closer to mock Him.

Now, surely now, the curses will begin to take their course. The heavy hand of God in judgment will come upon them! Yes, we see the sky is growing dark as midnight. Beware! The wrath of God is ready to fall. . . but it doesn't. Why?

You and I look in amazement at each other as we listen to Jesus painfully speak from the cross. It is at this critical moment that we begin to understand. We hear Jesus' quiet, powerful prayer to His heavenly Father, *"Father, forgive them, for they do not know what they are doing."* God hears His beloved Son, and the people receive a respite, a temporary suspension from impending judgment from God. Even though they are the agents of the most tragic day in history, the nation of Israel has been given one last opportunity to get things right.

Acts 28:26-27
"Go and say to this people: when you hear what I say, you will not understand, when you see what I do, you will not comprehend. For the hearts of these people are hardened, and their ears cannot hear, and they have closed their eyes—so their eyes cannot see, and their ears cannot hear, and their hearts cannot understand, and they cannot turn to me and let me heal them."

We are sitting in a room in a rented house located in the city of Rome. The apostle Paul is being held prisoner here for preaching the gospel. The year is A.D. 60. A large group of Jews has responded to Paul's invitation to hear the good news that the Messiah has come. He tells them about Jesus' ministry, His death, and His resurrection that occurred 30 years earlier. From morning until evening, we watch as Paul methodically goes through the Old Testament Scriptures, teaching and attempting to convince these Jews about Jesus. Some of the Jews believe, others do not; their arguing with one another is going nowhere.

You look at me and ask, "How is it that these Jews can't seem to see the truth that you and I as non-Jews see so clearly?"

Paul makes a final statement to the group by quoting from Isaiah 6:9-10. This Scripture describes the Jewish people as being so blind and hard of heart, that they have closed their minds and are unable to turn to Christ Jesus for salvation. Paul says these astonishing words to them:

Acts 28:28 (NIV)

> *"Therefore I want you to know that God's salvation has been sent to the Gentiles and they will listen!"*

We look at the crowd, then at Paul, and then back at the crowd surrounding him. How are they going to respond? This is a moment of great consequence—a crucial, pivotal moment of decision. But, one by one, the Jews begin to leave, and we can hear their voices fading away as they continue their meaningless debate.

Rejection not Reception
"He came into the very world he created, but the world didn't recognize him. He came to his own people, and even they rejected him."
John 1: 10-11

It is important for us to understand the significance of what has just taken place. Do you see a turning point? How does Paul say that the Gentiles will respond in Acts 28:28? ____________
What is the meaning of the words in this verse that Paul spoke to the Jews? ____________________
____

These words of Acts 28:28 bear great significance for two reasons.

- **First**

Who did the Jews say were responsible for the spilling of Jesus' blood at Jesus' trial in Pilate's court? ____

Peter and Paul preached until their deaths, which occurred sometime during the period of A.D. 64—68. The other apostles also proclaimed the gospel for close to 40 years. During this time, many of the men who stated, "*Let His blood be on us and on our children*!" would have died. It should be noted that the majority of the children of that generation also rejected God the Son during those 40 years, and like their fathers, faced no immediate consequences from God for their fathers' terrible pronouncement.

God's wrath did not instantly come down upon that generation as a direct result of Jesus' prayer to His Father as He hung on the cross. What was it that Jesus prayed? ____________________

____

Acts 28:28 is significant, because up until that point in time, the whole post-crucifixion generation of Jews was given the opportunity to believe in Christ the Messiah and repent of their sin. This would have made it possible for them to have taken their appointed place as God's chosen people in leading the nations of the world to God.

- **Second**

The book of Acts covers a period of almost 40 years. During this time, the gospel was presented first to the Jews, pressing them to believe. However, as was the case with the Jews living in Rome, only a few believed, while the majority did not. It should be noted that multitudes of Gentiles who heard the Gospel during this same period of time responded by believing the message of redemption in Jesus Christ.

Therefore, God chose to give this decree through Paul: "*Salvation has been sent to the Gentiles and they will listen!*

Acts 28:28 is extremely significant because this passage marks the moment in time in which God set aside the chosen nation of Israel and entrusted to non-Jewish Believers the honor of delivering God's message of salvation to the nations.

In their rejection of God's Son, the Jewish people turned their backs on what it meant to be a Jew, the chosen people of God. They lost God's blessing, and after nearly forty years had passed, God's wrath and the curses of Deuteronomy 28 became an imminent reality.

Again, let's imagine that you and I are a part of the following scene.

We are in Jerusalem standing in the midst of ashes, desolation, ruin, and death. This is the location where the great second temple once stood in all its grandeur. This temple symbolized the presence of God among His chosen people, but now the temple proper had been burned and destroyed. The year is A.D.70, and it has been 40 years since Jesus was crucified. The last 3 ½ years have been nothing short of horrific. We are told that this destruction came about as the result of a Jewish revolt against Rome. Temple authorities refused to offer sacrifices on behalf of the Romans and their emperor, and this, among other things, angered the Roman Emperor Vespasian. Therefore, he sent his son Titus to destroy the Jewish nation and their temple. Over 1,000,000 Jews perished and 95,000 were taken captive. Somehow, even though one out of every three Jews were killed, they managed to remain in Palestine until A.D. 135 when the Romans removed most all the Jews from their God-given land. This dispersion of the Jews is called the *Diaspora* which means "the body of Jews living among the Gentile nations."

Yes, the curses and judgment of God have indeed fallen upon His apostate people. *"Strike the Shepherd, and the sheep will be scattered."* (Zechariah 13:7) Jesus made it clear when He, the Shepherd, was stricken not only His disciples but also the *"lost sheep of the house of Israel"* would be scattered. The disciples were shortly recalled to Himself, Israel was not. (Matthew 26:31; Mark 14:27)

In summary, the Jews missed two opportunities: receiving Christ as their Messiah and King and the honor and privilege of taking the message of salvation through Jesus Christ to the nations.

It takes just one misguided generation to bring irreversible ruin to a nation.

McCandlish Phillips expresses this dereliction of duty so well.

> "It is no small thing for a Jew to refuse to be a Jew. It is to receive a commission from God and then tear it up and throw it aside as a thing of no value.
>
> God's intention of calling the Jews to obey Him and to receive His blessing was that the whole world might thereby see that it is good to serve the God of Israel. Instead, the Jews have given the world an entirely different demonstration. They have demonstrated the *curse* when they ought to have demonstrated the *blessing*. They have removed themselves as a people from the covenant-blessing pronounced by Moses and have placed themselves instead under the covenant-curse pronounced by Moses." [2]

This being said, we must remember that "*Christ died for us*" (Romans 5:8 NKJV), "*us*" meaning everybody. I, as a sinner, together with the Jews, am responsible for Jesus' death on the cross. The blessings and the curses also apply to me. If I receive Christ as my personal Savior, I receive blessings and eternal life! If I remain in my sin, I receive curses and judgment! The Word of God is spoken to all people. We have been forewarned.

"Chosen-ness"

I am amazed that as Believers, we can experience the same "chosen-ness" from God that the Jews did. Jesus said: "*You did not choose me, but I chose you and appointed you to go and bear fruit—fruit that will last.*" (John 15:16 NIV)

You are chosen. The God of Israel is the God of ____________________________ (write your name in that blank).

As a Believer, you have been singled out and chosen of God. How does this make you feel?_____

____

What are you chosen for and commissioned to do according to John 15:16?______________

____

My answer to this question goes back to what was covered in Lesson 2, God's plan for Abraham under Plot 3. I too am chosen by God, to love Him fervently as my God, and to be a spokesperson for Him. Perhaps, if I, like Abraham, do and be what God told Abraham to do and be so that "*All the peoples on earth will be blessed through you,*" just maybe some of the people of my generation will be blessed through me.

THE WANDERING JEW

A child never likes to hear a parent say: "I told you so." Do you think the people standing on Mount Gerizim and Mount Ebal really understood that God truly meant what He was telling them? After reading Deuteronomy 28, we can safely come to the conclusion that they certainly did. How much more clear could it be?

The word "curse" in the Hebrew language comes from the word *qalal*, which means "the opposite of blessing, it is the lowering to a lesser state, to be despised, to be little, to be insignificant, and to be of small worth." [KW]

Seven times we read in Deuteronomy 28:15-68. . ."until you are destroyed," "until you perish," or "until you are ruined." Through the centuries, generation after generation has died without knowing their Messiah. The hostility and prejudice against the Jews known as anti-Semitism was also born during this time. This was the lamentable "I told you so" of God.

The History of Israel

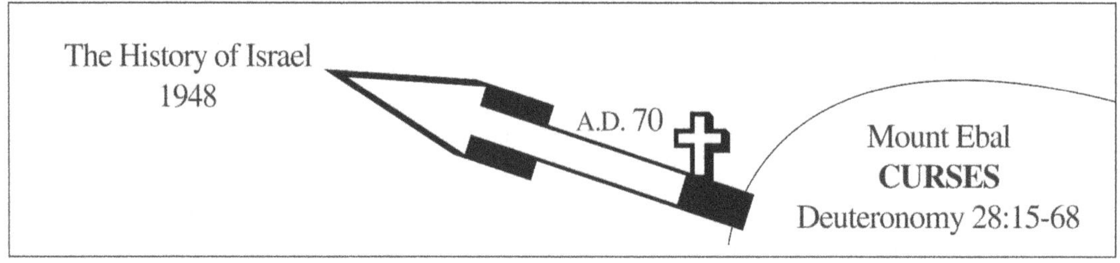

As a nation, the Jewish people ceased to exist in A.D. 70, practically speaking, and altogether in A.D. 135. Israel not only lost its status as a sovereign state, but it also lost its territory. Remarkably however, they never lost their nationality. They became unwelcome, homeless wanderers in many different nations for centuries, assimilating into many different cultures and languages, but always remaining Jewish and maintaining strong ties to their origin.

By studying the history of Israel from year 70 to 1948, it becomes evident that the curses of disobedience recorded in Deuteronomy 28 were prophetic, an exact historical outline of the tragic future that the Hebrew nation would face. Every vivid detail of this prophecy has been fulfilled. Amazing! What credence we should give to God's Word! It is absolutely trustworthy!

A Minimal Description of Maximum Suffering

- Deuteronomy 28:64
  "For the Lord will scatter you among all the nations from one end of the earth to the other."

With the exception of about 100 years during the Crusade Period, Jerusalem has been controlled by the Mohammedans since A.D. 637. In 1917, during the First World War, England defeated the Turks which brought the city under the control of a Christian nation.

The Crusades (1096 – 1270) was a holy war with papal sanction, involving military expeditions in which European Christians (in name only) attempted to recover the Holy Land (Israel) from the Muslims. "The Crusaders committed indescribable atrocities against Jewish communities, including torture, rape, and looting. As the Crusaders traveled toward the Holy Land, they destroyed whole communities of peaceful Jews." [3] All in the name of obtaining the "blessing" of God on their mission.

- Deuteronomy 28:65 (NIV)

  ". . .among those nations you will find no repose, no resting place for the sole of your foot."

Let's pause a moment to think what you would do if you were expelled from the country where you live? Where would you go? What would you take with you? How would you provide food, clothing, and shelter for your family?

About 16,000 Jews were expelled from England in 1290, and their descendants didn't return until the 17th century. In 1306, Jews living in France were arrested, their possessions were confiscated, and they too were expelled from the country. In 1492, the same year that Christopher Columbus discovered America, 200,000 Jews were expelled from Spain. Furthermore, in 1496, persecution and massacre followed the expulsion order of all Jews from Portugal. Jews were literally banished from dozens of European cities. [4] The Jewish people truly had no resting place.

- Deuteronomy 28:37 (NIV)

  ". . .you will become a thing of horror and an object of scorn and ridicule to all the nations where the LORD will drive you."

In 1215 Pope Innocent III "confirmed the shameful isolation of Jews from society at large, requiring among other things, that they wear a special badge [a yellow circle]. Sadly the Jews were increasingly confined to living in ghettos." [5] This was effective throughout the entirety of Europe.

- Deuteronomy 28:65-67 (NIV)

  "There the LORD will give you an anxious mind, eyes weary with longing, and a despairing heart. You will live in constant suspense, filled with dread both night and day, never sure of your life." "In the morning you will say, 'If only it were evening!' and in the evening, 'If only it were morning!'—because of the terror that will fill your hearts and the sights that your eyes will see."

The Jews have suffered persecution at the hand of so-called Christian nations for centuries. I use the term Christian as a system in name only, far from the biblical meaning of the word. Discriminatorily, the Jews were stereotyped as "Christ killers" and were directly targeted by three of the most devastating evils that have ever been invented by man, the Inquisition, pogroms, and the Nazi Holocaust, all of which were initiated by Christian nations so-called.

The Inquisition "a former tribunal in the Roman Catholic Church directed at the suppression of heresy." D

The Inquisition

The Inquisition began in the 12th century. "At this trial, the inquisitor had complete control as judge, prosecutor, and jury." [6] During this time, all Jews were considered heretics. The main intention of the Inquisition was to either convert the heretics to "Christianity" by torture, or to deem them irreconcilable. Irreconcilables would be turned over to the secular authorities for life imprisonment or to be burned at the stake. "In twelve years the Inquisition had condemned 13,000 *marranos* [Jews who were referred to as "swine"] for the secret practice of Judaism. In total, the Spanish Inquisition punished 341,000 people, more than 32,000 of whom were burned to death." [7]

Pogrom "an organized and often officially encouraged massacre or persecution of a minority group, especially one conducted against the Jews." D

Pogroms

Thousands of Jews were massacred or suffered the abuse of anti-Jewish riots in dozens of cities throughout Europe. I will give you only one example. "The Cossacks carried out pogroms against the Jews in 1648-49 without precedent for depravity or savagery. Thousands were tortured in the synagogues and decapitated with butcher knives. Entire communities were devastated in this wave of terror, and the Jews of Eastern Europe fell into despair." [8]

The Nazi Holocaust The Holocaust was the means by which Nazi Germany attempted to exterminate the European Jews and other "inferior people" during World War II. The Nazis called this program of genocide their "Final Solution."

The Nazi Holocaust

Hitler was obsessed with the idea of a perfect race. He attempted to eliminate all the "undesirables" within his reach in order to Germanize Europe and to develop it into a superior or master race.

> "The eradication of the Jewish race would be the act of social purification necessary to restore the uncorrupt past. . .The infamous concentration camps, originally created to break the spirits of Nazism's opponents, had even more ominous overtones for the Jews. In 1940 a new type of camp was developed, the largest being Auschwitz in Poland. Here the Nazis put into operation the 'final solution,' the extermination of the entire Jewish population of Europe. Men, women and children were transported to these 'death factories' and in a cold-blooded, calculated manner beaten, starved, shot, worked to death, utilized in medical experiments, and gassed. Reasonable estimates put the number of Jewish deaths in the 'holocaust' at six million." [9]

Deuteronomy 28:49 (NIV)

> *"The Lord will bring a nation against you from far away, from the ends of the earth, like an eagle swooping down, a nation whose language you will not understand, a fierce-looking nation without respect for the old or pity for the young."*

After reading this verse from Deuteronomy 28:49, it seems significant that the *eagle* was the Nazis' emblem.

Make no mistake

Even though God's wrath fell upon the Jews, He has never condoned or approved of man's vile, evil acts towards the Jews. In fact, Genesis 12:3 reads as follows, *"I will bless those who bless you* [Israel], *and whosoever curses you I will curse."* This verse is repeated many times throughout the Old Testament.

MEN AND WOMEN SENT FROM GOD

The Garden of The Righteous

Before we continue, we will pause to see something important and very beautiful—a garden called the Garden of the Righteous. This garden is a memorial located in Jerusalem at Yad Vashem.

Yad Vashem was established to memorialize each Jew murdered in the Nazi Holocaust during World War II. More than two-thirds of the names and life stories of the 6,000,000 victims have been recovered and are given a place in the Hall of Names. Thus, each precious victim has their *name* and *a place* in Israel in lieu of the unmarked graves they never had.

The words Yad Vashem literally mean "a place and a name" taken from Isaiah 56:5.

> "*And to them will I give in my house and within my walls a memorial and a name* [a yad vashem]. . .*that shall not be cut off*."

The following story was told to Jose Rodriguez, who had the opportunity and privilege of visiting this memorial. This story took place during the Holocaust and conveys the Jewish meaning of Yad Vashem, as taken from Isaiah 56:5

> "In the midst of the horrors of the Shoah, the Holocaust, a young man watched as his father was made to board one of the transports [taking him to a death camp.] As he did so, his father said to him: 'Remember, you have *a name* and a family, and you have *a place* in this world: *Eretz Yisrael*. And you must take care of your little brother.'
>
> You see, the purpose of Yad Vashem is not so much to remember the Shoah [Nazis Holocaust], but to remember its victims and its heroes. Its purpose is to give 'a name and a place', a memorial, to all those millions of known and unknown persons robbed of their very identities, and to affirm that even in death they have 'a place in this world'."

Golda Meir, Foreign Minister and Prime Minister of Israel compared the Righteous Among the Nations to drops of love in an ocean of poison.

In this same unique place in Jerusalem is another memorial named the Garden of the Righteous. The Righteous Among the Nations is a title used by the State of Israel to describe non-Jews who risked their lives, putting themselves and their families in danger, during the Holocaust to save Jews from extermination by the Nazis. These brave people are referred to as righteous gentiles by the Israeli. The Garden of the Righteous was created by Israel to commemorate the lives and acts of these valiant righteous gentiles.

A person who is recognized as Righteous Among the Nations is awarded a medal with his or her name on it, a certificate of honor, and the privilege of having their name added to the Wall of Honor located in the Garden of the Righteous at Yad Vashem.

I cannot help but include the names of just a few of the heroes in the company of the Righteous Among the Nations. [10] Some rescuers saved thousands, while others, just one precious person or a family. Some righteous gentiles will forever remain anonymous.

Righteous Gentiles

The Netherlands, Gertruida Wijsmuller-Meier, helped save about 10,000 Jewish children from Germany and Austria. Most of their parents died in extermination camps.

Germany, Oskar Schindler, a businessman who saved more than 1,000 Jews by employing them in his factory.

Switzerland, Carl Lutz, helped save tens of thousands of Hungarian Jews.

Portugal, Aristides de Sousa Mendes, issued 30,000 visas to people escaping the Nazis. Also, Carlos Sampaio Garrido, sheltered about 1,000 Jews in safe-houses in Budapest and gave them Portuguese documents to leave the country.

Republic of China, Ho Feng-Shan, provided thousands of visas to Jews in need during his tenure in the embassy of the Republic of China to Vienna during World War II.

In total, 24,811 (as of January 2013) men and and women from 45 countries have been recognized as Righteous Among the Nations, representing over 10,000 authenticated rescue stories. Our hearts swell with pride because of them.

"To reduce the holocaust to statistics is another way of dehumanizing the victims. Each one has a face, a unique human being." [11]

As I write these words, I am looking at a photograph taken in 1945 of a deep, open mass grave at Bergen-Belsen. The pit is filled with hundreds of rigid, starved bodies piled one on top of another. Each one of these innocent Jews had *a name* and *a place* that they called home in this world, but both were ripped away from them. Today their *names*, and some their pictures, adorn the memorial in Yad Vashem. They have *a place* in *Eretz Yisrael*, the Land of Israel, their homeland.

Believer, no matter what happens to you, always remember that you have *a name* and you have *a place* in Jesus' Kingdom, which no man can never, ever take away from you.

Unbeliever, you may have a name and a place somewhere in this world, but you do not have a name or a place in Jesus' Kingdom. Thankfully, God gives you opportunities every day to be born-again into His Kingdom.

JESUS CHRIST THE GLORY OF ISRAEL

Luke 2:32

LESSON **5B**

JESUS CHRIST THE GREAT PROPHET TO ISRAEL
Deuteronomy 18:15 Acts 3:22-23 John 6:14

Jesus is God's last word to Israel and to all men.

EVENT 3

PLOT 3: ISRAEL AND THE WORLD SYSTEM OF THE ANTICHRIST

THE DRY BONES LIVE

What treasures we have in the Old Testament. God gives the prophet Ezekiel a vision that transcends the history of Israel of the Old Testament and looks on to the future age of the end times. To be exact, it relates to the wandering Jew of the generations beginning with the destruction of their nation until the times in which you and I live. During that time the Jew lived as unburied bones scattered throughout the nations. The vision expresses the astounding re-birth of the nation Israel taking place in the formative years of the World System of the Antichrist. Please read Ezekiel 37 in your Bible.

Ezekiel 37:11-14

> 11 *Then He said to me* [Ezekiel], *"Son of man, these bones represent the people of Israel. They are saying, 'We have become old dry bones—all hope is gone. Our nation is finished.* 12 *Therefore, prophesy to them and say, 'This is what the Sovereign LORD says: O my people, I will open your graves of exile and cause you to rise again. Then I will bring you back to the land of Israel.* 13 *When this happens, O my people, you will know that I am the LORD.* 14 *I will put my Spirit in you, and you will live again and return home to your own land. Then you will know that I, the LORD, have spoken, and I have done what I said. Yes, the LORD has spoken!'*

At this point in time, how do the people of Israel see themselves? (verse 11) ____________

____

From bones *"scattered everywhere"* in verse 2, God changes the metaphor to the nations representing ______________________ of exile. (verse 12)

Imagine a map of the world. Now imagine seeing each nation open up like a grave with old dry bones coming to life and rising out of them. Visualize the bones becoming complete bodies, people; they all start moving toward the land of Israel.

What is God's intention for these people? Verses 13-14 ____________________________

____

Which verses of this prophecy have already been fulfilled? __________________________
A predetermined day called "that day" has dawned, and a word comes forth from the throne of God in heaven.

Isaiah 11:11-12 (NIV)

> *"In that day the LORD will reach out His hand a second time to reclaim the remnant of His people. . .He will raise a banner for the nations and gather the exiles of Israel; He will assemble the scattered people of Judah from the four quarters of the earth."*

Amos 9:15 (NIV)

> *"I will plant Israel in their own land, never again to be uprooted from the land I have given them, says the LORD your God."*

The heavy hand of the Lord upon Israel is lifted. God's curse has run its course. He has determined that the time has come to prepare His people to receive spiritual salvation and to renew His covenant relationship with them. It is also God's time to prepare the chosen people for their ultimate goal: to rule, along with the non-Jewish Believers under the kingship of Jesus during His Thousand-Year Kingdom on earth and beyond into eternity. End-time prophecy takes on new significance as God takes the first step toward this ultimate goal for His people. Against all odds, God works a miracle, the re-creation of the State of Israel.

We are going to see God planting an unswerving resolve in the hearts of the Jewish people to return to their homeland. I cannot overstate just how significant the return of the Jewish people to their homeland is for the initiation of end-time prophetic Events. "God's prophecy-clock" is ticking.

In this lesson we will study:

Three Fulfilled Prophecies Concerning Israel
Five Unfulfilled Prophecies Concerning Israel

THREE FULFILLED PROPHECIES CONCERNING ISRAEL

As you study the fulfilled prophecies, carefully observe the ways in which God's dealing with the Jews has changed. Decades of alienation has changed to a very obvious demonstration of His protection and favor towards them. At this time, Israel has not yet turned to God for their redemption, but they are oh so close!

As you study the following prophecies concerning Israel, write *yes* with the *date* in the spaces provided.

1. The Jews will return to their homeland. Fulfilled ________ date ________
2. Israel will become a nation. Fulfilled ________ date ________
3. Jerusalem will return to the sovereignty of Israel. Fulfilled ________ date ________

Many Believers, who saw these events take place, are still living, myself included!

FULFILLED PROPHECY ONE: THE JEWS WILL RETURN TO THEIR HOMELAND

Even though the Jews have been oppressed and scattered throughout the nations of the world, they have been divinely preserved as a people group by the very God they do not understand. Long before the Jews became a homeless, wandering people, God declared He would return the Jews to their homeland, to once again become a sovereign nation. (Isaiah 11:11-12; Ezekiel 36-37; Amos 9:15; Romans 11: 25-27)

The Jewish people have survived. They are going home!

GOING HOME!

Let's try to identify ourselves with the Jews at this important turning point in their history. Nearly 2,000 years have passed since the Jews lost their homeland and sovereignty. At this point in our lesson, God's chosen people are on their way back to their homeland and statehood. Picture it this way.

What if all the people in the U.S.A. were conquered by another nation? Many of them were killed, and the rest of them were either taken to the land of their victors or forced to flee to different parts of the world. Generations came and went until almost 2,000 years had passed. All the while, these Americans were never permitted to return in mass. In fact, many efforts were made to exterminate them, because they were so despised. But then, world authorities declared that American's could return to their former homeland. Many obstacles were put in their way making it very difficult for them to return, but they finally prevailed.

How do you think you would feel under these circumstances? Imagine arriving at a port city with only one suitcase in hand (if you are fortunate). You are arriving at what was formerly known as the United States of America, along with thousands of other fellow, but unfamiliar Americans. These Americans are coming from a hundred different nations, and most of them do not even speak the English language. Upon arriving, you find that unfriendly people are living in your ancient homeland. Likewise, hostile neighboring nations want to see you dead. What if this was your reality? How would you feel?

A National Home

In 1922 after World War I, the League of Nations approved Palestine as the National Home for Jews. At that time, some Jews returned to Palestine.

On November 29, 1947, at the end of World War II, the United Nations approved the division of Palestine to allow for a Palestinian and a Jewish State. This was God's doing. As a result of God's promptings, many weary, brokenhearted Jewish people from across the world returned with great effort to the very homeland God had promised them in the book of Genesis.

The most unusual passport ever issued

A passport is a document issued by governments to certify the identity and citizenship of an individual. This document allows individuals to travel abroad. In this case, displaced Jews did not have a national government, and therefore, no passport, and no legal documentation to migrate to Israel.

At the end of World War II, the British governed Palestine. So what was Britain to do with the hundreds of thousands of improperly or undocumented Jews seeking to enter Palestine?

"During the restrictive period of the British Mandate, [many Jewish] immigrants were supplied with passports that read:" [1]

> "Mr. __________________________ has been found suitable by the Jewish Community of Palestine for repatriation to the Holy Land. Its authority:
>
> 1. Ezekiel 37:25: "And they shall abide in the land I have given Jacob my servant. . .and they shall abide therein forever more."
> 2. Isaiah 54:7: "With great mercies shall I gather thee."
> 3. The Balfour Declaration, issued November 2, 1917.
> 4. The League of Nations Mandate for Palestine.

This is truly remarkable! Have you ever heard of a passport authorized by God's Word! Well, you have now. Thousands upon thousands of Jews returned to their homeland coming from as many as 100 different nations, with as many languages and customs. Very few had a passport of any kind, and the British issued severe restrictions on Jewish immigrants due to hostility and pressure from Arab countries. In fact, many Jewish refugees were actually turned away from the very shores they so yearned to reach; they were returned to camps set up for displaced persons in Europe. Nevertheless, secret networks among the Jews in Palestine were organized making it possible for thousands of belabored Jews to arrive to their new home. . .and freedom.

THE *ALIYAH*. . .THE RETURN

The return to Palestine (Israel) was called the *aliyah*, which means "to ascend" in English. Whenever the Bible says "*going up*" to Jerusalem or to Mount Zion it is because Mount Zion is in Jerusalem, and is spiritually the highest place that a person can go. Whenever anyone goes to Jerusalem, they always *go up* to Jerusalem *(Isaiah 2:2-3; Luke 2:41-42; 19:28; John 2:13; 5:1, Acts 25:1).* Jews who immigrate to Israel from any country in the world are said to be making *aliyah* to the land of Israel. They are "*ascending*." [2]

The spiritual understanding of Aliyah

In a spiritual sense, the term *aliyah* is symbolic of a person ascending to a higher place in God, attaining a deeper knowledge and revelation of God than he had previously experienced. Believers "are on a spiritual journey, departing from the ways of the world and entering into the ways of God. As we grow spiritually, one step at a time, we desire to finish the course which God has laid before us and ascend to the eternal city of God, Mount Zion." [3] God is drawing

Israel back to Himself. First, God brings Israel to their promised land, and then He will redeem them and place His Spirit within them.

Psalm 24:3-4 (NIV) "Who may ascend [aliyah] the hill of the Lord? And who may stand in His holy place? He who has clean hands and a pure heart, who does not lift up his soul to an idol or swear by what is false."

On average, 23 Israelis per hour (both during the day and at night) arrived in Palestine in the first three years (1949-1951). Far from a complete list, here are a few facts pertaining to Jews who *made aliyah* or returned to Israel after World War II. The following is accumulated information from multiple sources across the years.[4]

100,000
The Youth Aliyah began in 1934 by Henrietta Szold who was originally from Baltimore. The mission of the Youth Aliyah was to bring back "the sons of Israel," homeless children from as many as 72 different countries (most of their parents were killed in the holocaust during World War II.) In December 1960, a twelve-year old girl named Shiarifa arrived at the airport in Lidia. She was the 100,000th child to be rescued by the Youth Aliyah. Upon her arrival to Israel, she was met by various officials along with a woman by the name of Ethel Mossek, who as a little girl was the very first child to be rescued by Henrietta Szold.

100,000
By the end of 1948, 100,000 individuals being held in displaced persons camps throughout Germany, Austria, and Italy returned to Israel.

30,000
In 1948, 30,000 "illegal persons" who had been held in British prison camps in Cyprus from 1939 to 1948 returned to Israel.

47,000
From 1949-1950, the entire Jewish community in Yemen "*made aliyah.*" These Jews are said to be one of the oldest Jewish communities in the world having gone to Yemen in 625 B.C. to escape the captivity of King Nebuchadnezzar (at the time when God gave Daniel the end-time prophecies that we are studying). For centuries, these Jews had lived in virtual slavery. In fact, they were not permitted to leave the country until 1949. In order to leave Yemen, the government officials forced them to either forfeit their property or sell it for very little money. Additionally, these very religious Jews were forced to pay taxes on their precious Old Testament scrolls which they refused to relinquish, as well as a tax for each person.

These Yemeni Jews literally dragged themselves for hundreds of kilometers to the British Protectorate in Aden. A 75 year old man along with his 106 year old father walked 160 miles to the airport in Aden where Israelis were airlifting their Jewish brothers back to Israel. C-54 Skymasters, flown by American pilots, who were sent by a Jewish organization in North America, took these valiant Jews home to Israel.

Other Jews include **350,000** from Romania (1948-1980); **All** from Yugoslavia; **36,000** from Bulgaria (1948-1949); and **65,000** from Poland (by 1956); and **225,000** from Arab countries (same time period.) In the 1970s **200,000** Soviet Jews arrived in Israel and between 1990-1995 another **650,000**.

An Ethiopian official in the court of the queen of Ethiopia, was introduced to Christ and baptized by Philip after having gone to Jerusalem to worship. (Acts 8:26-40) Could he have belonged to the Beta Israel Jews?

125,000

Between the years 1984 – 2013, 125,000 Black Ethiopian Jews known as Beta Israel (the House of Israel) were airlifted in several operations to Israel. On May 24, 1991 during Operation Solomon, 14,324 Ethiopian Jews threatened by rebel groups taking over the country, were airlifted in just 36 hours on 34 airplanes stripped of their seats to accommodate maximum capacity. Planning to carry 760 passengers, one Boeing 747 actually transported 1,122 people. (This set a record!) These Ethiopian Jews are thought to have established themselves in Ethiopia around the time of King Solomon of Israel, almost 1,000 years before Christ. In August 2013 as the final two flights arrived in Israel with 450 people, the last of this ancient segment of Jews, the chairman of the operation said: "We are closing a 3,000-year-old circle." [5]

2,300

From 1953–1956, 2,300 Jews from India returned to Israel. The skin of these Jews had turned dark like that of the Indian people, as their ancestors had been there since the 4th century. These Jews were isolated or "out of touch" with Jews that lived in other countries. However, they felt moved to go up to Israel as a result of an irresistible feeling that the Messiah would be coming soon.

2,000

Chinese Jews wanted to go up to Israel. Ten of them successfully arrived, but five of the ten were very sick. Consequently, the others were not permitted into the country. But such was the spirit of *aliyah*, that Israeli doctors were sent to the Institute of Tropical Diseases in London to find a remedy for this sickness. Afterward, several doctors were sent to China in an attempt to cure the Jews who were sick. Eventually, all 2,000 went up to Israel. Read Isaiah 49:12 (NKJV and NASB) *Sinim* refers to a distant oriental region thought to be China.

Isaiah 49:12 (NKJV) "Surely these shall come from afar; Look! Those from the north and the west, and these from the land of Sinim [China]."

You may be wondering what the Israelis did with the thousands of orphaned children mentioned above. Special towns were constructed for these children. One of these well-known children's towns was Ben Sheman, located near the Lidia airport. Dr. Siegfried Lehmann, director of this unique town, informed a commission from the United Nations in 1947: "Our children learn to weave, to sew, and to spin yarn; they raise sheep and learn welding. They have come from a great number of prison camps and camps for displaced persons. They trust no one. Under Hitler's regime, in order to survive, they learned to steal and to lie. It takes some of them three months, six months, or a year to learn to trust us." [6] The 1948 battle for statehood roared all around this special town but it was never attacked.

Others reported that children placed in large camps after World War II were commonly "put to bed with a slice of bread to hold. If they wanted more to eat, more was provided, but this particular slice was not to be eaten—it was just to hold." [7] By grasping the bread in their hands, it became possible for these fearful children to fall asleep. They were assured that there would be something to eat when they woke up in the morning.

The Jewish people have survived and have *ascended* to their homeland to now gain sovereignty.

Fill in the blanks on the page of this lesson: FULFILLED PROPHECIES CONCERNING ISRAEL

1. The Jews will return to their homeland. Fulfilled __Yes__ date __1945 onward__

What attribute of God most impressed you as you read this account of the Jews returning to their homeland? ______________________________

FULFILLED PROPHECY TWO: ISRAEL WILL BECOME A NATION

May 14, 1948

At dawn of May 14, 1948, the flag at the British headquarters in Jerusalem was lowered. Since 1917, upon defeating the Turks during World War I, Palestine had been governed by a British Mandate. But in May of 1948, General Sir Alan Cunningham boarded the last British ship setting sail from Palestine, leaving the Israelis, Palestinians, and surrounding Arab nations, to the inevitable event of war.

At exactly 4:00 p.m., on May 14, 1948, in the exhibition hall of the art museum in the costal city of Tel Aviv (at the time, Jerusalem was under Arab siege and cut off to the Jews), a small man stood before his peers. Outside, a great crowd had formed, and men with Sten guns watched the streets and the roofs. David Ben-Gurion called the meeting to order. The crowded audience of 200 people stood and sang "Hatikvah," the Jewish national anthem, accompanied by the Palestine Symphony Orchestra. For seventeen minutes, David Ben-Gurion read the Declaration of Independence of the State of Israel in Hebrew from the scroll they had endorsed. What a breathtaking moment when this future prime minister read the following words, "We. . .hereby proclaim the establishment of the Jewish nation to be known as the State of Israel." There was much applause and heart-felt weeping.

Deuteronomy 33:29 (NASB) "Blessed are you, O Israel; Who is like you, a people saved by the Lord, who is the shield of your help, and the sword of your majesty! So your enemies shall cringe before you, and you shall tread upon their high places."

Twenty years later in 1968, "once again in this historic room, with the paper he read then, before him, Ben-Gurion, now 81 and retired after serving as prime minister of Israel for most of its life, remembered that day: 'My head was not on the proclamation but on the war that was coming. I saw people dancing, but I could not dance. I knew by 12:00 a.m. they [the Arab nations] would be coming. At 4:00 a.m., they woke me up, and I talked [by radio] to America, and then, as I was speaking, they started bombing, and I told America the attack had started.'" [8]

May 15, 1948

"At 5:00 p.m. [one hour after the reading of the establishment of the State of Israel] invasion columns of six Arab nations [Egypt, Saudi Arabia, Trans-Jordan, Iraq, Syria, and Lebanon] outnumbering Israel's forces ten-to-one could be seen on the move. The next morning the first Arab bombers hit the Tel Aviv airport at 5:25 a.m. on May 15, 1948. But a year later, in spite of 6,000 dead, the loss of the Jewish quarter in Old Jerusalem [including the Temple Mount], and Jordan's seizure of the West Bank, Israel had clearly survived its birth. Isolated kibbutz [agricultural] settlements had somehow held off whole battalions of attackers, and Jewish forces actually added about 1,000 more square miles to their territory than the United Nations plan envisioned." [9]

"The Bee Battle," one of God's many miracles.

Deuteronomy 7:20-23 (NIV)

> *"Moreover, the LORD your God will send the hornet among them until even the survivors who hide from you have perished. Do not be terrified by them, for the LORD your God, who is among you, is a great and awesome God. The LORD your God will drive out those nations before you, little by little. . .But the LORD your God will deliver them over to you, throwing them into great confusion until they are destroyed."*

In an attempt to keep the peace between the Jews and the Arabs, during the British tenure, the British limited the Jews to very few weapons. When the well-armed Arab nations struck the Israelis, the Jewish people were armed with little more than broom sticks and anything else that they could find to utilize as a weapon: but God supplied them with all that they needed.

> The Arab legions had modern arms; coming from the east they bore down on the city of Tel Aviv. Thousands of swarms of bees had their nests in the forests of Petah Tikvah, a suburb of the city. When the Arabs entered the forest, hundreds of millions of very angry bees rose up and attacked the army from one extreme to the other. The soldiers threw down their weapons, to fight off the bees. They finally had to throw down all of their equipment to run as fast as they possibly could with this vast army of bees in angry pursuit. Without weapons the Israelis easily won that victory. The Israelis also claimed the much needed discarded weapons. [10]

This is very interesting in light of Deuteronomy 7:20-23 where God told the Israelites to not be afraid when it was time for them to enter the Promised Land to conquer the wicked, idolatrous nations. Is this déjà vu or what?

But, the story doesn't end there.

> Another miracle that brought down the northern enemy forces made up of soldiers from Syria, Iraq, and Lebanon was disease. On the eve of the "Battle of the Bees," this huge army was camped in the Jordan Valley when dysentery hit them. They were so weak that they couldn't withstand the Israeli forces that came against them armed with, you guessed it, the equipment thrown off by the Arabs that were trying to outrun the bees. The Israelis drove their enemy back to where they had come from, capturing village after village, and obtaining great quantities of abandoned provisions and ammunition. [11]

The Jews were not only in their homeland, but they became the free nation that God had promised to establish for them. He performed miracle upon miracle to preserve His people. This is very important because it reveals that God, from this war forward, began to protect and fight for this nation to accomplish His eternal plans for them.

Fill in the blanks on the page of this lesson: FULFILLED PROPHECIES CONCERNING ISRAEL

2. Israel will become a nation. Fulfilled ___Yes___ date ___May 14, 1948___

What attribute of God most impressed you as you read this account of Israel becoming a nation?

FULFILLED PROPHECY THREE: JERUSALEM WILL RETURN TO THE SOVEREIGNTY OF ISRAEL

The following verse is the key end-time prophecy concerning Jerusalem. **Circle** the word "until," which refers to the timing.

Luke 21:24

> *"They* [Jews] *will be killed by the sword or sent away as captives to all the nations of the world. And Jerusalem will be trampled down by the Gentiles* [non-Jews] *until the period of the Gentiles comes to an end."*

This verse is referring to the destruction of Jerusalem by the Roman Empire in A.D. 70. Since this event took place, Jerusalem continued to remain under the control of Gentile nations. The Romans called the land Palestine until it became Israel in 1948.

After World War I, Palestine became a British Mandate, and it was populated by both Jews and Arabs. "In 1919, under a ruling by British officials in Palestine, Jerusalem regained its status as a capital city. During the following three decades, numerous Jews, whose ancestors had been barred from the city, settled in and around Jerusalem. A new city, whose population was predominately Jewish, was constructed west of the site of the old city. Following the Arab-Israeli War of 1948-49, the new city was allotted to the Jews, while the old city remained in Muslim hands." [12] At the time of their declaration of statehood, only a small, isolated Jewish population lived in the Old City. Both the Old City and the Temple Mount were under Jordan's control from 1948 until 1967.

The Six-Day War

Isaiah 31:5

> *"The LORD of Heaven's Armies will hover over Jerusalem and protect it like a bird protecting its nest. He will defend and save the city; he will pass over it and rescue it."*

Another war began on June 5, 1967. "What were the odds against Israel? A quick glance at the figures—46 million in the surrounding Arab countries, 97 million total [includes Arab countries not bordering Israel], against 2.6 million Israelis—might lead one to believe that the Arab states would have little trouble in overwhelming Israel, except that twice before, in 1948 and 1956, they had tried to do so and failed." [13]

The Six-Day War was outstanding in its brilliance. The retreat of the enemy following their defeat was so successful that the United Nations called for a cease-fire to stop the Israelis' victorious advance into the Arab countries that had attacked them.

Jerusalem at last

On June 7, 1967 "Israeli commandos prepared a dawn attack into the Old City itself [eastern Jerusalem]. Most of the Jordanian troops defending it had slipped away, leaving only sniper resistance as one Israeli unit entered through St. Stephen's Gate. By 10:00 a.m., the conquerors stood before the great boulders of the Wailing Wall, the only remnant of the Second Temple [the temple during Jesus' time on earth], that for 1,897 years has been the symbol of Jewish national hope—and despair. For all the sensational, and far more important military victories won in Sinai, nothing so elated the Israelis as the capture of the biblical city of Jerusalem. Said the tough commando leader who took the Wall: 'None of us alive has ever seen or done anything so great as he has done today.' And there beside the Wall, he broke down and wept." [14] The Defense Minister Moshe Dayan said, "We have returned to our holiest of holy places, never to depart again." [15]

The prophecy of Luke 21:24 has been fulfilled.

Fill in the blanks on the page of this lesson: FULFILLED PROPHECIES CONCERNING ISRAEL.

3. Jerusalem will return to the sovereignty of the Jews. Fulfilled <u>Yes</u> date <u>June 7, 1967</u>

Notice where 1948 and 1967 are located on **Timeline One** (located at the end of Part One of this book.)

The fulfillments of these three prophecies bear great importance. Their fulfillment means that the end-time prophecies have indeed been set in motion. After almost two thousand years, the prophecies concerning the questions asked by Jesus' disciples in Matthew 24:3 are now beginning to take place.

Matthew 24:3

> "*Tell us, when will all this happen? What sign will signal your return and of the end of the world?*"

Some of us were living at the time that these three prophecies were fulfilled. Just think about what this means for all of us who are living during this time in history! Do you understand the significance of these events? When God gives a prophecy, it will be fulfilled literally. For years, many Bible scholars thought that these prophecies pertaining to Israel were merely figurative, not literal. They just couldn't understand how the Jews would ever return to their homeland.

We must never limit God by our imperfect and finite knowledge. God literally fulfills all Bible prophecy. In our study of prophetic Events, we must remember this no matter how shocking the prophecy seems to be. Prophecies concerning Israel are being fulfilled against all odds. As Believers, we can rest assured that all end-time prophecies will be fulfilled, and they will be fulfilled in a relatively short period of time once they begin. The fact that God fulfills biblical prophecy is why we enjoy studying it.

FIVE UNFULFILLED PROPHECIES CONCERNING ISRAEL

Watch for the following prophetic events concerning Israel that have **not** yet been fulfilled (as of 2015) but will be fulfilled during the World System of the Antichrist. The first four will take place within a 3 ½ year period. As these events take place, keep track of them by utilizing the following spaces.

1. Antichrist will confirm a covenant (treaty) with Israel Fulfilled ________ date ______

2. Israel's temple will be rebuilt Fulfilled ________ date ______

3. Invasion of Gog's army Fulfilled ________ date ______

4. Salvation of the Jews Fulfilled ________ date ______

5. Christian Jews will be persecuted for Jesus' sake Fulfilled ________ date ______

Believers will see all of these events take place, with the exception of numbers 4 and 5. When number 4 takes place, we will be too busy being raptured to watch the salvation of the Jews take place, although we know it will be happening. Likewise, the persecution of the Christian Jews will take place after we are in heaven.

UNFULFILLED PROPHECY: THE ANTICHRIST WILL MAKE A COVENANT (TREATY) WITH ISRAEL

The Antichrist will confirm a covenant (treaty) with Israel (and others) that will last for a period of seven years. (Daniel 9:27) This covenant will take place approximately 3 ½ years before the Rapture occurs. Because the nations of the world are at that time, embroiled in wars, Israel lives under the constant stress of danger. This covenant will be made solid and lasting by the ruler of the world, the Antichrist, and will guarantee conditions of peace and safety for Israel.

Look for the location of the seven-year covenant on **Timeline One** (located at the end of Part One of this book).

UNFULFILLED PROPHECY: ISRAEL'S TEMPLE WILL BE REBUILT

The temple where Jesus taught was destroyed by Titus and his Roman army in A.D. 70. The following end-time Scriptures speak of this future temple: Daniel 9:27; Matthew 24:15; 2 Thessalonians 2:4; Revelation 11:1-2. Scripture indicates that the end-time temple will be built in the same location where the temple that was destroyed in A.D. 70 once stood.

The Problem
The Dome of the Rock, an important Muslim holy site built by Caliph Abdel Malik in A.D. 691, is located on the Temple Mount and supposedly sits on the exact site where the Jewish temple

once stood. The southern part of the Temple Mount is also home to the al-Aqsa mosque the third most holy site.

The city of Jerusalem is perhaps the oldest and best-known of the religious cities on earth. In fact, there are three major world religions that have religious sites in Jerusalem: Judaism, Christianity and Islam.

As previously mentioned, the Muslims, who tend to be very hostile toward the Jews, have two religious buildings on the Temple Mount. Likewise, Roman Catholics, Orthodox Christians, and others have many ancient religious sites located in and around Jerusalem. They too are very protective of their sites. Israel still does not have a temple as their central place of worship even though the Temple Mount has been in Israel's possession since 1967. This is because the Jewish people made a promise to protect all the religious sites in Israel regardless of their religious ties. Muslims were given custody of the Temple Mount creating an impossible situation for the Jewish people to rebuild their temple.

What do you think needs to happen in order for Israel to rebuild their temple? ____________

____

A solution

Among the many possible answers, perhaps you came up with the most logical, convenient, and simple solution: the three major religions that have religious sites in Jerusalem could make an agreement that would give permission for the Jews to rebuild their temple.

Initially, this sounds like a fairly easy and adequate solution to the problem. However, due to the unique circumstances and tensions that exist in Jerusalem, this solution would require an authoritative figure that would be respected by all three religions to oversee or administer such a treaty.

The authoritative figure would need to call on all of the religious and political leaders involved to make a treaty that would allow for the rebuilding of the Jewish temple on the Temple Mount. The treaty would not only result in the rebuilding of the temple, but it would also need to bring about changes or effects that would benefit each of the entities involved in the treaty.

Daniel 9:27 (NIV) "He [the Antichrist] will confirm a covenant with many [Jews and others] for one 'seven' [seven years]."

This agreement explains the treaty referred to as "*a covenant*" that the Antichrist confirms with Israel and the others in Daniel 9:27.

How is that for a solution? A solution will in fact become a reality. Perhaps this will occur similarly to the way just described.

One more thing, what if one of these leaders secretly decides that he wants the Jewish temple as his throne from which to rule the world? Now, that is something to think about!

Clarence Wagner believes the restoration of the temple is near:

> ". . .all the signs are there that the temple's time is near. And the main sign is that this city [Jerusalem] is once again a thriving metropolis—over [800,000] people and the capital of a rebuilt, restored Jewish State, just as the prophet said it would be in the last days. So the day of His return has got to be drawing very, very near." [16]

When the Israelis rebuild their temple, they will revert back to their old sacrificial system, as they still do not believe that Jesus is the Christ, the perfect sacrifice for all sin. **Look** for the location of "Temple Rebuilt" on **Timeline One** (located at the end of Part One of this study book).

UNFULFILLED PROPHECY: INVASION OF GOG'S ARMY

About half way through the period of the seven-year covenant between Israel and the Antichrist, Israel will experience an invasion that will far surpass any invasion that they have thus far experienced. Ezekiel 38 and 39 describe this horde of warriors that will attack Israel from practically every direction of the compass. It is necessary for you to read these two chapters in your Bible to get the full picture.

In an atmosphere of presumed peace through the treaty, the Jews will rebuild their temple. However, shortly after the temple is rebuilt, Israel will be invaded by a coalition led by a man named Gog. Ezekiel 38:9 portrays this gigantic army like advancing storm clouds covering the land of Israel. The Jews will helplessly watch as their inevitable annihilation approaches.

Zechariah 12 makes clear God's great victory over these invaders of Jerusalem. *"On that day I will make Jerusalem an immovable rock. . .the people living in Jerusalem remain secure. . .the Lord will defend the people of Jerusalem. . .on that day I will begin to destroy all the nations that come against Jerusalem."* (Zechariah 12:3, 6, 8-9)

At the eleventh hour, King Jesus will appear in the clouds of heaven at the Rapture. The catastrophic events of Ezekiel 38:19-23 describe God's destruction of Gog's army and seem to coincide with the physical disturbances of the 6th Seal which also describes the Rapture. (Revelation 6:12-17)

Ezequiel 38:20

> *"All the people on earth—will quake in terror at my presence. Mountains will be thrown down; cliffs will crumble; walls will fall to the earth."*

Revelation 6:12, 14-15

> *"There was a great earthquake. . .and all of the mountains and islands were moved from their places. . .everyone. . . cried to the mountains and the rocks, 'Fall on us and hide us from the face of the one who sits on the throne."*

The Rapture will be accompanied by God's fury against the armies of Gog. The Lord will cause a massive earthquake centered in Israel. (Ezekiel 38:19). Great panic and confusion will spread throughout the ranks of the enemy causing them to attack one another. This will result in great bloodshed. Deadly diseases, flooding rains, great hailstones, and burning sulfur will rain down on

Ezekiel 39:7-8
"In this way, I will make known my holy name among my people of Israel. I will not let anyone bring shame on it. And the nations, too, will know that I am the Lord, the Holy One of Israel. That day of judgment will come, says the Sovereign Lord. Everything will happen just as I have declared it."

these armies until they are completely destroyed. Due to their sheer size and great numbers, it will take seven months to bury the dead, and their weaponry will provide Israel with seven years of fuel.

This magnificent demonstration of God's power that will be shown during the appearance of Christ at the Rapture and the destruction of Gog's army, will serve as a warning to the people of the earth. You would think that it would deter earth people from continuing down the path to destruction that it will have chosen. But tragically, even though the nations will stand in awe of the greatness of God, they will not bend their knee to Him. Their loyalty will lie with the evil one, the Antichrist. Therefore, they must drink from the cup of God's wrath that will soon fall upon them.

What a different response from Israel!

Through all of the death and destruction raining down on Gog's huge army, the people of Israel will look up and see their Savior, Jesus Christ, in the clouds of heaven at the Rapture. All of the calamity taking place around them will pale in comparison to the light of His glorious face. Israel will repent of their sin and centuries of unbelief.

Ezekiel 39:22 (RSV)

"The house of Israel shall know that I am the LORD their God, from that day forward."

The salvation of Israel at the climax of the invasion of Gog, places this invasion at the time of the Rapture. We will be studying the timing of Israel's salvation and its connection to the Rapture in the next lesson.

Three invasions of Israel

There are three invasions of Israel in the last seven years. This can be very confusing. They are:

- Gog and his armies
- Antichrist and his armies
- Antichrist and the Ten Kings and their armies at Armageddon

The following diagram clarifies when each invasion takes place. The Scriptures describe the invasions.

LAST SEVEN YEARS

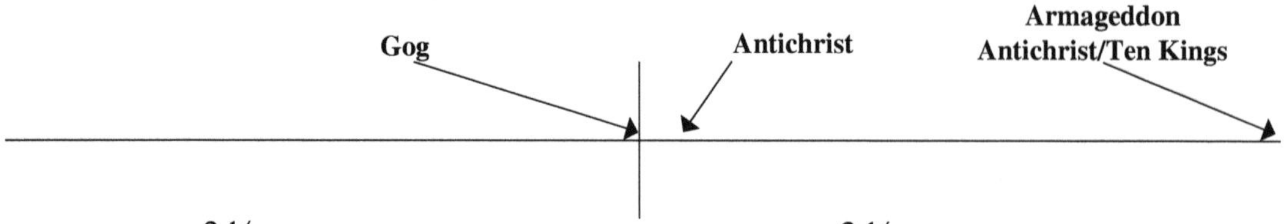

Gog **Antichrist** **Armageddon Antichrist/Ten Kings**

3 ½ years		3 ½ years
Ezequiel 38 and 39	Zechariah 13:8-14:2	Zechariah 14:3-15
Zechariah 12	2 Thessalonians 2:4	Revelation 19:11-21
		Revelation 16:17-21
		2 Thessalonians 2:8

A helpful clue to differentiate between these three invasions is to take notice of what happens to the city of Jerusalem in each case.

- **Gog:** The people of Jerusalem remain secure (Zechariah 12:1-9). No destruction to Israel (Ezekiel 39:4- 5). The Lord destroys Gog's army (Ezekiel 38:17-22).
- **Antichrist:** Jerusalem will be overcome and fall into the hands of the enemy (Zechariah 14:1-2).
- **Antichrist and Ten Kings at Armageddon:** Jerusalem will be delivered, the enemy will be totally destroyed (Zechariah 14:3-15).

UNFULFILLED PROPHECY: SALVATION OF THE JEWS.

Ezekiel 36 and 37 prophesy the return of the Jews to their homeland where the Lord will restore them spiritually. **Underline** the "I wills" of God in the following verses.

Ezekiel 36:24-27

> 24 *"For I will gather you up from all the nations and bring you home again to your own land.*
> 25 *Then I will sprinkle clean water on you, and you will be clean. Your filth will be washed away, and you will no longer worship idols.* 26 *And I will give you a new heart, and I will put a new spirit in you. I will take out your stony, stubborn heart and give you a tender, responsive heart.* 27 *And I will put my Spirit in you so that you will follow my decrees and be careful to obey my regulations."*

This Scripture is speaking of the spiritual new birth that awaits the nation Israel. Circle the sentence indicating that their salvation from sin will occur after they are restored to their homeland. God will wash away their sin and give them a new heart. He will place His Holy Spirit within them, and the Holy Spirit will give them the power they need to live a life that will glorify Him.

This is the Jew's promise from God. It will be fulfilled. When this takes place, Israelis will be spiritually prepared for their future ministry during Christ's Thousand-Year Reign on the earth.

Find "Israel Saved" on **Timeline One** (located at the end of Part One of this book). If you are a Jew, you may write your Event **3** on the line by the asterisk (* _3_).

UNFULFILLED PROPHECY: CHRISTIAN JEWS WILL BE PERSECUTED FOR JESUS' SAKE.

These newly, born-again Jewish Christians will not be Raptured, but they will remain on the earth as witnesses for Jesus for approximately 3 ½ years. Shortly after the defeat of the armies of Gog at the Rapture, the Antichrist will break his covenant with the Jews and will invade Jerusalem. The Antichrist will ruthlessly persecute the Jews, but they will remain faithful and true to Jesus. At the end of this period, Israel will be delivered from persecution by King Jesus at His Second Coming. Then, at that time, Israel will be exalted and will reign with King Jesus in His kingdom.

In the following Scripture, the Lord is speaking to the apostle John. **Circle** the numbers indicating the amount of time that the Christian Jews in Jerusalem will be victimized at the hand of the Antichrist.

Revelation 11:2-3

> *"But do not measure the outer courtyard* [of the rebuilt temple], *for it has been turned over to the nations. They will trample the holy city* [Jerusalem] *for 42 months* [3 ½ years]. *And I will give power to my two witnesses, and they will be clothed in burlap and will prophesy during those 1,260 days* [3 ½ years]."

During these 3 ½ years, two-thirds of the Jewish nation will die. The remaining one-third will remain under harsh oppression due to the Beast and his followers.

Zechariah 13:8

> *"'Two-thirds of the people in the land will be cut off and die,' says the Lord. 'But one-third will be left in the land.'"*

Daniel 7:25

> *"He* [the Antichrist] *will defy the Most High and oppress the holy people of the Most High. He will try to change their sacred festivals and laws, and they will be placed under his control for a time, times, and half a time* [3 ½ years]."

At this present time

The Jewish nation is still walking in spiritual blindness. They have returned to their homeland, and they have become a sovereign nation. Their beloved city of Jerusalem has been restored to them. They too are a part of the developing World System of the Antichrist, as are all of the countries of the world. The next prophetic Event that will take place for the Jews will be the creation of the seven-year treaty with the Antichrist.

What does fulfilled prophecy concerning the Jews mean in regard to end-time prophetic Events?

___

___

You may have said something like: this means that all end-time prophecies are in the process of being fulfilled, and their fulfillment will occur precisely as God has told us they will in His Word.

How has this lesson affected you? ___

___

___

Be alert! Watch for the fulfillment of the coming prophecies concerning Israel.

Timeline covered in Lessons 5A and Lesson 5B

Important dates in Israel's history:

1400 B.C. yr. 30 60 70 135 —— 1948

SYSTEM OF THE ANTICHRIST

Year 1400 B.C. the reading of the blessings on Mount Gerizim and the curses on Mount Ebal.
Year A.D. 30 the Jews reject and condemn their Messiah, Jesus, to death.
Year A.D. 60 salvation and the responsibility of spreading the good news given to the Gentiles.
Year A.D. 70 the Jewish nation and temple destroyed by Rome.
Year A.D. 135 the Jewish nation sent into exile among the nations.

Events still future in Israel's history:

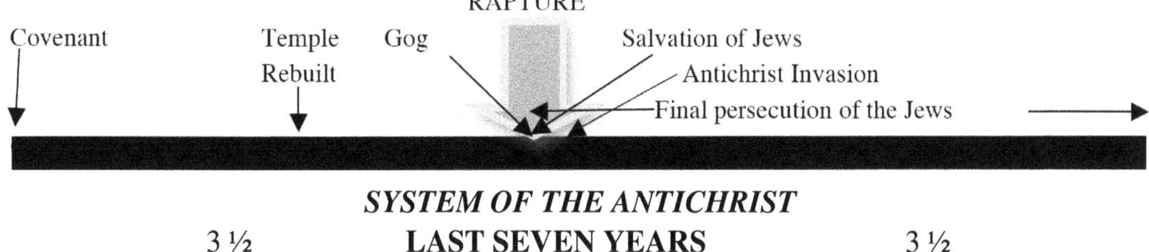

SYSTEM OF THE ANTICHRIST

3 ½ **LAST SEVEN YEARS** 3 ½

JESUS CHRIST THE GREAT PROPHET TO ISRAEL

Deuteronomy 18:15; Acts 3:22-23; John 6:14

LESSON 6A

JESUS CHRIST ENTHRONED KING FOREVER
Psalm 29:10

"The ebbings and flowings of this lower world, and the agitations and revolutions of the affairs in it, give not the least shake to the repose or to the counsels of the Eternal Mind."
—Matthew Henry

EVENT 4

THE RAPTURE—POINT OF IMPACT!

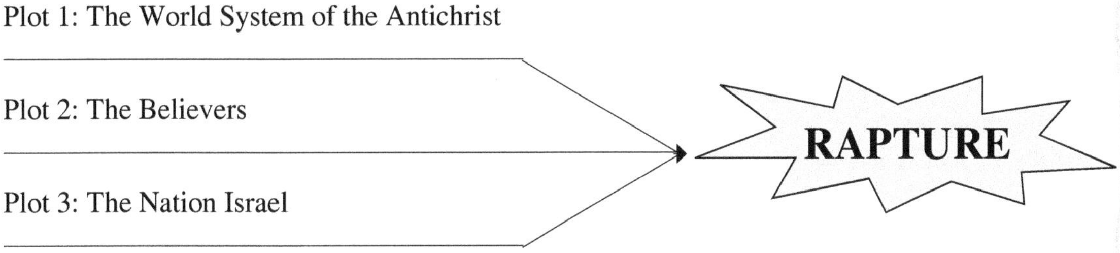

Plot 1: The World System of the Antichrist

Plot 2: The Believers

Plot 3: The Nation Israel

RAPTURE

The three plots are converging and they will meet at their *point of impact* when the Rapture occurs.

Lessons 6A and 6B are pertinent to the understanding of the Rapture. If you can grasp the prophecies concerning the convergence of these three "plots" and their effect on each other, you will have a good understanding of the things that will happen at the time of the Rapture. In this case, the term *convergence* means that each plot is moving toward or approaching the same point, from different directions.

Interestingly, the New Testament teachings to the church do not specify the timing of the Rapture of the Believers. Rather, this timing is clearly presented in the prophecies concerning Israel. In other words, as Believers, we can only know the *time* of our "*gathering together to Him*" through prophecies concerning Israel. That is why it is indispensable to study the end-time prophecies concerning Israel.

Of course we clearly understand that we "*do not know the specific* day or hour" of the Rapture. The exact time is and will remain unknown (Matthew 24:36). However, because of the multiple references to the time factor in the Scriptures, it is apparent that the Lord wants us to be well-informed about the timing of end-time Events so that we are not caught unprepared.

Matthew 24:36 "However, no one knows the day or hour when these things will happen, not even the angels in heaven or the Son himself. Only the Father knows."

You will see how the converging of the three plots describes some of the most exciting drama found throughout the entire Bible. As you work through this lesson, bear in mind that Israel holds the key to unlocking the primary prophecies of the end times.

In this lesson we will study:

The Seventy-Week prophecy of Daniel 9:24-27
The Last Seven Years – The Seventieth Week

THE BELOVED PROPHET

God was the love of Daniel's heart, and Daniel was "*greatly beloved*" by God. (Daniel 9:23) God loved and trusted Daniel so much that He revealed to Daniel His divine purposes and mysteries. Who was this exceptional man, Daniel?

The Old Testament tells us about the days when Israel turned their backs on God by corrupting themselves in the worship of idols. God, therefore, delivered them into the hand of the powerful king of Babylon who destroyed the city of Jerusalem and the temple of the Jews. Daniel, who may have been only 15 years old at the time, was among the early captives taken to Babylon. He was elevated to high positions in the government of four kings of powerful empires because of his unwavering loyalty to God. When Daniel was 80 years old, and still in captivity, he read Jeremiah's prophecy.

Jeremiah 29:10-13

> [10] *"This is what the Lord says: 'You will be in Babylon for seventy years. But then I will come and do for you all the good things I have promised, and I will bring you home again.* [11] *For I know the plans I have for you,' says the Lord. 'They are plans for good and not for disaster, to give you a future and a hope.* [12] *In those days when you pray, I will listen.* [13] *If you look for me wholeheartedly, you will find me. I will be found by you,' says the Lord."*

Daniel was shocked. "Why, the seventy years are almost here! I will seek the Lord!" So, in an attitude of great humility before the Lord, Daniel fasted and put on rough burlap and sprinkled himself with ashes. He reached out to God for understanding with the confidence that these Scriptures gave to him. But Daniel received much, much more. God gave to Daniel a picture of the history of Israel which led up to Jesus' First Coming and all the way to Jesus' Second Coming.

This prophecy in Daniel 9, along with other prophecies given to Daniel, reveal to us the end-time situation in which we are living today. How pertinent they are to our understanding of the things we see developing around us and those things just beyond the horizon in our very near future! All studies of prophecy must include Daniel's prophecies and this one in particular.

THE KEY

Daniel 9:24 is the key to interpret the whole prophecy of Daniel 9:24-27.

Daniel 9:24 (NKJV)

> "*Seventy weeks are decreed for your people and for your holy city, to finish the transgression, to make an end of sins, to make reconciliation for iniquity, to bring in everlasting righteousness, to seal up vision and prophecy, and to anoint the Most Holy.*"

Upon speaking to Daniel, God states that He has determined seventy weeks that concerns "*your* ____________________" and "*your* ______________________________" that is to say, the Jews and Jerusalem. Underline *your* both times it is used in verse 24. It is all about the Jews, not the New Testament Church. This is the key to interpret this prophecy and we will focus our interpretation on this fact as God has intended.

GOD'S PROMISE TO ISRAEL

Please read Daniel 9:4-19 in your Bible. As you read Daniel's prayer to God you will notice that Daniel upholds God's righteous judgment on Israel and acknowledges Israel's great sin against God in his prayer for forgiveness. Daniel is apprehensive because he sees that Israel is still "*full of wickedness.*" As Daniel sees it, their problem is sin. If God will not release His people from bondage and return them to their homeland because of the sin in their hearts, then they would never return. So Daniel pleads with God, in view of God's faithful mercies, to turn His furious anger away from Israel, to forgive them, and to return His people to their homeland.

So, you see, this is all about sin, the sin of Israel. The prophecy of the seventy weeks is God's answer regarding the sin of Israel. Even though the Jews abandoned idolatry while in captivity, they did not completely turn away from their sin against God. In like manner, when Jesus came to Israel as their King, they did not repent of their sin and turn to Him. Down through the years to this day, Israel has not turned to Jesus and away from their sin. But God informed Daniel that a day was coming when Israel would repent, with a capital "R", and would leave their sinful ways forever.

Underline each phrase in verse 24 beginning with the word "to" that expresses a promise from God to the Jews. I found six.

> 24 *"Seventy 'sevens' are decreed for your people and for your holy city, to finish transgression, to put an end to sin, to atone for wickedness, to bring in everlasting righteousness, to seal up vision and prophecy and to anoint the most holy.*

God is saying to Israel: "On a specific day that I have planned, Daniel, your people will turn to Me and will experience the spiritual transformation of being born again.

- I will take away their transgression; it will no longer exist.
- I will bring an end to their sin; they will no longer be held in bondage to it.
- I will cover their iniquity; they will be cleansed from their guilt. Therefore, the wall of separation between My people and Me will be removed and will never be raised again."

"Not only that, the day that I take away My people's sin:

- I will bestow upon Israel My everlasting righteousness; their spiritual transformation will allow them to have a right relationship with Me through their faith in My Son, Jesus. Israel will enter into the Age of Righteousness.

- I will not give prophetic revelation anymore; My people will have full and direct knowledge of My will; therefore, there will be no more need for My messengers, the prophets.

- I will anoint the Most Holy, My Son, Jesus, the Holy One of Israel. His Kingdom will come, and He, the King of kings and Lord of lords, will reign forever and ever. Israel, My people, will reign with the Most Holy for all eternity."

The purpose of the seventy-week prophecy is to reveal to Daniel that a day will come when Israel will thoroughly repent of their sin, be completely pardoned, and forever live for God.

THE SEVENTY-WEEK PROPHECY

Daniel 9:25-27 (NIV)

> 24 *"Seventy 'sevens'* [weeks] *are decreed for your people and for your holy city, to finish transgression, to put an end to sin, to atone for wickedness, to bring in everlasting righteousness, to seal up vision and prophecy and to anoint the most holy.*
>
> 25 *Know and understand this: From the issuing of the decree to restore and rebuild Jerusalem, until the Anointed One, the ruler, comes, there will be seven 'sevens'* [weeks], *and sixty-two 'sevens'* [weeks]. *It will be rebuilt with streets and a trench, but in times of trouble.*
>
> 26 *After the sixty-two 'sevens'* [weeks], *the Anointed One will be cut off and will have nothing. The people of the ruler who will come will destroy the city and the sanctuary. The end will come like a flood: War will continue until the end, and desolations have been decreed.*
>
> 27 *He will confirm a covenant with many for one 'seven'* [week]. *In the middle of the 'seven'* [week] *he will put an end to sacrifice and offering. And on a wing of the temple, he will set up an abomination that causes desolation, until the end that is decreed is poured out on him."*

AN INTERPRETATION

This is an interpretation of Daniel 9:24-27 in the form of an imaginary conversation between God's heavenly messenger, Gabriel, Daniel, you and me. (You may find it interesting to know what you are going to say.) This dialogue begins with Daniel 9:20 when Gabriel is sent by God to explain the meaning of this vision.

It is late afternoon as you and I watch Daniel agonizing in prayer. We feel like intruders listening to him confess his sins and that of his people, the Jews, but he knows that we are there. Our hearts are drawn to this old man as we hear him plead with God for the destroyed city of Jerusalem with such depth of emotion.

"Oh, that we could pray like that," was in our thoughts.

Daniel still hadn't said, "Amen," when we feel a rush of air and hear a powerful voice, "*Daniel, I have come here to give you insight and understanding.*" This glorious *man* appears so suddenly that you and I are frightened.

Daniel, with a calm voice, turns to us and says, "It's alright, this is Gabriel who has appeared to me before in a vision."

"Yes, Daniel, the moment you began praying, God gave the command to come to you and to explain the meaning of your vision for you are very precious to God," Gabriel kindly affirmed. That really got our attention because this vision has always been hard for us to figure out.

Gabriel proceeds to explain, "Daniel, God knows the burden you feel for the sin of your people, but one day, your people will look on the Messiah, in all His splendor, and will repent. Seventy weeks are determined for your people and for your holy city. . ." Gabriel continues to explain all that God was going to do for Israel to put away their sin and to make them righteous before Him. He also talks about seven weeks and sixty-two weeks.

As Gabriel speaks we shift our feet back and forth. We elbow each other to speak up. Finally, you blurt out, "Excuse me for interrupting, but we just don't understand what you are saying, Gabriel. We have read God's word enough times, but we don't grasp how all the things you are saying can possibly take place in just seventy weeks. Why, it has been hundreds of years since this was supposed to happen."

Daniel laughs and says to us, "I understand it perfectly. This is prophetic terminology. The word *weeks* in the Hebrew language is *shabua* which means periods of seven. That is, each week is really a period of seven years. In other words, these *weeks* are not seven-day weeks, rather, they are seven-year weeks:

- 1 week (or period of seven) represents 7 years (1 X 7 equals 7).
- 70 weeks (or periods of seven) represent 490 years (70 X 7 equals 490).

Gabriel is using a way of marking time that we Jews sometimes use. The time period of 70 weeks is not a literal 70 weeks, but rather a literal 490 years. But go ahead, Gabriel, tell me the rest of the prophecy."

"This is going to be fascinating stuff," I whisper to you.

Gabriel describes how God will give a command through one of the kings that will permit the Jewish people to return to their homeland to rebuild Jerusalem. Some had already received permission to return to build the temple. But Gabriel explains that this particular command will be very significant in that from the time this command is issued, in seven weeks (49 years) Jerusalem and the temple will be rebuilt. Then, after the following sixty-two weeks (434 years) the Messiah, Jesus, will manifest Himself in Jerusalem as the King of the Jews.

Daniel responds to this statement with an audible gasp. His eyes shine with wonder, "I actually know when my Lord, the King will come!"

But his joy is short lived as Gabriel continues to say, "But He will be killed."

To this Daniel groans and questions, "How can that be?"

Your voice conveys great sadness as you respond to Daniel. "Daniel, your people refused to recognize Jesus as the Son of God, their Savior, and delivered Him up to be crucified by Roman soldiers."

"No, no," he cries, "That cannot be. We have waited centuries for Him to come."

You put your hand on his shoulder as you say, "*He came to His own, and His own did not receive Him.*" You pause to let that sink in before continuing, "*But as many as received Him, to them He gave the right to become children of God, to those who believe in His name.*"

"I would have believed in Him, I would have received Him!" Daniel exclaims.

"Yes, Daniel, *you* would have, but I have more distressing news," says Gabriel, "God will give your people time to repent at the request of His Son while dying on a cross, but they will not. Disaster will come upon them as suddenly as a flood. Jerusalem and the temple will be destroyed."

I speak up to tell Daniel how Titus, a Roman prince, assailed the city for three and a half years and finally broke through to carry out a great slaughter. I also let him know how they burned the city and completely leveled the temple with only one original wall of the temple complex remaining.

"It is God's just punishment! Our rejection of God is why we are here now in this foreign land as captives for almost seventy years. Jerusalem and the temple were destroyed, we were violently taken from our land, and now, it will happen again because of the hardness of our hearts," Daniel replies in dismay.

"Your people will be scattered among the nations for a very long time, but they will not be destroyed," continues Gabriel. "During that long period of time there will be war, misery, and desolation." He pauses in deep thought. "Your people will go through terrible suffering." Then his voice rises to proclaim, "But the day will come when God will bring them back to their homeland, then soon afterwards, the seventieth week will begin."

Daniel asks anxiously, "How will the last week begin and what will happen afterward?"

Expectantly, we look at Gabriel. What will he say?

"The coming ruler from Rome at that time will have supreme power over the world. He will confirm a covenant and make valid a treaty with your people and others for a period of one week, seven years. However *after half this time, he will put an end to the sacrifices and offerings* in the newly built temple. *As a climax to all his terrible deeds, he will set up a sacrilegious object that will desecrate the temple, until the fate decreed* by God *for this defiler is finally poured out on him."* (Daniel 9:27)

With this, Gabriel leaves us. He does not answer Daniel's second question—what will happen afterward? Our dialogue has ended; we lovingly embrace Daniel, and we go our separate ways. You and I return to our study to find out what will happen afterward.

THE INTERVAL OF TIME

In this prophecy, God gave Daniel a broad outline of future, specific Jewish events that are to take place within a seventy weeks' time frame. This is referred to as the *prophecy of seventy weeks*. The series of events began with the decree of King Artaxerxes Longimanus, King of Persia, to Nehemiah in 445 B.C. to rebuild Jerusalem (Nehemiah 2:1-8) and extends to the end of this Present Age. In other words, this time period contains certain events pertinent to Israel until the Second Coming of King Jesus.

The specific events to occur in the first sixty-nine of the seventy weeks, have already taken place. These sixty-nine weeks covered a span of 483 years, ranging from the time of Nehemiah, an Old Testament prophet, until the year A.D. 32 [1] on the day of Jesus' triumphal entry into Jerusalem. This was the day that Jesus publicly and officially presented Himself as Israel's Messiah. Christians still celebrate this day as Palm Sunday.

Daniel 9:26 also gives two more prophecies that are to closely follow the conclusion of the sixty-ninth week.

- First, the death of the Messiah, the Anointed One. This prophecy was fulfilled when Christ was crucified for the sin of the world just five days after His triumphal entry into Jerusalem.
- Second, the destruction of Jerusalem and the temple. This was carried out by the Roman armies in year A.D. 70.

In year A.D. 70, Israel's historical standing as a sovereign nation in Palestine ceased. The surviving Jews were scattered throughout the world. There is a very long space of time between the fulfilled sixty-nine weeks that have already occurred and the seventieth week that will take place in our not so distant future. The Jews, as well as ourselves, are currently living between the sixty-ninth and the seventieth week.

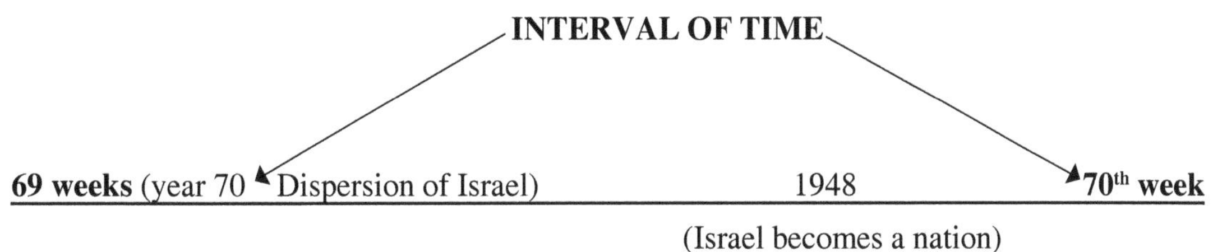

According to Scripture, two significant things must happen before the seventieth week of this Present Age begins.

- First of all, the Jewish people must return to their homeland and Israel must become a sovereign nation. This took place in 1948 (see diagram above).

- Secondly, the World System of the Antichrist must be established with a representative of Rome dominating this global government. This is currently in the process of becoming a reality.

The seventieth week, the end of this Present Age and the Second Coming of Christ, will be very near when these two things occur. As previously stated, the first prerequisite concerning Israel has already taken place and the second one is in the process of taking place.

The realization of these two prophecies makes the conditions right for the seventieth week to take place. So prophetically speaking, we are astonishingly close to the last seven years of this Present Age. When the seventieth week begins, we can say: "Hey, we only have seven more years of life on earth as we now know it!"

At this point in our study, we need to look back at Lesson 3 when we learned about the statue which speaks about the second significant prerequisite, the World System of the Antichrist. The statue in Daniel 2 portrays a succession of world empires that ends with the establishment of the world rule of the Antichrist. This was symbolized by the feet of iron representing Rome and the clay representing the Ten Kings. You will remember the interval of time between the *legs*, the expired Roman Empire, and the *feet*, the end-time confederation of a Roman Empire and the Ten Kings represented by the ten toes. These two prophecies reveal unmistakable consistency.

Daniel 2
THE WORLD SYSTEM OF THE ANTICHRIST

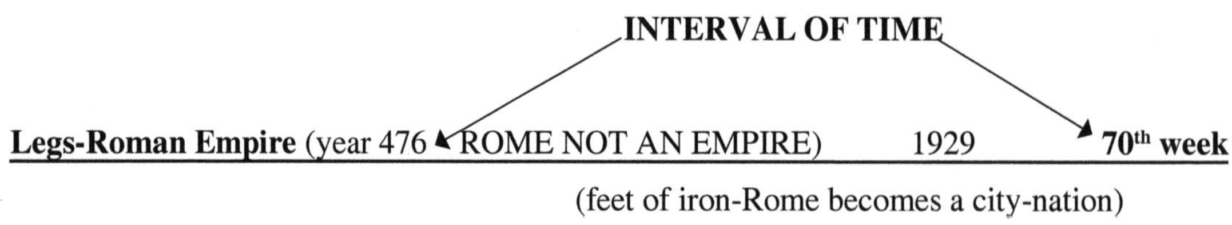

Daniel 9:24-27
ISRAEL A SOVEREIGN NATION

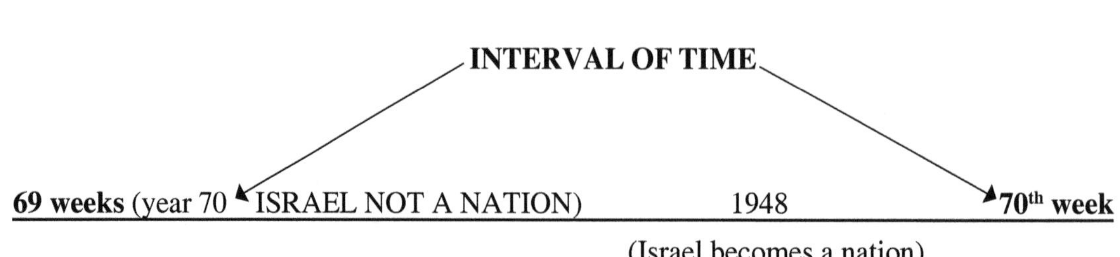

The symbol *iron legs and feet* represent Rome. "Rome becomes a city-nation" in 1929 as seen in the diagram above will not be explained in this lesson, but will be fully explained in Part Two of this book. At the present time, Ten Regions, represented by the ten toes of the statue, have been formed, but not fully developed to the point of having a ruler or king over each region

Things are really getting interesting!

THE LAST SEVEN YEARS - THE SEVENTIETH WEEK

Part One of this book presents a chronology of prophetic Events that are currently happening and rapidly moving toward future Events. At this point in our study, we are looking specifically at the last seven years of our Present Age decreed by God in Daniel 9:27. Remember, these seven years take place during the World System of the Antichrist.

Clarification

The last seven years, commonly referred to by those who study and teach biblical prophecy, comes from Daniel 9:20-27. Please keep in mind that this time period of seven years refers to prophetic events that apply to Israel, not to the church. Some interpreters see Daniel's prophecy of the last week as referring to the church and the Great Tribulation spoken of in Matthew 24. Nowhere in the Bible does it say that the Tribulation is confined to this seven year period. In fact, there is no definite time frame given for the Great Tribulation mentioned in Matthew 24, and it is reasonable to assume that it will cover a much longer period than seven years.

How will we know when we enter the last seven years?

Daniel 9:27 (NIV) provides us with an important clue that we can use to determine when we have in fact entered into the last seven years. **Read** the verse again and then fill in the blanks.

> "*He will confirm a covenant with many* [Jews and others] *for one 'seven'* [seven years]. *In the middle of the 'seven' he will put an end to sacrifice and offering. And on a wing* [of the temple] *he will set up an abomination that causes desolation, until the end that is decreed is poured out on him.*"

He confirms a _______________ with the ___________ and others for _____________ years. When this event takes place, we will know that there are only __________ years left until Jesus comes to establish His Thousand-Year Reign on the earth.

Who is "he" in 9:27?

Verse 26 is obviously predicting the destruction of Jerusalem and the temple by Titus the Roman prince (who later became emperor) and his armies in year A.D. 70. In verse 27 the pronoun *he* seems to be referring back to verse 26 the "*ruler who will come*" which grammatically is the antecedent of the word *he.*

> 26 *The people* [Romans] *of* ***the ruler who will come*** *will destroy the city and the sanctuary. The end will come like a flood: War will continue until the end, and desolations have been decreed.*

> [27] ***He will confirm a covenant with many for one 'seven'* [week].** *In the middle of the 'seven'* [week] *he will put an end to sacrifice and offering. And on a wing of the temple, he will set up an abomination that causes desolation, until the end that is decreed is poured out on him."*

Verse 27 projects us into the far future when "*the ruler who is to come*" will make a seven-year treaty between Israel and others. Based on this information, we can look for a ruler from Rome, which is referred to in other Scriptures as the Antichrist, to be the "*he*" of verse 27. This fits the other end-time visions of Daniel 2 and 7 which we will study in Part Two of this book.

The important thing to understand from this Scripture is that the Antichrist will be involved in a seven- year covenant that has implications for Israel and others.

Disruption of the Treaty

Read verse 27 and write the two things that the Antichrist does in the middle of the seven years.

1. ______________________________

2. ______________________________

Mid-way through these seven years the Antichrist will put a stop to the Jew's animal sacrifices and grain offerings. Underline this phrase in Daniel 9:27. He will also set up his statue to be worshiped within the temple compound.

The fact that the Antichrist "*will put an end to sacrifice and offerings*" at the half way point of the seven years tells us that the Jews will have begun to make animal sacrifices and offerings. The word used here for *sacrifice* is the Hebrew word *zebach* meaning "to slaughter, kill, sacrifice and is used primarily to describe the killing of animals for sacrifice." [KW] As a nation, Israel has not made animal sacrifices since the year A.D. 70 when their temple was destroyed. They will not do this in any location apart from their temple site.

Verse 27 implies that Israel will have rebuilt their center of worship, the temple. Apparently the Antichrist has no problem with this even though he is forcing all the other people of the world to worship him exclusively. Hmmmm. This looks suspicious. Why this exception?

The act of stopping the Jews from performing their worship to God in the temple during the middle of the week will be a hostile, threatening action on the part of the Antichrist. Now what is he up to?

Ezekiel 43:7
"...this is the place of my throne and the place where I will rest my feet."

Bear in mind that the eventual rebuilding of the temple is extremely important

The temple will be the place where Christ establishes His throne at the time of His Second Coming, marking the beginning of His Thousand-Year Kingdom on the earth. (Ezekiel 43:7) The temple is also the location where the Antichrist will attempt to set up his throne and rule the world in an act of defiance toward God. Are you beginning to comprehend the reason for the approaching turmoil and conflict that will be coming?

The two plots concerning the Antichrist and Israel are clearly merging together.

Timeline

Find "Covenant/Treaty" on **Timeline One** (located at the end of Part One of this book). This is the seven-year covenant, or treaty, that the Antichrist will sanction with Israel, and others, that will apparently allow for the rebuilding of the Jewish center of worship, the temple. Notice where it says "Temple Rebuilt" and "Israel Saved" on Timeline One. At this point, we are approaching the time of the Rapture.

THE ANTICHRIST MAKES HIS MOVE

The Antichrist will need to come up with a strategy that will allow the Jews to build their temple. He will deceitfully make his move as the supposed benefactor to the Jews by confirming a treaty with the Israel and all those affected which will result in the rebuilding of the temple in Jerusalem. The Antichrist will make this covenant for only seven years. Why such a short time? Perhaps he is thinking that it will take the Jews at least that long to rebuild their temple. He has plans for the temple.

SEVEN-YEAR COVENANT/TREATY

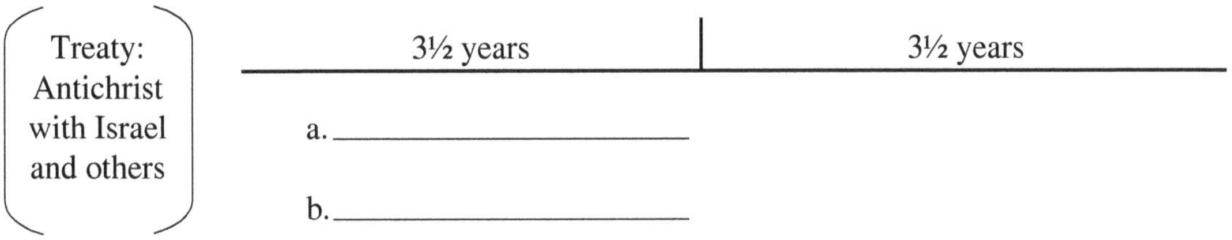

Treaty: Antichrist with Israel and others	3½ years	3½ years
	a. ______________________	
	b. ______________________	

Write *Temple rebuilt* on line **"a"** in the diagram above.

ISRAEL MAKES ITS MOVE

The temple will have been rebuilt and functioning. The Jews will return to their animal sacrifices during the first 3 ½ years of the treaty. From their point of view, how do you think they will feel when they do this? Almost 2,000 years have passed since the temple was destroyed preventing them from offering sacrifices to the God of Israel. What jubilation will be theirs when that first sacrifice is made! They will be able to have a sacrificial lamb again at their Passover feasts. From their perspective, their religious system will again be fully compliant with Old Testament requirements.

What will the renewing of the sacrifices reveal about the attitude of Israel toward Jesus Christ?

____

Does this indicate that the Jewish people will be *saved* or *not saved* during the first 3 ½ years of the seven-year period? ("Saved" implies being spared from spiritual death by belief in Jesus Christ and His work on the cross.)

Write your answer either *Israel saved* or *Israel not saved* on line **"b."** in the diagram above titled: "Seven-Year Covenant/Treaty."

If you answered *Israel not saved*, you are absolutely correct. During the first 3 ½ years of this seven- year period, Israel will certainly be in a state of unbelief regarding the death and resurrection of Jesus.

What takes place that will turn the Antichrist against his pretended ally, Israel, and stop them from making their sacrifices?

(We will answer this question in Lesson 6B.)

JESUS CHRIST ENTHRONED KING FOREVER

Psalm 29:10

LESSON 6B

JESUS CHRIST THE CLEANSING FOUNTAIN
Zechariah 13:1

Sorrow not despairing sinner. Drink from the open, cleansing, life-giving fountain that never will run dry.

EVENT 4

THE RAPTURE—POINT OF IMPACT

In order to interpret the Bible, we must ask questions. The right questions usually lead to the right answers. At this point in our study, Israel is approaching the middle of the seven-year treaty. Here are the two questions that we must ask ourselves to better understand the salvation of Israel, which will also lead us to the time of the Rapture: how will Israel be saved, and when will Israel be saved?

Zechariah 13:1 (RSV) "On that day there shall be a fountain opened for the house of David and for the inhabitants of Jerusalem to cleanse them from sin and uncleanness."

In this lesson we will study:

- The Salvation of Israel
  - How Israel will be saved
  - When Israel will be saved
  - When the Rapture will take place

THE SALVATION OF ISRAEL

HOW ISRAEL WILL BE SAVED

The Lord reveals *how* Israel will be saved in three key Scriptures: Revelation 1:7; Matthew 24:30-31; and Zechariah 12:10 – 13:1. These three passages are speaking about the Rapture, the Event when Jesus appears in the clouds of the sky to gather together all the born-again members of His Body, the church, to transport them to heaven.

Let's study these three verses one by one to answer the question, "How is Israel saved."

REVELATION 1:7

The context of Revelation 1:7

The book of Revelation, beginning with chapter 4 to the end of chapter 22, is a precise account of end-time Events that will occur during and after this Present Age. It is about the final victorious consummation expressed by the following words found in Revelation 1:7, "*He is coming*." This statement is the primary theme of the book of Revelation. It includes:

- the appearance of Christ at the time of the Rapture
- the glorious manifestation of Christ at His Second Coming to rule the earth
- world conditions surrounding both of these appearances.

Revelation 1:7 is an expressive description of Christ's appearance at the Rapture. We begin with verse 5 so that you can clearly see that Jesus is the person referred to in verse 7. **Circle** the word *see*.

Revelation 1:5-7 (NIV)

> [5] *". . .Jesus Christ, who is the faithful witness, the firstborn from the dead, and the ruler of the kings of the earth. To him who loves us and has freed us from our sins by his blood,* [6] *and has made us to be a kingdom and priests to serve his God and Father—to him be glory and power for ever and ever! Amen.*
>
> [7] *Look, he is coming with the clouds, and every eye will see him, even those who pierced him; and all the peoples of the earth will mourn because of him. So shall it be! Amen."*

Make four observations from these verses.

1. ______________________________
2. ______________________________
3. ______________________________
4. ______________________________

Who is the person that Revelation 1: 5–7 is talking about? ______________
Where does He appear in verse 7? ______________
Underline the first phrase that reveals how many will *see* Him. ______________
Fill in the blanks: e__________ e________ w__________ s__________ H__________.
Who do you think the people are in the phrase "*even those who pierced Him*"? __________
What do we call this Event? ______________

The word "see"

The Greek word *optomai* is used in Revelation 1:7 for the English verb *to see. Optomai* means "to *gaze* with wide-open eyes, as at something remarkable and is used alternately with *horao* which means to "stare and to discern clearly" [S] "*Horao* is the physical act 'to see.' It especially indicates the direction of the thought to the object seen; a perception or an understanding of something as a result from visually seeing the object." [V]

The *remarkable thing* the Jews and earth people are gazing at with wide-open eyes is King Jesus. The Greek word *horao* indicates that these same two groups of people *see* with understanding. What a difference these two Greek words make in our understanding of this verse! These same Greek words are used in Matthew 24:30.

I might add here that earth dwellers will have good cause to mourn at this time. We will learn why later on in our study.

MATTHEW 24:30-31

The context of Matthew 24:30-31

In this chapter, Jesus' disciples were admiring the temple, and they pointed out its great beauty to Jesus. Jesus responded by stating that the temple buildings, along with the entire city of Jerusalem would be destroyed. This unexpected response must have shaken the disciples to their very core.

Moments later, Jesus was sitting on the Mount of Olives overlooking Jerusalem and the temple. The temple would have been situated to the west of where He was sitting. Only days before, Jesus had entered Jerusalem to present Himself as the Messiah and King. He was welcomed by multitudes of cheering and applauding people. Before the week would end, Jesus would be agonizing on a cross to pay the penalty for the sin of the whole world. From where He was sitting, Jesus could practically see the very place where this would happen.

Perhaps Jesus' thoughts took Him far into the future, to the distant day when He would return to Jerusalem to rule the world and to be worshipped in the temple that will be rebuilt upon the very site in front of Him.

Still disturbed by Jesus' prophecy concerning Jerusalem and the temple, the disciples went to Jesus, where He sat alone, and asked two important questions recorded in Matthew 24:3.

1. Tell us, when will these things happen?
2. What will be the sign of your coming and of the end of the age?

The rest of Matthew 24 is Jesus' detailed answer to these two questions. He finishes His discourse with Matthew 24:30-31 which is His appearance at the Rapture during the end times. **Circle** the word *see.*

Matthew 24:30-31

> [30] *"And then at last, the sign of the Son of Man is coming will appear in the heavens, and there will be deep mourning among all the peoples of the earth. And they will see* [optomai – horao] *the Son of Man coming on the clouds of heaven with power and great glory.* [31] *And he will send out his angels with the mighty blast of a trumpet, and they will gather his chosen ones from all over the world—from the farthest ends of the earth and heaven."*

Make four observations from these two verses.

1. ____
2. ____
3. ____
4. ____

Who is the Son of Man? ____________________Where does He appear? ____________

____

_______________________________ Circle the two places that tell us where Jesus appears. Is the Son of Man visible to all people? _________ Who sees Him? ____________________
____
___________ Does this include the Jews? __________ What Event are these verses talking about? ____

ZECHARIAH 12:10–13:1

The context of Zechariah 12:10-13:1
First of all, let me introduce you to Zechariah, in case you do not know who he was. Zechariah was both a priest and a prophet. He was born into captivity in Babylonia, during Israel's exile from Palestine (586 B.C.). Israel was in exile because the people fell into idolatry and departed from God's rule. After the Babylonian Empire fell to the Persians, Zechariah was one of the 50,000 Jews who were permitted to return to Jerusalem to rebuild the destroyed temple.

Initially, the rebuilding of the temple did not go very well. As a result, God called the young man Zechariah to be His spokesman to the discouraged Jewish people. God gifted Zechariah with eloquence. He spoke like a poet. Interestingly, Zechariah "is probably the most Messianic [about Christ], apocalyptic [symbolic language], and eschatological [about the end times] of all the Old Testament books." [1] Zechariah's enthusiastic messages were very encouraging, and they motivated the people to rebuild the temple. Zechariah reminded the Jewish people that God had great plans for their nation in the light of the coming Messiah. As a result, the book of Zechariah provides us with specific, key predictions about Jesus' three appearances:

Chapters 9 – 11 . . . . . Christ's First Advent and rejection
Chapters 12 – 13 . . . . Christ's appearance at the Rapture
Chapter 14 . . . . Christ's Second Coming. . .and into the Thousand-Year Kingdom

"*. . .the word of the Lord came to the prophet Zechariah. . .*" (Zechariah 1:1) "That the word of the Lord '*came*' to Zechariah is indicative of the vitality of the divine word in the Old Testament. God's word not only 'comes,' it also 'comes true.'" [2] That is to say, God's word is always fulfilled.

Zechariah 12 and 13 reveal what the conditions on earth will be like for Israel immediately before and after the Rapture appearance of Jesus. The Jewish nation will see Jesus when He appears at the Rapture to remove from this world all Believers belonging to His church. However, before the Rapture takes place, the nations under the leadership of Gog will invade Israel. (Ezekiel 38, 39) The terrible nature of this situation will cause the Jewish leaders to turn to God seeking His deliverance (Zechariah 12:5). When the Jewish people are at their most desperate and vulnerable moment, God will crush the enemy, and King Jesus, the Deliverer, will appear in the clouds of the sky.

Psalm 3:8 (RSV) "Deliverance belongs to the Lord; thy blessing be upon thy people."

Zechariah 12:10 -13:1 is a vivid, heart-warming picture of Jesus' appearance to the Jews in their great distress, at the time of the Rapture. **Circle** the words *look on* in Zechariah 12:10.

Zechariah 12:10 – 13:1 (NIV)

> (12:10) *"And I will pour out on the house of David and the inhabitants of Jerusalem a spirit of grace and supplication. They will look on me* [intently], *the one they have pierced,*
>
> *and they will mourn for him as one mourns [to tear the hair and beat the breasts, to wail] for an only child, and grieve bitterly for him as one grieves for a firstborn son.* [11]
> *On that day the weeping in Jerusalem will be great, like the weeping of Hadad Rimmon*
> *in the plain of Meggido.* [12] *The land will mourn, each clan by itself, with their wives by themselves: the clan of the house of David and their wives, the clan of the house*
> *of Nathan and their wives,* [13] *the clan of the house of Levi and their wives, the clan of*
> *Shimei and their wives,* [14] *and all the rest of the clans and their wives.*
>
> (13:1) *On that day a fountain will be opened to the house of David and the inhabitants of Jerusalem, to cleanse them from sin and impurity."*

Draw a box around the word "*Jerusalem*" each time it is used. **Underline** "*the house of David*" each time it is used. These key words identify the people group in these verses. Who are the people that these verses are talking about? ____________________________________.

Who do "*they*" and "*Me*" refer to in verse 12:10? Write your answer in the following blanks. "They" (________________________) will look on "Me" (__________________) the one they have pierced.

Jesus is the speaker in Zechariah 12:10 (NIV): "*they will look on* me, *the one they have pierced.*" These same words of Jesus were written close to 600 years later when the apostle John wrote them in Revelation 1:7, in the New Testament: "*every eye will see him, even those who pierced him*"—the Jews.

Why will the Jews mourn "*on that day*" (12:11) when they see Jesus? Maybe you have already figured it out. Good for you if you did!

Let's look at Zechariah 13:1. According to this verse, what will happen "*on that day*"? ________
____

What is this "*fountain*" that will cleanse the Jews from their sin? ____________________
____.

These verses repeat the words "*on that day.*" What specific day or Event are these words referring to? ______________________________

Jesus' sudden appearance in the clouds at the Rapture will be shocking to the people of Israel. They will *optomai* "*gaze* with wide-open eyes, as at something remarkable." They will *horao* "stare and discern clearly" who Jesus is. As they look at Jesus, all prejudices, misunderstandings, stubbornness, ignorance, and unbelief will be shattered in a moment of awesome recognition.

The Jews great error for which they will mourn "He came into the very world He created, but the world didn't recognize Him. He came to His own people [the Jews], and even they rejected Him." John 1:10-11

Their blind eyes will be opened to the truth. Jesus Christ the Savior is (and always has been) their promised Messiah.

Upon seeing the Lord Jesus, the Jewish people will immediately be smitten with remorse and anguish because for centuries they have refused to acknowledge Jesus as the Son of God. Notice how the nation as a whole will repent with great mourning, "*the land will mourn.*" (Zechariah 12:12 NIV) How is their mourning expressed in 12:10? ________________________________

____

The depth of the nation's repentance is compared to the grief-stricken mourning of parents who have lost their firstborn and only son. The nation gathers in close, intimate family groups in penitential grief. Overwhelmed husbands and wives will separately lament in true repentance. This national repentance will be an individual response to Jesus Christ. (Zechariah 12:12-13)

Read Isaiah 53 as possibly being the very words of the Jewish nation as they express their repentance and mourning at this time. The multiple use of *we* and *our* reveal how personal it is. This is an acknowledgement of the true meaning of Jesus' death. I will give you a few moments to read it.........Wasn't that remarkable! What depth of meaning the circumstances of Zechariah 12:10 lend to this confession voiced by Isaiah!

A fountain will be opened

The "*open fountain*" spoken of in Zechariah 13:1 most likely is referring to the pierced side of Jesus Christ. Among a great crowd of Jews, the apostle John stood transfixed by the sight of Jesus's death on the cross. As he watched, a Roman soldier drew near and pierced Jesus' side with a spear. Blood and water came out. Looking at the multitude, John utters in despair: *"They will look on the one they have pierced."*

John 19:34-37 (NIV)

> "...*one of the soldiers pierced Jesus' side with a spear, bringing a sudden flow of blood and water. The man [the apostle John] who saw it has given testimony, and his testimony is true. He knows that he tells the truth, and he testifies so that you also may believe. These things happened so that the scripture would be fulfilled: 'Not one of His bones will be broken'* [Psalm 34:20] *and, as another scripture says, 'They will look on the one they have pierced.'"* [Zechariah 12:10]

The Jewish nation as a whole did not repent at the time when they saw Jesus hanging on the cross as indicated in Zechariah 12:10–13:1. The apostle John only quoted a part of Zachariah 12:10–13:1. This type of prophecy found in John 19:37 is known as partial fulfillment prophecy. That is to say, Zechariah's prophecy was partially fulfilled at the cross. The Jews looked at Jesus on the cross, but did not repent. As a result, we can know with complete certainty that Zechariah 12:10-13:1 will be completely fulfilled in the future when all of Israel will look up at Jesus in the clouds of the sky "*on that day*"—"*they will look on* me, *the one they have pierced,*" and they will believe!

"*To Him who loved us and washed us from our sins in His own blood. . .*" (Revelation 1:5 NKJV) Figuratively speaking, Jesus' blood will be like an open fountain to the Jewish nation, bathing their souls, cleansing and purifying them from all sin. What a loving act of grace!

William Cowper "There is a fountain filled with blood drawn from Immanuel's veins. And sinners plunged beneath that flood lose all their guilty stains.

E'er since by faith I saw the stream Thy flowing wounds supply, Redeeming love has been my theme and shall be till I die."

On that day

The phrase, "*On that day,*" (verse 11) refers to the day when the Jews will see Jesus in the clouds of the sky at the time of the Rapture. THE JEWS WILL SEE HIM whom they pierced, AND THEY WILL BELIEVE. "*On that day*" is a specific, predetermined day that God has appointed.

When this happens, you, John and Daniel in heaven, and I will say: "Today, God has fulfilled His Daniel 9:24 promise. '*I will take away their transgression; I will bring an end to their sin; and I will cover their iniquity.*' The first half of the verse has been accomplished *today.*" The second half of Daniel's verse is soon to follow. "*To bring in everlasting righteousness, to seal up vision and prophecy and to anoint the most holy.*"

A two question quiz

The following two questions are based on Revelation 1:7; Matthew 24:30-31; and Zechariah 12:10–13:1.

1. What do we call the appearance of Jesus in the clouds of the sky when all peoples (especially the Jews) will see Him? ____.

2. How will Israel be saved?

    Israel will be saved when they see ______________________.
    They will see Jesus at the time of the ___________________________.
    Therefore, the Jews will be saved at the time of the ____________________________.

Let's put some things together

- **Revelation 1:7** ties the salvation of Israel to the end-time appearance of Jesus Christ.
- **Matthew 24:30-31** ties the salvation of Israel to the appearance of Jesus Christ at the Rapture, the gathering together of the Believers to Himself.
- **Zechariah 12:10–13:1** clearly explains how the Jews will be saved. The Jews will be saved by seeing Jesus in person. They will believe that Jesus is their Savior and they will repent with great emotion when they see Him.

You have discovered *how* the Jewish Nation of Israel will be saved. They will become the Jewish-Christian Nation of Israel when they see Jesus and by placing their faith in Him at the Rapture.

But wait! We are not quite finished learning about these two plots. There is more.

WHEN ISRAEL WILL BE SAVED AND WHEN THE RAPTURE WILL TAKE PLACE

BELIEVERS AND ISRAEL CONVERGE

John 16:13
"When the Spirit of truth comes, he will guide you into all truth... He will tell you about the future."

When Will Israel Actually See Jesus?
Scripture tells us that Israel will be saved upon seeing Jesus at the time of the Rapture. But does it give us the exact moment or time when this will happen? This is a very important question to ask, because if Scripture tells us when, the moment Israel will see Jesus, we can also determine when the Believers of the end times will be Raptured! Remember we are not predicting the exact day and hour. We are looking at the Scriptures that God has given us in order that we are not caught unaware.

1 Thessalonians 5:2, 4

> *"For you know quite well that the day of the Lord's return will come unexpectedly, like a thief in the night. . .But you aren't in the dark about these things, dear brothers and sisters, and you won't be surprised when the day of the Lord comes like a thief."*

Galatians 3:26-28 (Philips)
"For now that you have faith in Christ Jesus you are all sons of God. All of you who were baptized 'into' Christ have put on the family likeness of Christ. Gone is the distinction between Jew and Greek [non-Jew], slave and free man, male and female—you are all one in Christ Jesus! And if you belong to Christ, you are true descendants of Abraham, you are true heirs of his promise."

Proceed with discernment
Be very observant. Use logic and problem solving skills as you look to the Holy Spirit for guidance while attempting to interpret these prophetic events. Examining the Scriptures and letting them reveal their meaning to you is a thrilling experience. God has given us information in His Word so that we can understand it. . .so that YOU can understand it.

Romans 11:25-27
We now turn to Romans 11, which also indicates that Israel's salvation will be directly connected to the Believer's rapture. As we study this passage, we will specifically focus on "the timing / the when" of Israel's salvation and "the timing / the when" of the Rapture.

Romans 11 explains that God did not permanently "*cast away*" His people, Israel, for rejecting His Son the Messiah. Rather, God "*set Israel aside*" so that non-Jews could have the opportunity of hearing the Gospel and being saved. The majority of individuals who make up Jesus' true church, referred to as the Body of Christ, are believing Gentiles. The few Jews who have chosen to believe in Christ as Savior also belong to the church. They are our brethren in Christ.

Romans 11:25–27 (NIV)

> [25] *"I* [the apostle Paul] *do not want you to be ignorant of this mystery, brothers,. . .Israel has experienced a hardening in part until the full number of the Gentiles has come in.*
>
> [26] *And so* [when that happens [3]] *all Israel will be saved, as it is written: 'The deliverer* [Christ] *will come from Zion; he will turn godlessness away from Jacob* [the Jews].
> [27] *And this is my covenant with them when I take away their sins.'"*

The Jewish people have lived in spiritual blindness and hardness of heart since the time of Jesus' First Coming almost two thousand years ago. There have been very few Jews who have believed and received salvation through Jesus Christ. But remember, as previously stated, the few Jews who have received salvation through Jesus belong to the church. (Romans 11:5-7) The blindness of the vast majority of the Jews will continue *until* the very last person of the Gentiles receives salvation to complete the church, the Body of Christ.

Full number is the Greek word *pleroma* which means "a complete number" or "a total number." [KW]

The phrase *"the full number,"* found in Romans 11:25 means "filled up," like a "no vacancy" sign at a motel. In this case *"full number"* is referring to the completion of the church. Jesus knows who that last person to receive Him as their Savior will be.

What Event will take place when that last person giving his or her believing heart to Christ finishes their prayer of repentance with the words: "Thank you Jesus. Amen"? ________________

Yes, the Rapture will take place! Jesus will appear in the clouds of the sky. What will happen to the Jews living at the time when this takes place as stated in Romans 11:26? ______________

The words in verse 26 have the following meaning:

> "The 'full inclusion' (*pleroma*, literally 'fulness') of the Jews is to be understood in the same sense as the 'full number' [*pleroma*, 'fulness'] of the Gentiles' in verse 25. The large-scale conversion of the Gentile world is to be followed by the salvation of 'all Israel'; this salvation involves their 'full inclusion'." [4]

The fountain will be open, and Israel will be plunged beneath the cleansing flood. Their sins will be washed away when they see Jesus. God, in His wonderful grace, will fulfill His promise to give the Jewish Nation a Deliverer, a Savior. His name is Jesus.

The Rapture of the Believers is the glorious Event that brings salvation to Israel. So as you can see, Believers and Israel will come to a point of impact at the time of the Rapture.

Evangelize. . .evangelize. . .evangelize!

Have you captured the great significance of leading people to Christ? Jesus' words in Matthew 24:14 reveal that during the end-time persecution, many Believers will not only stand firm in their faith, but will, by God's grace, advance the gospel throughout the nations to reach the very last person for Christ.

> *"This good news of the kingdom will be proclaimed to men all over the world as a witness to all the nations, and then the end will come."* (Phillips)

What unspeakable joy it would be to lead that very last soul to Jesus! How overwhelming to consider the possibility of being the instrument God uses to complete the Body of Christ to usher in the Rapture, and to bring about the salvation of Israel! Someone will be that witness. Will you be that person? Now that's something to think about!

...the rapture of the saints, or 'of the church,' is an entirely Scriptural expression, and describes vividly the instantaneous removal of those who are in Christ, whether living or dead, at the word of the Returning Lord." [5]

WHEN WILL THE RAPTURE TAKE PLACE?

Let's take another look at these seven years on our diagram. At some point within these seven years, Israel will see Christ, they will believe in Him, and they will be saved. But, where? When will the Rapture take place?

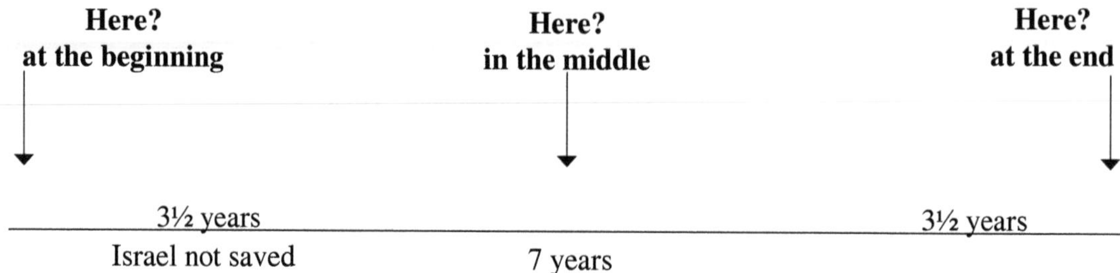

3½ years 3½ years

Israel not saved 7 years

Let's follow the Scripture to see where it will lead us. Remember, we have already learned that Israel will not be saved during the first 3 ½ years of the seven-year treaty with the Antichrist. Consequently, we can be sure that the Rapture will not take place during the first 3 ½ years.

PERSECUTION OF CHRISTIAN ISRAEL

The following prophecies speak about the persecution of Israel that will take place immediately after Israel receives salvation.

Read the Scriptures below to discover how long this persecution of the Jewish nation will last?

Zechariah 13:8-9 (NIV)

> [8] *"In the whole land* [Israel], *' declares the* LORD, *'two-thirds will be struck down and perish; yet one-third will be left in it.*
> [9] *This third I will bring into the fire; I will refine them like silver and test them like gold. They will call on my name, and I will answer them; I will say, 'These are my people,' and they will say, 'The* LORD *is our God.'"*

Daniel 7:25 (NIV)

> *"He* [the Beast/Antichrist] *will speak against the Most High and oppress his saints* [Jews] *and try to change the set times and the laws. The saints* [Jews] *will be handed over to him for a time, times, and half a time."*

"*A time*" equals one year, "*times*" indicates two years, while "*half a time*" refers to one-half of a year. The total is 3 ½ years.

Revelation 11:2 (NIV)

> *"They* [the nations] *will trample on the holy city* [Jerusalem] *for 42 months."*

42 months equals 3 1/2 years.

There are five vital questions that we should ask ourselves after reading these verses from Zechariah, Daniel, and Revelation. **Circle** the following words in the verses above: *struck down, perish, oppress, handed over, trample.*

1. What is happening to Israel in these verses? ______________________________________
____

2. Who is persecuting Israel? ____

3. Looking at the terminology used to refer to Israel in these verses, is the nation Israel saved at this time?
Yes ______________ No ______________

4. A significant question: How long is Israel persecuted by the Antichrist? ______________

5. In which half of the seven-year period is Israel saved and persecuted for their faith in Jesus Christ? the first half _______________ or the second half ______________

Jesus warns the Jews when the Antichrist will move against them.
Jesus quoted Daniel 9:27 in Matthew 24:15-16. Jesus did this to warn the Jews *when* the Antichrist, referred to by his image "*the abomination of desolation*," will turn against Israel during his evil reign in an attempt to kill them all.

Matthew 24:15-16 (NIV)

> *"So when you see standing in the holy place* [temple] *'the abomination that causes desolation'* [waste, ruin], *spoken of through the prophet Daniel—let the reader understand—then let those who are in Judea flee to the mountains."*

Daniel 9:27 (HCSB)

> *"He will make a firm covenant with many for one week, but in the middle of the week he will put a stop to sacrifice and offering. And the abomination of desolation will be on a wing of the temple until the decreed destruction is poured out on the desolator."*

By quoting Daniel, when does Jesus tell Israel that the Antichrist will break his covenant with them and that they must flee a horrible persecution? ________________________________

BELIEVERS, ISRAEL AND THE ANTICHRIST CONVERGE

Without a doubt, the Antichrist will angrily witness the breathtaking phenomenon of the Rapture and the conversion of the Nation Israel to Christ. With rage, the Antichrist will desperately make his move to regain control of the emotionally shaken world because of the realization that the Wrath of God has come upon them. 2 Thessalonians 2:4 tells us what the Antichrist will do next.

2 Thessalonians 2:4

> "*who* [the Antichrist] *opposes and exalts himself above every so-called god or object of worship, so that he takes his seat in the temple of God, displaying himself as being God.*"

Write down the three things that the Antichrist will do.

1.____

2.____

3.____

Within a short time after the Rapture, this "exalter of himself" will march into Jerusalem to stop Jewish worship. He will rush to the temple, storm into the Holy Place, and proclaim himself to be God. He will consider himself to be above God, above any other so-called god, and above any other thing that serves as an object of worship. All the world will bow down to worship their marvelous, false god. . .well, not quite all. The Antichrist will immediately have one earthly opponent and only one, the Jewish Christians. God's people, the Jews, will be the only ones left on earth who will proclaim Christ, as the Antichrist will attempt to sweep the earth of any visible traces of Christianity. He sees the need to do something about the Jews. The persecution begins.

THE ANSWER!

When will the Rapture take place during this seven year period? **Circle** the correct "Here."

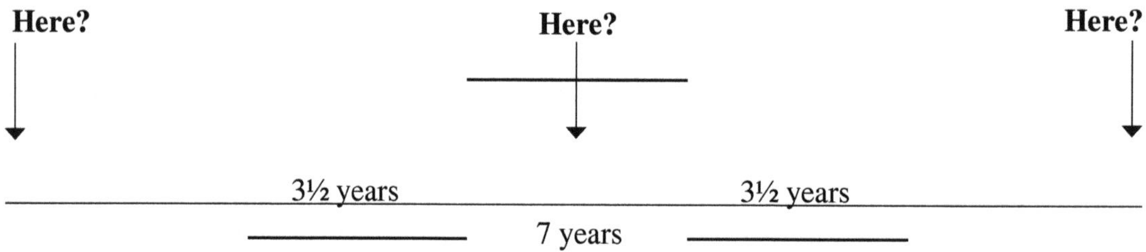

- The Rapture will not occur at the *beginning* of the seven years. During this time, Israel will join in a covenant relationship with the Antichrist and return to their old system of animal sacrifices, indicating that Israel will not yet be saved at the beginning of the seven-year treaty. Scripture also specifically states that the persecution of Israel by the Antichrist will last for the duration of 3 ½ years, not the whole seven-year period. **Write** "Israel not saved" under the first 3 ½ years.

- The Rapture will not occur at the *end* of the seven-year period, because we would need to tack on an additional 3 ½ years to allow for the fulfillment of prophecies regarding the 3 ½ year persecution of Israel at the hand of the Antichrist. The prophecy is a 7 year period. Not a 10 ½ year period. Therefore, the Rapture cannot occur at the end of the seven years.

A Hermeneutical or interpreting principle of prophetic Scripture prohibits the act of arbitrarily adding more time to the seven years. Extending this period of time would violate the principle of interpretation already confirmed by fulfillment. Because the first 69 weeks of this 70 week prophecy found in Daniel 9 were fulfilled exactly as decreed at the time of Jesus' First Coming, the part of the prophecy concerning the last week, the Seventieth Week, or last seven years, must also be fulfilled exactly as decreed. It will only last for the duration of seven years and no more. The interpreter cannot add to or subtract from a set time given in prophecy.

- **Write** "Israel saved" under the second 3 ½ years in the diagram above.

- The logical answer for the timing of the Rapture is in the middle of the seven-year period. This allows us to maintain an interpretation without creating a contradiction.

- **Write** the words "The Rapture," on the line below the middle "Here" in the diagram above. This is located at the mid-point of the seven years.

Check out "Israel Saved" and "The Antichrist Sits as 'God' in the Temple" and the way these events correlate to the Rapture on **Timeline One** (located at the end of Part One of this book.)

Summing it up

- Israel will join in a seven-year covenant/treaty relationship with the Antichrist.
- Israel is "not saved" during the first 3 ½ years of the seven-year treaty.
- Israel will see and believe in Jesus Christ about the middle of the seven year period.
- Israel will see Jesus at the Rapture.
- Israel will be "saved" throughout the second 3 ½ years of the seven-year treaty.
- Therefore, the Rapture will occur in the middle of the seven years.

Congratulations! You have discovered when the Rapture will occur according to the Scriptures.

You have seen how the three plots will merge together, coming to a full point of impact at the time of the Rapture.

Plot 1
The Antichrist will continue his diabolical reign for the last 3 ½ years of the Seventieth Week. As he controls the willing hearts and minds of the peoples of the world, great suffering will come to all. Throughout the last 3 ½ years of the seven-year period, the people on earth will bear the Wrath of God in all of God's fury. We will study this terrible judgment in another lesson.

Plot 2
Believers living in the end times will suffer greatly for their faith in Jesus Christ, but they will be gathered to Jesus at the time of His appearance at the Rapture. These glorified Believers will be filled with wonder and great joy on their actual arrival in heaven to see and experience the. . .you will have to wait until another lesson to read the end of this sentence.

Plot 3

Israel will remain on earth during the last 3 ½ years of the Seventieth Week. During this time, these new-born Christian Jews, because of the new found love they dearly hold for Jesus, will face extreme suffering for their faith. Joy will fill their souls as they endure the fires of affliction, pain, and distress.

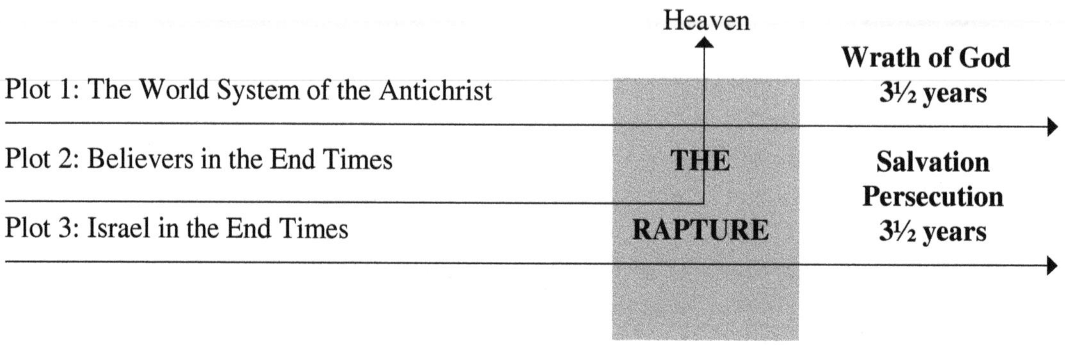

Heaven

Wrath of God
3½ years

Plot 1: The World System of the Antichrist

Plot 2: Believers in the End Times

THE RAPTURE

Salvation Persecution 3½ years

Plot 3: Israel in the End Times

JESUS CHRIST THE CLEANSING FOUNTAIN

Zechariah 13:1

LESSON **7A**

JESUS CHRIST THE RESURRECTION AND THE LIFE
John 11:25

Jesus is Resurrection. He is Life.
This is who He is. It is His name.

EVENT 4 THE RAPTURE AND RESURRECTION DAY

For Believers the Rapture is one of the most spectacular and desired of all events. You, as a Believer, will experience it.

In this lesson we will look at five different aspects of the Rapture.

- The Ascension of Jesus
- The Promise of Jesus' Return
- The Certainty of the Believer's Resurrection
- The Resurrection
  - Why the Need for a New Body?
  - How will the Body be Resurrected?
  - When Will the Rapture / Resurrection Day Occur?
  - What Happens at Death?
- The Rapture / Resurrection / Glorification Process

THE ASCENSION OF JESUS

Luke 9:51 (NIV)

> "*As the time approached for him to be taken up to heaven, Jesus resolutely set out for Jerusalem.*"

Jesus had just so much time on earth to complete the work of redemption. He knew that the appointed hour for His departure from this world was fast approaching. The cross now stood between Him and the time of His exaltation in heaven. ". . .*who for the joy set before him endured the cross, scorning its shame, and sat down at the right hand of the throne of God.*" (Hebrews 12:2 NIV)

After unimaginable suffering, Jesus accomplished His work on the cross and victoriously rose from the dead. From time to time, Jesus appeared to and disappeared from His disciples during a 40-day period. How do you think the disciples would have felt when these appearances stopped, if they hadn't literally and visibly witnessed Jesus' departure from the earth?

____

Do you think that they would keep wondering when He was going to appear to them again? Maybe they would have puzzled over what had become of Him. Would they feel insecure in their faith as the days passed? Jesus chose to affirm their faith with a visual exodus from earth. The disciples were permitted to see Him ascend to heaven.

The apostle Luke gives the account of Jesus' ascension and the promise of His future return in Luke 24:50-51 and Acts 1:1-2; 9-11. As you read the following Scripture notice the emphasis on the words *taken up*, the action, and *into heaven*, the destination. "*Taken up*" is expressed by two different Greek words, but they both mean "to be lifted up from the ground as was our Lord at His ascension." [KW]

Underline *taken up* and *into heaven* in the following verses. **Write** four observations from Act 1:9-11. This will help you to see in your mind the action taking place.

Luke 24:50-51

> *"Then Jesus led them to Bethany, and lifting his hands to heaven, he blessed them. While he was blessing them, he left them and was taken up to heaven."*

Acts 1:1-2; 9-11

> [1] *"In my first book* [the book of Luke] *I told you, Theophilus, about everything Jesus began to do and to teach* [2] *until the day he was taken up to heaven after giving his chosen apostles further instructions through the Holy Spirit.*
>
> [9]*. . . he was taken up into a cloud while they were watching, and they could no longer see him.* [10]*As they strained to see him rising into heaven, two white-robed men suddenly stood among them.* [11] *'Men of Galilee,' they said, 'why are you standing here staring into heaven? Jesus has been taken from you into heaven, but someday he will return from heaven in the same way you saw him go!'"*

Your Observations

1. ______________________________
2. ______________________________
3. ______________________________
4. ______________________________

Observations

Luke 24:50-51

Jesus had been walking up the Mount of Olives toward Bethany with His disciples giving them important instructions. At a certain spot, He lifted His hands to heaven and He blessed them. The very last words that the disciples heard from Jesus' lips were His gracious blessing on them.

The Venezuelans have a lovely tradition. When people would say good-bye to us, they would say, "Bendicion (Blessing)." Okay. . .whatever? Finally, some kind-hearted soul noticed our look of bewilderment and told us that people were asking for our blessing. For example, when a child is leaving the house, he will ask for his parents blessing, and Mom or Dad will respond with their blessing. This very touching tradition is an act of love and reveals an affectionate bond between the two individuals.

Your heavenly Father blesses you far beyond any human blessing; He has blessed you with every possible spiritual benefit. *"Blessed be the God and Father of our Lord Jesus Christ, who has blessed us with every spiritual blessing in the heavenly places in Christ."* (Ephesians 1:3 NKJV) You are a blessed child.

While Jesus was blessing them, He started to ascend and soon vanished from their sight. How would you have felt if you had been there that day and had seen this most amazing thing? Speechless? Awe-struck? How high did Jesus get before disappearing from sight? Acts 1:9___

____

Acts 1:9-11

As the disciples were straining to see Jesus, they suddenly experienced another remarkable sight right there among them. Two, white-robed angels convey to the disciples a promise. What is the promise? ______________________________How will He return? ______________________________The promise is a declaration of a true and actual return of Jesus. How? Scripture says *"in the same manner."* Jesus ascended into heaven in His resurrected body and will sometime in the future visibly appear again in the *"clouds"* of heaven. Jesus' appearance in *the clouds* is one of the distinctive characteristics of the Rapture passages.

Matthew 24:30 "And they will see the Son of Man coming on the clouds of heaven with power and great glory."

Luke gives the account of Jesus departure from the disciple's point of view. What do you think Jesus was thinking about when He ascended? Was He focused on heaven or on the earth as He was leaving this world? I would like for you to meditate on an unusual and imaginative narration of the Ascension.

Alexander Patterson, in his book The Greater Life and Work of Christ [1] dramatically presents Jesus' view of His disciples, Jerusalem, Israel, and the world as He ascends to heaven. It will undoubtedly give you something to think about.

> The ascension of Jesus is simply described by one of the witnesses: *"He lifted up His hands, and blessed them. And it came to pass, while He blessed them, He parted from them, and was carried up into heaven, and a cloud received Him out of their sight."* He was hidden from their sight, but they were not hidden from His. He looks down upon the little company at His feet. They are His flock. They heard His voice and followed Him. He remembers none of their failures or faithlessness. They are inexpressibly dear to Him. They are the nucleus of the church, they were entrusted with His truth for all the world and all the age. He is leaving them as sheep among wolves. They are to face untold dangers for His sake, and to suffer joyfully and at last to die, some of them as He died, because of their love for Him. But they are to be kept true and to finish their course in triumph and to meet Him in glory.
>
> As He rises, a larger scene meets His view. Jerusalem was spread out before Him. It has crucified Him. But He had cried, *"Father, forgive them,"* as His blood flowed out, and the prayer sealed with His heart's blood will be answered. It was the City of David, and He remembered His promise to David that his seed, Jesus, should sit on his

J.I. Packer "Jesus' ascension was his Father's act of withdrawing him from his disciples' gaze upward (a sign of exaltation) into a cloud (a sign of God's presence). This was not a form of space travel, but part two (the Resurrection being part one) of Jesus' return from the depths of death to the height of glory." [2]

throne. Jerusalem was the site of His Father's house. Temple and city must and will be redeemed.

He rises still higher. The land of Israel is all before Him. He had walked its roads and preached and healed from village to village. Under the open sky He as Jehovah had promised Abraham this land in possession forever. He has sealed that covenant afresh with His blood. He remembers Israel's early love, their following Him into and through the wilderness. He calls to mind all the long line of faithful men and women who had kept His truth. For a time His people are to be hardened, but He knows, they are to "*look upon Him whom they have pierced*," and to receive Him as their Messiah.

As He ascends, a still larger scene meets His eye. The world He made and has just redeemed rolls at His feet. Surely He paused to gaze upon it. Successively its cities swarming with people and all its lands with their many tribes of men pass in review before Him. To save this world He came. It is His by creation and now by redemption. It was all in His mind as He hung upon the cross. He took all its load of sin upon Himself and reconciled all by one sacrifice. He had left His heart's life-blood in its soil. He thinks of the coming centuries of wars and famines and gospel proclamation. He knows that out of every nation and tongue and tribe and people they shall come to sit down with Him in His Kingdom; and after some ages have passed, "*the earth shall be full of the glory of the Lord as the waters cover the sea.*"

Mark 16:19 "When the Lord Jesus had finished talking with them, he was taken up into heaven and sat down in the place of honor at God's right hand."

Hebrews 1:3 "When he had cleansed us from our sins, he sat down in the place of honor at the right hand of the majestic God in heaven."

Jesus' ascension was the visible sign of the conclusion of His physical presence on earth. Jesus returned to heaven in His resurrection body to begin His ministry from the position of power at the right hand of His Father. (Hebrews 1:3) "*All authority in heaven and on earth has been given to*" Jesus. (Matthew 28:18) Jesus was restored to the glory which He had with the Father before the world existed. (John 17:5)

Jesus' ascension has opened "*a new and living way. . .right into the presence of God.*" (Hebrews 10:19-22) All men, and especially God's children, are welcome to come to His all-powerful "*throne of grace*" to receive mercy and find grace to help in the time of need. (Hebrews 4:16 NKJV)

THE PROMISE OF JESUS' RETURN

Just as He had promised, "*I will not leave you orphans; I will come to you.*" (John 14:16-18) The Lord did return to earth to abide in His disciples through the presence of the Holy Spirit. However, Jesus has promised "*I will come again, and receive you to Myself.*" (John 14:3 NASB) Jesus will come again to take, gather together, all His followers to Himself. "*Yes, I am coming soon.*" (Revelation 22:20) His promise given through the angels at His ascension was looking to the day when He will come for His own at the Rapture soon to be followed by His Second Coming with His own to establish His Kingdom on earth

THE CERTAINTY OF THE BELIEVER'S RESURRECTION

Resurrection (*anastasis* Greek) is a rising of the body from the grave; a returning to life. The Bible teaches us that all Believers who have died will rise again at the Rapture. This is called the Resurrection Day. (1 Thessalonians 4:13-18; 1 Corinthians 15:23)

Ever since Jesus' ascension, all born-again Believers have looked for and longed for this glorious future event—Jesus' return. Why? Because all those that have died trusting in the Lord as their Savior from the Old Testament times and all those who have died in Christ during the Church Age and all those victorious Believers who will be alive at His coming will participate in the Rapture Event. Pause and think about it!

I Corinthians 15:22-23
"Just as everyone dies because we all belong to Adam, everyone who belongs to Christ will be given new life. But there is an order to this resurrection: Christ was raised as the first of the harvest; then all who belong to Christ will be raised when he comes back."

In our immediate surroundings at the Rapture, we will see with our own eyes the resurrection of the bodies of the dead who placed their faith in God's saving grace through Jesus Christ! We will also see the glorious transformation of those loyal followers of Christ who are living at the time of this great day!

People of the Bible Longed for the Resurrection Day

Consider these expressions of faith in a day of resurrection by these Old Testament Believers. It had not been revealed to them when the Resurrection Day would take place; they just knew that some far and distant day it would happen.

Job

"But as for me, I know that my Redeemer lives, and he will stand upon the earth at last. And after my body has decayed, yet in my body I will see God! I will see him for myself. Yes, I will see him with my own eyes. I am overwhelmed at the thought!" (Job 19:25-27 NIV)

Isaiah

"But those who die in the Lord will live; their bodies will rise again! Those who sleep in the earth will rise up and sing for joy! For your life-giving light will fall like dew on your people in the place of the dead." (Isaiah 26:19)

Daniel

"*As for you* [Daniel], *go your way until the end. You will rest, and then at the end of days, you will rise again to receive the inheritance set aside for you."* (Daniel 12:13)

Martha

In John 11:23-27 Martha affirmed this same belief when her brother Lazarus died. Jesus said to her, "*Your brother will rise again.*" "*Yes,*" Martha said, "*he will rise when everyone else rises, at the last day.*" Martha is stating here the same belief in a resurrection that all Old Testament Believers held.

Jesus' Declaration

Then Jesus gave His wonderful declaration and the basis for the resurrection: "*I AM the Resurrection and the Life*!" What an impact these words must have made on Martha; they are rich with meaning. Jesus is saying that He not only has the power to raise the dead body but that He is the very *power* that gives it life. Jesus imparts life, maintains life, and will restore the body to life.

Jesus continues to say, "*Anyone who believes in me will live, even after dying.*" Here Jesus, in reference to one's dying, is speaking of the separation of the spirit and the soul from the body. "*Everyone who lives in me and believes in me will never die.*" The spirit and the soul do not die, but continue to live in a specific place—in heaven!

"*Do you believe this, Martha?*" "*Yes, Lord,*" she told him, "*I believe that you are the Christ, the Son of God, who was to come into the world.*"

Do you believe that if you should die before Jesus comes again, that by Jesus' power on Resurrection Day you will be raised from the grave? ______ This is a good moment, like Martha, to make your personal declaration of faith.
I believe that ____

____

THE RESURRECTION

WHY THE NEED FOR A NEW BODY?

When we think about heaven and life that never ends, we can readily understand that a resurrection of the old body would be very unsuitable to live eternally. Let's see what the Bible says about the old, earthly body.

1 Corinthians 15:50 (RSV)

> *"I tell you this, brethren: flesh and blood cannot inherit the kingdom of God, nor does the perishable inherit the imperishable."*

Fill in the blanks from the verse above: Flesh and blood, the physical body, cannot inherit the kingdom of God. Is the body we live in: adequate ___________ or inadequate ___________ for living in heaven? Nor does the ______________________, that which decays, inherit the __________________, that which will never decay and will exist forever.

During His earthly ministry, did the people that Jesus resurrected live forever, or did they eventually die again? ____________________________. Why didn't they live forever? ________

____.

I'm sure you answered something like this: even though they were resurrected, they still lived in the old, perishable, earthly body; therefore, they eventually died again.

We could also call the Rapture and Resurrection Day—Glorification Day! *"Our bodies are buried in brokenness, but they will be raised in* *glory*. *They are buried in weakness, but they will be raised in strength* [power]." (1 Corinthians 15:43) Your glorified body will be a creation of beauty and perfection.

HOW WILL THE BODY BE RESURRECTED?

Quickened

But, we ask, how is the body resurrected? Quickened! The answer lies in the word *quicken.*

1 Corinthians 15:35-38 (NIV)

> [35] *"But someone may ask, 'How are the dead raised? With what kind of body will they come?' [36]How foolish! What you sow does not come to life unless it dies. [37]When you sow, you do not plant the body that will be, but just a seed, perhaps of wheat or of something else. [38]But God gives it a body as he has determined, and to each kind of seed he gives its own body."*

The fascinating Greek word *zoopoieo* is used in verse 36 to express *"come to life."* It is translated in the King James Version as *quickened.* This word *quickened* in the New Testament is used primarily of raising the dead to life and generally used in reference to salvation. *Quicken* is the power of God and means *to vitalize* (to endow with life; to invigorate), *reanimate* (to fill with life), *to make alive.* It is like a man with cardiac arrest. He dies, and someone using a defibrillator zaps (*quickens*) him back to life. It is a "kick start" back to life.

This *quickening* has already taken place in the Believer's soul and spirit. We call this being born-again by the Spirit of God. We are a new creation in Christ because this *quickening* has brought about a basic change in our soul and spirit. (2 Corinthians 5:17) *"Even when we were dead in sins,* [He] *hath quickened us* [made alive spiritually] *together with Christ."* (Ephesians 2:5 KJV) Wouldn't it be interesting if we asked people if they have been *quickened*? Has your soul and spirit been *quickened* by the Spirit of God? That might get their attention.

But our body must pass through the process of death before it will be *quickened.* Let's look at Romans 8:11 (NIV): *"And if the Spirit of him who raised Jesus from the dead is living in you, He who raised Christ from the dead will also* [quicken] *give life to your mortal bodies through his Spirit, who lives in you."*

The Expositor's Bible Commentary explains this in the following manner.

> "The Spirit's future work on behalf of the saints will be to [*quicken*] "give life" to their mortal bodies. . . The life bestowed by the Spirit, in that coming day, is beyond the power of death or any other agency to vitiate [corrupt, spoil] or destroy. It is the very life of God, blessedly spiritual and indestructibly eternal." [3]

How long will it take to be changed by this *quickening* process? Read 1 Corinthians 15:51-52 (NIV) and circle the answer.

> *"Listen, I tell you a mystery: We will not all sleep* [die], *but we will all be changed—in a flash, in the twinkling of an eye, at the last trumpet."*

"We have a building from God, a house [body] *not made with hands, eternal in the heavens..."* (2 Corinthians 5:1 NASB)

Two Characteristics of our Resurrection Body:
1) God is not taking the old constituent parts of our body to build our new one, but He is building it completely new. It will be a product made directly by God. It is now being made in heaven for us and will come from heaven.
2) It will be eternal both in duration and in quality which means that it cannot be lost, broken up or destroyed. [KW]

The change to a new glorified body at the Rapture will happen instantly. The Greek word for "twinkling" is *rhipe* which signifies in this case a blink of the eye, "the shortest possible moment of time, and with a startling suddenness." [4]

WHEN WILL THE RAPTURE / RESURRECTION DAY OCCUR?

Matthew 24:29-31 (NKJV)

> [29] *"Immediately after the tribulation of those days the sun will be darkened, and the moon will not give its light; the stars will fall from heaven, and the powers of the heavens will be shaken.* [30] *Then the sign of the Son of Man will appear in heaven, and then all the tribes of the earth will mourn, and they will see the Son of Man coming on the clouds of heaven with power and great glory.* [31] *And He will send His angels with a great sound of a trumpet, and they will gather together His elect from the four winds, from one end of heaven to the other."*

1 Corinthians 15:51-52 (NIV)

> [51] *"Listen, I tell you a mystery: We will not all sleep* [die], *but we will all be changed—* [52] *in a flash, in the twinkling of an eye, at the last trumpet. For the trumpet will sound, the dead will be raised imperishable, and we will be changed."*

1 Thessalonians 4:16-17 (NIV)

> [16] *"For the Lord himself will come down from heaven, with a loud command, with the voice of the Archangel and with the trumpet call of God, and the dead in Christ will rise first.* [17] *After that, we who are still alive and are left will be caught up together with them in the clouds to meet the Lord in the air. And so we will be with the Lord forever.*

According to Matthew 24:29, when will the Rapture and Resurrection Day take place? _____ ____. **Underline** it.
What announces this great day? Matthew 24:31 ______________________________
1 Corinthians 15:52 ______________________________ 1 Thessalonians 4:16 ___________ ______________________________________. **Circle** each phrase in the Scriptures above.
Matthew clearly indicates that the Rapture, Resurrection Day, will take place after the Great Tribulation of the Believers living at that time.

Like the constant mention of the clouds, each of these Scriptures indicate that the sound of a trumpet will announce the Rapture Event. The body of Christ has been completed (Romans 11:25), the Nation of Israel has been saved, and the trumpet blast appears to mark the end of sinners response to the gospel call for salvation. God in His foreknowledge does not give any indication of people coming to Christ from this time forward. To the contrary, during the last 3 ½ years mankind *"cursed the name of God. . .They did not repent of their sins and turn to God and give him glory."* (Revelation 16:8-11)

Listen, dear Believer, for the trumpet (*salpigx,* Greek). This word means that the sound will be a loud, shaking vibration, "a quavering, a reverberation" [5] that will surround and envelope the whole earth.

WHAT HAPPENS AT DEATH?

The answer to this question is essential to your understanding of the Rapture process.

Spirit, Soul, and Body

Have you had the shocking experience of looking into a casket at the body of a loved one? Shocking, because it just isn't them! It impresses you that something is missing. There lies their body but the most vital part of them is absent. Their person, that which makes them *them,* is gone.

What does the Word of God tell us about who we are? In the following verse, circle the three parts that compose our being.

1 Thessalonians 5:23 (NKJV)

> *"Now may the God of peace Himself sanctify you completely; and may your whole spirit, soul, and body be preserved blameless at the coming of our Lord Jesus Christ."*

According to this verse. . .
What was lying in the casket of your loved one? ______________________
What was missing in the casket of your loved one? ______________________

Paul prays that your whole person, the immaterial part of you and the material part of you, as created by God, be preserved or kept safe until Jesus comes again. The word for *preserved* in the Greek language is *tereo* meaning "to guard (from loss or injury) by keeping an eye on it." [S] What a heart-warming truth! God is keeping an eye on the body of each of His deceased loved ones.

"Whole spirit, soul, and body," the word "*whole*" is the Greek word *holokleros* meaning "complete in every part; entire." [S] Because the body is included in your sanctification and safe keeping, we see an implication here. The resurrection of the body from the dead is to be reunited to its spirit and soul so that man may live forever in a glorified body. Death will separate the soul and spirit from the body for a while, but ultimately, the Believer will be a complete, glorified person at the Rapture. The bodies of Believers (perhaps their DNA?) lying in the grave are under the watchful eye of our Lord.

Let's look at two Scriptures

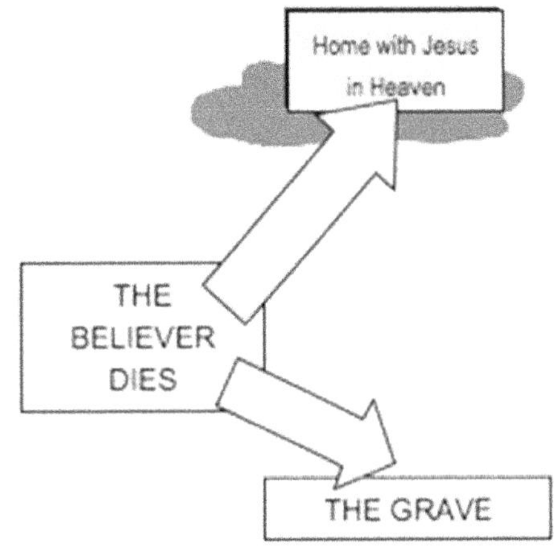

Genesis 3:19 (NIV)
"By the sweat of your brow you will eat your food until you return to the ground, since from it you were taken; for dust you are and to dust you will return."

2 Corinthians 5:6, 8-9
"So we are always confident, even though we know that as long as we live in these bodies we

William Barclay "We call this world the land of the living; but it would in fact be more correct to call it the land of the dying. And through Jesus Christ we know that when death comes we do not pass out of the land of the living; we pass into the land of the living. Through Jesus Christ we know that we are journeying, not to the sunset, but to the sunrise."[5]

are not at home with the Lord. . .and we would rather be away from these earthly bodies, for then we will be at home with the Lord. So whether we are here in this body or away from this body, our goal is to please him."

When Believers die their spirits and souls do not lose consciousness nor do they pass through some dark valley. Rather, they instantly go to be with Jesus in heaven. However, their bodies lie in the grave and deteriorate. Sadly, when Unbelievers die, their bodies are also placed in a grave but their spirits and souls go to the abyss. (Psalm 9:17)

Write "soul/spirit" and "body" in the proper arrow of the diagram above. How real is this living hope of the believer's destination to you? Are you living for that day? When your loved ones see you in the casket, will they have total assurance that you are home with Jesus?

THE RAPTURE / RESURRECTION / GLORIFICATION PROCESS

The most clear and concise teaching on what takes place at the Rapture is found in 1 Thessalonians 4:13-18. We will study *who* is affected by the Rapture and the series of *actions* that describe this awesome Event.

1 Thessalonians 4:13-18 (NIV)

> 13 *"Brothers we do not want you to be ignorant about those who fall asleep, or to grieve like the rest of men, who have no hope.* 14 *We believe that Jesus died and rose again and so we believe that God will bring with Jesus those who have fallen asleep in him.*
>
> 15 *According to the Lord's own word, we tell you that we who are still alive, who are Left till the coming of the Lord, will certainly not precede those who have fallen asleep.*
>
> 16 *For the Lord himself will come down from heaven, with a loud command, with the voice of the archangel and with the trumpet call of God, and the dead in Christ will rise first.*
>
> 17 *After that, we who are still alive and are left will be caught up together with them in the clouds to meet the Lord in the air. And so we will be with the Lord forever.* 18 *Therefore encourage one another with these words."*

A statement of faith

This classic teaching about the Rapture process in verse 14 begins with a statement of faith that substantiates another statement of faith. A Believer cannot and does not select which Scriptures he believes in and what he does not believe in. A true, born-again Believer believes *all* the Bible is God's infallible word, and therefore, it cannot err.

Fill in the blanks from verse 14 and tell the Lord that you believe every word of it while you are writing.

"I believe that ______________________________ and so I believe that __________
____."

It is of great value for a follower of Jesus Christ to state his beliefs often and with conviction. Every new teaching from the Word of God should be integrated into your personal belief system, that which defines who you are and guides your every thought and act.

For example, as I say with all the conviction of my soul: "I believe that Jesus died and rose again," I am confirming a personal decision to believe this statement which means that I put my *trust* in what it says, I *adhere* to it like glue, and I *rely* totally on it for all that it signifies. These three actions give us the definition of the Bible word *believe*, *pisteuo* in the Greek, "to trust, to adhere to, and to rely on." [6] One who believes in the revealed truths of the Bible is a steadfast *pistos*, (Believer.)

THE "WHO" PART

Read again 1 Thessalonians 4:13-18. Look for two groups of Believers mentioned in this Scripture.

Group 1

Who are they?

verse 13 those ______________________________

verse 14 those ______________________________

verse 15 those ______________________________

verse 16 the ______________________________

clarification

I would like to clarify a term used in these verses. "*Fallen asleep*" is a figure of speech known as a euphemism which softens a harsh reality and is used by a sensitive speaker. In this Scripture *asleep* means "dead" and stated as dead in verse 16. Today we generally say, "passed away," or for a born- again believer we say, "He or she went home to be with the Lord."

Do the participants of Group 1 have a body? __________ yes __________ no

Group 1 consists of those who are home with Jesus in heaven. This group does not have a body; their persons at this moment consist of spirit and soul.

Group 2

Who are they?

verse 15 ______________________________

____

verse 17 ______________________________

Group 2 consists of those Believers on earth who have not died but have lived up to the time of the coming of the Lord at the Rapture. "*We who are still alive, who are left till the coming of the Lord.*"

THE "ACTION" PART

What does Jesus do? Look at verse 16 and fill in the blanks. Try to visualize this.

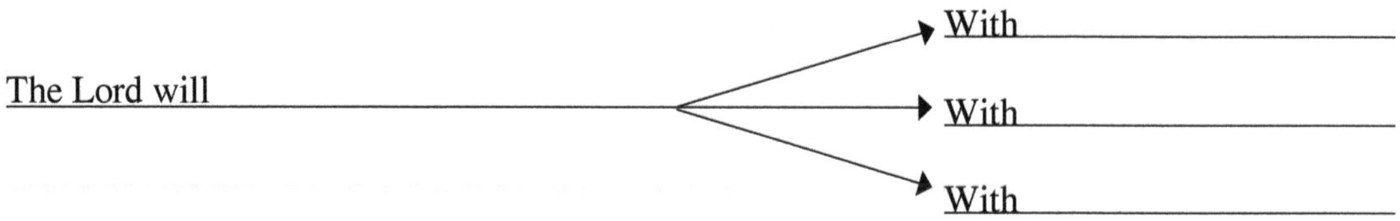

The Command
First, King Jesus gives a *command* of incitement, that is, His order stirs to action the dead.

The Archangel
Secondly, the voice of the archangel could very well be the command spoken in another Rapture passage, Revelation 14:14-16. Possibly, "*and another angel came out of the temple*" is the archangel who delivers the Father's order to bring home all the saints of God.

Revelation 14:14-16 (NKJV)

> [14] *"Then I looked, and behold, a white cloud and on the cloud sat One like the Son of Man, having on His head a golden crown, and in His hand a sharp sickle.* [15] *And another angel came out of the temple, crying with a loud voice to Him who sat on the cloud, 'Thrust in Your sickle and reap, for the time has come for You to reap, for the harvest of the earth is ripe.'* [16] *So He who sat on the cloud thrust in His sickle on the earth, and the earth was reaped."*

The Trumpet of God
Finally, *God blows His trumpet, the last trumpet.* The first trumpet was sounded by God when He descended upon Mt. Sinai to enter a covenant relationship with Israel.

Exodus 19:13, 16, 18-19 (NKJV)

> [13] *"When the trumpet sounds long, they* [the Israelites] *shall come near the mountain.* [The gathering or assembly of God's people.] [16] *Then it came to pass on the third day, in the morning that there were thunderings and lightnings, and a thick cloud on the mountain; and the sound of the trumpet was very loud, so that all the people who were in the camp trembled.* [18] *Now Mount Sinai was completely in smoke, because the LORD descended upon it in fire. Its smoke ascended like the smoke of a furnace, and the whole mountain quaked greatly.* [19] *And when the blast of the trumpet sounded long and became louder and louder, Moses spoke, and God answered him by voice."*

When the people heard the trumpet sound what were they to do? verse 13 ____________ ____ Then God's advent. His glorious presence descended upon the mountain in fire and cloud. Great phenomena shook the whole mountain.

From the Mt. Sinai occasion, God established The Feast of Trumpets, or Rosh Hashanah, to be one of the seven holidays for the Jewish people. These seven feasts are celebrated at different times of the year and are all prophetically related to Christ's redemptive ministry. "Four of the seven holidays occur in the spring of the year. . .the events which the four spring feasts of the Lord typify in the Hebrew Scriptures [Old Testament] have been fulfilled in the Messiah. . .The final three holidays occur in the fall of the year within a brief period. . .As the first four holidays depict events associated with Messiah's first coming, these final three holidays depict specific events associated with His second coming." [7]

The Feast of Trumpets, the fifth feast, points to the return of King Jesus at the Rapture and the subsequent period of judgment on the world. One of the most informative studies you will ever find on this subject is the book <u>The Feasts of the Lord, God's Prophetic Calendar from Calvary to the Kingdom</u> by Kevin Howard and Marvin Rosenthal. (see end note 7)

On Rosh Hashanah the ram's horn, the shofar, was sounded "to call the Jews to repentance. It was a call to the dead to arise and live again, to wake up from sin to regeneration through repentance. Its purpose was to remind the Lord that He was in covenant relationship with His people Israel and to deal gently with them, not according to their merits but according to His gracious promises specially made to Abraham and to the patriarchs of old." [8]

The trumpet, as you can see, was not blown by a human at Mt Sinai. It was the trumpet of God! Again the trumpet of God will sound, the last trumpet, and all of God's people, both dead and alive will be assembled to meet King Jesus in the Shekinah glory-cloud in the heavens. (1 Corinthians 15:52)

At the sound of the trumpet of God, the nation of Israel will see Christ and repent, and the God of forgiveness will cover them with His grace.

At the sound of the trumpet of God, Unbelievers will tremble and suffer all the consequences brought about by their choice to abandon God and to worship the Antichrist for the great day of God's wrath has come, and who is able to stand? (Revelation 6:17)

What action takes place with Group 1?
In verse 14 we read that the dead will accompany Jesus when He appears at the Rapture. What part of their person is in heaven at this time? their _____________ and ______________.

In verse 16, the last phrase, what will happen to the third part of their being?

____

So, we see that Jesus will bring the spirit and soul of all those in heaven with Him to be reunited with their resurrected bodies.

What action takes place with Group 2?
After the dead in Christ rise from the grave, *"Then, <u>together</u> with them* [simultaneously], *we who are still alive and remain on the earth will be <u>caught up together</u> in the clouds to meet*

"...to meet the Lord in the air." To leave a place and go to meet one who is coming toward you. It involves responding to an action of another. [KW]

the Lord in the air. Then we will be with the Lord forever. So encourage each other with these words."

Everyone meets in the clouds, in the air. Remember the cloud of Acts 1:9, 11 *"After saying this, he was taken up into a cloud while they were watching, and they could no longer see him. . . Jesus has been taken from you into heaven, but someday he will return from heaven in the same way you saw him go!'*

"Caught Up"

Harpazo: Jude 23; Acts 23:10; John 6:15; John 10: 12, 28, 29

The term *Rapture* is not found in the Bible but is used doctrinally to identify the event. Its meaning comes from two Bible phrases: *caught up* and *gathering together.* The Greek word used for this phrase is *harpazo* and conveys the idea of taking something or someone for oneself by force suddenly exercised. Synonyms of the word are: *pluck, pull, snatch, take (by force), grab.* [V]

Other verses in the Bible may help us to understand the action taken at the Rapture. "To snatch or catch away, is said of the act of the Spirit of the Lord in regard to Philip, Acts 8:39; of Paul being caught up to Paradise, 2 Corinthians 12:2, 4; of the Rapture of the saints at the return of the Lord, 1 Thessalonians 4:17; [V] Jesus says that no one can *snatch* His sheep out of His hand, John 10:28.

Jesus' power is displayed at the Rapture by snatching up millions of Believers to Himself either from the grave or from their situation of persecution and forcefully removing them from earth by transporting them to heaven.

"Gathering together"

The author of the book of Mark describes this "*gathering together"* in the following manner.

Mark 13:27 (NKJV)

> *"And then He will send His angels, and gather together His elect from the four winds* [the four points of the compass] *from the farthest part of earth to the farthest part of heaven."*

The Greek word for *together* is *episunago* which means "a complete collection." [S] In Mark *gather together* means "an assembling together" at one place. [S] This word conveys to us that at the time of the Rapture all Believers in their new bodies will rise from every point of the compass of the earth and heaven to assemble in the clouds at the gathering point, the point of attraction, the gathering center—King Jesus!

HOW TO LIVE IN ANTICIPATION OF THE RAPTURE

1 Corinthians 15:54, 57-58 (NASB)

> [54] *"But when this perishable will have put on the imperishable, and this mortal will have put on immortality, then will come about the saying that is written, "DEATH IS SWALLOWED UP in victory.*

57 "Thanks be to God, who gives us the victory through our Lord Jesus Christ. 58 Therefore, my beloved brethren, be steadfast, immovable, always abounding in the work of the Lord, knowing that your toil is not in vain in the Lord."

Underline the following words in the verses above and look them up in a dictionary: steadfast, immovable, and abound. How does this inspire you to live for this outstanding moment of history?

Steadfast ______________________________

Be Steadfast!

Immovable ______________________________

Be Immovable!

Abound ______________________________

Abound in the Work of the Lord!

JESUS CHRIST THE RESURRECTION AND THE LIFE

John 11:25

LESSON **7B**

JESUS CHRIST OUR SAVIOR
John 4:42

A great multitude. . .crying out with a loud voice, "Salvation belongs to our God who sits upon the throne, and to the Lamb!"
Revelation 7:9-10

EVENT 4
THE RAPTURE

THE WHITE-ROBED MULTITUDE IN HEAVEN

THE DAY YOU EXPERIENCED THE RAPTURE

When the Rapture occurs, each Believer will be living in their own set of circumstances; but all will have one thing in common. All will be enduring persecution at the hand of the Antichrist. The following scenario is an imaginative scene at the time of the Rapture with you as the main character. It is based on Psalm 13:1-2, Matthew 24:29-31, 1 Corinthians 15:51-53, 1 Thessalonians 4:13-18, and Revelation 6:12-17.

Just for a moment, place yourself in the position of one of the many triumphant Believers living in the Great Tribulation. You have steadfastly proclaimed Christ. By His grace and through His provision and strengthening, you have remained firm in your faith. You have survived the worst testing ever experienced by followers of Jesus. That is saying a lot.

Late in the afternoon, you have covertly entered the cemetery and are standing beside the grave of your loved one whose life was so cruelly destroyed by the followers of the Antichrist. Exhausted, your arms hang listlessly, and your head bows in sorrow. In your hand you clutch a few wild flowers picked along the way to lay lovingly on the grave. Your lonely heart is faint within you; you hunger and thirst from the unbearable heat of the sun. So much suffering! You cry to God, "Oh Lord, how long. . ."

Your prayer is suddenly cut short by a roaring sound beneath your feet. The earth violently heaves upward throwing you to the ground! Earthquake! A huge, huge earthquake! The sun! Where did it go? It is black. You whisper, "Can it be?" In the darkness you see the moon, red like blood! You call out, "Oh Lord, can it be?" Your once fainting heart now is racing with anticipation! Suddenly, you hear a long blast of a trumpet that grows louder and louder. You look up and joyfully exclaim, "Yes, oh yes! It's the trumpet of God!"

The sky splits apart. You hear a mighty shout from the archangel. YOU SEE HIM! King Jesus is coming down in the clouds shouting a command. The earth trembles anew, you brace yourself as you listen to a deep rolling rumble coming toward the surface. The grave at your feet splits open! You can hardly believe your eyes! The remains of your precious loved one are impacted by her spirit and soul jolting her to life...a new glorified body! You are speechless!

In the next instant, YOU ARE CHANGED! GLORIFIED! You are free! You are transformed into the image of Christ! Glory! Awe! Praise! Love! Joy! Things are happening so fast. You reach for your beloved. Arm in arm you ascend together. As you go higher and higher, you see a great multitude from all over the world rising. Clouds surround you; they transport you. Arms extended, the King, your Savior, majestically waits your arrival in the air. Oh, what joy! King Jesus leads us home.

The glorious procession enters heaven. We hear thousands upon thousands of heavenly beings shouting:

> *"Who may ascend into the hill of the LORD? And who may stand in His holy place? He who has clean hands and a pure heart, who has not lifted up his soul to falsehood, and has not sworn deceitfully. He shall receive blessing from the LORD and righteousness from the God of his salvation. This is the generation of those who seek Him, who seek Thy face—even Jacob.*
>
> *Lift up your heads, O gates, and be lifted up, O ancient doors, that the King of glory may come in! Who is the King of glory? The LORD strong and mighty. The LORD mighty in battle. Lift up your heads, O gates, and lift them up, O ancient doors, that the King of glory may come in! Who is this King of glory? The LORD of hosts, He is the King of glory."* (Psalm 24:3-10 NASB)

With King Jesus in the lead, the redeemed of the earth approach the throne of God and . . .

The Rapture has taken place and the Jews have been saved according to the Scriptures. What happens next? Revelation 7 continues the account:

- Revelation 7:1-3: preparations for the Wrath of God of the last 3 ½ years.
- Revelation 7:4-8: the sealing of the 144,000 Christian Jews saved at the Rapture who serve their Lord Jesus on earth during the last 3 ½ years.
- Revelation 7:9-17: raptured Great Tribulation Believers, from every nation and tribe and people and language, stand before the throne of God and the Lamb.

In this lesson we will study:

The White-Robed Multitude in Heaven
A Closer Look at the Last Martyrs of the Church
The Characteristics of a Martyr
Safe at Last

THE WHITE-ROBED MULTITUDE IN HEAVEN

This is not a new Event, rather, it is a continuation of your Event 4 the Rapture and Resurrection Day. Look for The White-Robed Multitude to the left of the Judgement Seat of Christ on **Timeline Two** (located at the end of Part One of this book.)

Revelation 7:9-12

> 9*After this I* [the apostle John] *saw a vast crowd, too great to count, from every nation and tribe and people and language, standing in front of the throne and before the Lamb. They were clothed in white robes and held palm branches in their hands.* 10 *And*

they were shouting with a mighty shout, "Salvation comes from our God who sits on the throne and from the Lamb!"
[11]*And all the angels were standing around the throne and around the elders and the four living beings. And they fell before the throne with their faces to the ground and worshiped God.* [12] *They sang,*

"Amen! Blessing and glory and wisdom and thanksgiving and honor and power and strength belong to our God forever and ever! Amen."

1. How large is this multitude? (verse 9) ______________________________

2. Who forms this multitude? (verse 9) ______________________________

3. Do these people look like overcomers? ______________________________

4. Where do they stand? (verse 9) ______________________________

Read about the throne room of heaven in Revelation 4 to better understand the magnitude of what this location means.

You, as a part of this great multitude, are standing in a great place of honor—before the throne of God. This will be your first, close-up look into the face of your beloved Savior. What will all of you be saying to Jesus? (verse 10) ______________________________
______________________________. Your first words are an expression of profound gratitude for your salvation. You fully comprehend that you owe both the preservation of your faith through the Great Tribulation and your deliverance from persecution, to the grace of God.

5. The great multitude is standing before God's throne. Where are the heavenly beings standing in relation to the multitude? (v.11) ______________________________.
Try to picture this magnificent scene in your mind.

6. What do all the heavenly beings do at this moment? (v.11) They ______________________________
______________________________.

Identifying the multitude
Revelation 7:13-14 (NIV)

[13] *Then one of the elders asked me, "These in white robes—who are they, and where did they come from?"* [14] *I answered, "Sir, you know."*

And he said, "These are they who have come out of the great tribulation; they have washed their robes and made them white in the blood of the Lamb."

Observe how God wants to make sure that readers of the book of Revelation understand who this multitude is. It is this reason, that the conversation between the heavenly elder and the apostle John is recorded.

Revelation 3:4-5 (NIV) "They will walk with Me, dressed in white, for they are worthy. He who overcomes will, like them, be dressed in white..."

Take note of what the elder says about these people in verse 13. **Circle** the words in verse 14 that tell us from where those wearing white robes have come. Then fill in the following blanks.

"*These are they who have come out of the* ________________________ *they have washed their robes and made them white in the blood of the Lamb.*"

The individuals who make up this multitude are clearly identified and distinguished as victorious overcomers. That is, these are the Believers who endured and survived the Great Tribulation right up to the moment of the Rapture.

Harriet Beecher Stowe "Even in this world they will have their judgment-day; and their names, which went down in the dust like a gallant banner trodden in the mire, shall rise again all glorious in the sight of nations." [1]

Without a doubt, the martyrs of the fifth seal who died during the Great Tribulation under the oppression of the World System of the Antichrist form a part of this special group. They also "*came out of the great tribulation,*" not alive, but martyred. They too, are dressed in white robes. (Revelation 6:9-11)

Out of all of the millions from all the ages who have been resurrected and glorified at the Rapture, this group is singled out. Why is it that God will honor this group at this time?

Throughout church history, there have been many dreadful persecutions of the church. However, the severity of the persecution that will take place during the end times will far surpass them all. Yes, these Tribulation Believers lovingly and loyally bear it all for Jesus' sake in His name.

A CLOSER LOOK AT THE LAST MARTYRS OF THE CHURCH

"These are they who have come out of the great tribulation. . ."
Let's analyze the mind and heart of the martyr. What qualities do you think a martyr should have?

____

____

____

I wish that I knew what you just wrote, so that I could add your insights to mine. The topic of martyrdom is a serious matter. Let's look at its meaning in the Greek language.

The biblical meaning of "martyr"

Many years ago, I was looking for the meaning of *martyr* in a Greek dictionary. To my total surprise it read: "for MARTYR see WITNESS." Strange. These are two, very different words. Right? However, I followed the directions and looked up the word *witness.*

Lo and behold, the Greek word *martus* or *marturion* is the translation for *martyr*, *witness*, and *testimony*. These three words in English are expressed by just one word in the Greek language, *martyr.* Notice how the following Scripture reads when we include the Greek word alongside the English translation.

Acts 1:8

> *"But you will receive power when the Holy Spirit comes upon you. And you will be my* [martus, martyrs] *witnesses, telling people about me everywhere—in Jerusalem, throughout Judea, in Samaria, and to the ends of the earth."*

Did that shake you up a bit? It shook me up. I thought of Scripture after Scripture where we read "witness" and "testimony," that uses the Greek word *martyr.* Believers that come out of the Great Tribulation will have the heart of a martyr/witness in all the sense that the word implies.

Consider the Bible definition of *martyr.* Let your mind dwell on it and your soul absorb its meaning:

Vine's Greek Dictionary: [V]

- Witness/Martyr – *(martus* or *martur)* both of these words indicate one who can or does [declare, affirm] what he has seen or heard or knows.

- Testimony – *(marturion)* is mainly subjective, having to do especially with the [the speaker's] personal experience.

Hebrew-Greek Key Word Study Bible: [KW]

- Martyr/ Witness – *(martus)* In reference to Scriptures which refer to those who have died for Christ (Acts 22:20; Revelation 2:13; 17:6) these verses. . .should not be understood as if their witness consisted in their suffering death but rather that their witnessing of Jesus became the cause of their death.

- Testimony – *(marturion)* The meaning is that the [speaker] bases what he says on his own direct knowledge coincident with reality, and the gospel is preached as a narrative of actual and practical truth, a declaration of facts.

The Believer witness/martyr is one who affirms his belief in the Gospel even to the point of personal suffering. This suffering can take the form of emotional distress, economic consequences, social discrimination, physical discomfort or abuse, and may even result in death. The Believer will witness, declare, and affirm what he has seen, heard, or knows, even though his witness for Jesus may cause his death. The Believer chooses humble obedience and allegiance to the Word of God and to the Truth, which is Jesus Christ. (John 14:6)

Do you remember, at the end of the first lesson, what my pastor told me as a new believer? He did a great job of summing up the meaning of the word *martyr.*

> "Kathy, as you think of your future as a foreign missionary, you must always be ready to preach, pray, or die at a moment's notice."

Obviously, I am still alive. However, Jesus' command, "*you will be my witnesses* [martyrs]," (Acts 1:8) is just as binding today for an elderly, slow-motion witness, as it was for a young, energetic witness. We are witnesses unto death, whether we die a natural death or one that is forced upon us.

THE CHARACTERISTICS OF A MARTYR

Herb and I served Christ as missionaries with The Christian and Missionary Alliance. In 1892, the founder of this mission, Dr. A.B. Simpson, wrote out what he considered to be the essential characteristics of a missionary. I believe these distinguishing traits can help us to truly understand the heart of a genuine follower of Christ in any age. However, they are especially true of end-time Christian martyrs. The following is a list of some of these characteristics.

1. We want men and women who are thoroughly converted and know it.

2. We want men and women who are fully consecrated to God, sanctified by the blood of Jesus Christ and filled with the Holy Spirit.

3. We want people so saved from themselves that they are at leisure to work for the good of others and are not fighting an everlasting battle to keep their own salvation.

4. We want men and women who are burning with the love of people and longing to lead others to Christ.

5. We want men and women who can live simply, endure hardship, deny themselves, and put up with every discomfort. We want Christian soldiers who can travel with a backpack and sleep in their boots without grumbling, glad they can do it for Christ's sake. We can enjoy "things" but we must not be bound or hindered by "things." As it says in 1 Timothy 6:17 (NKJV), *"God, who gives us richly all things to enjoy."*

6. We want men and women who are easy to get along with, who have died to self and self-will, who can keep sweet and can submit themselves to their leaders. . .until they have become qualified leaders themselves. We want those who are adjustable, good-natured, ready to meet persecution and insult without getting angry, who can live the gospel of Christ among the people to whom they are sent even as their Master did.

7. We want men and women who trust the Lord for their physical needs and are able to stand exposure, hardship, and do real work for God. Christ is able to give this kind of victory. . .and if we trust Him, He will enable us to do all things, to endure all things that His providence may lay upon us.

8. We want men and women who know the Lord so well that they can have His joy under all circumstances; who will not be afraid of loneliness or privation; who ask no greater recompense than the privilege of serving and pleasing Him, and who go out not wanting sympathy but rejoicing in the name of missionary and the privilege of enduring suffering and even shame for Christ who died for them.

We can use this list of characteristics to evaluate our own lives. Examine each item, and ask yourself, "Does my life display this characteristic?" Then, prayerfully make a declaration that goes something like this: "I will permit the Holy Spirit to develop this Christian quality in my life," or "I see this virtue in my life, but I will allow the Lord to strengthen and refine it." By doing this, you will be able to stand steadfast and true to the Lord in the day of evil. This list should not limit the characteristics that the Holy Spirit wishes to display in your life, but it is a good starting point.

This is not a study about the history of the church or of missions, but if it was, I could mention other countless, faithful, witnesses/martyrs whose hearts are in sync with the heart of the apostle Paul. "*Yes, everything else is worthless when compared with the infinite value of knowing Christ Jesus my Lord. For His sake I have discarded everything else, counting it all as garbage, so that I could gain Christ and become one with Him.*" (Philippians 3:8, 9) To know Christ and to make Him known.

I will live my life as Christ Jesus lived His.
"Let this mind be in you [me] which was also in Christ Jesus..." (Philippians 2:5 NKJV)

Our first years in Venezuela were very difficult. Our ministry had been suppressed for four years. I just couldn't seem to go any further. Reaching out to Jesus, I cried, "Lord, I would rather be in any other place but here!" In great distress I waited before Him on my knees.

His answer came to me softly, "*What other place*?" Well yes, what other place was I thinking of? This is the place He has put us. That is all He said, but it was enough. With those words the Lord removed the heavy burden from my shoulders. He *freed* my hands from the wearisome basket of worries I was clutching. In distress I called, and He delivered me.

I learned two things from Jesus' reply to my discouraged heart. First, a Believer can be in only one geographical place and be in the perfect will of God. Herb and I were in that place. God had no other place for us at that time. What peace came with this discovery.

Psalm 81:5-7 (RSV)
"I hear a voice I had not known: 'I relieved your shoulder of the burden; your hands were freed from the basket. In distress you called, and I delivered you...'"

Secondly, never throw in the towel in your time of hardship. Your trial may seem like forever, wearily walking down a dark, dingy ally with no end in sight and no light at the end of this tunnel. The ever-present temptation—just give up! But, you don't. You take one more step. Suddenly, a corner appears out of nowhere. You turn the corner, and everything changes. Deliverance has come! You begin to tremble at the thought of how close you were to the corner and almost gave up! Dear Believer, never, ever give up because every situation has an end, and it may be just one step away.

Our "corner" came shortly after the Lord's liberating answer to my prayer. The floodgates of heavenly blessing on our service had opened.

More often than not, reaching the world for Christ results in long periods of great suffering and hardship (in some parts of the world more than others, in some ages of history more than others.) The following, took place several years ago. [2]

> "Bill Easton, a missionary with Evangelical World Crusade in Colombia, South America, along with his wife and little, six-year old son, were just beginning a youth

meeting with two young women and three young men. Suddenly, several policemen burst into the room and began examining their Bibles and hymn books. They declared them to be 'evil books that should be burned.'

Matthew 24:9
"Then you will be arrested, persecuted, and killed. You will be hated all over the world because you are my followers."

Matthew 24:14
"And the Good News about the Kingdom will be preached throughout the whole world, so that all nations will hear it; and then the end will come."

After beating Easton and the three young men with the butt of their rifles, they took them to the police station. After hours of torture, indecent abuse, forced to drink 'water' from the open sewer flowing in the ditch alongside the street, and being forced to burn their Bibles and hymn books, the men were led into a field. With rifles pointed at them ready to be fired, Easton and the young men knew this was the end. Fervently they prayed. Unexpectedly, they were ordered back to the police station.

At the station, the torture began all over again. Commanding their victims to preach and sing Christian songs, the officers laughed and mocked them with contempt. Afterwards, Easton reported that the willingness of one of the young disciples to suffer for Jesus' sake impressed him deeply. The official asked young Saul what he thought of the missionary and his propaganda. Saul's face shone with the Spirit of Christ as he proclaimed his belief in the teachings of the Bible and his undying loyalty to the faithful missionary. Saul's face was smashed by the officer's fist. Two more times the official asked the same question, and two more times Saul gave the same answer. Each time his face was brutally beaten.

Finally, all eyes turned to Easton as the interrogator snarled, stressing each word, 'And you! Who are you?'

'I am,' replied Easton, 'a humble servant of the Lord Jesus Christ.'"

What a precious and powerful answer! I can just imagine the angels rejoicing as they surrounded these faithful witnesses, tightening their grip on these four men that were entrusted into their care. This is the spirit of martyrdom. This is the spirit of Christ. You might like to know that Easton, and his three young disciples, were eventually released!

Safe at last

Revelation 7:15-17 (NIV)

> [15] *Therefore, they are before the throne of God and serve Him day and night in His temple; and He who sits on the throne will shelter them with His presence.* [16] *Never again will they hunger; never again will they thirst. The sun will not beat down on them, nor any scorching heat.* [17] *For the Lamb at the center of the throne will be their shepherd; He will lead them to springs of living water. And God will wipe away every tear from their eyes.'"*

Do you think that verse 16 is referring to the conditions that the Great Tribulation Believer will suffer on earth? If so, what are some of the conditions that they will endure?

___

These verses disclose one of the most beautiful and touching scenes in the entire Bible. The words "*He_who sits on the throne will shelter them with His presence*" literally means: "*God will spread His dwelling over them.*" These are very protective words.

Your enemies will persecute you. However, when you arrive safely in heaven, *the Lamb at the center of the throne* will guide and care for you as your Shepherd forever. Your thirst will be quenched with *living* water, and He will tenderly comfort you. What will it feel like when the hand of God wipes away your tears? *You will never, ever suffer again!*

So now you know why this multitude stands before God's throne arrayed in white with palm branches, symbols of victory. And what a victory!

We look forward with anticipation to your next Events that will take place. . . in heaven.

JESUS CHRIST OUR SAVIOR

John 4:42

LESSON 8A

JESUS CHRIST OUR REWARDER
Revelation 22:12

God has graciously promised to recognize all service that is rendered as an expression of love to Him, and is within the gracious plan of life He has for every child of His. [1]

EVENT 5

THE JUDGMENT SEAT OF CHRIST

IN HEAVEN

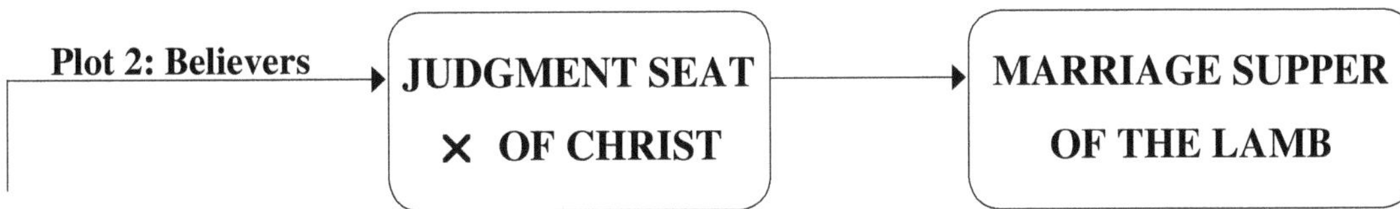

You made it! Awesome! You are in heaven. You are in the presence of your Holy God. As William Barclay so beautifully puts it: "Here in this world and amid the things of time, our awareness of the presence of God comes and goes; but in heaven we will be permanently aware of that presence." [2]

You are seeing the realities of God's heaven and are beginning life in a whole new dimension. It makes you want to throw away all the old chapters of your earthly life story and. . .HOLD ON, WAIT A MINUTE, NOT SO FAST! There is something that you are going to experience that has everything to do with your life on earth. You must come into the courtroom of your heavenly Judge, to appear at the Judgment Seat of Christ. Come reverently.

Treasure in Heaven

As a new Believer I was intrigued by Jesus' teachings regarding *treasures. "Do not lay up for yourselves treasures on earth. . .but lay up for yourselves treasures in heaven."* (Matthew 6:19-20 NKJV) I could understand the pitfalls of amassing money and things on earth that don't last and certainly weren't going to heaven with me. But, how could I store up *treasures* in heaven?

Jesus is concerned with our investments. The definition of *invest* is "to spend or utilize (time, money, or effort) for future advantage or benefit." [D] That's what most people do. Jesus' intention for His followers is to do the same but looking to a future beyond death and with a different goal.

At death earthly investments end up in a garage sale, in someone else's pocket, in the trash, etc. But something far different takes place with a Believer who invests in things that have eternal value. You will meet again in heaven whatever you invest on earth whether it be time, money, or effort, to do God's work. Jesus calls this investment *"treasures in heaven."*

If you invest your $20 tithe, you will meet this investment in heaven. If you invest your time in helping young kids to know Christ, you will meet it in heaven. If you invest time and effort praying for lost souls and the needs of people, you will meet it in heaven.

By supplying the needs to God's servants, we enter into the role they play in God's agenda, and thus, He who keeps accounts will reward us correspondingly. (Matthew 10:40-42; 2 Corinthians 8:1-5)

Let me make this even clearer with this example. *Voice of the Martyrs* (founder Richard Wurmbrand) works with underground churches and front-line workers in many different countries. These workers are enduring the temporal hardships of arrest, harassment and beatings for the reward of leading others into an eternal relationship with Jesus Christ. Each worker will one day meet in heaven every investment they have ever made. These precious brothers and sisters in Christ, ask for the investment of Believers of the free world. They beseech us with their resolve, "Give us the tools. We will pay the price!" If you provide Bibles, literature, bicycles, even horses, you will meet your investment in heaven at the Judgment Seat of Christ. This is what Jesus meant by *"lay up for yourselves treasures in heaven."*

Event 5: The Judgment Seat Of Christ: Born Again Believers Only
Find the "Judgment Seat of Christ" on **Timeline Two** (located at the end of Part One of this study book.) Write Event **5** on the line by the asterisk (*_5_). Remember this is for the Believer only.

We will study in this lesson:

What Does a Day of Judgment Mean?
The Two Judgments
The Place of Accountability – The Judgment Seat of Christ
When Does the Judgment Seat of Christ Take Place? Who will Be There?
The Standard or Measure by Which You Will Be Judged

WHAT DOES A DAY OF JUDGMENT MEAN?

We have learned that there are *two resurrections* from the dead: Believers who will be raised to eternal life and Unbelievers who will be raised to eternal damnation. There are also *two inescapable judgments*, one for Believers and another for Unbelievers.

Many years ago, a medical doctor showed me a tape that had registered the heartbeat of an individual who was in the process of dying. I could see where the needle jumped with each palpitation. It appeared to be more or less regular until the tape revealed that the heart was in real trouble. The needle was not jumping as high and moved erratically. Finally, the line flatten out altogether. I could actually see the very instant death occurred; the exact moment this individual's soul left its body and entered eternity. For days, even weeks, my mind kept going back to that unescapable moment—death.

Revelation 22:12 (NKJV) *"Behold, I am coming quickly, and My reward is with Me, to give to every one according to his work."*

Hebrews 9:27

> *". . .just as each person is destined to die once and after that comes judgment."*

Acts 17:30-31 (NASB)

> *"God is now declaring to men that all people everywhere should repent, because He has fixed a day in which He will judge the world in righteousness through a Man whom He has appointed, having furnished proof to all men by raising Him from the dead."*

Hebrews 9:27
Life on earth ends when a person ________________________.

Does this mean annihilation, nonexistence? Yes ___________ No ___________.
What follows death? ____________________________________.

Acts 17:30, 31 (NASB)
God has "*fixed a day*" to do what? ____.
If God had a wall-calendar, could we say that He would have a specific day circled for judgment? How *fixed* do you think *fixed* is? The dictionary says that *fixed* means "not subject to change or variation." [D] Who do you think "*a Man*," the appointed judge, is? ________________.
In light of this awesome day, what is the one word message God has for all men everywhere?
____________________________ .

Because Hebrews 9:27 says that *all* people will die and *all* of them will come to judgment, what difference will turning to God in repentance make? Does the difference lie in the fact that there will be a judgment for those who have truly repented and turned from their sin to God, and a separate judgment for those who have never repented or turned to God in the manner that God's Word instructs us? Are there two judgments? Yes, indeed there are!

Bruce Milne
"To die in faith, even when that faith is exercised in one's final conscious moments, is to die justified, clothed in the perfect righteousness of Christ and assured of full acquittal at God's judgment seat." [3]
(Luke 23:43; Romans 5:1; 8:1, 33-34.)

THE TWO JUDGMENTS

THE JUDGMENT SEAT OF CHRIST

The Judgment Seat of Christ is the name of the judgment of Believers. It could just as easily be called the Reward Seat of Christ or the Award Ceremony of Christ. This Event takes place in heaven after the Rapture. All Believers of all the ages will stand before King Jesus to give an account of themselves for all the things they have done in this life both good and bad. King Jesus will evaluate their life and give them their due rewards, or loss of rewards, according to how they fulfilled God's will for them. The Believers status throughout the Eternal Age will be known at that time.

This judgment has nothing to do with your final destiny. That was decided on earth when you placed your faith and trust in Jesus Christ as your Savior and Lord. You will have arrived at your final and eternal destination—to be with the Lord forever! Where He is, you are. <u>This is not a judgment of condemnation.</u>

2 Corinthians 5:10 (NIV)

> *"For we must all appear before <u>the judgment seat of Christ,</u> that each one may receive what is due him for the things done while in the body, whether good or bad."*

Romans 8:1

> *"So now there is no condemnation for those who belong to Christ Jesus."*

THE GREAT WHITE THRONE JUDGMENT

The Great White Throne Judgment is the name of the judgment of the Unbeliever, those who remain in their unrepentant state of sin. With heartfelt concern for your eternal destiny, I would like to address you personally if you are an Unbeliever. You must understand that all people are born with a sinful nature into the human race, and therefore, you are condemned. John 3:18 (NIV): *"Whoever believes in Him is not condemned, but whoever does not believe stands condemned already because he has not believed in the name of God's one and only Son."* This is why you must be born-again into God's family. This judgment at the throne of God has to do with sin and consequent eternal punishment of those who have never entered into God's family.

There is no injustice or grounds for complaints. You can choose the judgment and the consequences that you would rather face—the Judgment Seat of Christ or the Great White Throne Judgment.

Jesus speaks to Believers "For the Son of Man will come in the glory of His Father with His angels, and then He will reward each according to his works. (Matthew 16:27 NKJV)

Jesus speaks to Unbelievers "And the dead were judged by what was written in the books, by what they had done." (Revelation 20:12 RSV)

Revelation 20:11-15 (NIV)

> *(11) Then I saw a great white throne and him who was seated on it. The earth and the heavens fled from his presence, and there was no place for them. (12) And I saw the dead, great and small, standing before the throne, and books were opened. Another book was opened, which is the book of life. The dead were judged according to what they had done as recorded in the books. (13) The sea gave up the dead that were in it, and death and Hades gave up the dead that were in them, and each person was judged according to what they had done.*
>
> *(14) Then death and Hades were thrown into the lake of fire. The lake of fire is the second death. (15) Anyone whose name was not found written in the book of life was thrown into the lake of fire.*

What are Unbelievers judged "according to?" verse 12 ______________________________

____

What happens to Unbelievers? verse 15 ______________________________

Recently I was given a Bible that had belonged to a deceased individual. I enjoyed reading the occasional underlining of a verse and the notes written in the margin in response to the verse until I came to Matthew 18:9 which spoke of "*the fire of hell*." The note read: "This is figurative. Hell is separation from God." Hell is certainly a separation from God, but there is no indication anywhere in the Bible which gives us to understand that "*the fire of hell*" is not literal. However, if that is not the case, what dreadful reality does this symbol represent?

The difference between the two judgments

> The Believer will be *rewarded* according to his works. (Matthew 16:27 NKJV)
> The Unbeliever will be *judged* by his works. (Revelation 20:12 RSV)

We are studying the prophetic Events in chronological order, so we will discuss the Great White Throne Judgment in a later lesson. The Judgment Seat of Christ is the judgment that we are considering at this time.

THE PLACE OF ACCOUNTABILITY—THE JUDGMENT SEAT OF CHRIST
The most complete teaching on the Judgment Seat of Christ is found in one Bible verse, so let's take a close look at it.

2 Corinthians 5:10 (NIV)

> *"For we must all appear before the judgment seat of Christ, that each one may receive what is due him for the things done while in the body, whether good or bad."*

"Appear"
I would like to call your attention to the word *appear* (some translations read *manifest*). Sometimes when the Greek is translated into English we do not see the precise meaning. In English we would understand "*we must all appear*" to mean, we must all make an appearance. By the way, the word *must* makes it mandatory.

The Greek word *phaneroo* has a deep and beautiful meaning of our word translated *appear*. The words to *"appear before"*, "in the Scriptural sense of the word, is more than to make an appearance. "A person may make an appearance in a false guise or without a disclosure of what he truly is; but to be manifested, ["*to appear*"] in this verse means "to be revealed in one's true character." This is the meaning of *phaneroo*." [V]

When you stand before the throne of Christ, you will appear in your true character. As Christ sees you, so will you be. He, and all who are present, will gaze at your being and see the spiritual life that you have attained in this world. This spiritual development is what concerns our Lord today. What will be seen? Think long and hard about this coming reality.

Romans 8:29 says that God's great purpose for His children is to be molded into the likeness of His Son, that is, to have His inward likeness. As you stand before the tribunal of Jesus Christ, He should be able to look at you as if He were looking in a mirror, and say, "Yes, I definitely see the likeness."

"The judgment seat of Christ"
The magnitude of this occasion "requires *omniscience* [to know all things] and *omnipresence* [to be everywhere present] to comprehend and witness all that has been thought, said, and done by every creature. [It requires] "*infinite justice* and *entire freedom from all partiality*, as well as an *inherent right* to fix the eternal destinies of undying souls." [4] Only Jesus can fairly weigh the elements that affect a believer's life, decisions, motives and opportunities with the standards and expectations stated in His Word.

Jesus is called the "*righteous judge*". (2 Timothy 4:8 NKJV) This does not only mean that He will judge righteously or justly, it also means that righteousness and justice flow from the moral attributes or traits of His very being. Jesus is altogether righteous. Jesus is absolute justice. Rest assured you will be treated fairly with His infinite compassion because, as you well know, He also lived on this earth and understands what it is to be human.

1 John 2:28
"And now, dear children, remain in fellowship with Christ so that when he returns, you will be full of courage and not shrink back from him in shame."

"things done in the body"

"Death is life's defining moment. It is the point where the final touch is put on each person's life portrait. The masterpiece is signed and the paint dries, never to be changed again. It is finished. Forever fixed, for better or for worse."[5]

Now we are getting down to the "nitty-gritty." Some Believers seem to think that when they die they will be changed immediately into a super-spiritual being. They are ignorant of the fact that the things they do in this life will have a direct bearing on their life in eternity.

Reflecting on this accountability and responsibility makes me realize how casually we live our lives. Even the smallest act God calls us to do may have unimaginable eternal outcomes for another person. . . . and oh, what consequences for us at the Judgment Seat of Christ if we choose to obey or ignore His commands. Who we are and what we do is what life it is all about.

Let me share an example of this from my own personal experience. Herb and I were assigned to an administrative and teaching ministry at the Bible School in Colombia, South America to prepare men and women for the ministry. One of the classes that I taught was Bible prophecy. Invariably one or more students would ask to talk to me outside the classroom about prophetic matters. This was difficult for me as I had umpteen other classes and responsibilities, but I tried to comply.

Eunice was an Indian girl from one of the tribes of Colombia and an excellent student. After prophecy class she asked to speak to me, but I told her how that particular day was so crazy that maybe later we could talk. This was a little out of character for me as I valued each student's interest in the Word of God and tried to help them in any way I could. A week or so passed by and again she approached me after class. In her soft spoken way she asked me to give her some time. "Whew, Eunice, you just don't understand what a tight schedule I have," went through my mind. Again I put her off with a promise to meet with her soon. It never happened. The third time she approached me I couldn't find it in me to put her off so I told her to meet me in the chapel after my next class. I went to the chapel, and there she was waiting for me. Expecting that she was going to talk about the prophecy class, I thought, "Oh, I hope she doesn't have too many questions."

Here is what she said, and it wasn't about prophecy at all. "Dona Katalina (my name in Spanish), back home I have been a leader of the youth and am very active in my church. Everyone looks up to me." Then she hung her head and said so softly that I could barely hear her, "But I have never prayed for salvation. I do not know Jesus as my Savior. Through my studies here at the Bible Institute I see my need. Help me to receive pardon for my sins."

"Oh my! Lord, forgive me," was my cry as I wept in my soul.

Eunice became a new, blood-washed, born-again child of God in the next few minutes. Imagine all the "what if's" that went through my mind. A deaf ear to the voice of the Holy Spirit is a very dangerous thing. The Believer must have an unbroken awareness of God.

I am deeply impressed by the following definition of ungodliness from Jerry Bridges' book, Respectable Sins, written to Christians.

> ". . .living one's everyday life with little or no thought of God, of God's will, of God's glory, or of one's dependence on God. You can readily see, then, that someone can lead a respectable life and still be ungodly in the sense that God is essentially irrelevant in his or her life." [6]

Charles G. Finney explains ungodliness as neglecting God.

> "It is the omission of duty to God; the withholding from Him of worship, love, confidence, and obedience. It is the withholding from God that which is His due." [7]

"Life on earth is a prologue, just an introduction, to the real story that begins with our transfer to heaven. What happens in that prologue, matters forever. The fact that others will cast their crowns at Jesus' feet will remind all, that they too could have brought Him more glory had they lived more for Him and less for themselves. No act of kindness and love will be overlooked, all will be enshrined for eternity." [8]

"whether good or bad"

This has to do with your purposes, motives, what you accomplish, what you spend your time doing, and on what you focus your attention.

The judgment seems to be a black and white issue as we look at the meaning of the words in Greek. The word for *good* is *agathos* which means "beneficial, benevolent, profitable, and useful." [KW] The word for *bad* is *phaulos* which means "worthless, mediocre, unimportant" and even "wicked, foul, vile." [KW]

All of your past deeds, good and bad, will confront you at the Judgment Seat of Christ and will be judged. In talking about this time of judgment, Paul tells us in 1 Corinthians 4:5 (NIV):

> *"Therefore judge nothing before the appointed time; wait until the Lord comes. He will bring to light what is hidden in darkness and will expose the motives of men's hearts. At that time each will receive his praise from God."*

This will be an evaluation of your life by the Lord himself. You will see what your life really was like from His point of view. It is as though you and the Lord will walk together back through all the scenes of your life, and He will point out to you the real nature of what you did and what you said. All your beneficial, benevolent, profitable, and useful deeds will be displayed. All your unrepented worthless and evil deeds which harmed yourself and others will be exposed.

It is so important in your Christian development, that you allow the Lord to let you see yourself the way you really are. You should not fight back and refuse to acknowledge that Jesus is right about things. The mark of spiritual progress is always the awareness we increasingly have of all the possibilities and potential for evil that lie in our hearts.

Psalm 10:4 (NKJV) "God is in none of his thoughts."

He has no room in his life for God. He thinks that God is not concerned with his daily affairs. He has no sense of God's presence nor of his ultimate accountability to Him.

2 Corinthians 13:5 "Examine yourselves to see whether you are in the faith; test yourselves. Do you not realize that Christ Jesus is in you—unless of course, you fail the test?"

This test involves a fruitful, dedicated life to Christ and unswerving loyalty to Him and all His teaching.

All sincerely confessed sin will be forgiven and remembered no more...not even at the Judgment Seat of Christ. (Jeremiah 31:34; Hebrews 10:17)

Our sins are like a computer cluttered up with thousands of words. God hits "delete"...gone, all of them.

Even the stain is gone!

"If we confess our sins to Him, He is faithful and just to forgive us and to cleanse us from every wrong." (1 John 1:9)

Notice the last sentence of 1 Corinthians 4:5. "*At that time each will receive his praise from God.*" "The Lord wants that moment before the Judgment Seat of Christ to be a moment of joy not a moment of disclosure that will shame you, or of facing things that you refused to face in life. The Lord will have the joy of showing you many things that you thought were failures that were really a success, and things that you did that no one heard anything about will be brought to light and vividly displayed before others." [9]

WHEN DOES THE JUDGMENT SEAT OF CHRIST TAKE PLACE? WHO WILL BE THERE?

Luke 14:14 (NIV) answers both of these questions ". . .*you will be repaid at the resurrection of the righteous.*"

What is the name of the Event when all the righteous dead are resurrected? _______________

All of God's people, who are dead, both in the Old Testament and New Testament ages, will be brought back to life at the "*resurrection of the righteous*" which occurs at the Rapture. 1 Thessalonians 4:14-17 tells us that when the Rapture takes place "*the dead in Christ will rise first.*" All the dead in Christ! Their bodies are resurrected and joined with their spirit and soul. This is called the First Resurrection.

According to Luke 14:14 the next Event to immediately follow the "*resurrection of the righteous*" will be the repayment or reward which is known as the Judgment Seat of Christ. **Circle** the word "at" and then read the verse again emphasizing this little word "at".

All Unbelievers, of all ages, will be resurrected at the Second Resurrection. The apostle John, writer of the book of Revelation, places an interval of a 1,000 years between the two resurrections. The First Resurrection will occur during the sixth seal (Revelation 6:12-17; Matthew 24:30-31), at the Rapture; and the Second Resurrection will take place at the Great White Throne Judgment (Revelation 20:11-13) after Jesus' Thousand-Year Reign on earth. (Revelation 20:1-10)

Write First Resurrection and Second Resurrection in their appropriate places.

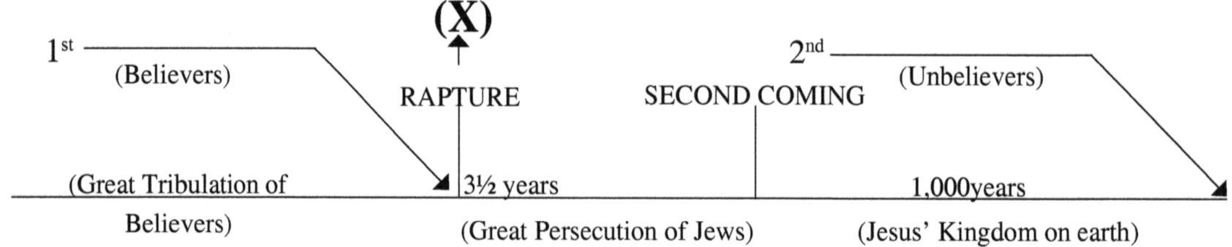

The resurrection of the righteous, which is the First Resurrection takes place at the Rapture; therefore, the Judgment Seat of Christ, represented by the **(X)**, will take place immediately following the Rapture. The "*righteous*" includes all those in the Old Testament who lived by faith for God's glory, who were looking ahead to their reward (Hebrews 11:24-26) and all of those who belong to Christ's Body, the church. Jesus Christ will be the focal point. It is Jesus who will bring all His children to His reward ceremony. Not a single Believer that He intends to be there will be left behind! You will find yourself a part of a huge, glorious multitude! Now that's something to think about!

THE STANDARD OR MEASURE BY WHICH YOU WILL BE JUDGED

This lesson is about the Judgment Seat of Christ. To be judged or evaluated implies a known standard or measure to which the object of the judgment is to be held. In our human courts, the laws of the land are the standard or basis of judgment. If the degree of reward in heaven is based on the Believer fulfilling God's purpose here on earth, then knowing what God expects is essential. God's standard is very clear: the Believer must fulfill His divine purpose.

THE STANDARD
Ephesians 2:10 (NIV)

> *"For we are God's workmanship, created in Christ Jesus to do good works, which God prepared in advance for us to do."*

All of God's will for you, with regard to serving Him, is contained in this verse. For this you were created as a new person in Christ Jesus. Only you can accomplish the works that God has prepared for you to do. He has appointed you to do specific work for Him. Sometimes, it is a very teeny, tiny thing. Sometimes, it is a great big thing. To accomplish all these works will take a life time. Awesome!

You are God's masterpiece, His creative work of art. The purpose of this *new* you is for you to do God's work on earth.

> God is working out your life so that He might have a display case in which His own grace—the glory of His character and being—can become evident through you. He is teaching you, training you, bringing you along, applying the paint in exactly the right places, producing a marvelous masterpiece to be put on display. You can now step into and experience the good works for which you were created. [10] (Ray Stedman, *Authentic Christianity)*

In a Psalm expressing love and gratitude the psalmist humbly claims his servitude to God. *"O Lord, I am your servant; yes, I am your servant, born into your household; you have freed me from my chains."* (Psalm 116:16) This is who we are; God's servants born into His family.

A good question
Should the Believer be considered a *volunteer*? For example, the Lord asks you (possibly through the leaders of your church) to work in some area of ministry. Can you . . .

- volunteer to do the work?
- not volunteer?
- volunteer, but quit when you feel like it?

Something doesn't feel right with those questions does it? What is the difference between a *volunteer* and a servant?

- Does a volunteer have a Master? Does a servant?
- May a volunteer say when he will do the work or how he will do it? May a servant?
- May a volunteer say, "I don't want to do that kind of work?" May a servant?
- May a volunteer grumble about his job? May a servant?

If God has planned work for us to do, can we volunteer to do it? Not by any means! We just do it!

Nahum Diaz

Let me give you an example of a servant who loved and served his Master all his life. At the Bible School in Colombia our apartment was located on the second story over classrooms and the chapel. Travelers were constantly passing through so we were able to give them a safe place to eat and rest. One morning I went down to the front veranda of the building and there, sound asleep, sitting on a bench, was the beloved and elderly Nahum Diaz. He had washed his one pair of socks and they were drying on the arm rest beside him.

Voluntary [D] "arising from one's own free will; acting on one's own initiative... normally controlled by or subject to individual volition... proceeding from impulse; spontaneous"

The Master has given each one of His children a "pathway." He has said, "*Follow Me and I will make you fishers of men.*" At the age of nineteen, Nahum Diaz began to walk in his "pathway" to do the works that God had prepared for him to do. This pathway took him on the trails high into the Andes Mountains; it descended into the fertile valleys; it followed the jungle rivers of Caqueta during a time of great persecution and opposition to the Gospel and it's messenger. It was incredibly dangerous. He never married, nor had a home. He had no preparation for the ministry other than a solid discipleship by a missionary. But remarkably, Nahum had thousands of *spiritual* children and gave dozens of pastors and Christian workers to God's ministry in Colombia.

Nahum had a great awareness of God's call to win souls for Christ, but he also knew that he was not a preacher. God revealed to Nahum his life pathway, and the following tells what he did for the rest of his life.

Armed with Bibles, New Testaments, and Christian literature, Nahum traveled from home to home working as a farmhand by day and teaching the gospel in the evenings. With his well-worn Bible he would explain and teach with gentleness and patience until he was sure that the family had become part of the kingdom of God. When Nahum entered a home, he did not leave until the occupants had been converted to Christ, had a Bible, knew how to pray, and had learned some hymns by heart.

Those who knew Nahum intimately said that he did not speak about the Savior to everyone he met in his travels, nor did he give Christian literature to just anyone. It was as if *Someone* was telling Nahum to whom he should talk or to whom he should give literature. Nahum's secret for his devoted servant-hood was discovered by his niece's children. They were curious as to where Nahum would disappear to after breakfast, and what he was doing. Finally, they found him in his secret place, kneeling in the shade of a tree reading the Bible aloud and praying.

Sometimes he would remain there about thirty minutes, other times, two hours. He would then return to the house and to the work of the day. His custom was to begin everyday seeking the Presence of that *Someone*, and asking, "Where is Your pathway today, my Master?"

After having ministered for many years, Nahum began keeping a record, from 1946 to 1970, of the homes and places he visited, the date, and how many had given their lives to Christ. If you read his ledgers with care, you will discover the number of souls that came to Christ to be 4,190. [11]

After reading this, I, like you, am saying, "I too, am a humble servant of the Lord Jesus Christ. Show me *my* pathway, dear Master." I would love to be near Nahum Diaz when he stands before the Judgment Seat of Christ.

JESUS CHRIST OUR REWARDER

Revelation 22:12

LESSON 8B

JESUS CHRIST OUR MASTER

2 Timothy 2:21

The Christian's goal is honor, the honor conferred by God; his principle is holiness; his aim is service, usefulness to his Master Christ; his watchword is be prepared, ready at every moment to perform kind and charitable actions.[1]

EVENT 5

HOW DO I PREPARE FOR THE JUDGMENT SEAT OF CHRIST?

IN HEAVEN

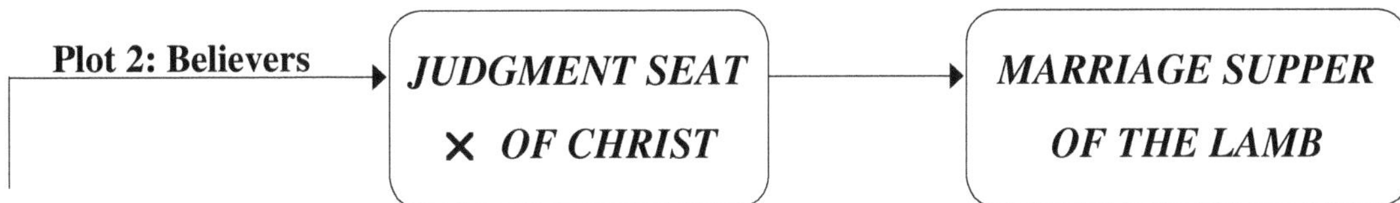

C.S. Lewis
"It is since Christians have largely ceased to think of the other world that they have become so ineffective in this one."

The main purpose of this lesson is to help you to live your life effectively in this world because you are aware of the great significance that the Judgment Seat of Christ holds for you in the next.

In this lesson we will study:

- Your Servant Relationship to Jesus
- Power From on High
- God Enables You
- Your Grace-Gift
- The Secret of How Not to Lose What You Have Worked for
- A Word of Encouragement

YOUR SERVANT RELATIONSHIP TO JESUS

Perhaps you are thinking, "How can I prepare myself to be ready for that day of rewards?" Think of it this way. When we take a new job it is essential to know some things. Who is my employer? How is my relationship to him connected to doing my job? What is my job? What is the compensation for doing my work? God's reward system involves a working relationship between Himself and His servants. The rewards or loss of rewards depends on how well you understand and fulfill your relationship to the Lord Jesus Christ. This relationship is a fundamental ingredient for the reward process at the Judgment Seat of Christ.

THE MASTER

Jesus describes Himself as our Master. We are His servants. In the New Testament, the title *Master* is translated from several Greek words, each one has a different meaning. The following are some of these words describing who Jesus is in His relationship to you. [V] Notice in the Scripture how the Bible writers use these titles to describe their relationship to Jesus.

Our Master Jesus, is either Lord of all or not Lord at all.

1. Sovereign (*despotes*) signifying absolute ownership and unrestricted power

   "our only Master [despotes] *and Lord* [kurios] *Jesus Christ."* (Jude 4 NASB)

   As a Believer, I recognize Jesus as my Owner; therefore, I bow before His divine power and supreme authority. Jesus is my Master/Sovereign Lord.

2. Chief, Commander, Overseer (*epistates*) used by the disciples in recognition of Jesus' authority

   The disciples said to Jesus, who was sleeping in a fishing boat filling with water during a fierce storm, "*Master, Master* [*epistates*], *we are perishing!' And being aroused, He rebuked the wind and the surging waves, and they stopped, and it became calm."* (Luke 8:24 NASB)

   Did you see the connection between the authority Jesus exerted over the storm and the disciples calling on Him using the term *epistates,* Chief, Commander with authority not only over humans but also over nature? Jesus is my Master/Commander.

3. Teacher (*didaskalos*)

   ". . .you have only one teacher [didaskalos]." Matthew 23:8

   Jesus is my Teacher. Jesus is my Master/Teacher.

4. Lord (*kurios*) one who exercises power and is supreme in authority (controller) [S]

   "Remember that you also have a Master [kurios] *in heaven."* (Colossians 4:1)

   He who exercises power and authority over my life is seated in heaven, the supreme place of power and authority. Jesus is my Master/Lord.

5. Guide, Leader (*kathegetes*) to go before; a teacher

   ". . . One is your Leader [kathegetes], *that is, Christ."* (Matthew 23:10 NASB)

   My commitment is to follow the Way, my only Guide, my true Leader and no one else. Jesus is my Master/Leader.

Each expression of the word *Master* represents Jesus' relationship to you. A very good practice is to address Jesus in prayer or conversation as Master. This is who He is. He is your Master. Let this meaning sink down into your soul. Now, let's see the other side of the coin—who you are in your relationship to the Master.

For God to name a person "His servant" is the greatest privilege He could bestow.
1. My servant Abraham (Genesis 26:24)
2. My servant Moses (Numbers 12:7)
3. My servant David (1 Kings 11:32)
4. My servant Job (Job 1:8)
5. My servant

____

(your name)

THE SERVANT

Needless to say, if Jesus is your Master, then you are His servant. In the New Testament, Believers in Jesus willingly called themselves His servants to express their absolute devotion to Jesus. There are different Greek words used for *servant* but the most common is *doulos* in reference to Christ's servants.

Doulos
"a slave, one who is in a permanent relation of servitude to another, his will altogether consumed in the will of the other." [KW]

Underline "permanent relation" in the above definition of a biblical servant. The dictionary definition of the word permanent: (1) fixed and changeless, lasting, meant to last indefinitely (2) not expected to change in status, condition, or place. [D]

How do you see your present relationship with the Lord Jesus in the light of these definitions of who you are and who He is? ____

____

____

My statement
From the very beginning of my Christian life, I recognized Christ as my One and only Master. This is my adopted life purpose statement. . .*I bind myself to God's authority, acknowledging His supremacy, and devoting myself to His glory and service alone.*

Hebrews 13:20-21 "Now the God of peace...equip you in every good thing to do His will, working in us that which is pleasing in His sight, through Jesus Christ, to whom be the glory forever and ever. Amen."

POWER FROM ON HIGH

We have learned that God has a standard by which the Lord Jesus will judge believers: *"to do good works, which God prepared in advance for us to do."* (Ephesians 2:10 NIV) We have also learned that God has a time and place of accountability, the Judgment Seat of Christ where all His followers will be judged by this standard. (2 Corinthians 5:10)

Our loving Lord does not make demands upon us without equipping us with the means to do His will. God enables His children with all that they need to accomplish the good works which He prepared in advance for them to do. *Enable* means "to supply with the means, knowledge, and opportunity to be and to do something." [D]

How you use this enabling, your talents, gifts, abilities, and opportunities, will be brought into account at the Judgment Seat of Christ. The Scriptures clearly reveal that God formed your being according to His divine blueprint and chose you to be His child before the earth even existed. (Psalm 139; Ephesians 1:4) He designed your physical body, gave you a unique personality, and gifted you with certain natural talents and abilities. In other words, He made you to be who you are today. He knows you intimately, and is with you everywhere. God has achievement and purpose in mind for you. Therefore, He is constantly working on your spiritual development because He receives glory or dishonor according to your relationship of obedience to Him.

GOD ENABLES YOU

1 Corinthians 12:4-6 (NIV)

> 4 *"There are different kinds of gifts, but the same Spirit.*
> 5 *There are different kinds of service, but the same Lord.*
> 6 *There are different kinds of working, but the same God works all of them in all men.*

When you are born again of the Holy Spirit, God does some special things for and in you. He enables you to be a channel of grace to His people and to the world through supernatural grace-gifts. This Scripture helps us to focus on how this takes place.

That the three Persons of the Trinity are mentioned gives great importance to this matter. Remember, the Trinity is a union and where one is, all are present and working. **Circle** the three persons of the Trinity in the verses above.

The word *different* in all three verses means both "differing in kind, many varieties" and also "in the portion given, to some a greater amount and to others a lesser amount."

THE SPIRIT GIVES GIFTS

> ***"There are different kinds of gifts, but the same Spirit."***

Gifts

The gifts that are bestowed are miraculous powers, spiritual abilities, grace-gifts (results of God's grace). These are capacities given to us to serve as channels of grace through which the Lord will work to bring blessing and spiritual benefit to our fellow believers and to the lost world.

The Holy Spirit

The Holy Spirit bestows different gifts in different allotments, and He also bestows certain gifts to certain people, not the same to all. "*All these are the work of one and the same Spirit, and he gives them to each one, just as he determines.*" (1 Corinthians 12:11) Is there any mention of race, position, economic status, or gender as a basis upon which the Spirit chooses to bestow His grace-gifts and ministries? Not at all. It is very important that we as members of the Body of Christ do not hinder or limit an individual's use of the grace-gifts that the Holy Spirit has assigned him or her. Will some leaders in our churches have to give an account at the Judgment Seat of Christ for hindering God's work by prohibiting certain believers to exercise their Spirit-given gift?

Grace-gifts do not take the place of what we would call normal Christian activities such as witnessing, praying, giving, teaching, etc. but are in addition to these activities. The grace-gifts are specific gifts given to specific believers for specific spiritual purposes. As you use your grace-gift, this will become very clear.

Now this may sound a bit strange, but one of the problems some may have in serving the Lord with a special grace-gift is—not particularly wanting that special grace-gift from the Lord. "A little girl acknowledged a gift from her aunt with these words, 'Thank you for your present. I have always wanted a pin cushion, but not very much.'" [2] Look honestly into your heart to see if you are saying to the Lord, "Thank You for Your spiritual gift. I have always wanted a grace-gift, but not very much." In order for a born-again believer to fulfill his purpose in life he must have a genuine, joyful commitment, and an "at your disposal" attitude toward God. As in all spiritual things, our free will can choose to use the grace-gift or neglect its use. You have a wonderful gift with which to serve your loving Lord. What you do with it will be revealed at the Judgment Seat of Christ.

There is no complete list of all God's gifts but you can find some of the gifts listed in 1 Corinthians 12:8-11; Romans 12:3-8; and Ephesians 4:11-13.

THE LORD JESUS GIVES OPPORTUNITIES

"There are different kinds of service, but the same Lord."

Service

The word for *service* here in the Greek language is *diakonia* which signifies "serviceable labor, and involves compassionate love towards the needy within the Christian community. Every business, every calling, so far as its labor benefits others is a *diakonia*." [KW] It is always to or for others. There are many types of ministries or service. Some may seem small things to us, but any work that Jesus gives us to do has significance to Him.

The Lord Jesus

The Lord Jesus opens doors of opportunity to use your grace-gifts. You should be looking for these divine opportunities as one who leans forward in anticipation, alert to the call of your Master. Jesus will bring us to that opportunity to do something that He wants done.

You may be asking, "How do I hear His promptings? How do I recognize what Jesus wants me to do?" Here is some excellent advice.

> "God has access to your thought life in a way that no other person has. He can influence your actions by guiding your thoughts. As you read His Word and fellowship with Him in prayer, He is given access to your thoughts to a degree which is impossible when you are tearing around with your daily duties. The person who is serious about discovering God's will for his life should be as consistent in his Bible reading as the pianist who is serious about making a career of his music is in his daily practice. If you are not, you need to question the depth of your desire to know God's will for you." [3]

Think of where you worship, you have grace-gifts to be a channel for God to your fellow believers. Think of where you work, you are a channel of grace and blessing to your fellow workers. Think of your home, you are a channel of grace and blessing to your family. Think of spiritually lost people in a spiritually darkened world, you are a channel of grace to bring them to a loving Father.

The book, *How to Know God's Will*, by Charles W. Shepson, is among the best concerning this very important matter of knowing God's will in all aspects of our life.

> "In some ways it makes more sense to ask God for discernment than it does to ask for direction in a specific instance. The former will serve you well in each instance of decision-making you face. The latter is only for one particular instance." [4]

What a great piece of advice regarding the practice of discerning the open doors of opportunity to use your spiritual gifts.

Full Time Servants of Christ

When Herb and I retired from missionary service we felt so out of touch with how things work here in the United States. We had come back for furloughs during the years, but that year was occupied with family and ministry. So, for 41 plus years we were what you might say, left behind in the workings of things. It seemed like we needed everything all at once that may have otherwise taken years to acquire for most people: a house, car, computer, bank account, credit card, church, barber, doctor, dentist, insurance, etc. We needed the *diakonia* of individuals to meet multiple needs. We entered into a dependence on others as we entered into North American society. When an insurance agent helped us to find the right insurance for us we thanked him and told him how he had ministered to us. Even though he was a Christian, he had never thought of it that way. We told the realtor who helped us find and purchase our house how grateful we were to him for his ministry to us. He, not being a believer, tilted his head and looked at us very thoughtfully. Our comment gave him something very new to think about. So, on and on this went. Every person was a source of help to supply our needs. Some supplied a physical need, others a material need, and others a spiritual need. We felt ministered to by all these servants of society.

Our eyes were opened to something very precious. The Lord says to Believers in Colossians 3:17: *"And whatever you do, whether in word or deed, do it all in the name of the Lord Jesus, giving thanks to God the Father through him."* (NIV)

Our job, our occupation, is a ministry and service that the Lord Jesus gives us to perform for Him. This is a spiritual heart attitude that quietly reaches out from our spirit to others. We can let Christ's love flow from us and envelop the person receiving the service our employment provides for them. For example, as a cashier in a grocery store you may serve every customer in the name of Jesus without speaking a word. Christ's servant-cashier is a channel by which the physical and material needs of others is supplied. What a glorious power would be unleashed in our world if all God's children lived as a channel of grace in their everyday job. Your presence in your neighborhood, in the classroom, office, shop, fast-food restaurant, as a general manager, service representative, printer, you bring Jesus Christ into the scene of your activity.

Will not this part of your life, the activity that takes up most of your time on earth, be looked at and assessed by Jesus at His Judgment Seat?

I love this illustration by Ron Hutchcraft.

"As the senior minister of a megachurch, Pastor Highland could never learn the names of all the people who attended. He knew that, but one day he heard a memorable introduction from Hazel, a weekly regular. As he was shaking hands at the church door, the pastor asked her the get-acquainted question, 'What do you do?'

He expected to hear an occupation for an answer. Instead he listened to Hazel's insightful reply. 'Oh, pastor,' she said, 'I'm a disciple of Jesus Christ, cleverly disguised as a machine operator!'

Now there's a lady who knows who she is. Her friends and coworkers would probably just say, 'Hazel? Oh, she's a machine operator.' To which Hazel might reply, 'No! That's just my clever disguise! My job simply puts me in a position to direct other Machine operators to Jesus Christ!" [5]

What is your clever disguise (your job)? ______________________________
What do you supply to others? ______________________________
What area of need does this meet? Physical _______ Material _______ Spiritual _________
Do you do your work *in the name of the Lord Jesus*? ______________________________

If you haven't done so already, perhaps this would be a good time to dedicate your job to God, this important opportunity from Jesus. Claim the following promise for yourself and don't give up.

Galatians 6:9-10 (NIV)

> *"Let us not become weary in doing good, for at the proper time we will reap a harvest if we do not give up. Therefore, as we have opportunity, let us do good to all people, especially to those who belong to the family of believers."*

Jesus promised that He would give His followers opportunities to use their grace-gifts. When He gave the Great Commission, He affirmed, "*And be sure of this: I am with you always, even to the end of the age.*" (Matthew 28:20) Jesus is our companion along life's way, but these words have an even greater significance. The Gospel according to Mark explains what Jesus meant by this promise:

Mark 16:19-20

> *"After the Lord had spoken to them* [the disciples] *He was taken up into heaven and He sat at the right hand of God. Then the disciples went out and preached everywhere, and the Lord worked with them and confirmed His word by the signs that accompanied it."*

Jesus was right there working with His disciples giving them opportunities of ministry to use their grace-gifts. "*Even to the end of the age*" indicates that He was speaking to all of His disciples of all the centuries until He comes again. What a companion!

GOD THE FATHER BRINGS RESULTS

> ***"There are different kinds of working, but the same God works all of them in all men."***

Working

This gets even more exciting. *Working* in the Greek language is *energema.* Of what word in English does this Greek word remind you? _________________. Yes, and that is what it means, "energy." It is the energy, or divine power of God the Father that flows through your grace-gift when it is God directed. It brings God-intended results. He has said:

Isaiah 55:9-11

> [9] *"As the heavens are higher than the earth, so are my ways higher than your ways and my thoughts than your thoughts.* [10] *As the rain and the snow come down from heaven, and do not return to it without watering the earth and making it bud and flourish, so that it yields seed for the sower and bread for the eater,* [11] *so is my word that goes out from my mouth: It will not return to me empty, but will accomplish what I desire and achieve the purpose for which I sent it."*

Each summer I would return to my former job with the phone company in Omaha from Bible college where I was preparing for missionary service. So full of joy, after my first year experience at college, I just had to share Jesus with my fellow workers, but as a new Believer, I didn't have a clue as to how to use the Bible. Aha!. . . a plan. In my evangelism class we were provided a notebook ring holding little cards with about fifty Bible verses printed on them. I had brought them home with me to practice memorizing them.

Every morning and afternoon I would invite a co-worker to accompany me on coffee break. I then proceeded to flip through the ring of verses reading as many as possible in *fifteen minutes.* No commentary, just reading them. Every one of those co-workers were very polite, and as the days passed, at each coffee break, I'm sure they were probably watching to see who my next "target" would be. I just knew God was going to bring them all to Christ. The summer ended with no one expressing their desire to receive Jesus as Savior. I returned to Bible college still believing that someone must have been touched by all those zillions of Bible verses.

Twenty years later one of my "targets" wrote a letter to me stating that since that time she had given her life to Christ and had never forgotten my witness and that of another Christian in the office.

Sometimes we stew and fuss thinking that we are accomplishing so little for the Lord. Well, maybe twenty years later you will receive a letter or communication from someone revealing that God's powerful energies were indeed released to work in them or in their circumstance through your grace-gift. More than likely, when you stand before King Jesus at His Judgment Seat, He will point behind you and say, "Turn around, I want you to see what your loving obedience did for all those people." You turn and see. . . and weep for joy.

". . .as the Scripture said, 'From his innermost being shall flow rivers of living water.' But this He spoke of the Spirit, whom those who believed in Him were to receive. . ." (John 7:38-39 (NASB) This is referring to the Holy Spirit who flows through us as living water; under His continuous guidance and power. This *living* water means not only living but causing to live, vivifying and quickening. It speaks of the energizing, regenerating power of God the Father.

The Lord Jesus told His disciples before ascending to heaven that they would be "*clothed with power from on high.*" (Luke 24:49 NASB) *Power* here is another Greek word *dunamis.* What word in English does this Greek word remind you? ______________________. Yes, we get the words dynamo and dynamite from this word *dunamis.* The mighty power of God envelops Jesus' disciples like a robe.

So you see it is the energy of God the Father that works for results through us as we utilize our spiritual gifts. He will work through some of His servants in greater degree, and in others to a lesser degree, but glory to God, Kingdom work will be done.

1 Corinthians 3:9 (RSV)
"For we are fellow workers for God."

Two Believers Empowered By God
Jeff
All five of our boys (Jeff, Scott, Dan, Ben, and David) received Christ as their Savior as young children. Each one loves and lives for Jesus. For lack of space, I can only share about one. Jeff gave his heart to the Lord when he was five years old while living in Colombia, South America. We immediately saw a little "spark" of one of his gifts—evangelism. He had such a concern and compassion for people's souls. On one occasion he told a man passing by that he was going to hell because the man was doing something Jeff perceived to be wrong. The man continued walking up the street but was so moved by the words of this little boy that he returned to the campus to ask one of the Bible School students who this little gringito was and why he said what he did. The student, who had seen the incident, answered both questions.

At the age of eight, Jeff led his playmate, a little Colombian boy, to the Lord.

The spark flared into a flame, and to change the metaphor, the flame became "*rivers of living water*" flowing from his soul. After serving many years as a missionary, Jeff is now serving as a pastor in Minnesota. Every week it is amazing to see the turbulent river of troubled souls flowing into his office, and in turn, flowing out as cleansed rivers of living water—new-born children of God.

To many, it is thought that Jeff is overworked and needs more down time. But not to Jeff. He is filled with joy and energy when he leads a soul to Christ. If a few days go by and he hasn't been able to lead someone to Christ, he gets restless in his soul and feels a compelling need to share the salvation story.

It is important to note that Jeff fully surrenders his life daily to King Jesus. Because of this, God can work in and through him to accomplish the good works which He prepared in advance for Jeff to do. One day Jeff will humbly stand before his Lord at the Judgment Seat of Christ where the results will be revealed about his wonderful grace-gifts. I can't wait for that Day!

1. ______________________________
2. ______________________________
3. ______________________________

Fern

This example is about Fern who received Jesus as her personal Savior when she was forty-nine years old. With all the enthusiasm of a new believer, she started attending the Women's Missionary Prayer Fellowship with the ladies of her church. An offering was taken every week for missionaries. The offering didn't amount to very much, but Fern was fascinated with this way of supplying the needs of the missionaries sent out to reach the world for Christ.

A "spark" was born in her heart as she gave as generously as she could with great joy for God's work. The Lord opened the door for service as she was asked to be the treasurer of the little group. Regardless of not knowing exactly how this all worked, she accepted. The Lord's blessing came with that acceptance. God gave Fern discernment on how to do this ministry. Purses opened wide, and the money started flowing into the treasury.

The "flame" grew and, yes, became "rivers of living water" flowing through this dear lover of God. She lived on a small pension, but, my guess is that eighty percent of it was given to the Lord for missionary work. She loved to give. It was her greatest joy. The Bible says that the Lord loves a cheerful giver. (2 Corinthians 9:7-8) What a love relationship these two had! I am going to delight in seeing my mom stand before her Lord at the Judgment Seat of Christ.

1. ______________________________
2. ______________________________
3. ______________________________

Your observations

You undoubtedly noticed the three lines after Jeff's and Fern's stories. Read the stories again looking for the action of God the Holy Spirit in giving the *grace-gift* (line 1); the opportunities of *service* provided by God the Lord Jesus (line 2); and the power of God the Father in effecting the *results* (line 3). Write on the line provided what you perceive to be the workings of each person of the Trinity according to our study verses from 1 Corinthians 12:4-6.

YOUR GRACE-GIFT

The Shoe Fits So Put It On

- You are a channel of God's grace.

- You have a special spiritual grace-gift all your own. It was bestowed upon you at your new-birth. You may have multiple grace-gifts. The gift fits your personality and situation in life. It flows in a most natural way in and through your life, even though its source is supernatural.

- Your service is a ministry, a calling that will benefit all those you serve. All grace-gifts are related to the good news of the gospel and the ministration of it in one form or another.

- You may or may not see them, but there will be results produced by divine energy that comes from God the Father. Your input will be one of the stepping stones towards the completion of God's work in someone's life.

- Commands of the Lord to you:
  "Do not put out the Spirit's fire." 1 Thessalonians 5:19 (NIV)
  "Fan into flames the spiritual gift God gave you. . ." 2 Timothy 1:6
  "Do not neglect the spiritual gift you received. . ." 1 Timothy 4:14

- God is keeping a very detailed record of all we do for Him. Prepare to stand before the Lord at the Judgment Seat of Christ to give an account of how you used your grace-gift. Make sure it will be the greatest day of your life.

If you do not honestly know what your grace-gift is, seek the Lord in this matter. He wants you to know. Perhaps talking to your pastor or Bible teacher, and in prayer together, you can discover the grace-gift that is ready to "spark." Surrender your life completely to the Lord, and trust Him to enable you for ministry. Become active. Take opportunities to serve the Lord as the doors open to you. Follow the Lord's guidance in different kinds of ministries until you realize, "Yes this is it! This is my special grace-gift!"

If you do know your grace-gift, it might be a thrilling experience for you to take pencil and paper, and together with the Lord, do the exercise with your life that you did with the stories of Jeff and Fern based on 1 Corinthians 12:4-6. You will be confirmed, encouraged, and empowered.

I Corinthians 3:13-15 (NIV) "...his [Believer's] work will be shown for what it is, because the Day [Judgment Seat of Christ] will bring it to light. It will be revealed with fire, and the fire will test the quality of each man's work. If what he has built survives, he will receive his reward. If it is burned up, he will suffer loss; he himself will be saved, but only as one escaping through the flames."

THE SECRET OF HOW NOT TO LOSE WHAT YOU HAVE WORKED FOR

2 John 1:8 (NIV)

> *"Watch out that you do not lose what you have worked for, but that you may be rewarded fully."*

What do you think could cause you to lose your reward for faithful service? ______________

____

Even though you readily accept the Bible concept of the Lordship of Christ as your Master and you as His servant, there is one more ingredient in order to assure your reward and status in Christ's coming Kingdom. Unfortunately some Believers miss this great and wonderful truth and much of their work for Christ will be burned up at the Judgment Seat of Christ.

Many things can prevent you from receiving your full reward, but they all radiate from one center—the flesh or self-life, that is to say, all the aspects of life that pivot around *me*. God created us with self-hood; we have a distinct identity. Self may also be referred to as *ego* which makes us conscious of our existence as an individual, unique and distinguishable from others.

Starting point—Adam

Understanding his individuality, Adam, the first man, was not impeded in any way by self, or ego, to fellowship with his Creator God. However, when Adam sinned against God, his selfhood, or ego, became egocentric. This means that his ego, or self, became the center, object, and norm of all experience. Man is incredibly self-centered. Self is the egocentric king that reigns over his entire life and subjects all things to itself. Let's call it "king-self."

Romans 8:8 (NASB) "Those who are in [controlled by] the flesh cannot please God."

After he had disobeyed God, Adam's nature was corrupt and sinful. Hostility, insubordination, and unacceptable actions characterized this sinful, fleshly nature. Adam removed himself from under the rule of God and placed himself under the power of the dominion of sin, self, Satan, and death. We call this rule of sin "the kingdom of darkness." All of Adam's children, the whole human race, are born with this sinful, egocentric nature into the kingdom of darkness. We call this nature the "old Adamic nature" that we received at birth.

Galatians 3:3 "How foolish can you be? After starting your Christian lives in the Spirit, why are you now trying to become perfect by your own human effort [the flesh]?"

Receiving Christ as Savior will result in Christ enthroning Himself where king-self once reigned. Jesus is the replacement for the self-life. The Bible teaches the Believer that Jesus is his Master, his Lord, and that he is a humble servant of Jesus. However, this must become a reality in your experience. God has not taken away your free-will; He permits you to will according to your desire. Your king-self, through your free-will, may want to continue to rule at the center of your being. Its manifestations are self-reliance, self-effort, self-seeking, self-pity, self-sufficiency, self-determination, my ideas, my way, what I think, what I will do, not do. . .this list is getting long and boring. Christ cannot reign from the center of your life if king-self is in charge. The good news is that Jesus provided the way to total freedom from its tyranny.

Christ died on the cross of Calvary for your sin, my sin, and the sins of the whole world that we may receive forgiveness and eternal life. But there is a second significant meaning of Jesus' work on the cross. Your king-self, that is, your Adamic nature, DIED ON THE CROSS WITH JESUS AND HAS NO POWER TO REIGN IN YOUR LIFE.

I have been crucified with Christ

Remember this verse? *"My old self has been crucified with Christ. It is no longer I who live, but Christ lives in me. So I live in this earthly body by trusting in the Son of God, who loved me and gave himself for me."* (Galatians 2:20) Many Believers have committed this verse to memory.

Look at the words! **Underline** each phrase. When was I crucified with Christ? Christ died 2,000 years ago. I wasn't even born yet. What does this mean? Let's see how this plays out.

We are going to examine Romans 6:1-14. It is necessary to our study to understand the meaning of the term baptism. The Greek word for *baptism* is *baptisma* meaning "*to dip or submerge* something into something else; *to place* a person or thing into a new environment or surrounding or *to join* something to another thing in order to alter its condition or relationship to the former environment or condition." [6]

In Romans 6 you will see that you have been baptized into Christ Jesus which means that God "placed you into Christ." At the cross God removed you from being a person in Adam to being a new person in Christ. Every time baptism is mentioned, think *placed into, joined to*, or *in union with.*

THE "ROMANS 6" WAY OF LIFE

IN CHRIST I AM DEAD TO SIN

Underline the word "joined" in the following verses. Keep in mind the meaning of joined in the above definition of baptism.

Romans 6:1-3

> *"Well then, should we keep on sinning so that God can show us more and more of his wonderful grace? Of course not! Since we have died to sin, how can we continue to live in it? Or have you forgotten that when we were joined with Christ Jesus in baptism, we joined him in his death?"*

This Scripture makes it clear that the Believer cannot continue in sin because he has ____________ to sin. Jesus died on a cross. Therefore, if the Believer has been placed into Christ, where did he die to sin? With Jesus on the _________________. The "we" in these verses refers to the Believer's self-ego, or the king-self of his Adamic nature, which controls the center, object, and norm of all experience. By the divine actions of Jesus on the cross, the Believer has unquestionably died to sin.

F. B Meyer [7] "God has treated the likeness of my sinful self, when borne by the sinless Christ, as worthy of His curse, how terrible in God's sight it must be for myself to hug it and embrace it and live in it."

IN CHRIST I HAVE A NEW LIFE

The words "*united with him*" in the following Scripture have an awesome significance. The Greek word is *sumphutos* which means "planted together." [V] "Growing at the same time, a being combined and united one with another." [KW] "Growing together in such an intimate way that it means an essential union. . .union by growth." [9] A good illustration of this kind of union is Siamese twins who are joined together in the mother's womb, grow together, and sometimes share the same organs. We are joined with Christ. Jesus did the dying, the being buried, the resurrection and we are in Him, receiving all the benefits.

F. B Meyer [8] "Next to seeing Jesus as my sacrifice [for sin], nothing has revolutionized my life like seeing the effigy of my sinful "self" upon the sinless, dying Savior... God has nailed the likeness of my self-life to the cross."

Romans 6:4-5

> *"For we died and were buried with Christ by baptism. And just as Christ was raised from the dead by the glorious power of the Father, now we also may live new lives. Since we have been united with him in his death, we will also be raised to life as he was."*

These verses declare that we ________________, and were ________________ with ________________ by ____________________ (being joined with Jesus.) Because Jesus was ____________________________________ therefore we may ________________.

King-self, the Adamic nature, died with Jesus on the cross; it was buried. The power of *self* has been canceled, annulled. It has lost its power over you.

"*So we too might walk in newness of life.*" (NASB) Here comes the great transformation. You are still in Christ when he was ________________ from the dead. He rose with a new, glorified body without the old body's limitations and demands.

2 Peter 1:4
"These are the promises that enable you to share His divine nature and escape the world's corruption caused by human desires."

What happened to the Believer? Christ was raised from the dead through God's glorious power. This power also works in you. God does not raise king-self, the old Adamic nature, from the dead. That is one of the benefits you receive from Jesus' death on the cross. He died to release you from the power of sin and self-rule. You live a changed, new kind of life. This life has a new, divine nature which gives you a new power source for your life and a new desire to please God. Christ has been enthroned in the center of your being. You have come back to the condition of Adam before his fall. Your ego, your unique personhood, free from egocentrism, can fellowship with and serve your Creator God in the freedom of unimpeded love and purity. Jesus is your Master; your self-hood is His servant.

IN CHRIST I HAVE A NEW MASTER

Romans 6:6-7

> *"We know that our old sinful selves were crucified with Christ so that sin might lose its power in our lives. We are no longer slaves to sin. For when we died with Christ we were set free from the power of sin."*

This is powerful truth. At your spiritual rebirth Christ's crucifixion, burial, and resurrection became operative in your life. You have been removed from the "reign of sin and death" and transferred to the "reign of Christ."

Ephesians 2:6-7

> *"For he raised us from the dead along with Christ and seated us with him in the heavenly realms because we are united with Christ Jesus. So God can point to us in all future ages as examples of the incredible wealth of his grace and kindness toward us, as shown in all he has done for us who are united with Christ Jesus."*

Self has lost its throne; it has lost its power. We bow to a new and loving Master, the Lord Jesus. What do the old life and the new life look like?

Old Self Life	New Christ Life
Self-centered	Christ-centered
"King-self" my master	Christ my Master
I am a servant of self	My self-hood is a servant of Christ

THE CRUCIFIED LIFE

Romans 6:8-11

> [8] *"And since we died with Christ, we know we will also live with him.* [9] *We are sure of this because Christ was raised from the dead, and he will never die again. Death no*

> *longer has any power over him. [10] When he died, he died once to break the power of sin. But now that he lives, he lives for the glory of God. [11] So you also should consider yourselves to be dead to the power of sin and alive to God through Christ Jesus."*

All that we have seen to this point deals with what Jesus did for us. It is done, all for your benefit. Now it is your turn to take action. If you want to stand unashamed as your loving Savior processes your life and works at the Judgment Seat of Christ, you must live and work through the power of the Holy Spirit.

The following steps will help you to find this path to victory.
What are you told to do in verse 11? ______________________________

____

You must put all your faith and trust in believing this teaching from God's Word. Declare by faith believing that it is true and that it applies to you. When you do this, all that Jesus accomplished on the cross will become a functioning reality in your life.

Let me give you an example of considering yourself to be dead to the power of sin, but alive to God in Christ. This is the declaration of a very godly man, F.B. Meyer, when he came to this pivotal moment.

> "Christ and I are one. In Him I hung there. I came to an end of myself in Christ, and kneeling at His cross I took the position of union with Him in His death, and I consign [turn over permanently] my self-life to the cross. It was as though I took my self-life with its passions, its choices, its yearnings after perfection, its wallowing, its fickleness, its judgment of others, its lack of love for others—I took it as a felon, and said:
>
> 'You are cursed, you shall die. My God nailed you to that cross. Come. I put you there by my choice, by my will, by my faith. Hang there.'
>
> After that decisive moment in my life, I have ever considered that my self-life is on the cross, and that the death of Christ lies between me and it." [10]

Have you been to the cross? Have you seen yourself hanging there with Jesus? Have you felt the aloneness, the sorrow, the agony that Jesus felt on the cross?

YOUR DECLARATION

The first step
Agree with God by considering your "self" to be dead to the power of sin, and that you are alive to God in Christ Jesus just as it is taught in Romans 6. Will you make the following declaration or one similar to it, with all your heart to trust God and take Him at His word?

> My king-self has been crucified with Christ and no longer has dominion over my life. I am dead to the power of sin and self but alive to God in Christ. The life I live in the body, I live by faith in the Son of God, in all His redeeming power, who loved me and gave Himself for me. I am finished with who I was in the kingdom of sin. I will live exclusively under the reign of King Jesus.

Signed: ______________________________
Date: ______________________________

The second step
Refuse to let sin and self reign in your body.
Romans 6:12-14

> [12] *"Do not let sin control the way you live, do not give in to sinful desires.* [13] *Do not let any part of your body become an instrument of evil to serve sin. Instead, give yourselves completely to God, for you were dead, but now you have new life. So use your whole body as an instrument to do what is right for the glory of God.* [14] *Sin is no longer your master, for you no longer live under the requirements of the law. Instead, you live under the freedom of God's grace."*

Write the three "do not" commands from these verses.

1. ______________________________
2. ______________________________
3. ______________________________

"When you feel temptation in your body or your mind, then there are two things you are to do: First, remember that you don't have to obey sin. You just don't have to. You are free to refuse it. You are free to say, "No, you don't have the right to use that part of my body for a sinful purpose." And, second, remember His power is in you to enable you to offer that same part of your body to God, to be used for His purposes. Now, that may mean a struggle, because the strength of sin is very strong. When we start to turn away from evil in our bodies, the habits of our lives are so deeply engrained that oftentimes it is very difficult, and we struggle. But we have the power not to sin because we have God Himself within us—the living God." [11](Ray Stedman, *Authentic Christianity)*

Refuse to let "self" reign in your body by making a complete surrender to Jesus. . .offer yourself to God. Here are two prayer suggestions for your consideration as you surrender your life to God.

> My Lord and Master, I refuse to go on presenting any member of my body as an instrument to do evil things. I offer my mind, my eyes, my tongue, my hands, my feet, all of my body to You as instruments for your glory and to do the work that You have assigned me to do.

> My Lord and Master, I also want to dedicate to You, not only my body, but my entire life, all that I have, all that I will ever have, my future—everything that will ever concern my person. Take my all; I give everything to You to do Your will until that great Day when I stand before You in perfect glory. From this day forward, dear Jesus, You are not only my Savior but also my Master, my Lord. Behold your grateful servant.

More than likely, the works for God done only by human choice, self-effort and human planning will be burned up. King-self cannot do the works of God. Do you see that works done in the flesh will bring loss of reward at the Judgment Seat of Christ? If you do not understand this truth, you may live your whole life without eternal significance or consequence. This lesson is intended to help you to be fully rewarded rather than lose that for which you've worked.

IF YOU NEED A WORD OF ENCOURAGMENT, READ THIS

Perhaps through this study it has been revealed to you that your works for God could mostly burn up because they were performed through fleshly, self-effort. You may feel that the work you have done for God is basically lost because of doing them through your own initiative and power. Perhaps you fear the consequences this will bring to you at the Judgment Seat of Christ.

First, seek God's forgiveness. Then, make sure that you have given your king-self to God by acting upon the truth that you have died with Christ on the cross, been buried with Christ, and have risen with Christ to a new life with Him in charge. Do this as if this were the last day of your life. Live it whole-heartedly under Jesus' direction through the power of His Spirit. And if God should grant you more, live each day and hour completely consecrated to Him.

Second, I suggest that you bring your whole life's ministry to God's throne of mercy and ask Him to anoint it with the Holy Spirit, every word and deed that you ever did in the past. Ask the Lord to bring all of Christ Jesus' redemptive love and power upon those who sat under your ministry. Place your past works under the blood of Christ that they may be washed of your "self" and will somehow bring glory and honor to your Lord and Master.

When we came to Jesus and asked Him to forgive all of our sins, He went way back to the beginning to our very first sin and He wiped them all away as if they had never been. Can He not remove from each deed the tainted flesh so repugnant to Him and bring blessing and fruit from the ministry of the Word? Remember, He can bring beauty from the ashes of futile works. (Isaiah 61:3 NKJV)

The Locust
Joel 2:25 (NKJV)

> *"So I will restore to you the years that the swarming locust has eaten. . ."*

Because Israel had forsaken the Lord, He sent an army of locust to destroy the whole produce of that year and probably all that was stored away for the future. However, God promised to repentant Israel that the years of energy spent for nothing would be restored; the effects of the locust would be completely reversed.

The Well
Genesis 26:18 (NKJV)

> *"And Isaac dug again the wells of water which they had dug in the days of Abraham his father, for the Philistines had stopped them up after the death of Abraham."*

These important life-giving wells of water had been filled with rock, dirt, and debris. However, the dirt filled wells were reopened, cleansed and restored. God's blessing will not be hindered; wrong doing was reversed.

The Potter

Jeremiah 18:1-4 (NKJV)

> *"The word which came to Jeremiah from the Lord, saying: 'Arise and go down to the potter's house, and there I will cause you to hear My words.' Then I went down to the potter's house, and there he was, making something at the* [potter's] *wheel. And the vessel that he* [was] *making of clay was marred* [ruined] *in the hand of the potter; so he made it again into another vessel, as it seemed good to the potter to make."*

This was a beautiful illustration given to the rebellious people of Israel that they must allow God to mold them into the nation that would fulfill his plans. He had found defects in them that made them worthless to Him. His judgment was pending over them. But if they would repent He would start again and restore them by molding them into another vessel. The effects of worthlessness can be reversed.

"[Godly] repentance can always change the Lord's decree of judgment, for His threatenings are never unconditional." [12] Works of the flesh will burn up at the Judgment Seat of Christ; we are not there yet. God is able to restore the *"years the locust have eaten,"* to cleanse the clogged life-giving wells, and to reverse the effects of worthlessness.

I trust that the truth of these lessons on the Judgment Seat of Christ will inspire and spur you on toward love and good deeds. (Hebrews 10:24)

1 Corinthians 4:5 (NIV)

> ". . .*He will bring to light what is hidden in darkness and will expose the motives of men's hearts. At that time each will receive his praise from God.*"

Can you imagine what it will be like to receive praise from. . . God? Beyond comprehension!

JESUS CHRIST OUR MASTER

2 Timothy 2:21

LESSON 9A

JESUS CHRIST THE HEAD OF THE CHURCH
Ephesians 1:22-23

"If ever I reach heaven I expect to find three wonders there: first, to meet some I had not thought to see there; second, to miss some I had expected to see there; and third, the greatest wonder of all, to find myself there."[1]

EVENT 6

THE MARRIAGE SUPPER OF THE LAMB

IN HEAVEN

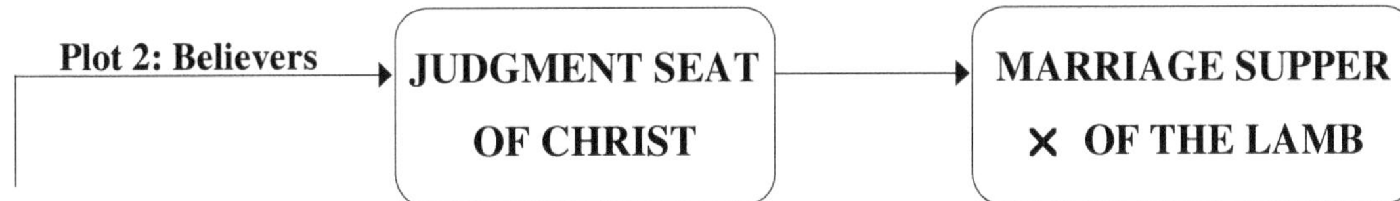

Your appearance as you anticipate this grand Event, is nothing less than regal. You stand in holiness, robed in righteousness. Everything displeasing to your Most Holy Lord has passed through the fire at the Judgment Seat of Christ. All your negatives have ceased to exist. You radiate the unhindered beauty of the righteousness of Christ. You have walked the Halls of Recompense, and have received many great and wondrous rewards for all you ever did in the name and for the glory of Jesus Christ.

You are unique, but you are also an intricate part of a countless multitude of glorified brethren, God's people from the Old Testament days, those of the church age, and of course most recently, that huge multitude of brethren from all nations, tribes, peoples, and tongues with whom you came to heaven. Altogether, you form the complete body of Christ, His glorious Bride.

Paul E. Billheimer has written an interesting and profound concept concerning the church as the Bride or Wife of the Lamb. Glory in the fact that God chose you to be a part of this select group.

> "If God knew from all eternity that the net result of all His creative activity, including the plan of redemption, would be only this tiny minority [of Believers], comparatively speaking, then it may be presumed that this small group was the object of all of God's previous plans, purposes, and creative enterprises.
>
> Therefore, it follows that it was for the sake of this small group that the universe was originated. It was for them that the inhabitants of outer space [the angels], were brought into being (Hebrews 1:14). It was for them that the earth and the world were formed. For their sake the Adamic race was born. To possess them, God Himself, through His Incarnation, entered the stream of history. This small group is called the church, the bride, the Lamb's wife (Matthew 16:18; Revelation 21:9).

Revelation 3:21 (NIV) "To him who overcomes, I will give the right to sit with me on my throne, just as I overcame and sat down with my Father on His throne."

> Creation has no other aim. History has no other goal. From before the foundation of the world until the dawn of eternal ages, God has been working toward one grand event, one supreme end—the glorious wedding of His Son, the Marriage Supper of the Lamb." [2]

This eternal Companion in God's eternal purpose is to share the Bridegroom's throne following the Marriage Supper of the Lamb (Revelation 3:21)."

Find the "Marriage Supper of the Lamb" on **Timeline Two** (located at the end of Part One of this study book.) Write Event **6** on the line by the asterisk (*_6_).

In this lesson we will study:

- Revelation 19:6-9: The Marriage Supper of the Lamb
- When Does the Marriage Supper of the Lamb Take Place?
- The Significance of the Marriage Supper of the Lamb
  - The First Lord's Supper
  - The Bride to be

REVELATION 19:6-9: THE MARRIAGE SUPPER OF THE LAMB

Read the following Scripture and make three observations from it.

Revelation 19:6-9 (NKJV)

> 6 *"And I heard, as it were, the voice of a great multitude, as the sound of many waters and as the sound of mighty thunderings, saying, 'Alleluia! For the Lord God Omnipotent reigns!*
> 7 *'Let us be glad and rejoice and give Him glory, for the marriage of the Lamb has come, and His wife has made herself ready.'* 8 *And to her it was granted to be arrayed in fine linen, clean and bright, for the fine linen is the righteous acts of the saints.* 9
> *Then the angel said to me, 'Write: Blessed are those who are invited to the wedding supper of the Lamb!' "*

Your observations

1. ______________________________
2. ______________________________
3. ______________________________

Perhaps you observed that this Event is recorded in only four brief verses, and even then, there is no description of what really takes place. Quite amazing! However, other Scriptures come to our rescue to help us understand this Event so rich in meaning.

THE BRIDE OF THE LAMB

Revelation 19:7 (NKJV)

> *"Let us be glad and rejoice and give Him glory, for the marriage of the Lamb has come, and His wife has made herself ready."*

The redeemed announce that the consummation of this longed for forever-union with their Lord as His betrothed, His wife, has arrived. As you visualize this, don't forget that you are a part of it.

The wife of Christ is composed of all God's people both from the Old Testament Age and the New Testament Age. Jesus speaks of the marriage supper of the Lamb in Matthew 8:11, when He says: "*many Gentiles will come from all over the world—from east and west—and sit down with Abraham, Isaac, and Jacob* [representative of all the Jews] *at the feast in the kingdom of heaven.*"

Throughout the Bible, God compares His relationship with His people as husband and wife. Actually, marriage, the deepest and most complete relationship of a man and a woman, is patterned after Christ's relationship to His Church. (See Isaiah 54:5; Ephesians 5:21-33) Marriage should be understood in this context. Sad to say, many people of our modern times mistakenly understand the marriage relationship to be abusive, lacking in moral values, with lightly esteemed and easily broken vows.

Many years ago, we obtained a little booklet by Norman B. Harrison.[3] I would like to share some of his thoughts on this subject. This will help you to understand why we as Believers are called the bride or wife of Christ. If you miss the meaning of this Biblical concept, your walk with Christ will be deficient, dull, and lacking in vitality.

"The marriage imagery conveys to us the highest concept of New Testament living—Jesus is ours, and we are His. To teach our inner vital union, Jesus used:

> the vegetable world. . .the branch joined to the vine. John 15:1-8
> the human world. . .the body united to the head. Ephesians 1:22-23
> the social world. . .two persons united in marriage, to live as one. Ephesians 5:31, 32

Marriage is two persons giving themselves unreservedly each to the other to live together in intimate companionship. The life of each centers in the other. It is a life of:

- **Separation**. At the marriage alter, solemn promises are made: 'I will, forsaking all others, cleave lovingly and loyally to him/her and to him/her alone.' Joined to one, separated from all others. When separation from others ceases, the marriage is headed for disaster. The Bible insists on separation from the world and its ideologies. '*Do not love this world nor the things it offers you, for when you love the world, you do not have the love of the Father in you.*' (1 John 2:15) We belong to Jesus and not to any other.

If you are faithful to your heavenly LOVER, you will be faithful to your earthly lover.

- **Affection**. Marriage is a love-bond. Love revolutionizes life. We do things, not from a sense of duty, but by the promptings of love. We want to! The love of our Lord draws out our love and loyalty. '*For the love of Christ controls us* [holds us firmly].' (2 Corinthians 5:14 NASB)

- **Devotion**. New Testament living is meant to be far more than being good. Life centers in a person, in utter devotion to that person. How often we have discovered the joy, the thrill of doing something to please the one we love. Do the same thing out of a sense of duty. . .the thrill is lacking. This explains why devotion to a church or a cause is no substitute for devotion to a Person, to our Lover. We have taken the most lovely Person into our lives, let us make it our aim to be well-pleasing to Him. '*Then the way you will live will always <u>honor</u> and <u>please the Lord</u>, and your lives will produce every kind of good fruit. All the while, you will grow as you learn to know God better and better.*' (Colossians 1:10)

Ruth Paxson "In Christ—how simple the words! How superb the truth! All Believers made one with the glorified Christ so that His position is their position; His possessions their possessions; His privileges their privileges; His power their power; His plenitude their plenitude."

- **Communion**. This is sharing in the highest and deepest sense. Christians confess to being too busy for times of communion with Christ. How shameful! How it hurts Him! How can we deny Him His heart's longing for daily communion? Married to Christ, let our communion be constant, sweet and satisfying. *'Mary. . .sat at the Lord's feet and was listening to what He said. . .Mary has made the right choice, and it will not be taken away from her.'* (Luke 10:39, 42 HSCB)

- **Future Perfection**. Jesus' love has a glorious goal in view. He purposes to present us to Himself in a degree of unmarred perfection. To present to Himself His bride '*as a glorious church without a spot or wrinkle or any other blemish. Instead she will be holy and without fault.*' (Ephesians 5:27)"

You will have all eternity to share with Jesus, the Great Lover of your soul, all that He is and has, and you will share with Him all that you are and have. What a remarkable future you have!

Clarification
In Revelation 21:9 the heavenly city New Jerusalem is referred to as "*the bride, the wife of the Lamb.*" This city is the community of the redeemed—the bride.

Colossians 3:9-10 "...for you have stripped off your old sinful nature and all its wicked deeds. Put on your new nature, and be renewed as you learn to know your Creator and become like Him."

YOUR GARMENT

Revelation 19:7-8 (NKJV)

> *"His wife has made herself ready. And to her it was granted to be arrayed in fine linen, clean and bright, for the fine linen is the righteous acts of the saints."*

What is the bride given to wear? ______________________________
What does "*fine linen*" symbolize? ______________________________
Where were these righteous acts done, in heaven or on earth? ______________________

Verse 7. . ."*His wife has made herself ready*" The preparing of herself for this great event began with her life on earth. As a child of God, all that you are, and all that you have done in this life, will determine your appearance in the garment you will wear. Perhaps, for all eternity?

Remember how God describes your works before you became a child of God? "*For all of us have become like one who is unclean, and <u>all our righteous deeds</u> are like a filthy garment.*" (Isaiah 64:6 NASB) If this is how God views your *righteous* deeds, your very best good works, then throw in all of your *sinful* deeds and that filthy garment turns into an unspeakably filthy rag. That is how God and all of the heavenly beings saw you walking around on earth. . .before Christ.

But God cleansed you from all unrighteousness when you were born again into His family. You were helpless to cleanse yourself, it was the Lord Himself who removed your sin and cleansed your soul through His blood. *"You have stripped off your old sinful nature and all its wicked deeds. . .and. . .put on your new, divine nature."* (Colossians 3:9-10; 2 Peter 1:4) You are a new person under a new Director. Your inward desire is to manifest your love and loyalty in obedience to your new Master in fulfilling the work He gives you to do through the power invested in you by the Holy Spirit. All your righteous acts here on earth are, figuratively speaking, "weaving your heavenly garment."

Verse 7. . ."made herself ready" This is probably referring to the Judgment Seat of Christ where all her deeds of the flesh were burned with the fire of judgment. That which remains are her righteous acts, her garment of fine linen. Will these garments of fine linen differ one from another? Probably. Our righteous deeds vary greatly one from the other. At the Judgment Seat of Christ it is plain for all to see that the works done for Christ are different in number, in quality, in motive, in sacrifice, in love. What is important to understand is that these works are assigned to us by the Father. The doing of them is under the management of the Holy Spirit. This is all that counts. Therefore, each individual will receive his or her very own special garment of glory.

WHEN DOES THE MARRIAGE SUPPER OF THE LAMB TAKE PLACE?

In Heaven

Look at **Timeline Two**, the Judgment Seat of Christ has ended, tears are dried, awards given, and all eyes turn in joyous anticipation to the next significant Event for King Jesus and His followers—the Marriage Supper of the Lamb.

On Earth

Continue to look at **Timeline Two**. Observe that the Wrath of God is taking place on earth. This judgment of God begins at the Rapture and is concurrent with the Judgment Seat of Christ and the Marriage Supper of the Lamb in heaven. The worshipers of the Beast have come face to face with God's undiluted wrath, known as the Trumpet/Bowl Judgments. (Revelation 8-9, 11, 15-16)

Yes, judgment falls on the vilest generation of all times. The climax and consummation of God's redemptive plan is finalizing. Utter defeat for the evil World System of the Antichrist is very near. The collapse of Satan's well designed plan is underway.

The multitude in heaven is just receiving the news that the ancient, evil city that has been the center of godless activities for centuries, the cause of countless martyrs for Christ, and the focal point of the World System of the Antichrist of the end times. . .HAS BEEN DESTROYED!

The 3 ½ year period of the Wrath of God is near its conclusion. Because of the ambitions of the Antichrist, he and the Ten Rulers of the world, have destroyed the harlot city. The apparent intentions of the Antichrist are to throw off his role as the religious leader of the great city and to transfer his seat of power to Jerusalem. This is referred to in Daniel 11:37.

Daniel 11:37 (NIV)

> *"He* [Antichrist] *will show no regard for the gods of his fathers or for the one desired by women, nor will he regard any god, but will exalt himself above them all."*

"His [the Antichrist] showing *no regard* for the gods of his fathers means that in order to gain absolute power in the religious realm, this king will have no respect for his religious heritage. He will set aside all organized religion (*nor will he regard any god*) and will set himself up (*exalt himself*) as the sole object of worship. Instead of depending on gods, he will depend on his own power (received from Satan, Revelation 13:2) and by that power he will demand worship of himself." [4]

2 Thessalonians 2:4 (RSV)

> ". . .*who* [Antichrist] *opposes and exalts himself against every so-called god or object of worship, so that he takes his seat in the temple of God* [in Jerusalem], *proclaiming himself to be God."*

The Antichrist is dominated by Satan's fixation to reign supreme over mankind and to be worshiped as the god of the earth from the Jewish temple.

The Antichrist and his ten cohorts begin to assemble their armies to march on Jerusalem leaving behind the most evil city on earth burning and in ruins. "*For God has put it in their hearts* [the ten rulers] *to execute His purpose by having a common purpose, and by giving their kingdom to the beast* [Antichrist], *until the words of God should be fulfilled.*" (Revelation 17:16-17 NASB) Revelation 19:2 (below) also attributes this judgment to God who uses man as His instruments of destruction.

Back to Heaven

Because of this news, the great multitude in heaven turn to one another rejoicing and exclaiming over the destruction of the city that "*was drunk—drunk with the blood of God's holy people who were witnesses for Jesus.*" (Revelation 17:6) Hallelujahs burst forth in a deafening sound of praise.

Revelation 19:1-8 (NIV)

> [1] *"After this I* [the apostle John] *heard what sounded like the roar of a great multitude in heaven shouting:*
>
> ***'Hallelujah!*** *Salvation and glory and power belong to our God,*
>
> [2] *for true and just are his judgments. He has condemned the great prostitute who corrupted the earth by her adulteries. He has avenged on her the blood of His servants.'*
>
> [3] *And again they shouted:*
>
> ***'Hallelujah!*** *The smoke from her goes up for ever and ever.'*

4 The twenty-four elders and the four living creatures fell down and worshipped God, who was seated on the throne. And they cried:

'Amen, ***Hallelujah!****'*

5 Then a voice from the throne, saying: 'Praise our God, all you His servants, you who fear him, both small and great!'

6 Then I heard what sounded like a great multitude, like the roar of rushing waters and like loud peals of thunder, shouting:

'Hallelujah! *For our Lord God Almighty reigns* [has begun to reign.]'

7 Let us rejoice and be glad and give him the glory! For the wedding of the Lamb has come, and his bride has made herself ready. . .'"

The biblical context of the Marriage Supper of the Lamb is this victorious, hallelujah celebration. All heaven is joyously celebrating the destruction of an ancient foe of the Lord's church. Many of these rejoicing are recent martyrs, and others are victims and martyrs throughout history.

Sequence of Events

Revelation 18 the destruction of the harlot city.
Revelation 19:1-5 the joy in heaven at the announcement of the destruction of the harlot city.
Revelation 19:6-10 the Marriage Supper of the Lamb
Revelation 19:11-21 King Jesus' Second Coming to earth and Armageddon.

Look at **Timeline Two** to find the Event that occurs after the Marriage Supper of the Lamb. What is it? ______________________________ Get ready for battle!

Before Jesus descends to earth to reign with His people, He will be joined together with them so that they can reign with Him. The church, including all people from every nation, tribe, people, and language, from all the ages, whether in heaven or on earth, has existed as the spiritual body of Christ. The church is now in one place in space and time. The unification of all the individuals in heaven into one massive body with Jesus takes place at the *table of the Presence*—the Marriage Supper of the Lamb.

Revelation 5:9-10 (NIV) "...because you were slain, and with Your blood You purchased men for God from every tribe and language and people and nation. You have made them to be a kingdom and priests to serve our God, and they will reign on the earth."

As we are following the chronological order, it is necessary to explain, at this point, the two exceptions to the group above. The first comprises a group of 144,000 Christian Jews, including two prophets who are fulfilling an extraordinary mission on earth during the Wrath of God period. The second is also a special group, "who-fear-your-name," who also minister during the Wrath of God. These two groups will receive their reward and inclusion when King Jesus comes to establish His Thousand-Year Kingdom on the earth. (Revelation 11:18) This will be reviewed in lessons to come.

THE SIGNIFICANCE OF THE MARRIAGE SUPPER OF THE LAMB

To understand the meaning of Event 6—The Marriage Supper of the Lamb, we need to go back many centuries to the last supper that the Lord Jesus celebrated with His disciples. Carefully watch how this evolves.

How It All Started

As you may remember, the Passover was celebrated in the Old Testament by the Jewish people. It was in recognition of the night when each Jewish family, then slaves to the Egyptians, was told by Moses to sacrifice a lamb and put its blood on the door posts of their house. Because the Pharaoh, the king of Egypt, would not obey God's command to release the Jewish people from slavery, the Lord warned Moses that He would send an angel to slay the firstborn of every family, from the firstborn of Pharaoh to the firstborn of the lowliest servant, even the firstborn of the animals.

Exodus 12:11—"This is the Lord's Passover" The name Passover is derived from the Hebrew verb *pacach* meaning to "pass over, to spare." KW

Every Jewish family killed a lamb, a substitute for their firstborn, and in an act of faith, put the blood, as they were told to do, above the door and on each side of it thus providing them protection from death. The family then gathered together and feasted on the roasted lamb. At midnight the messenger of death swept through Egypt and fulfilled God's judgment against Pharaoh and his people. Egypt suffered such a great loss that Pharaoh finally released the Israelites from their bondage.

The Lord commanded the Jewish people to commemorate this event annually. The Passover was the name given to this yearly festival. God wanted them to remember that they escaped this judgment through the blood of a sacrifice. Therefore, each year, in special communion with God, every family would join together to feast upon a sacrificial lamb that represented their substitute. The lamb without blemish was central to this feast. You will find this story of the Passover in Exodus 11 and 12.

THE FIRST LORD'S SUPPER

Jesus on the night of His betrayal wanted to keep the Passover with His twelve disciples. When Jesus and His "family" were seated at the table, Jesus indicated that there was a connection between the Passover and His future Kingdom. The Passover feast was to take on a whole new meaning. This night marked the last Passover feast and the first Lord's Supper. The Christian era was born.

Luke 22:15-16

> [15] *"Jesus said, 'I have been very eager to eat this Passover meal with you before my suffering begins* [16] *For I tell you now that I won't eat this meal again until its meaning is fulfilled in the Kingdom of God.'"*

Matthew 26:26-29 (NASB)

> [26] *"And while they were eating, Jesus took some bread, and after a blessing, He broke it, and gave it to the disciples, and said, "Take, eat; this is My body."*
> [27] *"And when He had taken a cup, and given thanks, He gave it to them, saying, "Drink from it, all of you;* [28] *for this is My blood of the covenant, which is poured out for many for forgiveness of sins.*
> [29] *But I say to you, I will not drink of this fruit of the vine from now on until that day when I drink it new with you in My Father's kingdom."*

What words in Luke 22:15 express Jesus' anticipation to eat the Passover with His disciples before He suffers and dies? ______________________________ **Underline** the words in verse 16 implying that the true meaning of Passover is still future?

Circle the phrase in Matthew 26:29 that indicates when the true meaning will be fulfilled.

Notice the word *new* in Matthew 26:29, "*when I drink it* <u>*new*</u> *with you in My Father's kingdom.*" The Greek word *kainos* is the word for new and means "new as to form and quality, of a different nature. . .from what they were accustomed to."[V] William Barclay says: "A thing which is *kainos* is new in the sense that it brings into [existence] a new quality of thing which did not exist before."[5] That should inspire you to look forward to just what exactly Jesus meant by this word "new."

1 Corinthians 5:7 "Christ, our Passover Lamb, has been sacrificed for us."

Jesus is saying that He, with all His disciples, will celebrate the Passover with a whole new meaning in His Kingdom.

Christ's death on the cross was the final sacrifice and the true meaning of Passover. Jesus, the Lamb of God, died on the cross on Passover day.

The New Meaning of Passover

The focus of the Passover table was always on the sacrificial lamb. At the last Passover feast, Jesus intentionally changed the focus from the lamb to the bread and the cup. He did this because *He Himself was the true sacrificial Lamb* to be slain within a very few hours. Once He paid the price for our salvation on the cross, His death would never be repeated, and should not be repeated in any type of symbolic rituals. The sacrificial lamb, the animal, of Passover became obsolete. It served as a symbol of the true Lamb of God who was to come to die once for all.

Revelation 13:8 (NIV) "The Lamb slain from the creation of the world."

Jesus gave the Passover meal a new meaning. The bread represented His body soon to be sacrificed, and the cup symbolized His blood soon to be shed. Jesus, the sacrificial lamb, the Lamb slain from the foundation of the world, is present at every communion table. That was when and how the ordinance of the Lord's Supper was instituted.

Nevertheless, the Lord's Supper celebrated across the centuries is a "meanwhile" celebration a precursor of the reality to come.

THE BRIDE TO BE

The Judgment Seat of Christ is an Event that concerns the Believer as an individual. Very personal. The Marriage Supper of the Lamb is an Event involving the corporate body of Christ—the church. The focus will be on the group as a whole. We will take a closer look at this unique group which is expressed in God's Word as the "body of Christ, His church, His bride."

I Corinthians 12:13-14

> "*Some of us are Jews, some are Gentiles, some are slaves, and some are free. But we have all been baptized* [placed] *into one body by one Spirit, and we all share the same Spirit. Yes, the body has many different parts, not just one part.*"

At our new birth, we are placed, or immersed, into the body of Christ; we are added to it. We also refer to the body of Christ as the church.

> "The church consists of all who have been called out from the world, have been born of the Spirit of God and have by that same spirit been baptized into the body of Christ, thus belonging to Him and subject to His dominion and authority." [6]

The Holy Spirit is at work in every Believer bringing them into spiritual maturity and the likeness of Christ. The Spirit convicts every Believer of sin. He is their guide. He is their comfort in difficult situations. The Spirit works in every Believer the same as He works in you. But there is a sense in which you are incomplete here on earth. You are only able to relate to those of your local church, or in a very limited geographical area. But your eye, so to speak, is in India, your foot is in China, your ear is in France, your hand is in Ecuador. You experience *incompleteness.* You also experience isolation from those members of Christ's body of the past, and those of the future.

Ephesians 1:22-23 (Phillips) "God has placed everything under the power of Christ and has set him up as head of everything for the Church. For the Church is his body, and in that body lives fully the one who fills the whole wide universe."

The Spirit produces in you a sense of belonging to a family, a yearning to be with those like-minded, same goal oriented brothers and sisters, to be complete with them in the very presence of the "Head" of the body—King Jesus. Yes, King Jesus, more precious than tongue can ever express. And what of King Jesus' yearnings. They are expressed in His words, His prayer to His Father in John 17:20-24 (NKJV)):

> *"I pray. . .that they all may be one, as You, Father, are in Me, and I in You; that they also may be one in Us, that the world may believe that You sent Me. And the glory which You gave Me I have given them, that they may be one just as We are one: I in them, and You in Me; that they may be made perfect in one, and that the world may know that You have sent Me, and have loved them as You have loved Me.*
>
> *Father, I desire that they also whom You gave Me may be with Me where I am, that they may behold My glory which You have given Me; for You loved Me before the foundation of the world.*

Event 6 seems to be the finale of all that has gone before. The Marriage Supper of the Lamb definitely is a climax of all that has gone before, but it is more than that. It is a unifying starting point, like a new and perfect beginning of an eternity of glorious relationships in a God-directed forever existence. The Marriage Supper of the Lamb is the perfect, final, and complete union of Christ with all His followers of all ages.

Before the foundation of the world, God the Father chose men and women to be the bride of Christ in order to reign with King Jesus throughout all the ages to come. This Event will take place in heaven after the Judgment Seat of Christ and immediately before King Jesus' Second Coming.

Lesson 9B will take us into the heart of Jesus at the Marriage Supper of the Lamb.

JESUS CHRIST THE HEAD OF THE CHURCH

Ephesians 1:22-23

LESSON 9B

JESUS CHRIST THE GLORIOUS PRESENCE
Jude 24

"If we had a clear sight of this glory, would we have an eye for anything else? Would not everything else be an utter irrelevance? [1]

EVENT 6

THE CALL TO THE MARRIAGE SUPPER OF THE LAMB

IN HEAVEN

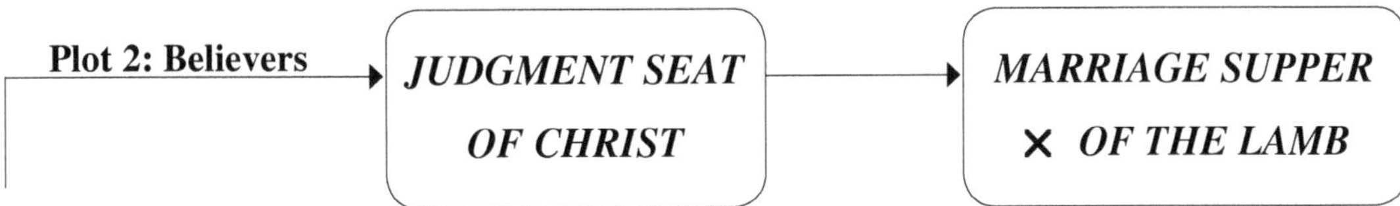

THE CALL TO THE ROYAL MARRIAGE FEAST

A parable told by Jesus in Matthew 22:1-14 is a picture of the mission of the church today in relation to the future Marriage Supper of the Lamb. **Read** this story and make five observations on the key nuggets of truth relating to our theme in this lesson.

Matthew 22:2-14 (NKJV)

> [2] *"The kingdom of heaven is like a certain king who arranged a marriage for his son,* [3] *and sent out his servants to call those who were invited to the wedding; and they were not willing to come.* [4] *Again, he sent out other servants, saying, 'Tell those who are invited, 'See, I have prepared my dinner; my oxen and fatted cattle are killed, and all things are ready. Come to the wedding.'*
>
> [5] *But they made light of it and went their ways, one to his own farm, another to his business.* [6] *And the rest seized his servants, treated them* [insolently], *and killed them.* [7] *But when the king heard about it, he was furious. And he sent out his armies, destroyed those murderers, and burned up their city.* [8] *Then he said to his servants, 'The wedding is ready, but those who were invited were not worthy.* [9] *Therefore go into the highways, and as many as you find, invite to the wedding.'*
>
> [10] *So those servants went out into the highways and gathered together all whom they found, both bad and good. And the wedding hall was filled with guests.*
>
> [11] *But when the king came in to see the guests, he saw a man there who did not have on a wedding garment.* [12] *So he said to him, 'Friend, how did you come in here without a wedding garment?' And he was speechless.* [13] *Then the king said to the servants, 'Bind him hand, and foot, take him away, and cast him into outer darkness; there will be weeping and gnashing of teeth.'*
>
> [14] *For many are called, but few are chosen."*

Your Observations
1. ____________________
2. ____________________
3. ____________________
4. ____________________
5. ____________________

Your observations are priceless and I am certain that you understand that this is a teaching about the great wedding supper in heaven. The first group called to the wedding feast is referring to the Jews and the second wider call to the non-Jews. We are going to work with the key components of this parable as they apply to our work as servants of Christ to call, or invite, people to the Marriage Supper of the Lamb.

OBSERVATIONS

Verses 2-4. . .God, the king, has prepared this great Event—the Marriage Supper of the Lamb. The servants, the followers of Christ, have diligently pursued for centuries the task of calling mankind to the great Supper. *"Come to the wedding!"* This assignment is almost completed.

Verses 5-6. . .**they made light of it.** Have you in your witnessing for Christ found this same indifferent attitude? People do not take the call seriously, others make light of it and turn to their priorities. Others react violently to the call. They have a different (Satan fed) philosophy or religion. So the door slams in your face, so to speak, or worse you suffer severe consequences for your compassionate efforts.

Verses 7-8. . . Jesus the Savior awaits at the table. Who will respond? Verse 7 is a harbinger of the final end of those that the furious King proclaims as *"not worthy."* They will burn.

Psalm 1:5 Sinners will not stand in the congregation of the righteous.

Verses 9-10. . .We press on far and wide. Our call is to the morally good and to the bad, the very wicked. All are called. All need salvation from sin and death. I have always thought how great it would be if God would put some kind of mark on those that will respond to the gospel call. Then we wouldn't have to waste any time or effort, and be able to go right to them. But our gracious Lord wants all people to have the opportunity to hear the call, at least once in their lifetime. So, we call them all. *"And the wedding hall was filled with guests."*

Verses 11-13. . . We would love to end right here on this high note. But Jesus adds one more important detail. Jesus focuses on the *garment.* A man was found without the garment provided by the King to all the called. The man had no excuse for he wore a "*garment spotted by the flesh*," (Jude 23), and his end was eternal damnation.

The garment. The King only gives the garment of righteousness to those that belong in the congregation of the Marriage Supper of the Lamb.

Isaiah 61:10 (NASB)

> *"I will rejoice greatly in the Lord, my soul will exult in my God; for He has clothed me with garments of salvation, He has wrapped me with a robe of righteousness. . ."*

All are invited to the Marriage Supper of the Lamb, but all must be clothed with the *"garment of salvation"* provided by God, the Father through His Son, Jesus Christ.

Verse 14. . .For many are called, but few are chosen.

And so, the Lord's table expands. Every month, for some every Sunday, Christian congregations unite together around the communion table of the Lord in obedience to His command. This is done literally all over the world in mega-churches, country churches, in small bamboo churches, churches in homes, shopping malls, mountains, jungles, deserts. Jesus is present with each cultural and language group. He understands every word, every expression of love and gratitude. He is waiting for the table to be complete.

In this lesson we will study:

Two Cherished Components of the Lord's Supper: Communion and the Presence of Christ
Christ's Reign Announced
The Purpose of the Marriage Supper of the Lamb
The Lord's Table is Complete
The Royal Marriage Feast

TWO CHERISHED COMPONENTS OF THE LORD'S SUPPER: COMMUNION AND THE PRESENCE OF CHRIST

COMMUNION

What fellowship, what communion of love for all believers everywhere is the communion table; that place which brings us into Jesus' presence in such a special manner. At His table we are immediately joined to our world family of true believers. "The unity which Jesus achieves is not by blotting out all racial characteristics; it is achieved by making all men of all nations into Christians. Our oneness in Christ is in Christ." [2] Yes, the group of disciples has greatly expanded.

There is a communal quality in the Lord's Supper foreshadowed in the Passover feast of the Old Testament as they celebrated in family groups. The great Bible teacher, A.W. Tozer, has said, "There is a sense in which the people of the Lord are a people apart, *belonging to each other* in a sense in which they don't belong to anyone else." [3]

Definition of "communion" [v] participation, sharing, fellowship, partnership, a having in common

The Lord's Supper has always been the symbol of Christian unity. This communion with the Lord is to be celebrated with other believers. Even though our primary fellowship is with the Lord, we fellowship with Him in community. "By being united to Christ, we become united to one another; and the Lord's Supper, as it symbolizes our common partaking of Christ, symbolizes also the consequent oneness of all in whom Christ dwells." [4]

1 Peter 2:9
"...for you are a chosen people. You are royal priests, a holy nation, God's very own possession. As a result, you can show others the goodness of God, for he called you out of the darkness into his wonderful light."

1 Corinthians 10:16-17
"When we bless the cup at the Lord's Table, aren't we sharing in the blood of Christ? And when we break the bread, aren't we sharing the body of Christ? And though we are many, we all eat from one loaf of bread [Christ], showing that we are one body."

When we sit in the presence of Jesus at the communion table, in that moment, we feel the love bond, the union, the closeness, the belonging to all our brothers and sisters in Christ around the world. We are all listening to the same words from Scripture, just in a different language. We are all partaking of bread and juice (which may have different components). We may be celebrating on a different day or hour, but we are all one in Christ, looking to the day when we will partake together in heaven as one huge group.

One can well imagine Jesus' pleasure as He has observed His people through the centuries coming together in unity with a sense of partnership, sharing the common bond of brotherhood at His table. Someone has said that the ground at the foot of the cross is level, so too is the participation together of the bread and the cup of Christ's presence. No one is greater, no one is inferior. All are precious in His sight.

All followers of Christ may participate at *the table of the Presence,* not just our spiritual leaders. This privilege is granted to us by virtue of our birth into God's family. It is our birthright.

But our number is not complete. There are those who have yet to hear the Gospel and receive Christ as Savior and consequently join us in our earthly communion service. Where are these unborn-again, potential Believers who are waiting to enter into the body of Christ? How many are still out there longing to hear the good news of a Savior? Let us not grow weary of our task when we are so close to fulfilling it. Let us press on in His power and grace to call the lost to "the table of the Presence."

THE PRESENCE OF CHRIST

The Presence in the Old Testament

A table overlaid with pure gold called "*the table of the Presence*" was located in the Holy Place in both the tabernacle and the temple of the Old Testament. (Numbers 4:7) Twelve loaves of bread, one for each of the twelve tribes of Israel, were laid on this table every week in this most holy place. The priests, representing God's people, ate this bread. Each aspect of the tabernacle, and later the temple, symbolized the person and ministry of Christ Jesus.

This bread was literally called "Bread of face" or "*the Bread of the Presence*" (Exodus 25:30) because it represented God's face or presence. There are two Hebrew words expressed here, *paniym* meaning "face" and *panah* meaning "to turn" giving the sense of "the Face turns to face the bread." [S] Also the same Hebrew word for *face* is used for God's "presence." *God's face* is interchangeable with the expression "God's presence." Christ's face, His presence comes to the bread. He is there in person.

Let's look at some other Scriptures using this term. Presence is capitalized because it means either God or Christ and will be used in this way in the rest of this lesson.

Numbers 6:24-26 (NIV)

> *"The Lord bless you and keep you;*
> *the Lord make His face shine upon you and be gracious to you;*

the Lord turn His face toward you and give you peace."

Exodus 33:14-15 (NIV)

> *"The Lord replied, 'My Presence* [literally, face] *will go with you, and I will give you rest.'*
> *Then Moses said to Him, 'If your Presence* [literally, face] *does not go with us, do not send us up from here.'"*

Exodus 25:30
"Place the Bread of the Presence on the table to remain before me at all times."

In Venezuela we learned how our deaf brethren showed their disagreement in an argument and didn't want to discuss it any more. They simply turned around with their back to the other person involved. That cut off all discussion! When the Scriptures state that God has withdrawn His presence, it means He has turned His face or hidden His face indicating His aversion, disgust or rejection.

The significance of Christ's presence symbolized by the bread lends to the fact that the priests of the Old Testament were to consume this bread. Here are some of the meanings given to the "*bread.*"

Psalm 34:16
"But the LORD turns his face against those who do evil; he will erase their memory from the earth."

- The bread, the Divine Person Himself
- Christ, our bread, is the sustainer of life. "*I am the bread of life."* (John 6:35)
- "*The table of the Presence*" meant that the covenant-people possessed "His Presence" as their bread and their life.
- The priests eating the bread demonstrated that spiritual fellowship with Christ supports spiritual life.

The Presence: In the New Testament age

Let the words of A.W. Tozer [5] inspire you to some deep thinking of your own about the Presence at the communion table.

> "As we meet together in our individual congregations, Christ is literally present. But not physically present. As we take communion together, it would be a mistake to believe that Christ is physically present in the elements. But He is literally present. When we come to the Lord's Table, we do not have to try to bring His Presence. He is there! It is imperative that we recognize His Presence! God wants us to be able to sense the loving nearness of the Savior—instantaneously bestowed."

What if the priests of the Old Testament came into the Holy Place with a flippant, ho-hum manner, not recognizing the Presence, the Face of God? What if they consumed the bread of the Presence with known sin in their lives? This is something to think about.

One of the churches of the New Testament, Corinth to be exact, was coming to "*the table of the Presence*," the Lord's Table, with irreverence and many different known and tolerated sins in their lives. The apostle Paul told them that they were not recognizing the Presence. Paul made it clear that they were not to believe that the bread and juice were Christ's body, but they were required to believe that Christ was present.

Read the following Scripture carefully, and let the full meaning sink down into your soul concening the importance of recognizing His Presence at the communion table.

1 Corinthians 11:23 – 29 (Phillips)

> [23-25] *The teaching I gave you was given me personally by the Lord himself, and it was this: the Lord Jesus, in the same night in which he was betrayed, took bread and when he had given thanks he broke it and said, "Take, eat, this is my body which is being broken for you. Do this in remembrance of me." Similarly when supper was ended, he took the cup saying, "This cup is the new agreement in my blood: do this, whenever you drink it, in remembrance of me.*
>
> [26-27] *This can only mean that whenever you eat this bread or drink of this cup, you are proclaiming that the Lord has died for you, and you will do that until he comes again. So that, whoever eats the bread or drinks the wine without due thought is making himself like one of those who allowed the Lord to be put to death without discerning who he was.*
>
> [28-30] *No, a man should thoroughly examine himself, and only then should he eat the bread or drink of the cup. He that eats and drinks carelessly is eating and drinking a judgment on himself, for he is blind to the presence of the Lord's body.* [30] *"It is this careless participation which is the reason for many feeble and sickly Christians in your church, and the explanation of the fact that many of you are spiritually asleep."*

Baptism emphasizes that I am in Christ. The Lord's Supper emphasizes that Christ is in me. His Presence is emphasized in both.

Because these people carelessly observed the Lord's Presence they were in great spiritual trouble. They did not commune with an awareness of the Presence. The purpose and meaning of communion becomes vague to them; its value is diminished. We may attend every communion service, but unless Christ's presence is real and vital, loved and sought, the partaking is futile and insignificant.

A.W. Tozer "Wherever people are gathered together in the Name, there also is the Presence."

The ordinances of baptism and the Lord's Supper have significance. The one recognizes our new life in Jesus, the other sustains our new life in the presence of Christ until the actual fulfilment at the Marriage Supper of the Lamb. The Believers who observe both of these ordinances as an act of love will be the ones who will most benefit at the Marriage Supper. How could it be otherwise?

CHRIST'S REIGN ANNOUNCED

We return now to the point in time of the "Hallelujahs" which were given at the beginning of Revelation 19. These "Hallelujahs" are a celebration by the redeemed in heaven giving glory to God for the destruction of the evil city on earth that had caused so much death. Heavenly beings recognize that the System of the Antichrist has come to an end. The fourth "Hallelujah" is a declaration that Christ has begun His reign.

Revelation 19:6 (NIV)

> *"Then I heard what sounded like a great multitude, like the roar of rushing waters and like loud peals of thunder, shouting,*
>
> ***'Hallelujah! For our Lord God Almighty reigns!'"***

Can you imagine yourself standing with this countless multitude of holy ones shouting: "*Hallelujah! For our Lord God Almighty reigns*"? It is going to happen! Here in this Scripture God even tells you the words you will be saying. Think about it and marvel.

"Almighty," this word in the Greek language is *pantokrator* which means "the One who has dominion over all things, the Ruler of all." *Our Lord God Almighty reigns*! The great multitude proclaims that the Lord Jesus Christ, the Ruler of all, reigns as a given fact. He is ready to bring His kingdom to the earth.

THE ROYAL MARRIAGE FEAST

Revelation 19:9 (NKJV)

> *Then he said to me, "Write: Blessed are those who are called to the marriage supper of the Lamb!" And he said to me, "These are the true sayings of God.*

Blessed are those who are called to the marriage supper of the Lamb! "This beatitude conveys the thought that to be included in the celebration of the union with Christ for all eternity is the highest of all blessedness." [6]

We are called. The moment has arrived as we stand collectively ready as the bride of Christ washed in His blood, purified by fire, and holy. You will now read an imaginative description of the heavenly supper. Just remember that this all will take place in a wonderful and many times more profound manner than this finite, limited possibility expressed in the following. My friend, I hope that you are alone as you read. You would do well to commit your mind and heart to the Lord's presence. It is a holy moment.

The unifying starting point. . .the new and perfect beginning

The Judgment Seat of Christ is concluding. King Jesus presents you to Himself in your final moral state. He takes your righteous deeds and clothes you with your robe of righteousness, a wondrous garment of a material like fine linen, glowing bright and clean.

In your new glorified body, you stand in purity, robed in righteousness, "*radiant, without stain or wrinkle or any other blemish, but holy and blameless.*" (Ephesians 5:27 NIV)

With tender care, King Jesus gently places you in your special place within this huge forever-family, which now in perfect unity, forms a circle around King Jesus. Every heart beats as one, given to this moment of unhindered communion and fellowship with the very real and awesome Presence.

All eyes fasten on the majestic person of the King. You watch, hardly able to breath because of the overwhelming effect of the moment. You know what is about to happen. The Lord Jesus Himself holds the new bread and the new wine in His nail scarred hands and, as you weep with unspeakable joy, lifts them high above His head. He gives thanks, and He speaks; His voice resonating with emotion.

"On earth, my beloved, you came together around My table, and in sweet fellowship with My spiritual Presence, you fed upon Me. I told you in My Word that I would not eat this bread nor drink of this cup until these "meanwhile observances" find their fulfillment in the kingdom of My Father. . . IT IS FULFILLED!"

Ten thousand times ten thousand, and thousands of thousands of angelic beings call to one another.

> *"Holy, holy, holy is the Lord Almighty."* (Isaiah 6:3 NIV)
> *"Worthy is the Lamb, who was slain, to receive power and wealth and wisdom and strength and honor and glory and praise!"* (Revelation 5:12 NIV)

"How earnestly I have desired to eat this supper with you, all of you! You have waited, I have waited. I told you in My Word that 'whenever you eat this bread and drink this cup, you proclaim the Lord's death until He comes.'. . . I HAVE COME!"

And then, oh, the wonder of it all. The Lord of Glory walks toward you. . .you fall to your knees. The Lord of all Creation, the Lamb slain from the foundation of the world looks down upon you with infinite, unfathomable love. He holds out to you the new bread and the new wine. You take with trembling hands this marvelous gift of His love. "***Take, eat, drink; this is My body which was broken for you, My blood that was shed for you***." He rests His hands upon your shoulders never removing His gaze from your eyes as you partake in the Presence of your King.

King Jesus lifts up His countenance and smiles on the whole multitude, the complete body. In awe you realize that your Master had served and shared with all the brethren in that same moment. Oh, the joys of His greatness!

With powerful voices, the angels shout!

> *"To Him who sits on the throne and to the Lamb be praise, and honor and glory and power, for ever and ever!"* (Revelation 5:13 NIV)

The Lord of Glory opens His arms and gently summons His bride with the words. . .

"Now enter into the joy of your Lord, inexpressible and full of glory!"

The Marriage Supper of the Lamb. You are invited. Your place is prepared.

I think that I will just tiptoe out of your presence to leave you with your most sacred thoughts.

What was the one thing you needed from this lesson?

___

___

___

JESUS CHRIST THE GLORIOUS PRESENCE

Jude 24

LESSON 10

JESUS CHRIST THE WISDOM OF GOD
1 Corinthians 1:24

"The Bible which has anticipated world events so accurately can well bring heavenly wisdom to bear upon personal problems of our lives!" Norman B. Harrison

SIMULTANEOUS EVENTS AT THE RAPTURE

The task of the interpreter of Bible prophecy is challenging, but it is also a rewarding and joyous experience. In working with prophecy concerning future events, the joy for me is the realization that God has allowed man to know about these things and that every event will take place.

Individual prophets of the Lord rarely give us the whole picture of a prophetic event. This is the challenging part. I would like to share with you how this works. First and foremost, you need an open mind in your approach to the Scriptures so that the Holy Spirit can reveal meaning. Those who are cemented in their position of a particular prophetic interpretation will have difficulty in observing what God's Word says. Most Believers who have studied prophecy do hold to a particular line of thought, naturally, but an honest interpreter in pursuit of truth is always alertly observant and eager to see truth. A teachable spirit is priceless and will be rewarded. It is indispensable to Bible interpretation to let the Word speak!

2 Timothy 2:15 (RSV) "Do your best to present yourself to God as one approved, a workman who has no need to be ashamed, rightly handling the word of truth."

Having said that, let's say we decide to do a study on how and when Israel will be saved. The following box represents the whole Bible. The "X marks" represent the passages about all future events in the Bible from Genesis to Revelation.

× × × × × × × × × × ×
× × × × × × × × × × ×

Circle five "X marks" but not in sequence. The circled "X marks" represent Scriptures that refer to "how and when Israel will be saved," some are in the Old Testament and some are in the New Testament. None of the "X marks" give us all the details on our subject of study.

What do we do at this point to have a complete picture of all the information the Bible gives on this subject? We focus our attention on all the circled "X marks."

This is called a comparison of parallel passages. By this we mean that the parallel passages talk about the same thing. They are usually scattered all through the Bible. Parallel passages throw a great deal of light not only on the same event but also help us to understand the sequence of the facts. For example, to study the life of Christ, we must study the four Gospels which are parallel passages.

To interpret is to explain the meaning of something. Parallel passages help to do that. One of the most important rules of interpreting the Scripture is: *Scripture interprets Scripture.*

Lesson 10 is a result of gathering together the "X marks" on certain topics to arrive at certain conclusions. Remember if a conclusion can be contradicted by Scripture, it is not the right conclusion. "Differences are insignificant unless the differences constitute contradictions. According to logic, a system that contains a contradiction cannot be true." [1]

Keep in mind that the prophecies of God are not weird, mythical symbolism written for anyone and everyone to give them their favorite meaning. The prophecies of God have literal meaning.

Deuteronomy 29:29 (NKJV) "The secret things belong to the LORD our God, but those things which are revealed belong to us and to our children forever, that we may do all the words of this law."

The Lord has lovingly and graciously provided us with these prophecies that we may know the end-time Events. Here is a good illustration to help us understand how God can give such accurate information on things that haven't happened yet. I am referring to God's foreknowledge.

> You are standing on the sidewalk watching a parade. You can only see what is passing directly in front of you. God is standing on a very tall building watching the same parade, but from His view point He can see the beginning and the end of the parade at the same moment of time. Therefore, He can describe in detail anything in the long parade that He wishes. God lives in the realm of eternity with no limitations, whereas we live in time with all its limitations. For us, as human beings, the parade has a beginning and an end. The parade that God sees, expressed in human terms, extends from a non-beginning into an unending future. In other words, the parade is eternal.

Hopefully, this brief discussion concerning prophecy will give you a window of understanding on this vital subject.

SIMULTANEOUS EVENTS AT THE RAPTURE

We may think of the Rapture as an Event which only affects the Believer. This diagram will help you to visualize *six* important Events that take place at the time Jesus appears at the Rapture. In order to understand just one end-time Event, it is necessary to garner information from many different books of the Bible. I will make a brief resume of this information; but, you will enjoy participating in the study of one or two passages of Scripture.

The numbering on this diagram is not in sequence nor does the arrangement of the Events have any meaning. The numbering and placement of the Events serve only in the capacity to help us differentiate one Event from another. These all take place simultaneously at the Rapture which will occur in the middle of the Seventieth Week of Daniel's prophecy to the Jews.

SIMULTANEOUS EVENTS AT THE RAPTURE

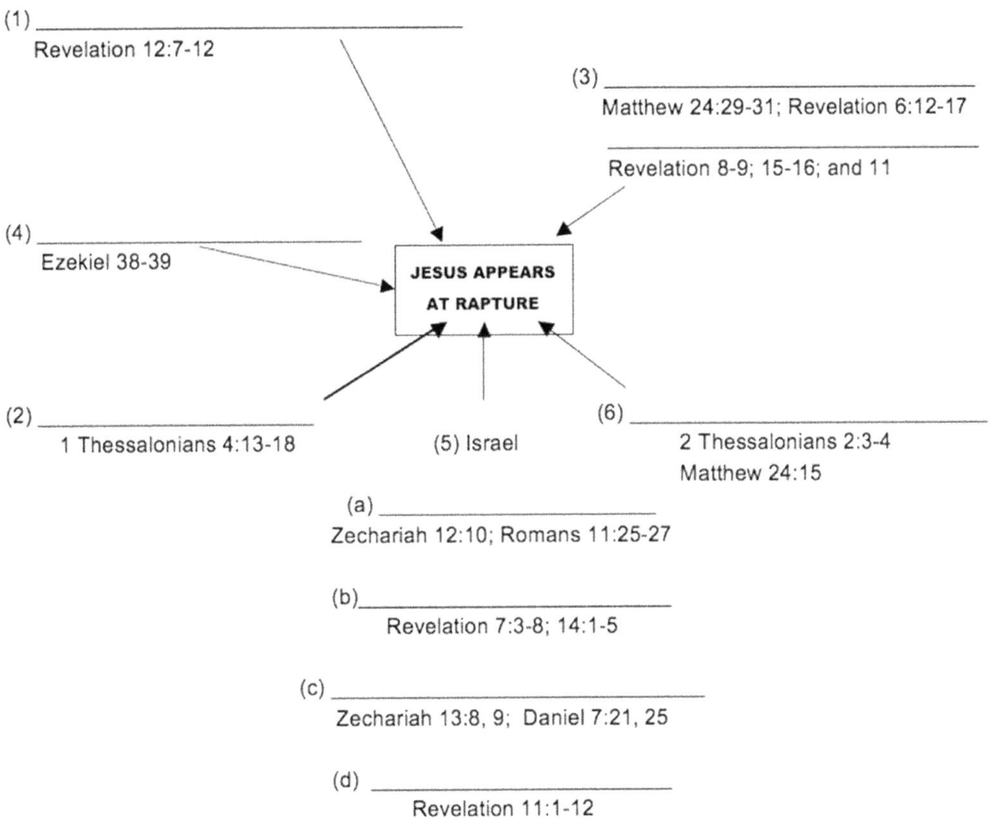

Read the description of each of the following Events. **Write** the name of the Event on the line beside its corresponding number of this diagram "Simultaneous Events at the Rapture."

THE HALF-WAY POINT OF THE LAST SEVEN YEARS

SIX MAJOR EVENTS

1. WAR IN HEAVEN

"*War broke out in heaven*!" (Revelation 12:7 NKJV) This battle in the sky is very important in order for the Rapture process to take place, an Event we do not want to overlook.

Angels. . .good and bad
You need to have a clear understanding regarding the spirit world that populates the aerial spaces all around us in order to comprehend the angelic activity revealed in the end-time prophecies. God created a company of spirit beings called angels who possess superhuman intelligence and power, but with limitations. In the apostle John's vision in Revelation 5 we are

allowed to see the throne room of God. In this vision, he tells us the angels in God's presence number "*thousands upon thousands, and ten thousand times ten thousand.*"

Matthew 4:8-9 "Next, the devil took him [Jesus] to the peak of a very high mountain and showed him the kingdoms of the world and all their glory. 'I will give it all to you,' he said, 'if you will kneel down and worship me.'"

The Scriptures also reveal to us a sinister, spiritual force composed of Satan and evil angels who are constantly battling against God their Creator. Ezekiel 28:12 describes Lucifer, also known as Satan before his fall: "*You were the model of perfection, full of wisdom and perfect in beauty.*" *Perfect* is the Hebrew word *kaliyl* which signifies that Lucifer has as much wisdom and beauty that a created being could possibly possess. However, he does not have all-knowledge, nor is he present everywhere, or all-powerful.

Lucifer (Satan) and an innumerable host of angels, rebelled against God. These utterly evil creatures are now engaged in malignant activities to alienate mankind from God, mainly through deception. They desire to corrupt man and confine him to Satan's rule. Always keep in mind that Satan is an egomaniac consumed with a lust to be worshiped. He even tried to get Jesus to worship him.

Where are the bad angels?
The book of Revelation reveals that these evil angels, or demons, are found in three different locations. Two groups are confined and unable to work against mankind. . .until the end times. The world will get very well acquainted with them at that time as we will see in another lesson.

Revelation 12:9 (NKJV) "So the great dragon was cast out, that serpent of old, called the Devil and Satan who deceived the whole world."

Group 1 These demonic creatures are kept under lock and key in the bottomless pit. They have a king over them. His name is Abbadon in Hebrew and Apollyon in Greek. (Revelation 9:1, 11)

Group 2 Two hundred million evil spiritual beings are confined in the Euphrates River region of Iraq. They will be led by four malicious angels. (Revelation 9:13-21)

Group 3 This horde of evil beings is not confined. (Luke 8:31) Their leader is Satan. His names are found in Revelation 12:9 and are used throughout Scripture. **Write** his names on the following blanks. ______________________, ______________________ (Genesis 3:1), ______________________, and ______________________.

Satan's center of operation
When people think about Satan's habitation or where he comes from to work havoc on the world, most people think he and his demons come up out of ____________.

The place where Satan has his center of operations has everything to do with this "*war in the skies.*" **Underline** his location in the following verses

Ruth Paxon "In Christ we inherit not only all the love of God but all the hate of the devil."

Ephesians 2:1-2 (NIV)

> "*As for you, you were dead in your transgressions and sins, in which you used to live when you followed the ways of this world and of the ruler* [Satan] *of the kingdom of the air, the spirit* [Satan] *who is now at work in those who are disobedient.*"

Ephesians 6:12

"For we are not fighting against flesh-and-blood enemies, but against evil rulers and authorities of the unseen world, against mighty powers in this dark world, and against evil spirits in the heavenly places."

I'm sure you found the location of their headquarters and where Satan and his myriads of wicked angels operate: the kingdom of the ______________; the unseen and dark ________________ and in ____ which is the sky, air or the atmosphere! Satan does not operate out of Hell. Hell, the lake of fire, is his final destination.

Jesus relates a very interesting story in Luke 16. In that story he tells us that a beggar, apparently a faithful servant of God, died. Now take careful notice of this: "*the angels carried him to Abraham's bosom,*" to the place of the righteous dead before Christ's ascension to heaven. It is significant that in this story, Jesus reveals a most precious truth: angels carried the souls and spirits of the righteous dead to Abraham's bosom and after the ascension of Jesus, at this present time, to God's presence in heaven. Jesus would not have included this fact in His story if it were not true, as He did not indulge in fictitious flippancies.

"These angelic guardians of the righteous escorted the spirit of Lazarus [the beggar] to the realms of bliss, for they knew the route." [2]

G.H. Lang remarks that "in various ways they [angels] serve in life the heirs of salvation (Hebrews 1:14); here we learn that they guide and protect them after death. How shall the [Believer] know the route to Abraham's bosom [now heaven]? Who shall protect his soul on the way from attacks by evil spirits?" [3]

"Heaven and Earth are separated by an immense stretch of the Enemy's territory. And through this territory the believer's spirit must pass to return to God. That is the theological explanation of why angels take us to heaven." [4]

In light of the Enemy's territory, the air around the earth, and the escort by angels to take the deceased Believer to his home in God's heaven, do you see the importance of removing Satan and his host from his base of operation at the time of the Rapture? If one Believer needs an escort, how much more the millions from all around the world that will rise to meet the Lord in the air during the Rapture.

Satan ejected from the heavens

Revelation 12:7-9, 12 (NIV)

[7] *And there was war in heaven. Michael and his angels fought against the dragon, and the dragon and his angels fought back.*

[8] *But he was not strong enough, and they lost their place in heaven.* [9] *The great dragon was hurled down—that ancient serpent called the devil, or Satan, who leads the whole world astray. He was hurled to earth, and his angels with him.*

[12] Therefore rejoice you heavens and you who dwell in them! But woe to the earth and the sea, because the devil has gone down to you! He is filled with fury, because he knows that his time is short."

Verse 7. . .Where is this battle fought? ______________________ Who are the warriors? ______________________

Enormous proportions of spiritual forces are involved in this colossal battle in the heavens. Michael is an angel of high rank and is the chief guardian angel of Israel. (Daniel 10:13, 21; 12:1; Jude 9)

1 John 4:4 (RSV) "Little children, you are of God, and have overcome them; for he who is in you is greater than he who is in the world."

Verse 8. . . Why do Satan and his angels loose this battle? ______________________

As a personal application, this fact should give all Believers great hope and encouragement in their difficulties, temptations, and suffering. Our enemy is not strong enough, and SATAN WILL BE COMPLETELY DEFEATED! It all started with Satan's defeat at Calvary.

verses 8-9. . . What do these evil ones lose, and where do they end up? ______________________

____

Verse 12. . .As Satan and his cohorts pick themselves up from being splattered all over the earth, figuratively speaking, what kind of mood is he in and why? ______________________

____

When will this battle be fought?

This battle will in all probability take place at the Rapture. The remaining verses of Revelation 12 inform us that when Satan is thrown down from his stronghold to the earth, he then focuses his rage on Christian Israel. Notice the length of time of this satanic persecution in the following verses, and that some of the Jews are divinely protected for 3 ½ years. **Circle** the timing given in the following verses.

Revelation 12:13-14 (NKJV)

> *"Now when the dragon* [Satan] *saw that he had been cast to the earth, he persecuted the woman* [Israel] *who gave birth to the male Child* [Jesus]*. But the woman was given two wings of a great eagle, that she might fly into the wilderness to her place* [prepared for her]*, where she is nourished* [cared for and fed] *for a time and times and half a time from the presence of the serpent* [Satan]."

The length of time in which this takes place is given by the saying: *a time* = one year; *times* = two years; *half a time* = one half of a year. In other words, 3 ½ years.

These protected Jews most likely are the 144,000 who have been sealed by God for their preservation and care. (Revelation 7:1-8) By this time, the population of Israel will have been decimated by the Six Seals of Revelation 6 and Matthew 24 as will all the nations.

Place an "X" on the time line below indicating when Satan will be cast down to the earth during the "War in Heaven."

Last 7 years of this Present Age ________________________________

3 ½ years 3 ½ years

Write "War in Heaven" by the number (1) on the diagram entitled "Simultaneous Events at the Rapture" at the beginning of this lesson.

2. THE RAPTURE

The titanic battle we have just witnessed will empty the heavens of all malignant spirits. The passageway from earth to heaven will be clear. Jesus will now appear in the clouds of the sky to snatch His suffering ones out of the Great Tribulation.

Before reading the following, I would like to make clear to you that figures of speech are very common in Bible prophecy. A figure of speech is "an expression in which words are used, not in their literal sense, but to create a more forceful or dramatic image." [D] The Lord may have other reasons as well. Keep in mind that these symbolic terms have literal meaning. In this study, I would like to point out two of these expressions: *falling stars* and *powers* that accompany the Rapture Event.

Stars

Stars in the Bible may be used in a literal sense, but in their figurative sense, they can represent Christ, as the Morning Star (Revelation 22:16); people (Genesis 37:9-10); false teachers (Jude 13); and *angels* (Judges 5:20; Revelation 9:1-2). Our emphasis here is on the symbolic use of the word *stars* to mean angels.

Figures of speech always have literal meaning.

Powers

Powers and principalities in the Scriptures usually refer to Satan's kingdom. Therefore, we shall see in the following verses that *powers*, as well as the other descriptive words used here, refer to Satan and his evil angels.

Ephesians 6:12

> *"For we are not fighting against flesh-and-blood enemies, but against evil rulers and authorities of the unseen world, against mighty powers in this dark world, and against evil spirits in the heavenly places."*

See also the use of the word *powers* referring to Satan and his host in Ephesians 1:21; 2:2; Romans 8:38; Colossians 2:15; 1 Peter 3:22.

Observe how your understanding of the following verses concerning the Rapture will expand with the figurative use of the words *stars* and *powers* symbolizing evil angels. Another way of interpreting the falling *stars* is that the meaning is found in a mixture of the literal with the figurative. In other words, both celestial bodies and evil angels are meant in the following Scriptures. *Powers* definitely refers to Satan and his vast host of evil angels.

Cosmic chaos

Mark 13:24-25 (NKJV)

> *"But in those days, after that tribulation, the sun will be darkened, and the moon will not give its light; the stars of heaven will fall, and the powers in the heavens will be shaken."*

Could this cosmic disturbance during the Rapture process be a description of the mighty angelic warriors at war in the heavens? We can only imagine the tremendous clash (like megatons of explosives) when these two powerful forces meet. They will violently affect the heavens when Satan and his great host are thrown out of heaven!

Revelation 12:7, 9 (NIV)

> *"And there was war in heaven. . . The great dragon was hurled down. . . He was hurled to earth, and his angels with him.*

Mark 13:25

> *". . .the stars will fall from the sky, and the powers in the heavens will be shaken"*

Revelation 6:13

> *"Then the stars of the sky fell to the earth like green figs falling from a tree shaken by a strong wind."*

Luke 10:18

> Jesus says *"I saw Satan fall from heaven like lightening!"*

Revelation 6:14

> *"The sky was rolled up like a scroll, and all of the mountains and islands were moved from their places."*

No wonder Leon Morris comments: "In vivid and forceful language John is describing the complete break-up of this cosmic system." [5] What a battle! The Unbelievers of this world are terrified by these catastrophic events.

Revelation 6:15-17

> *"Then everyone—the kings of the earth, the rulers, the generals, the wealthy, the powerful, and every slave and free person—all hid themselves in the caves and among the rocks of the mountains. And they cried to the mountains and to the rocks, 'Fall on us and hide us from the face of the one who sits on the throne and from the wrath of the Lamb. For the great day of their wrath has come, and who is able to survive?"*

Jesus appears in the heavens at the Rapture.

Mark 13:26 (NKJV)

> *"Then they will see the Son of Man coming in the clouds with great power and glory."*

The Grand Procession

After several years in Venezuela, Herb and I were able to return for a visit to Colombia where we had served the Lord for twenty years. On the outskirts of the city where many years of our ministry took place, we spotted a dear Believer who was also a policeman. He came quickly on his motorcycle to greet us and told us that he was going to escort us through the busy traffic to our destination. So before we could say, "No way," off we went with sirens and flashing lights. At every busy street corner he stopped all traffic and then would catch up with us to roar ahead of our vehicle. What an experience! We felt like V.I.P.'s; a sensation of being very special as people along the way tried to see who these very important people were. We laughed and enjoyed this once-in-a-life-time experience all the way.

But one of these days, all of us Believers are going to experience the most magnificent, royal escort ever! The angels will deliver God's children, unimpeded, to the waiting Christ in the clouds of heaven. Multitudes of the risen dead reunited with their souls and spirits that have descended from heaven with the Lord, and thousands of living Believers from all over the earth will be escorted to meet their Savior—the most glorious procession ever.

Mark 13:27 (NKJV)

> *"And then He will send His angels, and gather together His elect from the four winds* [four points of the compass], *from the farthest part of earth to the farthest part of heaven."*

Place an "X" on the time line below indicating when the Rapture will take place.

Last 7 years of this Present Age ____

3 ½ years 3 ½ years

Write "The Rapture" by the number (2) on the diagram entitled "Simultaneous Events at the Rapture" at the beginning of this lesson.

3. THE GREAT TRIBULATION ENDS AND THE WRATH OF GOD BEGINS

The Great Tribulation Ends

Actually, two victories over Satan will be won, one in the sky and one on earth. Michael and his angels win the battle in the heavens, so who defeats Satan on the earth? Look at verses 10-11 below and write your answer here ____

____

Revelation 12:10-11

> (10) *"Then I heard a loud voice in heaven say: 'Now have come the salvation and the power and the kingdom* [the dominion and reign] *of our God, and the* [sovereign] *authority of His Christ. For the accuser* [Satan] *of our brothers, who accuses them before our God day and night, has been hurled down.*

(11) *They overcame him by the blood of the Lamb and by the word of their testimony; they did not love their lives so much as to shrink from death.*

Your answer should be something like this: these who will overcome Satan on earth will be Believers who suffer for Christ's sake during the Great Tribulation.

These overcomers, along with all the resurrected dead, rise to meet the Lord of Glory in the heavens. Millions of angels who fought against Satan and his hosts will parade through the skies with all the victorious redeemed. Christ Jesus, in a triumphant show of power, will sweep the world clean of all who are His blood-bought children up to that moment. It seems with both the announcement in verse 10 of the arrival of Jesus' kingdom and the marvelous display of the Rapture, Jesus is telling the world, "I will return shortly to establish My Kingdom!"

The first words of the raptured multitude upon their arrival in heaven: "Salvation belongs to our God, who sits on the throne, and to the Lamb." (Revelation 7:10)

The Believer is free at last from the oppression and scorn of the world. The Rapture has brought an end to the Great Tribulation of the Believer. Hallelujah! But now. . .

The Wrath of God Begins

The Wrath of God will be your study in the next lessons. This introduction will give you a basic explanation of this Event and when it will take place.

What is the Wrath of God?

The Wrath of God is a series of seven catastrophic judgments known as the Trumpet/Bowl judgments which are found in Revelation 8-9; 15-16; and 11. God's merited wrath will come down on the World System of the Antichrist and all that belong to it.

The Word of God tells us that each Unbeliever will stand before God at the Great White Throne where the Unbeliever will receive judgment as a sinner and will face the consequences of his sins and unrepentant state. (Revelation 20:11-15) So then, why this collective judgment of mankind on earth?

The reasons are as follows:

A question When God "abandons" mankind to their lusts, vile passions, and debased mind, do they become better or worse? (Romans 1:24, 26, 28 NKJV)

- Mankind as a whole will have come to the place of *despising and totally rejecting salvation* through the substitutionary death of Jesus. Unbelievers will deliberately and willfully cut themselves off from their eternal salvation. Therefore, they will be in a hopeless state because "*There is salvation in no one else! God has given no other name under heaven by which we must be saved.*" (Acts 4:12)

- The people of the world at this time will *deny God's rightful place in their lives, having replaced Him with the Antichrist* whom they will serve and worship. The world will be in a state of total rebellion against God. Therefore, the collective mass of spiritual anarchists will be subject to the fierceness of God's wrath. This is a collective judgment. The Great White Throne Judgment is on an individual basis.

- *Unsurpassed evil* will reign upon the earth. God's written Word will be meaningless to man, who may very well destroy copies of the Bible.

- The zeal of the ungodly is so intense that *they will persecute all who stand for righteousness.* Unbelievers will view as an enemy anyone who does not belong to their system. Therefore, in their minds, he deserves to die. The Harlot-city, which has spawned the Antichrist and will become the center of operations for the World System of the Antichrist, is described as "*drunk with the blood of the saints, the blood of those who bore testimony to Jesus.*" (Revelation 17:6) This figure implies that her atrocious acts are done with the joy of a drunkard in his liquor. We are told in Revelation 14:10 (NKJV) that the ungodly inhabitants of the earth will "*drink of the wine of the wrath of God which is poured out full strength into the cup of His indignation.*" God will repay this evil, especially in the third judgment where He will turn the rivers into blood. God will literally give them blood to drink. (Revelation 16:5-6)

Revelation 16:5-6
"You are just, O Holy One, who is and who always was, because you have sent these judgments. Since they shed the blood of your holy people and your prophets, you have given them blood to drink. It is their just reward."

- There is one more reason for this period of divine wrath. Unbelievers will experience the cost and consequences of God's devastating judgments for 3 ½ years. As we will soon see in our study, it is stated that when the judgments are in full effect, *man will not repent.* These words imply the possibility of repentance. God desires that the severity of the 3 ½ years of judgment of man's wickedness will cause him to reflect on what an eternity under His judgment would be like. The Wrath of God judgments are meant to open rebel-man's spiritual eyes bringing him to his knees in repentance.

The Time of the Wrath of God

The following Scripture describes the Sixth Seal which is the Rapture and the moment in time when all people will see Christ. (Revelation 1:7; Matthew 24:30-31; Zechariah 12:10) When they *see* the face of the One who sits upon the throne, all the ungodly people of the world will be terrified of *something* and they will announce correctly that this *something* has come.

Read the following Scripture to discover what it is they realize has arrived. What do they understand has come? ______________________________ **Underline** it.

Revelation 6:12-17 (Phillips)

> "*Then I* [John] *watched while He* [Jesus] *broke the sixth seal. There was a tremendous earthquake, the sun turned dark like coarse black cloth, and the full moon was red as blood. The stars of the sky fell upon the earth, just as a fig tree sheds unripe figs when shaken in a gale. The sky vanished as though it were a scroll being rolled up, and every mountain and island was jolted out of its place.*
>
> *Then the kings of the earth, and the great men, the captains, the wealthy, the powerful, and every man, whether slave or free, hid themselves in caves and among mountain rocks. They called out to the mountains and the rocks:*
>
> *'Fall down upon us and hide us from the face of Him who sits upon the throne, and from the wrath of the Lamb! For the great day of their* [God and His Son] *wrath has come, and who can stand against it?'*"

During the Sixth Seal, which takes place at the midpoint of the last seven years, the people of the world realize that the Wrath of God has come upon them. So how many years will the Wrath of God last? ____________________.

The Seventh Seal is composed entirely of the seven Wrath of God judgments. This is how it will look.

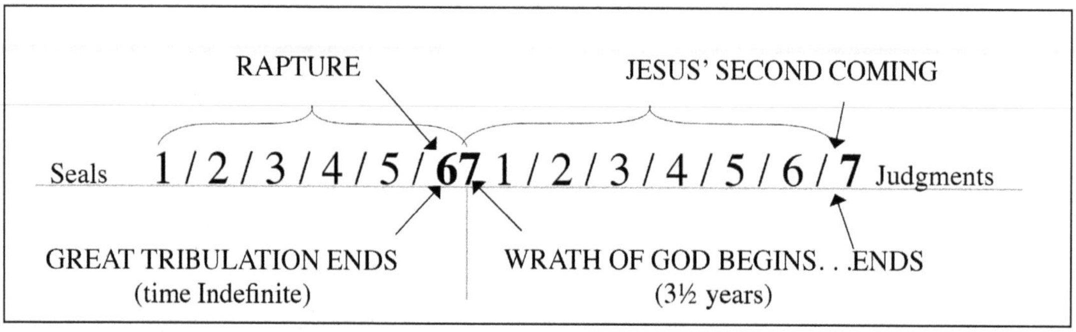

RAPTURE — JESUS' SECOND COMING

Seals 1 / 2 / 3 / 4 / 5 / **67** 1 / 2 / 3 / 4 / 5 / 6 / **7** Judgments

GREAT TRIBULATION ENDS (time Indefinite) — WRATH OF GOD BEGINS. . .ENDS (3½ years)

BASIC DIFFERENCES BETWEEN THE GREAT TRIBULATION AND THE WRATH OF GOD:

THE GREAT TRIBULATION	WRATH OF GOD
1. Correct biblical term for this interval of time described in Matthew 24 and Revelation 6	1. Correct biblical term for this period of time described in Revelation 6:16-17; 8-9; 15-16; 11
2. Prolonged period up to the 6th Seal	2. The 7th Seal contains 7 Trumpet/bowl Judgments
3. Time: indefinite	3. Time: 3 ½ years
4. Takes place before the Rapture	4. Begins immediately after the Rapture
5. Ends at the Rapture	5. Ends at the 2nd Coming of Christ
6. Cause of calamities: Antichrist/ Unbelievers	6. Cause: God directed calamities
7. Affects people of the world and Believers	7. Affects people of the world and Christian Jews
8. Believers present	8. Believers absent
9. Jews not saved	9. Jews saved
10. Development of the World System of the Antichrist and ensuing reign of the Antichrist	10. Reign of the Antichrist

Place an "X" on the time line below indicating when The Great Tribulation ends and The Wrath of God begins.

Last 7 years of this Present Age ____

3 ½ years 3 ½ years

Write "The Great Tribulation Ends" (top line) and "The Wrath of God Begins" (bottom line) by the number (3) on the diagram entitled "Simultaneous Events at the Rapture" at the beginning of this lesson.

4. GOG'S ARMY DESTROYED

The Jews will have entered into a covenant relationship with the Antichrist and others and will immediately launch into rebuilding their temple. At this point in time, the Jews will have finished building their temple and will have begun the ritual of animal sacrifices.

The Antichrist will have plans well under way to invade Israel and to proclaim himself as "God" in their temple. However, an apparent rival of the Antichrist tries to beat him to the draw. In Ezekiel 38 and 39 we read about a man referred to as Gog, chief prince of Rosh, who will attack Israel with a sizable army. A comparison of the names given in Ezekiel 38:3-6 with their ancient names in Genesis 10:1-3 will identify these nations involved with Gog. If you look at the map of the "Ten Regions of the World" at the end of Lesson 3A page 45, you will notice that Gog and his army mainly come from Regions 5 and 7. The nations from Region 7 have been long-standing enemies of Israel.

Perhaps Gog through a power play of his own will seek to block the plans of the Antichrist and establish himself in the recently built temple of the Jews in Jerusalem. This invasion by Gog will be far too great for the Jews to handle. God, through supernatural intervention, will defeat this army in a stupendous fashion. You can review this Event in Lesson 5.

When will this invasion take place?
Read carefully Ezekiel 38 and 39 in your Bible. Notice the wording in the following verses that indicates when this invasion will take place. **Underline** the key phrases which refer to the time.

The Lord speaks to Gog (Ezekiel 38:8, 16 NASB)

> 8 *"After many days you* [Gog] *will be summoned; in the latter years you will come into the land* [Israel] *that is restored. . .*
>
> 16 *"It will come about in the last days that I will bring you* [Gog] *against My land, so that the nations may know Me when I am sanctified through you before their eyes, O Gog."*

Observe in verse 8 that Gog will "*come into the land that is* ____________________." This gives us a time factor. The invasion of Gog's army will take place after Israel has been "*restored*" in their land which took place in 1948. Therefore, the conditions are right for this to happen.

"*After many days,*" "*in the latter years,*" and "*in the last days,*" are prophetic terms for the end times. This Event portrayed in Ezekiel 38 and 39 is very difficult to place in the chronology of end-time Events. However there are clues to indicate that it takes place at the time of the Rapture. Once again, the prophecies concerning the salvation of Israel serve as a north star to guide us. Let's review what we know about how and when Israel receives Christ as Savior.

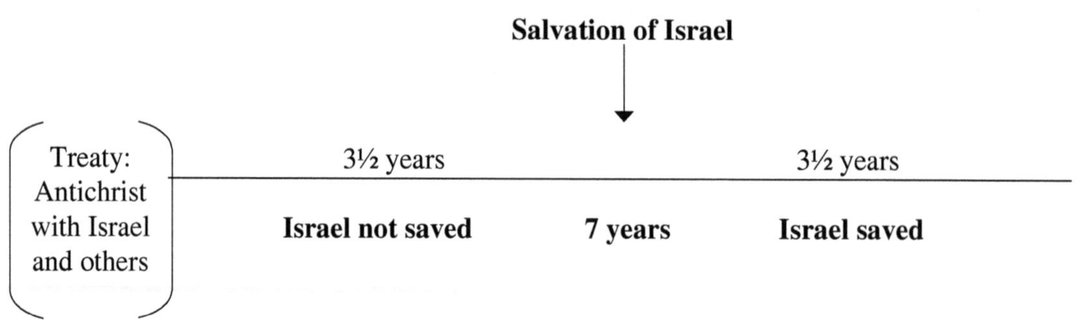

We have discovered from God's Word that Israel will be saved at the midpoint of their last seven years.

- Israel is not saved during the first 3 ½ years of the last seven years of this Present Age. Israel is saved throughout the last 3 ½ years of this Present Age.
- Israel will be saved when they see Jesus.
- They will see Jesus at the Rapture.
- This means that Israel will be saved at the time of the Rapture.
- Therefore, the Rapture will take place at the midpoint of the last seven years.

What do you see in the following verses which indicate that Israel will be saved at the conclusion of this battle of Gog and his armies? ______________________________

____

Ezekiel 39:21-22, 29 (NIV)

> [21] *"I will display my glory among the nations, and all the nations will see the punishment I inflict and the hand I lay upon them* [Gog's army].
>
> [22] *"From that day forward the house of Israel will know that I am the LORD their God.*
> [29] *"I will no longer hide my face from them, for I will pour out my Spirit on the house of Israel, declares the Sovereign LORD."*

Underline what God will do to Israel that affects their relationship with Him in verse 29. Does God pour out His Spirit on people who do not recognize Christ as their Savior? Yes ________ No __________.

Underline the time factor in verse 22.
What does *that day* mean? ____.

These two verses indicate that the Jews are saved *on that day* at the climatic defeat of the armies of Gog. We know that Israel's salvation takes place at the midpoint of the last seven years; therefore, we can place this invasion of Gog's armies at the midpoint of the last seven years.

Place an "X" on the time line below indicating the invasion and defeat of the armies of Gog.

Last 7 years of this Present Age ______________________________
3 ½ years 3 ½ years

Write "Gog's Army Destroyed" by the number (4) on the diagram entitled "Simultaneous Events at the Rapture" at the beginning of this lesson.

5. ISRAEL

a. Salvation

The Jews will be faced with the unbelievable odds of Gog's army coming at them from all directions. The Lord Jesus will appear in the sky at the Rapture and God will pour destruction on Gog's army. These two things result in Israel's belief in and acknowledging of Jesus Christ as their Savior.

In Lesson 6 we studied that Israel will see Jesus and receive Him as their Messiah/Savior at the Rapture. This takes place in the middle of the seven year covenant between the Jews and the Antichrist. Keep in mind that this Event, the Jews salvation, is the watershed for many end-time prophecies in the sense that the interpreter is able to place other Events before or after their salvation experience. You have probably noticed that the 3 ½ year period mentioned many times in Scripture refers to the second half of the Jewish/Antichrist seven year covenant. Many prophetic Events fall into place when we understand when Israel is saved.

Place an "X" on the time line below indicating when Israel is "saved."

Last 7 years of this present age ______________________________
3 ½ years 3 ½ years

Write "Salvation" by the number (5a) on the diagram entitled "Simultaneous Events at the Rapture" at the beginning of this lesson.

b. 144,000 sealed

Israel, at this point in time, has been converted to Christ. The terrible judgment of the Wrath of God is about to explode upon the earth. The book of Revelation, in very descriptive language, informs us that four angels stand at the four corners of the earth and are prepared to unleash the storms of God's judgment upon a world of appalling wickedness. Another angel commands the four angels not to harm the earth, sea, or trees *until* 144,000 Jews have received God's seal on their foreheads.

Revelation 7:1-4

> *"Then I* [John] *saw four angels standing at the four corners of the earth* [four directions of the compass], *holding back the four winds so they did not blow on the earth or the sea, or even on any tree. And I saw another angel coming up from the east, carrying the seal of the living God. And he shouted to those four angels, who had been given the power to harm land and sea, 'Wait! Don't harm the land or the sea or the trees* <u>*until*</u> *we*

Israel will...

- be born-again... "And I will give you a new heart, and I will put a new spirit in you."
- love God, the Son, with all their heart ..."I will take out your stony, stubborn heart and give you a tender, responsive heart."
- walk humbly in God's pathway...I will put my Spirit in you so that you will follow my decrees and be careful to obey my regulations." (Ezekiel 36:26-27)

have placed the seal of God on the foreheads of His servants.' And I heard how many were marked with the seal of God—144,000 were sealed from all the tribes of Israel."

Who else will have a mark on their foreheads at this time? ______________________________

This is very striking because the peoples of the earth also will have a seal referred to as the mark of the Beast/Antichrist upon their foreheads or right hands. Anyone who will refuse this evil mark will not be able to buy or sell. Believers who refuse this mark suffer greatly. We know this because of a statement in Revelation 7:16 that describes them in heaven immediately after the Rapture as never again knowing hunger or thirst, or homeless conditions that caused them to suffer from the elements of nature during the Great Tribulation.

The special privilege of God's seal
Revelation 14:1-5 gives a beautiful account of how special these 144,000 Jews are to God.

Verse 1a. . . *"Then I* [John] *saw the Lamb standing on Mount Zion, and with him were 144,000. . ."*

Just as Jesus promised to always be with the Believer (Matthew 28:20), in the same manner, Jesus' presence will be manifested to these 144,000 Jews following their salvation experience in Jerusalem. Observe that the place mentioned in this verse is on earth, not in heaven, on _____ ______________________________ which is another name for Jerusalem.

Verse 1b. . . *"who had his* [Jesus] *name and his Father's name written on their foreheads."*

They will have the name of God and Jesus on their foreheads, which symbolizes a seal of protection under God's ownership. We observe that the 144,000 will not be harmed by the fifth judgment during the Wrath of God judgment. (Revelation 9:4)

Verses 2-3. . .*"And I heard a sound from heaven <u>like</u> the roar of mighty oceans waves or the rolling of loud thunder. It was <u>like</u> the sound of many harpists playing together. This great choir sang a wonderful new song in front of the throne of God and before the four living beings and the twenty-four elders. No one could learn this song except the 144,000 who had been redeemed from the earth."*

In verse 1 we are told that the 144,000 Jews are on the earth on Mount Zion, not in heaven. But a magnificent sound of music is heard from heaven coming directly from the throne room of God. This new song from heaven will be given to the 144,000 which only they can sing. There have been countless composers of sacred music down through the ages, but can you imagine what it would be like if a song came directly from God's throne room, and you, along with a very select group, were the only ones who could sing it? Amazing!

Verse 4a. . .*"These have kept themselves as pure as virgins . . ."* (NLT) *"These are those who did not <u>defile</u> themselves with women, for they kept themselves pure."* (NIV)

Sexual imagery is used in the Scripture to denote spiritual purity, those faithful to God, or it can indicate the opposite which is spiritual defilement, those who turn away from God to idol worship and the vices of the world. Since God's Word never condemns marriage but rather blesses it, this probably refers to the 144,000 Jews as keeping themselves free from disgraceful wickedness so prevalent at this time.

The 144,000 will reject the world religious system of the Beast by refusing to worship the Beast. Perhaps they will also be in disagreement with the leaders of Israel who will enter into a seven-year covenant relationship with the Antichrist.

Verse 4b. . . *"following the Lamb wherever he goes. They have been purchased from among the people on the earth as a special offering to God and to the Lamb."*

While the entire world is filled with wonder and exclaims: "*Who is like the Beast*?" the 144,000 will offer themselves wholeheartedly to Christ as His witnesses whether this means life or death.

Verse 5. . . *"They have told no lies; they are without blame."*

In God's sight they are not guilty of falsehood and are above reproach. Satan's whole system is one gigantic deception, truth is totally absent, but these faithful Jews will not be deceived by it, nor will they submit to it. Considering the dreadful times in which they live, these are extraordinary and valiant servants of God!

Defile:
The Greek word *moluno* is the word for "*defile*." "*Moluno* denotes to besmear, as with mud or filth, to befoul. It is used in a figurative sense, of a conscience defiled by sin, 1 Corinthians 8:7; of believers who have kept themselves (their 'garments') from defilement, Revelation 3:4; and of those who have not soiled themselves by adultery or fornication, Revelation 14:4." [v]

Place an "X" on the time line below indicating when the 144,000 Jews receive God's seal.

Last 7 years of this Present Age ______________________________

3 ½ years 3 ½ years

Psalm 60:12
"With God we shall do valiantly; it is he who will tread down our foes."

Write "144,000 sealed" by the number (5b) on the diagram entitled "Simultaneous Events at the Rapture" at the beginning of this lesson.

c. Persecution

The Devil is filled with fury because he knows that he only has 3 ½ more years of freedom. The Believers have escaped from his cruelty; therefore, the dragon's evil gaze targets the only ones remaining who stand for God—the Christian Jews.

Underline the words in the following verses that indicate persecution of the Jews.

Revelation 12:12-13

> *"Therefore, rejoice, O heavens! But terror* [woe] *will come on the earth and the sea, for the devil has come down to you in great anger, knowing that he has little time. When the dragon* [Satan] *realized that he had been thrown down to the earth, he pursued the woman* [Israel]. . ."

Satan is a creature of "unimaginable meanness, malice, fury, and cruelty directed against God, against God's truth, and against those to whom God has extended His saving love." [6]

Zechariah 13:8-9

> *"Two-thirds of the people in the land* [Israel] *will be cut off and die,' says the LORD. 'But one-third will be left in the land. I will bring that group through the fire and make them pure. I will refine them like silver and purify them like gold. They will call on my name, and I will answer them. I will say, 'These are my people,' and they will say, 'The LORD is our God.'"*

Daniel 7:21, 25

> *"As I watched, this horn* [the Antichrist] *was waging war against God's holy people* [Jewish Christians] *and was defeating them. . .He* [the Antichrist] *will defy the Most High and oppress the holy people* [Israel] *of the Most High. . .They will be placed under his control for a time, times and a half a time* [3 ½ years]."

The Antichrist and the people under his rule will carry out a cruel persecution of the Jewish nation. Two-thirds will perish. The emphasis placed on sealing the 144,000 may indicate that they are the one-third who are preserved through the last 3 ½ years.

This will be Israel's finest moment in history. Israel will shine forth the mercies and patience of God, fervently love and honor the Son of God, and willingly live or die for the One they had rejected for centuries.

Place an "X" on the time line below indicating when the persecution of Israel begins.

Last 7 years of this Present Age ____

3 ½ years 3 ½ years

Write "Persecution" by the number (5c) on the diagram entitled "Simultaneous Events at the Rapture" at the beginning of this lesson.

6. THE ANTICHRIST IN THE TEMPLE

Even though this is not a simultaneous Event with the Rapture, it is so close in time that it seems appropriate to include it here for chronological clarity. Within a very short time period after the defeat of Gog at the Rapture Event, the Antichrist will invade Jerusalem to make the fantastic declaration that he is "God" in the temple. [7]

Apparently the Antichrist will return from Jerusalem to his headquarters in the "*harlot city*" from where he rules the world. (You will be able to identify this "*harlot city*" in Part Two of this study book.) But he does leave several thousand troops in control of Jerusalem and the rest of Israel. The Antichrist will also set up his statue within the confines of the temple site. Probably in the court adjacent to the temple proper where there will be ample space to worship it.

Place an "X" on the time line below indicating when the Antichrist will enter the Temple of the Jews to proclaim himself to be God.

Last 7 years of this Present Age ____
3 ½ years 3 ½ years

Write "The Antichrist in the Temple" by the number (6) on the diagram entitled "Simultaneous Events at the Rapture" at the beginning of this lesson.

5d. THE TWO WITNESSES

The Antichrist's conquest of the world and his rule is not without opposition and difficulties during the last 3 ½ years of this present age. Two Jews in Jerusalem have been endowed by God with great power and authority and will bring calamity after calamity on the earth causing great destruction and ruin. These judgments in all probability are the seven Trumpet/Bowl Judgments of the Wrath of God.

We will come back to their dynamic story in another lesson.

Place an "X" on the time line below indicating when the two witnesses begin their ministry.

Last 7 years of this Present Age ____
3 ½ years 3 ½ years

Write "The Two Witnesses" by the number (5d) on the diagram entitled "Simultaneous Events at the Rapture" at the beginning of this lesson.

"X MARKS"
All the "X marks" of every Event in this lesson should be located in the middle of the seven year period (the Seventieth Week of Daniel's prophecy.) Consult **Timeline One** and **Two** (located at the end of Part One of this study book) to observe that all the events in this lesson occur where the Rapture appears on the Timeline. Hopefully you are getting a firm grasp and understanding of end-time Events in regard to their relation to one another.

We have arrived at the point in time in our study of end-time prophetic Events when God seems to say to the world, "Enough! I will give you one last chance. You haven't responded to My call to repentance by My loving acts of grace. Now you will have one last chance to hear and to respond to My call to repentance by My wrathful acts of judgment."

JESUS CHRIST THE WISDOM OF GOD

1 Corinthians 1:24

LESSON 11

JESUS CHRIST THE HOPE OF GLORY
Colossians 1:27

"'Christ in you, the hope of glory!' The future is a hope and not a dread. Bereavement loses its despair, and death loses its sting." [1]

PREPARATION FOR THE STUDY OF THE WRATH OF GOD

THE DAY I LEARNED AWESOME RESPECT

When I was a little girl I was usually nice and sweet, but there was another side to Kathryn; she could be very obnoxious and stubborn. I had one of the most loving and gentle dads that a child could be blessed with. However, love and gentleness are not the only characteristics required in the formation of the lives of children. A life transforming day when I learned awesome respect was a day the "other Kathryn" came out.

In reality, I do not remember what I did to engage this particular characteristic of a good parent. But I do remember my dad firmly holding my hand as we rapidly descended to the basement. I was so shaken and frightened by my dad's anger, righteous indignation to be sure, that when he looked at me, he saw fear and repentance written all over my face. He understood that in this instance, there was no need to apply his hand to my "seat of education." The sternness of his face and his firm, direct to-the-point words, would be sufficient. They were! I learned two things that day: one, that wrong doing always bears consequences, and two, an awesome respect for the one appointed to hold me accountable.

As we move into the study of the period of history known as the Wrath of God, you must understand who your heavenly Father is. You will be looking at His stern countenance, hear His direct to-the-point words and stare wide-eyed at His awe-inspiring actions. If you can grasp the deep meaning from Exodus 34:6 (NIV), you will be prepared for these studies. Please read slowly; and with awesome respect submit yourself to the balanced truth of God's loving perfections and His terrible wrath.

> *"...The Lord, the Lord, the compassionate and gracious God, slow to anger, abounding in love and faithfulness, maintaining love to thousands, and forgiving wickedness, rebellion and sin. Yet He does not leave the guilty unpunished..."*

This lesson is to prepare you for the study of the judgments of The Wrath of God; therefore, we will cover five specific points of discussion to accomplish that purpose. These judgments for Unbelievers are called the Trumpet/Bowl Judgments and are found in Revelation 8-9, 15-16, 11.

In this lesson we will discuss:

1. God's Justice
2. Cataclysmic Events

3. Supernatural Beings—Agents of the End Times
4. Symbols
5. Repeat the Prophecy!

1. GOD'S JUSTICE

Have you ever questioned God's actions? Can you think of an instance that seemed harsh and perhaps unreasonable in your opinion? Jot it down here. ______________________________

____

____

God is always right and always fair. If I do not understand His ways or actions, the shortcoming is in me, my understanding, not in God.

How this truth has helped me through many *gymnastics* of soul and mind to deal with the hard things of life! I read somewhere, and unfortunately can't recall where to give just credit, but my memory comes up with something like this:

> "There are things that I know that I know. (all kinds of things)
> There are things that I know that I don't know. (scientific, technological, biological, etc. things)
> And there are things that I don't know that I don't know." (? things)

Guess which statements apply most to our knowledge of the workings of the All-Knowing Holy One?

People want to hold all things to their idea of fairness; they believe that even God must be subject to their concept or at least to some universal standard of fairness. When man faces obstacles, injustice, or tragedy, this unwritten "law of fairness" is set in motion. The question is, can man be absolutely fair? If he cannot, then how can he establish a law of fairness? Let's take some time here to investigate a few words from the dictionary that define fairness. [D] **Read** them first with humans in mind; then read them with God in mind.

Fair can imply any of the following definitions:

- **Just**

stresses being in accordance with a code of what is legally or ethically right and proper

- **Impartial**

emphasizes lack of favoritism in deciding an issue

- **Unprejudiced**

means without preconceived opinions or judgments, especially those adverse to a person or thing and not soundly based

- **Unbiased**

implies straightness of judgment or behavior, in the absence of self-interest, prejudice, or emotionalism

- **Straightforward**

suggests what is frank and honest rather than devious

- **Objective**

implies detachment that permits a person to observe and judge without undue reference to his own experience and without indulgence of his sympathies

By definition, can man ever formulate a true standard of what is fair? Not in a million years, not ever! Can God? Absolutely, or He wouldn't be God.

It is imperative to understand the attributes of God in light of the display of His wrath in the final seven judgments of mankind. God transcends all created things; yet, He is personally involved with all created things and has graciously revealed Himself so that man may know Him in His perfections (attributes). God is perfect, lacking in nothing, flawless, in a state of undiminished or highest excellence. He is. . . perfect. Fairness and justice are two of His perfections. God is always right in what He says and does.

Psalm 89:14 (NKJV) "Righteousness and justice are the foundation of Your throne; mercy and truth go before Your face."

Therefore, God sets the standard of fairness and justice. All things must be held to and measured by His standard. This truth should really take a heavy burden off our shoulders as we try to figure out all this stuff. We can look to a perfect God who is one hundred percent right in what He does and says.

To aid our understanding of God's wrath during the 3 ½ years known as The Wrath of God, here are two helpful quotations. They refer to the wrath of God throughout history as it is recorded in the Bible. Each quotation is full of insight and truth.

Ray C. Stedman
"I must point out that many people greatly misunderstand this phrase "the wrath of God." For some the phrase "the wrath of God" suggests that God is a cranky, vengeful deity who is given to uncontrolled outbursts of violent temper. But such a view of God's wrath only reveals the limitations of our understanding. The Bible never speaks of the wrath of God that way.

According to the Scriptures the wrath of God is actually the outworking of God's moral integrity. God has created the universe with certain moral laws, which operate much like the physical law of gravity. When human beings refuse to yield themselves to God, they run up against the moral laws of His universe. When people violate God's moral laws, the result is pain, sorrow, and wounding. It is God's way of saying to humanity, 'Look, you must face reality. You were made for Me. If you use the gift of free will I have given you to violate My will, I won't stop you, but you will have to bear the consequences of your actions.'" [2]

Revelation 15:3 (NIV) "Great and marvelous are your deeds, Lord God Almighty. Just and true are your ways, King of the ages."

The Believer's Study Bible
"The word most often employed to designate God's anger is *orge* [Greek word], defined as the eternal disposition of settled anger in the very essence of God's nature against the destructive forces of evil in the universe. Men make themselves the object of that wrath when they sin and become a part of the destructiveness of evil. The concept of wrath includes God's present displeasure with evil as well as the ultimate confinement and defeat of all evil in the eternal state of hell (Matthew 8:12). Wrath is as much a part of the character [perfections] of God as is love. A God who does not exercise wrath against injustice is an immoral God. A universe in

which evil exists unchallenged and ultimately unvanquished is inconceivable and could not be ruled by a good God of holy love. Essential to a good God of love is His wrath against evil." [3]

It would be a good thing for you to clarify in your mind and heart exactly where you stand on this important topic of God's fairness and justice. **Write** down your statement of belief. ________

____

____

My personal statement of belief:
I believe God makes all His decisions according to His perfections. I believe that He will never commit an error of judgment in fairness or justice. I submit myself to His divine actions regarding my personal life and to all my Father's methods in dealing with mankind.

2. CATACLYSMIC EVENTS

The first four judgments of The Wrath of God affect the environment and the universe. (Revelation 8, 16) Demonic forces are released upon mankind in the fifth and sixth judgments. (Revelation 9, 16) The seventh judgment brings us into the consummation and establishment of Christ's kingdom on earth. (Revelation 11)

End-time prophecy reveals to us that there will be great upheaval on earth and in the heavens. As you study The Wrath of God, perhaps you will think, "How can this be?" Or, you may think that the earth and mankind would be destroyed many times over if this were to have a literal meaning. Sensible thinking.

All the calamities of the cosmos during The Wrath of God judgments come by orders from the heavenly throne of God, the place of supreme authority and control**.** The catastrophes of the first four judgments are not caused by man-made disasters, from pollutants and abuses of nature, nor are they caused by nature itself. God not only causes the phenomena, but controls it to accomplish only what He intends. As someone has said, God performs these judgments with the same ease with which we perform our ordinary everyday tasks. Look up some of these Scriptures: Joshua 10:12-14; 2 Kings 20:9-11; Exodus 14; Matthew 8:23-27. These wondrous acts do not surprise Believers; we expect God to do supernatural things.

There are no limitations or boundaries for the God of creation and sustainer of the universe.
Colossians 1:16-17 (NIV)

> *"For by Him* [Jesus] *all things were created; things in heaven and on earth, visible and invisible, whether thrones or powers or rulers or authorities; all things were created by Him and for Him. He is before all things, and <u>in Him all things hold together</u>."*

To *"hold together*" means that Jesus Christ not only is the Creator of all things, He is also the cohesive, the glue that holds things together. He is the unifying principle, the center that holds all creation together. The Lord Jesus is conserving and preserving creation from self-destruction and chaos.

Hebrews 1:3 (NIV)

"The Son is the radiance of God's glory and the exact representation of His being, sustaining all things by His powerful word."

If you were sustaining all things, nothing excluded, how would you picture that in your mind? A little difficult imagining that isn't it? However, that is what Jesus is doing. The words "*sustaining all things*" mean that Jesus is actively preserving; but also carrying creation towards its goal, its divinely ordained destiny. How does He do this according to Hebrews 1:3? ________
____.

There seems to be an apparent return to some normality after each judgment.
Like the plagues of Egypt, it is probable that God begins and terminates each judgment in a decisive manner. Because of this definite beginning and end of each episode, it will be very evident that a divine power is at work. Naturally, the earth will suffer damaging changes, and a great number of people and creatures through death will be gone forever because of the scope of the judgments. A return to "new-normal" conditions and a slight break between judgments will allow opportunity for reflective thinking and true repentance or, the opposite, a hardening of the heart in defiant opposition to God.

God will maintain the heavens and earth during the great destruction He brings upon them. He will have a hands-on management of what will occur, its duration and extent.

3. SPIRITUAL BEINGS—AGENTS OF THE END TIMES

Supernatural beings, angels and demons, are always involved in the affairs of man, but at this point in our study, they are very active. Therefore, it is necessary to briefly focus our attention on them. We can divide these created spirits into three groups.

Psalm 103:20-21 "Praise the Lord, you angels, you mighty ones who carry out His plans, listening for each of His commands. Yes, praise the Lord, you armies of angels who serve Him and do His will."

- **God's angels**

God's angels are powerful beings. They are active in nature, nations, and good ministries for mankind, and especially, all that pertains to born-again Believers. All angels were created as moral, highly intelligent beings. They have a free will, and like the first man, Adam, were on probation and tested. Those who remained obedient to their Maker and Lord have been confirmed in a state of holiness and goodness. They are loyal to God and carryout His commands in unquestionable obedience. "Their beneficent services are a constant reproach to the demons of Satan, who are ever seeking to destroy the work of God and distort His natural providence." [4]

- **Apostate evil angels**

These angels are called demons and evil spirits in the Bible, and Satan is their prince. These angels were created holy at the same time as the good angels. When they were tested, they disobeyed God and were confirmed in evil; good is totally absent from their nature. "Their minds are permanently set to oppose God, goodness, truth, the kingdom of Christ, and the welfare of human beings, and they have real, if limited, power and freedom of movement, though in Calvin's picturesque phrase 'they drag their chains wherever they go and can never hope to overcome God.'" [5]

It is important to remember that Satan can be resisted. "Submit yourselves, then, to God. Resist the devil, and he will flee from you. Come near to God and He will come near to you." (James 4:7-8 NIV)

- **The Cherubim and the Seraphim**

These angels seem to hold a very high rank in the order of angels and are the most extraordinary of these created spiritual beings. They are first seen guarding the way to the tree of life against sinful man's intrusion into God's paradise, the Garden of Eden. They seem to always be near God's manifested glory, the throne, the mercy seat, worshiping and serving their Holy Creator. What will it be like to see these magnificent creatures? (Genesis 3:24; 2 Kings 19:15; Ezekiel 10:1-22; Revelation 4:6-11; 5:6, 8-14; Isaiah 6:2-3, 6)

ANGELS, GOD'S MINISTERING SPIRITS

Angels and their counterpart are extremely active but not always openly mentioned in the Scriptures. They are like the wind. We see the results caused by the action of the wind but we can't see the wind itself. The book of Acts is an interesting study in opposing spiritual forces as revealed in the work of the Holy Spirit and the opposition of Satan. God permits us to see the work of angels time and time again throughout the book of the Revelation.

Church history is a record of the acts of God and the acts of the arch enemy, Satan. You are definitely a part of these spiritual battles. Good angels have been commissioned by God to serve His followers. (Hebrews 1:13-14)

The Believer's body-guards "For He will command His angels concerning you to guard you in all your ways; they will lift you up in their hands, so that you will not strike your foot against a stone." (Psalm 91:11-12 NIV)

> "And it appears from many Scripture intimations that this is a peculiarly important branch of their work. We understand that by means of the good angels the demons are restrained and defeated in their designs to injure the children of God. Were it not so, we do not see how, for one moment, we could be safe from these foul spirits, who are invisible, sly, and overpoweringly numerous. The Christian owes profound and unceasing gratitude to God for this provision of His providence in appointing good angels as our defenders." [6]

John refers to angels over 70 times in the book of Revelation allowing us to observe their important actions as God's ministering servants at work. The following Scriptures reveal just a few instances of their participation in the end-time Events.

- Angels accompany King Jesus at the Rapture and will gather the Believers. (1 Thessalonians 4:16; Matthew 24:31)

- Angels accompany King Jesus at His Second Coming. (Matthew 25:31 NKJV)

- A particular angel was sent to the apostle John to communicate to him the book of Revelation. (Revelation 1:1; 19:10; 22:16)

- Myriads of angels worship God and the Lamb of God. (Revelation 5:11; 7:11) What will it be like when we will not only get to observe the worship of millions of angels, but will actually blend our voices with theirs in perfect worship of God and King Jesus! Remarkable!

- An angel puts the seal of God on the foreheads of the 144,000 Christian Jews. (Revelation 7:2-3)

- Michael, the archangel, and his angels will war and overcome Satan and his angels. (Revelation 12:7-9) An angel will lay hold of Satan and bind him with a great chain, cast him into the bottomless pit, and shut him up with a seal where he will remain until the end of Christ's Thousand-Year Reign on earth. (Revelation 20:1-3)

- Seven angels will sound their trumpets and pour their bowls of wrath upon the inhabitants of earth. (Revelation 8-9; 15-16; 11:15) "The most potent and destructive forces of creation have been delegated to the use of angels, for the punishment of sin at the last day." [7] Therefore, during the Wrath of God, the greatest cataclysmic eruptions ever known to mankind will be performed by spirit beings.

- Another mighty angel announces that when the seventh trumpet sounds there will be no delay. Immediately, the mystery of God, as foretold by the prophets, will be fulfilled, that is to say, King Jesus will return to establish His eternal reign. (Revelation 10)

THE FURY OF THE DRAGON DURING THE WRATH OF GOD

Revelation 12:9, 12

> *"This great dragon—the ancient serpent called the devil, or Satan, the one deceiving the whole world—was thrown down to the earth with all his angels. But terror will come on the earth and the sea, for the devil has come down to you in great anger, knowing that he has little time."*

Fury, he is filled with fury! Satan has gained such great things through the World System of the Antichrist, soon to be lost at the Second Coming of King Jesus!

> "Will it mean nothing to Satan that his rule over the world for so many millenniums is wrested from him and conferred upon Christ and the Christians whom he hates with such violent hatred? Can he be indifferent to the prospect of those very saints whom he persecuted and sought to destroy on earth becoming the judges of the world that belongs to him and the fallen angels? Could this not account for his special hatred toward the Christians of the present time. . .challenging their every step onward and upward with his diabolical assaults?" [8]

Such an unspeakably evil creature knows neither remorse nor repentance. Stealing, killing, destroying consumes him. (John 10:10) All the strength of Satan, fired by his fury, tenaciously holds on to his power over mankind through his servants, the Antichrist and the False Prophet. The people of the world in willful allegiance follow him into the Wrath of God to their destruction.

The last days are truly a spectacular drama of spiritual powers. But the outcome has already been decided, so fix your eyes upon Christ, who sits at the right hand of God, in whose name we overcome and with whom we are made worthy to reign.

4. SYMBOLS

It is very important for you to understand symbolic meaning in Scripture, especially in the prophetic books of the Bible. Readers of the book of Revelation, for example, discover such extraordinary language that they sometimes give up on it as incomprehensible; they determine the book to be mythical. If you have felt this way, I trust that this brief treatment of symbolic language will help you to understand how profound truths are enhanced when conveyed by this type of expression.

First of all, God does not speak in mysterious terms that only the *initiated elite* can comprehend. The Lord is a lover of straightforward, honest speaking. *"Simply let your 'Yes' be 'Yes,' and your 'No,' 'No"* (Matthew 5:37 NIV) Would He, then, give some of the most important information affecting mankind in totally incomprehensible language? Of course not! The Lord reveals His truth through His Holy Spirit who illuminates our minds.

Symbols are comparisons or representations which have a literal meaning. For example, the term *beast* a name for the Antichrist is used by the prophet Daniel in the Old Testament and the apostle John in the New Testament. The Antichrist will not be an animal with iron teeth and bronze claws (Daniel 7:19) just as our Lord Jesus is not a literal lamb, door, bread, or light. (John 1:29; 10:7, 9; 6:35; 8:12) However, the characteristic or function of the symbol, which is something very familiar to the Bible writer, is a comparison or representation of the same characteristics or function of the thing he is talking about.

The term *beast* portrays to the average person a powerful, ferocious, scary animal, that if not in the wild, should be locked in a cage. With that in mind, think about why this name "*the beast*" was chosen to depict the Antichrist. God purposefully chose this symbol to compare the coming king of the world with the characteristics of a brutal beast who "*crushed and devoured its victims and trampled underfoot whatever was left*." (Daniel 7:19 NIV) Figurative language can reveal truth in an effective manner. It not only speaks to the intellect but also engages the emotions of the soul.

Let's take a couple of symbols used by Jesus to see how accurate symbols can be.

"I am the door." (John 10:9) What is the function of a door? ____________________________

____

How does your answer make a *door* such a good comparison with Jesus? ____________________

____

The meaning of the symbol lies in the function of a *door*. A door gives or prevents access to a place. Jesus says He is the door, meaning that through Him, people are given exclusive access to God and to eternal life.

"I am the bread of life." (John 6:48) What is bread used for? ____________________________
How does your answer make *bread* such a good comparison with Jesus? ___________________

____

The meaning of the symbol, again, lies in the function of *bread.* Bread nourishes and sustains physical life. Jesus is nourishment to man's soul. He is the provision for all his spiritual needs. Jesus gives eternal life.

In regard to studying end-time prophetic Events, it is necessary to distinguish between the literal and the figurative. Here are some good guidelines:

- "Take the passage in its most simple, direct, and ordinary meaning unless there are compelling reasons to do otherwise." [9] If the Scripture passage says that the ocean is turned into blood, there is no compelling reason to consider blood to be something other than blood such as "the sunset reflecting on the water turned the ocean red."

- Every symbol has a literal meaning. The symbol stands for a reality.

- Because end-time prophecy deals with the very real, but invisible spirit world, you will meet situations very different from our physical world. Do not ignore them as fiction or myth.

In these studies I will try to give a helping hand in understanding the expressively rich symbolism in the book of Revelation. For those of you who have read Revelation many times, I firmly believe that you would prefer to leave it just the way it is with all its symbolism.

5. REPEAT THE PROPHECY!

Very puzzling. . .something is wrong here. . .I am confused. Maybe you have felt this way as you have read the seven Trumpet/Bowl judgments in the book of Revelation. You have read about all six trumpets in Revelation 8 and 9 then chapter 10 interrupts the sequence, and you finally find the seventh and last trumpet judgment in chapter 11. Everything seems to wrap up with the seventh angel when he will blow the seventh trumpet; the judgment of the Wrath of God will be complete, and the Lord Jesus and His kingdom will have arrived. Wonderful!

Revelation 11:15 (NIV)

> *"The seventh angel sounded his trumpet, and there were loud voices in heaven which said: 'The kingdom of the world has become the kingdom of our Lord and of His Christ, and He will reign for ever and ever.'"*

But as you move on to chapters 12. . .13. . .14. . . instead of the Kingdom of Christ these chapters throw you back into the things that take place during the World System of the Antichrist. Hmmm. . .Now it gets really confusing. Chapters 15 and 16 go through another whole string of judgments described as bowls. If King Jesus came when the seventh trumpet was blown, why are you now back into what appears to be the same judgments with a different name? You thought that you were all done with the judgments. And more importantly, Jesus' Kingdom hasn't arrived, it is still future. This makes some people want to throw up their hands and say, "Who can understand the book of Revelation; it seems to be all scrambled up."

The answer is surprisingly simple, but can be easily missed. When we study a book of the Bible we must always consider the scope (what the book covers) and the plan (the arrangement of the book) so we can see the writer's order of thought. Let's go to chapter 10 which interrupted the trumpet judgments to see what this is all about. Our intention here is not to study chapter 10 verse by verse but to discover the key to help us to understand the arrangement and deliberate order, or chronology, of the book of Revelation.

First of all, **read** the following Scripture then answer the questions. Use your best interpretive perceptions.

Revelation 10 (NIV)

> 1 *Then I saw another mighty angel coming down from heaven. He was robed in a cloud,*
> *with a rainbow above his head; his face was like the sun, and his legs were like fiery*
> *pillars.* 2 *He was holding a little scroll, which lay open in his hand. He planted his right*
> *foot on the sea and his left foot on the land,*
>
> 3 *and he gave a loud shout like the roar of a lion. When he had shouted, the voices of*
> *the seven thunders spoke.* 4 *And when the seven thunders spoke, I was about to write;*
> *but I heard a voice from heaven say, "Seal up what the seven thunders have said and*
> *do not write it down."*
>
> 5 *Then the angel I had seen standing on the sea and on the land raised his right hand*
> *to heaven* 6 *And he swore by Him who lives forever and ever, who created the heavens*
> *and all that is in them, the earth and all that is in it, and the sea and all that is in it, and*
> *said, "There will be no more delay!"*
>
> 7 *But in the days when the seventh angel is about to sound his trumpet, the mystery*
> *of God will be accomplished* [finished], *just as He announced to His servants the*
> *prophets."*
>
> 8 *Then the voice that I heard from heaven spoke to me once more: "Go, take the scroll*
> *that lies open in the hand of the angel who is standing on the sea and on the land."* 9
> *So I went to the angel and asked him to give me the little scroll. He said to me, "Take*
> *it and eat it." It will turn your stomach sour, but in your mouth it will be as sweet as*
> *honey."* 10 *I took the little scroll from the angel's hand and ate it. It tasted as sweet as*
> *honey in my mouth, but when I had eaten it, my stomach turned sour.*
>
> 11 *Then I was told,* ***"You must prophecy again about many peoples, nations, lan-***
> ***guages and kings."***

Sometimes the prophets saw the vision given to them by God and at other times they actively participated in the vision itself. John not only watches the action take place in this vision, but he also participates in it.

verses 1-2. . .How does the appearance of this angel compare with society's idea of what angels look like? ____________________

Although angels are disembodied spirits they often appeared in bodily form in the Bible. Many times they seemed to look like everybody else in regard to clothing, etc. Even today's angels appear like people of our day. "Do not forget to entertain strangers, for by so doing some people have entertained angels without knowing it." (Hebrews 13:2) The bodily position of this mighty angel seems to indicate that he is gigantic in stature. What did he have in his hand? __________

verse 6. . .What did the angel so emphatically declare? ____________________

Circle this phrase in verse 6 above.

verse 7. . .The angel tells John what will take place when the seventh trumpet is blown. To help you understand what the *mystery of God* is that is finished, let's look directly at the actual moment when the seventh trumpet is blown.

Revelation 11:15

> *"The seventh angel sounded his trumpet, and there were loud voices in heaven which said: 'The kingdom of the world has become the kingdom of our Lord and of His Christ, and He will reign for ever and ever.'"*

According to Revelation 11:15, what will take place when the seventh angel blows his trumpet?

____

____

The *Mystery of God* has come to a fulfillment. The evil kingdom of the Antichrist and the Ten Kings has been terminated, and the world has become the Kingdom of our King, Jesus Christ.

There is a definite finality, a conclusion, here in 10:7. The word *accomplished,* finished, is the Greek word *teleo* which means "end, goal; to make an end or accomplishment, to complete anything, not merely to end it, but to bring it to perfection or its destined goal, to carry it through." [KW] This, my friend, is the very same word used by Jesus when He hung on the cross to accomplish redemption for all mankind, "*It is finished* [teleo] *and bowing His head, He gave up His spirit*" (John 19:30)

The seventh trumpet judgment is the Second Coming of Jesus Christ! The Wrath of God judgments will have ended, Christ comes to reign upon the earth! Just wait till we study this!

verses 8-10. . .What is John told to do? verse 8 ____________________

What is he supposed to do with it? verse 9 ____________________

Does he obey? verse 10 ______________ What strange thing happened to him? ____________

____

The Greek word for *eat* is *katesthio* which means "to consume by eating, to devour; of a prophet, eating up a book, is suggestive of spiritually eating and digesting its contents (Revelation 10:9; Ezekiel 2:8-3:3; Jeremiah 15:16)." [V]

Genesis 6:6 (NIV) "So the Lord was grieved that he had made man on the earth, and His heart was filled with pain." ...it broke His heart.

This symbolic action of eating the little scroll signifies that the prophet needed to internalize the message received from God in order to deliver it effectively. "The true preacher of God's word will faithfully proclaim the denunciations of the wicked it contains. But he does not do this with fierce glee. The more his heart is filled with the love of God the more certain it is that the telling forth of 'woes' will be a bitter experience. The wickedness of man grieved God at His heart (Genesis 6:6), and the true preacher of God's Word enters to some degree into this suffering." [10]

verse 11. . .What is John told to do now? ____________________
Who does this prophecy affect? __________, __________, __________
and __________.

Do you think the message of the *"little scroll"* given to John is a repetition of the Trumpet judgments that he had just given? __________

The *kings* of verse 11 more than likely refers to the Ten Kings of the World System of the Antichrist, at the time this will take place.

"You must prophecy again." *Again* is the Greek word *palin* and means "anew, once more, oscillatory repetition." [S] *Oscillatory* is the adjective for oscillate which means "to swing back and forth" like a fan, or a swing in the backyard tree. Therefore, John is instructed to *swing back* to repeat (give anew, once more) the prophecy he has just given and then to *go forth*, or forward, from there.

I think that you are doing a good job of observing. Have you figured it out? The little scroll given to John by the angel contains the Seven *Bowl* Judgments. The Seven Bowl Judgments are the repetition of the Seven Trumpet Judgments. They are one and the same.

John read the open scroll, consumed it, as it were, and now he will reveal its contents at the proper place in his writing of the book of Revelation. Chapters 14 through 16 are the repetition of Chapters 7 through 11. So the repetition is parallel and talks about the same things but with different symbols.

Repeat the Prophecy!
The prophets many times repeated the same message but used different symbols and gave additional information in the repetition. Listen to the words of a renowned Bible interpreter, Milton S. Terry.

> ". . .we should naturally presume that the seven vials [bowls] of the seven last plagues in Revelation 16 are intended to correspond with the seven woe-trumpets of chapters 8 and 9. The striking resemblances between the two are such as to force a conviction that the terrible woes [referred to] by the trumpets are substantially identical with the plagues [referred to] by the vials [bowls] of wrath. A contrary opinion would make the case a remarkable exception to the analogy of prophecy, and should not be accepted without the most convincing reasons." [11]

Repeated dreams and visions have the same meaning or significance but the repetition will reveal even more details.

> "The repetition under different symbols was the divine method of intensifying the impression, and indicating the certainty of the things revealed." [12]

To understand that the book of Revelation repeats itself has the same effect for us as a powerful floodlight in a very dark place. Now it makes sense. In Appendix A, an outline of the structure and chronology of Revelation will be presented. The very title *Revelation* tells us that God wants us to understand this book. *Revelation* in the Greek language is *apokalupsis* which means to reveal, to uncover, to remove a veil like opening the curtain on a theatre stage, or taking a lid off to reveal what is inside a pan.

We will see new details in the repetition of the seven judgments; therefore, we will need to study both of the narrations of the Trumpet judgments and the Bowl judgments together as one complete prophecy.

A PARALLEL CHART OF THE SEVEN TRUMPETS AND SEVEN BOWLS OF THE WRATH OF GOD

Explore the Book [13] written by J. Sidlow Baxter, expresses great insight in his analysis of the structure of the book of Revelation. I am in total agreement that the Trumpet and Bowl judgments are parallel judgments based on his analysis of looking at *where* they take place. My analysis differs slightly, in some respects, to Baxter's.

Again, I believe that you will enjoy discovering things for yourself. So I am leaving blanks for you to fill in as you look up these verses on your own. The answers will be provided afterwards so that you can check your work. This is not a difficult exercise, but it is enlightening.

Look up each Scripture reference in your Bible, and find where, the place, each judgment occurs. **Write** your answer on the blank provided. I am using the Revised Standard Version.

THE WRATH OF GOD

The Seven Trumpets Chapters 8-9,11 (RSV)	The Seven Bowls Chapters 15-16 (RSV)
1. on the ______________ (8:7)	1. upon the ______________ (16:2)
2. into the ______________(8:8)	2. into the ______________ (16:3)
3. on ____________ and ____________ ________________ (8:10)	3. into the ____________ and ________ ______________________ (16:4)

4. the _________, _____________ and ___________ (8:12)

5. the _____________________________ ______ (9:1, 11)

6. at the ______________________ (9:14)

7. in ________________________ (11:15)

Proclamation from heaven (11:15)

". . .and there were loud voices in heaven saying:

"The kingdom of the world has become the kingdom of our Lord and of His Christ, and he will reign forever and ever."

"and there were flashes of lightning, loud noises, peals of thunder, an earthquake and heavy hail." (11:19)

4. on the ___________ (16:8)

5. on the __________________________ __________________________ (16:10)

6. on the __________________________ __________________ (16:12)

7. into the _______________ (16:17)

Proclamation from heaven (16:17)

". . .and a great voice came out of the temple, from the throne, saying,

"It is done!"

"Then there were flashes of lightning, loud noises, peals of thunder, and a great earthquake such as had never been since men were on the earth, so great was that earthquake." (16:18)

The answers will vary depending on which words your Bible version uses.

Trumpets

1. on the earth
2. into the sea
3. rivers, fountains or springs of water
4. the sun, moon, stars
5. the bottomless pit or abyss
6. river Euphrates
7. in heaven

Bowls

1. on the earth
2. on the sea
3. rivers, fountains or springs of water
4. the sun
5. on the throne of the beast
6. river Euphrates
7. into the air

We see clearly that the Bowl Judgments are the repeated prophecy as according to Revelation 10.

A summary of the reasons for concluding that the Bowl Judgments are a repetition of the Trumpet Judgments.

- The book of Revelation speaks of Seven Seals which are opened by Jesus. (Revelation 5:5) Six of these Seals are opened in Chapter 6.

Jesus opens the *Seventh Seal* which contains the Seven Trumpet judgments in Revelation 8:1: "*When the Lamb* [Jesus] *broke the seventh seal on the scroll. . .*" The opening of the Seventh and final *Seal* is mentioned only this one time because it includes the Seven Trumpet and Bowl Judgments. There are only seven Wrath of God judgments, not fourteen.

- In Revelation 10:6-7 we are told specifically that when the Seventh Trumpet sounds no more time will pass, Jesus' Kingdom will come immediately.

- In Revelation 10:11, John is told to give the prophecy again, to repeat it.

- The place affected or the action that takes place by both Trumpet and Bowl Judgments is the same.

- Studying the two judgments together gives a complete picture of what is going to happen during The Wrath of God.

This interpretation of the structure of Revelation is the key to understanding this remarkable book. As was mentioned, you will see an outline of the chronology of Revelation in Appendix A. How blessed we are that God has prepared us by revealing to us exactly what He intends to do in the end times.

A suggestion

This morning, following the words in my Bible, I listened again to the Seven Trumpet Judgments narrated with sound effects on a CD. I am deeply moved in my soul every time I listen to these CD's of the book of Revelation. To me, it all becomes more of a reality, like being there. I have also done this in a small group Bible study. The effect is breathtaking.

I recommend this way of listening to the Scriptures. There are many Audio CD's of the Bible. The one we have on the New Testament is: The Word of Promise, New Testament (New King James Version) 20 CD Set.

With this orientation, you are prepared to study the Event known as the Wrath of God.

JESUS CHRIST THE HOPE OF GLORY

Colossians 1:27

LESSON **12**

JESUS CHRIST EVERLASTING LIGHT

Isaiah 60:19 - Revelation 21:23

The Lord will nudge the sun and moon aside to replace them with Himself. Darkness, gone forever!

THE WRATH OF GOD

THE FIRST FIVE TRUMPET/BOWL JUDGMENTS

My aunt Arlien had the habit of screaming whenever a sudden, loud noise occurred. One evening she went with the family to her granddaughter's high school concert. A hush came over the theater as the curtains began to open. The deep silence continued as the audience looked expectantly at the young musicians who remained absolutely still. Then, a young man, way in the back of the orchestra, abruptly crashed the cymbals together! Yes, you guessed it—my aunt let out a piercing scream. The rest of the family was reduced to about a foot tall in their seats.

You will participate in a scene in heaven which opens with the most dramatic moments of silence that has ever been experienced with unmatched significance. No singing, no praises. The millions of angelic beings are silent. The innumerable multitude of the redeemed stand in awestruck silence observing every movement. In the intensity of the absolute silence you see. . .we'll get to what you see in just a moment. But first. . .

In this lesson we will pause from our joyous *blending-together* experience of the Marriage Supper of the Lamb in heaven to view the tragedy of earth. We go back to the Rapture which occurred well over three years ago. While we Believers experience incredible joys in heaven, Unbelievers, and the Jewish Christian nation, are involved in a violent, intense struggle on the earth; they are entering the last 3 ½ years of this Present Age known as the Wrath of God.

THE UNBELIEVER (NOT BORN-AGAIN)—EVENT 3

Your birth was Event 1. God brought you into this world because He has a purpose for you. However, you have not given your life to Him through repentance and faith in the Savior, Jesus Christ. You, along with everyone else at the end of this Present Age, were born into the World System of the Antichrist which we refer to as your Event 2.

At this present time, the "Wrath of God" is still in the future. You still have time to make this life-changing decision which will redirect your eternal future. But if you chose to remain in the kingdom of darkness and to follow the Antichrist, you will suffer the consequences of this judgment. This will be your Event 3. Keep in mind that this study book is about the Prophetic Events of "your" life.

Locate The Wrath of God on **Timeline Two** (located at the end of Part One of this study book.) **Write** Event **3** on the line by the asterisk (*_3_) located just above the 1st Trumpet/ Bowl Judgment.

THE CHRISTIAN JEW—EVENT 4

You are most blessed. You will be born-again at the Rapture, but in God's plan, you are permitted to remain on the earth to shine as a witness for Him through the darkest time of your nation's history. Perhaps you think the holocaust was that time, and yes, it was indeed a horrendous period of your history. However, most who died in the holocaust, died for themselves. During the Wrath of God you will live or die for Christ Jesus. This may be difficult for you to understand at this point in your life; nevertheless, it has been prophesied by God, and it will come to pass. Consider and come to Christ today. Don't wait for the Rapture to be born-again. No one is guaranteed another day.

Your birth was Event 1. You were born into the World System of the Antichrist which we refer to as your Event 2. Locate the Rapture on **Timeline Two** (located at the end of Part One of this study book). You will receive Christ Jesus as your Savior at that time, therefore, write Event **3** under the Rapture on the line by the asterisk (*_3_). Now find the Wrath of God which will be your next Event on **Timeline Two**. **Write** Event **4** on the line by the asterisk (*_4_) located above the "1st Trumpet/Bowl Judgment.

Oh, how I wish I could personally witness the great conversion of Israel, but I, along with my fellow Believers, will be on our way to meet King Jesus in the air and then on to heaven.

THE BELIEVER

You are safe in heaven at this point in time, but you need to know what God has revealed about the "Wrath of God." Our mission right now is to bring as many as we can into the Kingdom of God so they will not have to suffer the sinner's judgment; "*It is a terrible thing to fall into the hands of the living God.*" (Hebrews 10:31) As you study this lesson, and the reality of it sinks in, I am certain that you will experience a new call to be a witness for God to those who are perishing and who, unfortunately, don't even understand their need of Jesus.

Locate the Wrath of God on **Timeline Two** (located at the end of Part One of this study book.) **Write** Unbelievers - Event 3 on the line by the asterisk (*________) located beneath and to right of the Rapture.

THREE MAIN PURPOSES FOR THE WRATH OF GOD JUDGMENTS

First of all, The Wrath of God Judgment will serve to punish the followers of the Antichrist for their inhumane persecution and murder of God's people during the Great Tribulation.

Second, the Wrath of God is an outpouring of God's undiluted wrath on the final, reprobate generation of this Present Age. Reprobate signifies those who are calloused in their consciences, totally given over to sin. Rebel-man will have rejected God and in His place will have chosen Satan's man, the Antichrist.

Third, it will serve as a last call or opportunity for people to repent of their sins and to receive salvation through Jesus Christ.

THE OPENING OF THE SEVENTH SEAL

In your mind's eye, I would like for you to envision the opening of the Seventh Seal. To help you accomplish this, the preparations in heaven for the Trumpet/Bowl Judgments are spoken of as if you were relating them in person as you see them happen. The vision of this Event was given to the apostle John in approximately A.D. 95, but you will be present in heaven when it actually takes place. We will bounce back and forth between the parallel Scriptures of Revelation 8:1-7 and 15:1-16:2.

The Scriptures are in italics to differentiate them from *your* commentary.

Revelation 8:1-7 and 15:1-16:2

> *Then I saw in heaven another marvelous event of great significance. The Lamb broke the seventh seal on the scroll, there was silence throughout heaven for about half an hour.*

In the intensity of the absolute silence I watched as. . . *the seven angels who stand before God were given seven trumpets. Seven angels were holding the seven last plagues, which would bring God's wrath to completion.*

I saw before me what seemed to be a glass sea mixed with fire. And on it stood all the people who had been victorious over the beast and his statue and the number representing his name. I recognized them as the martyrs of the Fifth Seal slain by the beast. Their cry to God for justice, at that time, is now to be answered. *They were holding harps that God had given them.* My heart swells within me to see how lovingly the Father singles them out.

Then. . . the most beautiful music that I have ever heard filled the vastness of heaven. *They were singing the song of Moses, the servant of God, and the song of the Lamb:*

> *"Great and marvelous are your works, O Lord God, the Almighty. Just and true are your ways, O King of the nations. Who will not fear you, Lord, and glorify your name? For you alone are holy. All nations will come and worship before you, for your righteous deeds have been revealed."*

The prayer of the martyrs of the Fifth Seal "O Sovereign Lord, holy and true, how long before you judge the people who belong to this world and avenge our blood for what they have done to us?" (Revelation 6:10)

I looked and saw that the Temple in heaven, God's Tabernacle, was thrown wide open. The seven angels who were holding the seven plagues came out of the Temple. They were clothed in spotless white linen with gold sashes across their chests. Then one of the four living beings handed each of the seven angels a gold bowl filled with the wrath of God, who lives forever and ever. The Temple was filled with smoke from God's glory and power. No one could enter the Temple until the seven angels had completed pouring out the seven plagues.

Another angel with a gold incense burner came and stood at the altar. And a great amount of incense was given to him to mix with the prayers of God's people as an offering on the gold altar before the throne. Every anguished cry to God from those imprisoned, tortured, starved, and martyred, and all the prayers of the suffering saints of the Great Tribulation, fill the gold incense burner. The last prayer had already been received. *The smoke of the incense mixed with the prayers of God's holy people, ascended up to God from the altar where the angel had poured them out.*

Luke 21:22 "For those will be days of God's vengeance, and the prophetic words of the Scriptures will be fulfilled."

In one swift motion the angel *filled the incense burner with the fire from off the altar and threw it down upon the earth; and thunder crashed, lightening flashed, and there was a terrible earthquake.* The flaming censer is hurled with devastating force. I hear piercing screams of sheer horror throughout the earth. The terrors of the Wrath of God are just beginning.

Then the seven angels with the seven trumpets prepared to blow their mighty blasts. Then I heard a mighty voice from the Temple say to the seven angels, "Go your ways and pour out on the earth the seven bowls containing God's wrath.

Six angels holding their trumpets look toward the first angel who raises his trumpet to his lips and blows a long frightening blast. *The first angel blew his trumpet. . .* The first angel empties the first bowl to the last drop upon the earth. *So the first angel left the Temple and poured out his bowl on the earth. . .*

Take Courage

Incense Revelation 5:8 "...golden bowls filled with incense, which are the prayers of God's people."

Incense is a symbol of Jesus as our intercessor. Jesus takes the prayers of the Believer and by the fragrance of His name (merits and perfections) causes them to ascend to God. Without Jesus' intercession not a single prayer would ever ascend to the throne of mercy.

In this Present Age, we may feel that prayers for justice have no effect, but God tenderly stores them in golden bowls. He has not forgotten them. Every despairing cry to God for justice from those who have suffered injustice, abuse, martyrdom, as well as voiceless cries from aborted babies, victims of every kind of evil, and those who suffered for righteousness sake. . .every cry will be avenged. The day of final reckoning for all the injustices committed down through the ages will take place at the coming Great White Throne Judgment. God will spell out His judgment to all evil doers like a judge sentencing the offender: "For this and this and this, you will receive this."

Romans 2:5 explains that God may not bring immediate punishment for each wrong doing or sinful act. However, this verse reveals that man is storing up for himself God's anger and wrath for a time designated when God will settle accounts.

One day, driving past the house of a man who was well-known for hoarding, I noticed that his two car garage was crammed full of trash from floor to ceiling. It was to the point that he couldn't close the garage door. I looked at the windows of his two story house. All I could see were old boxes. I couldn't tell if the discarded piles of useless junk in the yard was spillage from the house or the other way around.

It made me reflect that this sad situation had probably begun with one item that the owner had stored in the corner of the garage, but over the years had become a huge stockpile of worthless, decaying waste as a result of a man's uncontrolled cravings. What will be the outcome of this property so full of rot and decay?

In like manner, the end-time generation will have stored up a tragic stockpile of God's wrath. Extreme punishment is inevitable. The Wrath of God is not the final reckoning, but is the out pouring of God's wrath on the most unspeakably wicked and depraved people of all the generations of mankind. In due course, each individual person from all the ages will also receive a final judgment at the Great White Throne of God for all the unrepentant sins they have amassed for themselves.

Romans 2:5-6
"But because of your stubbornness and your unrepentant heart, you are storing up wrath against yourself for the day of God's wrath, when His righteous judgment will be revealed. God will give to each person according to what he has done."

TRUMPET AND BOWL JUDGMENTS—ONE AND THE SAME

You will notice many similarities in these two visions. New and vital information is given in the repetition of the prophecy. The first four judgments affect the environment and the universe, the fifth and sixth unleash the demon world, and the seventh is the consummation and the establishment of Christ's Kingdom upon earth. From beginning to end, the Wrath of God only covers a 3 ½ year period of time.

The interpretation that we will study presents the Trumpet/Bowl Judgments as simultaneous events. The two complementary narratives blend together into one judgment.

It looks like this:

1	2	3	4	5	6	7
1st Trumpet	2nd Trumpet	3rd Trumpet	4th Trumpet	5th Trumpet	6th Trumpet	7th Trumpet
1st Bowl	2nd Bowl	3rd Bowl	4th Bowl	5th Bowl	6th Bowl	7th Bowl

Another fact to observe

If you will look at **Timeline Two** you will notice that there is no break between the wars, famine, disease, and death of the Six Seals and the First Trumpet/Bowl Judgment. The Wrath of God judgments immediately follow the Sixth Seal. . .and are all contained in the Seventh Seal.

As you examine these catastrophic events, try to grasp their enormity by visualizing them in your mind. Be alert in your observation; think of significance and meaning. May the Lord help each Believer to rescue as many as possible from the Wrath of God before it is too late.

Timeline Two (located at the end of Part One of this study book) locates the Trumpet/Bowl Judgments. All the following Scriptures are from the New International Version of the Bible.

THE SEVENTH SEAL—THE WRATH OF GOD

JUDGMENTS ON THE WORLD EMPIRE OF THE BEAST

(THE LAST 3 ½ YEARS)

FIRST TRUMPET
Place: on the earth

Revelation 8:7

[7] *The first angel sounded his trumpet, and there came hail and fire mixed with blood, and it was hurled down* ***upon the earth*** *a third of the earth was burned up, a third of the trees were burned up, and all the green grass was burned up.*

FIRST BOWL
Place: on the earth

Revelation 16:2

[2] *The first angel went and poured out his bowl* ***on the land*** **[earth]**, *and ugly and painful sores broke out on the people who had the mark of the beast and worshiped his image.*

Observations

A third of the earth . . . Can you conceive of a third of our earth burned up? Whether the third will be concentrated in one huge part of our world or interspersed throughout the earth is not revealed.

Hail. . .The food source will be affected. Referring to the hail, what do the words "*hurled down upon the earth*" suggest to you? ____

Fire. . .There will be destruction of property, vegetation, and forests. "*Fire* can refer to supernatural combustion. . .heavenly in origin and nature. . .to execute judgment." [M] Have you seen the terrifying sight of forests and grass-lands burning? Just think of the magnitude that one-third of this world represents.

Blood. . . The slime and smell of blood covering the ground will be intolerable.

Sores. . .16:2 gives the *time* of these judgments as during the reign of the Beast/Antichrist by mentioning those who are affected by the sores. What people are not affected? ___________ ______________________________. What does *ugly* suggest? __________________________ __________________________. Not a pretty sight! As this sickness spreads, hospitals will be overwhelmed, cities, business, transportation, schools will be paralyzed.

The only people not affected are the Christian Jews and the possibility of some who have not taken the mark of the Beast.

SECOND TRUMPET
Place: the sea

Revelation 8:8-9
[8] *The second angel sounded his trumpet, and something like a huge mountain, all ablaze, was was thrown* ***into the sea****. A third of the sea turned into blood,* [9] *a third of the living creatures in the sea died, and a third of the ships were destroyed.*

SECOND BOWL
Place: the sea

Revelation 16:3
[3] *The second angel poured out his bowl* ***on thesea****, and it turned into blood like that of a dead man, and every living thing in the sea died.*

Observations

The Trumpet Vision, 1/3 of the water turned to blood, 1/3 of all living creatures die, and 1/3 of the ships destroyed. **The Bowl Vision** expands the judgment to all living things in the sea. The repetition of the prophecy increases the judgment.

Mountain. . .List three descriptive things pertaining to "*the mountain*."

- ________________________ By appearance, John can only describe it as a mountain.
- ________________________ This could possibly be a celestial body like an asteroid which have "characteristic diameters between one and several hundred miles and orbits lying chiefly between Mars and Jupiter." [D] Or, this could be a burning meteor. Just think of the panic if people see it coming. The origin of the "*mountain*" is not stated.
- ____ Which sea (Pacific, Atlantic) is not revealed.

Ships. . .The destruction of the ships indicate violent commotion of the sea. This turbulence is probably caused by the impact of the "*mountain*." Can you imagine the height of the waves this would cause?

Blood. . .The sea covers three fourths of the earth's surface. Think of the vast area that one-third represents and also the depth of the ocean that would be filled with blood. How is the blood described in 16:3? ____ Truly, the ocean is turned into a malodorous cesspool. Can we even imagine the smell from the number of the carcasses of sea creatures floating on the seas or thrown up onto the beaches?

Satanic involvement. . .You are probably saying to yourself, "Why don't people turn to God immediately? I certainly would!" Let me remind you of some things:

- God sends to these people, on their way to destruction, a powerful delusion so that they will believe the lies of Satan. The reason for this is because they refuse to love and accept the truth that would save them. (2 Thessalonians 2:9-11)

- Mankind at this point is delusional. The dictionary defines *delusion* as referring "to false belief held without reservation as a result of self-deception, the imposition of another, or mental disorder. . .often associated with harm." [D] One of the disastrous results of this delusion is that inhibitions are thrown to the wind; their delight is in wickedness.

- The Antichrist comes to do the work of Satan with counterfeit power, signs, and miracles. He will successfully use every kind of deception to win the souls of mankind. Deceit is mentioned time and time again in reference to the Antichrist. (2 Thessalonians 2:9-11)

- The powers that Satan has been allowed to exercise are way beyond anything we know about as humans. He has power over people to inspire them to do violence and evil (Job 1:13-17), however, he cannot force them to do things against their will. He has power to affect nature such as storms (Job 1:19); power to afflict people with disease (Job 2:7; Luke 13:11-16); power over the supernatural and any occult practices. This is seen in his working through the magicians of Egypt who turned water into blood, rods into serpents, and exercised power over animal life (Exodus 7:11, 22; 8:7)

- We understand from Scripture that during The Wrath of God, Satan, through the Antichrist, is doing all he can to counteract the supernatural disasters of God's judgment by his own miracles and wonders. This show of power is convincing and successful in maintaining his firm grasp on mankind.

THIRD TRUMPET
Place: rivers and springs of water

Revelation 8:10-11

[10] The third angel sounded his trumpet, and a great star, blazing like a torch, fell from the sky on a <u>*third*</u> *of* ***the rivers and on the springs of water—*** *[11] the name of the star is Wormwood. A* <u>*third*</u> *of the waters turned bitter, and many people died from the waters that had become bitter.*

THIRD BOWL
Place: rivers and springs of water

Revelation 16:4-7

[4] The third angel poured out his bowl on the ***rivers and springs of water****, and they became blood. [5] Then I heard the angel in charge of the waters say: "You are just in these judgments, you who are and who were, the Holy One, because You have so judged; [6] for they have shed the blood of your saints* [holy people] *and prophets, and you have given them blood to drink as they deserve. [7] And I heard the altar respond: "Yes, Lord God Almighty, true and just are your judgments."*

Observations

Star . . . "The word 'star' is also used as a figure of speech for angels. This symbolic usage is most obvious in the book of Revelation (Revelation 8:10-11; 9:1-2)." [1] Notice in 16:5 that an angel has power over the water. What is said of this angel? ____________________ ____________

In Revelation 14:18 we read of an angel who has charge (power) over fire. Revelation 7:2 speaks of angels that have power to harm the land, trees, and the sea and are at the time of this vision actively engaged in carrying out the Trumpet/Bowl Judgments.

Wormwood. . . Wormwood was a plant in Palestine whose characteristic was a bitter taste. It was used at times to make an intoxicating drink. Gall was a bitter, poisonous herb. Wormwood and gall are closely associated in the Old Testament and used figuratively to mean: wrong-doing that results in bitterness and poisons the soul. Also the judgments of God, as a result of injustice, idolatry, immorality, and wickedness, are compared to wormwood and gall which are extremely bitter.

Isn't it interesting that gall and vinegar (sour wine) were offered to Jesus on the cross but when He realized that it had gall in it, He refused the drink. Later He drank from a sponge filled with vinegar only. (Matthew 27:34, 48) Could this be an indication that Jesus refused the gall because of its association with wrong doing? He Himself was without sin. What do you think?

The Star Wormwood. . .The angel of the waters intensifies the judgment from bitter to blood. He makes earth dwellers drink the bitter, poisonous waters as a judgment. Then he makes them literally drink nauseating blood. What is the result? 8:11 ______________________________.

"The punishment fits the crime". . . **16:6** The angel of the waters proclaims the righteousness of God in punishing the peoples of the earth. Such is their due—they deserve it! They are paid with the same coin! Why did they deserve to drink blood? 16:6 ______________________________ ____.

Revelation 17:2, 6 states that ". . *.the inhabitants of the earth were made drunk* [maddened] *with the wine of her* [harlot city, seat of the evil world empire] *fornication. . .I saw that the woman was drunk with the blood of those who bore testimony to Jesus.*"

I heard the altar respond. . .**16:7** The response from the altar represents the victims of the Fifth Seal martyred during the Great Tribulation whose prayers are now being answered. (Revelation 6:9-11) They respond to the words of the angel of the waters. "*Yes, Lord God Almighty, true and just are your judgments.*" Yes, yes, yes!

Jeremiah 23:15 (NKJV) "Therefore thus says the Lord of hosts concerning the prophets: Behold, I [God] will feed them with wormwood, and make them drink the water of gall; for from the prophets of Jerusalem profaneness [ungodliness] has gone out into all the land"

FOURTH TRUMPET

Place: sun, moon, stars

Revelation 8:12-13

12 *The fourth angel sounded his trumpet, and a third of* ***the sun*** *was struck, a third of* ***the moon****, and a third of* ***the stars****, so that a third of them turned dark. A third of the day was without light, and also a third of the night.*
13 *As I watched, I heard an eagle that was flying in midair call out in a loud voice: 'Woe! Woe! Woe! to the inhabitants of the earth, because of the trumpet blasts about to be sounded by the other three angels!'*

FOURTH BOWL

Place: sun

Revelation 16:8-9

8 *The fourth angel poured out his bowl* ***on the sun****, and the sun was given power to scorch people with fire.*
9 *They were seared by the intense heat and they cursed the name of God, who had control over these plagues, but they refused to repent and glorify Him.*

Observations

The luminaries. . .The sun, moon, and stars will suddenly be struck a powerful blow; diminishing their light by a third. This word for *struck* or *smite* in the Greek language is *plesso* and has a curious meaning: "to mould or shape (through the idea of flattening out); to pound; a single blow with the fist." [5] It seems to indicate that the luminaries were struck a terrific blow. This "single blow" involves a great number of heavenly bodies that shine their light upon the earth. What a thing to behold! Incomprehensible!

Partial light. . .What words from 8:12 indicate volume of light? ____________________
Which two words indicate time? ______________________________

The reading seems to imply both a lack in the volume of light and also a shortening of time that the luminaries give their light. Earth's visibility is reduced by one-third like turning a dimmer switch. It is further stipulated that darkness reigns over a third of the day and a third of the night. This results in a twilight effect along with a period each day and night of total darkness.

Effects. . .The effects of this judgment are beyond comprehension. So many essentials for the existence of life are affected such as temperature, weather, gravity, tides, and psychological effect. The Lord sustains the universe, or it would be destroyed instantly.

The sun. . .We must not miss the words "*was given power.*" (16:8) In spite of the partial darkness, God, in a special manifestation of divine intervention, empowers the sun to burn men with a fierce heat, fire. And they all turned to God in great repentance. No! What did they do? (16:9) ______________________________ and what did they not do? __________
____

Does this verse indicate that mankind will recognize where these calamities are originating? ________

What do you think would immediately happen if the Unbelievers would feel regret and remorse for their waywardness, and turn to God in repentance? ______________________
Yes, the judgments would stop! God would joyously embrace mankind like the father of the prodigal son who portrays God's unending love for man.

Luke 15:20
"But while he was still a long way off, his father saw him and was filled with compassion for him; he ran to his son, threw his arms around him and kissed him."

Darkness and fire. . .This fourth judgment, more than any other, is a direct appeal to the people of the world to repent. Their negative response and insistent rejection has great significance to God; therefore, He told John to include this fact in the narrative. Everlasting condemnation is described by the Lord Jesus in the Bible as a place of never-ending darkness and fire. Earth dwellers are forewarned in this judgment of strange darkness and scorching heat which plainly foreshadows the consequences lying just ahead of them.

Jesus, while on earth, told some Jews, who, as God's chosen people, should belong to His Kingdom, that because of their lack of faith and their blind unbelief, they would be "*cast out into outer darkness*" where there would be "*weeping and gnashing of teeth.*" (Matthew 8:12 NKJV)

Jesus also said: "*So it will be at the end of the age. The angels will come forth, separate the wicked from among the just, and cast them into the furnace of fire. There will be wailing and gnashing of teeth.*" (Matthew 13:49-50 NKJV)

The vision of the "flying eagle". . .**8:13** Let's go on an interpretation expedition. The first phrase of this verse reveals who the messenger is and where he delivers his message; the rest of the verse is the message.

First, we will focus on who the messenger is and where he delivers his message. The apostle John is watching the judgments take place in a vision. A loud voice from the sky causes him to look up.

Revelation 8:13

> "*As I* [John] *watched, I heard an eagle that was flying in midair call out in a loud voice. . .*"

Is an eagle actually speaking a message from God? Let's see what we can discover by looking at three other verses in the book of Revelation. Remember, Scripture interprets Scripture.

Revelation 4:6-7

> "*In the center, around the* [God's] *throne, were four living creatures. . .the first living creature was like a lion, and the second was like an ox, the third had a face like a man, the fourth was like a flying eagle.*"

Revelation 14:6

> "*Then I saw another angel flying in midair, and he had the eternal gospel to proclaim to those who live on the earth—to every nation, tribe, language and people. . .*"

Revelation 19:17

"And I saw an angel standing in the sun, who cried in a loud voice. . ."

What similarities do you see in 4:6, 14:7, and 19:17 regarding "*an eagle that was flying*" and the term "*in midair*?" **Circle** or **underline** them.

midair. . . This word means in the middle. It is the part of the sky where the sun reaches the *meridian* (the highest point or zenith). This makes it possible for the eagle to be heard by all "*the inhabitants of the earth*."

Write where the eagle of 8:13 is flying. ____.
What is the location of the angel in 14:6? ____________________________________.
Write the angel's position in 19:17. ____.

"an eagle that was flying". . .Two questions. Do you think that the "*eagle*" is an angel? ________
Do you think that it is likely that the "*eagle*" was the heavenly being designated as the fourth living creature in 4:7? ____________

Many Bible scholars see the four living creatures of Revelation 4:6 as the cherubim of Ezekiel chapters 1 and 10, especially 10:20, where the cherubim are referred to as "*the living creatures*." It is stated in Revelation 15:7 that "*one of the four living creatures gave to the seven angels seven golden bowls filled with the wrath of God*"—the very bowl judgments we are studying.

The "*flying eagle*" could very well be the fourth living creature of Revelation 4:7 which is "like a flying eagle."

The message. . .I think the vision of the "*flying eagle*" recorded in 8:13 should move us to the very depths of our soul. It is filled with pathos and reveals extreme concern for those who dwell on the earth. The apostle John sees this eagle flying in the heavens expressing deep sorrow and grief, "*Woe! Woe! Woe to the inhabitants of the earth*," because of what the next judgments will bring upon them.

The word "*woe*" is an interjection, an exclamation like *oh my!* It is an utterance of extreme sorrow or pain. "All uses of *ouai* (Greek word) express an intensity of emotion." [M] Unbelievers have been warned; they have made their choice; they will reap the consequences.

What comes next is truly terrifying. . .
The next three judgments are very different from the first four**.** As you have discovered, to get a full picture we are placing the narrations of the Trumpet and Bowl Judgments side by side and are interpreting them as one judgment not two.

Read this whole narrative. Try to envision the action as it takes place. **Circle** key words and **underline** phrases that you think are important.

FIFTH TRUMPET
Place: The Abyss/The Bottomless Pit

Revelation 9:1-12
[1] *"The fifth angel sounded his trumpet, and I saw a star that had fallen from the sky to the earth. The star was given the key to* ***the shaft of the Abyss*** [Bottomless Pit]. [2] *When he opened the Abyss, smoke rose from it like the smoke from a gigantic furnace. The sun and sky were darkened by the smoke from the Abyss.* [3] *And out of the smoke locusts came down upon the earth and were given power like that of scorpions of the earth.* [4] *They were told not to harm the grass of the earth or any plant or tree, but only those people who did not have the seal of God on their foreheads.*
[5] *They were not given power to kill them, but only to torture them for five months. And the agony they suffered was like that of the sting of a scorpion when it strikes a man.* [6] *During those days men will seek death, but will not find it; they will long to die, but death will elude them.*
[7] *The locusts looked like horses prepared for battle. On their heads they wore something like crowns of gold, and their faces resembled human faces.* [8] *Their hair was like women's hair, and their teeth were like lions teeth.* [9] *They had breastplates like breastplates of iron, and the sound of their wings was like the thundering of many horses and chariots rushing into battle.* [10] *They had tails and stings like scorpions, and in their tails they had power to torment people for five months.*
[11] *They had as king over them the angel of the Abyss, whose name in Hebrew is Abaddon, and in Greek, Apollyon.*
[12] *The first woe is past; two other woes are yet to come."*

FIFTH BOWL
Place: The Throne of the Beast

Revelation 16:10-11
[10] *The fifth angel poured out his bowl on* ***the throne of the beast****, and his kingdom was plunged into darkness. Men gnawed their tongues in agony and* [11] *cursed the God of heaven because of their pains and their sores, but they refused to repent of what they had done.*

Observations

Verse 1. . .The abyss, the key, the star
We studied in Lesson 1 that the abyss (or Hades) describes an immeasurable depth. It is:

- the abode of Unbelievers who have died until the Great White Throne judgment (Revelation 20:11-15)
- a prison for certain demons (Revelation 9:1-2, 11)
- the place from which the Antichrist will ascend (Revelation 11:7; 17:8) [2]

The **key** to the abyss (Hades) has an interesting story in the book of Revelation. **Read** what Jesus says in Revelation 1:18:

> *"I am the Living One; I was dead, and behold I am alive for ever and ever! And I hold the keys of death and Hades* [the abyss, the bottomless pit]."

Jesus says that He has the *keys* to ______________________________________.
No one goes into the abyss, nor does anyone come out of it, without the permission of Jesus who holds the key.

Revelation 9:1: "*The star was given the key to the shaft of the Abyss.*" Who gives the *key* to the star? __________________.

Some believe the star to be Satan. However, Revelation 20:1-3 identifies the star. Who has the key to the abyss according to this Scripture? ________________________.

Revelation 20:1-3

> *"And I saw an angel coming down out of heaven, having the key to the Abyss and holding in his hand a great chain. He seized the dragon, that ancient serpent, who is the devil, or Satan, and bound him for a thousand years. He threw him into the Abyss, and locked and sealed it over him. . ."*

The *star* is an angel, a very powerful one. Jesus gives the key to the abyss to the angel of Revelation 9:1 and the angel uses it again in chapter 20 to imprison Satan in the abyss.

Did you notice the apparent close proximity of earth and the abyss in 9:1-3? Read them carefully.

Verse 2. . .What happens when the angel opens the abyss and what is the effect? ____________
____.

Verse 3. . .I shudder to even say the words—the pit is open. Millions of demons are released. These are not Satan's demons who freely and actively move about the world. These demons, described as "*locusts*," have been confined to the abyss for thousands of years.

Locusts. . .Where do the "*locusts*" come from? verse 3 ____________________________ ____ and the smoke came out of the _________________________ verse 2. As the smoke drifts across the whole world like volcanic ash, the "*locusts*" drop down from it to the earth.

Probably the reason John describes the demons as locusts is because of the great similarities. Locusts travel in huge columns stretching for miles. The sound of their millions of wings makes a terrifying noise. They are destructive beyond belief. However, John soon discovers, these are not an insect, but rather, intelligent beings. They obey instructions given to them, they distinguish between those they are to afflict, and those they are not to harm, and they have lived in some kind of organized kingdom dominated by a king.

As these creatures are visible to John they will more than likely be visible to their victims during the fifth judgment. Because the generation that lives during the Wrath of God has completely turned its back on God to embrace the pleasures of Satan, God will let them experience first hand the "goodness" of the demon world. What will the people of the world see? Let's examine the description given by John.

John uses similes to compare what he sees in the vision to things that are in his range of knowledge. Similes are many times identified by the words *as* and *like*. Read 9:7-10 from the text above and fill in the blanks with the words *as*, *like* and accompanying words or other words which indicate the comparison.

9:7 the locusts ____________________ horses prepared for battle
on their heads they wore ______________________ crowns of gold
their faces __________________ human faces

9:8 their hair was ____________ women's hair
their teeth were ____________ lion's teeth

9:9 they had breastplates ____________ breastplates of iron
the sound of their wings was ______________ the thundering of many horses and chariots rushing into battle

9:10 They had tails and stings ______________ scorpions

What a description! We see a combination of animal and human likenesses.

Their assignment

Who are these demons to harm? verse 4 ________________________________
____.

Notice in 9:5 that the demons are not to kill men, but to torture them for how long? _______
What is their agony compared to in this verse? ______________________________

Who were exempted from this plague according to 9:4? ______________________
These are the 144,000 Jews who bear on their foreheads *"the seal of the living God."* This seal "is an emblem of ownership, security, and destination, in the sense that these belong to God and the seal secures them from destruction." [V]

The Fifth Trumpet/Bowl Judgment lasts five months of the 3 ½ year duration of the Wrath of God. This may give us an indication that each judgment extends over several months.

The circumstances
To understand the circumstances of this judgment, let's read again the Fifth Bowl 16:10-11.

> [10] *The fifth angel poured out his bowl on the throne of the beast, and his kingdom was plunged into darkness. Men gnawed their tongues in agony and* [11] *cursed the God of heaven because of their pains and their sores, but they refused to repent of what they had done.*

In verse 10, what does the "*throne*" of the beast mean? ______________________________
Yes, this is the place, the seat of government, where Satan through his puppet, the Antichrist, reigns over the world and the Ten Kings. You will discover where this is and who it implies in Part Two of this book.

What happens to the kingdom of the Beast (which includes the entire world) when this judgment strikes? ____. From our study of 9:2, what causes the darkness? ______________________________.

To add to the calamity, the demons will carry out their torment in darkness which lasts five months. We do not know the size of these demons, if they are large or small. The Unbeliever at first cannot see the demons, but he will hear them dropping from the smoke. Plop, plop! First in the distance, then louder and closer come the agonized cries of the tormented stung by these creatures. Gradually they emerge through the gloom of the darkness; the victim will see the horrible creatures. There is no escape.

The comparison of the sting of the demons is likened to a scorpion sting which is extremely painful and can be repeated several times because unlike a bee the stinger remains in the tail of the scorpion. The venom feels like fire in the veins and nerves.

In 16:10, **underline** the phrase that describes the consequences of the sting. We see man's great desperation expressed in 9:6? "*During those days men will seek death, but will not find it; they will long to die, but death will elude them.*" The King James Version says, "*death shall flee from them*"—"death keeps running away from them." [3]

9:11. . .They had a king over them, the angel of the Abyss. His name in Hebrew is _______________ which means "destruction" and in the Greek ______________________ meaning "the destroyer." Could it be that long ago this evil angel led this particular group of evil angels in a separate fall, distinct from Satan's fall? No doubt, King Apollyon leads this horde.

Keep in mind that the abyss is also the place where the dead, the souls of those remaining in their sin, are kept until the Great White Throne Judgment. What a horrible place to be confined!

Contrast: angels and demons
Demons have chosen to follow Satan. They seek to torment, enslave, and destroy mankind. The *angels of God* have chosen a totally different mission—to bring God's grace, goodness, and protection and help to mankind.

Contrast: The Lord Jesus, and Satan and Apollyon
Both *Satan* and *Apollyon*, leaders of demons, have the purpose and goal to oppress and to destroy. Our *Lord Jesus* is so different. He is the Savior. His purpose and goal is to bring abundant life and eternal life to all men; for that He paid a great price. King Jesus' rule is to free man, to lift him up, and set him on a very high plain of living.

John 10:10
"The thief's [Satan's] purpose is to steal and kill and destroy. My [Jesus'] purpose is to give them a rich and satisfying life."

Contrast: The wicked, earth dwellers and the overcomers in Christ
Again, *earth dwellers* curse and denounce the God of heaven with abusive language, and they refuse to repent of what they have done. (Revelation 16:11)

How different the *overcomers* in Christ! Just before the narration of the Bowl Judgments we see them in heaven standing by the sea of glass. (Revelation 15:2-4) Their hearts swell with adoration as they lift their voices in a mighty chorus of praise to God.

- These martyrs had been victorious over the beast (political victory). (Revelation 13:7-8)
- They did not bow down to the image of the beast (religious victory). (Revelation 13:14-15)
- They refused to receive the apostate mark of the beast (economic victory). (Revelation 13:16-17)
- They stood upon the solid Rock and died for Him.

At the end of this lesson you can find a chart of the Trumpet/Bowl Judgments that corresponds to this lesson.

To conclude this Fifth judgment, I would like to share the following commentary which is very appropriate to what you have just studied. You will appreciate this reading from a man of spiritual insight.

Revelation 15:2 (NIV)
"And I saw what looked like a sea of glass mixed with fire and, standing beside the sea, those who had been victorious over the beast and his image and over the number of his name."

> "Hell and hell-torments are not the mere fictions which some have pronounced them. Neither are they as remote from this present world as men often dream. There is a fiery abyss, with myriads of evil beings in it, malignant and horrible, and there is but a door between this world and that. Heaven is just as near; but heaven is above, and hell is beneath. Mortal man and his world lie between two mighty, opposite, spiritual spheres, both touching directly upon him, each operative to conform him to itself as he yields to one or the other, to be conjoined eventually to the society on high, or to companionship with devils and all evil beings beneath.
>
> To doubt this is to [make a] mistake concerning the most momentous things of our existence, and to have all our senses closed to the most startling realities of our lives. As we are heavenly in our inclinations and efforts, and open and yielding to things Divine, heaven opens to us, and spirits [angels] of heaven become our helpers, comforters, protectors, and guides; and as we are devilish in our temper, unbelieving, defiant of

God, and self-sufficient, the doors of separation between us and hell gradually yield, and the smoke of the pit gathers over us, and the spirits [demons] of perdition come forth to move among us and to do us mischief [injury]. And at the last, as the saints of God are taken up out of the world on the one side, the angels of hell with their malignity and torments are let in on the other."

On the Apocalypse by J.A. Seiss, a Lutheran minister (1823-1904) [4]

You will continue with the Sixth Trumpet/Bowl Judgment in the next lesson. We are now very close to the end of this Present Age.

JESUS CHRIST EVERLASTING LIGHT

Isaiah 60:19 – Revelation 21:23

The Seven Trumpet /Bowl Judgments—Revelation 8-9, 15-16, 11

Environment and Universe				Demon World		Consummation
1st	**2nd**	**3rd**	**4th**	**5th** **WOE**	**6th** **WOE**	**7th** **WOE**
8:7; 16:2	8:8-9; 16:3	8:10-11; 16:4-7	8:12-13; 16:8-9	9:1-12; 16:10-11	9:13-20 16:12-16	11:15-19 16:17-21
Where? on the earth	the sea	rivers and springs of waters	1/3rd of the sun, moon, stars	bottomless pit/throne of the beast		
What happened? hail, fire, blood, sores	1/3rd of sea turned to blood	1/3rd bitter, then turned to blood	1/3rd were darkened	demons released		
Results? 1/3rd earth, 1/3rd trees, all grass burned up, severe and malignant sores on men	all creatures in sea die, 1/3rd of ships destroyed	many people died	1/3 of day and night had no light; sun scorched people with fierce heat; blaspheme God, refuse to repent	darkness; people stung, tormented by demons, in great pain for 5 months; curse God, refuse to repent		

LESSON 13

JESUS CHRIST THE SUNRISE FROM ON HIGH
Luke 1:78 (NASB)

"We look for His coming as men look for the dawn." [1]

THE WRATH OF GOD

THE SIXTH TRUMPET/BOWL JUDGMENT

> **Prepare**: to make ready beforehand for a specific purpose or for some event, occasion, or the like.
> **Ready**: prepared or available for service or action. [D]

As a young woman looking toward a future ministry somewhere in God's big world, I was very impressed by the motto of the St. Paul Bible College in St. Paul, Minnesota (now Crown College.) *There are prepared places for prepared people.* The principle of this motto was that each student who diligently acquired basic ministry skills and spiritual formation could step forward confidently in faith to be led by God to the work that God had prepared for him to do. As students, we were made ready to go to our prepared place on the mission field, in the homeland, as church planters, pastors, Christian workers, wherever God wanted us to work in His harvest field.

I have always liked that word *prepare*. It refers to doing something now which will affect the future. This word becomes quite awe-inspiring when it relates to God. With the definitions of *prepare* and *ready* in mind thoughtfully examine the following verses.

Prepare

Amos 4:12

"Prepare to meet your God. . ."

John 14:2

In speaking of heaven, Jesus says, *"I am going to prepare a place for you. . ."*

Matthew 25:34

"Come, you who are blessed by My Father, inherit the kingdom prepared for you from the creation of the world."

Matthew 25:41

"Then the King will turn to those on the left and say, 'Away with you, you cursed ones, into the eternal fire prepared for the devil and his demons."

1 Corinthians 2:9 (NIV)

"However, as it is written: 'No eye has seen, no ear has heard, no mind has conceived what God has prepared for those who love Him'—but God has revealed it to us by His Spirit."

Ready

Matthew 24:44

"You also must be ready all the time, for the Son of Man will come at an hour when least expected."

Luke 22:33

"Peter said, 'Lord, I am ready to go to prison with you, and even to die with you.'"

1 Peter 3:15

"If someone asks about your Christian hope, always be ready to explain it."

Psalm 92:5 (NIV)
"How great are your works, O Lord, how profound your thoughts!"

Fascinating words *prepare* and *ready*. They make one so aware of God's planning far in advance for things that will affect every human being. To understand this aspect about God brings peace and stability. Many people see things as coincidence, but Believers see the hand of their great God in all things. His work is so evident and yet so incomprehensible.

W.E. Vine

> "The steps taken by God in the carrying out of His plans have been eternally predetermined both as to time and mode of accomplishment. Nothing can change them, nothing can thwart them. His acts are the expressions of His character. His immutability shines out in the [actions] of His providence. God's designs are as unalterable as His nature; His modes of procedure vary, His plans never change." [2]

God's long-time plan to bring people into His kingdom and Satan's efforts to thwart that plan can be compared to two parallel lines closing in at a vanishing point. God with His holy ones will converge with Satan's hosts and the armies of the nations at the vanishing point—Armageddon, the final conflict of this Present Age. There is no doubt who will be the victor for no power in creation can overcome the Sovereign of the Universe.

The 6th Trumpet/Bowl Judgment is man's last opportunity to turn to God. Rebel-man will be living in the last hours of this Present Age. We can only marvel at the goodness, tolerance, and loving patience of God which gives earth people time to repent of their excessive wickedness. But not once during these unimaginable disasters does man cry out to God for forgiveness and mercy.

Just so you and I are on the same page, **look** for the Wrath of God on **Timeline Two** (located at the end of Part One of this study book). Find the 6th Trumpet/Bowl Judgment.

The 6th Trumpet/Bowl Judgment covers:

The Judgment in Itself

The Preparation for Christ's Second Coming and Armageddon.

THE SIXTH JUDGMENT OF THE WRATH OF GOD

SIXTH TRUMPET	**SIXTH BOWL**
Place: Euphrates River	**Place: Euphrates River**

Revelation 9:13-21

[13] *Then the sixth angel blew his trumpet, and I heard a voice speaking from the four horns of the gold altar that stands in the presence of God.* [14] *And the voice said to the sixth angel who held the trumpet, "Release the four angels who are bound at the* ***great Euphrates River****".* [15] *Then the four angels who had been prepared for this hour and day and month and year were turned loose to kill one-third of all the people on earth.* [16] *I heard the size of their army, which was 200 million mounted troops.* [17] *And in my vision, I saw the horses and the riders sitting on them. The riders wore armor that was fiery red and dark blue and yellow. The horses had heads like lions, and fire and smoke and burning sulfur billowed from their mouths.* [18] *One-third of all the people on earth were killed by these three plagues—by the fire and smoke and burning sulfur that came from the mouths of the horses.* [19] *Their power was in their mouths and in their tails. For their tails had heads like snakes, with the power to injure people.* [20] *But the people who did not die in these plagues still refused to repent of their evil deeds and turn to God. They continued to worship demons and idols made of gold, silver, bronze, stone, and wood—idols that can neither see nor hear nor walk!* [21] *And they did not repent of their murders or their witchcraft or their sexual immorality or their thefts.*

Revelation 16:12-14 (NIV)

[12] *The sixth angel poured out his bowl* ***on the great Euphrates****, and its water was dried up to prepare the way for the kings from the East.* [13] *Then I saw three evil spirits that looked like frogs; they came out of the mouth of the dragon, out of the mouth of the beast and out of the mouth of the false prophet.* [14] *They are spirits of demons* [demonic spirits] *performing miraculous signs* [miracles], *and they go out to the kings of the whole world, to gather them for the battle on the great day of God Almighty.*

"Prepare the way" This is an end-time term referring to both the first and second Coming of the Lord. Like saying, "Roll out the red carpet," or preparing the streets for a parade. (see Isaiah 40:3-4 1st Coming of Jesus; verse 5 forward, Jesus' 2nd Coming)

Make five observations:

1.______________________________

2.______________________________

3.______________________________

4.______________________________

5.______________________________

Observations

9:13. . . gold altar. Again reference is made to this place where the prayers of God's people rise up before God for His justice to be done. (Revelation 6:9-11; 8:3) A voice instructs the sixth angel what to do after he blows his trumpet. Try to visualize the action that takes place.

9:14-15. . . four angels. Make three observations about the four angels from these two verses.
1.____
2.____
3.____

Who do you think bound these angels? ______________________Who do you think gives the command to release them? ______________________ Apparently, this is not the same group of demons that came out of the abyss during the 5th Trumpet/Bowl Judgment. This is another group of fallen angels that God has held in confinement (for centuries) at the Euphrates River. When we read the description of their hideous army, how thankful we can be to our gracious Lord for preventing them from attacking mankind down through the ages.

These demon-angels committed a sin so hideous that God mercifully imprisoned them in order to keep them away from mankind. . .until this moment. Presumably, both Peter and Jude are referring to this group of angels.

Jude 6

> *"And I remind you of the angels who did not stay within the limits of authority God gave them but left the place where they belonged. God has kept them securely chained in prisons of darkness, waiting for the great day of judgment."*

2 Peter 2:4 (NKJV)

> "*For God did not spare the angels who sinned, but cast them down to hell* [tartaroo], *and delivered them into chains of darkness, to be reserved for judgment. . ."*

These evil angels are chained in a place called *tartaros* in the Greek language.

> **Hell. . .** "The verb *tartaroo*, translated 'cast [them] down to hell' in 2 Peter 2:4, signifies to consign to Tartarus, which is neither Sheol nor Hades [abyss] nor Hell, but the place where those angels whose special sin is referred to in this passage are confined 'to be reserved unto judgment;' the region is described as 'pits of darkness.'" [V]
>
> "The language of 2 Peter 2:4 may mean not simply that the angels are imprisoned awaiting sentence, but that they are kept in restraint until they are released to become instruments of judgment." [3]

Revelation 9:14 tells us that four angels are bound at the ______________________ ________. This indicates the probable location of their imprisonment in gloomy dungeons of darkness.

PREPARED AND KEPT READY!

Write the definition of *prepare* from the top of the first page of this lesson to complete the following statement. These angels have been bound by God; they have been "made ready ____ ____."

For what specific purpose or event have they been prepared? Revelation 9:15 ____________ ____

This verse also tells us that angels will be released at an exact ____________, ____________, ____________, and ____________.

What do you learn about God from this fact? ______________________________ ____

God has every prophetic event planned and prepared right down to the very hour. God is in control. These evil angels are *ready* for action.

If the people of the world would have repented during any of the former judgments, would this judgment have taken place? ____________. There would be no need for it. In repentance they would have remorsefully asked God's forgiveness and stopped worshiping the deceiver, the Antichrist.

Great River Euphrates
Two things happen at this location during the 6th Trumpet/Bowl judgment.

9:14-16. . .Four angels are ____________________at the river Euphrates who are ____________ to lead a huge ________________ of __________________________ troops. It is very difficult to wrap our minds around the magnitude of this army. . .and these are demons!

16:12. . .The water of the Euphrates River will ____________________ in order to prepare ____.

9:15, 18. . . **a third of mankind.** Have you noticed that a stipulated fraction of mankind is affected in each of God's judgments? Each time the number represents a minority not the majority. The earth's population presently numbers approximately 7 billion people.

- At the least, *one-fourth* (1,750,000,000) of mankind is killed during the Six Seals (Revelation 6:8) cutting the population to 5,250,000,000.

- Another *one-third* (1,750,000,000) die during this 6th Trumpet/Bowl judgment (Revelation 9:18) again reducing the population to less than 3,500,000,000.

- However, an *unspecified number* of people also die during the 3rd Trumpet/Bowl judgment (Revelation 8:11); therefore, the population has been further reduced.

- *Seven thousand* will be killed by an earthquake in Jerusalem (Revelation 11:13) just before the 7th Trumpet sounds. During the 7th Trumpet/Bowl judgment who knows how many millions will die by the worst earthquake ever.

It is safe to say that before Armageddon the world population will be reduced to less than 3 billion. And after the armies of the nations are slain at the final conflict of this present age it will be even less.

9:17-19. . .horses and riders. These demons look like monstrosities from an extremely wild imagination, but how else would a demon look? They are evil and when made visible to the human eye, they are horrifying. Rebel-man "*continued to worship demons. . .*" (9:20) Why would anyone want to worship such creatures?

Notice the similarities of these demons to those of the Fifth judgment (Revelation 9:7-10).

Fifth -From the Abyss Revelation 9:7-10	Sixth -From the Euphrates River Revelation 9:17-19
verse 7 The locusts looked like horses prepared	verse 17 The heads of the horses
verse 9 They had breastplates	verse 17 their breastplates were
verse 10 in their tails they had power	verse 19 The power of the horses was in their tails

Unlike the Fifth judgment, it is not dark in the Sixth judgment. It is likely that rebel-man clearly sees this horde of demons thundering across the globe mounted on horse-like creatures belching flames of fire and smoke from their mouths produced by burning sulfur. The breastplates of these hideous horsemen share the colors coming from the horse's mouths—fiery red, blue, and sulfurous yellow. In this wild outbreak, these beasts with lion-like heads bear down on men, women, and children with absolute cruelty. At the end of the rampage, more than 1,750,000,000 people will have been burned to death or will have died from asphyxiation, while simultaneously being inflicted with injury from the snake-like tails of the demonic horses. This will take place! It is unspeakably sad.

We are not told in the Scriptures what becomes of the demons of the Fifth and Sixth judgments after they have done their designated work. Possibly, they are confined to the abyss.

Verses 20-21. . .The people still refused to repent. These two verses expose the moral condition of rebel-man throughout the course of this 3 ½ year period of The Wrath of God. People will live in deplorable spiritual conditions—everyday and every night. **Write** the things that the people will not stop doing in verses 20 and 21.

____

____

A. W. Tozer remarks, "The deep disease of the human heart is a will broken loose from its center, like a planet which has left its central sun and started to revolve around some strange body from outer space which may have moved in close enough to draw it away. When Satan said, 'I will,' he broke loose from his natural center, and the disease with which he has infected the human race is the disease of disobedience and revolt." [4] Murders, magic arts, sexual immorality, and thefts flow out of these spiritually diseased hearts as a natural result of their new center—demonic perversion.

Rebel-man has reverted back to the times before the Flood. "*Now the earth was corrupt in God's sight and was full of violence. God saw how corrupt the earth had become, for all the people on earth had corrupted their ways.*" (Genesis 6:11-12 NIV) What are the two main words in these verses that describe world culture? ______________________ and ______________________.
Life is unrestrained by any moral code whatsoever. We see here a total lack of inhibitions; mankind is out-of-control.

"When people fail to respond to God's gracious invitation and set themselves in opposition to His purposes, then they become the prey of horrifying demonic forces. They suffer the consequences of their choice. . .God is not mocked." [5]

"There is a twofold evil in idol worship: it robs the true God of His glory (Romans 1:23) and it leads to consorting [to be united] with evil spirits." [6]

Verse 20. . .They continued to worship demons and idols. Here is an in-your-face statement revealing the fact that mankind has turned from God to worship demons. How deceived can mankind be? Their main object of worship is the Antichrist and his image. (Revelation 13:4, 12; 19:20) More than likely, rebel-man tries to placate the attacking demons by worshipping them. In Strong's Greek dictionary we find a fascinating definition of this word *worship* which describes how earth people worship the demons.

> *Proskuneo* is the Greek word for *worship* in verse 20. It means: to *kiss*, like a dog *licking* his master's hand; to *fawn* or *crouch to*, that is, (figuratively or literally) prostrate oneself in homage, do *reverence* to, *adore*. [S]

Believers do not *fawn* over their God, meaning to seek favor or attention by flattery and slavish behavior, nor do we *crouch* or cringe in fear. Believers, at times, do prostrate themselves in loving adoration to their God. It has been granted to us "*to come boldly* [with confidence] *to the throne of grace, that we may obtain mercy and find grace to help in time of need.*" (Hebrews 4:16 NKJV) We bow before our Lord in humility, but with dignity as His children. Believers worship God in love, reverence, and in heart-felt adoration.

PREPARATION FOR THE BATTLE OF ARMAGEDDON

SIXTH BOWL Revelation 16:12-16 (NIV)

> [12] *The sixth angel poured out his bowl on the great river Euphrates, and its water was dried up to prepare the way for the kings from the East.*

> [13] *Then I saw three evil spirits that looked like frogs; they came out of the mouth of the dragon, out of the mouth of the beast and out of the mouth of the false prophet.* [14] *They are spirits of demons* [demonic spirits] *performing miraculous signs* [miracles], *and they go out to the kings of the whole world, to gather them for the battle on the great day of God Almighty.*
> [15] *"Behold, I come like a thief! Blessed is he who stays awake and keeps his clothes with him, so that he may not go naked and be shamefully exposed."*
> [16] *Then they gathered the kings together to the place that in Hebrew is called Armageddon.*

Observations

These observation questions will help you to picture in your mind the things that take place in the Sixth judgment. Stay alert!

Verse 12. . .Two things take place at the Euphrates River during the Sixth Trumpet/ Bowl judgment:

Trumpet (9:14-15) Evil angels were released with the purpose of ____________________.

Bowl (16:12) The water ____________________________ with the purpose of____________
____.

Where is the Euphrates River? If you fly almost directly east from Jerusalem, you will arrive at Baghdad, Iraq located on the Euphrates River. The head of the Euphrates River is in the mountains of eastern Turkey and continues to flow 1,780 miles through the middle of Iraq and ultimately into the Persian Gulf. This is the location of the Sixth Trumpet/Bowl Judgment. It is an ancient site with a great deal of history.

Verse 13. . . From where do these three evil (disgusting) spirits that look *like* frogs come?
____
____

Read in 1 Kings 22:19-23 a similar story in the Old Testament of how God uses a lying spirit in the mouths of false prophets for a divine purpose—the downfall of wicked King Ahab.

What are these frog-like creatures called in verse14? ______________________________

Does this clarify beyond the shadow of a doubt that the Beast (a man) and the False Prophet (a man) are controlled and possessed by demons? ________________ Remember these evil men appear before the Rapture so we Believers must not be deceived by their amazing appearance or performance.

Verse 14. . .What is the mission of these foul creatures? ___________________________
____

What do the demons do to make themselves very convincing to the rulers and leaders of the world? (verse 14) ____. These miracles will have evil significance in Satan's plan to bring the armies of the world into conflict with the hosts of heaven.

How many kings and how many regions of the World System of the Antichrist will be represented at Armageddon? ________

In speaking of the end times, 1 Timothy 4:1 (KJV) refers to "*seducing spirits*." This type of demon is used of Satan to lead people astray, to entice, or lure them to do evil. From man's beginnings, Satan has exercised his powerful influence upon man to cause changes in his character, thoughts and actions (Genesis 3). More than likely, these demons will enter into evil men who are willing to give them a human body with which to carry out their dirty work.

Demons cannot force humans to do anything against their will, but they can convince and deceive them to gain their cooperation which can eventually lead to demon possession. Probably these Ten Kings will not need much convincing as they are trying to survive the worst holocaust mankind has ever experienced. Their world has been devastated time and time again by God's judgments.

Verses 16. . .Where are the armies of the nations going to gather? ____________________
This battle will take place somewhere in Israel possibly on the plain of Meggido. The Greek derivative of the Hebrew word *Armageddon* means "the mountain of Megiddo." There is no mountain at this site but the ancient fortress city of Megiddo sits on a hill overlooking the Plain of Esdraelon and the Valley of Jezreel to the east. The eastern part of the Valley of Jezreel divides Galilee from Samaria. Megiddo is north of Jerusalem and can be found on any map of Israel.

In Bible times Megiddo was a crossroads for trade routes as well as movement of international armies. Many battles were fought in this valley. "As recently as 1918 the strategic importance of Megiddo was evident when the allied forces under Allenby (English General) entered northern Palestine through the Megiddo Pass to wrest it from the Turks." [7] This took place during World War I. Today it is still a very strategic site in that it is easy to get to from the coast on the west with roads also coming to it from the north, south and east. Megiddo is practically the center of the world, accessible and spacious for the gathering of the armies of the nations.

Verse 14. . .to gather them for the battle on the great day of God Almighty. Mankind actually intends to battle against God. Satan and his demons are not omniscient (know all things), but they do know the Scriptures. That was evident when Satan quoted Scripture in his endeavor to tempt Jesus to sin. (Matthew 4:6) Satan, knowing that his time is short and that King Jesus is on the verge of His return, assembles the worlds leaders with their armies, along with his vast supernatural army of evil, to a showdown with God.

Revelation 1:8 "I am the Alpha and the Omega—the beginning and the end." says the LORD God. "I am the one who is, who always was, and who is still to come—the Almighty One."

Picture in your mind armies departing from each of the Ten Regions of the world, representing every language and nation, to engage in a titanic battle at the center of the earth, Israel. *"Then I saw the beast and the kings of the world and their armies gathered together to fight against the one sitting on the horse* [King Jesus] *and his armies."* (Revelation 19:19)

Verse 14. . .the great day of God Almighty. What a marvelous description of the last day of this Present Age. "*Great* distinguishes it from lesser days. And it is the day *of God*, not of man or even of the Antichrist. It is associated with the culmination of the divine purpose." [8] *Almighty* (*pantokrator* Greek) "means the All-Powerful One, the All-Mighty One, the One who has dominion over all things, the Ruler of all."

God's power is supreme! All this clamoring, cesspool of evil gathered in one geographical spot amounts to nothing, absolutely nothing.

When this Day draws to a close, all things will be new; the old will have entirely passed away!

Verse 15. . . In the midst of this turmoil while all evil is combining forces against God, Jesus breaks into the middle of this vision with a special message like an interruption of "Breaking News" on television. For this reason the Revised Standard Version of the Bible places Jesus' words in parenthesis.

> *("Lo, I am coming like a thief! Blessed is he who is awake, keeping his garments that he may not go naked and be seen exposed!")*

What are His first four words? (verse 15) ____________________
To whom do you think Jesus is speaking? ____________________

Isaiah 61:10 "I am overwhelmed with joy in the LORD my God! For he has dressed me with the clothing of salvation and draped me in a robe of righteousness."

like a thief
What does *like* a thief mean? ____________________

Jesus applies this unusual but very good comparison to both the Rapture and to His Second Coming. (see Matthew 24:42-44; Luke 12:39-40; 1 Thessalonians 5:2, 4; 2 Peter 3;10; Revelation 3:3) The comparison lies in the fact that a thief arrives suddenly and unexpectedly. Therefore, Believers must always be spiritually ready for His coming. "*So you also must be ready, because the Son of Man will come at an hour when you do not expect Him.*" (Matthew 24:44)

King Jesus sees the need to give the Christian Jews in Israel a personal word to encourage them not to give up. "I am ready to come! I'll be there at any moment!" Like a husband responding to an urgent phone call from his wife saying, "I am just leaving the office! I'll be arriving any minute! Hang in there!"

Stay awake! Keep your garments!
This is a call to encourage the flagging, burdened spirits of His persecuted people who are now under the threat of annihilation. It is as if King Jesus is saying:

"I know the persecution is acute and the world is despicably immoral. Be alert! Those of you who are watching for me are going to be so blessed! Don't give up! Be ready for My coming! When you received Me as your Savior, you threw off your old, sinful self like an old, dirty garment fit only for the rubbish, and you put on your new, regenerated self like a new robe, pure and clean. Do not throw off this beautiful, spiritual garment; keep it close or when I come you will be ashamed at being caught without it *unprepared.*

Listen for the sound of the Seventh Trumpet. IT IS MY COMING!"

The next and final Trumpet/Bowl Judgment is His Second Coming!

THE KINGS FROM THE EAST

The Trumpet narration of the Sixth judgment reveals to us that at a specific time four evil angels are released at the Euphrates River to carry out their deadly mission. At the moment this release occurs, the Bowl narration states that through the intervention of an angel, the waters of the Euphrates River will dry up.

Revelation 16:12

> *"The sixth angel poured out his bowl on the great river Euphrates, and its water was dried up to prepare the way for the kings from the East."*

The English Revised Version gives a literal translation:

> *"And the sixth poured out his bowl upon the great river, the river Euphrates; and the water thereof was dried up, that the way might be made ready for the kings that come from the sunrising."*

Why is the river dried up? ____

Remember the definition of prepare? *Prepare* means "to make ready beforehand for a specific purpose or for some event, occasion, or the like." It is apparent that by God's will and for His purposes the river is dried up. We have learned from the Trumpet Judgment that the demons are released from this region.

The Ten Kings will be bringing their armies from every point of the compass to Armageddon in Israel. Why would this one river be so significant when the majority of the armed forces of the Ten Kings have greater obstacles to get to Israel, for example, oceans to cross? God does not dry up the oceans. This one short statement seems to be communicating a truth of great consequence. Because of the importance given to each locality where the Trumpet/Bowl Judgments take place; this location at the Euphrates River also must have special significance.

Who are the "*kings who come from the east,*" literally, "*the kings that come from the sunrising.*" If we look carefully at the wording, their context, and their significance we will see an amazing reality. The following is an interpretation which I believe to be a very credible one.

AN INTERPRETATION

I believe that it will be easier to follow the study of the "*kings from the east*" by stating this interpretation at the beginning of this process of interpretation rather than at the conclusion.

Interpretation
The Sixth Bowl Judgment is speaking of the preparation for King Jesus' Second Coming. The phrase, "*the kings from the East*," include King Jesus and all the Believer-kings that accompany Him from heaven and will reign with King Jesus for a thousand years. The point of entry will be the region of the Euphrates River at sunrise.

Jesus' Coming will look something like this
At a predetermined moment, the world will witness the most breath-taking, glorious scene ever! The Euphrates River is dried up; the prison house of demons has been emptied; the royal way of the kings is prepared. Just as the sun breaks the horizon at the river, out of its brilliance emanates King Jesus. *"Suddenly, the glory of the God of Israel appeared from the east. The sound of His coming was like the roar of rushing waters, and the whole landscape shone with His glory."* (Ezekiel 43:2)

The sky fills with majesty—King Jesus with His royal host! The Believer-kings dressed in white linen, astride white horses ride in His wake. The earth cowers and trembles at the roar of millions of wings like a thousand thunder storms as angelic beings advance swiftly over the land. This glorious host comes like the wind; their feet scarcely touching the ground. [9] Their destination—the Mount of Olives. This is the Great Day of God Almighty!

ANALYSIS OF KEY WORDS: THE EAST, THE EUPHRATES RIVER, KINGS

THE EAST

Revelation 16:12 (NIV)

> *"The sixth angel poured out his bowl on the great river Euphrates and its water was dried up to prepare the way for the kings from* ***the East****."*

These words in verse 12 literally read: "*the way of the kings from the dayspring* [sunrising]." *Dayspring* refers to the early dawn or daybreak when the sun's first light begins to fill the earth. The words for *east* and *dayspring* are one and the same word in the Greek language. We are looking for Jesus' Coming from the *east.* The following word studies are from Vine's Greek dictionary. [V]

East
Anatole, primarily a rising, as of the sun and stars, corresponds to *anatello*, to make to rise, or, intransitively, to arise, which is also used of the sunlight, as well as other objects of nature. In Luke 1:78-79 which reads: "*because of the tender mercy of our God, by which the rising sun* [Dayspring] *will come to us from heaven to shine on those living in darkness and in the shadow of death, to guide our feet into the path of peace.*" *Anatole* is used metaphorically of Christ as "the Dayspring," the One through Whom light came into the world, shining immediately into Israel, to dispel the darkness which was upon all nations. The east in general stands for that side of things upon which the rising of the sun gives light.

Dayspring

Anatole, literally a rising up (cp. *anatello*, to cause to rise), is used of the rising of the sun and stars; it chiefly means the east, as in Matthew 2:1-2 which reads: *'Where is the one who has been born king of the Jews? We saw His star in the east* [anatole-the dayspring] *and have come to worship Him.'*

Dawn

Diaugazo, signifies to shine through (*dia*, through, *auge*, brightness); it describes the breaking of daylight upon the darkness of night. 2 Peter 1:19 *"And we have the word of the prophets made more certain, and you will do well to pay attention to it, as to a light shining in a dark place, until the day dawns and the morning star rises in your hearts."* Metaphorically in 2 Peter 1:19, of the shining of the spiritual light into the heart. A probable reference is to the *"Day"* to be ushered in at the Second Coming of Christ: *'until the Day gleam through the present darkness, and the Light-bringer dawn in your hearts.'*

Again and again we see the word east/dayspring in relation to things related to Jesus' First and Second Comings. For example, wise men saw His star in the east/dayspring (Matthew 2:2, 9) The illustration of Christ's Coming at the Rapture *"as the lightening comes from the east/ dayspring. . ."* (Matthew 24:27) An angel ascended from the east/dayspring (the rising of the sun) with the seal of God to put on the 144,000 Christian Jews. (Revelation 7:2)

But where is the east? Where does the "dawn" begin?

We know where *north* is, at the North Pole. We know where *south* is, at the South Pole. Starting at the North Pole, one can only move to the south. From the South Pole, one can only move to the north. But where does the *east* begin?

God tells us in Isaiah 41:8-9 that He brought Abraham and the people of Israel from *"the ends of the earth, its farthest corners."* By this He is speaking of the Euphrates River valley where He called Abraham to go to the Promised Land of Israel. The word *ends* in Isaiah 41:9 in the Hebrew language *qatsah* means "a termination. . .border, brink, edge, end." [S] We can say that it is the "edge of the world" figuratively speaking.

Psalm 19:6 uses the same word *qatsah* when it poetically speaks of the sun: *"It rises at one end* [qatsah] *of the heavens and makes its circuit to the other."* Circuit means "any path or route, the complete traversal of which without local change of direction requires returning to the starting point." [D]

The Hebrew people seemed to frequently view the area known as the Euphrates River valley as "the ends of the earth" as a figure of speech for the farthest point of their world; that being said, it would also be the point from which things begin.

The "glory" of God departs

In the Old Testament, prophetic book that bears his name, Ezekiel reveals to us that the Lord God removed His presence from the temple because of the spiritual adultery of His people; they were overwhelmingly given to idolatry. Israel's *Glory* left them. We will briefly look at this because it has a great deal to do with the Lord's Second Coming. God's presence, spoken of as *His glory*, dwelt in the Holy of Holies in the innermost part of the temple, and now it departs from the temple step by step. We begin there.

1. God's presence moves from the mercy-seat of the Most Holy Place and proceeds to the doorway of the temple proper.
   "*Then the glory of the God of Israel rose up from between the cherubim, where it had rested, and moved to the entrance of the temple* [house]." (Ezekiel 9:3)

2. God's presence continues to the courtyard.
   "*. . .the cloud of glory filled the inner courtyard. . .Then the glory of the Lord rose from above the cherubim and went over to the door of the temple. The temple was filled with this cloud of glory, and the courtyard glowed brightly with the glory of the Lord.*" (Ezekiel 10:3-4)

3. God's presence moves to the eastern gate of the outside wall.
   "*Then the glory of the Lord departed from over the threshold of the temple and stopped above the cherubim. While I watched, the cherubim spread their wings and rose from the ground. . .They stopped at the entrance to the east gate of the Lord's house, and the glory of the God of Israel was above them.*" (Ezekiel 10:18-19 NIV)

4. God's presence abandons Jerusalem and stands over the Mount of Olives.
   The glory of the Lord went up from within the city and stopped above the mountain east of it." (Ezekiel 11:23 NIV)

The *Glory* of Israel had departed. The temple was destroyed by the Babylonians. Since that time, 586 B.C., God's glory has not been present even when the temple was later rebuilt. Jesus entered that temple during His life on earth, and, in a sense, God's glory entered with Jesus who is "*the radiance of God's glory*" (Hebrews 1:3 NIV), but the glory departed with Him whenever He left the temple. God's *Glory* was crucified in Jerusalem, was resurrected, and ascended to heaven. The temple, of Jesus' days on earth, was also destroyed in the year 70.

During the end times, the Antichrist will establish a covenant with the Jews which apparently allows for the rebuilding of the third temple. Ezekiel tells us that when this takes place the Glory of the Lord will return the same way He left, in reverse order. He will come to the mountain east of the temple which is called the Mount of Olives and will enter by the east gate and proceed to the Most Holy Place. Ezekiel sees this Great Day of the Almighty. Listen to his words.

> "*Then the man brought me to the gate facing east, and I saw the glory of the God of Israel coming from the east. His voice was like the roar of rushing waters, and the land was radiant with His glory. The vision I saw was like the vision I had by the Kebar River, and I fell facedown. The glory of the Lord entered the temple through the gate facing the east. Then the Spirit lifted me up and brought me into the inner court, and the glory of the Lord filled the temple.*

> *While the man was standing beside me, I heard someone speaking to me from inside the temple. He said: 'Son of man* [Ezekiel], *this is the place of my throne and the place for the soles of my feet. This is where I will live among the Israelites forever.*" (Ezekiel 43:1-7)

Circle the places referring to the reverse order of God's glory returning to the Temple.

16:12 "*The sixth angel poured out his bowl on the great river Euphrates and its water was dried up to prepare the way for the kings from the East.*" Jesus will come from the East.

THE EUPHRATES RIVER

16:12 "*The sixth angel poured out his bowl on the* **great river Euphrates** *and its water was dried up to prepare the way for the kings from the East.*"

This is the divinely chosen location for this Trumpet/Bowl judgment to take place. As we have seen in the Sixth Trumpet, four captive, evil angels have been released from this area leading a horde of demons to slay millions of people. A short time lapse is probable between this massacre and the coming of King Jesus; both with the same starting point or location—the Euphrates River.

In speaking of the messianic reign of Christ, Psalm 72:8 and Zechariah 9:10, both using the very same words, tell us that Jesus' kingdom will encompass the whole earth. **Underline** from where it begins.

Psalm 72:8

> "*May he* [Jesus] *reign from sea to sea, and from the Euphrates River to the ends of the earth.*"

Zechariah 9:10

> "*His* [Jesus'] *realm will stretch from sea to sea and from the Euphrates River to the ends of the earth.*"

Why is this location chosen for the point of entry of King Jesus on the Great Day of God Almighty? Perhaps because of its importance to God as the place of beginnings.

- This is believed to be the vicinity where the human race began. (Genesis 2)
- The first sin was committed here. (Genesis 3)
- The first murder took place here. (Genesis 4)
- The flood that destroyed the earth began in this area. (Genesis 6-8)
- The nations of the world originated here. (Genesis 10)
- First attempt of world government and a world religion apart from God began here. (Genesis 11)
- Diversity of languages began here. (Genesis 11)
- The beginning of the Jewish nation, God's chosen people, began here. (Genesis 12 – 50)

- The Jewish nation was held in captivity here. (2 Kings 17 – 25)

Perhaps the reason that *the Euphrates River Valley,* will be chosen as the port of entry to receive King Jesus at His Second Coming is because of the many significant failures that took place here. The restoration of the earth from the effects of the Trumpet/Bowl Judgments will begin here. It will be a new and glorious beginning which will not fail. This new beginning, in the person of Jesus Christ, closes the door on old failures; His arrival brings a perfect divine order to the world. Old things will pass away, all things will become new.

From here King Jesus and all the holy ones with Him press on to their destination: "*On that day His feet will stand on the Mount of Olives, east of Jerusalem. . .*" (Zechariah 14:4) What does Ezekiel 43:4 tell us will happen next? ____

Ezekiel 43:4 (NIV) "The glory of the Lord entered the Temple through the gate facing the east."

The dried up Euphrates River will be the place where Jesus' feet will touch the earth. The imprisoned demons have been cleared out of this whole area. This reminds us of the war in heaven when Michael and his heavenly army cast Satan and his demonic army out of the sky. Having done that, the heavens were *prepared* for the ascension of the victorious procession of saints at the time of the Rapture. The dried up Euphrates River is also cleared of a concentration of demons *to prepare the way* for the descent of Christ's victorious army of saintly kings.

16:12 "*The sixth angel poured out his bowl on the great river Euphrates and its water was dried up to prepare the way for the kings from the East.*" Jesus will appear at the genesis of the history of mankind, the Euphrates River valley.

THE KINGS

16:12 *The sixth angel poured out his bowl on the great river Euphrates and its water was dried up to prepare the way for* ***the kings*** *from the East.*

2 Timothy 2:12 (NKJV)

"*. . .if we endure, we shall also reign with Him.*"

The word in this verse for *reign* in the Greek language is *sumbasileuo* and means "to rule or reign in union with, together with as co-regent, or king." [S]

Our identity with Christ brings us into a sharing of hardships with our Savior. We will suffer persecution, misunderstanding, adversities, and criticism for Jesus' sake. "*Yes, and everyone who wants to live a godly life in Christ Jesus will suffer persecution.*" (2 Timothy 3:12) Now, a crown of thorns, but if we persevere, then, in the Kingdom—a crown of glory!

Jesus "has given us royalty. Through Him we may become the true sons of God; and, if we are sons of the King of kings, we are of a lineage of which there can be none more royal." [10] "In the mind of God every believer shares complete identity with Christ from the cross to the throne.

According to the Word, we are crucified with Him, buried with Him, raised with Him, exalted with Him, and enthroned with Him (Romans 6 and Ephesians 2)." [11]

The following verses teach us the fact that we will reign with Christ in His kingdom.

Revelation 2:26

> *"To all who are victorious, who obey me to the very end, to them, I will give authority over all the nations."*

Revelation 3:21

> *"Those who are victorious will sit with me on my throne, just as I was victorious and sat with my Father on His throne."*

We have been delegated the position of kings in the kingdom of King Jesus. Just a question here in light of this remarkable future of ours: Does your life and my life have a godly, regal demeanor of a king or queen? Are our speech, activities, and attitude worthy of such a position? This is a good moment to reflect on these things.

16:12 "*The sixth angel poured out his bowl on the great river Euphrates and its water was dried up to prepare the way for* <u>*the kings*</u> *from the East.*" The King and the kings, loyal followers of King Jesus.

THE CONTEXT OF REVELATION 16:12 IN THE LIGHT OF THE PROXIMITY OF THE SECOND COMING OF KING JESUS

The Context

A true interpretation of Scripture always looks at the context of the passage under consideration. The context is the *womb* in which the passage lies, the surrounding words which give it meaning. In this case we are trying to discover the meaning of 16:12. The *womb* is the book of Revelation whose theme is the enthronement of Jesus Christ.

- Chapters 1-5 speak of Christ's enthronement in heaven
- Chapters 6-20 lead to King Jesus' enthronement on earth
- Chapters 21-22 reveal the Lord Jesus' enthronement in the new heaven and the new earth [12]

In the above outline of the book of Revelation notice the location of Chapter 16. Accordingly, toward what is chapter 16 leading? ____

If you will look at **Timeline Two** (at the end of Part One of this study book), you will see that the Wrath of God lasts ____________ years. What are the two Events that take place at the end of these 3 ½ years?

______________________________________ and ______________________________

The context reveals to us that Chapter 16 is in the section of the book of Revelation that is moving toward the Lord's enthronement on earth which will take place at His Second Coming.

We are presently studying the Sixth judgment of the Wrath of God; the Seventh, and last, judgment is the Second Coming of Christ and Armageddon. Jesus will come immediately after this Sixth judgment. In 16:15 Jesus triumphantly declares, "*I am coming*" and without delay He comes at the sound of the Seventh Trumpet of the Seventh Trumpet/Bowl judgments.

16:12 *The sixth angel poured out his bowl on the great river Euphrates and its water was dried up* ***to prepare the way*** *for the kings from the East.* The preparation for King Jesus' Coming with the Believer kings is the meaning of this verse.

The water is dried up, the way has been *prepared.* Oh, rebellious earthlings, the Lord God of heaven's armies is coming! Watch for Him in the eastern skies!

16:16. . .Then they gathered the kings together to the place that in Hebrew is called Armageddon. The Ten Kings with their fighting men are arriving daily from every point of the compass to the place called Armageddon. Satan with his powerful demons are already there. At the arrival of each military unit, roars of triumph rise up with back slapping all around. But with the arrival of the Antichrist and the False Prophet the roiling mass can hardly contain themselves. With one voice they cry out for hours, "Great is the Beast, god of this world! Who is like the Beast? Who can make war against him?"

The 144,000 Christian Jews watch with solemn thoughts as the armies grow until the land can hardly contain them; darkness covers the earth. But their spirits are victorious, but vigilant; each Believer wears his spiritual garment. The words: "'*Behold, I come like a thief,*' play over and over in their minds while their attention swings between the fast growing army and the east. Finally they turn their full attention to the east and watch in hope for the Sunrise.

JESUS CHRIST THE SUNRISE FROM ON HIGH

Luke 1:78 (NASB)

The Seven Trumpet /Bowl Judgments—Revelation 8-9, 15-16, 11

Environment and Universe				Demon World		Consummation
1st	**2**nd	**3**rd	**4**th	**5**th **WOE**	**6**th **WOE**	**7**th **WOE**
8:7; 16:2	8:8-9; 16:3	8:10-11; 16:4-7	8:12-13; 16:8-9	9:1-12; 16:10-11	9:13-20 16:12-16	11:15-19 16:17-21
Where? on the earth	the sea	rivers and springs of waters	1/3rd of the sun, moon, stars	bottomless pit/throne of the beast	Euphrates river	
What happened? hail, fire, blood, sores	1/3rd of sea turned to blood	1/3rd bitter, then turned to blood	1/3rd were darkened	demons released	four angles released to lead demonic army, kill 1/3 of people	
Results? 1/3rd earth, 1/3rd trees, all grass burned up, severe and malignant sores on men	all creatures in sea die, 1/3rd of ships destroyed	many people died	1/3 of day and night had no light; sun scorched people with fierce heat; blaspheme God, refuse to repent	darkness; people stung, tormented by demons, in great pain for 5 months; curse God, refuse to repent	Dragon, beast and false prophet summon all kings to battle against God at Armageddon	

LESSON **14**

JESUS CHRIST KING OF THE NATIONS
Revelation 15:3-4

"My Jesus, my King, my Life, my All, I again dedicate my whole life to Thee."

David Livingstone, Missionary to Africa
(His prayer on the last day of his life.)

THE TWO WITNESSESS AND THE SEVENTH TRUMPET/BOWL JUDGMENT

Wondrous things have just taken place. I am a Jew, but not an ordinary Jew, because the traditional, ordinary Jew doesn't exist anymore. Now, we the people of Israel are all Christian Jews, servants of the Lord Jesus Christ. Our Messiah, Jesus, appeared in the clouds of the sky. It was the most awesome, glorious thing that I have ever seen. In wonder we all looked at Him whom our forefathers had slain. Our hearts were broken in deep remorse because we Jews had denied Jesus for centuries. Repentance and regret immediately spread throughout our nation and drove us to our knees; every knee bowed to King Jesus. We begged forgiveness from the Savior, and Jesus mercifully brought grace and healing to our sin-sick souls. The Holy Spirit regenerated our spirits with His dynamic power and filled us with divine life. I feel so free! How I love Jesus!

Our salvation took place when Gog invaded our land with his huge army. Our Messiah King destroyed Gog at the same moment that He came to take all Christians, the resurrected dead and the living, back to heaven with Him. What an event that was! We are still recovering and burying the decaying bodies of Gog's defeated army. There are thousands of them strewn across our land causing a great stench. The Scriptures speak of this saying that it will take us seven months to find and bury them and to clean up our land. (Ezekiel 39:12)

Recently, two thirds of our population was killed by the treacherous traitor, the Antichrist, when he abruptly terminated our Seven-Year Covenant. His armies attacked and captured Jerusalem. *"Half the population* [was taken] *into captivity, and the rest* [was left] *among the ruins of the city."* (Zechariah 14:1-2) The Antichrist invaded our temple and set up his hideous statue which now stands in the outer court. The enemy has taken over our city and has filled it with unspeakable wickedness.

Many of us have been scattered, but there are 144,000 of us who have received God's seal; for that reason, we are confident in God's faithfulness to provide for our needs and protect us even though we are in bondage. We are so few and are facing a world full of blasphemers of God and worshipers of the Antichrist and even of demons. Though we are being humiliated, vilified, and suffer every abuse imaginable, we will never bow to the evil one. We will preach Christ, King of the nations, to the end. We remain the only light shining for Jesus in this world of great darkness.

We, my valiant companion and I, are the leaders. You are going to read our story. Never in history have two human beings been such powerful instruments of judgment in the hands of the living God. Our submission is absolute, as well as our steadfast trust in our Sovereign Lord. Come! Come with us and witness the awesome and alarming things that our Lord has commissioned us to execute upon the world in the next 3 ½ years.

In this lesson we will study:

Psalm 19:1-4 "The heavens proclaim the glory of God. The skies display his craftsmanship. Day after day they continue to speak; night after night they make him known. They speak without a sound or word; their voice is never heard. Yet their message has gone throughout the earth, and their words to all the world."

- **God's Last Witness to the World**
  The world has never been without a witness of God's truth and saving grace. Even creation spreads the knowledge of God before the eyes of mankind. If we learn anything in the Old Testament Scriptures, it is the fact that God raises up and empowers dedicated individuals in times of great spiritual necessity. Just look at the book of Judges which illustrates this fact. Even during the Wrath of God, this darkest hour of history, God will provide the world with a witness to fill its great spiritual vacuum caused by the Rapture of the Believers.

  In this lesson we will study from another perspective the 3 ½ years of the Wrath of God which is Event 3 for the Unbeliever. We will learn about the ministry of two Christian Jews known only as the "two witnesses." They will carry out a very powerful ministry in an extremely hostile world. (Revelation 11:1-14)

- **God's Last Judgment**
  We will also study in this lesson the Seventh and final judgment of the Wrath of God. The Seventh Trumpet/Bowl judgment includes both the announcement of Christ's eternal reign (Revelation 11:15-19) and His actual Second Coming which we will study in the next lesson.

GOD'S LAST WITNESS TO THE WORLD (Revelation 11:1-14)

THE AWESOME MINISTRY OF THE TWO WITNESSES

The Greatest Question To Ask God's Word: I am presently writing this question at the top of every page of my Bible as a guide to my daily reading. The question: *Why is it important to God that I know this?* Amazing results! Try it!

Their Story

Read then **write** down five facts from the following Scripture. To observe means to both concentrate on the words of the text over against a passive, uninvolved reading and the restating of specific parts of the text. Dialogue with these verses by asking the "observation w's" (Where? Who? When?).

Revelation 11:1-6

> [1] *"Then I* [John] *was given a measuring stick, and I was told, "Go and measure the temple of God and the altar, and count the number of worshippers.* [2] *But do not measure the outer courtyard, for it has been turned over to the nations. They will trample the holy city for 42 months* [3 ½ years].
>
> [3] *And I will give power to my two witnesses, and they will be clothed in burlap and will prophesy during those 1,260 days* [3 ½ years]. [4] *These two prophets are the two olive trees and the two lampstands that stand before the Lord of all the earth.* [5] *If anyone*

> *tries to harm them, fire flashes from their mouths and consumes their enemies. This is how anyone who tries to harm them must die.* [6] *They have power to shut the sky so that no rain will fall for as long as they prophesy. And they have the power to turn the rivers and oceans into blood, and to strike the earth with every kind of plague as often as they wish."*

Your Five Observations

1. ______________________________
2. ______________________________
3. ______________________________
4. ______________________________
5. ______________________________

I would enjoy a conversation with you concerning your discoveries. More than likely your observations led to searching questions about the meaning of the text. We will work together on the meaning.

At the half-way point of the Seventieth Week, the Seven Trumpet/Bowl Judgments of the Wrath of God and the ministry of the Two Witness will begin simultaneously. In other words, Revelation 11 chronologically covers the 3 ½ years beginning at the Rapture and ending with the Second Coming of Christ and Armageddon. The action of the entire chapter takes place in Jerusalem and focuses on God's witness to the world through the Nation Israel.

The Setting

Revelation 11:1-2

> *"Then I* [John] *was given a measuring stick, and I was told, "Go, and measure the Temple of God and the altar, and count the number of worshippers. But do not measure the outer courtyard, for it has been turned over to the nations. They will trample the holy city for 42 months* [3 ½ years]. "

Observations

The "*temple of God*" is speaking of the Jewish place of worship; therefore, the city where this chapter takes place is ______________________. What part of the temple site was not to be measured? ______________________. Why was it not to be measured? ______________________________________. The time period of this chapter is ______________________ or ____________ years.

From these two verses we have gathered together some basic information, and as we add it to what we have learned so far, we realize that we are looking at the time period called the Wrath of God. This being the case, **circle** the correct "3 ½ years" on the chart below and write "Two Witnesses" on the line provided.

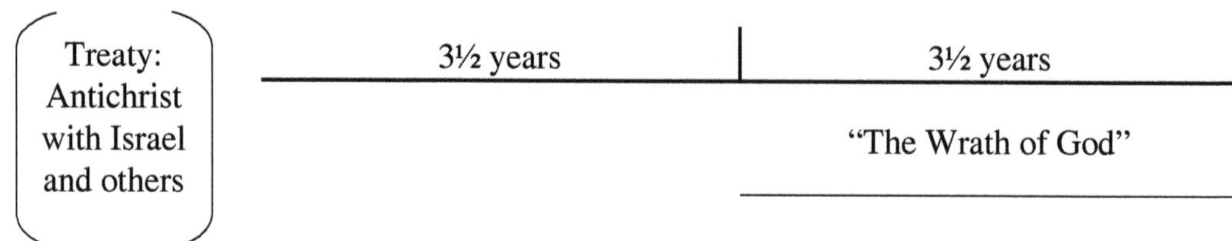

Keep in mind, that the visions revealed to John in the book of Revelation will, in fact, be played out in real life on God's time-clock.

Verse 1. . . ***measure*** **the temple of God and the altar, and count the number of worshippers.**

Definitions
Temple. . .*naos* (Greek) refers to the sanctuary, the Holy of Holies and the Holy Place.
Altar. . . *thusiasteron* (Greek) the huge altar of sacrifice in the court of the priests.
Worshippers. . . God's people.

John not only sees all that takes place in the vision, he also participates in it. The *measuring* John is told to do seems to indicate that God is going to protect and preserve all that comes within the confines of this measurement. This would indicate that the newly-built temple was not to be destroyed. The measuring is similar to God's sealing of the 144,000 Jews, which has just occurred, for His protection and divine care. The counting of *"the number of worshippers,"* indicates that a large number of Jews, worshippers of God, are within the confines of the inner courts of the temple proper. Perhaps this is where the two witnesses and some of the 144,000 will be confined to live throughout the entire 3 ½ years. A large number of Jews will have been taken captive during the surprise attack by the Antichrist's international army, while other Christian Jews who survive will flee to *"the wilderness,"* a place prepared by God. **Circle** the number of years of their safe keeping specified in the verse located in the margin.

Revelation 12:14 "But she [a remnant of Israel] was given two wings like those of a great eagle so she could fly to the place prepared for her in the wilderness. There she would be cared for and protected from the dragon [Satan] for a time, times, and half a time [3 ½ years.]"

By the way, you no doubt circled the "second-half 3 ½ years" in the diagram above which is the correct answer.

Verse 2. . . But do not measure the outer courtyard, for it has been turned over to the nations. God permits the armies of the Antichrist and other enemies of Israel to use this outer courtyard. This outer courtyard will probably be the final location and place of worship of the abominable image of the Antichrist. (Daniel 9:27; Matthew 24:15; Revelation 13:14-15)

The temple mount during the days of Jesus

At this point, you need to know how the Jewish temple was laid out. A barrier or partition divided the temple proper from the outer courtyard which was named the Court of the Gentiles (non-Jews). Gentiles were permitted access to this outer courtyard, but they were prohibited from passing beyond the barrier into the inner courts of the temple proper. Only Jews were permitted to go into these courts. In the Old Testament, and in the times of Jesus in the New Testament, signs were posted warning that no Gentile go beyond the barrier into the inner courts of the temple under penalty of death. Gateways permitted the Jews to pass back and forth through the barrier.

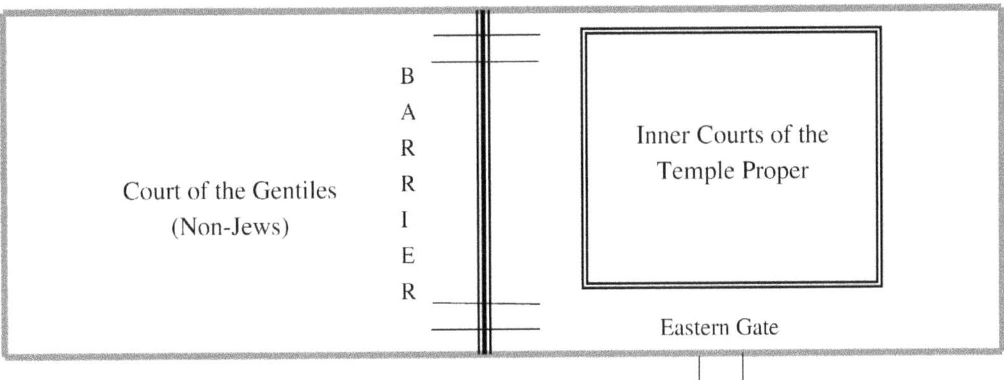

The temple mount from A.D. 691 to the present time

In A.D. 691 the Muslim Caliph 'Abd al-Malik erected a shrine, the Dome of the Rock, over what has been considered the foundation stone of the Jewish temple. Muslims also believe that their founder Muhammad ascended to heaven from this place.

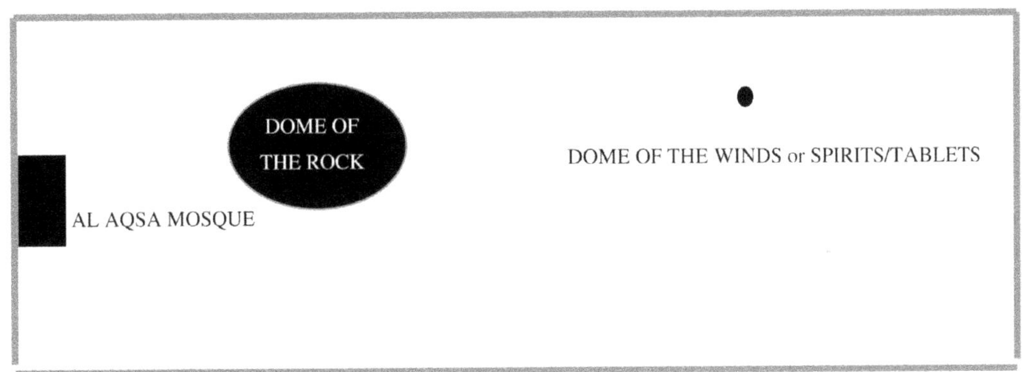

It is believed by many Jews that the Muslim Dome of the Rock is located in the outer courtyard, Court of the Gentiles, and that the actual location of the ancient Jewish Temple destroyed in A.D. 70 was situated where a small sixteenth-century Muslim cupola is located at this time. This landmark was named, possibly to maintain its original identity, "the Dome of the Winds or Spirits" and "the Dome of the Tablets" These ancient names may possibly be referring to this spot as the place where God's Spirit was positioned, and *Tablets* could refer to the Ten Commandments located inside the Ark of the Covenant. Dr. Asher Kaufman, a professor of physics at the Hebrew University of Jerusalem's Rachah Institute, gives very convincing evidence that places the true location of the temple at the site of the "Dome of the Spirits/Tablets." In other words, this little dome may be the very place where the Holy of Holies was located.

Al Aqsa Mosque was built in A.D. 715 on the south side of the temple mount.

An interpretation of the temple mount at the rebuilding of the Jewish temple

The Seven-Year treaty made with the Antichrist, Israel, and others seems to indicate permission given to the Jews to rebuild their temple on the temple mount. This implies an agreement with Muslim leaders, which are the *others* involved in the treaty. The temple is built on the site of the "Dome of the Spirits/Tablets," and a wall with doorways is constructed separating the temple from the Dome of the Rock and Al Aqsa Mosque. The diagram below is based on this interpretation.

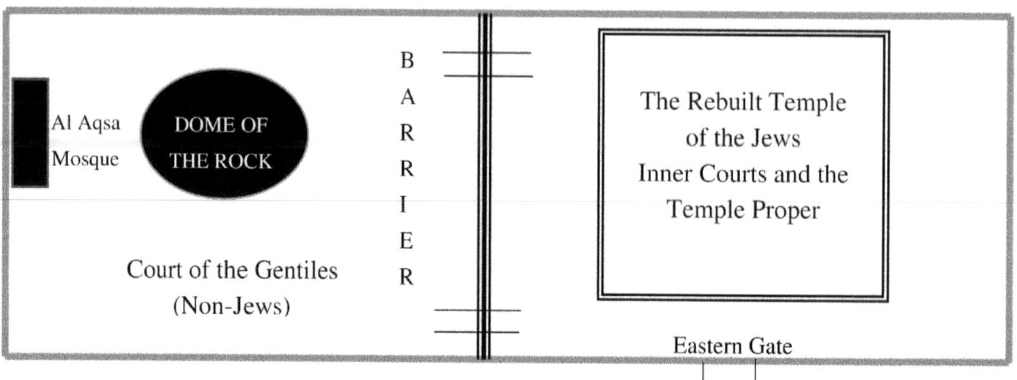

Look at the diagram above. What does Jesus see upon His arrival to the temple mount at His Second Coming? ______________________________

Ezekiel 43:1-6 gives the vision of the glory of God, in the person of King Jesus at His Second Coming, returning to the temple coming *"from the way of the east,"* and *"into the temple by way of the gate which faces toward the east."* Ezekiel 43:7-8 are the words of King Jesus as He enters the temple. **Underline** any words that concur with your answer to the above question.

Ezekiel 43:7-8 (NKJV)

> [7] *"He said to me "Son of man,* [Ezekiel], *this is the place of My throne and the place of the soles of My feet, where I will dwell in the midst of the children of Israel forever. No more shall the house of Israel defile My holy name, they nor their kings, by their harlotry* [spiritual unfaithfulness] . . .
>
> [8] *When they set their threshold by My threshold, and their doorpost by My doorpost, with a wall between them and Me, they defiled My holy name by the abominations which they committed; therefore I have consumed them in My anger."*

Ezekiel 43:8 tells us when King Jesus returns and enters the temple He will find that there is only a wall between the Temple and a place where idol worship is conducted with doorways connecting the two.

Verse 2. . . But do not measure the outer courtyard, for it has been turned over to the nations. They will trample the holy city for 42 months. What will the armies of the nations do to the *"holy city,"* Jerusalem? ______________________________

____

Underline the time given in verse 2. What does the word "*trample*" indicate to you in regard to the situation of the Jews during this time? ______________________________

Zechariah 14:1-2

> *"Watch, for the day of the Lord is coming when your possessions will be plundered right in front of you! I will gather all the nations to fight against Jerusalem. The city will be taken, the houses looted, and the women raped. Half the population will be taken into captivity, and the rest will be left among the ruins of the city."*

trample or tread [D] to treat harshly or ruthlessly, contemptuously; crush forcibly; oppress; subdue; violate; destroy.

The "*holy city*" will be crushed and violated. God will have delivered Israel from annihilation by destroying the armies of Gog at the time of the Rapture. But shortly after, the Antichrist will abandon the treaty with Israel, invade Jerusalem and declare himself "God" in the temple proper. The statue of abomination will be placed by the Antichrist in the Court of the Gentiles. After accomplishing this, it appears that the Antichrist will return to the "*wicked city*" where he continues to rule the world. But he will leave a large military presence to occupy Jerusalem. Zechariah 14:1-2 speaks of this invasion of Jerusalem that Jesus warned Israel about in Matthew 24:15-22.

The Jews in the Temple "will be like sheep in a sheepfold with wolves howling and prowling all around its walls." [1]

There will be worship of the Most Holy God in the Temple of the Christian Jews on the one side and idol worship by the nations of the world of the most evil image of all time on the other. The inner courts of the temple seem to be off limits to the occupiers of Jerusalem. The temple proper will be like a tiny island of safety in the midst of a sea of malicious creatures. Legions of angels stand watch over God's chosen ones.

Their Description

Revelation 11:3-4

> [3] *"And I will give power to my two witnesses, and they will be clothed in burlap* [sack-cloth] *and will prophesy during those 1,260 days* [3 ½ years]. [4] *These two prophets are the two olive trees and the two lampstands that stand before the Lord of all the earth."*

Psalm 34:7 "For the angel of the Lord is a guard; he surrounds and defends all who fear him."

These two verses introduce two Jewish men who will have an unusual ministry during the seven Trumpet/Bowl judgments. What does God give these two witnesses in verse 3? ____________________

This word *power* in the Greek language is *exousia* (from another Greek word *exesti*), and means: "Permission, authority, right, liberty, the power to do anything. The words *exesti* and *exousia* combine the two ideas of *right* and *might*." [KW] We can expect a terrific outpouring of power and marvelous expressions of authority from these two witnesses. Extraordinary!

Maybe one of your observations was the peculiar clothing that these two men will wear. Burlap or sackcloth was a coarse, dark colored cloth made of goat hair. Sacks were made from it in Bible times.

There are three possible explanations for dressing in this manner.

- Burlap was worn by mourners. Figuratively, it carried the sense of severe judgment. (see Isaiah 50:3 and Revelation 6:12) The two witnesses could be wearing sackcloth as a sign of mourning because of the *desecration* and *defilement* of the temple by the Antichrist when he blasphemously declared himself to be "God" and set up his image to be worshipped there. In a sense, this is the worst of the worst in regard to defiling a holy place of God. Remember, this is where the Son of God will establish His throne during His reign of a thousand years.

Defile or desecrate [D] "to defile" ... to make filthy or dirty, unclean, contaminated.

- Their garment could also bear the meaning of contrition and self-humbling from their recent repentance at the appearance of Jesus at the Rapture.

- The third possibility could be that the armies assigned to Jerusalem by the Antichrist will force the Jewish captives to dress in this manner not only to humiliate them but also to distinguish them from the Gentile population. This would be reminiscent of Nazi Germany during World War II where all Jews were forced to wear the star of David on their clothing for easy identification.

When Jesus enters the temple, the glory of His presence will purify it and make it holy.

Notice in verse 4, the place of authority from where these two men confront the world. They "*stand before* ______________________________________." Observe the personal pronoun in verse 3 "______ *two witnesses.*" These words were written centuries ago but they tell us that God has these two particular men all lined up and prepared for their task. They could be living today.

Like all of God's people, you too are called, chosen, prepared and empowered to do special things for Him.

The witnesses will present to the world fiery messages on God's love, redemption, and judgment; and they will certainly protest against the imposter who claims to be God, but in fact, represents "the god of this age"—Satan. (2 Corinthians 4:4) How great is the mercy and love of God for mankind! This is God's last witness to the world; this is the world's last chance to turn to Him.

Notice again the length of time that these two witnesses prophesy: ____________________ or ____________________ **Underline** the time given in verse 3.

Their Power

Revelation 11:5-6

> [5] *"If anyone tries to harm them, fire flashes from their mouths and consumes their enemies. This is how anyone who tries to harm them must die.* [6] *They have power to shut the sky so that no rain will fall for as long as they prophesy. And they have the power to turn the rivers and oceans into blood, and to strike the earth with every kind of plague as often as they wish."*

God has given these two witnesses great assurance for their safety—"*anyone who tries to harm them must die.*" Notice the emphatic word "*must.*" *Dei* is the Greek word for *must* and "points to a compelling divine necessity. The death in question is inevitable." [2] Divine protection will be the confidence that inspires these valiant men in their dedication to the work that God gives them to do. They will be instruments of instant death for those who try to kill them.

This protection from God keeps them alive as they preach from the temple and throughout the streets of Jerusalem for a very long 3 ½ years. Other examples of evil people killed by the words or command of the prophets are found in 2 Kings 1; Acts 5:1-11.

Every Believer is "immortal" until his work is done. This truth brought me great comfort in some "scary moments" on the mission field.

The reason that the occupiers of Jerusalem hate and seek to kill these two men of God is found in verse 6. In your own words what is the reason: ______________________________

____

We can make the observation that these tormenting powers affect the entire world as suggested by the words: rivers, oceans, and the earth. The word "*power*" used twice in verse 6 is the same Greek word *exousia* as explained in verse 3. These two men will exhibit great authority and power.

The calamities to be performed by the two witnesses bear a striking resemblance to the judgments of the Trumpets/Bowls of the Wrath of God which will take place at this same time. Perhaps the two witnesses will be the human counterparts of the angelic beings that will let loose the judgments upon the earth. If this is the case, we see God working in perfect union with man as His agent on earth to accomplish His divine will. These two men, upon the Spirit's promptings and through His power, will call upon God to perform each judgment. This implies that the ministry of the two witnesses will be one of terrible judgment upon the people of the earth.

Psalm 5:11-12 (NIV) "But let all who take refuge in you be glad; let them ever sing for joy. Spread your protection over them that those who love your name may rejoice in you. For surely, O Lord, you bless the righteous; you surround them with your favor as with a shield."

Can you imagine the hatred that the people of the world will have for these two witnesses? Each time the prophets call to God for a calamity, the sound of a Trumpet will follow and a Bowl will pour out plagues on the earth. Enraged rebel-man will implore the Antichrist to call for the military in Jerusalem to kill the prophets of death. And try as they might, those who make the attempt are the ones who will wind up dead.

Throughout the chaos, death, disaster, and destruction, 144,000 jubilant voices will uplift the name of God in the presence of their enemies. (Psalm 23:4-5) Can you hear their victorious song ringing out over the city of Jerusalem?

God has wrapped His shield of protection and glory around His valiant servants as expressed in Psalm 5:11-12. "Their hope lies in the Lord, who will constantly guard His own '*as with a shield.*' '*You surround them*' may also be translated as '*you crown them.*' On the one hand, the Lord extends his protection and favor, likened to a '*shield.*' On the other hand, he bestows his royal glory on the godly." [3]

THE AWESOME DEATH AND RESURRECTION OF THE TWO WITNESSES

Again, I want to give you another opportunity to study the Scripture on your own. Learning to make observations is a very good exercise as it is the first step to interpret the Bible. Observation basically asks the question: What does the Scripture say?. . .and that leads us to meaning.

"Victories, Christian victories,... have never been substantiated by the criterion of saving the body from destruction, but rather by keeping the faith at cost of bodily life for the sake of "a better resurrection." [4]

Hebrews 11:35 (NIV) "Others were tortured and refused to be released, so that they might gain a better resurrection."

Revelation 11:7-10

> 7 *When they complete their testimony, the beast that comes up out of the bottomless pit will declare war against them, and he will conquer them and kill them.* 8 *And their bodies will lie in the main street of Jerusalem, the city that is figuratively called "Sodom" and "Egypt," the city where their Lord was crucified.* 9 And for three and a half days, all peoples, tribes, languages, and nations will stare at their bodies. No one will be allowed to bury them. 10 *All the people who belong to this world will gloat over them and give presents to each other to celebrate the death of the two prophets who had tormented them.*

Write your five observations on the lines below.

1. ____________________
2. ____________________
3. ____________________
4. ____________________
5. ____________________

How incredibly sad! Does Satan's puppet, the Antichrist, have more power than God's two witnesses? Has God abandoned His faithful servants to the cruelties of the wicked worshippers of the Antichrist? Inconceivable!

Their Mission Accomplished
Revelation 11:7

> *"When they complete their testimony"*

The work that God has appointed for these two courageous men has been completed. They have worked in perfect harmony with angelic beings in bringing judgment on mankind.

Again we meet this wonderful word *complete* or *finish*. Notice how the meaning of the Greek word, *teleo*, enhances our understanding of the phrase: *"when they complete* [*teleo*] *their testimony."* *Teleo* means: "To make an end or accomplishment, to complete anything, not merely to end it, but to bring it to perfection or its destined goal, to carry through." [KW] What does this reveal about the character and dedication of these two witnesses? ____________________

The two witnesses finish their work for the Lord just days before Jesus comes again. The end of this Present Age is that close!

Their Death
Revelation 11:7

> *"the beast that comes up out of the bottomless pit will declare war against them and he will conquer them and kill them."*

This phrase serves to confirm the identity of the Beast, or the Antichrist. The Beast will have already come back from the dead. In order to refresh our memories, I will again include the definition of the abyss/bottomless pit from where the Antichrist will ascend.

The abyss, bottomless pit, is depicted as an immeasurable depth. It is:

- the abode of Unbelievers who have died until the Great White Throne judgment (Revelation 20:11-15)
- a prison for certain demons (Revelation 9:1-2, 11)
- the place from which the Antichrist will ascend (Revelation 11:7; 17:8) [6]

The Bottomless Pit "The bottomless pit can be found nowhere else but in the molten interior of this earthly globe…This pit is described in Ezekiel 32:17-32 (KJV) as "the nether parts of the earth" [5] meaning the underworld of the dead.

The Antichrist, along with his master, Satan, and the False Prophet, are in the process of assembling the Ten Kings and their armies in the land of Israel to battle against God Almighty. In their evil council they decide that it is time "*to declare war*" on the two witnesses, the 144,000, and any other living Jew to "*conquer them and kill them.*" It is time to set up the permanent throne of the Antichrist in the temple of Jerusalem. It is time for the armies of the earth to conquer King Jesus and His Believer kings. It is time for the forces of Satan to defeat the angelic armies of heaven. Satan remembers that only 3 ½ years ago, Michael the archangel of God and his angels, threw him and his cohorts out of the heavens. Humiliating! Revelation 12:7-9) But this time they will not fail! Yes, the time has come to make the final move—one last gigantic battle!

One other item on the Antichrist's agenda before proceeding to Jerusalem is to destroy the capital city of the world from where he has ruled. He casts aside all pretense of religious ties. The Beast considers himself to be God. He himself *is* the religion of the world! The Ten Kings of the Ten Regions join with their supreme ruler in setting fire to the wicked "*harlot city.*" (Revelation 17:16-17; 18)

Meanwhile as the armies of the nations assemble in Israel, you, as a part of the glorified multitude in heaven, are being prepared to return to earth in company with your conquering King, Jesus Christ. You are receiving instructions concerning Armageddon and your place in the subsequent reign of Christ. There is much to learn.

Let's try to visualize the situation in Jerusalem and the world in general at this time. For three and a half years, no one has been able to kill the two witnesses or to stop them from tormenting the people of the earth with God's world-destroying, catastrophic judgments. Millions have died during six horrible catastrophes and earth people are bracing for the impact of the next one. All assassination attempts on these two Jews has resulted in the death of the assassins. Their situation is unbearable.

The Antichrist has decided to take matters into his own hands. It is announced that the supreme ruler of the world, the great imposter, is bringing all the kings and their powerful armies to march against Israel. The Antichrist will declare war on the two leaders in Jerusalem. And so the world holds its collective breath as it listens to the glowing reports of the world's mightiest men and their final solution. So much depends on this great mission.

The Antichrist has arrived in Jerusalem. He is calling out the two Jewish prophets! He did it! He did it! The Antichrist has slain the enemies of the world. They are dead! No more torment, no more death! All the kingdoms of the earth fall down and worship their great leader! And so goes the euphoria of the celebration. Three and a half days of drunkenness, orgies, and unspeakable wickedness.

Their Ridicule

Revelation 11:8-10

> [8] *And their bodies will lie in the main street of Jerusalem, the city that is figuratively called "Sodom" and "Egypt," the city where their Lord was crucified.* [9] *And for three and a half days, all peoples, tribes, languages, and nations will stare at their bodies. No one will be allowed to bury them.* [10] *All the people who belong to this world will gloat over them and give presents to each other to celebrate the death of the two prophets who had tormented them.*

What is the extent of those who view the prophet's bodies? verse 9 ____________________

____

How do they regard the bodies of the prophets? verses 9-10____________________

____

How long does this go on? verse 9 ____________________

What do they hold against the two witnesses? verse 10 ____________________

Who do you think wants to bury the two witnesses? verse 9 ____________________

How do you think they felt about losing their beloved leaders? ____________________

Spoken by two angels in Genesis 19:13 (RSV) "...for we are about to destroy this place [Sodom], because the outcry against its people has become great before the Lord, and the Lord has sent us to destroy it."

Verse 8. . .And their bodies will lie in the main street of Jerusalem; the city that is figuratively called "Sodom" and "Egypt," the city where their Lord was crucified. At this point in time of its occupation, Jerusalem is described by three significant terms.

Sodom was a city destroyed by God in the Old Testament. Sodom's characteristics: notorious wickedness, rebellion, extreme moral degradation. So wicked was this city, that the whole region cried out to God to do something about it. God compares Jerusalem with Sodom. He uses this term to express the evil that will permeate the city through the wicked actions of the occupying armies. If you are curious to know of what Sodom's greatest wickedness consisted, read Genesis 19:1-28 and you will probably say, "That is something to really think about in light of the obsession with sex in our world today."

Egypt was a country in the Old Testament that enslaved Israel and held them in bondage for 400 years. This term is used to convey the condition of the Christian Jews as they will be held in bondage throughout this 3 ½ year period.

The city where their Lord was crucified. How tender, that God says "*where their Lord was crucified,*" the "their" referring back to the two witnesses. These two valiant men in their struggle against sin resisted to the point of shedding their own blood. (Hebrews 12:4) They have truly followed in their Lord's footsteps.

Ridicule [D]
The attempt to arouse laughter or merriment at another's expense by making fun of or belittling him.

Their bodies will lie in the main street of Jerusalem. Down through the centuries Bible readers have wondered how people from all over the world could view the bodies of these two witnesses. Of course God knew all about the technologies of the end times. Even though the terrific judgments of these 3 ½ years will disrupt life in many ways, apparently the ability of technology will still be able to provide the answer to this prophecy. Does this indicate that this prophecy was meant to take place during this age of technology? Interesting thought.

The Lord spares us of the details of these 3 ½ days as to what was done to the rotting bodies of our two faithful *"unto death"* brothers in Christ. (Revelation 2:10) Can you imagine the jubilee when the spirits/souls of these two heroic men enter the gates of heaven? What a contrast between the celebration on earth and the one in heaven! The recently martyred Christian Jews are especially elated to see them.

Watch what God does! As the souls of the two witnesses stand before God's throne, He informs them that He has one more task for them that they are really going to enjoy. God sends His witnesses back to earth to get their bodies!

Their Resurrection

Revelation 11:11-12

> *"But after three and a half days, God breathed life into them, and they stood up! Terror struck all who were staring at them. Then a loud voice from heaven called to the two prophets, "Come up here!" And they rose to heaven in a cloud as their enemies watched."*

Write five observations from these two verses. Enjoy!

1. ______________________________
2. ______________________________
3. ______________________________
4. ______________________________
5. ______________________________

In the midst of the world's over-the-top celebration, the bodies of the two prophets suddenly sit up! They get to their feet and stand with glorified bodies before the very eyes of the terrified multitude. Then all the people *"heard a tremendous voice speaking to these two from Heaven, saying, 'Come up here!' And they went up to Heaven in a cloud in full view of their enemies."* (Revelation 11:12 Phillips)

At That Moment—*Earthquake*!

Revelation 11:13

> *"At the same time there was a terrible earthquake that destroyed a tenth of the city. Seven thousand people died in that earthquake, and everyone else was terrified and gave glory to the God of heaven."*

When the earthquake hits Jerusalem, the Antichrist will get out of there as fast as he is able. He will flee to the plains of Megiddo, Armageddon, to the security of his troops. His desire to rule the world and conquer the Lord is still undiminished. He is a complete egomaniac.

Liberation of Jerusalem

Verse 13. . .everyone else was terrified and gave glory to the God of heaven. The survivors are terrified. "This is a new note, for John [author of Revelation] has not [previously] spoken of sinners as being other than hardened by the judgments of God (*e.g.* 9:21). But these happenings were so striking and so clearly from God that even sinful men could not [refrain] from ascribing glory to him." [7] Jerusalem has been liberated of its oppressors. The temple still stands and the despairing 144,000 rejoice in the marvelous miracle they have just experienced.

GOD'S LAST JUDGMENT

THE SEVENTH TRUMPET/BOWL – THE ANNOUNCEMENT OF THE SECOND COMING OF JESUS CHRIST

SEVENTH TRUMPET Revelation 11:15-19

Place: Heaven

Revelation 11:15-19 The Announcement

[15] *"Then the seventh angel blew his trumpet, And there were loud voices shouting* ***in heaven****: 'The world has now become the Kingdom of our Lord and of his Christ, and he will reign forever and ever."*

[16] *The twenty-four elders sitting on their thrones before God fell with their faces to the ground and worshipped him.* [17] *And they said: "We give thanks to you, Lord God, the Almighty, the one who is and who always was, for now you have assumed your great power and have begun to reign.* [18] *The nations were filled with wrath, but now the time of your wrath has come. It is time to judge the dead and reward your servants the prophets, as well as your holy people, and all who fear your name, from the least to the greatest. It is time to destroy all who have caused destruction on the earth.* [19] *Then, in heaven, the temple of God, was opened and the ark of his covenant could be seen inside the temple. . .*

SEVENTH BOWL Revelation 16:17-21

Place: The Air

Revelation 16:17 The Announcement

[17] *"Then the seventh angel poured out his bowl into* ***the air****. And a mighty shout came from the throne in the temple, saying 'It is finished!'"*

Observations

The tone of these verses is one of *finality*. The final act on the world's stage as we know it today. The world will never be the same.

16:17. . . a mighty shout came from the throne in the temple [in heaven]. Who declares "*it is finished*?" ________________. These were the very words of Jesus on the cross. Both of these pronouncements have incredible meaning. By the way, what do you think "*a mighty shout*" from God would sound like?

Psalm 29:4 "The voice of the LORD is powerful; the voice of the LORD is majestic."

16:17. . . It is finished. The world under the power of Satan, man's rebellion against God, the kingdoms of this world have come to an end—God's new order, His perfect rule through His Son Jesus, has now begun; it is now factual. Jesus' Thousand Year Reign has begun.

11:15. . . there were loud voices shouting in heaven. At the sound of the 7th Trumpet the angels erupt into shouting because they realize that the Rock of Daniel 2:34-35, and 44 will fall at this time on the world empires, and His Kingdom will cover the whole earth. . . crushing all these kingdoms into nothingness. Christ's Kingdom will stand forever and ever.

Today during a sports event, even though the game has not quite ended, the spectators can see that victory is inevitable. They stand to their feet and claim the victory, "We won! We won! We won!" In like manner, the angels, like astute, discerning observers, *detect the point* in this conflict of the ages when the finality of complete victory sets in and unhesitatingly and exultantly proclaim the triumph of our Lord and of His Christ.

11:16. . . The twenty-four elders. In heaven these spiritual leaders of the church of Jesus Christ, of both Old Testament and New Testament, rejoice that the answer has finally come to the thousands and thousands who have prayed in faith, "*Thy Kingdom come, thy will be done on earth as it is in heaven.*" I'm sure that you and I will also fall on our faces with heartfelt thanksgiving to worship Him.

Revelation 1:4 "Grace and peace to you from the one who is, who always was, and who is still to come..."

11:17. . . Lord God, the Almighty, the one who is and who always was. This expression is used in other places in the book of Revelation. Read the verses in the margin. Underline the repeated phrase in each verse but is missing in this verse. Why do you think it is missing at this point in time? ____

____

Revelation 1:8 "I am the one who is, who always was, and who is still to come—the Almighty One"

Has the omission of five words ever had such significance? Jesus is all set to come! As in a drama on a great stage, the actors are all in their places ready to perform. The curtain begins to rise.

Revelation 4:8 "Holy, holy, holy is the Lord God, the Almighty—the one who always was, who is, and who is still to come."

11:18. . . The nations were filled with wrath, but now the time of your wrath has come. The Dragon, Satan, stirred up the wrath of the nations into a white-hot rage against the Believers and the Jewish people. As we have seen, rebel-man's persecution of God's people was one of the causes of the 3 ½ years of God's wrath towards them. The terrors of the Wrath of God have come to an end. God's enemies are about to receive the conclusive and *full* impact of God's terrible wrath.

11:18. . . It is time to judge the dead and reward your servants the prophets, as well as your holy people, and all who fear your name, from the least to the greatest. It is time to destroy all who have caused destruction on the earth. This verse lists three coming events;

Revelation 20:4 "And I saw the souls of those who had been beheaded for their testimony about Jesus and for proclaiming the word of God. They had not worshipped the beast or his statue, nor accepted his mark on their forehead or their hands. They all came to life again, and they reigned with Christ for a thousand years."

Herbert- "God's mill grinds slow but sure."

Revelation 15:3-4 "Great and marvelous are your works, O Lord God, the Almighty. Just and true are your ways, O King of the nations. Who will not fear you, Lord, and glorify you name? For you alone are holy. All nations will come and worship before you, for your righteous deeds have been revealed."

that will take place on God's timetable. Observe the word "*time*" used twice in this verse. *Kairos* is the Greek word for *time.* It "signifies a fixed or definite period" [V] because of the "necessity of the task at hand." [KW] The designated moment has come for God to accomplish the following three things:

- **Time. . .for the judging of the dead**. This is the judgment of those who are the *nekros*, the dead who have no hope of eternal life with God. This will take place at the Great White Throne Judgment as related in Revelation 20:11-15

- **Time. . .for rewarding God's servants**. The Believers have been resurrected at the Rapture and have received their rewards in heaven and are now at the point of coming back to earth with King Jesus. Therefore, this occasion of rewards is referring to the two prophets (witnesses), all the faithful 144,000 Christian Jews, and the resurrected Christian Jews who were martyred during the last 3 ½ years. Their resurrection and rewards ceremony will take place at the beginning of the Thousand- Year Reign of Christ. (Revelation 20:4)

- **Time. . .for *destroying* those who *destroy* the earth.** More than likely, this is specifically referring to the Antichrist, the False Prophet (Revelation 19:20), the Ten Kings (Revelation 19:11-15), and Satan, and all the demonic hosts of evil (Revelation 20:10).

  "*Who destroy the earth*" speaks of the destruction, ruin, waste and devastation these evil ones have caused throughout the earth. God will now reciprocate by paying them back in like manner. They will be destroyed; the Antichrist, the False Prophet and the Ten Kings at Jesus Coming; Satan and all fallen angels one thousand years later at the conclusion of Jesus' Thousand-Year Kingdom on earth. God has not forgotten the smallest injustice by any one of them.

THE SECRET OF THE TWO WITNESSES

These two spiritual giants will be human beings just like us. What is the secret of their great confidence in God? It is the "oil" that will flow through them. (Revelation 11:4) Oil is one of the biblical symbols for the Holy Spirit. And you, like them, can withstand harmful, satanic attempts on your physical and spiritual life when "*you are clothed with power from on High*". . .until your special work on this earth is completed, *teleo*. (Luke 24:49 RSV)

To be sure, the message and unwavering conviction of the two witnesses will be—Jesus Christ is Lord. (Philippians 2:11) This declaration of faith is non-negotiable. As a missionary to peoples beyond our shores, our life-giving message was Jesus Christ our Savior and Sovereign Lord. This is the mark of a Christian. As you hold Jesus up before others as Savior and Sovereign Lord, Jesus power will be released in your life and witness.

The following story is true and relates so well to the ministry of the two Hebrew witnesses. Observe what this courageous witness for Christ accomplished in a most spontaneous and natural way in his supposedly last minutes of life.

Christ's kingdom will be composed of Believers from every nation. "What a thrill, to live in this certainty! *Disciples will be made of all nations.* Though the work be hard, the end will justify every sacrifice. Tears shed on earth will be pearls in heaven. They that go forth with weeping, carrying the seed of the Gospel, '*Shall indeed come again with a shout of joy*,' bringing their sheaves [harvest] with them (Psalm 126:6).

E.P. Scott, a pioneer missionary to India, in one of his journeys to an unreached area, came upon a savage band on a war expedition. They seized him and pointed their spears at his heart. Feeling utterly helpless, not knowing what else to do, he drew out the violin he always carried with him and began to play and sing, in the native language: "All Hail the Power of Jesus' Name."

As the music and words of the song rang out, he closed his eyes, expecting death at any moment. But when nothing happened, even after the third stanza, he opened his eyes and was amazed to see that the spears had fallen from the hands of his captors, and tears filled their eyes. They invited him to their homes, and for several years he labored among them, winning many to Christ.

Amy Carmichael "We have all eternity to celebrate the victories, but only a few hours before sunset to win them."

I like to think of this experience as a parable of the coming kingdom. Those who bring the good tidings may not always be delivered from the spears of the enemy. Nevertheless, the name of Christ will someday prevail to the ends of the earth, and He shall be crowned Lord of all!" [8]

These are the powerful words that conquered the warrior's hearts. As you read, think about how the Holy Spirit impressed upon these sin darkened hearts the glorious majesty of King Jesus and His divine right over their lives.

All hail the power of Jesus' name!
Let angels prostrate fall;
Bring forth the royal diadem,
And crown him Lord of all.

Let every kindred, every tribe,
On this terrestrial ball,
To him all majesty ascribe,
And crown him Lord of all.

Ye chosen seed of Israel's race,
Ye ransomed from the fall,
Hail him who saves you by his grace,
And crown him Lord of all.

O, that with yonder sacred throng
We at his feet may fall!
We'll join the everlasting song,
And crown him Lord of all.

And crown him, crown him, crown him, crown him, and crown him Lord of all!

Edward Perronet

Tomorrow. . . every knee shall bow and proclaim that Jesus Christ is Lord! He will be crowned Lord of all.

Timeline covered in Lesson 14

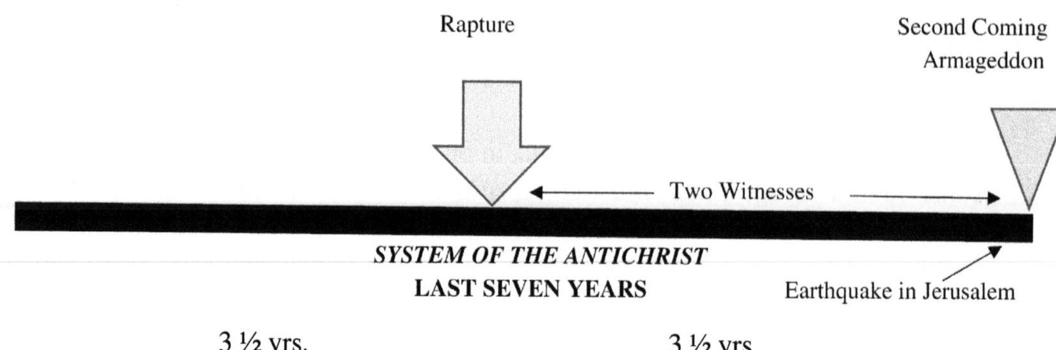

JESUS CHRIST KING OF THE NATIONS

Revelation 15:3

LESSON 15A | EVENT 7

JESUS CHRIST KING OF ALL KINGS AND LORD OF ALL LORDS
Revelation 19:16

No creature can stand before Him. All must bow before the overwhelming splendor of His presence.

THE SECOND COMING OF CHRIST AND THE ARMIES OF ARMAGEDDON

There have been many times in my ministry where I have felt the inadequacy of human expression and wished for the tongue of an angel. This is one of those times. A trait of a good interpreter of the Bible is the ability to step into the narrative and live it. This means that he is able to use all the five senses as well as the mind to comprehend the Scripture. He will see the action taking place; smell it; hear its sounds; and emotionally feel and experience the action of the account as it takes place, as an "I am there" feeling. In Lessons 15A and 15B I will depend heavily on your ability to visualize (in the spiritual-comprehension part of your mind) the biblical narratives of the Second Coming of Jesus Christ and Armageddon. Its glories, the devastation, the significance, the terror, and the majesty are truly transcendental, rising above common thought and expression.

"If our devotion of time and energy is more to what the world offers than to God's purposes, we may be among those needing repentance." [1]

You belong to one of the following three groups. **Circle** the Plot you belong to and discover what will be happening to you at the time of King Jesus' Coming and Armageddon. Hopefully, many of you have joined Plot 2—The Believers.

PLOT 1— THE WORLD SYSTEM OF THE ANTICHRIST

The Antichrist's Narrative

The world lies firmly in my grasp; I have total control of mankind. I have led the Ten Kings of my empire in the destruction of the harlot city. That ludicrous farce is not needed anymore. At my command the Ten Kings have obediently gathered a huge army and are looking to me, their supreme leader, to lead them into battle here in Israel. . .at, what do they call it? Oh yes, Armageddon.

Oh, great master Satan, you have given me two final tasks to accomplish, and these are the only obstacles that stand in the way for you to bring me to the heights of universal power over man and God. The first task I have taken care of; I have destroyed those two pesky, disgusting prophets. No one was able to kill them for 3 ½ years! The fools! The power of those Jews, I have to admit, was quite amazing. However, all the world saw the great power you gave me, my master, as they watched me slay those weaklings. It was rather disconcerting to see them come back to life and then disappear into heaven, but they're gone and out of the picture.

The earthquake that destroyed all my men in Jerusalem and my wonderful image in the court-yard on the temple mount was hard to take. But let the Jews bask in their liberation. It will be short lived as I have my armies ready to attack and take back the city. They don't stand a chance. My powers are greater than theirs.

So, here we are at this place called Armageddon, which engages me with the last and final obstacle—The Son of God. Uh, you will give me the victory as you have promised, your highness, master? Ah, yes indeed, this undertaking is nothing for you. The time has come, therefore, onward to victory. . .at Armageddon!

The Marriage Supper of the Lamb "… is a unifying starting point, like a new and perfect beginning of an eternity of glorious relationships in a God-directed for-ever existence." (from Lesson 9)

If you are not a born-again believer (and have survived thus far) find the Second Coming and Armageddon on **Timeline Two** (located at the end of Part One of this study book). **Write** Event **4** on the line by the asterisk (*_4_) below and to the left of "Armageddon." Review the following on both of the charts, Timeline One and Two:

- Event 1 where you marked your birth date.
- Event 2 which signifies that you were born during the time of The World System of the Antichrist.
- Event 3 will be the dreadful Wrath of God.
- Event 4 for you who will survive the Wrath of God, this lesson describes your participation at Armageddon.

PLOT 2—BELIEVERS

Zechariah 14:9 "The Lord will be king over the whole earth. On that day there will be one Lord, and His name the only name."

As a part of the great multitude of Christ's glorified followers in heaven, you have delighted in the Judgment Seat of Christ, and have been crowned, rewarded, and dressed in fine linen, white and clean. As the Bride of Christ you have been joined into a forever-bond with your Lord at the Marriage Supper of the Lamb. All of you who are called, chosen, and faithful have been conferred the position of kings and priests soon to reign with your Sovereign Lord on earth. (Revelation 17:14)

The Believer's Narrative

You have been receiving instructions concerning the departure from heaven and your ministry on earth. Having been informed of the vast human and demonic forces prepared to receive us in mortal combat, your excitement and joy runs high as we all understand the significance of this great Day of the Almighty. Christ Jesus the Lord, the King, has been crowned with many crowns. The time has come for Him to bring to completion the victory that He won on the cross and to sit on the throne of David in the temple of Jerusalem to rule the world in truth and righteousness.

reveille [D] —The sounding of a bugle early in the morning to awaken and summon persons in a camp or garrison.

The heavenly reveille begins with the sound of the Seventh Trumpet. Among the fervent acclamation and praise of heaven, the King's army assembles for battle. You will be participating in things that you never imagined yourself doing. Christ the King takes His position at the head of His heavenly hosts. This very day you will see Him perform great and mighty things in order to accomplish His eternal goals. What you are about to witness will fill you with awe and an overwhelming sense of gratitude to be positioned on Jesus' side of events.

Find the Second Coming and Armageddon on **Timeline Two** (located at the end of Part One of this study book). Write Event **7** on the line by the asterisk (*_7_) to the right of "2nd Coming of Christ Rev. 19."

PLOT 3—THE NATION ISRAEL

At this moment in time, the Christian Jews have been completely worn down because of their horrific suffering over the last 3 ½ years. Yet a more faithful and dedicated group of Christ-followers is unequaled. With infinite patience and loving trust they have committed their safe keeping to their heavenly Father. The miraculous earthquake which liberated the Christian Jews in Jerusalem was uplifting evidence of the imminent coming of King Jesus and their final deliverance. Their eyes constantly search the eastern skies for the sign of His Coming.

If you believe that you will be a Christian Israeli still alive on earth at the time of Jesus' Second Coming and Armageddon, you may write Event **5** on the line by the asterisk (*_5_) below and to the left of Armageddon on **Timeline Two** (located at the end of Part One of this study book). As a review, your Events are numbered like this:

- Event 1 – your birth
- Event 2 – you were born during the System of the Antichrist
- Event 3 – your salvation at the time of the Rapture
- Event 4 – your marvelous witness and possible martyrdom during the Wrath of God
- Event 5—your deliverance.

In this Lesson we will study:

Two Descriptions of Christ in the Book of Revelation
The Lord of the Church
Our Resplendent King
The Armies of Armageddon

TWO DESCRIPTIONS OF CHRIST IN THE BOOK OF REVELATION

THE LORD OF THE CHURCH (Revelation 1:13-16)

His Beauty

How do you picture Jesus in your mind? When last seen by the people of the world, Jesus hung, a lifeless body, on the cross. When last seen by His disciples, Jesus was clothed with a marvelous, glorified body.

From that time until the present, people have desired to know what Jesus looked like physically when He lived on earth. Psalm 45:2, a Messianic psalm, gives us the most informative picture we could possibly have of Jesus:

"*You are the most handsome of Adam's descendants.*" (ISV) "*You are the most handsome of all.*" (NLT)

The literal meaning of these words in the Hebrew language is: "*Beauty, thou art beautiful*" in other words, beauty itself in perfect beauty. Of all humans, Jesus was completely beautiful; he was "*altogether lovely*" (Song of Solomon 5:16). Jesus "*is the radiance of God's glory and the*

Let the beauty of Jesus be seen in me…His grace, His love, His purity.

exact representation of his being." (Hebrews 1:3 NIV) Jesus was the most handsome of all men of all times. How could it be otherwise? He is God.

The four Old Testament sacrifices demanded an animal without blemish. Jesus the Lamb of God was without blemish. In the sacrificial fire, the perfect animal was completely marred, and so was the Lamb, the most beautiful man who has ever walked upon the earth, in His sacrificial death.

1 Peter 1:18-19 (NIV) "For you know that it was not with perishable things such as silver and gold that you were redeemed from the empty way of life handed down to you from your forefathers, but with the precious blood of Christ, a lamb without blemish or defect."

Some have thought that Isaiah 53 is a picture of Jesus' physical appearance, but the content of the chapter shows it to be a description of Jesus in His sacrificial state. From the time Jesus went on trial before the Jewish leaders until He was nailed on a cross, He had been spit in the face, beaten with fists, repeatedly slapped, His beard torn out (Isaiah 50:6), tormented by being beaten while blindfolded, flogged mercilessly, and a crown of thorns put on His head. Isaiah 52:14 tells us that *"His face was so disfigured he seemed hardly human, and from his appearance, one would scarcely know he was a man."* Jesus was not born *disfigured.* Mob-like brutality disfigured Jesus so badly that His sagging body on the cross was bathed with blood from His head, upper body, hands, and feet.

Now add to Jesus' physical suffering the burden of bearing the sin of the whole world. *"God made him who had no sin, to be sin for us. . ."* (2 Corinthians 5:21 NIV) *"There was nothing beautiful or majestic about his appearance, nothing to attract us to him. . .we turned our back on him and looked the other way."* (Isaiah 53:2-3) No wonder Mary, at the tomb, did not recognize the risen Savior; He had a glorified body. His mutilated body had been healed, except for the scars of the cross which He intentionally bears as an eternal testimony of His great sacrifice. (John 20:27)

His Glory

In His exalted glorious state "*high and lifted up*" on the throne of His Father in heaven, Jesus is portrayed in Revelation 1:13-16 as inexpressibly beautiful! Breathtakingly majestic! The writer of Revelation uses earthly comparisons to help us visualize the displayed attributes of Jesus which, at His first advent, were veiled by His human body. **Circle** the words of comparison *as* and *like.*

Rule of thumb When "as" and "like" can be substituted for one another, they are a simile, a figure of speech which compares one thing with another.

Revelation 1:12-13, 20; 13-16

> 12 *". . .I saw seven gold lampstands.* 13 *And standing in the middle of the lampstands was someone like the Son of Man.* 20 *the seven lampstands are the seven churches."* [these are seven literal churches and also representative of all true churches.]
>
> 13 *"He* [Jesus] *was wearing a long robe with a gold sash across his chest.* 14 *His head and his hair were white like wool, as white as snow. And his eyes were like flames of fire.* 15 *His feet were like polished bronze refined in a furnace, and his voice thundered like mighty ocean waves. . .*16 *a sharp two-edged sword came from his mouth. And his face was like the sun in all its brilliance."*

This symbolic description portrays the attributes of Christ's deity, such as, His authority, power, omniscience, majesty, purity, holiness, and wisdom. In this vision Christ is portrayed as the High Priest and Sovereign Lord *"in the midst"* of His church. . .the heart, center, and life of His Body.

Upon reading the complete passage, including chapters 2 and 3, two concepts step forward. The first, King Jesus, in all His attributes seen in this vision, is present in every congregation that meets in His name, no matter how large or small. He praises them, He corrects them, He exhorts them, and He promises them eternal rewards. The second concept gained from this vision of Christ is that the church will never be overcome. No power, no threats, persecution, famine, or death, no assault by man or the devil has ever destroyed God's people. It has never happened and never will because there is no power in all creation that can extinguish the power of the Lord working in and through His church. (Romans 8:31-39)

The church "is victorious only in the Victor. Everything centers in His person." [2]

Among all the endearing relationships the Believer enjoys with Jesus, every Believer should have firmly impressed on his mind this picture of Jesus at this present time—The King—in all His majesty and splendor, His glory which was veiled by his humanity. And we get to know and serve Him.

"Then I saw" Each segment begins with: "I saw." Revelation 19:11, 17, 19; 20:1, 4, 11, 12; 21:1

OUR RESPLENDENT KING (Revelation 19:11-16)

The apostle John was writing the book of Revelation and had just finished writing verse 10 of chapter nineteen, when abruptly heaven opened to him in another vision. It revealed King Jesus at His Second Coming which is described in 2 Thessalonians 2:8 as *"the splendor of His coming"*. Each segment of this account begins with the words: *"Then I saw."* You may wonder what it was like for John to have actually *seen* this unimaginable vision. You can see it too as you visualize the narrative. But bear in mind, in the future when this takes place, you will be living the reality as a participant in the Second Coming of Christ!

We need to think together, so again, I ask you to make five observations from the upcoming verses. There are so many things to see that you may want to make more observations on a separate notepaper.

This time I would like to influence your observations concerning the way you see Jesus in this Scripture. Let me tell you a story. One Easter, Herb and I visited a cathedral. We walked directly to the main display which was a deteriorating plaster figure of Christ lying in a coffin with a see-through plastic cover. It was the most pathetic thing I had ever seen. The figure had bloody wounds painted all over it and a crown of thorns on its head. The body was emaciated. My eyes were drawn to the face which portrayed in death utter defeat and helplessness. People knelt before the casket weeping and worshipping the figure. I was dismayed at the unbiblical concept that these people held of the Lord. Year after year they carry this coffin through the streets at Easter. This is their understanding of who Jesus is.

Upon reading the story in the text, you can better understand the sense of fulfillment and joy that a missionary experiences when he or she teaches the biblical concept of Jesus to people who have never heard the Word of God; and then, to watch their eyes shine as the Holy Spirit enlightens their understanding.

We were told that there was another statue of Jesus sitting on a throne as King. Good, let's go see that one! But to our disappointment, we saw the same bloody, thorn-crowned, emaciated figure sitting on a throne. The only changes were a long purple cloth wrapped around its waist, a scepter in its hand, and eyes open looking pathetically towards the heavens. This is not the Christ of the Bible!

Do you have a Biblical concept of Jesus?

Now that you have been *influenced*, make your observations based on a true representation of King Jesus from God's Word. Perhaps you would like to include some thoughts on what the symbolism suggests. Be sure to notice the predominant tone or atmosphere of the following verses.

Revelation 19:11-16

> [11] *"Then I saw heaven opened, and a white horse was standing there. Its rider was named Faithful and True, for he judges fairly and wages a righteous war.* [12] *His eyes were like flames of fire, and on his head were many crowns* [diadems]. *A name was written on him that no one understood except himself.* [13] *He wore a robe dipped in blood, and his title was the Word of God.* [14] *The armies of heaven, dressed in the finest of pure white linen, followed him on white horses.* [15] *From his mouth came a sharp sword to strike down the nations. He will rule them with an iron rod. He will release the fierce wrath of God, the Almighty, like juice flowing from a winepress.* [16] *On his robe at his thigh was written this title: King of all kings and Lord of all lords."*

Your observations
1. ______________________________
2. ______________________________
3. ______________________________
4. ______________________________
5. ______________________________

KING JESUS

Check out other instances of heavenly horses. 2 Kings 2:11; 6:16-17; Psalm 68:17

Verse 11. . .a white horse was standing there. If you know anything about horses, you would have loved to have seen the look on the apostle John's face when in his vision heaven burst open, and there, right in front of him, was this huge, magnificent horse pawing and prancing, nostrils flaring. I cannot give you an explanation for this *ethereal* horse (you will be mounted on one also.) However, from the nature of the action to follow, it seems to be *real*. Who is the undisputed rider of this horse? ____________________

In another lesson we studied about the Great Tribulation which includes the Six Seals and takes place before the Rapture. The vision of the First Seal portrays a white horse and rider which are definitely symbolic along with his evil companions (war, famine, disease, and death) on the other three horses of Revelation 6:1-8.

Do not confuse King Jesus regally mounted on His white horse here in Revelation 19:11 with the rider of the white horse of Revelation 6:1-2. Do you remember what the rider of the First

Seal represents? ____

__________________ These two riders are two very different persons. Their only similarity is a white horse. The rider of the First Seal represents both the World System of the Antichrist and the person of the Antichrist.

Revelation 6:1-2 "As I watched, the Lamb broke the first of the seven seals on the scroll. Then I heard one of the four living beings say with a voice like thunder, 'Come!' I looked up and saw a white horse standing there. Its rider carried a bow, and a crown [stephanos] was placed on his head. He rode out to win many battles and gain the victory."

JESUS' NAMES AND TITLES

Verse 11. . . Its rider was named ____________________ and _________________. What would it be like to have as the highest leader in government a person that is categorically trustworthy? Or one in whom falsehood is non-existent? King Jesus is the Truth and He is to be trusted absolutely!

Verse 11. . .for He judges fairly and wages a righteous war. Jesus has, by His shed blood, opened the pathway to God. Until this moment of time, the door of salvation has stood open for man to approach God's "*throne of grace*," (Hebrews 4:16) and to find mercy and forgiveness of sin through Jesus, "*the perfect sacrifice for our sins*." (Hebrews 9:14) Based on God's foreknowledge that no one will turn to Him at this time, the door of salvation has closed; the line has been drawn. Those that are on the inside are eternally secure in their salvation; those who are on the outside are eternally lost.

"*For He judges fairly*" indicates that the time has come for King Jesus to descend to earth to judge the world in righteousness. Perfect truth, fairness, justice, and mercy will be executed with absolute integrity in His Kingdom**.** No wrong doing will escape the eyes "*which were like flames of fire*." The time has come for Christ to make war against the Antichrist, who gives a human face to unrighteous. Beware you blind, depraved men of the earth who oppose God Himself; the just Judge is coming!

Look closely at verse 15. Who will King Jesus "*rule with an iron rod*?"_______________ We will take up this subject in Lesson 16—the Judgment of the Nations.

Verse 12. . . A _________________ was written on him that no one understood except himself. Can we fully comprehend the meaning of any of the names of Jesus? Do Jesus and His Father enjoy an intimate depth of understanding of their many names that is beyond our limited, human comprehension? Even with the best help that Bible scholars have to offer, "The mind fails to grasp the innermost significance of the Person of Christ, which eludes all efforts to bring it within the terms of human knowledge. Only the Son of God can understand the mystery of his own being." [3]

Perhaps we will one day share this unknown name of Jesus. Take note of the promise given to the overcomers in Revelation 3:12 (RSV): "*I* [Jesus] *will write on him the name of my God, and the name of the city of my God, the new Jerusalem which comes down from my God out of heaven, and <u>my own new name</u>.*"

Verse 13. . . his title was the ______________________________. Words, for one thing, are the expressions of the will. Christ's words are expressions of the will of His Father.

(John 17:8) Jesus is the perfect expression of God. (John 1:1) His words are living and active. (Hebrews 4:12) They are so powerful that with them He spoke the creation into existence. (Genesis 1:1-27; John 1:3) Jesus' title is the Word of God because He *speaks* the will of God.

Beware, all those who are waiting to war against Him! *"From his mouth came a sharp sword to strike down the nations. . . He will release the fierce wrath of God, the Almighty, like juice flowing from a winepress." God, the Almighty* literally means "God of the armies" expressing "the Lord's sovereign rule as king and commander *over every created force. . .*" [4] Just think of all that statement encompasses.

Verse 16. . . on his robe at his thigh was written this title: ______________________________ ________ and ____ On Jesus' head *"were* ***many*** *crowns."* These are diadems signifying his boundless sovereignty as king over all kingdoms. All earthly kings will be deposed. King Jesus assumes His rightful position on earth. He is now the *only* King of the *only* Kingdom. Jesus has been Lord to His church, now He becomes Lord of all.

Using the following words, would you like to join me at this time to confidently declare Jesus as our praiseworthy King?

> *"Now to the King eternal, immortal, invisible, the only God, be honor and glory forever and ever. Amen."* (1 Timothy 1:17 NASB)

Verse 13. . .He wore a robe dipped in blood. The blood is Christ's own blood. The Greek word for *dipped* is *bapto* and means to "dye by dipping." This signifies that King Jesus is clothed in a robe dyed by dipping in blood. This is not the blood of His enemies. That is still future at this point in time.

John 8:23-24
He said to them, "You are from below, I am from above; you are of this world, I am not of this world I told you that you would die in your sins, for you will die in your sins unless you believe that I am he [the Christ.]

The apostle John was told by one of the elders in Revelation 5 to look at Jesus: "*Stop weeping! Look, the Lion of the tribe of Judah, the heir to David's throne, has won the victory. He is worthy to open the scroll and its seven seals."* When John looks he saw: "*a Lamb standing, as though it had been slain*," a sacrificed lamb still bearing the marks of His crucifixion. (Revelation 5:6 RSV) Before your descent to earth, you will look with awe at your powerful King, the Lion, ready to take possession of His inheritance, and you will also behold Him as the sacrificial Lamb, arrayed in a crimson robe dyed with His own blood.

His crimson robe is an everlasting remembrance of His blood-bought right to the throne of the universe. To us, who will reign with Him, it serves as a constant reminder that He is our Savior-King. His blood has forever separated us to Himself. However, to the waiting armies of the world, it serves as a testimony of their willful rejection of the blood that was shed for them; they could have had eternal life, but they have chosen the way of death.

Patterson expresses King Jesus' appearance before the assembled powers of earth in the following manner:

> "[Jesus'] garments are stained with blood. It is the blood of Calvary and of his saints, which this guilty world has shed. It is the blood this apostate world has trampled underfoot, and counted it an accursed thing. This blood of Calvary is now the most awful witness of the guilt of man. It has never been repented of by the world. Every rejecter of Christ has thereby, as well as by his affiliation with the enemies of God, become a guilty accessory after the fact." [5]

All sinners are responsible for the crimson robe worn by King Jesus.

THE ARMIES OF ARMAGEDDON

THE KING'S ARMY

Verse 14. . .The armies of heaven, dressed in the finest of pure white linen, followed him on white horses. Satan's forces assembled in Israel will most certainly involve not only humans but also demons. What a colossal war is about to take place! King Jesus' army most certainly not only includes angels, who counteract the demons, but also includes glorified Believers as this verse implies.

These glorified Believers of heaven's armies are mentioned earlier in this same chapter.

Revelation 19:8

> "*She* [the Bride of Christ] *has been given the finest of pure white linen to wear. For the fine linen represents the good deeds of God's holy people.*"

Underline the words from this verse that correspond exactly to the glorified Believers of King Jesus' army in verse 14. Who are these people in 19:8? ______________________________ ______________

No one can mistake the wearer arrayed in "*the finest of pure white linen*" to be other than the Bride of Christ who now reigns with King Jesus. Where He goes, they go.

Jude 1:14-15
"Listen! The Lord is coming with countless thousands of his holy ones to execute judgment on the people of the world."

At this moment, our magnificent God and King sits on His great white charger. You too are mounted on a white horse. With a valiant heart, you are eager to follow the King into the greatest battle that has ever taken place. King Jesus, the redeemed saints of all the ages, and millions of angelic beings make up the heavenly army, and what an army it is!

This would be a good time to thank God for His loving-kindness for choosing you to belong to the army of heaven and not to the one on earth which will soon be consumed by vultures.

THE INVITATION AND THE PREDICTION

Revelation 19:17-18

> *"Then I saw an angel standing in the sun, shouting to the vultures flying high in the sky; "Come! Gather together for the great banquet God has prepared. Come and eat*

the flesh of kings, generals, and strong warriors; of horses and their riders; and of all humanity, both free and slave, small and great."

Do you ever read ahead in a book to find out the outcome of some chilling situation? That is exactly what these verses do. How does this invitation to the vultures foretell the outcome of Armageddon? ____

This banquet will basically take place geographically in Israel involving the international forces of the Antichrist and the Ten Kings. It will also include many across the world who will suffer death due to the forces of nature that will be unleashed as never before seen in the history of mankind.

Notice the irony. In the first part of Revelation 19, we are told that all of the glorified Believers in heaven are invited to the Marriage Feast of the Lamb, at which they will collectively enjoy communion with their Savior. In the latter part of this same chapter, we read about the great army of the Antichrist which will be gathered together at another *feast*, but in this instance, they will be the menu.

THE ANTICHRIST'S ARMY

Revelation 16:13-14

> *"And I saw three evil spirits that looked like frogs leap from the mouths of the dragon* [Satan], *the beast, and the false prophet. They are demonic spirits who work miracles and go out to all rulers of the world to gather them for battle against the Lord on that great judgment day of God the Almighty."*

Revelation 19:19

> *"Then I saw the beast and the kings of the world and their armies gathered together to fight against the one sitting on the horse and his army."*

Psalm 2:2-3
"The kings of the earth prepare for battle; the rulers plot together against the Lord and against his anointed one [Jesus]. 'Let's break [God's] chains,' they cry, 'and free ourselves from slavery to God.'"

Read the two verses above, **underline** and then **write** what the purpose is for this gathering of God's enemies. ____

Identify the assembled characters on earth in Revelation 19:19. The ____________________, and the ____________________________________, and their ______________________.

We know who the beast, the Antichrist, and the Ten Kings are, but it is necessary, at this point in our study, to understand the utter depravity of the souls of the men who belong to this evil intentioned army. Jesus is coming to reign, but they do not welcome Him. Man stands with Satan to such a degree that he is willing to battle against God with the objective of overcoming God's universal reign. Man's mind is consumed by demonic deception.

The souls of these men have reached the point of a reprobate, totally given over to sin. Reprobate is described by such words as rejected, a castaway, loathsome, and an utterly vile person. A reprobate has an "abominable mind, a mind to be abhorred by God and man." [KW] This is a mind that does not distinguish between right and wrong. It is rejected by God.

Reprobates are those who caused God to destroy every living being outside of Noah's ark.

Genesis 6:5-7 (NIV)

> *"The Lord saw how great man's wickedness on the earth had become, and that every inclination of the thoughts of his heart was only evil all the time. The Lord was grieved that he had made man on the earth, and his heart was filled with pain. So the Lord said, "I will wipe mankind, whom I have created, from the face of the earth—men and animals. . ."*

Neglect:
To fail to give proper attention to; to be careless of; habitual lack of concern; to make light of something as unimportant.

Romans 1:18-32 is especially applicable to these reprobates. God said three times:

- ". . .*God gave them over* [abandoned them] *in the lusts of their hearts to impurity*" (verse 24)
- ". . .*God gave them over* [abandoned them] *to degrading passions"* (verse 26)
- *"And just as they did not see fit to acknowledge God any longer, God gave them over* [abandoned them] *to a depraved* [reprobate] *mind. . .*" (verse 28)

Such are the men gathered to fight against God. But, how did they get this way? In their sinful state they crossed the *unseen line.*

Bear with me, dear friend. This poem pierces my heart every time I read it. It certainly is cause for serious reflection. Men are not always aware, in their neglect of God, that they have crossed an invisible, fatal line.

Hebrews 2:3 (NKJV)

> *"How shall we escape if we neglect so great a salvation. . .?"*

Let not your tombstone bear the inscription, "____________________________ crossed God's hidden line, therefore, God gave him/her over to ______________________________ ___________________"

The Hidden Line
Dr. J. Addison Alexander

"There is a time, we know not when,
A place we know not where,
That marks the destiny of men,
For glory or despair.

There is a line by us unseen,
That crosses every path;
The hidden boundary between
God's patience and His wrath.

To pass that limit is to die,
To die as if by stealth;
It does not quench the beaming eye,
Or pale the glow of health.

The conscience may be still at ease,
The spirits light and gay;
That which is pleasing still may please,
And care be thrust away.

But on that forehead God has set
Indelibly a mark—
Unseen by man for man as yet
Is blind and in the dark.

And still the doomed man's path below
May bloom as Eden bloomed—
He did not, does not, will not know,
Or feel that he is doomed.

He knows, he feels that all is well,
And every fear is calmed;
He lives, he dies, he wakes in hell,
Not only doomed but damned.

Oh, where is this mysterious bourne [boundary]
By which our path is crossed;
Beyond which God Himself hath sworn,
That he who goes is lost?

How far may men go on in sin?
How long will God forbear?
Where does hope end and where begin
The confines of despair?

An answer from the skies is sent;
'Ye that from God depart,
While it is called today, repent,
And harden not your heart

Judas, upon making his decision to betray Christ, stepped across the hidden line. (John 17:12)

For the multitudes at Armageddon this is their last night on earth. Judgment will come in the morning.

JESUS CHRIST KING OF ALL KINGS AND LORD OF ALL LORDS

Revelation 19:16

LESSON 15B

JESUS CHRIST THE GLORY
James 2:1

Mine eyes have seen the glory of the coming of the Lord; He is trampling out the vintage where the grapes of wrath are stored; He hath loosed the fateful lightning of His terrible swift sword; His truth is marching on.

Julia Ward Howe

EVENT 7

THE SECOND COMING OF CHRIST AND ARMAGEDDON

We will study in this lesson:

- The Seventh Trumpet/Bowl Judgment
  - The Heavenly Vision—The Throne of God
  - The Second Coming of King Jesus and Armageddon
  - The Filling
  - Vindicated
  - The Great Kneeling Down

THE SEVENTH TRUMPET/BOWL JUDGMENT

SEVENTH TRUMPET
Place: in heaven (the temple)

Revelation 11:15, 19

[15] *Then the seventh angel blew his trumpet. . .*
[19] *"Then, in* ***heaven****, the temple of God was opened and the ark of his covenant could be seen inside the temple. Lightning flashed, thunder crashed and roared, and there was an earthquake and a terrible hailstorm."*

SEVENTH BOWL
Place: in the air (the temple)

Revelation 16:17- 21 (NASB)

[17]*"Then the seventh angel poured out his bowl into the* ***air****. And a mighty* [megas] *shout came from the throne in the temple, saying,*

'It is finished!'

[18] *And there were flashes of lightning and sounds and peals of thunder; and there was a great* [megas] *earthquake, such as there had not been since man came to be upon the earth, so great* [megas] *an earthquake was it, and so mighty.* [19] *The great* [megas] *city was split into three parts, and the cities of the nations fell. Babylon the great* [megas] *was remembered before God, to give her the cup of the wine of His fierce wrath.* [20] *And every island fled away, and the mountains were not found.* [21] *And huge* [megas] *hailstones, about one hundred pounds each, came down from heaven upon men; and men blasphemed God because of the plague of the hail, because its plague was extremely severe* [megas]."

Observations

Where is the temple of God in Revelation 11:19? ______________________________
Where is the ark of the Covenant located? ______________________________
Where did the "*mighty shout*" come from in 16:17? ______________________________
Underline the words *in heaven, temple of God, ark of his Covenant*, and *temple* in 11:19.
Underline the words *the throne in the Temple* in 16:17.

16:17-21. . .You noticed something interesting in these verses, the insertion in brackets of the Greek expression *megas* which means "exceedingly great" in English. The Lord speaking through his servant John uses this series of superlatives to impress us with the excessive or powerful degree and intensity of the things mentioned. There are seven. Find them and **circle** them. The different Bible translations use synonyms such as great, mighty, tremendous, severe, enormous, and exceedingly severe for the seven *megas*. All this catastrophic phenomena takes place at Jesus' Second Coming.

Underline the phrases that speak of the magnitude of the earthquake (notice it is singular not multiple earthquakes.) Think about it. Also, what magnitude of a storm would it take to produce 100 pound hailstones?

Revelation 11:19 and **Revelation 16:17**
The apostle John did not write his typical *"I saw"* used some 38 times in the book of Revelation. Rather in 11:19 he says: *"could be seen."* We are going to consider these two verses as a vision given to mankind followed immediately by the catastrophic phenomena that accompanies Christ at His Second Coming. Revelation 16:18-21 should be read with Revelation 19:11-18. This episode will be given in narrative form.

THE HEAVENLY VISION—THE THRONE OF GOD (Revelation 11:19 and 16:17)

Satan has reached the moment in time to execute his ultimate goal: the battle to once and for all defeat King Jesus and to replace God's Eternal Kingdom of Righteousness with his demonic, unrighteous rule over the world.

The miraculous resurrection of the two Jewish prophets and the devastating earthquake in Jerusalem have just taken place.

Psalm 2:2-3 "The kings of the earth prepare for battle..."

Hundreds of thousands have gathered from the Ten Regions of the world for the final conflict. The place has been selected at Megiddo on the Plain of Esdraelon in Israel. There is such a great multitude that their camps stretch from 180 to 200 miles in length. (Revelation 14:20) A vast army indeed! They see the debris across the land still visible from the defeat of Gog and his armies 3 ½ years earlier; it makes them shudder at the sight of such complete destruction.

In our imagination, you and I are going to sneak into the enemy's camp to watch them in their last minutes on earth. We can see the Antichrist rallying the eager troops with his bravado, great speeches, and false promises. He reeks with the foul smell of his decayed soul. The False

Prophet stands at his side gazing at him with that ever-present-sickly-pious smile on his face. The time for Jesus' Second Coming is minutes away so we don't want to stick around here for very long.

The last five minutes

It is almost dawn. Suddenly, the world is illuminated by a startling sight. We look up at the sky and see the temple of God in heaven. Jaws drop, all eyes are riveted on the ark of the covenant—the very throne of God! Then we hear a mighty shout coming from God's throne saying, "***It is finished***!"

1 Samuel 4:4 "...the Ark of the Covenant of the Lord of Heaven's Armies, who is enthroned between the cherubim."

The heavens close as abruptly as they opened, the vision is gone, and darkness prevails once more. In fear and uneasiness men whisper, terror choking their words, "What was that?" "It was the throne of God!" "What does it mean?" "We are doomed!"

Meanwhile, the Christian Jews in Jerusalem know exactly what this glorious vision signifies. Jesus had recently told them "*Look, I will come as unexpectedly as a thief! Blessed are all who are watching for me. . .*" (Revelation 16:15) They are so few now. They encourage one another saying, "See! This is His sign that He is coming! Hold fast! Be faithful! The King is coming!"

The vision will be discernible to the Antichrist's followers and to the Jews alike. To the believing Jews it means life. Their King is coming to deliver them from their enemies. To the Unbelievers it will be a warning of doom.

Hebrews 9:24, 11-12 "He [Christ] did not go into the earthly place of worship...He has entered that great, perfect sanctuary in heaven... Once for all time He took blood into the Most Holy Place, but not the blood of goats and calves. He took His own blood, and with it He secured our salvation forever."

The vision consists of a single focal point in heaven—the heavenly ark of the covenant inside the temple. All earth people are looking at the throne of God in His heavenly temple. This revelation, at this moment of time, is stunning.

What, exactly, will earth dwellers see? What significance does this vision have at this moment of time? Can it be that when the people of the earth will see the ark of the covenant in the temple of God, they will be looking directly at the blood of Jesus on the mercy seat? Absolutely!

As the high priest sprinkled the mediatory blood of sacrifice, the atonement for sin, on the mercy seat in the Old Testament, accordingly on Easter morning Jesus ascended to heaven where He entered the true and perfect temple. He proceeded directly to the Holy of Holies, to the ark of the covenant, the very throne of God, and placed His sacred, mediatory blood, the perfect sacrifice for the sin of mankind, upon the mercy seat. (Exodus 25:22; Hebrews 9:11-14, 24-26)

This vision is a public manifestation of God's faithfulness and fulfilling of His covenant promises to redeem mankind. What mankind would not believe has been revealed to them in the most conclusive manner possible at the end of this Present Age.

And as earth people look, they hear a mighty shout from the Throne, saying: "***It is finished***!"

This is God's declaration that this Present Age has terminated; a new order begins. The heavens close as abruptly as they opened, the vision is gone, and darkness prevails once more. The door

Revelation 21:3 (NASB) "And I heard a loud voice from the throne, saying, "Behold, the tabernacle of God is among men, and He shall dwell among them, and they shall be His people, and God Himself shall be among them."

is closed! Mankind will face the consequences of their own choosing. Earth dwellers have rejected the shed blood of God's Son and they have shed the blood of God's children, as a consequence, they must now shed their own unholy blood. The King of kings and Lord of lords is on the way to establish His Kingdom on the earth!

THE SECOND COMING OF KING JESUS AND ARMAGEDDON

The last page of this lesson is the completed chart "The Seven Trumpet and the Seven Bowl Judgments—Revelation 8-9, 15-16, 11."

The following narration takes place as one divine Event. These verses, taken from different versions of the Bible, describe these catastrophic events: Zechariah 14:4; Psalm 18:15; Isaiah 24:18b-20; Ezekiel 43:2; Psalm 18:12 (NIV); Revelation 19:15; Zechariah 14:12; Revelation 19:20; Revelation 19:21; also 2 Thessalonians 2:8. The Scriptures are in italics.

two minutes
After seeing this heavenly vision, the realization of impending death certainly will penetrate even the most unbelieving heart. Satan knows this, so he urges the Antichrist to divert the focus back to himself. The Antichrist quickly responds, and a shout goes up, drawing the attention of the masses out of their state of shock back to their original plan of action. Their deafening chant resonates mile after mile throughout the battle lines: "*Who is as great as the beast? Who is able to fight against him?*" (Revelation 13:4) The entire army is ready for battle and turns to face the east.

0 minutes
The sun is just ready to break the horizon. . .a long, loud trumpet blast is heard. It is the Seventh Trumpet! The "who" question of their chant is resolved. The seventh angel empties his Bowl into the air.

The signal is given and the massive army surges forward. Their blood curdling yells reach the ears of the Christian Jews in Jerusalem. The first warriors breach the city gates. The Jews valiantly throw themselves into the seemingly hopeless battle. And then. . .the pendulum swings.

The earth beneath the fighting mass literally "*splits apart, making a wide valley running from east to west.*" The escaping Jews rush away from the invaders through this valley to safety.

Thunder crashed and rolled across the continents. The atmosphere of earth is charged by thousands of violent electrical storms! The entire earth reels and rocks with the impact of a great earthquake—the most devastating since people were placed on the earth!

The harlot city, referred to as Babylon, split into three sections separated by deep cracks. This is God's final touch of judgment on the ruins of the wicked city. Cities around the world crumble, creating mountains of rubble where once they stood!

Gigantic tsunamis roll over the islands causing them to disappear completely. "*The bottom of the sea could be seen, and the foundations of the earth were laid bare. . .at the blast of the breath of His nostrils.*" The mountains seem to twist, turn, rise, fall. . . until they implode; not a mountain can be found!

"Destruction falls like rain from the heavens; the foundations of the earth shake. The earth is broken up. It has utterly collapsed; it is violently shaken. The earth staggers like a drunk. It trembles like a tent in a storm. It falls and will not rise again, for the guilt of its rebellion is very heavy."

Our descent. . .*"Then the Lord my God will come, and all his holy ones with him."* (Zechariah 14:5)

The Euphrates River is dried up; evil has been removed; the royal way of the kings is prepared. Just as the sun breaks the horizon at the river, out of its brilliance emanates King Jesus. *"Suddenly, the glory of the God of Israel appeared from the east. The sound of His coming was like the roar of rushing waters, and the whole landscape shone with His glory."*

Earth and sky fill with majesty. Almighty God King Jesus! The Believer-kings dressed in white linen, astride white horses riding in His wake. The earth cowers and trembles at the roar of millions of wings like a thousand thunder storms as angelic beings advance swiftly over the land. This glorious host comes like the wind; their feet scarcely touching the ground. Their destination—the Mount of Olives. This is the Great Day of God Almighty!" [1]

"*Out of the brightness of His presence clouds advanced, with hailstones and bolts of lightning.*" Hailstones weighing one hundred pounds fell from the sky onto the people below! Rebel-men curse God as they die from the savage blows!

The armies of the world are terrified at the sight of the entire eastern sky ablaze with the brilliance of the Lord of glory! In the blinding light they panic and begin slaying one another. The "*sharp sword from the mouth*" of King Jesus smites the enemy. The rebels "*become like walking corpses, their flesh rots away; their eyes rot in their sockets, and their tongues rot in their mouths.*" The battlefield appears like a great winepress of God's wrath; the blood of the ungodly runs like a river, mile after mile.

The presumed, more-than-mortal Antichrist, and his accomplice the False Prophet cringe and quake. The splendor of King Jesus pins them to the spot. With the breath of His mouth they are consumed; their great power wasting away into nothingness. "*The beast* [the Antichrist] *was captured, and with him the false prophet who did mighty miracles on behalf of the beast—miracles that deceived all who had accepted the mark of the beast and who worshiped his statue. Both the beast and his false prophet were thrown alive into the fiery lake of burning sulfur*" . . ."where torment never ceases and from which none return." [2]

"And the vultures all gorged themselves on the dead bodies." The souls of the dead descend into the bowels of the bottomless pit to wait for their final judgment. Every demon is swept up and cast into the abyss.

The vultures "For them it is a banquet unsurpassed—all kinds of flesh, from that of the kings and mighty men down to that of horses and slaves." [3]

"Then I [John] *saw an angel coming down from heaven with the key to the bottomless pit and a heavy chain in his hand. He seized the dragon—that old serpent, who is the devil, Satan—and bound him in chains for a thousand years. The angel threw him into the bottomless pit, which he then shut and locked so Satan could not deceive the nations anymore until the thousand years were finished. Afterward he must be released for a little while."* (Revelation 20:1-3)

Plot 1, the World System of the Antichrist, has been utterly destroyed, *never* to rise again.

"The world has now become the Kingdom of our Lord and of his Christ, and he will reign forever and ever." (Revelation 11:15)

And as suddenly as it all started, it was finished.

THE FILLING

The Stone Kingdom
"*But the stone that struck the image became a great mountain and filled the whole earth.*" (Daniel 2:34-35)

The power of evil has been removed from the earth and the effect from this is immediately felt world-wide. What do you think the world will feel like in the total absence of satanic power? __

____

Numbers 14:21 (NKJV) "but truly, as I live, all the earth shall be filled with the glory of the Lord."

The reservoir of putrid, sickening, slime from which mankind drank for centuries has been completely drained and the pure, holy, life-giving, energizing waters of perfect goodness, like a torrent, flood not only the reservoir of earth, but the entire universe. It is the glory of King Jesus!

The Prince of Peace has come! His peace fills the earth. The Giver of Joy has come! He fills the earth with joy. The Truth has come! He fills the earth with truth. Perfect Goodness has come! He fills the earth with goodness. The Life has come! He fills the earth with life and health. Jesus "*fills all things everywhere with Himself.*" (Ephesians 1:23)

VINDICATED!

But most of all, I like to think that in the face of all. . .

the scoffers, atheists, doubters, skeptics, cynics, unbelievers. . .

the vile, the corrupt, the immoral, the murderers, indulgers in witchcraft, idolaters, liars. . .

the proud, the self-aggrandizing, the hypocrites, the foul mouthed blasphemers of the Holy God, and all who neglect or ignore the goodness of God and His most worthy Son Jesus, the Father, and the Son, and the Holy Spirit have been vindicated. God is who He is and mankind has been convinced of that. . .!

THE GREAT KNEELING DOWN!

Philippians 2:9-11

> *". . .God elevated him to the place of highest honor and gave him the name above all other names, that at the name of Jesus every knee should bow, in heaven and on earth and under the earth* [the abyss], *and every tongue confess that Jesus Christ is Lord, to the glory of God the Father."*

This is the long awaited moment you, and I, and all true worshipers of God will cherish forever. Every knee will bow at Jesus' name and every tongue will confess in truth that "*Jesus Christ is Lord, to the glory of God the Father.*" What a glorious moment this will be. I dare say that you and I will find ourselves not only kneeling but prostrate in adoration before His majesty. We will hardly be able to contain our joy.

> "On the lips of those who belong to God, this will be a willing, continuing, and loving declaration of allegiance and adoration. For those who have rejected Him, the confession will be unwilling but irresistible, a compelled acknowledgment of Jesus Christ as the sovereign Lord of the universe by those under His immutable judgment. . .Even the damned demons, including Satan, will have no choice but to agree with and confess the reality that Jesus Christ is Lord." [4]

Jesus the King is enthroned upon the praises of His creation. An earthly king basks in the adulation of his subjects, but to the contrary, Jesus' subjects bask in the radiated glories of their divine Monarch.

You will actually see the fulfilling of God's purpose for His creation which is to recognize and confess the lordship of His Son. Because Jesus was incarnated as a man, sinful humankind has considered Him just that and nothing more. But the core of the Christian faith is the acknowledgment that Jesus Christ as God and Man is Lord of all.

> "To proclaim the sovereign lordship of His Son is the greatest glory that can be given to God the Father. . .that is the supreme objective and fulfillment of the Father's divine will as He demonstrates His perfect love for the Son." [5]

Revelation 5:13

> *"And then I heard every creature in heaven and on earth and under the earth and in the sea. They sang: "Blessing and honor and glory and power belong to the One sitting on the throne and to the Lamb forever and ever."*

Timeline covered in Lesson 15A and 15B

SECOND COMING

RAPTURE

"WRATH OF GOD"

SYSTEM OF THE ANTICHRIST
LAST 3 ½ YEARS

ARMAGEDDON

JESUS CHRIST THE GLORY

James 2:1

The Seven Trumpet /Bowl Judgments—Revelation 8-9, 15-16, 11

Environment and Universe				Demon World		Consummation
1st	**2nd**	**3rd**	**4th**	**5th**	**6th**	**7th**
				WOE	**WOE**	**WOE**
8:7; 16:2	8:8-9; 16:3	8:10-11; 16:4-7	8:12-13; 16:8-9	9:1-12; 16:10-11	9:13-20 16:12-16	11:15-19 16:17-21
Where? on the earth	the sea	rivers and springs of waters	1/3rd of the sun, moon, stars	bottomless pit/throne of the beast	Euphrates river	heaven/air
What happened? hail, fire, blood, sores	1/3rd of sea turned to blood	1/3rd bitter, then turned to blood	1/3rd were darkened	demons released	four angles released to lead demonic army, kill 1/3 of people	proclamation from heaven, rumblings, lightening, thunder, devastating earthquake, hail storm
Results? 1/3rd earth, 1/3rd trees, all grass burned up, severe and malignant sores on men	all creatures in sea die, 1/3rd of ships destroyed	many people died	1/3 of day and night had no light; sun scorched people with fierce heat; blaspheme God, refuse to repent	darkness; people stung, tormented by demons, in great pain for 5 months; curse God, refuse to repent	Dragon, beast and false prophet summon all kings to battle against God at Armageddon	Babylon, cities of the world destroyed, death, islands and mountains disappear. **SECOND COMING!**

LESSON **16A**

JESUS CHRIST THE LORD GOD OMNIPOTENT REIGNS
Revelation 19:6 (NKJV)

His crimson robe declares He came to save.
His royal diadems—He's here to reign.

EVENT 8

CHRIST'S THOUSAND YEAR KINGDOM

THE KING HAS COME!

As you read the prophetic Scriptures, perhaps you have been inclined to see your earthly existence as reality and the prophecies of your future life as vague and unreal. To be sure you live by faith and fervently cling to the hope of heaven. But when you come to this point in your life, faith has become sight; hope has become substance. You have been a participant and witness of marvelous prophetic Events: the Rapture, the Judgment Seat of Christ, and the Marriage Supper of the Lamb. You have descended from heaven to earth at King Jesus Second Coming and witnessed the Rock crushing the rebel leaders of the world and their great armies at Armageddon. The Lord of Glory has begun His reign upon the earth. At this moment, you are geared up with all the vital energies of never-ending life coursing through your glorious new body to fulfill the assignment given to you by King Jesus. But let's not get ahead of ourselves.

Lessons 16A and 16B are important for you because knowing about future prophetic realities will motivate you to refocus on and adjust your *obedience meter* to your command center—Jesus. Your pathway in this life is custom designed by your loving heavenly Father. God wants you to live your life in the light of understanding and preparing for your part in the perfect reign of God when Jesus returns to establish His Kingdom. Be deliberate and intentional in keeping yourself immovable in your convictions regarding Bible truths and principles, in persisting to fulfill God's divine purpose for your life, and in sticking like glue to the person of the Holy Spirit, (meaning an awareness of His presence that will permit Him to guide, instruct, convict you of sin, and to mold you into the image of Christ.)

In this lesson we will study:

- King Jesus Returns to Reign
    - Satan's Confinement
    - The Resurrection of the Martyred Christian Jews
    - The Judgment of the Nations

KING JESUS RETURNS TO REIGN

King Jesus has come to earth, Armageddon is past, but we need to understand three more events mentioned in Scripture that take place at Jesus' Second Coming: the confinement of Satan, the resurrection of the martyred Christian Jews, and the judgment of the nations. **Write** these three events in their proper location on the following diagram. The first two events are found in Revelation 20. This chapter can be read in chronological order.

THOUSAND-YEAR REIGN OF KING JESUS

SATAN'S CONFINEMENT

We learned in Lesson 15B that at this juncture, the world has been cleansed of the Antichrist and the False Prophet by having them thrown alive (meaning body, soul, and spirit) into the lake of fire. Thousands of souls, including the Ten Kings and their international army, were cast into the abyss or bottomless pit

W.C. Stevens wrote this story about a little friend of his.

> A little six-year old orphaned girl was listening to her Auntie read Revelation 20:1-3, which speaks of the expulsion of Satan from the world. At this age, most children have God's gift to take the things of Scripture as real and as the truth. She had a very vivid concept of the Devil. She asked her Aunt to turn down the corner of that page in her Bible. Frequently the child would be seen in her little rocking chair, and even though she was unable to read, she sat with the Bible open in her lap at this page, rocking to and fro with an expression of delight on her face as she contemplated the time when Satan would be locked up in the bottomless pit and no one on earth would be troubled by him any more for a whole thousand years. [1]

If I were given the opportunity to start a world-wide movement, I think that I would start a movement among all the Believers in the world to "dog-ear" Revelation 20:1-3 in their Bible, and to read it often as reality and truth. That should put a smile on our face and a hope in our heart!

Revelation 20:1-3

> [1] *"Then I saw an angel coming down from heaven with the key to the bottomless pit* [abyss] *and a heavy chain in his hand.*
> [2] *He seized the dragon—that old serpent* [Genesis 3:1], *who is the devil, Satan—and bound him in chains for a thousand years.*
> [3] *The angel threw him into the bottomless pit, which he then shut and locked so Satan could not deceive the nations anymore until the thousand years were finished. Afterward he must be released for a little while."*

Observations

In Lesson 12, the Wrath of God, we were introduced to this mighty angel (star) who is possessor of the key to the bottomless pit. *"Then the fifth angel blew his trumpet, and I saw a star that had fallen to earth from the sky, and he was given* [by Jesus (Revelation 1:18)] *the key to the shaft of the bottomless pit."* (Revelation 9:1)

Why do you think that the bottomless pit needs a key? ________________________________

____

Looking at the inhabitants of the abyss will help you with your answer.

The abyss is depicted as an immeasurable depth. It is:

- the abode of Unbelievers who have died until the Great White Throne judgment (Revelation 20:11-15)
- a prison for certain demons (Revelation 9:1-2, 11)
- the place from which the Antichrist will ascend (Revelation 11:7; 17:8) [2]

Your answer may have been similar to mine. The key indicates confinement and because this bottomless pit is full of evil demons, the most dreadful of all intelligent beings, we can be grateful that this particular horde cannot be turned loose on mankind today. However, during the Fifth Trumpet/Bowl Judgment, God will release these demons to carry out His purpose.

Now Satan and his minions have been added to the population of the abyss. The dreadful abyss becomes the holding cell of Satan and his demons during the thousand-year reign of Christ.

What four words in Revelation 20:1-3 tell us that Satan has been restrained?

- (verses 1-2) He was ________________________ with a great chain (indicates that he cannot function)
- (verse 3) The angel threw him into the ________________________________ (removal from earth and its atmosphere)
- (verse 3) The angel ________________________ and ____________________________ it (his prison cannot be opened)

What is the duration of Satan's confinement? ______________________________ **Underline** the duration each time it is mentioned in Revelation 20:1-3.

What is the reason given for Satan's confinement? ________________________

____

According to verse 3, what will take place at the end of the thousand years of Satan's imprisonment?

____

What are the three main things that Revelation 20:1-3 teaches us? Keep in mind who, where, how long.

1. ____
2. ____
3. ____

The time of Satan's confinement begins at Armageddon. At this same time King Jesus will be enthroned in Jerusalem.

The reign of Satan which has extended from Adam until Armageddon has ended. Hallelujah!

Isaiah 24:21-23 (NIV) gives an amazing resume of these particular events.

> [21] *"In that day* [the day of the Second Coming of Christ and Armageddon] *the Lord will punish the powers in the heavens above* [Satan and all his evil angels] *and the kings of the earth below* [The Ten Kings]
>
> [22] *They will be herded together like prisoners bound in a dungeon; they will be shut up in prison* [the abyss] *And be punished after many* days [Satan in Revelation 20:10; and the Ten Kings at the Great White Throne Judgment]
>
> [23] *The moon will be abashed, the sun ashamed; For the Lord Almighty will reign on Mount Zion and in Jerusalem, and before its elders, gloriously."* [Christ's Thousand-Year Kingdom]

Living on the earth without Satan's interference will provide the most unusual and glorious freedom humans have ever experienced since the great fall. Unredeemed people born during Christ's Thousand- Year Reign will still have sinful natures, but the incitement to sin will be greatly minimized by Satan's absence as we shall see later.

The following are the three main teachings that I found in Revelation 20:1-3:
1. Who and where: Satan is bound in the abyss, including all demons.
2. How long: The duration of their confinement is one thousand years. This is important in that it coincides with the length of Christ's reign of one thousand years on earth.
3. Result: Satan does not have access to the world and therefore cannot deceive the people of the nations.

THE RESURRECTION OF THE MARTYRED CHRISTIAN JEWS

A problem

The Jewish nation will see Jesus and believe in Him as their Savior at the time of the Rapture, but remain on earth to proclaim the Word of God. The following 3 ½ years will be a time of incredible persecution for the Christian Jews. Thousands will be killed resulting in their souls and spirits ascending to heaven and their bodies committed to the grave.

The problem. When will these faithful-unto-death souls in heaven receive their new glorified bodies? Also, the same question stands for those Christian Jews living at the time King Jesus returns to earth at the Second Coming.

Read the following verses and make your customary observations. I really hope you are enjoying examining the Scriptures on your own.

Revelation 20:4-6

> [4] *"Then I saw thrones, and the people sitting on them had been given the authority to judge.*

[Then I saw] *the souls of those who had been beheaded for their testimony about Jesus and for proclaiming the word of God. They had not worshipped the beast or his statue, nor accepted his mark on their forehead or their hands. They all came to life again, and they reigned with Christ for a thousand years.*
5 *This is the first resurrection. (The rest of the dead did not come back to life until the thousand years had ended.)* 6 *Blessed and holy are those who share in the first resurrection. For them the second death holds no power, but they will be priests of God and of Christ and will reign with him a thousand years."*

Your observations
1. ______
2. ______
3. ______
4. ______
5. ______

Observations

Believers enthroned
Verse 4. . . Then I saw thrones, and the people sitting on them. In John's vision, he not only saw thrones, but also saw people sitting on them. These are not phantom people, these are real people—Believers, all who accompanied King Jesus at His Second Coming. John sees victorious Believers who have been exalted to Christ's victorious throne and are beginning their reign with Christ on earth just as King Jesus had promised. Perhaps as John scanned over these enthroned saints, he saw you. . .yes, you.

Revelation 3:21 "Those who are victorious will sit with me on my throne, just as I was victorious and sat with my Father on his throne."

Martyred Christian Jews enthroned
Now the apostle John sees another group, the worthy host of Jewish martyrs. In this vision he sees the whole process of their exaltation and glorification; from their disembodied souls in heaven, to their resurrection, to their reign with King Jesus in His Thousand-Year Kingdom on earth.

Verse 4. . . Then I saw the souls The apostle John saw, the disembodied souls of Christian Jews in heaven that had not yet been exalted and glorified.
How were they killed? ______ Why were they killed? What did they do and not do? ______
______
______

These were beheaded for their loyalty to Christ during the persecution of the Jews by the Antichrist. The act of beheading people in other parts of the world is not uncommon. Possibly it will be the choice of execution by the Antichrist because it is so gruesome and degrading, instilling fear into any dissenters. However, this will not impede these courageous Jews in announcing their faith in Jesus Christ. The choice given to the people of the world will be bow and worship the Antichrist, or die. These Christian martyrs choose physical death without hesitation. They know that they will be resurrected by the power of God in His timing.

In Revelation 14:9-13 the Lord warns of the dire eternal consequences of receiving the mark of the Beast. Listen to what follows this warning: *"This means that God's holy people must endure persecution patiently, obeying his commands and maintaining their faith in Jesus."* The Holy Spirit continues to speak: *"Write this down: Blessed are those who die in the Lord from now on. Yes, says the Spirit, they are blessed indeed, for they will rest from their hard work; for their good deeds follow them."*

When "*blessed*" (*markarios* Greek) is used for "those who persevere in trial (James 1:12; 1 Peter 3:14; 4:14) *markarios* takes the form of a pronouncement. That is, though the present situation of those facing trials is difficult, they are encouraged by the prospect of future consolation and reward (blessing) from God and thus are able to face the present with courage and hope." [M] They are blessed indeed!

1 Corinthians 15:22-23 "Just as everyone dies because we all belong to Adam, everyone who belongs to Christ will be given new life. But there is an order [series, or succession] to this resurrection: Christ was raised as the first of the harvest; then all who belong to Christ will be raised when he comes back."

Verse 4. . . They all came to life again. That the martyred Jews are resurrected and will reign with Christ is very clear in this Scripture. Their resurrection implies a new, deathless body. These faithful Christian-Jews experience a physical resurrection of their bodies just as Believers did at the time of the Rapture as described in 1 Corinthians 15:51-53 and 1 Thessalonians 4:13-18. It could very well be that the Jewish experience follows the same pattern as that of the Rapture. The martyred Christian-Jews will rise from the grave first and then the surviving Jews, those who are alive at Jesus' Second Coming, will be clothed with their new, immortal body and will reign with Christ and all their fellow Believers.

Their new body

"They are buried as natural human bodies, but they will be raised as spiritual bodies. (1 Corinthians 15:43-44) The glorified body "will have a spiritual way of functioning similar to the way heavenly bodies function in contradistinction to earthly bodies. This spiritual body is imperishable yet utterly real body—one of a different order and having different functions from the earthly body; it is a body given by God himself—a body glorified with eternal life." [3]

Problem of time element solved

Read carefully the last part of verse 4 to notice the time element: *They all came to life again, and they reigned with Christ for a thousand years.* The dead Christian Jews were resurrected just as King Jesus begins His Thousand-Year Reign. Placing this resurrection at Jesus' Second Coming.

Verse 5. . .the first resurrection. These Jewish martyrs are the last, to our knowledge, of the resurrected Believers, therefore, finalizing the First Resurrection. In Lesson 1 we saw a list of all who belong to the First Resurrection. To refresh your memory we will look again at the list of participants.

Participants:

- Jesus Christ was the first to rise from the dead. (1 Corinthians 15:20; Acts 26:23)

- All Believers, Old and New Testament Ages and the Present Age, who have died before the time of the Rapture. This resurrection occurs during the Rapture process which occurs 3 ½ years before King Jesus' Second Coming. (1 Thessalonians 4:13-18; 1 Corinthians 15:23)

- The two Christian-Jewish witnesses of Revelation 11:7-12. This occurs at the end of the great persecution of the Jews just 3 ½ days before Jesus' Second Coming.

- The Christian-Jewish martyrs at the time of Jesus' Second Coming when He sets up His earthly Kingdom. (Revelation 20:4-5)

Verse 6. . . those who share in the first resurrection. This includes all the Believers listed above. **Read** verse 6 and **fill in** the following blanks. This exercise is adapted to you because it is about you. You are one of millions, but keep in mind that each statement is to be taken personally.

Revelation 20:6

> *"Blessed and holy are those* who share *in the first resurrection. For them the second death holds no power, but they will be priests of God and of Christ and will reign with him a thousand years."*

God's royal declaration of who you are:

Blessed and Holy One who has fully separated himself from the ways of the world and is fully satisfied in God.

__________________ and __________________ is __________________ ______________ (your name) who shares in the first resurrection. For you the ______________________________ holds no __________________, but you will be a __________________ of God and of Christ and will reign __________________________ a ____________________________________."

This is one of those special moments to acknowledge the unfailing love of God that has been extended to you and me that permits us to be a part of this glorious, holy, royal host. **Read** God's imperial declaration, verse 6, over and over until it sinks down into your heart and soul.

Who are the "*The rest of the dead*" who "*did not come back to life until the thousand years had ended* [the Second Resurrection]" in verse 5? ______________________________ ____________ We will find out who these are in the study of the Judgment of the Nations.

How many years separate those of the final group of the First Resurrection and those of the Second Resurrection? ______________________________________ The Second Resurrection or "the resurrection of damnation (Daniel 12:2) is so horrible that its resurrected life is called "death" as opposed to the resurrected life inherited by believers." [4] What kind of life will it be to live in a lake of fire?

Second death "This lake of fire is the second death." (Revelation 20:14) As regards human beings, this is the final abode for all those whose names are not written in the Lamb's book of life.

THE JUDGMENT OF THE NATIONS

Look for this Event on **Timeline Three** (located at the end of Part One of this study book). What Event does the Judgment of the Nations chronologically follow? _______________ ____. Not all the people of the world were present at Armageddon, but all approved and supported the war against the Lord and the Christian Jews of Jerusalem. A great number of the nations survived the catastrophic events of the Second Coming. Zechariah 14:16 says: *"every one that survives of all the nations that have come against Jerusalem."* King Jesus has established His reign on earth so we ask, "What will be done with these followers of the now deceased Antichrist?" Jesus has explained this in His teaching concerning the Kingdom in Matthew 25:31-46. We call this intriguing event the Judgment of the Nations.

This judgment is not found in the book of Revelation. It is prophesied by Jesus in His fifth and final discourse in the book of Matthew. This end-time teaching of Matthew 24 and 25 is called the Olivet Discourse because it was given on the Mount of Olives, located east of the temple mount. These two chapters speak of the Great Tribulation, the Rapture, parables of exhortation to be ready for Jesus' Coming, and ends with the Judgement of the Nations at King Jesus' Second Coming.

The gathering of the nations

Something remarkable is taking place. King Jesus is gathering together the survivors of the catastrophic events that took place at His Second Coming and Armageddon. You are present and observe that earth's population has been greatly reduced as these ragged and beaten followers of the former Antichrist are assembled before the Lord of the earth. Their fearful eyes are fixed on the King, some appear to be ashamed, but most of them emanate animosity along with their fear. You listen in as the Lord begins to speak to them; you are expecting to see the immediate destruction of the whole rebellious lot.

Matthew 25:31-33

> 31 *"But when the Son of Man comes in his glory, and all the angels with him, then he will sit upon his glorious throne.* 32 *All the nations will be gathered in his presence, and he will separate the people as a shepherd separates the sheep from the goats.* 33 *He will place the sheep at his right hand and the goats at his left."*

We will pause here to make some observations. These verses give the setting regarding *when* and *where* this judgment takes place, and *what* happens to those involved.

Time

When does this judgment take place? verse 31 ___________________________________ ___________________________________This end-time event is the key to the interpretation of this judgment. It is very important to place events in their chronological order so as to interpret them in their historical context. This enables us to understand their meaning. It is apparent that this judgment takes place at the beginning of Jesus' earthly reign.

Place
Where does this judgment take place? verse 32 ______________________________

What happens
What does King Jesus do with this multitude? verses 32-33 ______________________
____

Who are these people? Verse 32 people of all ______________________________
Did you notice the figure of speech (a simile, identified by the word "as") of a shepherd dividing his flocks and herds to illustrate this end-time event? **Circle** the word "as" in verse 32.

"The description given here is not a parable, but a picture, a vision of the future. It does not liken the kingdom of God to anything, but describes 'the literal son of man, in his literal person, at his literal coming to a literal judgment. . ." [5]

Jesus prophesied this judgment of the nations during His earthly ministry and placed it at His Second Coming when He will establish His Kingdom on the earth. "*All the nations will be gathered in his presence*" refers to those who survive the catastrophic events of the Second Coming of Christ. This means both "*sheep*" and "*goats*" were followers of the Antichrist. This judgment occurs in Jesus' physical presence. Just as a shepherd easily distinguishes between sheep and goats, King Jesus knows which ones are blessed and which ones are doomed. He points His finger at each individual, and one by one they are separated into one of two groups. It seems curious to you that the *sheep* on His right are those whom you had noticed to appear to be ashamed. Having been singled out, they hang their heads with evident discomfort, humiliation and a sense of foreboding. Their group is incredibly small compared to the group of *goats* on the left.

Please observe the significance of the words underlined in the continuation of Matthew 25. Also notice the title Jesus gives to Himself. Observe King Jesus' startling words to the two groups.

Matthew 25:34-46
King Jesus speaks to those on His right hand, the sheep

> [34] *"Then the King will say to those on his right, 'Come, you who are blessed by my Father, inherit the Kingdom prepared for you from the creation of the world.* [35] *For I was hungry, and you fed me, I was thirsty, and you gave me a drink. I was a stranger, and you invited me into your home.* [36] *I was naked, and you gave me clothing. I was sick, and you cared for me. I was in prison, and you visited me.'*

The sheep reply

> [37] *Then these righteous ones will reply, 'Lord, when did we ever see you hungry and feed you? Or thirsty and give you something to drink?* [38] *Or a stranger and show you hospitality? Or naked and give you clothing?* [39] *When did we ever see you sick or in prison and visit you?'*

King Jesus responds to the righteous ones

[40] Then the King will say, 'I tell you the truth, when you did it to one of the least of these my brothers and sisters, you were doing it to me!'

King Jesus speaks to those on His left hand, the goats

[41] Then the King will turn to those on his left and say, 'Away with you, you cursed ones, into the eternal fire prepared for the devil and his demons. [42] For I was hungry, and you didn't feed me. I was thirsty, and you didn't give me a drink. I was a stranger, and you didn't invite me into your home. I was naked, and you didn't give me clothing. I was sick and in prison, and you didn't visit me.'

The goats reply

[44] Then they will reply, 'Lord when did we ever see you hungry or thirsty or a stranger or naked or sick or in prison, and not help you?'

King Jesus responds to the cursed ones

[45] And he will answer, 'I tell you the truth, when you refused to help the least of these my brothers and sisters, you were refusing to help me.'

Their actions determine their destiny

[46] And they will go away into eternal punishment but the righteous will go into eternal life."

How does Jesus refer to Himself in verse 34? ____________________________

When all earth-people representing every nation will have been gathered before Him at His return, King Jesus will separate out of them a group that needs to be dealt with because of their special relationship to Him. This separating process is like a shepherd dividing sheep from goats. It is plain to see that this division is based on the *actions of individuals* and not of nations as a whole even though every nation is represented.

WHO DO THE SHEEP AND THE GOATS REPRESENT?

This is a very difficult question, and we must pay very close attention to some strange implications from this passage of Scripture. Keep in mind that all, both sheep and goats, are former participants of the World System of the Antichrist, but as civilians were not a part of the armies destroyed at Armageddon. We will look at some of the facts we have thus far gathered.

- First of all, we see that this gathering is divided into two parts, and that they have two different destinations. The end result for the sheep is to enter immediately into the eternal Kingdom of Christ whereas all the goats will eventually be sent to eternal punishment—to the *"eternal fire prepared for the devil and his demons"* (verse 41).

- We notice that the destiny of the sheep and goats depends on one thing: if they fulfilled acts of mercy to Jesus' suffering followers, whom He calls His *"brothers and sisters"* (verse 40), during the time of great persecution. As the sheep identify with the suffering brothers and sisters by providing them with food, drink, clothing, shelter, and care, Jesus says that they were doing this dangerous service to Him, which was equivalent to identifying themselves with Him. The opposite is true of the goats.

- Salvation is never gained by doing good works. It is always obtained by faith in the saving work of Jesus Christ. This particular group called "*sheep*," who are the surviving followers of the Antichrist, seem to have a spiritual relationship to Jesus. It appears that it was *expected* of them to help those who were suffering persecution for Jesus' sake.

- In verse 34, the sheep are called ____________________ and in verse 37 ____________ ____________________. These terms "*blessed*" and "*righteous ones*" are used in God's Word only for those that have been born again by the blood of Christ. The sheep show surprise and do not seem to expect this turn of events which gives them entrance into Christ's Kingdom. They had been doing acts of mercy because their conscience compelled them to do so, but they expected nothing in return.

AN INTERPRETATION OF THE IDENTITY OF THE SHEEP AND GOATS

To understand the meaning of the Judgment of the Nations we must understand who the *sheep* and the *goats* are, as well as the identity of Jesus' "*brothers and sisters.*"

THE SHEEP

Who are the sheep?
The *sheep* are Believers who leave the faith and follow after the Antichrist in fear but not conviction. Nevertheless, they deny the Lord because of fear much like Peter did. (Matthew 26:69-75) Because of their status with Him, Jesus deals with them in a special way. Their final destination must be determined.

Why do we identify the *sheep* to be Believers? Look carefully at Matthew 25:34, 37, and 46. How does Jesus identify them? verse 34 ____
verse 37 ____verse 46 ________________
____

Three terms of identification
Verse 34 "blessed by my Father, heirs of the Kingdom"
Jesus unequivocally identifies the "*sheep.*" The phrase "*you who are blessed by my Father, inherit the Kingdom prepared for you from the creation of the world*" are expressions used only for a true, born-again follower of Christ. These two expressions indicate that the Believer is chosen and blessed of God before the creation of the world, and his name is written in the Lamb's Book of Life from the foundation of the world. (Ephesians 1:4; Philippians 4:3; Revelation 3:5; 17:8; 20:15; 21:27) God in His omniscience knows from eternity who will receive Christ as their personal Savior. All Believers have an allotment, or inheritance, in Christ's One Thousand-Year

Kingdom on earth which will continue into the future new world of glory. (1 Corinthians 6:9-10; Colossians 1:12; 3:24)

Verses 37, 46 "The righteous ones"

"*As the Scriptures say, 'No one is righteous—not even one.*" (Romans 3:10) The sheep are called "*the righteous ones*" in verses 37 and 46, therefore, it is obvious that even though they initially will give their loyalty to the Antichrist, they, indeed, had previously received the righteousness of Christ. They did this through repentance of sin and faith in the Lord Jesus which is the only way to a right relationship with God. (2 Corinthians 5:21)

By their disloyalty to Christ and their allegiance to the Antichrist, they will eliminate themselves from participating in the Rapture, and place themselves in a dangerous situation of possibly losing their salvation altogether. Having been left behind to suffer the Trumpet/Bowl Judgments was their "*stern discipline.*" "*Stern discipline awaits him who forsakes the path.*" (Proverbs 15:10)

Revelation 11:18 "...It is time to judge the dead and reward your servants the prophets, as well as your holy people, and all who fear your name, from the least to the greatest."

"and all-who-fear-your-name group"

One other possibility to identify the *sheep* as Believers lies in the wording of the announcement of the arrival of Jesus' Kingdom found in the Seventh Trumpet/Bowl Judgment in Revelation 11:18. It tells us that when King Jesus assumes His power and has begun to reign that He will reward "*your servants the prophets* [the two witnesses], *as well* as *your holy people,*" those faithful Christian Jews who survive the great persecution during the Wrath of God period of 3 ½ years. The verse goes on to include another group in the rewarding of those from this same time period, "*and all who fear your name.*" The Greek word *phobeo* is the word translated *fear* and means "to fear, be afraid; to show reverential fear of the Lord." [V] More than likely, these are the *sheep, the righteous ones.*

The *sheep* of Matthew 25 and the *all who fear your name* of Revelation 11 are one and the same and are identified as Believers who follow along and blend in with the crowd of Antichrist-lovers for convenience sake. I will call them disloyal-to-Jesus-Believers.

Disloyal-to-Jesus-Believers

After the Rapture occurs, during the Wrath of God, these disloyal-to-Jesus-Believers perform many secret, sacrificial acts of mercy on behalf of Jesus' "*brothers and sisters,*" the persecuted Christian Jews. In view of the distress and dangers during this period of judgment, it is clear that Christian Jews will have great difficulty surviving. The world dictator will be carrying out every conceivable act of violence in order to exterminate them.

The endeavors of the disloyal-to-Jesus-Believers who find ways to assist these suffering victims by their merciful actions place their lives in jeopardy. These actions reveal that they secretly align themselves with God's people which, in God's view, is equivalent to identifying themselves with Jesus. Their clandestine valor to provide food, a cup of water, give a shirt or coat, or shelter in a hiding place, and somehow sustain their imprisoned brothers and sisters in Christ, endears them to God's heart. King Jesus restores them as He did Peter (John 21:15-19), and He receives them into His eternal Kingdom. The fact that the sheep will live by Jesus' standard of expectancy, even at great risk to their own lives, reveals that they are related to Christ and are qualified to enter His Kingdom.

> "The compassionate actions of the "sheep" nations are *not* said to be the basis of their being "righteous." Their righteousness is the *cause* of their tender ministrations, not a *result* of it. Only as we see this passage from this point of view does it fit into the whole teaching of Scripture on salvation by grace through faith." [6]

God in His sovereign will displays mercy to these disloyal-to-Jesus-Believers who succor His chosen people. Apparently the sheep did not realize their denied Savior was watching their performance of righteous acts. It was accounted to them for righteousness. (Galatians 3:6)

A biblical precedence is found in the story of Rahab. (Joshua 2; 6:22-25; Hebrews 11:31; James 2:25) Notice Rahab's statement of faith in Joshua 2:11. Also the Kenites (1 Samuel 15:6). In Lesson 5 we saw a contemporary and touching illustration as reflected in the "Garden of the Righteous." These were compassionate people but it is unknown if they were Believers.

Hebrews 11:31 (NKJV) "By faith the harlot Rahab did not perish with those who did not believe when she had received the spies with peace."

> "This garden is a memorial located in Jerusalem at Yad Vashem. 'The Righteous Among The Nations' is a title used by the State of Israel to describe non-Jews who risked their lives, putting themselves and their families in danger, during the Holocaust to save Jews from extermination by the Nazis. These brave people are referred to as 'righteous gentiles' by the Israeli. The Garden of the Righteous was created by Israel to commemorate the lives and acts of these righteous gentiles.'" [7]

Mathew 10:42 Even a cup of water given *"to one of My disciples"* will be rewarded.

Matthew 25:31-46 has through the centuries inspired multitudes to perform merciful acts of love to help those in need. And rightly so, because this was taught and modeled by Jesus as the fruit of the Christian life. However, we must be mindful of the fact that the Judgment of the Nations is a specific event, at a designated time and place. The focus is on merciful acts, or the lack of them, to help the persecuted Jewish Believers survive the 3 ½ years during the Trumpet/Bowl Judgments.

A warning: do not be tempted, as a Believer, to take liberties with your holy God by receiving the mark of the Beast in order to escape persecution and possible death. God sees the motive behind every action. Likewise, do not think that you can fool the enemy; his power over the people of the world will be extremely controlling.

THE GOATS

The *goats* are made up of two groups of survivors: the apostate-Believers and the Unbelievers.

Group One—Apostate-Believers

Some of the *goats* on Jesus' left will be apostate-believers who will knowingly deny Jesus in order to give their allegiance and worship to the Antichrist and fully support his cause. These are probably the "*fearful*" or "*cowards*" of Revelation 21:8 and, if this is the case, they stand at the head of the list. The Greek word for these people is *deilia,* "to be fearful." "That

Revelation 21:8 "But cowards, unbelievers, the corrupt, murderers, the immoral, those who practice witchcraft, idol worshipers, and all liars—their fate is in the fiery lake of burning sulfur. This is the second death."

spirit is not given us by God. This word denotes cowardice and timidity and is never used in a good sense." V

> "John [author of Revelation] is not speaking of natural timidity, but of that cowardice which in the last resort chooses self and safety before Christ, and fears the threats of the beast [Antichrist] rather than trusts the love of Christ. God did not give his people such a spirit of cowardice (2 Timothy 1:7)." [8]

King Jesus holds these apostate-believers to the same standard as the sheep because they, like the sheep, have had a saving relationship with Christ. It is obvious that they have the same opportunity given to the *sheep* to be restored to Christ by identifying with God's suffering children. However, these apostates fail to meet the Lord's expectations. During the persecution, these apostates turn their backs on the anguish of their estranged brethren even though they know that the lives of these suffering saints depend on their compassion.

These are judged by their failure to extend mercy to "*My brothers and sisters*" and thus to Christ Himself. They confirm that they have severed their ties to Jesus by of their actions. Like Judas they condemn themselves by aligning with evil and will receive the same condemnation and banishment from the King's presence. They will be sent to the eternal fire where the devil and his angels will ultimately be located. "*And they will go away into eternal punishment*" (Matthew 25:46)

"For a Christian to be unkind to a Christian is not only wrong, it is monstrous." [9] (Galatians 6:10 NASB)

A valuable truth

Let's pause for a moment to focus on a valuable truth: to decline to help or to deny a brother in the Lord that which he needs is to deny the Lord Jesus. "*I tell you the truth when you refused to help the least of these my brothers and sisters, you were refusing to help me.*" (Matthew 25:45) In the light of this Scripture, we must consider all our merciful acts of kindness to our fellow Believers as actually doing it to Jesus. To withhold our help to our brothers and sisters in Christ is to withhold it from Jesus. Unthinkable!

The next time God gives you the opportunity to place your gift of love in the hands of your needy brother or sister, look into their face and you will behold the face of your dear Savior. It may be someone you will never actually *see,* possibly far away in another country. Now that's something to think about!

John 3:18 (NKJV) "He who does not believe is condemned already, because he has not believed in the name of the only begotten Son of God."

Group Two—Unbelievers

A large number of Unbelievers will make up the major part of the *goat* crowd. Without a doubt they will deny Christian Jews assistance to survive persecution and will most likely commit outrageous acts of violence against them. They apparently, however, will not be judged by the same standard as those related to Christ. Because they will not have confessed Jesus as their personal Savior, Jesus will not expect acts of mercy from these wicked Unbelievers.

It is apparent that these Unbelievers are permitted to remain on earth during Jesus' Thousand-Year Kingdom. These are the people that Christ will rule with a *"rod of iron"* and will ultimately rebel against King Jesus when Satan is released at the end of the thousand years. (Revelation 19:15; 20:7-10)

JESUS CHRIST THE LORD GOD OMNIPOTENT REIGNS

Revelation 19:6 (NKJV)

LESSON **16B**

JESUS CHRIST THE FULLNESS OF GOD
Colossians 2:9

King Jesus fills the whole universe. . . with Himself

EVENT 8

KING JESUS ESTABLISHES HIS KINGDOM

In this lesson we will study:

Event 8: King Jesus Establishes His Kingdom
- Christ's Kingdom Defined
- The Inhabitants of the Kingdom
- The Placement of Jesus' Followers on Thrones of Authority
- King Jesus Divides the World into Kingdoms

EVENT 8: KING JESUS ESTABLISHES HIS KINGDOM

Christ's Thousand-Year Kingdom will be your final Event on this earth. Find where this Event occurs on **Timeline Three** (located at the end of Part One of this study book) and **write** Event **8** on the line by the asterisk (*_8_). For the Christian Jews this will be Event 6. For the Unbelievers who survive Armageddon this will be your Event 5.

TIME PERIOD OF CHRIST'S KINGDOM

Revelation 20:1-7

Satan is imprisoned for a thousand years (verses 2, 7). The Christian-Jewish martyrs reign with Christ for a thousand years (verse 4). All Believers that have accompanied King Jesus at His Second Coming will reign with Him for a thousand years (verse 6). How long is Christ's earthly reign on earth?—a thousand years! The term "*one thousand years*" is specified six times in this chapter indicating a literal thousand years.

CHRIST'S KINGDOM DEFINED

World history is moving toward the day when the reign of Satan and sinful man will be thrown down and replaced by the forever Kingdom of our God and His Son Jesus Christ.

Christ's visible thousand-year reign on earth has, unfortunately, been given the title "The Millennium." Which is more important the length of time something takes place or the event itself; and in this case, Christ's Kingdom reign on earth or the length of His reign? I would encourage you to use the term Christ's Thousand-Year Kingdom or Christ's Millennial Kingdom. This brings the person of King Jesus to the forefront, putting the emphasis in the right place. It also focuses on *His reign* rather than on a span of time. The important thing is that Christ will rule the world literally and gloriously. But of course, how else can God reign?

Daniel 7:13-14 (NIV) "In my vision at night I looked, and there before me was one like a son of man [Jesus], coming with the clouds of heaven. He approached the Ancient of Days [God the Father] and was led into his presence. He was given authority, glory and sovereign power; all peoples, nations and men of every language worshipped him. His dominion is an everlasting dominion that will not pass away, and his kingdom is one that will never be destroyed."

Henry Blackaby gives an important distinction of the word *kingdom* translated from the Greek word *basileia.*

> "God's kingdom does include His sovereign rule and authority over all things (Daniel 4:34-35), but this is not the dominant New Testament use of the term *basileia. Kingdom* in the New Testament refers to God's manifested reign in human affairs. Jesus taught that the kingdom is both a present spiritual reality and a future physical reality." [1]

The present spiritual reality

At the present time, Jesus reigns in the hearts of all Believers. Therefore, *"the Kingdom of God can't be detected by visible signs"* (Luke 17:20) such as a capital or a throne. Jesus informs us that we must have a spiritual birth in order to belong to His Kingdom. *"I tell you the truth, unless you are born again* [born from above], *you cannot see the Kingdom of God."* (John 3:3) Unbelievers do not recognize or experience such a Kingdom and the majority have never heard of it. Nevertheless, Jesus' Kingdom is worldwide. The sun never sets on His Kingdom as revealed at the time of the Rapture when there will be representatives of Christ's spiritual Kingdom *"from every nation and tribe and people and language". (*Revelation 7:9)

A future visible, physical reality

This lesson presents the fulfillment of God's promise in Daniel 2:44-45: *"During the reign of those kings*—[referring to the Ten Kings of the Ten Regions of the world just destroyed at Armageddon]. . .*the God of heaven will set up a kingdom that will never be destroyed or conquered. It will crush all these kingdoms into nothingness, and it will stand forever."*

"The kingdom of the world has become the kingdom of our Lord and of his Christ, and he shall reign for ever and ever." (Revelation 11:15 RSV) From this point on, Christ will be the Absolute Ruler, First on the earth and then throughout all eternity. Keep in mind that Christ's Thousand-Year Kingdom *on earth* is not the final goal of God's plans. For you, things will only get better and better.

A definition of Christ's Thousand-Year Kingdom

Jesus will return to earth as King of kings and Lord of lords to reign over the nations in righteousness and peace from His earthly throne located in Jerusalem for a period of one thousand years. This type of government is called a theocracy which means that God Himself is the supreme ruler and "human rulers interpret and carry out the divine ruler's will." [2] King Jesus will govern directly in all human affairs. His will and laws will be absolute. Your part as a human ruler will be explained later.

King Jesus' earthly throne

The following Scripture is a beautiful description of Jesus' reign. I would like to give you the opportunity to discover the facts for yourself. Make five observations.

Micah 4:1-4 (see also Isaiah 2:2-4)

> 1 *"In the last days, the mountain of the Lord's house will be the highest of all—the most important place on earth. It will be raised above the other hills, and people from all over the world will stream there to worship.* 2 *People from many nations will come*

and say, 'Come, let us go up to the mountain of the Lord, to the house of Jacob's God. There he will teach us his ways, and we will walk in his paths.' For the Lord's teaching will go out from Zion; his word will go out from Jerusalem.

[3] The Lord will mediate between peoples and will settle disputes between strong nations far away. They will hammer their swords into plowshares and their spears into pruning hooks. Nation will no longer fight against nation, nor train for war anymore. [4] Everyone will live in peace and prosperity, enjoying their own grapevines and fig trees, for there will be nothing to fear. The Lord of Heaven's Armies has made this promise!"

Your observations:
1. ______________________________
2. ______________________________
3. ______________________________
4. ______________________________
5. ______________________________

I'm sure that you were delighted to discover some amazing things that will take place in King Jesus' Kingdom. Just makes you want it to come now.

Observations

Verse 1. . .Jerusalem will be the world's capital. *Highest of all* in the Hebrew language means "highest and supreme." [KW] The site of King Jesus' throne will be the highest place on earth, the summit. "It is as if God's dwelling place and his earthly temple are joined as one, an idea hinted at in certain hymns of worship (cf. Psalm 11:4; 46:4; 48:2)" [3] The topography of earth will be strikingly changed during Christ's Second Coming. It appears from the wording of this verse that the place of King Jesus' temple and throne will be thrust upward.

Psalm 48:1-2
"How great is the Lord, how deserving of praise, in the city of our God, which sits on his holy mountain! It is high and magnificent; the whole earth rejoices to see it! Mount Zion, the holy mountain, is the city of the great King!"

Verses 1-2. . . **Come, let us *go up* to the mountain of the Lord**. Do you remember the word *Aliyah* from Lesson 5? *Aliyah* comes from the Hebrew word *Alah* which means "to go up" or "ascend." This is the term that the Israelis used for the return of the Jews to Israel after World War II. The Jewish people were making *Aliyah*, going up to Israel. This word has great spiritual meaning in that "you are ascending to a higher place in God—a deeper knowledge and revelation of God—than where you were previously. You are growing in the knowledge of God and therefore God is taking you into a deeper understanding of knowing Him than you previously knew of Him." [4]

With people from all over the world we will *go up*, make *Aliyah,* to Jerusalem to see Christ's throne high and lifted up and the beauty of His temple. We will worship the King and hear the very words of God; "*there he will teach us his ways, and we will walk in his paths.*" (Micah 4:2)

What will it be like to hear His transcendent teachings which will take us into new and unknown territory? Our glorified minds, free from the residue of sin, will be better fit to absorb His wonderful words. Can you imagine yourself sitting in the very presence of Jesus; to be able to

In the here and now, read the Bible and you will be taught by God.

see the gestures He makes with His hands, His facial expressions as He teaches, his smile, a frown, a twinkle in His eye? We will be so ecstatic that we will call one another to come and join us to go up, to make *Aliyah "to the mountain of the Lord."*

We will hurry back to our country, where we serve the King, to interpret these truths and carry out the Divine Ruler's will for ourselves and for the generations born during this one thousand years.

Habakkuk 2:14 (NASB) "For the earth will be filled with the knowledge of the glory of the Lord, as the waters cover the sea."

Verses 3-4. . .The effect of King Jesus' teachings mentioned here is a world at peace. This thousand- year reign will not be a utopian, unspoiled state, because sinful man will be present. However, "this era will inaugurate a new relationship between God and humankind, Israel and the nations, and humanity and nature." [5]

The Lord Himself will keep law and order. *"He will rule* [shepherd] *them with an iron rod"* refers to His rule over the people of the world that are not Believers. (Revelation 2:27; 12:5; 19:15) The word for *rule* in this verse is "shepherd" (Greek *poimaino*) which indicates a huge difference between our understanding of an earthly, powerful despot and a Shepherd-King who cares deeply for the good of each individual. The earth will have never before experienced such justice and fairness.

Do the words of verse 3 carry the suggestion that unbelieving mankind will have disagreements and international differences? Will mankind still operate under God's permission to choose between right and wrong, to exercise his free will or choose not to obey God? I believe it does, but during the thousand years, King Jesus will keep mankind on a short leash and punish him when necessary. (Zechariah 14:17-19)

Wars will have been banished from the earth. There won't be recruiting offices to enlist men and women to join the military, nor factories to produce weapons of destruction. The prophet Micah assures us that there won't even be anything to fear because *"the Lord of Heaven's Armies has made this promise!"* He said so!

Genesis 1:30 "And I have given every green plant as food for all the wild animals, the birds in the sky, and the small animals that scurry along the ground—everything that has life."

Verse 4. . .**Everyone will live in peace and prosperity**. . .**for there will be nothing to fear**. Peace will be reflected in animal life (Isaiah 11:6-9). "No bloodshed shall then be needed by those creatures that are no longer carnivorous, but have returned to their original food, the green herb." [6] (Genesis 1:30) How delightful to run with cheetahs, cuddle with bears, ride an elephant, hand feed exotic birds, see the children playing among and leading wolves, lambs, leopards, baby goats, calves and lions in herds! Take a moment to imagine what you would like to do in the animal kingdom.

As the earth is restored from the upheavals of the catastrophic events of the Second Coming and Armageddon, prosperity will be reflected in nature. **Read** about the river that flows from the temple in Jerusalem throughout the land which will teem with fish and will nourish fruit trees of all kinds. (Ezekiel 47:1-12)

THE INHABITANTS OF THE KINGDOM

TWO GROUPS OF HUMAN BEINGS IN CHRIST'S KINGDOM

Unbelievers (with mortal bodies)

After the Judgment of the Nations, the surviving *unbelieving-goats* from every nation will continue to dwell on the earth. Their judgment is delayed for one thousand years. They will marry, reproduce and after a very long lifetime many will die. (Isaiah 65:20) Their bodies will return to the earth and their souls and spirits will be consigned to the abyss until the Great White Throne Judgment. How many generations will be born during the thousand-year period as a result of this group? How many millions of people will there be who will live under Christ's perfect reign but do not receive Him as their Savior? Pressure mounts as the percentage of Unbelievers increases. Very interesting.

Mickelsen has a good point when he says:

> "There will be no atheists or agnostics. The knowledge of God will be universal. But obedience could still come only by conformity rather than by conviction. Satan's being loosed [at end of the 1,000 years] for a short time would differentiate between the ones who serve God out of conviction and the ones who serve Him out of compliance." [7]

These are the ones that will need to be ruled with the "rod of iron."

Glorified Believers

You belong to this group of human beings. The difference is that you will live in your new body that is designed for the Kingdom age and beyond. . .forever.

"It will function normally and naturally in the material earthly realm as well as it does in the heavenly sphere. This is what Christ's "spiritual body" did during the forty days after His resurrection when He appeared to His disciples." [8]

Think of your new body in terms of Christ's resurrected body as described in the Gospels. Notice His apparent coming and going from earth to heaven. It will seem strange to us to live as a glorified being with those who are not. But, by this time, we are getting used to strange things. We just spent several years in heaven living with awesome heavenly beings.

THE PLACEMENT OF JESUS' FOLLOWERS ON THRONES OF AUTHORITY

Revelation 20:4

> *"Then I saw thrones, and the people sitting on them had been given the authority to judge."*

Prophecy will not always be future.

Throne
The characteristic feature of a royal throne was its elevation; Jehovah's throne is described as "high and lifted up" (Isaiah 6:1) A throne is a symbol of supreme power, honor and dignity. [9]

Prophecy of distant wonders will turn into reality. As you study your future responsibility in Christ's Kingdom, please think in terms of the certainty of your personal involvement. The following all applies to you.

The moment has arrived for your assignment in Christ's Thousand-Year Kingdom. You belong to the most elite of all time. No human being has ever risen to this level of existence. "*You are a chosen race, a royal priesthood* [king-priests], *a holy nation, God's own people.*" (1 Peter 2:9 RSV) You are "a priesthood called to royal dominion, clothed with royal dignity." [KW]

King Jesus speaks to all His followers from His throne in Jerusalem. "I now confirm the promises that I made to you in My Word:

If you *die with Me*, you *will also live with Me*. If you *endure hardship*, you *will reign with Me*. (adapted from 2 Timothy 2:11-12)

Those who are victorious will sit with me on My throne, just as I was victorious and sat with My Father on His throne. (Revelation 3:21)

I was *slaughtered*, and My *blood has ransomed people for God from every tribe, and language and people and nation. And* I *have caused* you *to become a Kingdom of priests for our God. And* you *will reign on the earth.*" (adapted from Revelation 5: 9-10)

With His face raised to heaven, King Jesus vigorously affirms, "Today My promises have been fulfilled!"

"At My Judgment Seat I gave you rich rewards for all that you did in your life of service for Me. At that time, I gave you your inheritance in My Kingdom; your royal status and position were confirmed. Today you will take possession of your inheritance and you will begin to reign."

King Jesus spreads His arms wide in an all-inclusive embrace as He continues: "At the Marriage Supper all of you were collectively joined to Me in a forever-union. Together we have returned to earth and together we will reign for a thousand years. . .and beyond."

Your Royal Position In Christ's Kingdom

King Jesus is the supreme ruler and will govern directly in all human affairs. (Isaiah 9:6-7) His will and laws will be absolute. The Believer's job will be to carry out the Divine Ruler's will in the area assigned to him.

> "Because Christ is the leader, some might call it a theocracy, but that would overlook the role of Christ's people. This is instead a new theocratic, democratic, participatory rule by people who are united because they died and rose together with Christ. They have returned together to achieve the full effects of their union in Christ. This union and rule will continue until the final battle (Revelation 20:7-10)." [10]

As ruler

To all Believers who have been victorious and have obeyed Him, to them King Jesus will give authority over the nations to rule with the same authority that He received from His Father. (Revelation 2:26-27) This indicates authority of the highest degree. Unbelievers must adhere to the Believers will and commands.

The Lord does not assign us a task and withdraw from us. His desire is to express Himself through us.

Authority (*exousia* Greek)
"Permission, authority, right, liberty, power to do anything. *Exousia* denotes executive power. *Exousia* also means justified, rightly supra-ordinated [invested] power." [KW]

Rule (*poimaino* Greek)
"To shepherd, tend. It implies the whole office of the shepherd, guiding, guarding, folding of the flock [to place or keep in a fenced enclosure], as well as leading it to nourishment." [KW]

Your authority as a ruler has to do with directing Unbelievers in the implementation of the ways and laws of God. I like the fact that King Jesus gives us the ability and strength to rule as well as the right to reign.

As judge

Glorified Believers are given the authority to judge. (Revelation 20:4; 1 Corinthians 6:2)

Judgment (*krima* and *krino* Greek)
"Judicial authority, power of judging. It also means to consider something with deep thought in order to make a decision." [KW]

Your position as judge has a great deal to do with settling Unbelievers' disputes and wrong doings.

As priest

The priesthood of God's followers dates back to the Old Testament. Exodus 19:6 "*you will be my kingdom of priests, my holy nation*" makes it clear that God's intention was to establish a people for Himself to work with Him as ministers of holiness. In the New Testament this intention is again stated for all Believers in this Present Age in 1 Peter 2:9 "*You are royal priests, a holy nation, God's very own possession.*"

The Priesthood of the Believer
"It is essential to remember that in the New Testament the word 'priest' is used in the singular only of Jesus and in the plural only of all believers. There is no such things as an order or 'caste' of 'priests', and Christian ministers should not be called, or allow themselves to be called, 'priests'." [11]

In the Kingdom Age, you will also be one of the "*priests of God and of Christ.*" (Revelation 20:6; 1:6; 5:10; 1 Peter 2:5) I would like to give you the opportunity to review the qualifications and service that God expects of a priest according to His Word in Malachi 2:5-7. This will give you an idea of what your priestly duties imply during Christ's Thousand-Year Kingdom as well as what it should be today.

Levites, a tribe of Israel, set apart for service to God; Israel's priests were also from this tribe.

Malachi 2:5-7

> [5] *"The purpose of my covenant with the Levites was to bring life and peace, and that is what I gave them. This required reverence from them, and they greatly revered me and stood in awe of my name.*
> [6] *They passed on to the people the truth of the instructions they received from me. They did not lie or cheat; they walked with me, living good and righteous lives, and they turned many from lives of sin.*
> [7] *The words of a priest's lips should preserve knowledge of God, and people should go to him for instruction, for the priest is the messenger of the Lord of Heaven's Armies."*

What thoughts from this Scriptures are especially meaningful to you? ____________________

____

____

Your priestly duties involve the spiritual part of your rule: instructing Unbelievers in the knowledge of God and providing a practical ministry to meet their needs; leading glorified Believers under your care in thanksgiving, prayer, and fellowship. I think that one of the greatest responsibilities will be to lead Unbelievers to a saving knowledge of Christ, however, we do not know if any will respond.

You at all times have access into the holy presence of King Jesus to guide you in your ministry, just as you do today. I hope you have sensed the beauty of your coming reign with your Savior-King. It will be the productive quality of life that you have always strived toward, dreamed of, and truly desired.

KING JESUS DIVIDES THE WORLD INTO KINGDOMS

You will always belong to your people group.

This fact is priceless, but what does it mean? This part of our study definitely involves deduction and logical conclusions based on key Bible verses.

DIVIDING THE WORLD BY NATIONS, TRIBES, PEOPLE, AND LANGUAGES

Even on the new earth, nations will exist as we see mentioned in the last two chapters of Revelation which describes the new heaven and the new earth. (Revelation 21:24, 26; 22:2) In what form will nations exist? When you die and go to heaven, or if you are raptured to heaven, will you, and all other Believers, lose your national identity, or your spoken language, or your family relationships?

These questions are easily answered in the following description of this glorious multitude in heaven.

Revelation 7:9

> *"After this I saw a vast crowd, too great to count, from every nation and tribe* [kindreds] *and people and language, standing in front of the throne and before the Lamb."*

Circle the words in the following verse that point out differences among the people of the world during the Kingdom age.

Daniel 7:14

> *"He* [King Jesus] *was given authority, honor, and sovereignty over all the nations of the world, so that people of every race and nation and language would obey* [serve] *him."*

The terms *nations, people, and language* comprise differences, but not division in the sense of conflictive factions. They are used over and over again in the book of Revelation. (see Revelation 1:7; 5:9; 7:9; 10:11; 11:9; 13:7; 14:6; 17:15)

Nation
"A people, usually the inhabitants of a specific territory, who share common customs, origins, history, and frequently language or related languages. [D]

Nations

According to Daniel 7:14 individual kingdoms or nations will continue. Jesus also speaks of cities over which some of His faithful followers will rule. (Luke 19:17, 19) The Jews are a nation, on the contrary, non-Jewish Believers are not a nation, but rather, are representatives of *all* the nations. Since Believers will rule the nations of the world, is it not reasonable to think that glorified Believers will return to rule in their country of origin?

Languages

Our oldest son, Jeff, (tongue in cheek) loves to tell people that the language of heaven will be Spanish. He is a little partial in that he, and his four brothers, spent his entire childhood and teenage years in South America.

In the Thousand-Year Kingdom, we most certainly will speak in our own language. If everyone should speak or praise God at the same time, it would sound like the day of Pentecost greatly multiplied. It is conceivable, even necessary, that we would understand one another. This ability will bring delightful communion in harmony and unity.

Listen to the description of the sound when the heavenly multitude speaks. To John it was like *"the sound of many waters and like the sound of mighty peals of thunder"* (Revelation 19:6; 14:2) What's more, Jesus speaks all the languages of the world and, He can speak them all at the same time. *"And his* [Jesus] *voice was like the sound of many waters."* (Revelation 1:15)

Family groups

On entering into heaven by death or at the Rapture, one of the top ten things we will want to do is to be reunited with our loved ones. Is it reasonable to think that these family units will be assigned to the same area in Christ's Kingdom? Why would that not be so?

Revelation 7:9 (KJV) "After this I beheld, and, lo, a great multitude, which no man could number, of all nations, and kindreds, and people, and tongues, stood before the throne, and before the Lamb, clothed with white robes, and palms in their hands."

Notice the word "kindreds" is used in the King James Version of Revelation 7:9 because it indicates "a group of related persons: a family, clan, tribe, or the like" [D] and has the same meaning as tribes.

Is it not possible that glorified Believers will be assigned to the nation of their origin to rule in family groups? It would seem logical that the Kingdom age will have as its basic social structure the former nuclear family (parents and their children) and its extended family. However, we must remember that these reigning family groups will be made up of glorified Believers only. Also, individual family members will have different assignments according to their spiritual growth and service to the Lord in this life. Unbelievers will probably live in their family groups, that is, those who have survived to this point. (see "families of the earth" Zechariah 14:17-18 NKJV)

Social Structure

Just a word here regarding our position and duties as they take on a different role during the Kingdom age. World society, concerning the Believer, will be structured differently compared to the way we live today. Jesus gives us a hint at some of the changes to come in the following Scripture which have implications regarding our rule.

Underline what you consider to be Jesus' most significant statements in the following Scripture.

Luke 20:34-36

> "*Marriage is for people here on earth. But in the age to come* [Christ's Thousand-Year Kingdom], *those worthy of being raised from the dead* [at the First Resurrection] *will neither marry nor be given in marriage. And they will never die again. In this respect they will be like angels. They are children of God and children of the resurrection.*"

Of course the Kingdom society will involve new and greater things than we can comprehend in this Present Age. Hopefully, this study inspires you to look forward with great expectation to the wonders of your future in Christ's Kingdom.

Israel

Israel is a nation made up of tribes, twelve to be exact. It is interesting that God sealed 144,000 Jews of the twelve tribes at the beginning of the Wrath of God which means that all Israel is represented in their last trial. The tribe of Dan is not in the list in Revelation 7, however it is listed in the millennial Scriptures of Ezekiel 48. The Israelis will take possession of an enlarged territory which lies between the Nile River of Egypt and Euphrates River of Iraq. Each tribe will have an allotment.

Guess who will reign over each tribe in Christ's Kingdom? Read Matthew 19:27-28 to discover the answer. (see also Luke 22:28-30).

Underline the words in the following verse that gives the time of their reign.

Matthew 19:28

> *"I assure you* [12 disciples] *that when the world is new* [restored] *and the Son of Man sits upon his glorious throne, you who have been my followers will also sit on twelve thrones, judging the twelve tribes of Israel."*

An enlightened, born-again glorified Israel will delight in their King. Their hearts will swell with joy because Jehovah has at last fulfilled His promise to them:

Isaiah 9:7 (NASB)

> *"There will be no end to the increase of His government or of peace, on the throne of David and over His kingdom, to establish it and to uphold it with justice and righteousness from then on and forevermore. The zeal of the Lord of Hosts will accomplish this."*

Jerusalem
And from that day the name of the city will be 'The Lord Is There'—Yahweh Shammah (Ezekiel 48:35)

King Jesus will sit on the throne of His ancestor David on the mountain of the Lord in Jerusalem. Did you notice the word *"increase"* in Isaiah 9:7? **Circle** the words *"no end to the increase"* and **underline** what will continually increase or grow. I would like to challenge you to expand your thinking on the greatness and glory of Christ's eternal Kingdom through the poetic thoughts of F.C. Jennings[12] based on this verse.

> "His kingdom ever grows. . .Indeed, being divine, this is inevitable, for nothing that is of God can possibly stagnate. Stagnation is the mark of death; growth is the surest evidence of life. Stagnant water we call "dead" water, while the running waters of a spring are termed "living." So with His Kingdom there is never stagnation; of its increase there is no end."

We are considering the very moment King Jesus begins His reign. Starting at His throne in Jerusalem, Christ's Kingdom begins to spread. It spills over the boundaries of the nation of Israel. It spreads throughout the world to the boundaries of the New Earth; and yet it increases—yes, continuing into the New Heaven. F.C. Jennings continues:

> "The boundaries of this kingdom is the earth. But still it 'increases,' and where can it now extend? There is to be no 'end' to its increase, then it must have a boundless limitless sphere, as the Kingdom of the Son of God. Earth is too small now. His peace, power, and presence fills all. Even the rule as Son of Man is too limited. The universe without any bounds—an idea that no finite mind can embrace—is finally, after the millennial reign, the ever-increasing kingdom of Him who for us died upon the tree."

You

At this point in time, you stand at the dawn of a thousand years. You look toward the horizon of a devastated world from the effects of the judgment at the Second Coming of King Jesus, and you see the Spirit of God hovering over the face of the earth. The paradise of God will be restored. Your heart thrills with the prospect of working with Christ; His inner presence ever guiding your mind and heart.

You have your assignment. You know exactly what King Jesus wants you to do. You are ready.

JESUS CHRIST THE FULLNESS OF GOD

Colossians 2:9

LESSON 17A

JESUS CHRIST THE HOLY ONE
Acts 3:14

The wicked one with all impurities are swept up like so much trash and dumped from God's dust pan into the furnace.

THE END OF EVIL

Something to think about
In Lesson 16B it was mentioned that we will always belong to our people group which includes continuing to speak our native language. However, did you know that our vocabulary is going to take a big hit in loss of words? Many words will also be greatly altered with our expanded understanding of their meaning, such as the word *eternity*. Our finite minds have a great deal of difficulty freeing our thinking from the bonds of time. We even tend to explain eternity by saying, "Eternity is a very long *time*" (oxymoron)

From Heaven's View, [1] by T.W. Hunt and his daughter Melana Hunt Monroe, is a unique study. The last four pages of this book present enlightening thoughts about our future heavenly language, such as, the expanded meaning of words and words that will be dropped from our vocabulary altogether. "Put on your thinking cap," (an old saying) and contemplate what our language will be like in the New Heaven and the New Earth. An analysis of eternal vocabulary reveals how very different life is going to be. The authors referred to, give a list of words that will cease to exist. Very uplifting!

Make a list of words that you think might be terminated. As an example, I will show you some on my list.

Nouns	**Verbs**	**Adjectives**
police, hospitals, weeds, hunger,	hate, irritate, defy, criticize,	worthless, selfish, obstinate,
storms, homelessness, deception,	procrastinate, kill, steal,	arrogant, disfigured, corrupt,
religion, crime, grief, cemeteries	forgive, punish, destroy	disgusting, distressful, wicked

I think we will celebrate the absence of the word *evil* more than any other word on the list of eliminated words in our new vocabulary. Before entering into God's final and permanent Kingdom in the New Heaven and the New Earth, all evil, and all things contaminated by evil, will be destroyed. This is where our lesson begins—the end of evil.

The End of Evil
In this lesson the end of evil does not mean non-existence, but rather, to be inoperative, isolated as in eternal confinement. *"These shall be punished with everlasting destruction from the presence of the Lord and from the glory of His power."* (2 Thessalonians 1:9 NKJV) Everlasting destruction signifies perpetual destruction; a destruction that continues for eternity.

We will study in this lesson:

The Purpose of Christ's Thousand-Year Kingdom on Earth

THE PURPOSE OF CHRIST'S THOUSAND-YEAR KINGDOM ON EARTH

Revelation 20:7 makes an important statement prefaced by these words: "*When the thousand years come to an end.*" The Greek word *teleos* or "end" used in this phrase indicates that the Thousand-Year Kingdom has accomplished its purpose or goal. This means that God has specific objectives in mind for this end-time Event. What are some of those purposes?

Keep in mind that every child born during the Kingdom years is born of unbelieving parents, whose ancestors were former worshippers of the Antichrist and survivors of the Second Coming. These children are sinners at birth. The reality of the extent of the degradation of man's sinful nature comes into full view at the end of the thousand years when these earth people willingly respond to satanic enticements.

Alexander Patterson will introduce our thoughts to the intriguing subject of God's purposes for Christ's Thousand-Year Kingdom on Earth.

Warren Wiersbe on Christ's Thousand-Year Reign "It will be God's final demonstration of the sinfulness of sin and the wickedness of the human heart apart from God's grace." [3]

> The millennium is a demonstration by God that the world by obedience to God's will is thereby made a wholesome and happy place. It is also a trial of man, under the most favorable circumstances, as to his willingness to obey God. It is the belief professed by many that the present state of man in sin and misery, comes from his environment, and if all this could be changed, he would attain to a state of comparative perfection. All men will be given an opportunity to be tried during the millennial age. With Satan bound and absent from earth, and natural evils that cause temptation removed, and beginning with a relatively small and selected group of survivors from Armageddon, there is no reason, if this theory is correct, why mankind should not reach their ideal. In the millennium there is to be made the fullest demonstration of man's nature and ability under every condition for success. When it is over, nothing will have been left untried or untested. A thousand years will be long enough for the trial. Tragically the millennium is to end in rebellion. [2]

Purpose: Christ must reign until all His enemies have been put under His feet and destroyed.

God's plan is moving toward a perfect, sinless universe. Christ's Thousand-Year Reign is a vital part of this plan concerning end-time Events. The Second Coming begins a new phase in which King Jesus will ascend unimpeded to His rightful place of lordship where He will impose His will and exercise His power to destroy every foe.

1 Corinthians 15:24-26 (RSV)

> *"Then comes the end, when he* [Christ] *delivers the kingdom to God the Father after destroying every rule and every authority and power. For he must reign until he has put all enemies under his feet. The last enemy to be destroyed is death."*

At the point in time just before Christ's millennial reign begins, what earthly enemy *rulers*, *authorities*, and *powers* have been destroyed and when did this happen? ________________

____

Who are the spirit enemy *ruler* and his *authorities* and *powers* still functioning up to the beginning of the millennial reign of Christ? ________________________________

What is the last enemy? ______________________

In the here and now of this Present Age, and much more so during the personal reign of the Antichrist, it may appear to us that evil is gaining ground and will triumph. Not so! To the first question above you most likely answered with great delight that at King Jesus' Second Coming the Antichrist, the False Prophet, and the Ten Kings with their armies will be destroyed at Armageddon. Praise the Lord!

We will soon see in this lesson what happens to Satan and his nasty host of demons which will answer the second question. And finally the end of Death.

John MacArthur, Jr. "The perfect millennial kingdom will testify through all eternity that Jesus Christ is the supreme sovereign, who alone can bring absolute harmony and peace to a world even while it is still infected by sin." [4]

Purpose: Christ's temporal thousand-year reign will bring closure to world history. Mark Hitchcock provides insight on the noteworthy purpose for Christ's temporal thousand-year reign which will bring closure to world history.

> ". . . the best and ultimate reason why there must be a literal millennium is that only in a literal millennium do we have a meaningful culmination of world history." [6]

The reasoning here is that God's original purpose for man "was to bring all things under the dominion of humankind and to submit all things to Himself through human beings." [7] (Genesis 1:26-27) This is finally accomplished in the closing chapter of world history during the thousand-year reign of King Jesus through His loyal followers. It took a long. . .a very long time.

John MacArthur, Jr. "An earthly millennial kingdom is the only and necessary bridge from human history to eternal glory." [5]

Purpose: Christ's Thousand-Year Kingdom is the final word at the Great White Throne Judgment. This to me is outstanding among the purposes of God and the temporal reign of His Son. I think you will agree with me that G.E. Ladd expresses this thought in a very clear and concise manner.

> "It is God's concern so to deal with men in righteousness and judgment that 'every mouth may be stopped, and the whole world held accountable to God' (Romans 3:19). If then there is yet to be in the sovereign wisdom of God an era in history when evil is restrained, when righteousness prevails as it never has before in this age—if there is to be a time of social and political and economic justice when men dwell together under the government of Christ in peace and prosperity—if before the final judgment God grants to men a time when their social environment is as nearly perfect as possible, and yet after such a period of righteousness, the hearts of unregenerate men prove still to be rebellious against God, in the final judgment of the great white throne every mouth

will indeed be stopped and every excuse voided, to the vindication of the glory and the righteousness of God."

"The millennial reign of righteousness is the <u>backdrop</u> for the last judgment. . ." [8]

W.E. Vine "Even the personal presence of Christ, and the establishment of His kingdom will not accomplish the regeneration of the human heart." [9]

The personal presence of King Jesus and godly instruction beautifully modeled by Christ's glorified servants will provide every condition for a thousand years to convince earth people to willingly turn in repentance to God and to voluntarily submit their lives to the lordship of King Jesus.

Every eye of every person standing before God in judgment will look, as it were, at the backdrop behind His Great White Throne. They will see displayed there a thousand years of earth-people's squandered lives, untouched by the nail prints in King Jesus' hands.

SATAN ON THE LOOSE

You have faithfully served Christ in His Kingdom for a thousand years. Who would have thought it possible to live on this earth for that long a time? But of course, your life is endless. Millions of Unbelievers have been born to the remnant of the former followers of the Antichrist. They seem to think that a perfect world makes them a perfect person. That is far from the truth. Through the years you have seen manifestations of the earth people's sinful nature. Even though King Jesus holds them in line, they remind us of the saying: "A man convinced against his will is of the same opinion still." [10] You sense the constant, underlying discontent and unrest.

A thousand glorious years have come to an end. Suddenly, the unthinkable happens. Our ultra-sensitive spirits can feel evil invading the atmosphere; dreadful, vile spirit-beings are everywhere. Satan and his demon forces have returned! To our dismay, we see the earth people turning to the enemy as if they were their great liberators. King Jesus summons all glorified Believers back to Jerusalem. An immense encampment takes shape around the beloved city. A battle is brewing. A historic event is about to take place.

Read the following verses which make known the most unthinkable rebellion against God that has ever taken place on earth. **Underline** the phrases that express the vast number of earth people who align themselves with Satan. Please make your five observations or questions. Questions are a type of observation because you can't ask a question unless you have observed something.

Revelation 20:7-9

> [7] *"When the thousand years come to an end, Satan will be let out of his prison.* [8] *He will*
> *go out to deceive the nations—called Gog and Magog—in every corner of the earth. He will gather them together for battle—a mighty army, as numberless as sand along the seashore.* [9] *And I saw them as they went up on the broad plain of the earth and surrounded God's people and the beloved city. But fire from heaven came down on the attacking armies and consumed them.*

Your observations
1. ______
2. ______
3. ______
4. ______
5. ______

Again, I would like to say that it would be such a delight for me to be able to sit down with you over a cup of coffee to discuss your observations.

Observations

Verses 7-9. . . After one thousand years in the bottomless pit, Satan still holds to his incredibly illegitimate ambition. His all-consuming objective is to exalt himself above God and to destroy God's Son, Jesus Christ. Satan sought to accomplish his overreaching goals through the person of the Antichrist. "*He will exalt himself. . .He will even sit in the temple of God, claiming that he himself is God.*" (2 Thessalonians 2:4) The Antichrist will have accomplished the first objective during the World System of the Antichrist, but his claims will have resulted in his eternal destruction in the lake of fire.

Isaiah 14:12-14 are words spoken to the king of Babylon, but are also believed by many to apply to Satan in his original state as a powerful cherubim. This Scripture helps us to understand the basis for the animosity between God and Satan. In order to comprehend the consequential significance of the consummation of evil, we must grasp the meaning of Isaiah 14:12-14 in its correlation with Revelation 20:7-9. Through this Old Testament Scripture, God permits us to look into the black heart and evil mind of Satan himself. We see the ruthless ambition which drives Satan's actions as he comes roaring out of his thousand-year incarceration.

Isaiah 14:12-14 (NASB)

> [12] *How you have fallen from heaven, O star of the morning, son of the dawn! You have been cut down to the earth, you who have weakened the nations!*
> [13] *But you said in your heart, I will ascend to heaven; I will raise my throne above the stars of God, and I will sit* [enthroned] *on the mount of assembly in the recesses of the north.* [14] *I will ascend above the heights of the clouds; I will make myself like the Most High."*

Let's think together as we develop an interpretation of Isaiah 14:13-14.
We will look at the meaning of the key words of this Scripture out of which an interpretation will emerge. **Circle** the five "I wills" in the Scripture above.

1. **I will ascend to heaven**. . .In Jesus' ascension He "*passed through the heavens*" (Hebrews 4:14 RSV). Jesus "*ascended higher than all the heavens, so that he might fill the entire universe with himself.*" (Ephesians 4:10) Then Jesus "*sat down in the place of honor beside the throne of the majestic God in heaven.*" *(Hebrews 8:1)* Satan's ambition is not only to imitate but to surpass the Lord Jesus.

Ezekiel 43:12 (NKJV) "The whole area surrounding the mountaintop is most holy." Holiness surrounds the millennial temple.

Psalm 48:1-2 (NKJV) "Great is the Lord, and greatly to be praised in the city of our God, in His holy mountain. Beautiful in elevation, the joy of the whole earth, is Mount Zion on the sides of the north, the city of the great King."

2. **I will raise [set] my throne above the stars of God**. . .Heaven is the abode of the angels. Satan's desire is to subjugate and to reign over his former peers—the angels of God. What a mighty stronghold this would be! In this case, we are using the figurative meaning of *stars* which are to be identified as angels.

3. **I will sit on the mount of assembly in the recesses [sides] of the north**. . . *mount of assembly* signifies "the place of solemn meeting between God and His people in the temple at Jerusalem" [11] *In the recesses or sides of the north* indicates an exact location of the temple placing it on the side of Mount Moriah, north of Mount Zion in Jerusalem. This is the location where God has chosen to enthrone His Son, where King Jesus will conduct the affairs of the world, and where He will communicate with His people during His Thousand-Year Reign. Psalm 48:2 speaks of this location.

   Satan has never swayed from his consuming desire to rule over both angelic powers and mankind. He wants it all. Satan's ambition is to *"sit in the temple of God, claiming that he himself is God"* on the holy mountain where King Jesus will rule the world from His millennial temple in Jerusalem. (2 Thessalonians 2:4) The description in this verse is very specific in telling us exactly where Satan presumptuously intends to enthrone himself.

4. **I will ascend above the heights of the clouds [cloud]**. . .The word *clouds* used here is singular, not plural, in the Hebrew it reads—*thick cloud mass* . Undoubtedly Satan is referring to "*the cloud of the Lord*," (the Shekinah) which was the manifestation of the presence of the glory of God. (Exodus 40:38)

   The cloud is described in Ezekiel's vision of God's glory. (Ezekiel 1:4, 27) Ezekiel saw "*a whirlwind. . . a great cloud with raging fire engulfing* [enfolding] *itself, and brightness was all around it.*" Then Ezekiel sees a man sitting on a throne within the cloud. "*From the appearance of His waist and upward I saw, as it were the color of amber with the appearance of fire all around within it; and from the appearance of His waist and downward I saw, as it were, the appearance of fire with brightness all around.*"

   Awesome! "*The cloud of the Lord*" looks like fire enveloped by a cloud. This manifestation of God's presence and glory protected Israel from Pharaoh's army during Israel's escape from Egypt; it covered the mountain where the Law was given to Moses; it led Israel through the desert; it covered and filled the tabernacle and remained above the mercy seat; it filled Solomon's temple in a magnificent manner. (Exodus 14:24; 24:15; Leviticus 16:2; Numbers 9:15-23; 2 Chronicles 5:13-14)

   Next, and still future, Ezekiel tells us that the glory of the Lord will fill the millennial temple at the Second Coming of King Jesus. (Ezekiel 43:5) This is the vision that torments the malevolent mind of Satan as he tears helplessly at his bonds for a thousand years in the bottomless pit. The vision of the "cloud of glory" spurs him on to unmatched perseverance toward his goal. His ranting reaches the most remote recesses of the abyss: "*I will ascend above the heights of **the cloud!***"

5. **I will make myself like the Most High**. . . This says it all. The word *like* embraces everything that God is in relation to His limitless power and all-encompassing dominion. Satan told our parents in Eden the same thing: "*you will be like God.*" (Genesis 3:5) The Antichrist believed the same lie. (2 Thessalonians 2:4) Having read the five "*I wills*," it is apparent that Satan really thinks that he can be like God. Satan literally lifts up his pride-filled heart against God to contend for the place of universal supremacy.

   John Wesley once said of a certain type of person: "He imagines himself to be what he is not, and therefore, setting out wrong, the farther he goes, the more he wanders out of the way." [12] What a fitting description of Satan!

   The Scriptures have established that Satan is utterly incorrigible.

The Antichrist "...who opposes and exalts himself above every so-called god or object of worship, so that he takes his seat in the temple of God, displaying himself as being God." (2 Thessalonians 2:4 NASB)

THE END OF EVIL

The *end of evil* when referring to evil beings, both evil spirts and man, is used here in the sense that all evil beings will be confined to a place of punishment forever. Their power to affect God's creation in the Eternal Age is abolished.

THE END OF EVIL—SATAN AND HIS DEMONS

We again turn to Revelation 20:7-10.

> 7 *"When the thousand years come to an end, Satan will be let out of his prison.*
> *8 He will go out to deceive the nations—called Gog and Magog—in every corner of the earth. He will gather them together for battle—a mighty army, as numberless as sand along the seashore.*
> *9 And I saw them as they went up on the broad plain of the earth and surrounded God's people and the beloved city. But fire from heaven came down on the attacking armies and consumed them.*
> *10 Then the devil, who had deceived them, was thrown into the fiery lake of burning sulfur, joining the beast and the false prophet. There they will be tormented day and night forever and ever."*

Verse 7. . .**When the thousand years come to an end, Satan will be let out of his prison.** At an exact hour Satan is unleashed. Apparently Satan's demon army is released with him. Compare the time mentioned in verse 7 with Revelation 20:3 below.

Circle the *time* elements in the following verse.
Revelation 20:3

> "The angel threw him into the bottomless pit, which he then shut and locked so Satan could not deceive the nations anymore until the thousand years were finished. Afterward he must be released for a little while."

Lies are always spoken with the intention of deceiving. Satan "is a liar and the father of lies." He is, therefore, the greatest of all deceivers. (John 8:44)

Verse 8. . . **He will go out to deceive the nations—called Gog and Magog—in every corner of the earth. He will gather them together for battle—a mighty army, as numberless as sand along the seashore.**

The term "*Gog and Magog*" is used here as a figure of speech in reference to the earth people, all the nations as a whole who will come together in alliance with Satan. The invasion of Israel by Gog and Magog at the time of the Rapture involved only a few nations. (Ezekiel 38-39) The use of this term for the final invasion of Israel is because of the great similarities. Basically both invasions will be Satan inspired and conducted, however, this rebellion will be on a much greater scale.

Jessie Penn-Lewis The word "deceived" is, according to the Scripture, the description of every unregenerate human being, without distinction of persons, race, culture, or gender.[13]

Underline in verse 8 the words that indicate the size of the earth people's army. How does Satan get the people to join him in such a futile endeavor? ______________________________
____

How does one explain the magnitude of this deception taking place in such a short period of time? We shake our heads in disbelief. This reveals Satan's great ability, cunning ingenuity, and spiritual power over mankind. Romans 1 certainly fits these millennial Unbelievers.

Romans 1:21, 25 (RSV)

> *"for although they knew God. . .they exchanged the truth about God for a lie and worshipped and served the creature* [Satan is a created being] *rather than the Creator. . ."*

Verse 9. . .And they came up on the broad plain of the earth and surrounded the camp of the saints and the beloved city. (NASB)

You with all glorified Believers are prepared for battle. Our vast camp encircles the holy mountain of the Lord. Extraordinary! *All* of God's people representing every nation, tribe, peoples, and language are confronting in mortal battle *all* Unbelievers from every nation, tribe, people, and language. No one is left on the sideline. Decisions have been made, and the lines have been drawn. We are *in Christ*; they are *in Satan.* At the same time, this is an indescribably triumphant moment because the end of evil is near.

You see your beloved King Jesus high up on the ramparts of the temple looking toward the horizon. His countenance is so fearsome it makes you tremble. The violent insurrection has begun. King Jesus points to the four corners of the earth. You turn to look in each direction He is signaling. You see the devils first; they blot out the sky as they gleefully rush towards us. Then, you hear a vehement clamoring. You see on the horizon the degenerate and mutinous shapes of the last generation. They are hardly recognizable as human beings.

Do not fear. The child of God does not strive to gain victory… he stands in victory!

Satan's vast evil host attacks the holy land. Satan believes that he can at last exterminate God's people because they are assembled in just one place.

Verses 9-10. . . But fire from heaven came down on the attacking armies and consumed them. Then the devil, who had deceived them, was thrown into the fiery lake of burning sulfur, joining the beast and the false prophet. There they will be tormented day and night forever and ever.

The deceived souls of the earth people involved in this conflict go down to the abyss. The devil and his demons are cast "*into the eternal fire* <u>*prepared for*</u> *the devil and his demons.*" (Matthew

25:41) Take note in verse 10 the mention of their *joining the* ____________________ *and the* ______________________________ who have already been in this eternal fire for one thousand years.

And so ends the last war of earth's turbulent history. This is truly the war that ends all wars.

I think that you will agree that the significance of the finality of Satan's rule is beyond our finite human comprehension. Mankind has never known, since the fall of man, the total absence and influence of his evil empire. Satan will never corrupt God's creation again, NEVER. . .EVER!

However. . .evil still exists and must be dealt with.

JESUS CHRIST THE HOLY ONE

Acts 3:14

LESSON **17B**

JESUS CHRIST THE CONQUEROR
1 Corinthians 15:24-26

Christ has vanquished every foe of God and man. The last enemy to be destroyed is death!

THE END OF EVIL

THE GREAT WHITE THRONE JUDGMENT

CHRONOLOGY OF EVENTS AT THIS POINT IN TIME
Because of the rapidity in which events take place, it will avoid confusion to see them in sequential order.

1. Fire from heaven consumed unbelieving earth people at the last battle at the conclusion of the thousand-year reign of Christ. Their bodies are incinerated and their souls descend into the abyss.
2. As a result of this last battle, Satan and his demons were dispatched to the lake of eternal fire.
3. The bodies of all the unbelieving dead are resurrected and united with their souls and spirits. They collectively stand before God for judgment. This is called the Great White Throne Judgment.
4. Heaven and earth are destroyed immediately following the resurrection of the unbelieving dead.
5. Death and Hades (the abyss) are thrown into the lake of fire.
6. All Unbelievers are judged at the final judgment and cast into the lake of fire.
7. The New Heaven and the New Earth take the place of the old.

In this lesson we will study:

- The Throne
  - John's Vision of the Great White Throne Judgment
- The Judged
  - The End of Evil—The Heavens and the Earth
  - The End of Evil—All Unbelievers
  - The End of Evil—Death and Hades

Definition of the Great White Throne Judgment
This is the final divine judgment of mankind, and it takes place at the end of Earth's history. All the resurrected, unbelieving dead from every age, from every family, nation, and language will stand collectively before God. Each individual will be judged guilty based on his relationship to Jesus Christ. Every person will also be judged by his works, and accordingly, will be assigned a place in the lake of fire forever.

At this judgment, earth and heaven are destroyed, and death and Hades (the abyss) are thrown into the lake of fire.

Deuteronomy 6:4 (NASB) "Hear, O Israel! The Lord is our God, the Lord is one!"

"In the unity of the Godhead there be three persons, of one substance, power, and eternity; God the Father, God the Son, and God the Holy Ghost [Spirit]." The Westminster Confession of Faith (chapter 2 #3)

Look for The Great White Throne Judgment on **Timeline Three** (located at the end of Part One of this study book.) If you are an Unbeliever write Event **6** on the line by the asterisk (*_6_) located above the "throne."

Believer, you will be present at this Event as we shall see in this lesson, however, this Event is between God and all who do not have their name written in the Lamb's Book of Life.

THE THRONE

Revelation 20:11-12 (NASB)

> [11] *"And I saw a great white throne and Him who sat upon it. . .And I saw the dead, great and small, standing before the throne."*

Remember Ezekiel's vision of *"the man sitting on a throne within the cloud"* in reference to Satan's ambition? Here it is. The great throne of God which surpasses all thrones in magnitude and majesty. (Ezekiel 1:4, 27) Not only could Satan not *"ascend above the heights of the cloud,"* he wasn't even permitted to stand before the throne of God to be judged! At the last battle he was cast directly into the lake of fire.

This scene is the most solemn and conclusive moment of all time. Therefore, you and I will approach it with great reverence. The significance of the moment demands that *"Him who sat upon it"* applies to the Godhead: God the Father, God the Son, and God the Holy Spirit, the Trinity.

God the Father is man's Creator.
"Then the Lord God formed the man from the dust of the ground. He breathed the breath of life into the man's nostrils, and the man became a living person." (Genesis 2:7) All people were made by God and designed for intimate fellowship with God for all eternity. But these *risen dead* have spurned the Father, and unlike the prodigal son, never returned home to His loving arms. Every person standing before the throne in the presence of God the Father owes his existence to his Maker. But he has forfeited his birthright. His precious life was squandered, pointless, wasted. He has no second chance.

God the Son is man's Savior.
Jesus took man's place on the cross. His death, resurrection, and ascension opened the way to God for man's salvation. Every guilt-ridden person standing before the throne in the presence of his disregarded substitute—God the Son—will stand in shameful condemnation bearing the judgment of his own sin. He is without excuse.

God the Holy Spirit is man's Convicter.
Jesus said that when the Holy Spirit would come to earth, He would do the following, and He has faithfully done exactly as stated:

- The Holy Spirit speaks to both man's mind and conscious about his sinful condition and acts. The resulting sense of guilt is meant to draw him to the cross of Christ.

- The Holy Spirit constantly reminds each person of God's authority over his life and His righteous standards by which he was meant to live. The resulting sense of guilt is meant to bring man to forsake his self-centered independence and live his life in total dependence upon God.

- The Holy Spirit speaks to the heart of every human being telling them that without Christ they will die in their sins resulting in judgment. The resulting sense of guilt is to bring man to live, through Jesus, a life that is guided by the principle: I will one day give an account of myself to God.

All who stand before the Throne in the presence of God the Holy Spirit understands that he cannot say, "But, I didn't hear your voice speaking to me," because he knows that he didn't listen, really listen. Or worse, the sinner heard the voice of God in his heart but preferred "*to enjoy the fleeting pleasures of sin.*" (Hebrews 11:25). There are no grounds for appeal.

John 16:8
When the Holy Spirit comes, "he will convict the world of its sin, and of God's righteousness, and of the coming judgment."

JOHN'S VISION OF THE GREAT WHITE THRONE JUDGMENT

The apostle John is permitted by God to see the prophetic events in the book of Revelation in the form of visions. Bible visions transmit to the reader a sense of awe and wonder through his emotions, and they easily involve him in the dramatic scene through his imagination. The reader also recognizes through his intellect that he has been touched by profound truth expressed in the visions.

Try to visualize this magnificent scene as it unfolds. Observe the action as if you were actually present. Whether you are a Believer or an Unbeliever, you will definitely be present on that day.

Revelation 20:11-15 (RSV)

> [11] *"Then I saw a great white throne and him who sat upon it; from his presence earth and sky fled away, and no place was found for them.*
>
> [12] *And I saw the dead, great and small, standing before the throne, and books were opened. Also another book was opened, which is the book of life. And the dead were judged by what was written in the books, by what they had done.* [13] *And the sea gave up the dead in it, Death and Hades* [the abyss] *gave up the dead in them, and all were judged by what they had done.*
>
> [14] *Then Death and Hades* [the abyss] *were thrown into the lake of fire. This is the second death, the lake of fire;* [15] *and if anyone's name was not found written in the book of life, he was thrown into the lake of fire."*

Great White Throne Judgment
"In giving this truth to us, the Holy Spirit used the past tense, the historic tense of prophecy, as He does in other prophetic Scriptures. Nothing can change the facts of history after they have happened. Nor can anything prevent this future event which the Spirit has declared. In God's sight it has already taken place.
-S. Maxwell Coder

Observation questions

1. Who are the dead? verse 12 ____________________
2. Where did they come from? verse13 ____________________
3. Where are the dead standing? verse 12 ____________________

Revelation 20:5
"The rest of the dead did not come back to life until the thousand years had ended."

4. Do you think that the dead will have a body? Yes ____________ No ____________
5. When does this resurrection take place? Revelation 20:5 (margin) ________________
____

(Note) The last phrase in Revelation 20:5 *"This is the first resurrection"* refers back to the resurrected martyrs who *"lived and reigned with Christ for a thousand years"* Revelation 20:4.

6. What is recorded in the books? verse 12 ________________________________
7. On what basis are the dead judged? verse 13 ________________________________
8. What happens to the dead whose names are not found in the Book of Life? verse 15 ________
____
9. Are there any rewards given at the Great White Throne Judgment? Yes ________ No ________ This is clearly not the same judgment as the Judgment Seat of Christ. (2 Corinthians 5:10)
10. What happens to *Death* and *Hades* (the place of the souls and spirits of the unbelieving dead)? verse 14 ________________________________
11. After this judgment of God, will evil still exist? Yes ____________ No ____________

You may check your answers within the commentary given throughout this lesson.

THE JUDGED

THE END OF EVIL—THE HEAVENS AND THE EARTH

Revelation 20:11-15 (RSV)

> [11] *"Then I saw a great white throne and him who sat upon it; from his presence earth and sky fled away, and no place was found for them.*

The destruction of earth and heaven is foretold many times in Scripture and the New Heavens and New Earth promised.

Jesus:

> *"Heaven and earth will pass away, but My words shall not pass away."* (Matthew 24:35 NASB)

God through the apostle Peter:

> [7]*"And by the same word, the present heavens and earth have been stored up for fire. They are being kept for the day of judgment, when ungodly people will be destroyed.* [13] *But we are looking forward to the new heavens and the new earth he has promised, a world filled with God's righteousness."* *(2 Peter 3:7, 13)*

The "*day of judgment*" is the Great White Throne Judgment. Look at the timing in 2 Peter 3:7. The present ____________________and ________________ will be destroyed at the time of the Great White Throne Judgment when ____________________ will be destroyed.

Why will heaven and earth be destroyed?
One day three young men came to our house to use the photocopier. Two went into the back room to do the copying while the third sat chatting with me in the living room. They finished their work, "hasta luegos" were said, and that was it. Many months passed when one of the fellows came to our house and confessed that two of the young men had committed an immoral act in that back room. We were shocked! My first thoughts were that our house had been violated and needed a moral cleansing, so to speak, because it had been dedicated to God's use and for His glory.

When man sinned in the Garden of Eden, the evil corrupting power of sin that possessed his being began to spread throughout the earth like a mammoth polluting spillage which continued its destructive course until the entire universe was brought under the bondage of corruption and decay. The sin-tainted earth (the back room) defiled all of creation (the whole house.)

As a result of the fall of man:

- the curse of sin and death came upon all *men. "For all have sinned. . ."* (Romans 3:23 NKJV) "*you shall die*" (Genesis 2:17)
- all creatures and the very earth itself fell under the curse of God. (Genesis 3:14-19) "Against its will, *all creation was subjected to God's curse. But with eager hope, the creation looks forward to the day when it will join God's children in glorious freedom from death and decay."* (Romans 8:20-22)

The RSV version translates Romans 8:20 this way: "*the creation was subjected to futility,*" a condition of uselessness, pointlessness, and ineffectiveness. The universe is in bondage to corruption, decay, and ruin, and therefore, cannot fulfill the purpose for which God created it. During the Wrath of God judgment and Armageddon the whole topography of the earth will be affected by catastrophic events. During the thousand years of peace and prosperity it will have been restored to a very beautiful place to accommodate the Kingdom of Christ. However, earth will be tainted by the presence of sinful Unbelievers during this Kingdom period.

"There shall no more be anything accursed" (Revelation 22:3 RSV)
In the New Heaven and the New Earth no accursed thing will be in existence. All evil, and everything contaminated by evil, will be brought to an end. Therefore, all three affected by the fall of man, unbelieving mankind, the earth, and creation will be purged from God's presence.

Cursed man so desperately needs a savior; what's more, the cursed creation groans for redemption!

Then Jesus came *becoming* for our sake *an accursed thing*; God made the sinless One to be sin for us. *"Christ redeemed us from the curse of the law, having become a curse for us. . ."* (Galatians 3:13 NKJV; 2 Corinthians 5:21) "*For in him* [Jesus] *all the fullness of God was pleased to dwell, and through him* [Jesus] *to reconcile to himself all things, whether on earth or in heaven, making peace by the blood of his cross."* (Colossians 1:19-20 RSV)

Leitch
"Earth is out of harmony with God. The great harp of the universe has one of its strings out of tune, and that one discordant string makes a jar through the whole. All things in heaven and earth shall be reconciled when this one jarring string is keyed right and set in tune by the hand of love and mercy." [1]

How utterly amazing! When Jesus suffered on the cross, He willingly took upon Himself the curse and sins of mankind as well as all the corruption found in the entire universe. Unfathomable!

In spite of the curse and all the corruption He bore, Christ rose from the dead an incorruptible, spiritual body.

All men must die physically, but those who have received salvation through faith in Christ will be resurrected with an incorruptible, spiritual body.

Psalm 146:1-2 "Praise the Lord! Let all that I am praise the Lord. I will praise the Lord as long as I live. I will sing praises to my God with my dying breath."

Acts 2:24 "But God released [loosed] him [Jesus] from the horrors of death and raised him back to life, for death could not keep him in its grip."

All corruption has been removed from those that are "*in Christ.*" Inanimate things cannot make a moral choice of accepting or rejecting salvation. Therefore, corrupt creation will *die*, that is to say, be destroyed in order to give place to a resurrection, of sorts, to an incorruptible New Heavens and a New Earth.

The heavens and the earth vanish

The disintegration of the universe, including the earth, occurs after Jesus Second Coming and His Thousand-Year Reign immediately following the resurrection of the unbelieving dead. Here is how it will happen.

2 Peter 3:10 (NASB)

> "*But the day of the Lord will come like a thief* [unexpected], *in which the heavens will pass away with a roar and the elements will be destroyed* [dissolved] *with intense heat, and the earth and its works will be burned up.*"

The word *elements* means the very tiniest component of matter or the substance of matter. The Greek word means the basic parts or the building blocks of matter. The action here suggests that these elements can be torn apart. The Greek word for *destroy*, is *luo* meaning "to loosen or unloosen, break up, dissolve." This word was used by Jesus to set free a woman who had been bound by Satan for eighteen years; she was so crippled that she was bent double and couldn't stand up straight. (Luke 13:16) Likewise, the heavens and the earth will be set free from the curse. This earth will disintegrate with a terrible heat including everything man-made.

I would like for you to consider Jesus' present operating power concerning the universe disclosed in Colossians 1:17.

> "*He* [Jesus] *existed before anything else, and he holds all creation together* [so that created things will not break up or fall into chaotic conditions]."

How do you explain the disintegration of the universe in light of Jesus' operating power that sustains and maintains it in perfect balance? What will Jesus do? ______________________________

____

In simple terms, the Lord Jesus will withdraw His sustaining power of the universe resulting in the disappearance of creation. Jesus will stop holding it together. Incredible! No man-made power could ever cause such a magnitude of destruction. There will be nothing left. The death of the heavens and the earth gives place to all things new.

You are safe
God's unique dwelling place will be exempt because this is the location of His great white throne and the New Jerusalem. It is a good thing that you have a spiritual body that can adjust itself to a non-material environment as well as conditions of physical substance. In God's heaven you are safe in Jesus.

G.E. Ladd
"The resurrection body as described by Paul transcends present historical experience. A body suited to the life of the Kingdom [and beyond] must be different from the bodies of this age." [2]

Let me insert here that there is another place that will not be destroyed at this point in time, nor ever will be—the eternal lake of fire. Jesus told us about this place: "*the eternal fire prepared for the devil and his demons.*" (Matthew 25:41) This eternal lake of fire is presently somewhere in creation and will be forever.

God wants us to pause and think deeply about the catastrophic destruction of creation.

God's question

> *"In view of the fact that all these things are to be dissolved, what sort of people ought you to be?*

God's answer

> *Surely men of good and holy character, who live expecting and earnestly longing for the coming of the day of God.*
> *True, this day will mean that the heavens will disappear in fire and the elements disintegrate in fearful heat, but our hopes are set not on these but on the new heavens and the new earth which he has promised us, and in which nothing but good shall live.*" (2 Peter 3:11-13 Phillips)

Yet evil still exists. . . and must be dealt with.

THE END OF EVIL—ALL UNBELIEVERS

THE RESURRECTION OF THE DEAD

Revelation 20:12. . .I saw the dead, both great and small, standing before God's throne. This specifies that all the dead from all the ages stand before God's throne. It is important to observe that *only* the unbelieving dead are being judged. A little over a thousand years before this day, glorified Believers were raised from the dead, judged, and rewarded for their deeds, good and bad, at the Judgment Seat of Christ. (1 Thessalonians 4:13-18; 2 Corinthians 5:10) Believers will sit on thrones as judges, consequently, those that are the judges at this tribunal cannot be at one and the same time the judged. (Daniel 7:9-10) We can categorically declare that this judgement is not for Believers.

As someone has said, "the ground at the cross is level." Before God's throne all are equally guilty.

The Lord uses the terms "*both great and small.*" This is a use of human terms as God sees all men as equal. Robert H. Mounce expresses it well: "The point is that no one is so important as to be immune from judgment and no one is so unimportant as to make judgment inappropriate." [3]

Where do the dead come from?

Revelation 20:13. . .And the sea gave up the dead in it, Death and Hades [the abyss] gave up the dead in them. There are only two places where the bodies of the dead are buried, in or on the earth and in the sea. Therefore, at the time of the final judgment, the dead will be resurrected out of the earth and out of the sea. Hades will give up the souls and spirits of the unrepentant dead. It's just as simple as that.

Matthew 10:28 "But don't be afraid of those who want to kill your body; they cannot touch your soul. Fear only God, who can destroy both soul and body in hell [lake of fire]."

Death claims the body and Hades the soul and spirit. *Hades* is the Greek word for the bottomless pit or the abyss. "*Hades* never denotes the physical grave nor is it the permanent region of the lost. It is the intermediate state between death and the ultimate hell. . .or, the temporary destiny of the doomed." [KW] The fact that the dead are in Hades indicates that they died in their sins, and therefore, have never been born-again or *quickened* by the regenerating, life-giving action of the Holy Spirit.

Are the unbelieving dead resurrected as a spirit or do they have a physical body?

The very words stating that "*Death*" (which claims the body) will "*give up*" the bodies of the dead, obviously means that the grave surrenders the physical body from its captivity. The same words referring to Hades, "*gave up*" the dead, signifies that the abyss surrenders the spirits and souls of the persons confined therein.

Notice the following Scripture states that at a specific hour, the condemned dead "*will hear* ____________________ *voice*" and will rise bodily from an open grave.

2 Thessalonians 1:9 (RSV) "They shall suffer the punishment of eternal destruction and exclusion from the presence of the Lord and from the glory of his might."

"*Do not marvel at this; for the hour is coming in which all who are in the graves will hear His* [Jesus] *voice and come forth--those who have done good, to the resurrection of life, and those who have done evil, to the resurrection of condemnation.*" (John 5:28-29 NKJV) This is "*the resurrection of condemnation.*"

The moment has arrived for "*the resurrection of condemnation*"; all dead sinners will rise to face their final destiny. Their resurrected bodies will be reunited with their spirits and souls, and like their Christian counterpart, will be imperishable. The Unbeliever will burn forever and ever. . .but never be consumed.

A clarification: Split reference

So as not to be confused, I would like to call your attention to a feature of prophetic Scripture that hermeneutic scholars refer to as *split reference*. The prophecies of the two resurrections are often presented in the same verse and therefore appear to take place at the same time as presented in John 5:28-29. Another example is found in Daniel 12:2: "*some to everlasting life and some to shame and everlasting disgrace.*" This is a split reference.

Split reference means that "part of the prediction refers to one future event (near at hand) and another part of the prediction to another future event (more distant.)" [4] Isaiah 61:1-3 is an example illustrated by Jesus when He read this Scripture in a synagogue. (Luke 4:16-21) Jesus read verse 1, and halfway through verse 2, He stopped, rolled up the scroll, and said, *"Today this Scripture is fulfilled in your hearing."* Why did He stop midway? He stopped because verse 1, and the first part of verse 2, predicts Jesus' First Coming and beginning with the second part of verse 2 through verse 3 predicts His Second Coming. Jesus made it clear, that at that time, He was fulfilling only the first part of the prophecy.

Split Reference Another example of a split reference is Isaiah 9:6-7 where the first phrase, "For unto us a Child is born, unto us a Son is given," refers to Jesus' first coming and the rest of verse 6 and 7 speak of Jesus' Second Coming.

As has been mentioned, a thousand years transpires between the First Resurrection and the Second Resurrection.

THE BOOKS

Revelation 20:12-13. . .[12] books were opened. Also another book was opened, which is the book of life. And the dead were judged by what was written in the books, by what they had done. [13]. . . all were judged by what they had done.

What a wise and remarkable act by God to keep written evidence of each man's deeds in order to produce the hard facts to proud, hard to convince individuals and weak memories. God does not need books of records. Jesus said to each of the seven churches of Revelation 2 and 3 (NKJV): "*I know your works.*" He is all-knowing, and time is nothing to Him. He sees every self-serving act which falls far short of His standard of righteousness as if it were taking place in that very instant.

"If man were his own judge, who would be condemned? [5]

Proverbs 16:2 "People may be pure in their own eyes but the Lord examines their motives." Proverbs 21:2 "People may be right in their own eyes but the Lord examines their heart."

What is the basis for judgment according to verses 12 and 13? ____________________

____

What would be a possible or feasible number of sinful deeds recorded by one individual in his lifetime? Evangelism Explosion International [6] provides an interesting illustration that will help us not to underestimate the possibilities. An adaptation we have used in sharing the Gospel goes something like this:

> Suppose we have a friend that only sins three times a day due to something he says, thinks, or does. So few sins would make him look almost like an angel, nearly perfect. In one year how many sins would that be? Let's see. . .3 X's 365 = 1,095. Yikes! What if he lived to be 80 years old? 80 X's 1,095 = 87,600. What if a person was to stand before a judge with 87,600 violations of the law? What would the judge do to him? Put him in jail and throw away the key! And we are talking about someone who is nearly perfect! Our sins do add up.

Observe in the following verses that some people "*in that day,*" the final day of judgment, will believe that their religious works will be written in the books of recorded acts to be in their favor. But what will Jesus tell them on judgment day according to Matthew 7:21? They may have been doing their own works of righteousness, but they weren't actually doing ________

____________________________________.

Jesus will clearly state the root of their problem in Matthew 7:23. ____________________

These religious people had no relationship with Jesus. Without knowing Jesus as one's personal Savior, no matter what the results are of his ministry, he is still a sinner without hope of eternal life.

Matthew 7:21-23 (Phillips)

> 21 *"It is not everyone who keeps saying to me, 'Lord, Lord' who will enter the kingdom of Heaven, but the man who actually does my Heavenly Father's will.* 22 *In 'that day' many will say to me, 'Lord, Lord, didn't we preach in your name, didn't we cast out devils in your name, and do many great things in your name?* 23 *Then I will tell them plainly: 'I have never known you. Go away from me; you have worked on the side of evil!'"*

It is very clear that men and women write their own books, nothing is added or subtracted, and therefore, judgment is both fair and just. The Great White Throne Judgment of God is the time and place spoken of in Lesson 1 by Kyle M. Yeats: "He can put your own little puny life up against His blueprint of your life and record all the differences." Here is where the differences of the divine blueprint are exposed and compared.

Degrees of punishment

1 Peter 1:17 relates that God judges impartially *according* to each man's works. Works or deeds in the New Testament "usually denotes comprehensively what a man is and how he acts." [KW] Obviously, the words "*by what they had done*" include both good and bad deeds.

1 Peter 1:17 (RSV) " [The Father] who judges each one impartially according to his deeds."

Examine closely the following verses.

Romans 2:5-6

> *"But because you are stubborn and refuse to turn from your sin, you are storing up terrible punishment for yourself. For a day of anger is coming, when God's righteous judgment will be revealed. He will judge everyone according to what they have done."*

What do you think the last sentence means? ____________________

____

John 19:11 "So the one who brought Me to you has the greater sin."

The key expression here is "*according to*" which means "in accordance" or "in proportion to." This involves the law of retribution, to repay as deserved, to give back in return. As an example, God directs His judgment toward the harlot city of the Antichrist. Give close attention to the wording which demonstrates how this law of retribution plays out.

Revelation 18:5-7 (NASB)

> 5 *"For her sins have piled up as high as heaven, and God has remembered her iniquities.* 6 *Pay her back even as she has paid, and give back to her double according to her deeds; in the cup which she has mixed, mix twice as much for her.* 7 *To the degree that she glorified herself and lived sensuously, to the same degree give her torment and mourning. . ."*

Bruce Wilkinson with David Kopp have provided a study entitled A Life God Rewards. [7] This is a great life-adjusting study. It is directed to the Believer concerning his rewards at the Judgment Seat of Christ. It becomes very clear that your eternal reward (for the Believer) or your retribution (for the Unbeliever) is based on what you do on earth. The Bible is very clear about "your choices on earth have direct consequences on your life in eternity."

Other Scriptures on this subject are: Matthew 11:21-24; Luke 12:47-48; Luke 20:46-47; 2 Timothy 4:14; Revelation 2:23.

It is imperative to grasp the fact that an Unbeliever sins because he is a sinner; he is not a sinner because he sins. He absolutely must be born-again!

It is also imperative to grasp the fact that the *degree of punishment* given to every Unbeliever at the final judgment is based on what he or she has done in this life. However, the *place of punishment* is based on the reality that the Unbeliever is not listed as a citizen of God's Kingdom in the Book of Life.

A plea to the insincere, *double-minded* Believer

Insincere is a disingenuous person. A double-minded person is one who holds two different opinions; he sits on a fence lacking conviction. (James 1:8) Jesus says to you, "*I know all the things you do, and that you have a reputation for being alive—but you are dead.*" (Revelation 3:1)

Jesus speaks to those *"who have been enlightened, who have experienced salvation and received the Holy Spirit, who have known the wholesome nourishment of the Word of God and touched the spiritual resources of the eternal world and who then fall away, it proves impossible to make them repent as they did at the first. For they are recrucifying the Son of God in their own souls, and by their conduct exposing him to shame and contempt.*

Ground which absorbs the rain that is constantly falling upon it and produces plants which are useful to those who cultivate it is ground which has the blessing of God. But ground which produces nothing but thorns and thistles is of no value and is bound sooner or later to be condemned—the only thing to do is to burn it clean." (Hebrews 6:7-8 Phillips)

"How much more dreadful a punishment will he be thought to deserve who has poured scorn on the Son of God, treated like dirt the blood of the agreement which had once made him holy, and insulted the very Spirit of grace? For we know the one who said: 'Vengeance belongeth unto me, I will recompense.' And, again: 'The Lord shall judge his people.' Truly it is a terrible thing for a man who has done this to fall into the hands of the living God!" (Hebrews 10:29-31 Phillips)

"Wake up! Strengthen what little remains, for even what is left is almost dead. I find that your actions do not meet the requirements of my God. Go back to what you heard and believed at first; hold to it firmly. Repent and turn to me again. If you don't wake up, I will come to you suddenly, as unexpected as a thief." (Revelation 3:2-3)

If you receive Jesus as your Savior, look at God's wonderful promise to you. "I will give you a new heart, and I will put a new spirit in you. I will take out your stony, stubborn heart and give you a tender, responsive heart. And I will put my Spirit in you so that you will follow my decrees and be careful to obey my regulations." (Ezekiel 36:26-27)

THE BOOK OF LIFE

Revelation 20:12, 15. . . [12] Also another book was opened, which is the book of life. [15]. . .and if anyone's name was not found written in the book of life, he was thrown into the lake of fire.

All those who have their name recorded in the Book of Life are the redeemed, the righteous who have, by God's grace, been cleansed and born-again by the blood of Jesus Christ shed on the cross of Calvary.

"All who are victorious will be clothed in white. I will never erase their names from the Book of Life, but I will announce before my Father and his angels that they are mine." (Revelation 3:5)

Psalm 1:5 (RSV) "Therefore the wicked will not stand in the judgment, nor sinners in the congregation of the righteous."

The wicked are considered in the Bible as enemies of God and adversaries of His people. They do not continuously walk in God's paths of righteousness.

One of the most incredibly wonderful things to know is that my name is written in heaven—in the Lamb's Book of Life.

It is highly unlikely that the names written in the Lamb's Book of Life will be read alphabetically or even read at all during the Great White Throne Judgment. Having said that, I want to somehow impress your heart and soul with this scene as the most tragic moment in human history. For that reason, let's use our imagination to grasp the solemn moment when at the Final Judgment the "*books*" of each Unbeliever's deeds, which determine their degree of punishment, have been closed.

At this point, every eye shifts to the awesome *"Book of Life,"* where the place of punishment is determined.

Breathlessly, we watch as the divine Judge opens the Book of Life and begins reading aloud the recorded names in alphabetical order. He reads the first name and a joyful cry rings out, "Here, thank you Lord!" (This comes from one who is sitting on a throne.) And then He reads the second name and before a response can be given, we hear a terrible cry, "My name! My name! Oh Lord, you did not read my name!"

"***Your name. . .is. . .not. . .here, only a blank space where it should have been***."

Then at each blank space one by one the condemned are removed and thrown into the lake of fire. . . until only holiness remains.

Why do you think that the "*books*" were opened first before opening the *"Book of Life"* instead of the other way around? ______________________________

Upon seeing the endless list of sins that he has never placed under the atoning blood of Jesus for pardon and reconciliation to God, the Unbeliever can only admit to his sinful state. He knows with absolute certainty why his name is not recorded in the Book of Life.

Yet evil still exists. . . and must be dealt with.

THE END OF EVIL—DEATH AND HADES

Revelation 20:14. . .Then Death and Hades [the abyss] were thrown into the lake of fire. Personification is a figure of speech frequently used in the Bible. It means to give a thing, idea or quality human characteristics or attributes. Death is portrayed in the Bible as an enemy and intimately related to sin. (Romans 6:23) Death and Hades are thrown into the lake of fire which signifies that all things that bring death will be eradicated, and the very place where the unbelieving dead reside, will be consumed in the *second death.* How fitting!

"The last enemy to be destroyed is death." (I Corinthians 15:26) Finally, with absolute power and authority a command is given and Death and Hades are thrown into the lake of fire. You will be an eye witness to the end of all evil.

Evil does not exist. . . it has been dealt with.

Beloved Unbeliever, it is here that we part ways—forever. Your last Event ends in the *"lake of fire."* You will find this concluding point on **Timeline Three** (located at the end of Part One of this study book). Write Event **7** on the line by the asterisk (*_7_).

To close this lesson I would like to share some very solemn words from J.I. Packer on the subject of hell.

> "New Testament teaching about hell is meant to appall us and strike us dumb with horror, assuring us that, as heaven will be better than we could dream, so hell will be worse than we can conceive. Such are the issues of eternity, which need now to be realistically faced."
>
> "The purpose of Bible teaching about hell is to make us appreciate, thankfully embrace, and rationally prefer the grace of Christ that saves us from it. . .It is really a mercy to mankind that God in Scripture is so explicit about hell. We cannot now say that we have not been warned." [8]

JESUS CHRIST THE CONQUEROR

1 Corinthians 15:24-26

LESSON 18A | EVENT 9

JESUS CHRIST OUR ETERNAL HOME

John 14: 23 (NKJV)

Jesus so loves the obedient Believer that He and His Father make the spiritual temple in his heart their home.

THE NEW HEAVEN
THE NEW EARTH
THE NEW JERUSALEM

HOME

"An elderly missionary named Samuel Morrison who, after years in Africa, was returning to the United States to retire. As it so happened, he traveled home on the same ocean liner that brought President Teddy Roosevelt back from a hunting expedition. When the great ship pulled into the New York Harbor, the dock where it was to tie up was jammed with what looked like the entire population of New York City! Bands were playing, banners were waving, choirs of children were singing, multicolored balloons were floating in the air, flashbulbs were popping, and newsreel cameras were poised to record the return of the president.

Mr. Roosevelt stepped down the gangplank to thunderous cheers and applause, showered with confetti and ticker tape. If the crowd had not been restrained by ropes and police, he would have been mobbed!

At the same time, Samuel Morrison quietly walked off the boat. No one was there to greet him. He slipped alone through the crowd. Because of the crush of people there to welcome the president, he couldn't even find a cab. Inside his heart, he began to complain, *Lord, the president has been in Africa for three weeks, killing animals, and the whole world turns out to welcome him home! I've given twenty-five years of my life in Africa, serving You, and no one has greeted me or even knows I'm here.*

In the quietness of his heart, a gentle, loving voice whispered, '*But My dear child, you are not home yet!*'" [1]

Home! You have a citizenship in a country that is incredibly beyond your greatest hopes and dreams. That is what this lesson is about, your eternal home. It already exists, and if you were to die at any moment, your soul and spirit would go immediately to this magnificent city in heaven. The welcome you would receive, and Samuel Morrison finally received, would make Mr. Roosevelt's homecoming look so trivial that his wouldn't be worth mentioning.

Locate the New Heaven, the New Earth, and the New Jerusalem on **Timeline Three** (located at the end of Part One of this study book) write Event **9** on the line by the asterisk (*_9_). For Christian Jews this is Event 7.

The apostle John again sees new revelations from the Lord. We will divide the vision into two parts. It would be very profitable for you, at this point, to read the final two chapters of

Revelation in your Bible. Look for and make a list of the many repetitions; these are intentionally designed to impress you with their importance.

In this lesson we will study:

- God Promises Us an Eternal Home
- A Broad View of the New Heavens, New Earth, and New Jerusalem
  - A New Environment
  - A First Look at the New Jerusalem
  - A New Relationship with God
  - New Human Relationships
  - The New You

GOD PROMISES US AN ETERNAL HOME

"Be it ever so humble, there's no place like home" has been a motto in many homes. Home is a place of contentment, security, and peace. And yet, even in the most perfect home, at a moment's notice, sickness, failure, tragedy, or sorrow could change the motto to "There used to be no place like home." Why? It is because sin has infected every part of this world and robs us of our happiness. Consequently, this causes us to yearn for a better place, a better world. The Believer has found the remedy in God's promises for this homesickness, a home in a remarkable city. This will be your permanent home; you will never have to worry about foreclosure or eviction.

As you read the following Scriptures concerning your future home, **underline** all the phrases and words that refer to your heavenly home or country. **Circle** all the words that refer to your status in this world. Let the truth of these promises put a spring in your step and a smile on your face. It's all going to happen!

Jesus guaranteed promise:
John 14:2-3

> "*There is more than enough room in my Father's home. If this were not so, would I have told you that I am going to prepare a place for you? When everything is ready, I will come and get you, so that you will always be with me where I am.*"

These verses are speaking about Abraham, however, the spiritual meaning applies to all Believers.
Hebrews 11:9–16

> [9] "*When he reached the land God promised him, he lived there by faith—for he was like a foreigner, living in tents. . .* [10]*Abraham was confidently looking forward to a city with eternal foundations, a city designed and built by God. . .* [12]*So a whole nation* [the Jews] *came from this one man* [Abraham.] [13]*All these people* [from Abraham] *died still believing what God had promised them. They did not receive what was promised, but they saw it all from a distance and welcomed it. They agreed that they were foreigners* [strangers] *and nomads* [exiles] *here on earth.* [14]*Obviously people who say such things are looking forward to a country* [lit. fatherland, homeland] *they can call their own.*

[15]If they had longed for the country they had come from, they could have gone back. [16]But they were looking for a better place, a heavenly homeland. That is why God is not ashamed to be called their God, for he has prepared a city for them."

Foreigner
A foreigner is "located away from one's native country…situated in an abnormal [atypical] or improper place [out of place] …an alien; an outsider." [D]

Also observe the reference to the Judgment Seat of Christ:
1 Peter 1:17

"*And remember that the heavenly Father to whom you pray has no favorites. He will judge or reward you according to what you do. So you must live in reverent fear of him during your time as 'foreigners in the land.'*"

Notice the reference to the Great White Throne judgment:
1 Peter 2:11-12

"*Dear friends, I warn you as 'temporary residents and foreigners' to keep away from worldly desires that wage war against your very souls. Be careful to live properly among your unbelieving neighbors. Then even if they accuse you of doing wrong, they will see your honorable behavior, and they will give honor to God when he judges the world.*"

Take note of the reference to the Rapture.
Philippians 3:19–21

"*They* [Unbelievers] *are headed for destruction. Their god is their appetite, they brag about shameful things, and they think only about this life here on earth. But we are citizens of heaven, where the Lord Jesus Christ lives. And we are eagerly waiting for him to return as our Savior. He will take our weak mortal bodies and change them into glorious bodies like his own, using the same power with which he will bring everything under his control.*"

Citizenship
Citizenship "refers to the place where one has official status, the commonwealth where one's name is recorded on the register of citizens. Though believers live in this world, they are citizens of heaven." [2]

How many phrases or words did you underline? ______ How many circles do you have? ____
What do the words underlined teach you? ____

____

What do the circled words teach you? ____

____

We are strangers, pilgrims, and nomads in this world. A Believer has possessions in this world, perhaps a lot of them, but he steadfastly remains unattached to them. Unencumbered by a fettered heart, he is free to press on toward eternal treasures. "You can always tell one of God's pilgrims by his or her eyes. They are not fixed on the artificial glory of the world around them, but on the heavenly glory of the world before them. Their attention, affection, and ambition are fixed on the things of God in the heavenly realm, not the things of man here on earth." [3] (Colossians 3:1-2)

The Glorified Believer's Home

You came to the end of your faith journey here on earth at the time of the Rapture. What a spectacular welcome you received as you entered the City of God in all its loveliness. You are home now. The Lord Jesus led you to your special dwelling place, and there, a great sense of well-being flooded your soul as you thanked Him profusely and sighed, "Truly Lord, there's no place like home. The place for which I have always longed."

Since your arrival in heaven, you have been actively engaged in service, sometimes in heaven and sometimes on earth; reigning with and serving King Jesus during His Thousand-Year Reign on earth; witnessing the awesome events that ended all evil—Satan and his hosts, the earth, all the universe, all Unbelievers, Death, and Hades.

Your final prophetic Event, to be honest, will be beyond human comprehension and my ability to describe. As you study, keep in mind that in this life God looks upon you as His child destined to live in His City in a heavenly homeland. . .forever. In other words, He is expecting you.

The last two chapters of the book of Revelation describe your eternal home. You will probably feel like you are looking at it through a peep-hole in a door because you can only catch a hint of its glory.

Contemplation of these last chapters of the Bible will stir our hearts to not only observe these future wonders, it will also create a desire to know the meaning of what we look upon. In this lesson we will thoughtfully consider what we are permitted to know about our eternal home. With few words the Lord encompasses vast areas of our future existence. God knows that humans learn about new things by comparing them to what they already know; they proceed from the known to the unknown. Therefore, God has given prophetic visions in human terms. However, the *new* presented to us in this case is far beyond man's experience and language. We are in a realm totally unknown to mankind. Your wonderment will definitely cause your mind to speculate on the profound glories presented in this study.

A BROAD VIEW OF THE NEW HEAVENS, NEW EARTH, AND NEW JERUSALEM

I'm sure that you are eagerly looking forward to making your own five observations or questions as you read the following Scripture.

Revelation 21:1–5 (NASB)

> [1] *"And I saw a new heaven and a new earth; for the first heaven and the first earth*
> *passed away, and there is no longer any sea.* [2] *And I saw the holy city, New Jerusalem,*
> *coming down out of heaven from God, made ready as a bride adorned for her husband.*
> [3] *And I heard a loud voice from the throne, saying, 'Behold, the tabernacle* [dwelling;
> home] *of God is among men, and He shall dwell among them, and they shall be His*
> *people, and God Himself shall be among them,* [4] *and He shall wipe away every tear*
> *from their eyes; and there shall no longer be any death; there shall no longer be any mourning, or crying, or pain; the first things have passed away.'*
>
> [5] *And He who sits on the throne said, 'Behold, I am making all things new. And He said, 'Write, for these words are faithful and true.'"*

Your observations:
1. ______________________________
2. ______________________________
3. ______________________________
4. ______________________________
5. ______________________________

F.B. Meyer
"Did He make all things? Then He can unmake them, and be Himself evermore the same."

Look through the verses above and list the things that "*shall no longer be.*"

There shall no longer be ____________, ____________, ____________, ____________, ____________, ____________

(The old order is replaced with a new order. Evil, in all its forms, is gone.)

"BEHOLD, I AM MAKING ALL THINGS NEW"

A NEW ENVIRONMENT

Verse 1. . . a new heaven and a new earth. A roaring sound begins deep in the universe, intense heat smashes through galaxy after galaxy; each vanishing instantaneously. You tremble in awe and clasp the hand of your loved one next to you as you watch the destruction of the old heavens and the old earth. Space all around you is filled with the thunderous roar of millions of stars and millions of worlds evaporating into nonexistence. The sun, moon, and earth melt; all that you had ever known and experienced is dissolving. The deafening roar continues to sweep on and on through the universe until. . . there is nothing. . . silence. . .

2 Peter 3:10-12 (NKJV) "The heavens will pass away with a great noise, and the elements will melt with fervent heat; both the earth and the works that are in it will be burned up...the heavens will be dissolved, being on fire, and the elements will melt with fervent heat..."

You feel so small, so insignificant. You have just witnessed the magnificient power of the living God!

And then, (I can hardly speak of it for the incomprehensibility of it all) in a blaze of light, color, and unspeakable beauty, a new heaven fills a vast expanse. Your heart is thrilled as you see a new earth rise up from the nothingness; it is beautiful beyond expression.

"Look, there is no sea!" someone cries out in awe.

And then you hear myriads of angels singing the glories and praises of God; you spontaneously join in with the countless multitude of God's children from every nation and tribe and people and language to sing in joyful harmony.

> "*You are worthy, our Lord and God, to receive glory and honor and power, for you created all things, and by your will they were created and have their being.*" (Revelation 4:11 NIV)

Job 38:7 Again..."All the morning stars [angels] sang together, and all the sons of God shouted for joy."

That, dear Believer, is a resume of what you will see and experience; the Word of God declares this so. You were not alive to watch God create the first heavens and earth, but you will be this time around! But, hold on, we haven't finished seeing it all!

"New"

This is a key word pertaining to the Eternal Age, so much so that in 21:5 God says: *"Behold, I am making all things new."* The Greek word *kainos* is the word for *new* and means "new as to form and quality, of a different nature. . .from what they were accustomed to." [V] William Barclay says: "A thing which is *kainos* is new in the sense that it brings into the world a new quality of thing which did not exist before." [4] John MacArthur gives this definition of *new*: "Not new in the sense of time but something that is fresh in quality, kind, or form; something that replaces something else that has been worn out." [5]

Isaiah 65:17 "Look! I am creating new heavens and a new earth, and no one will even think about the old ones anymore."

This meaning applied to the *New* Heavens and the *New* Earth gives the understanding that they will be pristine, fresh, brand-new, breathtaking, of a whole different quality, and totally unknown to us. The Bible is a book of instructions that deals with sin in one way or another (2 Timothy 3:16.) What wonders will God's instructions deal with in a new environment of perfection and righteousness? The new earth will be untouched by evil and will provide a perfect environment with a whole new quality of life for God's glorified people. Nothing harmful or evil will ever exist there. Just think, you get to live there!

21:1. . . there is no longer any sea. Continents and nations have been separated by the oceans on the first earth which has been a good thing because mankind surely would have destroyed themselves by wars and conquests had there not been these difficult-to-cross barriers. No need for these barriers now in a perfect world of peace. In addition, death is no more; therefore, creatures will not be killed for food; so, no need for seafood.

A FIRST LOOK AT THE NEW JERUSALEM

21:2. . . And I saw the holy city, new Jerusalem, coming down out of heaven from God, made ready as a bride adorned for her husband. Astounding! The city where all of God's people dwell descends from God's heaven to the new earth! It would seem that the *city* connects God's heaven with the new earth.

Leviticus 26:11-12 "I will live among you, and I will not despise you. I will walk among you; I will be your God, and you will be my people."

21:3. . . And I heard a loud voice from the throne, saying, 'Behold, the tabernacle [dwelling; home] of God is among men, and He shall dwell among them, and they shall be His people, and God Himself shall be among them.

What does God emphatically repeat three times? ______________________________

This is one of the meaningful "trisagions" mentioned in Scripture. It is called a "trisagion" because it is a threefold expression of the Godhead in His tri-personal existence, and, in this case, it reveals to us the following truth:

1) *the dwelling* of God the Father *is among men*;
2) God the Son *shall dwell among them*;
3) God the Holy Spirit *shall be among them.*

(See other examples of a trisagion: Revelation 4:8; Isaiah 6:3; Matthew 28:19)

God's heaven and the earth existed separately from one another while sin reigned on the earth. Worship in heaven took place in the very presence of God and consisted of angels and the ever growing group of souls who joined them after their death on earth. Worship on the earth consisted of Believers earnestly worshipping by faith alone, their unseen, but very present God. With the descent of the New Jerusalem, the barrier between heaven and earth has been eradicated; glorified humans, angels, and God Himself live together in a heavenly/earthly realm. All are holy. Men and angels intermingle freely without limitations to esteem and glorify the object of their eternal adoration—the triune God!

A Trisagion Numbers 6:24-26 (NIV) 1) The Lord bless you and keep you; (the Father) 2) the Lord make His face shine upon you and be gracious to you: (the Son) 3) the Lord turn His face toward you and give you peace." (the Holy Spirit)

God cannot be defined. Any description of God will fall far short of who He really is. However, God does reveal Himself through the Scriptures and through His Son Jesus so that we can see (although limited by our humanness) who He is by His attributes. He is self-existent, no beginning, no end, and not dependent on anything for His existence. God is not confined to time or space; He is beyond them. Therefore, when God says that He will dwell with men, this means that He has chosen to manifest His presence to men. This signifies a new relationship with God. Awesome, profound. We can only wonder what that will really be like.

A NEW RELATIONSHIP WITH GOD

21:3. . .they shall be His people. The word *people* is plural and should be translated *peoples.* This indicates a diversity, variety, distinct races. In our minds, we can imagine God looking out over a sea of glorified Believers and seeing a representation out of every tribe, tongue, people, and nation. Here is the fruit of His Beloved Son's death on the cross. Here is the end result of all His messenger's labors who, during the church age in obedience to the great commission, carried the good news of salvation to the farthest corner of the earth. As an earthly king claims the people of his kingdom to be his alone, the great Sovereign declares, "These are My people!" Do you sense great privilege to belong to this assembly?

"Oh, the anguish of separation! We understand death for the first time when he puts his hand upon one whom we love." [6]

21:4. . . and He shall wipe away every tear from their eyes. God is love; He loves *us.* (1John 4:8) His love is profound and unlimited for each and every one of His own. You are the object of His love. The words of this verse reveal the closeness in the heart to heart relationship that you will enjoy with your Father. It is imperative to remember that God is present everywhere. This means that He can be in close communion with you, and me, and millions of people all at once and at the same time.

There will be a moment when God will take each beloved child into His arms to answer all their questions concerning the pain, hardship, grief, distress, conflict, suffering, tragedies, sickness, deep struggles of the soul that they faced on earth. He will not need to ask what they would like to have clarified. He already knows with a complete knowledge. He knows all there is to know about you and the things that greatly distressed you.

With profound affection, holding your eyes with His own, your Father will make clear to you His divine will for every situation encountered in your life on the old earth. You will wonder how you could have ever doubted your Father's goodness.

We are reminded of the Scriptures where Jesus "*saw a man blind from birth. His disciples asked him, 'Rabbi, who sinned, this man or his parents, that he was born blind?' 'Neither this man nor his parents sinned,' said Jesus, 'but this happened so that the work of God might be displayed in his life.'*" (John 9:1-3 NIV)

What unfathomable comfort when the very hand of God touches your eyes to wipe away your tears and take away all pain. Now that's something to long for.

21:4. . . and there shall no longer be any death. Death is thought about in many different ways, but the best way to think of it is that one day it will cease to exist.

Psalm 49:14 (NKJV) reads: "*Death shall feed on them.*" Among the three things that are never satisfied is the "*grave.*" (Proverbs 30:16) It opens its vicious mouth and swallows, and again opens its voracious mouth and swallows, never satisfied. But the tables will turn, "*He will swallow up death forever! The Sovereign Lord will wipe away all tears.*" (Isaiah 25:8; 1 Corinthians 15:54) Death and the grave are swallowed up and are spewed into the lake of fire!

No more death requires life without end! Its full meaning implies that no one and no thing will ever die in the Eternal Age.

NEW HUMAN RELATIONSHIPS

21:4. . .there shall no longer be any mourning, or crying, or pain; the first things have passed away.

What do you consider to be the main cause of *crying* or *pain* in this world? ________________

____

Weather, such as storms, fire, flood, earthquakes, and other natural phenomena can cause great suffering as well as can disease. But if your reply was *human beings* to the question above, I would certainly agree with you. Humans seem to be the greatest cause for sorrow in this world.

Mourning, crying, and pain no longer exist, therefore, you will *always* experience the opposite: joy, health, pleasure, contentment, happiness, satisfaction, cheerfulness, optimism, and well-being. Nothing exists that can cause sorrow or pain because "*the first things* [of the old earth] *have ___________________.*"

What does this mean in terms of human relationships? Simply speaking, human relationships will be based entirely on love which we could never fully experience on earth because of the impairment caused by sin. Everyone's minds and hearts will be in perfect harmony in the Eternal Age.

Let me ask you a question. In this Present Age, what actions are essential in building relationships with fellow Christians? Please list a few things that would appear at the top of your list to accomplish this.

____

____

Perhaps you stated something like this: a strong relationship with another Christian is made by sharing, caring, sorrowing together, helping, loving, listening to their problems, encouraging them in their difficulties, forgiving, bearing their burdens, rejoicing with them, correcting, returning kindness for unkindness, and praying with them.

Look closely at your list, and mine, **circle** the items that will not be relevant to our relationships in a perfect environment involving a perfect people in Christ. Think about what each term implies. Interesting isn't it. If you would like to think a little more about this, read 1 Corinthians 13. Believers rightly call this the love chapter. Love in this chapter is defined, for the most part, by what it is not; those things that undermine, interrupt and damage human relationships. Negative emotions and actions cause resentment, misunderstanding, suspicion, and prejudice, which in turn afflicts others with pain and crying. This will no longer occur in the Eternal Age

No doubt, since communication is so important in a perfect community, we will be able to understand one another's language. God imposed diverse languages upon man for much the same reason He made the seas to separate and keep them from destroying one another. Languages were also a restraint from uniting to build a world empire in rebellion against God. (Genesis 11:1-9) If you have ever traveled to a foreign country, you immediately encountered the language barrier. In the Eternal Age there will be no such hindrance to harmony. What freedom! What a joy it will be to explore and embrace this new way of life.

Friendship, brotherhood, companionship, bonding, and oneness will take on a new depth of meaning. This will be a new social arrangement. Each glorified Believer will communicate kindness and goodness to His fellow brother. Nothing done in the Eternal Age will be outside the perimeters of love because God's love will be the very atmosphere that we will breathe and exhale.

THE NEW YOU

You, along with all your brothers and sisters in Christ, will be Christ-like. Think about all the ramifications that statement implies. For one thing, in your eternal state you will be free from even the last "little germ" of sin. Dan Schaeffer gives us something to think about as he deals with *What will I be like*? *What was I really created for*? and *The new me*. Let me whet your appetite for some of the things he has explored.

> "How different will I be from, who I am now—and yet, also, how alike? It is an incredible thought that I will finally discover the real Dan Schaeffer, the person God always intended me to become. Many parts of the old Dan—my personality, my passions, my gifts and unique interests—will, I believe, remain—but they will undergo

> a metamorphosis far more dramatic than that demonstrated by the caterpillar that emerges from its transformation as a beautiful butterfly." [7]

Philippians 3:21 "He will take our weak mortal bodies and change them into glorious bodies like his own..."

What could be more thrilling for the human race than to become like Christ. (Phillipians 3:21; 1 Corinthians 15:49) Of course, we are talking about the attributes of Christ that He shares with us, not those supernatural attributes that belong only to the Godhead, such as, being everywhere present at one and the same time (omnipresence) or to know all things (omniscience) or having all power (omnipotence.) You will find an excellent study on this topic in the book From Heavens View. [8]

That being said, your glorified body will have more mobility like Christ's glorified body in that He could appear and disappear. (Mark 16:12; Luke 24:31, 36) It is apparent that Jesus traveled back and forth between earth and heaven during the forty days after His resurrection (John 20:17). But, you will never be in all places at one and the same time. Your mind will be set free from limitations and malfunctions giving place to a greater capacity to learn, to retain, and to grow in knowledge and wisdom. But, you will never have all knowledge. Your body will have perfect health resulting in an energetic, strong body which will never feel age or wear out. But, you will never be all powerful.

The indwelling Christ began a spiritual, life changing transformation in you when you received Him as your personal Savior and Lord. But it is beyond our comprehension to even imagine the degrees of holiness and glory that you and I will attain in our eternal state.

All this is to say that you will make a fine contribution to the new relationships among glorified humans and to the eternal goodness of the new culture that we all will enjoy.

JESUS CHRIST OUR ETERNAL HOME

John 14: 23 (NKJV)

LESSON **18B**

THE GODHEAD THE GLORY OF ETERNITY
Revelation 22:4

They will see God's face. All else is secondary and contained in this greatest of all blessings.[1]

EVENT 9

THE NEW JERUSALEM

In this lesson we will study:

An Invitation, a Promise, and a Warning
A Closer View of the New Jerusalem
The City of God

AN INVITATION, A PROMISE, AND A WARNING

An invitation, a promise, and a warning directed at contemporary readers of the book of Revelation is inserted at this point, thus revealing the loving, longing desire of God the Father for the salvation of mankind.

Revelation 21:6-8 (NASB)

> [6] *"And He said to me, 'It is done. I am the Alpha and the Omega, the beginning and the end. I will give to the one who thirsts from the spring of the water of life without cost.* [7] *He who overcomes shall inherit these things, and I will be his God and he will be My son.*
>
> [8] *But for the cowardly and unbelieving and abominable* [corrupt] *and murderers and immoral persons and sorcerers* [witchcraft] *and idolaters and all liars, their part will be in the lake that burns with fire and brimstone, which is the second death.'"*

Observations

21:6. . . It is done. All things pertaining to the Eternal Age have been completed and set into motion. "*I am the Alpha and the Omega* (the first and last letter of the Greek alphabet), *the beginning and the end.*" God is saying here that He is the Creator of all things, the Goal of all things, and everything in between from "a to z." Everything belongs to His rule, authority, dominion, and power. God fills the New Heaven and Earth with His glorious Self. No opposing forces exist to disrupt His newly created perfections.

AN INVITATION

21:6. . . I will give to the one who thirsts from the spring of the water of life without cost. This invitation is given to Present Age readers of the book of Revelation—to all who thirst for God. In order to receive this life-giving water, there must be a thirst, a recognition that you are a lost, lonely sinner. You need God's free gift of salvation. Jesus offered this *spiritual water* to the Samaritan woman in John 4:14 (NASB).

> "Whoever drinks of the water that I shall give him shall never thirst; but the water that I shall give him shall become in him a well of water springing up to eternal life."

Eternal Life is a deathless life as the Godhead possesses; a life of purity, righteousness, holiness. The Samaritan woman did believe in Jesus; she drank from the *Spring* and received eternal life. If you are a Believer, you can look for her among the glorified multitude in heaven and listen to her story. She will probably want to hear yours too.

A PROMISE

21:7. . .He who overcomes shall inherit these things [all this], and I will be his God and he will be My son. The word *overcome* is the Greek word *nikao* meaning "to overcome, to be victorious in a struggle." [M] The overcomer does not take the Christian life lightly, rather he sets his eyes on things *above* in order to pursue the things of God with a passion. The overcomer is single-mindedly loyal to Christ. The cross is before him and the world behind him; he has burned his bridges; he won't turn back.

"Victory implies a battle, for there can be no victory where there is no fighting. Salvation is free, but victory means sacrifice; to win the race means discipline. Be not deceived, victory means a battle, wounds and scars, disappointments and sacrifice, but in the end the glorious crown of victory." [2]

Revelation 21:7 is the realization of God's statement in Romans 8:16-17 (NASB).

> [16] *"The Spirit Himself bears witness with our spirits that we are children of God,* [17] *and if children, heirs also, heirs of God and fellow heirs with Christ, if indeed we suffer with Him in order that we may also be glorified with Him."*

The significance of these two verses is indeed breathtaking. We must take each word at face value. Regarding our earthly families, a child is an heir. If there is more than one child, each one is co-heir or joint-heir. Here it is stated that the Believer because he is "in Christ" is an heir of _______________ and fellow heirs with ________________________. What defines our joint participation with Christ? ____ _____. This suffering is to *nikao* "to overcome, to be victorious in a struggle."

After creating the New Heavens and the New Earth, God says to the overcomer, "You will now share with My Son in His inherited glory. Lift up your eyes, and behold the majesty and the beauty of My new creation. It all belongs to you." God lovingly enfolds each overcomer and says, "I will be your forever-Father, and you will be My forever-son" or, "I will be your forever-Father and you will be My forever-daughter." This, I think, will be the moment when we will experience the full reality of our oneness with our beloved Jesus. What higher honor could there ever be?

Underline God's declaration above in Romans 8:16 which pertains to you as a son / daughter. This may be an opportune moment to bow in prayer and thank God for the assurance of this upcoming moment in your life and voice your resolute intention to be an overcomer for Him.

A WARNING

21:8. . . But for the cowardly and unbelieving and abominable [corrupt] and murderers and immoral persons and sorcerers [witchcraft] and idolaters and all liars, their part [share] will be in the lake that burns with fire and brimstone, which is the second death.

God's great concern for mankind is revealed at this point in the vision. Right in the middle of describing the Eternal Age, God gives a warning to the Unbeliever by reminding him of his destination if he remains in his sin. The invitation and warning are so important to God that He repeats them two more times in this final message. (Revelation 21:27; 22:14-15)

These sinful characteristics have always been common to man but will greatly increase in the end times. Make no mistake, God's Word, the Bible, is not just for born-again Christians to obey. Its authority applies to all men.

"The authority of Scripture means that all the words in Scripture are God's words in such a way that to disbelieve or disobey any word of Scripture is to disbelieve or disobey God." [3]

the cowardly. . .These are apostates who fear persecution. They fear man more than they love God, therefore, they deny Christ. They are afraid to declare themselves as followers of God in a dangerous, wicked world culture. (Matthew 13:20-21; 10:28-33)

unbelieving. . .Those who have a state of mind in which they refuse or have an unwillingness to accept the truth that Christ is the Son of God, the Savior of mankind. These do not have, nor care to have, thoughts about God. They are insensible to God's presence in the affairs of mankind. (Mark 16:16; Psalm 10:4)

Psalm 10:4 (RSV) "In the pride of his countenance the wicked does not seek him [God]; all his thoughts are, "There is no God."

abominable. . .Disgusting, vile. Those who commit depraved and vile acts that are offensive and detestable to God. The Greek word for *abominable* is *abdelusso* which means "to render foul, to stink." [KW] God turns Himself away from these as one would turn away from a terrible stench. (Leviticus 18:22-23; 20:13) This word also includes religious rites and practices other than the God ordained. (Proverbs 28:9; Titus 1:16) The Abomination of desolation referring to the statue of the Antichrist is detestable to the Lord. (Deuteronomy 7:25-26; Matthew 24:15)

murderers. . .Those who unlawfully kill another human being. (Exodus 20:13; Romans 1:29)

immoral persons. . ."The Greek word is *porneia*, from which the English word *pornography* comes. It refers to all illicit sexual activity." [4] These persons prostitute themselves. They habitually indulge in seducing, perverting and morally corrupting others for their self-gratification. Prostitution, adultery, incest, and fornication are all expressions of immoral persons. (Exodus 20:14; Romans 1:26-28)

sorcerers [witchcraft]. . .Those involved in the occult, magic arts, voodoo, and necromancy (communication with the dead) to name a few. They use idols, images, charms, amulets, spells, and superstitious objects to obtain supernatural results or supernatural powers. These practices always involve demons from the spirit world. Today's world is rampant with things alluding to the demonic, especially in the entertainment world, such as books, video games, clothing, movies, and television programs. The Greek word used here is *pharmakeus* from which the word *pharmacy* comes, "originally referred to medicines in general but eventually only to mood and mind-altering drugs, as well as the occult, witchcraft, and magic." [5] Drugs open the way for demonic attacks and activity in the minds of drug users.

Liar's listeners "Remember that the listening ear shares the responsibility of the malicious tongue." [6]

Idolaters. . .Those who reject God as He is. Idolatry has many aspects, such as, to put a "sacred" object in the place of God. It can also mean to form our own idea of God apart from biblical revelation in order to fit our needs. It means to worship what God has made, the created, rather than the Creator. It always means to replace God with something else. (Exodus 20:3-4; Romans 1:23)

all liars. . .Those who habitually and purposefully deviate from the truth in order to deceive and mislead others. They frequently promote themselves by telling lies to impress others. Slander, false promises, and hypocrisy are forms of lying. (Exodus 20:16; Ephesians 4:24-25)

On a scale of 1 to 10 how prevalent do you see these sins in world culture today? (1 meaning not at all and 10 meaning extremely prevalent). Your answer: ____________________

According to Revelation 21:8, while the glorified Believers are enjoying the New Heaven and the New Earth, what will the inheritance of the sinner be? ______________________________

Unbeliever, the bad news for you is that God's forever Kingdom is for *members only*. The good news for you is that God will forgive all the sins listed above and make you a *member*, that is, make you His born-again son or daughter if you genuinely repent, believe, and permit Christ to be Lord of your life, no turning back.

In 1 Corinthians 6:9-11 the apostle Paul speaks to born-again followers of Christ naming most of the sins of Revelation 21:8 and says to them, "*Some of you were once like that. But you were cleansed; you were made holy; you were made right with God by calling on the name of the Lord Jesus Christ and by the Spirit of our God.*" Do not turn Christ away! Your forever-place of residence hinges on what you will do with Jesus!

A CLOSER VIEW OF THE NEW JERUSALEM

The observation part of our study will take the form of one of our imaginative narratives. Please read Revelation 21:9–22:5 in your Bible and then read the narration below. You will find in this Scripture more impression-making repetition so you will want to have a pencil and paper on hand to jot them down.

THE CITY OF GOD

At the present time, "the City of God, the heavenly Jerusalem" is located in heaven. Hebrews 12:22

Year A.D. 95

We are going back in time to approximately A.D. 95 when the apostle John receives The Revelation of Jesus Christ. In the closing chapters of the book of Revelation, John sees a vision of the City of God coming down from heaven to the New Earth. John is looking at an event that will occur in the very far future during the Eternal Age.

In the vision, a very powerful angel calls John to approach Him. You and I are going to tag along with John as he responds to the angel's command. We recognize the angel as one of the seven who poured out judgment on the earth during the Trumpet/Bowl Judgments. While we stand expectantly before him, the angel says he is going to show us the most unique sight ever to be seen—the City of God descending from heaven to the earth.

We know that the City of God, the New Jerusalem, is God's dwelling where He chooses to manifest His glorious Presence and where our Mediator, the Lord Jesus Christ, is enthroned with His Father. Likewise, we know that it is inhabited by an innumerable company of angels and the abode all those registered in heaven from the Old Testament age through the Present Age. (Hebrews 12:22-24)

Uncertain what we are going to see, we anticipate an extraordinary experience.

To see this vision we are taken to the top of an extremely high mountain. From that vantage point, the earth looks new; it is amazingly beautiful, and totally different in many aspects from the old. The mighty angel directs us to look up into the heavens. And then. . . we see it appear—the City of God, enormous in size, glorious in appearance! Colossal! Stunningly brilliant with the glory of God; the whole earth is illumined with His glory. We are dazzled by the multiple, crystal clear colors, like prisms reflecting the glory of the Father in every color imaginable.

Slowly the City of God descends and settles on the earth. "Why, heaven and earth are joined, they are one!" you exclaim.

The angel softly replies, "Yes, you are witnessing the fulfillment of God's purpose; His good pleasure is to bring together all things in heaven and earth under one Head. The old earth stood in direct opposition to God's heaven. God has reconciled, through His Son Jesus, the separation caused by sin and will restore the original harmony of creation under the headship of King Jesus."

> "Through sin endless disorder and disintegration have come into the world; but in the end all things will be restored to their intended function and to their unity by being brought back to the obedience of Christ." [7]

It's no wonder we were taken to an exceedingly high mountain for the size of the City is massive. To help understand its size, the angel measures it for us. It is square, rather it is a cube.

Ephesians 1:9-10 "God has now revealed to us his mysterious plan regarding Christ, a plan to fulfill his own good pleasure. And this is the plan: At the right time he will bring everything together under the authority of Christ, everything in heaven and on earth."

We are told by the angel that the length and width and height are equal; each measures 1,500 miles that equals 2,250,000 square miles!

You and I try to put this enormous size into terms that we can manage. Eager to contribute, John tells us that Jerusalem is 1,434 miles from Rome. But since we want something a little closer to home John is soon left out of our calculations. We decide that the measurements of the City would be comparable to the distance from Portland, Oregon to Minneapolis, Minnesota. Then from Minneapolis to the farthest tip of Texas, actually about 25 miles beyond into Mexico. From that point going west into the Pacific Ocean and back north to Portland. Gigantic!

But what really is stunning is the height. Commercial planes fly from 6.6 miles to 8.5 miles above sea level. Looking down from the plane's window the earth seems so very far away. NASA awards astronaut status for flights above 50 miles. Space starts at 62 miles. The international space station is approximately 220 miles from earth. The New Jerusalem goes beyond the space station another 1,280 miles. Incredibly high!

The angel points out the 12 foundation stones made of precious jewels. There are three stones on each side. "Each stone measures 500 miles in length," he informs us. We immediately turn to stare at the foundation stones which are mammoth in size. Each is fashioned from a single gemstone and each radiates a beautiful color—deep orange, reddish, transparent green and red, blues, translucent yellows, purple and violet. The name of one of the twelve apostles of Jesus is engraved on each foundation stone. According to the book of Acts, Matthias was elected to take the place of Judas. (Acts 1:12-26) Or, possibly the twelfth could be another apostle mentioned in the New Testament such as Paul, Barnabas, Andronicus or his wife Junia (Acts 14:14; Romans 16:7). From our vantage point we can't quite see who the twelfth is.

The City itself is gold, clear, and pure. Surrounding the City is a great, lofty wall made of a gem that we can see through. It has twelve gates, three on each side of the city. Each gate is made of a single pearl, and we can make out the name of one of the twelve tribes of Israel engraved on them. We see an awesome looking angel standing by each gate. Our angel guide tells us that these gates are never closed.

The angel directs our attention into the City itself. We look through the transparent walls and see a river of the water of life, clear as crystal, flowing from the throne where God and the Lamb are seated. The sparkling water flows right down the middle of a street made of pure gold. On each side of the river we see the tree of life that grew in the Garden of Eden. (Genesis 2:9)

Actually the whole place, even the New Earth on which the New Jerusalem sits, looks like a huge, awesomely beautiful park or garden—a paradise. The angel explains that it really is a paradise. He reminds us that the Lord has said in His Word that all His victorious children will eat fruit from the tree of life in the Paradise of God. (Revelation 2:7)

John turns to us and explains, "You see *paradise* is the Greek word *paradeisos* which means just what we are looking at, a gloriously beautiful garden."

The angel turns the conversation back to the tree of life which is spectacular in itself. He explains to us that the tree of life bears twelve crops of fruit, with a fresh harvest each month. Its leaves are used for the healing of the nations. You and I look at the angel a little perplexed. You tell him that you thought that there would be no sickness in the Eternal Age.

The angel replies with a question, "Where do you see the source of the river of life?"

"It flows from the throne of God and His Son Jesus," you quickly respond.

"And that is your answer," the angel says, "The Father and His Son are the source and sustainers of all life and from them comes this pure, life giving water. The roots of the tree of life which bears the fruit and the leaves are nurtured with life. God and His Son Jesus impart a quality of life that brings purity, holiness, vitality, health, and well-being into your new bodies and souls. Someday you will drink this water and eat this fruit and then you will understand. There is no sickness."

"I will tell you a secret." The angel smiles, "You will also partake of our bread, the bread of angels. It's delicious!"

"What!" we all respond at the same time. Then we recall that the Scriptures tell of how God fed Israel in the desert for forty years with *manna* and how Psalm 78:24-25 refers to *manna* as *bread from heaven*—angel's food. Because the people of Israel did not have glorified bodies, they became sick and tired of heavenly bread.

Psalm 78:24-25 "He rained down manna for them to eat; he gave them bread from heaven. They ate the food of angels! God gave them all they could hold."

The angel continues, "King Jesus told you that everyone who is victorious will eat of the manna that has been hidden away in heaven for you." (Revelation 2:17)

For a few moments we discuss how delightful this will be. . .to eat angel's food. Awesome! Then you ask the angel about another observation of yours. You are very perceptive and drinking in all that you can. "It appears that people of many races have poured out of the City and have established themselves in the New Earth. Who are these people?"

"These are God's people *called*, *chosen* and *faithful*. What you see are the faithful overcomers of all the ages from every nation and tribe and people and language. These chose to share the oppression of God's people instead of the fleeting pleasures of sin. They thought it was better to suffer for the sake of Christ than to own the treasures of the world for they were looking ahead to their great reward. (Hebrews 11:25-26) All glorified Believers have their place in the New Jerusalem as well as dwelling throughout the New Earth in people groups. The order of things in the Eternal Age will be very different."

"Look!" We follow the direction the angel is pointing to see the majestic site of the kings of the nations entering the New Jerusalem bringing their glory into it. A multitude enter with them to bring the splendors and honors of the nations in homage to the King of kings. What grandeur!

Nation... Ethnos, the Greek word, means "a multitude of people of the same nature." [8]

"Who are the kings?" you ask.

"Have you forgotten," replies the angel, "that all of God's children will receive their rewards and status at the Judgment Seat of Christ? While some have more glory and responsibility, all are loved the same. King Jesus' blood was shed for each one making them of immeasurable value. The kings and leaders will be appointed by King Jesus."

Then he adds, "All these nations live within the light of God's glory."

"Tell us more about this wonderful light." John asks the angel. "The City doesn't seem to need the sun or moon to give it light."

"That's right, because the glory of God emanates from the City, and the Lamb is its light. There is no night, therefore, there is no need for lamps or the sun."

Glory
"*Doxa* [Greek] embraces all which is excellent in the divine nature, coinciding with His self-revelation. It comprises all that God will appear to be in His final revelation." KW

The angel further explains, "You see, when the New Jerusalem comes down from heaven to the New Earth, God will permanently dwell among men. He will visibly manifest Himself through the brilliance of *Shekinah Glory*. 'Glory, like grace, is not an attribute. Glory is the aura emanating from God that contains the totality of all His attributes. Glory in God. . .will always involve a whole or a sum of all He is. . ." [9] God is the light of His creation.

John speaks with new understanding as he remembers. "The night that we disciples had our last supper with Jesus, He lifted His eyes to heaven and prayed with great passion*: 'Father, I desire that they also whom You gave Me may be with Me where I am, that they may behold My glory. . .'*" (John 17:24 NKJV)

You, John, and I spend some animated moments talking about the day that "*we will see Him as he really is*"—in all the splendor of His glory.

"Do you notice something else missing in the City of God?" asks the angel.

John promptly replies, "Yes, I see no temple in the City." John had noticed this detail immediately because the temple of Jerusalem was very important to the Jews, the place where God's presence met with His people.

"Correct," the angel said. "There is no temple for the Lord God Almighty and the Lamb are the temple."

Turning to the apostle John, the angel asks, "Do you recall what you wrote in your Gospel, John 2:19-21?"

John's eyes light up as he says, "Of course! The Jewish leaders told Jesus to do something to prove His divine authority. Jesus told them, 'Destroy this *temple*, and in three days I will raise it up.' Jesus wasn't talking about the temple in Jerusalem, but rather, by '*this temple*,' He meant His own body. After Jesus was raised from the dead we remembered and believed what He said."

"Also," I joined in, "This is kind of a side note, but during the Present Age, Believer's bodies are the temple of the Holy Spirit, therefore we are to shine as lights in this dark world." (1 Corinthians 6:19-20; Matthew 5:14)

You break excitedly into the conversation to say, "Now I understand! Jesus was always the true temple where God's holiness in its fullness dwells! There is no need for a *building* in the City because God and the Lamb *are the temple*."

John, with his great wisdom sums it up, "There will be no more false religions to lead people astray; no more man-made philosophies that resist the truth; no more blasphemous religious shrines; and no more things that "muddy" man's understanding of spiritual truths. It will be God and God alone in the Eternal Age."

That thought really inspired us. The angel looked very pleased with our grasp of truth.

And then. . .the angel looks directly at us to see the impact that his next words will have. His eyes are penetrating. "When you finally reach this Paradise. . . you will see God face to face! . . . His name, which expresses the totality of His perfection and beauty, will be written on your foreheads! You will reign forever and ever."

Completely overwhelmed by the thought of actually seeing the face of God we fall to our knees. Our hearts almost burst they are so very full of gratitude.

We are what we are by God's saving mercies. We are where we are by His infinite loving grace.

The angel turns directly to John and says, "*Everything you have heard and seen is trustworthy and true. The Lord God, who inspires His prophets, has sent His angel to tell His servants what will happen soon.*" (Revelation 22:6)

Time: The Eternal Age

You and I return to the Eternal Age, your last Prophetic Event. You are living the reality of God's prophetic Word. Everything is just as the angel told us, however, you discover and keep discovering much, much more.

I think the most awesome wonder of the New Heaven and the New Earth is that God fashioned them, not for Himself alone, but rather, to enjoy them together with us for all eternity.

Yes, eternity! For you, dear God, "*a thousand years are as a passing day, as brief as a few night hours.*" "What are ages to eternity? The drop is more in relation to the sea than time to the life of the Eternal One." [10]

THE GODHEAD THE GLORY OF ETERNITY

Revelation 22:4

LESSON **19**

JESUS CHRIST OUR COMING KING
Revelation 22:20

Jesus—"I am coming soon!

"Amen! Come, Lord Jesus!" We wait for You in commitment, love, obedience, and service.

THE PROPHETIC EVENTS OF YOUR LIFE

YOUR LINE - YOUR LIFE

YOUR LINE — YOUR LIFE

This is your opportunity to "map" out your life from beginning to end. This activity will help you to visualize exactly what God has projected for your future. There are two practical reasons for this study book: first, as you follow the Events as they happen, you will know where you are or will be; and second, you will know the alternatives.

This exercise is based on the supposition that you will live through all the Prophetic Events. Turn to the **Timeline charts** at the end of Part One. Please use a colored pencil. Draw a line from your first Event (your birth) through every Event until you reach your designated prophetic end. This is something like "follow the dots."

As your line progresses, think about all that happens during each Event.

Believer:
All your Events are Jesus Events. He personally walks with you through these Events…one after the other.

Plot 1 – Unbelievers
Events:
1 Birth
2 Born into the World System of the Antichrist
3 Wrath of God
4 Armageddon
5 Christ's Thousand-Year Reign on Earth
6 The Great White Throne Judgment
7 The Lake of Fire—The Second Death

Plot 2 – Believers
Events:
1 Birth
2 New Birth
3 Born into the World System of the Antichrist
4 Rapture
5 Judgment Seat of Christ
6 Marriage Supper of the Lamb
7 Second Coming and Armageddon
8 Christ's Thousand-Year Reign on Earth
9 The New Heaven, New Earth, and New Jerusalem

Plot 3 – Nation of Israel
Events:
1 Birth
2 Born into the World System of the Antichrist
3 Rapture—New Birth
4 Wrath of God—Persecution
5 Second Coming and Armageddon—Deliverance
6 Christ's Thousand-Year Reign on Earth
7 The New Heaven, New Earth, and New Jerusalem

Do you see God's plan for your life? Believer, do you see the flow ever forward toward perfection in God?

Presuppositions

> "People have presuppositions, and they will live more consistently on the basis of these presuppositions than even they themselves may realize. By *presuppositions* we mean the basic way an individual looks at life, his basic world view, the grid through which he sees the world. Presuppositions rest upon that which a person considers to be the truth of what exists. People's presuppositions lay a grid for all they bring forth into the external world. Their presuppositions also provide the basis for their values and therefore the basis for their decisions." [1]

When Jesus appeared to His disciples after His resurrection we notice that He was continually opening the disciple's minds so that they could recognize Him and to understand the Scriptures. When Jesus joined the two disciples walking from Jerusalem to Emmaus, "*God kept them from recognizing him* [Jesus]." As they walked, Jesus explained thoroughly to them the Scriptural meaning of His death on the cross. It was not until the three had sat down to eat supper that they were permitted to recognize Jesus. Perhaps they saw His nail scared hands as He. . .well let's read about it.

> "*As they sat down to eat, he* [Jesus] *took the bread and blessed it. Then he broke it and gave it to them. Suddenly, their eyes were opened, and they recognized him. And at that moment he disappeared. They said to each other, 'Didn't our hearts burn within us as he talked with us on the road and explained the Scriptures to us?* (Luke 24:16; 30-32; also 24:36-45)

My prayer for you, my friend, is that Jesus has opened your mind to understand the Prophetic Events of your life. But especially, I pray that your hearts have *burned within* you as we have walked with Jesus through His Word. Perhaps your presuppositions, your convictions, have been altered, adjusted, amended, or affirmed to provide you with an enriched grid whereby you will see life in accordance with God's world view, and your values and decisions will reflect those of a future reigning king or queen.

By the way, the word *burn* in Greek is *kaio* which means "to set on fire" [S] with emphasis "to keep on burning." [M] Now that's something to think about!

JESUS CHRIST OUR COMING KING

Revelation 22:20

TIMELINE 1

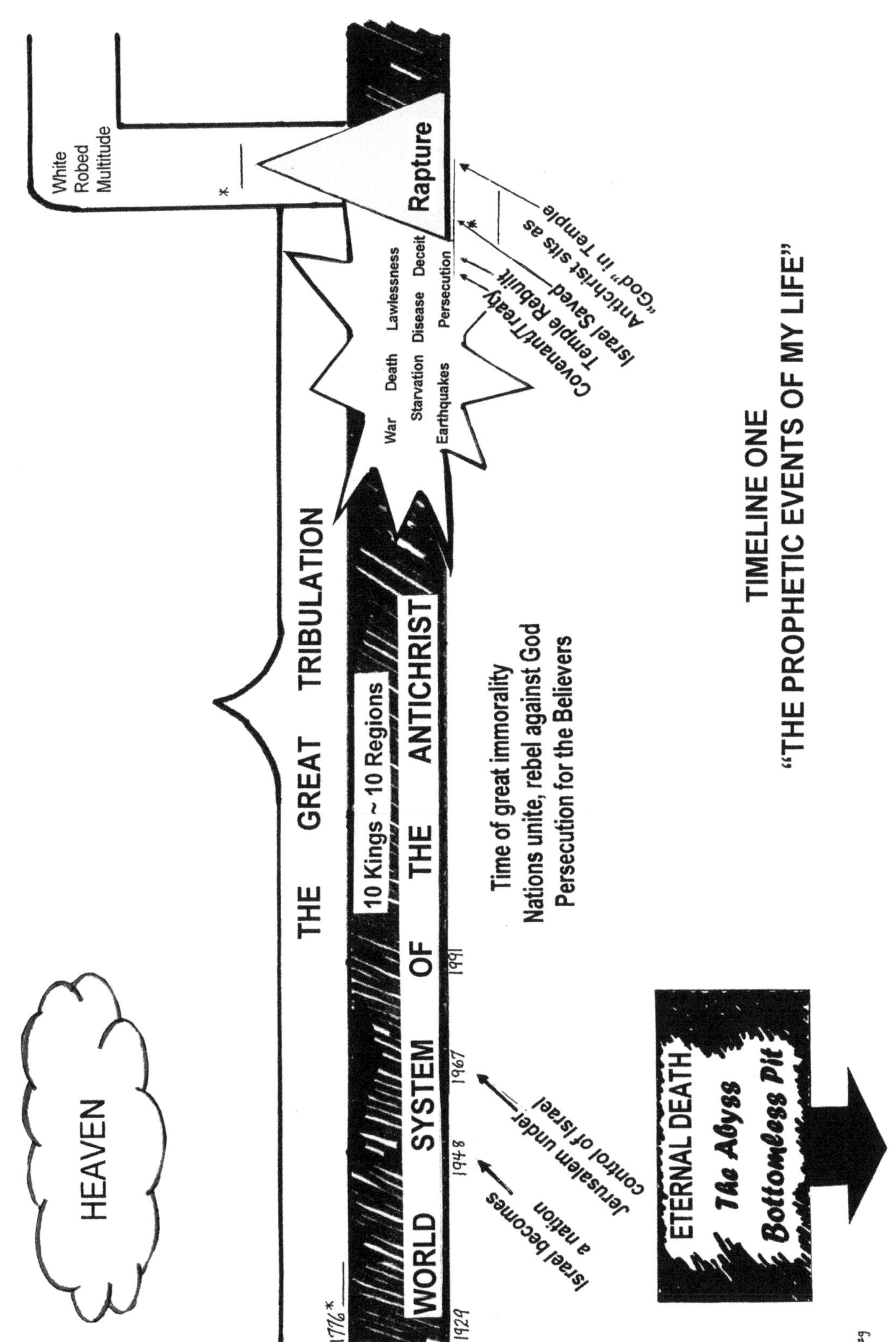
HEAVEN
THE GREAT TRIBULATION
WORLD SYSTEM OF THE ANTICHRIST
10 Kings ~ 10 Regions
White Robed Multitude
Rapture
War Death Lawlessness
Starvation Disease Deceit
Earthquakes Persecution
Covenant/Treaty
Temple Rebuilt
Israel Saved
Antichrist sits as "God" in Temple
Time of great immorality
Nations unite, rebel against God
Persecution for the Believers
←1776*
1929
1948
1967
1991
Israel becomes a nation
Jerusalem under control of Israel
ETERNAL DEATH
The Abyss
Bottomless Pit
TIMELINE ONE
"THE PROPHETIC EVENTS OF MY LIFE"

TIMELINE TWO

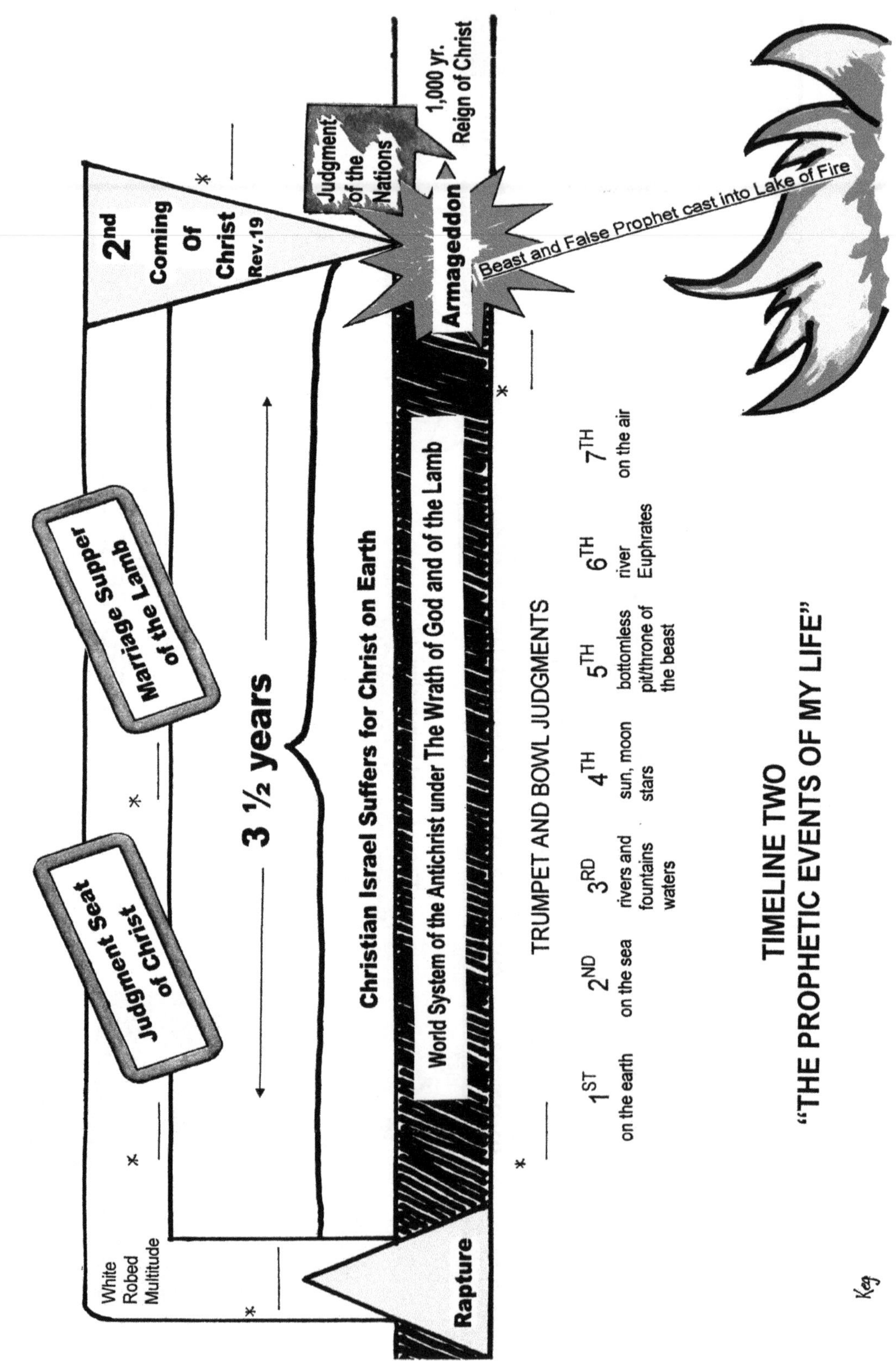

TIMELINE THREE

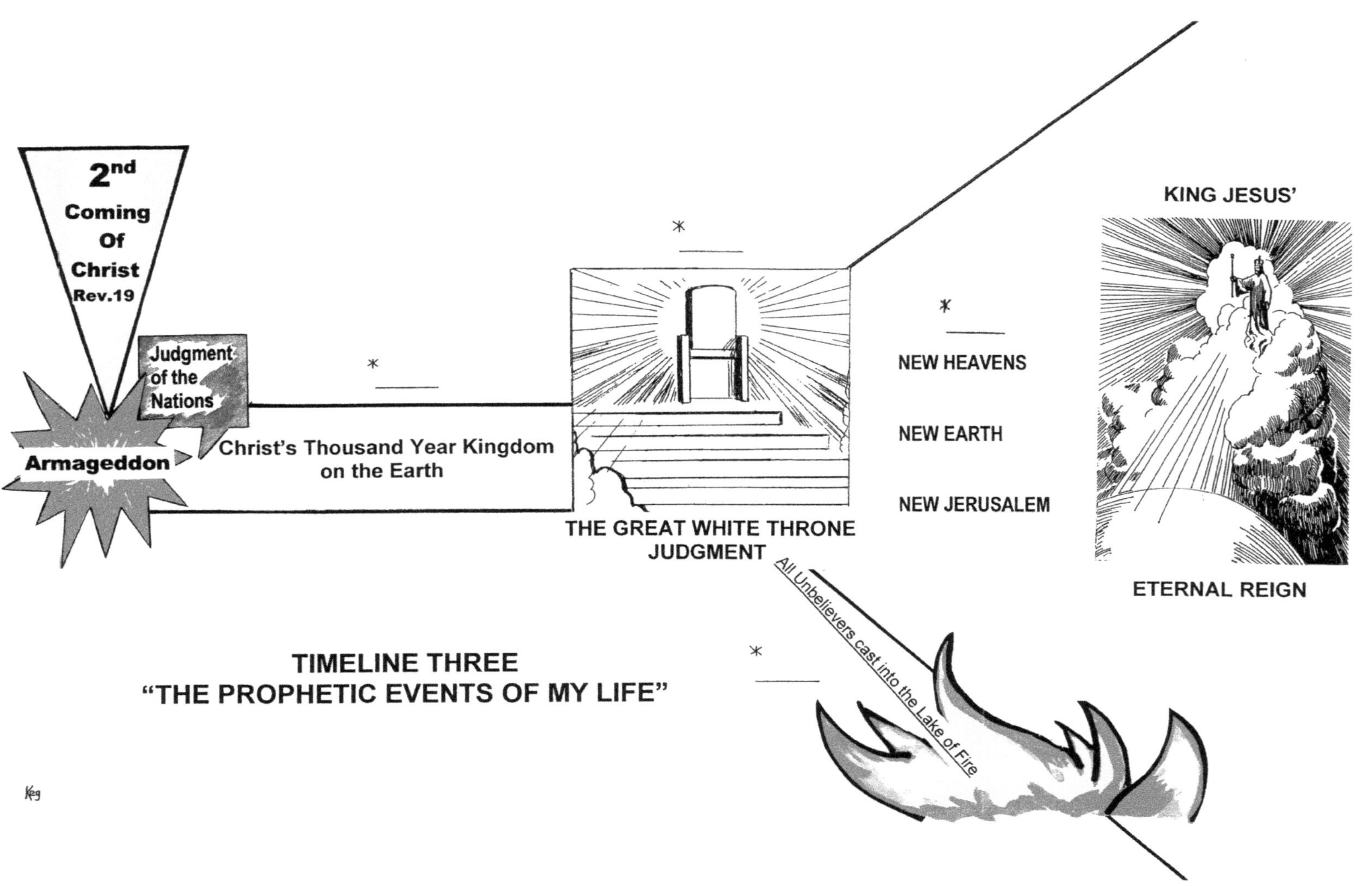

THE PROPHETIC EVENTS OF YOUR LIFE
BEYOND YOUR HORIZON

PART TWO

THE MYSTERY OF THE WORLD SYSTEM OF THE ANTICHRIST

MYSTERY

As a teenager, I loved to read mysteries. "Who-dunits" were the most fun because it gave the reader a chance to solve the mystery before the last chapter revealed that the butler did it.

Raymond Chandler said, "The ideal mystery was one you would read even if the end was missing." [D] That depth of intrigue certainly relates to "The Mystery of the World System of the Antichrist," however, the end is not missing. The Lord leads us through many books of the Bible unfolding this mystery in drama-like fashion through visions, clues, and symbols which all end with a breathtaking finale.

Many who read end-time prophecy and can't understand it, immediately place a label on it "Mystery—Known Only To The Experts." I use the word *mystery* in the sense of being perplexing to the point of being inexplicable. Let me explain things this way. Like the playwright, God is the mastermind who plans every scene, each script. He selects the actors and builds the backdrop. He allows us to read the program so that we may view the order of events permitting us to recognize the development of the storyline through each scene until we excitedly exclaim, "I see it, and I know the end!"

"The Lord our God has secrets known to no one. We are not accountable for them, but we and our children are accountable forever for all that he has revealed to us, so that we may obey all the terms of these instructions." (Deuteronomy 29:29)

This verse informs us that if God has revealed something in His Word it is certainly His intention that it be understood so that His revealed Word can become a part of our knowledge of the workings, purpose, and plan of God that we might obediently participate in it.

Mystery, in the biblical sense, means that man by his intellect cannot know the things of God. The word *mystery*, (*musterion,* Greek) emphasizes this fact.

John 16:13-14

> *"When the Spirit of truth comes, he will guide you into all truth. . .He will tell you about the future. He will bring me glory by telling you whatever he receives from me. . ."*

We hold this *truth* in our hands—the Word of God. Look to the divine Playwright to lead you to the understanding of the great mystery of end-time prophecies.

Having said all that, I would like to balance out our perception of the interpreter's task in dealing with prophetic Scripture. Three vital thoughts.

- **The heart of a true interpreter.**

"In dwelling on divine mysteries, keep thy heart humble, thy thoughts reverent, thy soul holy. . .What thou canst not prove, approve; what thou canst not comprehend, believe; what thou canst believe, admire and love and obey. So shall thine ignorance be satisfied in thy faith, and thy doubt be swallowed up in thy reverence, and thy faith be as influential as sight. Put out thine own candle, and then shalt thou see clearly the sun of righteousness." [1]

- **Characteristic of predictive prophecy.**

Scripture is progressive. "This progressive element is also present in predictive prophecy. Later revelation often discloses elements omitted from earlier revelation. Even so, the sum total of what God disclosed does not comprise a complete picture. The progressive character of prophecy gives us more materials. Yet ambiguity and enigma are not eliminated by greater quantity. It is true that the more we have to meditate upon, the easier it is to see dominant characteristics emerging." [2]

Revelation 17:6-7 (RSV) "...when I [John] saw her I marveled greatly. But the angel said to me, 'Why marvel? I will tell you the mystery of the woman, and of the beast with seven heads and ten horns that carries her."

- **Let the Word speak... no matter where it takes you.**

Our approach to the next five lessons

The next five studies, are all about the World System of the Antichrist. We will study its development, its deceitful actors, its devious activities, and its demonic intentions. You will study key Scriptures that will guide you to a clear, although not complete, understanding of these things. These studies are founded in the Word with little to no regard to contemporary events. Our purpose is to give a Bible basis for all things that pertain to the Antichrist.

It is important that you grasp the fact that each lesson will build on the clues gained from the preceding lesson. You live and participate in this drama whether you are a Believer or an Unbeliever. The curtain rises.

THE MYSTERY OF THE WORLD SYSTEM OF THE ANTICHRIST

Act One	Lesson 20	The Mystery of the Statue	Daniel 2
Act Two	Lesson 21	The Mystery of the Four Beasts	Daniel 7
Act Three	Lesson 22	The Mystery of the Beast	Revelation 13
Act Four	Lesson 23	The Mystery of the Harlot City	Revelation 17
Act Five	Lesson 24	The Mystery Solved	Revelation 17

LESSON **20**

ELOAH—GOD THE ADORABLE ONE THE WORSHIPFUL ONE
Isaiah 44:8

Is there an Eloah besides Me? Only God is worthy of adoration and worship.

THE MYSTERY OF THE WORLD SYSTEM OF THE ANTICHRIST

THE MYSTERY OF THE STATUE

God's Word grips the heart of man, any man, anywhere, any time. Let me illustrate this with the story of Julius Hickerson.

> "Julius Hickerson, a promising physician in the United States, felt God's call to be a missionary in Colombia, South America. After two years of evangelism there, he could see no visible results. Then he was killed in a plane crash in a remote village. Several years later, another missionary arrived at that village, unaware of the plane crash. To his surprise, everyone in the area had heard the gospel message, and groups of Colombians met regularly to worship. When he asked what had happened, the Colombians showed him a single book: a well-marked Bible in their own language—Julius Hickerson's Bible—which they had pulled from the crashed plane." [1]

How powerful! Man, the Bible, and the illumination of the Holy Spirit wonderfully combine to bring man to an understanding of Jesus, *"the way, the truth, and the life."* (John 14:6)

God instructs man through His Word. Every chapter, every paragraph teaches us something. Our study of the Prophetic Events of Your Life has taken us into the teachings of the prophets. This means that we are looking at literary language predominantly used in prophetic visions as you have noticed in Part One of this study book.

Jesus' parables in the four gospels are like mini-visions which engage our intellect through our imaginative faculties. In the same manner, as we contemplate these prophetic visions, things happen before our eyes in a very colorful, dramatic, expressive manner in our imagination. Biblical visions are one of God's methods of teaching divine truths.

Mickelsen explains this very well in his commentary on the meaning of John's expression *"I saw"* used over and over with the visions in the book of Revelation.

> "In each instance John tells about some specific thing, person, or place that he sees, and the reader begins 'to see' the vision. What is happening here is that our imagination has specific content for what we picture. *Imagination* must not be confused with *imaginary*. Something imaginary means that it exists only in our imagination. . .However, our imagination is a distinctive feature of our mind that has the power not only to create things that do not exist but also, more frequently, to call up a mental picture of what really exists in the world of reality. The more we 'look' at it, and think about it, the more the picture and the reality grow within us. This is true of every vision to which we give careful attention." [2]

Daniel Webster "I believe that the Bible is to be understood and received in the plain and obvious meaning of its passages; for I cannot persuade myself that a book intended for the instruction and conversion of the whole world should cover its true meaning in any such mystery and doubt that none but critics and philosophers can discover it." [3]

In our study of the statue of Daniel 2 let your discerning eye distinguish the abrupt beginning and end of the hues and shine of the metals that form the different parts of the body. The statue lends to our seeing the pomp, dominion, and majesty of powerful human empires ruling the world. Visualize the statue and hear the roar as the *Rock* comes hurtling through space like a magnificent asteroid to smash the statue, and feet first, this whole gigantic system of human power is crushed into nothingness.

This is the path we will take to discover the teaching, and the literal meaning in the following studies. Be prepared with an open mind to understand prophetic Scripture. Ask the Holy Spirit to illumine your mind so that you may comprehend, evaluate, and draw conclusions.

In the following studies of the kingdoms of this world we will study parallel Scriptures from Daniel and Revelation and then we will link them together to form a complete picture. These visions are the biblical basis to recognize and understand this end-time system. You will find great joy in your discoveries. Let the Word speak for itself to your open heart and mind.

Lessons 20 and 21 focus our attention on the numerous clues of our mystery presented in Daniel 2 and Daniel 7 concerning the World System of the Antichrist and its final leader. You will learn:

- when it will take place
- where to look for it
- its characteristics
- how it will end

In this lesson we will study:

The Dream Statue of Daniel 2
Four World Kingdoms
First Kingdom
Second Kingdom
Third Kingdom
Fourth Kingdom—Legs
Building the Kingdom of God
Fourth Kingdom—Feet and Toes
The Kingdom of God

THE DREAM STATUE OF DANIEL 2

King Nebuchadnezzar had conquered many nations, among them the Jewish Nation. After taking captive thousands of Jews, he selected some promising Jewish youths to be placed in an educational program to learn the Babylonian mysteries, language, literature, and wisdom. One night Nebuchadnezzar had a very disturbing dream so he called the wisest of the wise to not only interpret his dream but to also tell him the dream itself. An impossibility! The bad part was that the king promised them death if they failed. Daniel and his three Jewish friends as trainees were to perish also. However, these youths trusted in God and to Him they went in prayer. God revealed both the dream and the interpretation to Daniel who was still in his late teens or early twenties.

It has been said that God gives a nation the leadership it deserves.

The revelation and explanation of the dream brought Daniel to an understanding of a remarkable truth—God "*controls the course of world events; he removes kings and sets up other kings.*" (Daniel 2:21) As you do this study, let your mind absorb this teaching. God as absolute Sovereign governs the world according to His purposes which always lead toward the goal of establishing His perfect reign on the earth. Rest in the fact that God, today, is accomplishing His predetermined objective, and one day it is going to happen!

In Lesson 3 pages 37-40 Part One, we examined this vision given by God to the great Emperor Nebuchadnezzar of the Babylonian Empire. It is necessary for you to review that part of Lesson 3 before you proceed.

FOUR WORLD EMPIRES

The dream was of a statue which body parts represented the four world empires that would rule the world beginning in Daniel's day until the end of this Present Age.

FIRST KINGDOM

Daniel 2:37-38 (NASB)

> 37 "*You* [Nebuchadnezzar], *O king, are the king of kings, to whom the God of heaven has given the kingdom, the power, the strength, and the glory;* 38 *and wherever the sons of men dwell, or the beasts of the field, or the birds of the sky, He has given them into your hand and has caused you to rule over them all. You are the head of gold.*

To what specific world empire does the head of gold refer? ______________________________

The opinion of some historians is that Nebuchadnezzar, the head of gold, was one of the greatest men of ancient times and also extremely cruel. Did you notice in these verses from where his greatness came? Nebuchadnezzar's kingdom lasted about 21 years after his death. Belshazzar, the last king of the Babylonian Empire, invited a thousand of his nobles to a huge banquet and disgracefully drank wine from the gold and silver cups taken from the Jews temple in Jerusalem. These utensils were consecrated for the use of the Jewish priests in the worship ceremonies in the temple. Shock gripped the revelers as suddenly, they saw the fingers of a man's hand writing a message on the wall of the palace. Belshazzar's "*face turned pale with fright. His knees knocked together in fear and his legs gave way beneath him.*" (Daniel 5:5-6) None of the king's wise men could interpret the message, therefore, Daniel was brought to the king to explain the meaning.

However, before Daniel explained the message, he gave the reason for the appearance of the mysterious words written on the wall. From Daniel's message, can you discern the unquestionable truth that all monarchs, kings, and world leaders must recognize? In the following Scripture **underline** what you believe to be the fundamental guideline for all rulers of all ages regardless of their race, nationality, or religion. **Circle** the specific reason for Nebuchadnezzar's seven-year humiliation.

Daniel 5:18-28, 30

> 18 *"Your Majesty, the Most High God gave sovereignty, majesty, glory, and honor to your predecessor, Nebuchadnezzar.* 19 *He made him so great that people of all races and nations and languages trembled before him in fear. He killed those he wanted to kill and spared those he wanted to spare. He honored those he wanted to honor and disgraced those he wanted to disgrace.* 20 *But when his heart and mind were puffed up with arrogance, he was brought down from his royal throne and stripped of his glory.*
> 21 *He was driven from human society. He was given the mind of a wild animal, and he lived among the wild donkeys. He ate grass like a cow, and he was drenched with the dew of heaven, until he learned that the Most High God rules over the kingdoms of the world and appoints anyone he desires to rule over them.*

Isaiah 42:8
"I am the LORD; that is my name! I will not give my glory to anyone else, nor share my praise with carved idols."

You can read this fascinating story about Nebuchadnezzar's humiliation in Daniel 4. I'm sure that you observed that the arrogance of self-glory sets the stage for destruction.

Now read about the downfall of the Babylonian Empire as predicted in Daniel's words to Belshazzar. You can read the whole story in Daniel 5. Again, **underline** all the words that indicate to you the cause of the failure of Babylon's emperors from first to last. The following is a continuation of Daniel's message to the emperor.

> 22 *You are his successor, O Belshazzar, and you knew all this, yet you have not humbled yourself* [in your heart.] 23 *For you have proudly defiled the LORD of heaven and have had these cups from his temple brought to you. You and your nobles and your wives and your concubines have been drinking wine from them while praising gods of silver, gold, bronze, iron, wood, and stone—gods that neither see nor hear nor know anything at all. But you have not honored the God who gives you the breath of life and controls your destiny!* 24 *So God has sent this hand to write this message.*
> 25 *This is the message that was written: MENE, MENE, TEKEL, and PARSIN.* 26 *This is what these words mean:*
> *Mene means 'numbered'—God has numbered the days of your reign and has brought it to an end.*
> 27 *Tekel means 'weighed'—you have been weighed on the balances and have not measured up.*
> 28 *Parsin means 'divided'—your kingdom has been divided and given to the Medes and Persians.*
> 30*. . .That very night Belshazzar, the Babylonian king, was killed."*

God *"controls the course of world events; he removes kings and sets up other kings."* (Daniel 2:21)

Nebuchadnezzar's kingdom (modern-day Israel, Lebanon, Syria, and Iraq) is the first of four world kingdoms recognized by God. The last page of this lesson is a diagram of the Dream

Statue **Write** on the lines to the right of the head of the statue the following: **Nebuchadnezzar – Babylonian Empire (606– 539)**

SECOND KINGDOM

Daniel 2:39 (NASB)

"And after you there will arise another kingdom inferior to you. . ."

About 150 years before Babylon was conquered by the yet unborn King Cyrus, God addressed Cyrus as the new ruler with the ultimate intention that he release His captive people, the Jews, and to also bring judgment on unbelieving nations. **Read** this marvelous prophecy in Isaiah 45:1-7. *"I will do this so you may know that I am the LORD, the God of Israel, the one who calls you by name."* (verse 3) God knew all about Cyrus, even the name he would be given. "Cyrus was the first king of the Medo-Persians, and Darius the Mede was installed by him as king over the Babylon portion of the larger territory he controlled."[4] The chest and arms of silver represent these two nations whose empire lasted 200 years.

In a vision, Daniel saw a ram with two horns, one short and one long. The short horn symbolized the Medes and the long horn the more powerful Persians. Daniel 8:4 envisions the advance of this empire. **Underline** the words that indicate the decisive error committed by the rulers of this empire.

> *"I saw the ram butting westward, northward, and southward, and no other beasts* [nations] *could stand before him, nor was there anyone to rescue from his power; but he did as he pleased and magnified himself."* (Daniel 8:4-7 NASB)

Acts 14:16-17
"In the past he [God] permitted all the nations to go their own ways, but he never left them without evidence of himself and his goodness."

Long after Cyrus died, the great Medo-Persian Empire represented by the ram continued in its self- aggrandizement: *"he did as he pleased and magnified himself,"* thus, contributing to its collapse.

God *"controls the course of world events; he removes kings and sets up other kings."* (Daniel 2:21)

The Medo-Persian kingdom is the second world kingdom of four recognized by God. Go to the diagram of the Dream Statue. Perhaps you would like to write Medes on the left arm of the statue and Persia on the right arm. **Write** on the lines to the right of the chest and arms of the statue the following: **Medo-Persian Empire (539-331)**

THIRD KINGDOM

Daniel 2:39 (NASB)

"then another kingdom of bronze, which will rule over the earth."

The Grecians, led by Alexander the Great, a very young, dynamic warrior, defeated the Medes and Persians. His conquests swept across Asia Minor all the way to the northwestern portion of India. **Underline** the grave error of this emperor in the following paragraph and Scripture.

> "Alexander was so impressed with his own success that in the last year of his life he apparently believed that the appropriate way for his Greek subjects to recognize his greatness was to worship him as a god. However, he didn't have much time to enjoy this worship. Alexander died in Babylon on June 10, 323 B.C., at the age of only thirty-three. In thirteen years he had conquered most of the known world, and his military triumphs spread a Greek influence over the Near East that would last for a thousand years. It is because of Alexander the Great that the New Testament was written in Greek." [5]

Continuing the story of the *ram* and the *male goat*, Daniel 8:8 (NASB) speaks of Alexander's downfall.

> "*Then the male goat* [Alexander] *magnified himself exceedingly. But as soon as he was mighty, the large horn was broken; and in its place there came up four conspicuous horns toward the four winds of heaven* [the four directions of the compass]."

Acts 17:26 "From one man [Adam] he [God] created all the nations throughout the whole earth. He decided beforehand when they should rise and fall, and he determined their boundaries."

After the death of "*the large horn,*" Alexander's kingdom ended and was divided by his four generals into four parts before it was displaced by the Roman Empire.

How did Alexander the Great contribute to his downfall? ______________________________

God "*controls the course of world events; he removes kings and sets up other kings.*" (Daniel 2:21)

The Grecian kingdom is the third world kingdom of four recognized by God. Go to the diagram of the Dream Statue and **write** on the lines to the right of the belly and thighs of the statue: **Grecian Empire (331-146)**

FOURTH KINGDOM—THE LEGS

Daniel 2:40 (NASB)

> "*Then there will be a fourth kingdom as strong as iron; inasmuch as iron crushes and shatters all things, so, like iron that breaks in pieces, it will crush and break all these in pieces.*"

In turn, Rome defeated each of the four divisions of the Grecian Empire between the years 190 B.C. and 31 B.C. The Roman Empire in terms of present day countries extended from the Euphrates River in Iraq, all the coastal countries around the Mediterranean Sea to the Atlantic, and the coastal countries along the Atlantic of western Europe (including as far north as Scotland). It separated in A.D. 395 to form the Western Roman Empire with Rome as the capital and the Eastern Roman Empire with Constantinople as capital. The Western Roman Empire fell in the year 476 while the Eastern Empire lasted till 1453.

When Julius Caesar became emperor of Rome, he was the "Pontifex Maximus" or "Supreme Pontiff" (high priest) of the Etruscan religion that dated back to Nimrod of Genesis 10 and 11. [6] From Julius Caesar on, the title and office of "Pontifex Maximus" belonged to the emperor of the Roman Empire and each succeeding emperor, thus, uniting the head of this ancient pagan religion with the head of the Roman Empire. Julius Caesar carried both titles and was without a doubt the most powerful man on earth; he was held by the Romans to be a god. Observe the following information relating to his son.

> "During his lifetime, Caesar Augustus [Luke 2:1] did not support the veneration of himself as divine. Yet he asserted the deity of Julius Caesar, his adoptive father, and as his son permitted himself to be called the "Son of God," thus setting the stage for being deified after his death. Caesar Augustus also accepted the title of "Savior" and was honored for having brought peace to all the world. One inscription about him reads, "Divine Augustus Caesar, Son of God, Savior of all the world." [7]

Pontius Pilate, representing Rome as governor of Judea in Palestine, [Matthew 27:1-26; Luke 3:1] was handed the most significant decision ever placed in the hands of a human being—to crucify Jesus, Son of God, at the request of Jewish officials. He ordered Jesus to be crucified. Pilate attempted to disassociate himself from this unspeakable judgment by actually washing his hands of the whole affair!

First, the Roman government participated in the death of God's beloved Son, and then, for the next 300 years, carried out horrendous persecutions against God's beloved children. The constant requirement to worship the emperor forced the Believers to face the alternatives—apostasy (denial of their Lord) or death. By far, the majority valiantly chose the path of life through death. And yet, "by the end of the Imperial Persecutions (A.D. 313), Christians numbered about one-half the population of the Roman Empire." [8]

The Roman Empire died a slow death at the hands of the many tribes of Europe called *barbarians*. The term *barbarian* is used in the sense of its ancient meaning which applied to peoples that did not speak Greek or Latin. Rome was sacked in A.D. 410 and the Western Empire fell completely in A.D. 476.

God "*controls the course of world events; he removes kings and sets up other kings.*" (Daniel 2:21)

"Out of the ruins of the Western Empire arose the Papal Empire [along with the assumed title "Pontifex Maximus"], and Rome still ruled the world for 1000 years." [9] The political Roman Empire ceased, but the religious Roman Empire began to expand.

What was a repeated characteristic manifested by the emperors? ______________________

Absolute power mixed with pride, arrogance, and ambition is a formula for tragedy and great suffering. For any human being to consider himself to be God or a "god" is delusional or the height of arrogance.

None of the kings of the four kingdoms recognized God as He who "*controls the course of world events*" and who "*removes kings and sets up other kings*" to be rulers of the world.

God is Supreme, the only true Monarch. All others are appointed by the Most High God, and therefore, far inferior to Him—hardly a blip on history's radar screen.

Psalm 22:28
"For royal power belongs to the LORD. He rules all the nations."

The Roman Empire is the fourth world kingdom of four recognized by God. Go to the diagram of the Dream Statue. **Write** on the lines to the right of the legs of the statue the following: **Roman Empire (146 B.C.- A.D. 476)** Also **write** on the slanted arrow "**Political Roman Empire ceases A.D. 476**"

BUILDING THE KINGDOM OF GOD

A lapse of time between the ancient Roman Empire of the legs and the end-time Roman Empire of the feet was explained in Lesson 3A.

From the fall of the ancient Roman Empire in A.D. 476 and the establishment of the end-time Roman Empire, God has placed world empires on hold. At the present time, while powerful men rule the nations of the world, Jesus is building His Kingdom. God sent His Son, Jesus, to die on the cross for the sin of mankind during the rule of the ancient Roman Empire. From Jesus' cross to His future crown a period of divine grace has extended for centuries as Christ builds His Kingdom. . . one soul at a time.

Jesus
"I will build my church, and all the powers of hell will not conquer it."
(Matthew 16:18)

Believer, you belong to a holy nation. You have been separated from all other nations so that you might reflect the holiness of God. *"Consecrate yourselves and be holy, because I am the LORD your God. Keep my decrees and follow them. I am the LORD, who makes you holy. I have set you apart from the nations to be my own."* (Leviticus 20:8, 24) These words were spoken to Israel, but they certainly apply to the Christian.

Because of man's choice to rebel against his true King, he must remain under the tyranny of human government until God's perfect reign takes effect. Human governments are *meantime* governments; they occupy the time between the ancient Roman Empire and the end-time Roman Empire, the World System of the Antichrist.

The time lapse has ended. At this present time, the World System of the Antichrist is fast developing which will be the worst period of human government ever known or experienced,. *"But the one who endures to the end will be saved. And the Good News about the Kingdom will be preached throughout the whole world, so that all nations will hear it; <u>and then the end will come</u>."* (Matthew 24:13-14)

Go to the diagram of the Dream Statue. **Write** in the space between the legs of the statue and the feet: **The Church Age**. The Church Age will conclude when, "*The kingdom of the world has become the kingdom of our Lord and of his Christ, and he will reign for ever and ever.*" (Revelation 11:15)

FOURTH KINGDOM—FEET AND TOES

It is very obvious that this feet-and-toe empire will exist at the end of this Present Age. It will be as real and verifiable as the empires we have just studied. This interpretation sees this kingdom as the World System of the Antichrist of the last days.

None of the kings of the four kingdoms recognized God as the Supreme Ruler who "*controls the course of world events; he removes kings and sets up other kings*." Will the modern-day iron/clay kingdom follow this same pattern? Interesting question.

Daniel 2:41-44 (NASB)

> [41] *"And in that you saw the feet and toes, partly of potter's clay and partly of iron, it*
> *will be a divided kingdom; but it will have in it the toughness of iron, inasmuch as*
> *you saw the iron mixed with common clay.* [42]*And as the toes of the feet were partly of*
> *iron and partly of pottery, so some of the kingdom will be strong and part of it will be*
> *brittle.* [43] *And in that you saw the iron mixed with common clay, they will combine with*
> *one another in the seed of men; but they will not adhere to one another, even as iron*
> *does not combine with pottery."*
>
> [44] *And in the days of those kings the God of heaven will set up a kingdom which will*
> *never be destroyed. . ."*

Make four observations from the above Scripture.

1. ____
2. ____
3. ____
4. ____

A hermeneutic principle

A symbol may have more than one meaning. Its meaning is determined by the context in which it appears. The interpreter must consistently interpret the symbol by the obvious meaning given to it. This means that the interpreter cannot arbitrarily change the meaning of the symbol unless the biblical text changes its meaning. This principle will help you avoid confusion and will keep you faithful to biblical meaning. Please keep this important principle in mind as you work through these lessons.

Special attention is given the feet and toes of the statue. What is the element of continuity in both the legs and feet? ________________. What is the new element in the feet and toes which was not a part in the legs? ________________________________.

Every body part of the statue represented a world kingdom. What kingdom did the legs of iron symbolize? ____________________________________. What kingdom does the iron in the feet and toes symbolize? ____________________________________.
If every body part represents a kingdom, what do the <u>ten</u> toes symbolize? ______________________________. Because this feet-and-toes, end-time empire is depicted as one

kingdom, we shall see the ______________________________ (iron) united with ______________________________ (baked clay).

How I would love to see how you did on filling in the blanks! Don't be discouraged if you weren't able to tackle the "baked clay" part. If you studied Part One well of this book you should have done fine. Verify you answers, or fill in the unanswered blanks when the answer becomes evident.

Any interpretation of Scripture involves a close examination of key words. Please read the above Scripture once more (Daniel 2:41-44), and **circle** what you consider to be key words or phrases.

As you made your observations from Daniel 2:41-44 and circled the key words, perhaps some of you had difficulty finding the meaning of this Scripture. Take heart, as we study key words we will be able to gain insight into this very important, end-time prophecy.

The Composition of the "Feet and Toes" kingdom
Verse 41. . . "And in that you saw the feet and toes, partly of potter's clay and partly of iron, it will be a divided kingdom; but it will have in it the toughness of iron, inasmuch as you saw the iron mixed with common clay.

First of all, we need to pay close attention to just exactly what our eyes are seeing. The interpretation attracts our eyes to the head of the statue, which we now understand, and then our eyes are directed to slide downward as each new kingdom comes into view. Finally our focus is on the *feet* which are not referred to as a fifth kingdom but rather a continuation of the fourth with an added feature represented by the baked clay.

When speaking of our body, we generally refer to our *feet* (Daniel 2:33) not our *feet and toes*. It is just understood that toes are a part of the feet, that is, unless we want to specifically point them out. However, Daniel's interpretation of the statue places special emphasis on the toes as having their own importance. Because each body part represents a kingdom, how would that representation apply to our understanding of the toes? Think about it. Before you answer that question, look at verse 44 and **underline** the words that refer back to the toes.

> [44] *And in the days of those kings the God of heaven will set up a kingdom which will never be destroyed. . ."*

Yes, "*in the days of those kings.*" Notice the word "*kings*" is pluralized. The toes undoubtedly symbolize "*those* ____________________." How many toes are there? ____________. How many kings will form a part of the end-time kingdom? ________________. Each king rules a kingdom, therefore, each toe represents a kingdom. It is as simple as that!

Verse 41 also states that this kingdom "*will be a divided kingdom.*" This is certainly the case as we see a representative of the Roman aspect reigning with ten others. This kingdom is divided between eleven ruling entities.

Now you can verify your answers to the above exercise.

Iron is the element of continuity in both the legs and feet. Baked clay is the new element in the feet and toes which did not have a part in the legs. The legs of iron symbolize the Roman Empire. The Roman Empire is symbolized by the iron in the feet and toes.

The ten toes symbolize ten kings. Because this feet-and-toes end-time empire is depicted as one kingdom, we shall see the Roman Empire (iron) united with Ten Kings (baked clay).

We can reasonably draw the conclusion at this time that this end-time Roman Empire involves a nation and also that the Ten Kings involve nations. It is apparent that this end-time empire includes the entire world. Therefore, we conclude that the Ten Kings would necessarily represent ten regions of nations in order to embrace the whole world. This further leads us to conclude that as we look at the feet and toes of the statute we are looking at a Roman entity involved with a world federation of Ten Kings which will be in the act of ruling the world at the time King Jesus comes to earth to establish His Kingdom—*"in the days of those kings."*

The Characteristics of the Feet and Toes Kingdom

We are going to look at some very interesting aspects of this "mixed-doesn't mix" kingdom. Look closely at the underlined words to help your mind form a picture of this kingdom.

> [41]*. . .but it will have in it the toughness of iron, inasmuch as you saw the iron mixed with common clay.* [42]*And as the toes of the feet were partly of iron and partly of pottery, so some of the kingdom will be strong and part of it will be brittle.* [43] *And in that you saw the iron mixed with common clay, they will combine with one another in the seed of men; but they will not adhere to one another, even as iron does not combine with pottery."*

Verses 41-43 common clay. . . The Hebrew word for *common* or *potter's clay* is *tiyn* interchanged with *tiyt* which "has the idea of dirt to be swept away; mud or clay; mire" [S] "Most clays also contain silica and other foreign materials, and so graduate into common soil or earth. . . *Tiyt* is usually rendered 'mire' like our common word *mud*, for the fine deposit left from the evaporation of water. . .or washed up on the shore." [10] Other types of clay were used to make highly valuable and fine grades of pottery. Here we are speaking about clay of inferior quality, just mud.

The kingdoms have come a long way from gold to mud!

Verse 42 strong, brittle. . . *"And as the toes of the feet were partly of iron and partly of pottery, so some of the kingdom will be strong and part of it will be brittle."*

How is the iron described in this verse? ____________________. Verse 41 refers to the ________________________ of iron. Also verse 40 in speaking of the iron in the legs states *"as strong as iron; inasmuch as iron crushes and shatter all things, so, like iron that breaks in pieces, it will crush and break all these in pieces."*

How is the pottery described in verse 42? ______________________. Baked pottery is indeed delicate and fragile, very breakable.

Which of the two parts of the feet-toes kingdom strike you as the most powerful and dominate, the iron, Roman aspect, or the clay, Ten Kings? ______________________________

Verse 43 mixed, combine, seed of men, will not adhere, does not combine . . . *"And in that you saw the iron mixed with common clay, they will combine with one another in the seed of men; but they will not adhere to one another, even as iron does not combine with pottery."*

This verse clearly signifies that the Roman entity and the Ten Kings (in the sense of kingdoms) will *mix* or *combine* with one another in a political alliance. But we are told in the same verse that this alliance doesn't work very well. *"They will combine with one another in the seed of men."* The term "*seed of men*" is key to our understanding one of the vital characteristics of this end-time kingdom.

Agreements can be worked out among political leaders, but how can these same world leaders create a world consciousness, a global citizen? How can the people of the world be manipulated to reject the age-old ideology of nationalism? Nationalism is the fundamental "belief that nations would benefit from acting independently rather than collectively, emphasizing national rather than international goals." [D] It appears God in this Scripture is revealing one of the mechanisms that will be used to form a one world order—an undertaking to create world citizens by intermarriage between the nations.

Edward J. Young gives an excellent explanation of this phrase: *"they will combine with one another in the seed of men."*

> "This expression need not be limited to marriages. The figure of mixing by seed is derived from the sowing of the field with mingled seed, and denotes all the means employed by the rulers to combine the different nationalities, among which the *connubium* [Latin for marriage] is only spoken of as the most important and successful means. However this mixing together will fail." [11]

The Ten Kings represent each of their Ten Regions of the world. As they work to unify the world, an attempt is made to mix and blend together all the peoples of the world, former sovereign boundaries disappear. Because of the difficulties of attempting to mix the different races, cultures, ideologies, laws, languages, and religions, this world government will not be strong, but rather, weak like clay, ceramic clay.

In order to achieve a world citizen status, the system must develop by means of absolute uniformity which will lead to chaos. Every nation is made up of a distinct race, culture, ideology, economy, laws, and religion. For the controllers, no nation can prevail in any one of these areas over other nations, therefore, the measure is taken to neutralize all to establish one. This gigantic endeavor will be shaky and weak, like a ceramic pot about to fall off the edge of the table, that is, until the powerful, unbending "iron" leader comes on the scene to forcefully unify the world by his astounding appearance and severe measures. The "*iron*" remains strong, and the "*clay*" remains weak as we will soon see.

There are only two components of the end-time system of the Antichrist—Rome and Ten Kings. This is a very important fact to remember from this study of the "*feet and toes*" which represent the final kingdom appointed and foretold by God.

Go to the diagram of the Dream Statue and **write** on the lines to the right of the feet and toes of the statue the following: **Roman Empire _______ and World Federation of Ten Kings** ___________. We are not ready to write the dates quite yet.

THE KINGDOM OF GOD

Daniel's narration of the dream.
Daniel 2:34-35 (NASB)

> [34] *"You continued looking until a stone was cut out without hands, and it struck the statue on its feet of iron and clay, and crushed them.*
>
> [35] *Then the iron, the clay, the bronze, the silver and the gold were crushed all at the same time, and became like chaff from the summer threshing floors; and the wind carried them away so that not a trace of them was found. But the stone that struck the statue became a great mountain and filled the whole earth."*

Make five observations from these Scriptures.
1. ______________________________
2. ______________________________
3. ______________________________
4. ______________________________
5. ______________________________

Daniel's interpretation of the dream.
Daniel 2:44-45 (NASB)

> [44] *"And in the days of those kings the God of heaven will set up a kingdom which will never be destroyed and that kingdom will not be left for another people; it will crush and put an end to all these kingdoms, but it will itself endure forever.*
>
> [45] *Inasmuch as you saw that a stone was cut out of the mountain without hands and that it crushed the iron, the bronze, the clay, the silver, and the gold, the great God has made known to the king what will take place in the future; so the dream is true, and its interpretation is trustworthy."*

Make five observations from these Scriptures.
1. ______________________________
2. ______________________________
3. ______________________________

4. ______________________________
5. ______________________________

Having gone through this material in Lesson 3, and again in this lesson, I believe that your observations demonstrate your understanding of the Second Coming of King Jesus as represented by the "stone."

The Lord of Heaven's Armies says

> *"The day of judgment is coming, burning like a furnace. On that day the arrogant and the wicked will be burned up like straw. They will be consumed—roots, branches, and all. But for you who fear my name, the Sun of Righteousness will rise with healing in his wings. And you will go free, leaping with joy like calves let out to pasture. On the day when I act, you will tread upon the wicked as if they were dust under your feet."* (Malachi 4:1-3)

The Kingdom of the Righteous bursts from the gates of heaven! King Jesus descends to earth and blasts the statue so completely that not a trace is found. His coming at Armageddon is so powerful that the reverberation travels back through the governments and empires of time. . . back. . . back to the very first rebellion against God's rule and resulting establishment of human government at the tower of Babel. All is gone!

Go to the diagram of the Dream Statue and **write** on the lines to the right of the STONE the following: **King Jesus' Eternal Kingdom ____________.** And, yes, we are not ready to write the date quite yet.

We have learned from Daniel 2:

- There will be a lapse of time between the ancient Roman Empire and the end-time Roman Empire.
- The final world kingdom will be composed of Rome and Ten Kings.
- King Jesus will return during the reign of this kingdom to destroy it and end all human-lead kingdoms to establish His Kingdom on earth.

ELOAH—GOD THE ADORABLE ONE, THE WORSHIPFUL ONE

Isaiah 44:8

DANIEL 2

PROPHECY	HISTORY
Head *Gold*	
Chest and Arms *Silver*	
Belly and Thighs *Bronze*	
Legs *Iron*	
Feet and Ten Toes Iron and Baked Clay mixed	
STONE!	

Daniel 2 (statue)

LESSON 21

***EL OLAM*—THE GOD OF ETERNITY**
Psalm 90:2

"God extends beyond our furthest vision, whether we look backward or forward till it is lost to sight." [1]

THE MYSTERY OF THE WORLD SYSTEM OF THE ANTICHRIST

THE MYSTERY OF THE FOUR BEASTS

MONSTERS!

Almost every child has his dream monsters. These guys were usually hidden under our beds and when we fell asleep they crawled out and jumped into our dreams. Then we jumped into the safe haven of dad and mom's bed. If I were to ask you what your dream monsters were, I am sure that you would have an immediate reply about your own menacing monster specialty.

A really scary dream

> *"Earlier, during the first year of King Belshazzar's reign in Babylon, Daniel had a dream and saw visions* [in his mind] *as he lay in his bed. He wrote down the dream, and this is what he saw.*
>
> *In my vision that night, I Daniel, saw a great storm churning the surface of a great sea, with strong winds blowing from every direction. Then four huge beasts came up out of the water, each different from the others."* (Daniel 7:1-3)

A violent windstorm at sea, waves 50 feet high, powerful winds from all directions, clashing violently together, a column of rotating wind whips upward out of the sea enclosing and then spewing out four massive beasts one after the other. Brave Daniel stands his ground and when the vision ends he runs for his quill and ink to write down all that he saw.

This vision given to Daniel is another example of God's very creative methods to produce special effects in our minds and emotions with the purpose of teaching us His prophetic truths (they certainly help us to remember them also.) The giving of dreams and visions as *infallible* inspiration has ended with God's Word. All dreams and visions given to God's people must conform to God's written Word and are not on the same level, or equal to God's inspired revelation—the Bible.

This vision of the beast kingdoms terminating with God's eternal kingdom was given to 67 year old Daniel approximately 50 years after he had been taken captive to Babylon.

Numbers 12:6 (NIV) "When a prophet of the Lord is among you, I reveal myself to him in visions, I speak to him in dreams."

Parallel Visions

Daniel 2 portrays the kingdoms of the world with the dream statue in a rather majestic manner. The pompous statue seems to describe the grandeur of earthly empires from man's viewpoint. However, as we look at its parallel in Daniel 7, the repetition of the prophecy is from a whole different point of view—God's! This is an intentional representation of the ruthless rule of world rulers who are seen as beasts. The emphasis of this parallel vision is not on pomp nor military greatness, instead it portrays the insatiable greed of rulers to rise to the pinnacle of power at the expense of down-trodden people.

God gave man the command to *"fill the earth."* (Genesis 9:1) As mankind gradually spread throughout the world in God's providence, nations were formed; however, nations consuming other nations to form empires is not God's divine will for mankind. *"From one man he made every nation of men that they should inhabit the whole earth; and he determined the times set for them and the exact places where they should live."* (Acts 17:26 NIV) God establishes the boundaries of nations. What peace the world would enjoy, how many lives would be saved if man would only obey God's decrees!

Joyce Baldwin "World-rulers, glimpsed through the thin veil of imagery, all inspire terror, the more so as history progresses, for the worst is reserved for the end." [2]

World empires do not align themselves with God and good, but become pawns of evil to battle against their Creator King and His creatures. Even though the dictionaries define the word *beast* as "any animal except man" we cannot but agree with God that beastly characteristics are revealed in human empires. How can a foolish, sin-darkened heart rule the world in any other way? One-world empires are not of God's design. Keep this in mind as we study these empires and their outcome.

The purpose of Scripture in relating about these ancient empires is to reveal to us that there is one more world empire. God is also communicating the fact that all human governments and empires will be cast down. The only legitimate kingdom will come at the end of this Present Age—the Eternal Kingdom of Jesus Christ.

In this lesson we will study:

The Mystery of the Four Beasts
- The Four Kingdoms of this World
- The End-Time Fourth Beast
- The Kingdom of Our Lord Jesus Christ

THE MYSTERY OF THE FOUR BEASTS

THE FOUR KINGDOMS OF THIS WORLD

Take note that each empire is *like* a beast and that these beasts are wild beasts, incapable of being tamed. They are dangerous to man. The fourth beast was so dreadful that it could not be compared to any existing animal. This fourth beast will be the main focus of this study. **Circle** the simile *like* in each of the Scriptural descriptions of the first three empires.

THE LION EMPIRE

Daniel 7:4 (NIV)

> *"The first beast was like a lion, and it had the wings of an eagle. I watched until its wings were torn off and it was lifted from the ground so that it stood on two feet like a man and the heart of a man was given to it."*

The beast that represents Nebuchadnezzar, king of the Babylonian Empire, is a lion with eagle's wings, powerful pinions swift in flight. These symbols of strength, ferocity, and swiftness describe Nebuchadnezzar's conquering powers.

Daniel introduced Nebuchadnezzar to the true King of the nations when he interpreted Nebuchadnezzar's dream statue. It became very clear to Nebuchadnezzar that the God of Israel would ultimately destroy all arrogant, ruthless, human kingdoms and establish His perfect Kingdom by which all men would be blessed forever. Furthermore, Daniel 3 and 4 describe how God took great measures to reveal Himself to this pagan king.

Luke 18:14 (Phillips)
"For everyone who sets himself up as somebody will become a nobody, and the man who makes himself a nobody will become somebody."

Nevertheless, arrogance dominated Nebuchadnezzar's heart. Because of this, God removed him from his position of greatness for seven years declaring: *"Let his heart be changed from that of a man, let him be given the heart of a beast."* (Daniel 4:16 NKJV) The *heart* is an idiom referring to a man's soul which is the seat of his intellect, will, and emotions—so very different from a beast. The king's powerful wings, so to speak, were torn off. What would happen to an eagle if it suddenly lost its wings? Yes, it would have a very great fall to earth.

God's designated seven-year judgment finally came to an end. Unexpectedly, out in a field with his mouth full of grass, filthy, shaggy Nebuchadnezzar on his hands and knees "*looked up to heaven*." God returned to him his human heart; his sanity was restored. Nebuchadnezzar learned *"that the Most High rules over the kingdoms of the world and gives them to anyone he chooses."* (Daniel 4:32) Please read in Daniel 4:34-37, humbled Nebuchadnezzar's praises to God; they are magnificent.

The last page of this lesson is a comparative chart paralleling the World Powers of Daniel 2, the Statue and Daniel 7, the Four Beasts. Go to this chart and **write** in the center column between 1) Head and Lion**: Nebuchadnezzar – Babylonian Empire (606 – 539)**.

THE BEAR EMPIRE

Daniel 7:5

> *"Then I saw a second beast, and it looked like a bear. It was rearing up on one side, and it had three ribs in its mouth between its teeth. And I heard a voice saying to it, "Get up! Devour the flesh of many people."*

This bear "*rising up on one side*" represents the Medo-Persian Empire with Persian superiority. The three ribs, carried like trophies in its mouth, probably represent the three major kingdoms it conquered: Lydia (modern Turkey), Egypt, and Babylon (Iraq.)

Go to the chart of World Powers at the end of the lesson and **write** in the center column between 2) Chest-Arms and Bear: **Medo-Persian Empire (539 – 331)**.

THE LEOPARD EMPIRE

Daniel 7:6

> *"Then the third of these strange beasts appeared, and it looked like a leopard. It had four bird's wings on it back, and it had four heads. Great authority was given to this beast."*

The leopard represents Alexander the Great, and the Grecian Empire. If the two eagle's wings provided Nebuchadnezzar with great conquering speed imagine the doubled speed with four wings. Alexander the Great has been recognized as the most effective conqueror of all time given that his conquest from Greece to India was accomplished in only thirteen years. E.Michael and Sharon Rusten illustrate this fact.

> "Alexander's ambitions led him east. His greatest career accomplishment was when he defeated the Persians and as his prize controlled the splendid capitals of its empire. He reached India on his faithful old horse, Bucephalus in 327 B.C. At that point his weary soldiers refused to go any farther, and so Alexander turned back to the west." [3]

Thirteen years for a war horse is a very long time, but acquiring through conquest such a massive land area of the world, hardly a long time.

Kings and kingdoms are many times represented in the prophetic Scriptures by *horns* and *heads,* i.e. the Head of State. The *four heads* mentioned in this vision undoubtedly refer to the four Grecian generals who divided Alexander's kingdom after his death.

Go to the chart of World Powers at the end of the lesson and **write** in the center column between 3) Belly-Thighs and Leopard: **Grecian Empire (331 – 146)**.

THE TERRIFYING BEAST EMPIRE

Daniel 7:7

> *"Then in my vision that night, I saw a fourth beast—terrifying, dreadful, and very strong. It devoured and crushed its victims with huge iron teeth and trampled their remains beneath its feet. It was different from any of the other beasts, and it had ten horns."*

Daniel felt a curiosity about this beast inspired by terror and dread much like reading a horror story in an empty house at midnight during a terrific electrical storm. *"I, Daniel, was troubled by all I had seen, and my visions terrified me."* (verse 15) The bizarreness of the fourth beast prodded Daniel into asking someone in his vision about it. *"Then I wanted to know the true meaning* [exact meaning] *of the fourth beast, the one so different from the others and so terrifying."* (verse 19) You and I feel the same way, what is the exact meaning of this beast?

The presentation of the fourth beast is different also in the sense that it quickly moves to the end-time Roman Empire. Therefore, before we go any further, please go to the chart of World

Powers at the end of the lesson and **write** in the center column between 4) Legs – Terrifying Beast: **Roman Empire (146 B.C. – A.D. 476)**.

Because there is an immediate reference to the "*ten horns*," we can identify this beast with the end-time part of the statue—the feet and ten toes. For this reason, the commentary in the following study views the fourth beast as the system of the end times. This is not ancient history!

YOUR OBSERVATIONS—DANIEL 7

One of the purposes of Part Two is to engage your mind in the understanding and interpreting of end-time prophecy. The following is a narration of the vision of the fourth beast as Daniel saw it in the left- hand column and their corresponding interpretation in the right-hand column. Read them carefully with pencil in hand to underline, check, circle, draw connecting arrows, comment, compare to dream statue of Daniel 2, anything that will help you to understand this very important information about this end-time empire. Draw your own conclusions from your discoveries. Also, try to identify the symbols, who does what to whom. Pray for God's Spirit to enlighten you to understand Daniel 7:7-26.

NARRATION OF THE VISION	INTERPRETATION OF THE VISION
[7] . . .I saw a fourth beast—terrifying, dreadful, and very strong.	[23] . . .This fourth beast is the fourth world power that will rule the earth.
It devoured and crushed its victims with huge iron teeth and trampled their remains beneath his feet.	It will devour the whole world, trampling and crushing everything in its path.
It was different from any of the other beasts,	It will be different from all the others.
and it had ten horns.	[24] out of this kingdom ten kings will arise; (NASB)
[8] As I was looking at the horns, suddenly another small horn appeared among them.	Then another king will arise, different from the other ten,
Three of the first horns were torn out by the roots to make room for it.	who will subdue three of them.
This little horn had eyes like human eyes and a mouth that was boasting arrogantly.	[25] He will speak out [pompous words] against the Most High

[15] I, Daniel, was troubled by all I had seen, and my vision terrified me. [16] So I approached one of those standing beside the throne [of God] and asked him what it all meant. . .	[16] He explained it to me like this: [17] These four huge beasts represent four kingdoms that will arise from the earth. [18] But in the end, the holy people of the Most High will be given the kingdom, and they will rule forever and ever.
[21] As I watched, this horn was waging war against God's holy people and was defeating them.	[25] and oppress the holy people of the Most High. He will try to change their sacred festivals and laws, and they will be placed under his control for a time, times, and half a time.
[9] I watched as thrones were put in place and the Ancient One sat down to judge.	[26] But then the court will pass judgment, and all his power will be taken away and completely destroyed.
[10] . . .then the court began it session, and the books were opened.	

As a Bible teacher, I fairly ache to sit down with you in one big group to discuss what you have discovered. Usually one person will say, "I saw this!" and another will exclaim, "I saw that!". . .and we all learn what the Spirit has to say to God's people.

It is important for your peace of mind to understand that the visions of the Dream Statue and the Four Beasts confirm that all the kingdoms of the world will ultimately be given to King Jesus and His faithful followers.

Daniel 7:13-14, 27

> [13] *"As my vision continued that night, I saw someone like a son of man* [King Jesus] *coming with the clouds of heaven. He approached the Ancient One* [God the Father] *and was led into his presence.* [14] *He was given authority, honor, and sovereignty over all the nations of the world, so that people of every race and nation and language would obey him. His rule is eternal—it will never end. His kingdom will never be destroyed.*
>
> [27] *Then the sovereignty, power, and greatness of all the kingdoms under heaven will be given to the holy people of the Most High. His kingdom will last forever, and all rulers will serve and obey him."*

TIMELINE

Let's pause here to put things we learned from Part One into sequence. According to the interpretation presented, the following will be contemporaneous with this fourth empire:

- The feet-toe, ten-horned beast empire will emerge before the Rapture.
- This empire will rule the world through the Trumpet/Bowl Judgments at the time of the Wrath of God, the last 3 ½ years.
- Israel's greatest persecution will occur in the last 3 ½ years during this fourth empire.
- The powerful ministry of the two Jewish witnesses will take place in the last 3 ½ years of this empire.

The fourth empire ends with:

- the Second Coming of King Jesus and the battle of Armageddon
- the lake of fire which is the second death
- the establishment of Christ's Thousand Year Kingdom on earth

Look at **Timeline Two** (at the end of Part One) to help you form a visual idea of all that will take place during this end-time fourth kingdom.

THE END-TIME FOURTH BEAST

We will now engage ourselves with the clues relating to the "Mystery of The World System of the Antichrist."

THE DOMAIN OF THE FOURTH BEAST

Daniel 7:7, 23

> [7] *"Then in my vision that night, I saw a fourth beast—terrifying, dreadful, and very strong. It devoured and crushed its victims with huge iron teeth and trampled their remains beneath its feet. It was different from any of the other beasts, and it had ten horns."*
>
> [23] *"Then he said to me, "This fourth beast is the fourth world power that will rule the earth."*

Read verse 23 and **write** the two obvious facts.

1. ____
2. ____

Verse 23 states that the fourth beast is the fourth world power. In this case, the fourth beast symbolizes a world power, a world government, not the ruler. It clearly states that the earth is ruled by this kingdom.

When we think in terms of the geographical area controlled by the first three ancient kingdoms and the ancient Roman Empire there is a vast difference in the territorial size ruled by the

end-time fourth beast. What is the difference? ____
________________. **Underline** that part in verse 23.

The ancient world powers ruled portions of the known world; the fourth end-time kingdom is a system which rules the entire earth, not just part of it.

Keep in mind that the ancient Roman Empire received its name from the city of Rome, the starting point of its expansion. It was not referred to as the Italian Empire. Rome, the city-state, became the ruling power of the entire peninsula of Italy in 264 B.C. after a two and a half century conquest. The other three beast kingdoms began their conquest as nation states; to the contrary, ancient Rome began its conquest having the status of a city-state, one small city, geographically speaking.

THE "IRON" FEATURE OF THE FOURTH EMPIRE

With which of the kingdoms represented in the statue do the "*huge iron teeth*" of the Beast correspond? __________________ Because the beast vision is parallel to the statue of Daniel 2, it is safe to say that the iron teeth of the Beast refers to the ____________________ Kingdom of the end-time world power.

Did you observe the viciousness of this end-time empire expressed in verse 7? What are the three verbs used by Daniel to express the beast's actions with his iron teeth and his feet: ____________________ and _________________________ and ___________________
___________________________.

These are expressions of power without compassion. If it will devour the whole world, does that include your country? How will this affect your life? Now that's something to think about.

THE FOURTH BEAST IS "DIFFERENT"

"It was different from any of the other beasts. . ." (7:7) *"the one so different from the others. . ."* (7:19) *"which will be different from all the other kingdoms. . ."* (7:23 NASB) *"Then another king will arise, different from the other ten. . ."* (7:24)

Perhaps the word "*different*" stood out to you in your comparative study of the Narration and Interpretation of the vision because it is used so many times. This repetition indicates that God is emphasizing something important here.

Let me point out a very significant difference between the ancient Roman Empire and its three antecedents.

The three ruling empires prior to the Roman Empire did not solidify or assimilate the conquered peoples into a uniform culture and nation. The motivation of the first three empires was to extract the riches from the conquered lands. I am mentioning this because I want you to notice a pervasive mindset to which Rome aspired and has never lost.

> "Rome fused them into a heterogeneous mass of humanity with one emperor, one government, one military organization, a common body of laws and practices, a common language, common coinage, a central mail and transportation system, a common alphabet, and one culture.
>
> They were possessed by a firm belief that they were called upon to govern the world." [4]

Will the end-time beast express this same mentality? Interesting.

However, the use of the word *different* to describe the Beast seems to imply an even greater, fundamental difference. It is exceedingly different from the others. It is unlike and stands out or stands alone among the others. Its king will be different from the other kings.

This has great significance because we are to look for a Roman Kingdom which is entirely *different* from the norm. "In what way?" you ask. Keep studying.

THE "CLAY" FEATURE OF THE FOURTH EMPIRE

Daniel 7:24 (NASB)

> *"As for the ten horns, out of this kingdom ten kings will arise; and another will arise after them, and he will be different from the previous ones and will subdue three kings."*

The fourth beast has *"ten horns."* What do these "ten horns" represent? (verse 24) ____ ______________________________ What did the *"ten toes"* of the statue represent? __________________________

The horns of an animal are used to attack or defend itself. The Scriptures use horns as emblems of power and strength, and may refer to either kingdoms or individual kings. In this case, they symbolize powerful kings, or leaders.

According to verse 24, from where do these ten kings arise? ______________________ ___________.

They arise out of a system already established as a kingdom. Apparently this kingdom is composed of ten kingdoms, or regions, out of which will come their representatives, the ten kings. The fact that the world will be ruled simultaneously by ten kings in and of itself presents a very different kingdom.

ONE-WORLD GOVERNMENT OF TEN KINGS

To establish a one-world government would be an enormous undertaking. It would require leadership, cooperation, strategic planning, and secrecy among the world's leaders. The information prophetically given in the book of Daniel emphasizes Rome's involvement front and center.

Psalm 75:4-5, 10 (NASB)
"I said to the boastful, 'Do not lift up the horn; do not lift up your horn on high, do not speak with insolent pride.' And all the horns of the wicked He will cut off, but the horns of the righteous will be lifted up."

Ten Regions have been identified in our world today. There will come a point in time in the development of these Regions when Ten "Kings" will be elected—*"out of this kingdom ten kings will arise."* Do you believe this statement in God's Word to be true and factual?

Go to the chart of World Powers at the end of the lesson and **write** in the center column between Feet-Ten Toes in the left column and Ten Kings verse 24 in the right column: **The World System of the Antichrist: Confederation of Ten Kings.**

THE "LITTLE-HORN KING"

Daniel 7:8, 24

> [8] *"As I was looking at the horns, suddenly another small horn appeared* [came up] *among them. . .* [24] *Then another king will arise, different from the other ten."*

A new twist in our mystery drama

Notice the word "*suddenly*" meaning "abruptly, unexpectedly, without a warning." *"Another king"* will make a sudden appearance where? (verse 8) ________________________________ _________. This reveals a developing sequence in the formation of the final world order.

This king is *different* from ____. In what way?

Who is this king? If the only two components of the World System of the Antichrist are Rome and the Ten Kings, obviously, this new king represents the *iron*, Rome.

What is the biblical name of the world ruler of the end times? __________________________ _________ Yes, we can see that this king is equivalent to the Antichrist of the last days.

Verse 8 states that this king "*came up among them*" referring to the ten kings. The word *among* conveys the meaning that the *little horn* is an essential part of the group of ten, but not a leader of a region. Why is his appearance referred to as *suddenly*? In your review of Lesson 3, you will remember that the Antichrist is killed, and his soul and spirit go to the abode of sinners, the abyss. However, God permits the Antichrist to come back from the dead to rule the world. He was alive; he was dead; and now he is suddenly alive! Furthermore, this king represents a kingdom, the Roman Empire. The plot thickens.

Daniel 7:8, 24

> [8] *"Three of the first horns were <u>torn out by the roots</u> to make room for it.* [24]*. . .who will <u>subdue</u> three of them."*

Even with his more-than-remarkable coming back from the dead, the Antichrist is not without opposition. Apparently three of his associates forcefully object to his becoming the supreme leader of the world. What follows next? Verse 8 expresses how Daniel saw the action in the vision and verse 24 is the explanation given to Daniel by an interpretive angel. Let's look at the Hebrew meaning of the words.

"Torn out by the roots" is expressed by the Hebrew word aqar meaning "to pluck up, to hamstring, and figuratively to exterminate." [S] *To hamstring* can mean "to destroy or hinder the efficiency of (someone or something.)" [D]

"Subdue" is the Hebrew word shphal meaning "to abase, to lower, to make low, to humiliate, bring (cast, put) down." [S] "Its most important use is in the figurative sense of "abasement," "humbling," "humility." [5] *To abase* "refers principally to loss of rank or prestige." [D]

Armed with these definitions we can come to the evident conclusion that by his over-powering presence and authority, the Antichrist forcefully removes the three opposing regional kings from their position of power and replaces them. Does this action reveal that the *little horn king* is the Supreme Ruler?

We know that the three vacant positions were filled because at the time of Armageddon, ten kings will agree to give the Antichrist their loyalty, and together they will go to war against King Jesus at His Second Coming. (Revelation 17:13-14)

The World System of the Antichrist will be, biblically speaking, complete at this point in our drama. It is now a world federation—a union of states that recognize the sovereignty of a central authority while retaining certain lesser powers of government.

Go to the chart of World Powers at the end of the lesson and **write** in the center column next to Another King verse 24: **The Antichrist**

THE "LITTLE HORN-ANOTHER KING" STOMPS HIS FEET

Daniel 7:8

"This little horn had eyes like human eyes and a mouth that was boasting arrogantly."

As Daniel watches, the Antichrist rises to full power. Daniel seems to be looking straight into the horn's face. The Antichrist is not a supernatural being, but he is not a normal person either. Daniel tells us that his eyes are *like*, compared to, human eyes. Does *like* indicate that to Daniel something seems a bit inhuman about the person? It is said that the eyes reflect the soul, what does Daniel see in these eyes? **Write** down what you think he saw. Remember from where the little horn just arrived—the abyss, the abode of the dead and demons. ____________________

What are some things the Antichrist *"boasts arrogantly"* about? The fact that he comes back from the dead would more than likely fill the little horn with a sense of super-natural power and immortality. He will have an extreme sense of self-importance. He will blaspheme God (verse 25) and go so far as to claim that he himself is God and will demand that all people worship him as such. (2 Thessalonians 2:4)

If we were able to slip back in time to stand beside Daniel, with the little horn's arrogant boasts ringing in our ears, we would be able to look into his evil eyes and see his dark soul. They would undoubtedly be filled with arrogance, vainglory, pride, self-exaltation, contempt for all but himself—madness.

Daniel 7:21, 25

> [21] *". . .this horn was waging war against God's holy people and was defeating them.* [25] *He will. . .oppress the holy people of the Most High. He will try to change their sacred festivals and laws, and they will be placed under his control for a time, times, and half a time* [3 ½ years]*."*

Write three distinct facts from these verses.

1. ____
2. ____
3. ____

Daniel would recognize the words "*sacred festivals*" and "*laws*" to identify the "*holy people of the Most High"* as Jews. The time given refers to the last 3 ½ years.

What emotion Daniel must have experienced as he watched the "little horn" persecute his people and vilify his God!

These valiant Christian Jews are the *only* followers of Jesus on earth during this period of persecution. Do you sense their isolation? Time and time again, the Antichrist orders their death, but God miraculously defends one-third of these courageous Jews. *"Oppress"* in verse 25 literally means "to wear out." Have you ever experienced a protracted trial that causes your spirit to despair, tempts you to give up, and literally wears you out? This will be the situation of the Christian Jews. Their oppression consists of threats, near death experiences, daily struggle to meet physical needs, abuse and ridicule, even their God is blasphemed. What a terrific burden they bear for Christ.

Now watch what happens. Daniel says, *"I kept looking, and that horn was waging war with the saints and overpowering them until. . ."*

THE KINGDOM OF OUR LORD JESUS CHRIST

Destruction of the Beast

Daniel 7:22 (NASB)

[22] *"until the Ancient of Days came, and judgment was passed in favor of the saints of the Highest One, and the time arrived when the saints took possession of the kingdom."*

Daniel 7:26, 11 (NASB)

[26] *"But the court will sit for judgment, and his* [the Antichrist's] *dominion will be taken away, annihilated and destroyed forever.* [11] *Then I kept looking until the beast was slain, and its body was destroyed and given to the burning fire.*

King Jesus' Thousand-Year Kingdom

Daniel 7:14 (NASB)

> *"And to Him* [King Jesus] *was given dominion, glory and a kingdom, that all peoples, nations, and men of every language might serve Him. His dominion is an everlasting dominion which will not pass away; and His kingdom is one which will not be destroyed."*

Go to the chart of World Powers at the end of the lesson and **write** in the center column between Rock in the left column and Son Of Man Given Dominion in the right column: **King Jesus' Thousand-Year Kingdom.**

OUR COLLECTION OF CLUES

Thus far, we have collected some important clues toward solving "The Mystery of the System of the Antichrist." A picture is developing of the Fourth Beast, both the System and the Person. What we have learned from Daniel 2 and 7:

- There are only two components of the end-time System of the Antichrist—Rome and Ten Kings.
- This empire is different from all other empires.
- The *"terrifying"* beast represents a collective unit, composed of a group of ten interacting, interrelated kings.
- A new element is introduced in Daniel 7, the *"little horn,"* a king different from the Ten Kings and corresponds to the Rome (iron) part of the statue. He is portrayed as dominant and strong, with the power and authority to overthrow and replace three of the Ten Kings of the Ten Region Empire.
- Rome was a city-state which made it different from the other empires.
- The final world government will be a One-World Government; the representative *king* of Rome having preeminence over a Ten-King Federation.
- The *little horn* king is most certainly the Antichrist, the Beast, of the New Testament.
- The fourth and last kingdom will rule with ruthless force.
- King Jesus will return during the reign of this kingdom to destroy it and all human-led kingdoms in order to establish His Thousand-Year Kingdom on earth.

At this point in time, we must acknowledge that our world is divided into ten regions. Look at the map of The Ten Regions of the World at the end of Lesson 3. Check them out on the internet.

EL OLAM—THE GOD OF ETERNITY

Psalm 90:2

DANIEL 2 PROPHECY			DANIEL 7 PROPHECY	
DREAM 2:31-35	**INTERPRETATION 2:36-45**	**WORLD POWERS**	**INTERPRETATION 7:15-28**	**DREAM 7:1-14**
1) HEAD *Gold*	Nebuchadnezzar vs. 37-38		First Kingdom v. 17	LION v. 4
2) CHEST–ARMS *Silver*	After you, another kingdom will rise v. 39		Second Kingdom v. 17	BEAR v. 5
3) BELLY–THIGHS *Bronze*	Next, a third kingdom v. 39		Third Kingdom v. 17	LEOPARD v. 6
4) LEGS *Iron*	Finally, there will be a fourth kingdom v. 40		Fourth Kingdom v. 17	TERRIFYING BEAST v. 7
FEET-TEN TOES *Iron*–Baked Clay			Ten Kings v. 24 Another King v. 24	TEN HORNS v. 7 LITTLE HORN v. 8
ROCK	Indestructible Kingdom vs. 44-45		Everlasting Kingdom v. 27	SON OF MAN GIVEN DOMINION v 14

LESSON **22**

EL SHADDAI—GOD THE ALL-BOUNTIFUL ONE
Genesis 17:1

In El Shaddai, all fullness dwells, and out of His heart of love His own receive all things.

THE MYSTERY OF THE WORLD SYSTEM OF THE ANTICHRIST

THE MYSTERY OF THE BEAST

The purpose of this lesson is to know where to look for the Antichrist, to look in the right direction for his appearance. Jesus knows on the eve of His appearing at the Rapture people will speculate on His arrival. He knows this desire to foresee end-time things would also apply to the identity of the Antichrist, and as the end time draws nearer this desire would become even more prevalent. Jesus does not condemn this eagerness, but these topics should be approached with spiritual wisdom and understanding. In the case of Christ, God wants the Believer to always be watchful for Jesus' coming. In the case of the Antichrist, God does not want His children to be deceived by his appearance and the performance of false satanic miracles. Satan is the master of deception.

Therefore, with regard to the Antichrist, Jesus has given us an important warning providing us with discernment which will serve as a stabilizing influence to recognize this *false Christ*.

Matthew 24:23-24 (NASB)

> *"Then if anyone says to you, 'Behold, here is the Christ,' or 'There He is,' <u>do not believe him</u>. For <u>false Christs</u> and <u>false prophets</u> will arise and will show great signs and wonders, so as to mislead, if possible, even the elect."*

"Do not believe him." Please keep these verses in mind as you study this lesson.

On Your Toes! Important Clues!

We learned in the preceding lessons that there are only two components that make up the World System of the Antichrist—Rome and Ten Kings. This Lesson has many new clues, don't miss them! Read Revelation 13 in your own Bible before we begin our analysis.

At the end of this lesson you will find two comparative charts that you will complete during the course of this study. These charts will help you to proceed in the right direction.

Chart One: Comparative Chart of the Beast
Chart Two: The System of the Antichrist - Parallels From Daniel and Revelation

In this lesson we will study:

- A New Feature of the World System of the Antichrist
- The Beast before the Rapture
  - The Beast Rises to Power
  - The False Prophet

A NEW FEATURE OF THE WORLD SYSTEM OF THE ANTICHRIST

I am leaning heavily on your observational skills. Remember, we are looking for faithful-to-the-Scriptures consistency in our interpretation. Let the Word speak, and it will lead you to truth.

Approximately 700 years after Daniel's vision concerning world empires, the apostle John is given a parallel vision with new details. **Read** the following verses. Look for new information vital to our understanding of the World System of the Antichrist. **Underline** new key words that do not appear in the description of the Beast/Antichrist in Daniel chapters 2 and 7. **Circle** the simile *like.*

Daniel 7:2-7
2 "I, Daniel, saw
a great storm
churning the
surface of a great
sea...3 Then
four huge beasts
came up out of
the water...4 The
first beast was
like a lion...5
Then I saw a
second beast,
and it looked
like a bear...6
Then the third
of these strange
beasts appeared,
and it looked
like a leopard...7
I saw a fourth
beast—terrifying,
dreadful, and
very strong."

Revelation 13:1-2

> 1 *"Then I saw a beast rising up out of the sea. It had seven heads and ten horns, with ten crowns on its horns. And written on each head were names that blasphemed God.*
> 2 *This beast looked like a leopard, but it had the feet of a bear and the mouth of a lion! And the dragon gave the beast his own power and throne and great authority.*

Your Observations

1. ______________________________
2. ______________________________
3. ______________________________
4. ______________________________

Questions

1. What is the phrase in verse 1 and the words in the first sentence of verse 2 that gives us to understand that we are looking at a parallel of the vision of the beasts of Daniel 7?

verse 1______________________________

verse 2 ____________________, ____________________, ____________________.

2. Who gives power, his throne, and great authority to the beast?____________________

Who do you think this represents? ____________________

Observations

Verse 1. . . Then I saw a beast rising up out of the sea. This is the fourth beast formerly seen in a vision in Daniel 7. Let's look at the Greek meaning of *beast. Therion* means a "wild beast" and is a word that "brings out the predominance of the lower animal life." [KW] Keep in mind that this comparison to wild beasts, regarding their nature and actions, is God's assessment of this world power.

If Daniel was shocked by the appearance of the four beasts, what emotions would John have experienced in seeing this ten-horned, seven-headed, leopard-bear-lion monster coming up out of the sea? The three beastly empires of Daniel 7, represented by their animal symbols and characteristics, are applied to the Beast of Revelation 13. This clearly indicates that this Beast is a composite of all the beasts. Undoubtedly, this Beast will have the features of all human tyrannical empires. That is saying a lot!

Verse 1. . . It had seven heads and ten horns. I'm sure that you noticed in your observation this new clue—seven heads. Remember, kings and kingdoms are biblically symbolized by *horns* and *heads*. Horns are also used as emblems of great strength and power. Therefore, we can say that the ten *horns* signify ten __________________ and the seven *heads* signify seven __________________.

As was mentioned, according to the book of Daniel, there are only two components that make up the end-time kingdom—Rome and Ten Kings. We have learned that the Ten Kings (horns) represent ten kingdoms, or regions, of the world. Therefore, to which component do the "*seven heads*" (seven kings) belong? __________________________ Obviously, to Rome—Seven Roman Kings.

Go to CHART TWO. . .SYSTEM OF THE ANTICHRIST: PARALLELS FROM DANIEL AND REVELATION at the end of this lesson and fill in the blanks under **5) Revelation 13:1: the Beast**.

Verse 1. . . with ten crowns on its horns. And written on each head were names that blasphemed God. The crowns are diadems which are "always the symbol of kingly or imperial dignity." [V]

What wears the ten crowns or diadems in verse 1? ______________________ This conclusively identifies the ten horns as having the status of kings; they wear a king's crown.

What do the "*heads*" have on their heads? ____.
Yes, these Seven Roman Kings adorn their heads with blasphemous names.

Blasphemy "The act of claiming for oneself the attributes and rights of God." [D]

Blasphemy

Blasphemy is mentioned four times in chapter 13: one time in verses 1 and 5, and twice in verse 6.

Exodus 20:7 "Do not misuse the name of the Lord your God. The Lord will not let you go unpunished if you misuse His name."

Blasphemy is a very serious, anti-God offence. A spoken vilification, or irreverence concerning God, or that which belongs to Him, carried the penalty of death by stoning in the law of Moses. (Leviticus 24:13-16) A human claiming to be God is the worst form of blasphemy. When Jesus claimed His deity, the people sought to kill Him for the sin of blasphemy, claiming to be God. The following are two examples.

John 10:31-33 (NASB)

> *"The Jews took up stones again to stone Him. Jesus answered them, 'I showed you many good works from the Father; for which of them are you stoning Me?' The Jews answered Him, 'For a good work we do not stone You, but for blasphemy and because You, being a man, make Yourself out to be God.'"*

At Jesus' trial before His crucifixion He was accused of the serious sin of blasphemy.

Mark 14:61-64

> [61] *"Then the high priest asked him, 'Are you the Messiah, the Son of the Blessed One?'*
>
> [62] *Jesus said, 'I AM* [the 'I AM is here; or I am the LORD.] *And you will see the son of Man seated in the place of power at God's right hand and coming on the clouds of heaven.'*
>
> [63] *Then the high priest tore his clothing to show his horror and said, 'Why do we need other witnesses?* [64] *You have all heard his blasphemy. What is your verdict?' 'Guilty!' they all cried. 'He deserves to die!'"*

However, they were mistaken. Jesus *was* God, always was and always will be.

The Seven Roman Kings wear on their heads names that blaspheme God. A blasphemous name indicates a name or title representing deity. Jesus warns us in Matthew 24:5 (NKJV) that *"Many will come in my name, claiming, 'I am the Christ,' and will deceive many.*" These false Christs have for centuries come in Jesus' name claiming to represent Him on earth. Do you think that the *"blasphemous names"* these Seven Roman Kings wear on their heads is their claim to reperesent Jesus on earth? Interesting.

Verse 2. . . And the dragon gave the beast his own power and throne and great authority. No doubt in your examination of the above Scripture you underlined *dragon* as new and vital information in our quest to understand the World System of the Antichrist. If you answered *Satan* to the question: "Who do you think this represents?" You are absolutely correct.

Let's look at this new aspect to discover Satan's part in the World System of the Antichrist.

Read the following verses from Revelation 12. **Underline** the names of the dragon, notice his description, and most importantly, **circle** the words that identify him with the Beast of Revelation 13.

Revelation 12:3, 9 (RSV)

> [3] *". . . behold, a great red dragon, with seven heads and ten horns, and seven diadems upon his heads. . .* [9] *And the great dragon. . .that ancient serpent, who is called the Devil and Satan, the deceiver of the whole world. . ."*

First of all, if you were observant, you noticed that, in this case, the diadems are worn by the seven _______________ emphasizing their status as _________________. Thus confirming that the heads symbolize Seven Roman *Kings*.

The Beast always retains its two components:
- Seven Roman Heads ("*iron*" in Daniel 2 and the "*little horn-king*" of the fourth beast in Daniel 7)
- The Ten Horns represent Ten Kings ("*clay,*" ten toes in Daniel 2 and ten "*horns*" in Daniel 7)

Revelation 13 enlightens us as to the real force behind the World System of the Antichrist—the dragon, Satan himself. The shadow lurking in the background of Daniel's visions steps boldly onto center stage, no longer concealed. He was there all along.

The World System of the Antichrist will dominate the world with Satan's great *power*. The kings will rule the world from Satan's *throne* of great *authority*. No one can resist this deceitful system of evil.

When the Jewish leaders arrested Jesus in Gethsemane with the intention of killing Him, Jesus said to them, "*This is your hour, and the power* [authority] *of darkness*." (Luke 22:53 NKJV) These identical words are said in Revelation 17:12 (NKJV): *"The ten horns you saw are ten kings who have received no kingdom as yet, but they receive authority for one hour as kings with the beast."* The authority has been granted; the hour of darkness is upon us.

The World System of the Antichrist is complete with all its characters: Satan, Seven Roman Kings, and Ten Kings of Ten Regions. You are probably asking at this point, "Seven Roman *Kings* implies a kingdom." What kingdom do they reign over? We will discover the answer to that question in our study of Revelation 17.

Go to CHART TWO. . .SYSTEM OF THE ANTICHRIST—PARALLELS FROM DANIEL AND REVELATION at the end of this lesson and fill in the blanks on the right side under **4) Revelation 12:3: the red Dragon**.

THE BEAST BEFORE THE RAPTURE

The focus changes in 13:3. The emphasis turns from the *System-beast* as a conglomerate whole to the *Person-beast*, the *wounded head* referred to as "*the beast*." This will be obvious as we continue our study.

Chapter 13 is not written in chronological order. It is divided according to the three characters:
- that which deals with the Beast—the World System of the Antichrist (13:1-2)
- the person of the Antichrist (13:3-10)
- the works of the False Prophet (13:11-18)

We will study this chapter chronologically and will include related events studied in Part One of this book. This order of events is an interpretation.

THE BEAST RISES TO POWER

Revelation 13:3-4, 14 (NASB)

> [3] *"And I saw one of his heads as if it had been slain, and his fatal wound was healed. And the whole earth was amazed and followed after the beast;* [4] *and they worshipped the dragon, because he gave his authority to the beast; and they worshiped the beast, saying, "Who is like the beast, and who is able to wage war with him?*
> [14] *. . .the beast who had the wound of the sword and has come to life."*

What happens to one of the heads, one of the Roman Kings? Who is this Roman King? Make five observations from these three verses above. I'm sure that you will discover some astonishing things.

Your Observations

1. ______________________________
2. ______________________________
3. ______________________________
4. ______________________________
5. ______________________________

Observations

Revelation 13:3 "fatal wound" literally means – "smitten to death" KW

The apostle John was standing on the seashore of Patmos Island where he was being held prisoner for preaching the Gospel. As he gazed out over the ocean, God gave him a vision. John suddenly saw a strange and fearsome beast rise out of the water. One of the things that captivated his attention was the sight of one of the seven heads of the beast that had a terrible, fatal wound which had healed. It was apparent to John that the head had died but had come back to life and was now a part of this fearsome beast.

> "The wording of the English may be a bit misleading; it does not mean to say that one of the heads looked as though it was mortally wounded but really was not. The words are the same as those used of the Lamb in 5:6 [*"Then I saw a Lamb that looked as if it had been slaughtered"*] who actually had been slain." [1]

This head symbolizes a person, therefore, the wound does not necessarily mean that the actual wound that took his life was to his head. Rather, that one of the Seven Roman Kings was killed. Our question is, which one?

Verse 3. . .And I saw one of his heads as if it had been slain, and his fatal wound was healed. The words *"as if it had been slain"* in the Greek language is an action that has been completed in the past. That is to say that this head (king) had been killed before appearing to John in the vision.

This Roman King is identified in verse 3 as the Beast whom we refer to as the Antichrist. At the moment of death, his soul descends to the abyss and his body is laid to rest. The abyss is depicted as an immeasurable depth known also in the Bible as the bottomless pit.

Go to LESSON 22 CHART ONE. . .COMPARATIVE CHART OF THE BEAST at the end of this lesson. In the center column under **Revelation 13** fill in the blanks relevant to (**1. v.1**. and **v. 3**) and (**2. v.1**.)

Verse 14. . .**the beast who had the wound of the sword and has come to life.** We do not know how long the Antichrist remains in the abyss. But we do know that verse 14 states that he "*has come to life*." Both Revelation 11:7 and 17:8 inform us that the Beast will ascend out of the bottomless pit. God will permit the Beast to live again to fulfill His divine purposes.

"Jerome long ago expressed the true meaning, 'that we may not, according to the notion of some, think it to be a devil, or a demon, but one of those men in whom the whole of Satan is to dwell bodily." [2]

Verse 3-4. . . **And the whole earth was amazed and followed after the beast.** Can you imagine the great impact this will have on the world, even on Believers?

I was teaching this subject to a group of women and at this point a very perceptive young woman began to weep. She later wrote an email to a friend and sent a copy to me. She correctly identified the Antichrist, but I will edit out the part related to his identity because we will study this in another lesson. At that time, you will be able to fill in the blanks. The reason for this is that I want you to study the Scriptures and to discover their meaning for yourself. Just as she did.

The email

> "The Antichrist. . .
> We are finished studying Beth Moore's study of Revelation, and have moved on to 'End-Time Prophecy.' Yesterday, we were listening to a description of characteristics of the antichrist: a tremendous amount of power both politically and religiously, will deceive many (suggesting that the person will be trusted by the masses,) so on and so forth.
>
> People around me were whispering possible names under their breath, 'Maybe it's . . . . Could it be . . . . . .?'
>
> I, myself, have always pictured the antichrist as being some high power businessman. If you are a Wall Street guru, a president, prime minister or king, or the CEO of a world bank, you would probably know this person. But would the 'average Joe' know the guy? I thought, probably not.
>
> The _______________!

> I tried to catch my breath as I felt the world was collapsing around me. A picture formed in my mind. Millions of people falling to their faces to worship a ____________ raised from the dead. *'A miracle!'* The gravity of the image slowly began to take hold, and tears silently slid down my face. I couldn't stop them, my chest burdened with so much weight, trying to breathe.
>
> My previous image of the antichrist as being someone like Carpathia (from the Left Behind series), crumbled away. The image that was easy to deal with: Some powerful business guy takes over the world and does miraculous things. Those of us familiar with the book of Revelation will be expecting him. We will know the signs and be able to identify him for what he is, right?
>
> But what about this: what if the antichrist is someone like ______________________? He fits the characteristics. . .What if the antichrist is already dead? This one would only have to rise and walk out of his tomb in the _____________________. Millions would see it. It would be impossible for naysayers to claim this as a hoax.
>
> This would be the perfect set up for the ultimate deceit. How many people would toss away their Bibles and fall on their faces in utter worship of this person, 'miraculously' raised from the dead? They would glorify him. He will demand to be called God, and they will comply without as much as a backward glance. *Just think about it. . .* "

She is right, millions will abandon their faith in Jesus as Lord. The apostasy of 2 Thessalonians 2:1-3. Christians will be overwhelmed by the resurrection of this important religious person. They will be fooled by the miraculous deception of the Antichrist's great powers. Those who hold true to their faith in Christ will soon suffer great tribulation; some will pay with their lives or be imprisoned.

Verse 4. . .and they worshipped the dragon, because he gave his authority to the beast; and they worshiped the beast, saying, "Who is like the beast, and who is able to wage war with him?
Never before has the world seen a mere man come back to life! In their eyes he is greater than death! He is immortal! And so amid the adulation and worship of the astounded earth people, the Antichrist realizes his great ambition, to be worshipped as God. He will quickly rise to the position of supreme leader seated on a throne over the entire world. And in the dark recesses of the spirit world, Satan absorbs every word of praise as directed to himself. Remember the Restrainer, the Holy Spirit, is withdrawing His ministry of restricting evil in this world. (2 Thessalonians 2:6-8 and Lesson 3)

The Beast, the Antichrist, receives his authority from the demonic realm. Can you imagine a mere human invested with all the evil capabilities of Satan?

"The person without God… is a very scary creature." [3]

For this reason, the Antichrist is called "*the son of perdition*" (2 Thessalonians 2:3 NKJV) which "refers to the state after death wherein exclusion from salvation is a realized fact, wherein man, instead of becoming what he might have been, is lost and ruined." [KW]

To be sure Satan and the Antichrist have a working relationship even before the Antichrist's death and resurrection. This relationship will intensify at the time of the Rapture.

A matter of authority

Some people acknowledge the Bible, but man's authoritative ideologies hold sway over their souls. Do you live in submission to God's authoritative Word, the Bible, or to Man's authoritative ideologies? Keep in mind where the Antichrist's authority comes from—Satan. Do not place yourself under this authority.

The Offer of the Kingdoms of this World and all their Glory

The Beast stands, spiritually speaking, in the same place that our beloved Savior stood so long ago. "*Jesus was led by the Spirit into the wilderness to be tempted there by the devil.*" He was alone, without food or water. Satan came to Jesus with the same offer in the third temptation as he has now extended to the Antichrist.

While the devil was displaying the kingdoms of the world and all their glory to Jesus, he promised, *"I will give it all to you if you will kneel down and worship me."* Jesus sternly commanded Satan to "*get out of here*" and declared that He would only worship and serve the Lord as it is stated in the Scriptures. Satan skedaddled as fast as he could! (Matthew 4:8-11)

Satan "Satan, who is the god of this world, has blinded the minds of those who don't believe." (2 Corinthians 4:4)

Not so with the Antichrist. For centuries the "*heads*" have desired to rule the world. This *head*, so to speak, considers himself to be the "chosen one" and so he becomes both a fool and the embodiment of Satan. The Antichrist is given Satan's authority with the absolute power that the kingdom of darkness affords. See verses on Satan's delegated authority: 13: 2, 4, 5, 7, and 12.

Arrogant Blasphemer

Revelation 13:5 (NASB)

> "And there was given to him [the Antichrist] a mouth speaking arrogant words and blasphemies."

Scornful, abusive language towards God pours from the evil mouth of this reviler. He has no fear of God whom he *"opposes and exalts himself above all that is called God. . ."* (2 Thessalonians 2:4)

When the Antichrist bursts out of his tomb, he will come forth with maximum potential, master of the world, and altogether dedicated to Satan. His very being is energized with satanic power and authority. Satan's world-wide army of demons is at the Antichrist's disposal to feed him any secret intelligence made available by its invisible presence throughout the planet. The world is at the feet of its supreme monarch, so to speak.

THE FALSE PROPHET

At the resurrection of the Antichrist, the Second Beast (the False Prophet) immediately becomes the Antichrist's right-hand man until his destruction at King Jesus' Second Coming at Armageddon.

The Second Beast – The False Prophet

The "great prophet" [second beast] comes alongside the Antichrist and holds the world spellbound by his spectacular, miraculous signs. The False Prophet compels all earth people to worship both Satan and the Antichrist. Not only that, the False Prophet comes up with the hideous idea that all earth people *"be given a mark on their right hand or on the forehead. And no one could buy or sell anything without that mark, which was either the name of the beast or the number representing his name."* (13:16-17) But we will sort this out in the latter part of this lesson.

The Second Beast's description and his name

Revelation 13:11 (NASB)

"And I saw another beast coming up out of the earth and he had two horns like a lamb, and he spoke as a dragon."

Is this beast good (lamb) or evil (dragon?)

____

Matthew 7:15-16. "Beware of false prophets who come disguised as harmless sheep but are really vicious wolves. You can identify them by their fruit, that is, by the way they act."

Revelation 19:20

"And the beast was captured, and with him the false prophet who did mighty miracles on behalf of the beast—miracles that deceived all who had accepted the mark of the beast and who worshipped his statue. Both the beast and the false prophet were thrown alive into the fiery lake of burning sulfur.

Circle the name of the Second Beast.

Underline the two words that describe his miracles as to kind of miracle and their effect. Where does he end up?

____

____

____

Revelation 5:6

"I looked and I saw a Lamb [Jesus]...He had <u>seven</u> horns..."

<u>Seven</u> symbolically indicates that King Jesus has <u>all</u> authority, <u>all</u> power and strength... Omnipotence!

A False Prophet

The False Prophet appears to be a religious person well-known to the world when he takes his position alongside the risen Antichrist. The "*two horns*" symbolize great *strength* and *power*. Horns also symbolize kings, for that reason, there is a possibility that the False Prophet is one of the *"seven heads,"* one of the kings representing Rome. We will keep an open mind on this.

The False Prophet is spoken of as a prophet. His public image is likened to a lamb. The apostle John would immediately see this as an attempt to identify the False Prophet as a representative of Jesus, the Lamb of God. "*Lamb*" is used 29 times in the book of Revelation; as a name for Jesus it appears 28 times, and the one other reference designates the False Prophet here in verse 11. Earth people see this man as a spokesman for God, but the word *false* plainly indicates that this man is an imposter. God sees him as a *"beast."*

Jesus warns us to beware:
Matthew 24:24 (NASB)

> *"...<u>false prophets</u> will arise and will show great signs and wonders, so as to mislead, if possible, even the elect."*

"False prophet" is the name given by God to the second beast and is also mentioned in Revelation 16:13; 19:20; and 20:10. *False* in the Greek language is *pseudo* which means

"untrue, erroneous, deceitful, wicked, false, and liar." [S] Prophet is *prophetes* in the Greek language and means "someone who proclaims the truth with God's authority." [M]

Write your own definition of the False Prophet by combining the Greek meanings. ________

____

Someone who *"speaks with the voice of a dragon* [Satan]*"* clearly is not "someone who proclaims the truth with God's authority." You and I ask each other, "What does the voice of Satan sound like?" It sounds like the dreadful commands spewed out in the following verses:

Revelation 13:12-14 (NASB)

"And he exercises all the authority of the first beast in his presence. And he makes the earth and those who dwell in it to worship the first beast, whose fatal wound was healed.	What three things does the False Prophet *"make"* (require)? 1. ________________________
And he performs great signs, so that he even makes fire come down out of heaven to the earth in the presence of men.	2. ________________________
And he deceives those who dwell on the earth because of the signs which it was given him to perform in the presence of the beast, telling those who dwell on the earth to make an image to the beast who had the wound of the sword and has come to life."	3. ________________________

God's first commandment of the Ten Commandments is: *"You must not have any other god but me."* The second commandment is: *"You must not make for yourself an idol of any kind or an image of anything in the heavens or on the earth or in the sea. You must not bow down to them or worship them."* (Exodus 20:3-4)

Do you hear the voice of Satan loud and clear in the first and third requirements which cause men to violate God's commandments?

The False Prophet makes a show of supernatural power by making fire (possibly lightening) fall from heaven. The people of the world have witnessed the miraculous resurrection of the Antichrist and now the astounding miracles being performed by this supposedly great religious man is overwhelming proof to the earth people that they are who they say they are.

I would like to take a moment to point out the greatest difference between the miracles performed by the Antichrist and the False Prophet, and King Jesus. Be alert to these differences when the Antichrist makes his appearance.

- **King Jesus** performed miracles entirely focused on blessing mankind. These were acts of grace, mercy, and love redemptive in nature to release people from some type of bondage or danger, to provide for some kind of necessity, to benefit and help people in some manner. Jesus' miracles were salvational acts which pointed toward man's full deliverance, salvation, and preservation to be accomplished by the work of the cross. The power of God was the source of all Jesus's miracles, and still is.

- **The Antichrist** (and the False Prophet) will perform miracles for self-aggrandizement and to the benefit solely of himself. The purpose of his miracles will be to bring people under the bondage of his absolute control. It is this intention that makes these miracles a deception. (2 Thessalonians 2:9-10; Revelation 13:14) The delegated power of Satan will be the source of all the "lying wonders" performed by the Antichrist and the False Prophet.

This is an intentional, diabolical replacement of God. The scope of this rebellious sin is staggering in that it involves all the earth. . .except a few. Let's see who they are.

Revelation 13:15 (NASB)

"And there was given to him to give breath to the image of the beast, that the image of the beast might even speak and cause as many as do not worship the image of the beast to be killed."

Who do you think those who will not worship the beast are? What is the intention of the False Prophet toward these people?

____

____

WORSHIP THE IMAGE!

This image is the exact likeness of the Antichrist. The word used here for *image* in the Greek language is *eikon* meaning:

- "A bodily representation, an image as of a man made of gold or silver or whatever (Romans 1:23).
- Image, always assumes a prototype [original] that which it not merely resembles but from which it is drawn.
- Image includes and involves the resemblance of similitude [likeness.]" KW

Enforced Religion: Revelation 13:8, 12, 14, 15 (NIV)

Verse 8 *"All inhabitants of the earth will worship the beast. . ."*

Verse 12 The False Prophet. . . *"made the earth and its inhabitants worship the first beast* [the Antichrist]"

Verse 14 The False Prophet. . . *"ordered them to set up an image in honor of the beast* [the Antichrist]"

Verse 15 The False Prophet. . . *"was given power to give breath to the image of the first beast, so that it could speak and cause all who refused to worship the image to be killed."*

Go to LESSON 22 CHART ONE. . .COMPARATIVE CHART OF THE BEAST at the end of this Lesson. In the center column under **Revelation 13** fill in the blank corresponding to **4. vs. 8, 12, 14**.

The people of the world will unite together in an Antichrist religion which focuses on the worship of a created human being.

This image to be worshipped, that has some kind of life, will actually speak! Another shocking miracle. All eyes are riveted on this image, but what are they really seeing? They are looking at the exact likeness of the Antichrist, the "*abomination of desolation,*" which will be moved to the temple of the Jews in Jerusalem soon after the Rapture. (see Daniel 9:27; Matthew 24:15)

The *abomination of desolation* is God's name for this diabolical statue. To understand the serious significance of this title we will consult a Hebrew Lexicon [KW]

Abomination, *Shiqquwts* (Hebrew)
"The meaning is a disgusting thing, a filthy thing, an abomination, an idol, a detestable thing. The word is used to refer to idols themselves or anything associated with idolatrous practices. (2 Chronicles 15:8; Jeremiah 16:18; Ezekiel 5:11; 7:20) Because idol worshippers are wholly identified with idols, they, too, are detestable (Hosea 9:10). . . The Antichrist would establish a demonic, counterfeit worship in the temple sanctuary (Daniel 9:27; 12:11). *Shiqquwts* is a very strong word which shows how God feels. We need to learn His perspective (Deuteronomio 7:26)."

Deuteronomy 7:26 (NIV)
"Do not bring a detestable thing [image] into your house or you, like it, will be set apart for destruction. Utterly abhor and detest it, for it is set apart for destruction."

Desolation or Desolate, *Shamem* (Hebrew)
"To stun, to grow numb, to devastate, to stupefy; to be astonished, to be appalled; to be desolate, waste, ravaged, solitary, or depopulated; to destroy, to lay waste; to despair, to ruin oneself, to be destitute. It is something so horrible that it can leave a person speechless (Job 21:5)."

How would you like to kneel down before a statue like this? Even worse, to become detestable to God like this image!

You, no doubt, observed that 13:15 informs us that if any person does not worship the image, he will be killed. That is quite an incentive for worship! God explicitly forewarns that idol worshippers will be condemned to eternal punishment. Satan's rule through the Antichrist will be devastating for mankind.

Revelation 21:8
"But cowards, unbelievers, the corrupt, murderers, the immoral, those who practice witchcraft, <u>idol worshippers</u>, and all liars—their fate is in the fiery lake of burning sulfur. This is the second death."

God gives Believers a heads-up in 2 Thessalonians 2:2 not to fall apart or to be traumatized by false reports or shocking, unbiblical interpretations related to Christ's Coming. God does not want us to be thrown off balance and live in a state of anxiety when the time comes that we find ourselves surrounded by followers of Christ who leave the faith at the spectacular appearance of the Antichrist. At that time, lean on God's promise in Philippians 4:6-7 (Phillips).

"Don't worry over anything whatever; tell God every detail of your needs in earnest and thankful prayer, and the peace of God, which transcends human understanding, will keep constant guard over your hearts and minds as they rest in Christ Jesus."

THE MARK OF THE BEAST

Revelation 13:16-18

"He required everyone—small and great, rich and poor, free and slave—to be given a mark on the right hand or on the forehead. And no one could buy or sell anything without that mark, which was either the name of the beast or the number representing his name.

Wisdom is needed here. Let the one with understanding solve the meaning of the number of the beast, for it is the number of a man. His number is 666."

What does the False Prophet require of all inhabitants of the earth? What is the consequence mentioned here? What does it represent?

____
____
____
____
____
____

The implication

To carry out this order from the False Prophet who will control all financial systems, buying and selling, would require a central world bank that would regulate the flow of all commerce. This would also require a world political authority to give global governance to such a structure. According to this Scripture, a new global monetary exchange will be conducted through the unique mark given to each individual.

The mark

The key word in verses 16-18 is *mark* which in the Greek language is *charagma* meaning "engraving, impression, mark, symbol." [KW] The symbolic meaning indicates "ownership and loyalty."

> "Those who worship the beast have his brand of ownership on them, just as the followers of Jesus have the brand of God's possession on them." [4]

The difference between the mark, or name, of the beast and God's name written on His servants is that God's followers are not forced into receiving His name, rather, it is placed upon them because of their own free will to receive Christ as their personal Savior. *"And they will see His* [God's] *face, and his name will be written on their foreheads."* (Revelation 22:4; see also 3:12; 14:1)

A word of wisdom regarding the meaning of "666."

> "It requires special 'insight' to 'calculate the number of the beast, for it is a man's number 666 (Revelation 13:18). This alludes to Daniel 12:10, which refers to the knowledge of the end times that God will grant his people. John calls his readers to exercise extreme caution and divinely guided wisdom in interpreting this number." [M]

As we draw nearer to the appearance of the Antichrist, many Believers are concerned that because life in the modern world demands individual identification for practically all areas of life, that they may inadvertently receive the mark of the Beast by an imposed number or an implanted chip.

Who instigates this mark? ______________________. The mark of the Beast will take place when the Antichrist has risen to power and the False Prophet acting under his authority demands that all people receive this mark. At that time, we will definitely know who the Antichrist and the False Prophet are. God will make the mark of the Beast very clear to His followers. Rest upon this promise from His Word in Daniel 12:10 (NIV).

> *"Many will be purified, made spotless and refined, but the wicked will continue to be wicked. None of the wicked will understand, but those who are wise will understand."*

The *"name of the beast or the number representing his name"* will be fully understood by those who have godly wisdom, but woe to those who don't!

THE SYSTEM VERSUS THE BELIEVER

Jesus taught in His message to the church recorded in Matthew 24 that before His coming at the Rapture there would be a time of persecution. Jesus' message of the 6 Seals in Revelation 6 also confirms a time of suffering. Actually the Fifth Seal reveals the martyrs in heaven that will be killed during the Great Tribulation.

Read these verses from Matthew 24:9 and Mark 13:12-13 (NKJV).

> [9] *"Then they will deliver you up to tribulation and kill you, and you will be hated by all nations for My name's sake."*
> [12] *"Now brother will betray brother to death, and a father his child; and children will rise up against parents and cause them to be put to death.* [13] *And you will be hated by all for My name's sake. But he who endures to the end shall be saved."*

Revelation 13 informs us of the conditions in three major areas under the Antichrist that will bring adversity to the Believer. The Believer will not concede to the demands of the Beast or the False Prophet.

Circle the area of power with which the Antichrist dominates the world as revealed in the following verses.

1. Revelation 13:7 *"He* [the Antichrist] *was given authority over every tribe, people, language, and nation."*
   religion government finance

The Believer will not adhere to anti-God laws forced upon the world by ____________.

2. Revelation 13:4, 15 *"Men worshipped the dragon* [Satan] *because he had given authority to the beast* [the Antichrist], *and they also worshiped the beast. . .as many as do not worship the image of the best to be killed."*
   religion government finance

The Believer will not worship the Beast nor his ____________________.

3. Revelation 13:17 *". . .no one could buy or sell unless he had the mark, which is the name of the beast* [the Antichrist] *or the number of his name."*

religion government finance

The Believer will not receive the mark of the Beast which will bring him suffering in the area of all his ____________________________ matters.

At this point in time the Rapture takes place. All Believers will be delivered out of the Great Tribulation. Israel will be saved when the Jews see King Jesus at the Rapture. They remain on earth to witness for Christ during the last 3 ½ years.

THE BEAST AFTER THE RAPTURE

We are going to focus on three things in the following verses regarding the Antichrist's actions and the time of His unlimited rule of the world.

Time

Revelation 13:5 (NKJV)

> ". . .*and he* [the Beast] *was given authority to* <u>*continue*</u> *for forty-two months* [3 ½ years]."

How long will the Antichrist continue to govern the world with totalitarian power in the above verse? ______________________ The Beast is given full power and authority to continue to prosper and prevail for 42 months or 3 ½ years.

In former studies we learned that the Antichrist will reign over the world until Jesus comes to earth to establish His earthly Kingdom. At that time, *"the Lord Jesus will kill him with the breath of his mouth and destroy him by the splendor of his coming."* (2 Thessalonians 2:8) For that reason, the forty-two months, or 3 ½ years take place just before King Jesus' Second Coming.

Go to LESSON 22 CHART ONE. . .COMPARATIVE CHART OF THE BEAST at the end of this lesson. In the center column under **Revelation 13** fill in the blank relevant to **5. v.5**.

War on God's People

Revelation 13:7 (NKJV)

> *"It was granted to him* [the Beast] *to make war with the saints and to overcome them."*

The same fury against God and His people that Satan possesses stirs up rage in the Antichrist. God's faithful Believers have escaped Satan's attempts to exterminate them; they have been removed from the earth to their glorious home in heaven during the Rapture. This causes Satan to turn his wrath against Israel. He uses his eager puppet, the Antichrist, to attack Israel in an effort to kill all the Jewish Christians.

The Antichrist will not tolerate the Christ-loving Jew's worship of God. Their death is certain because all the earth is on his side. A mob mentality builds. The Antichrist's massive army eagerly marches on Israel to kill and destroy God's only witness on the earth. One-third of these faithful-to-Jesus Jews survive the sword but will be held captive, prisoners of hope. (Zechariah 13:8-9)

Beware earth people, the end is coming when King Jesus returns to earth to deliver the nation of Israel. Justice will be served. Those who will kill God's people *"with the sword"* will be killed with *"the sharp sword"* that will come from the mouth of King Jesus, the Lord of Righteousness. (Revelation 19:21)

Go to LESSON 22 CHART ONE. . .COMPARATIVE CHART OF THE BEAST at the end of the lesson. In the center column under **Revelation 13** fill in the blank relevant to **3. v.7**.

Blasphemy!

Revelation 13:5, 6 NASB

> [5] *"And there was given to him a mouth speaking arrogant words and blasphemies. . .* [6] *And he opened his mouth in blasphemies against God, to blaspheme His name and His tabernacle, that is, those who dwell in heaven."*

The Antichrist will wreak havoc on the Jewish nation then he will storm into the Jew's temple. He will proclaim himself to be "God," and will set up the dreadful statue of himself in the temple.

As the Beast sits in the most holy part of the Jew's temple and declares himself to be God, the forces of evil surge in his heart and he begins to vilify God. He blasphemes God's name, the very person of God! He rails against God's abode! He speaks evil of all of God's holy, redeemed people in heaven! Unrestrained impudence. . .unmatched insolence!

Antichrist's Blasphemous Assumption of the Role of God

Revelation 13:7-8

> *"And he* [the Beast] *was given authority to rule over every tribe and people and language and nation. And all the people who belong to this world worshipped the beast. They are the ones whose names were not written in the Book of Life before the world was made—the Book that belongs to the Lamb who was slaughtered."*

The Antichrist reigns with absolute power for 3 ½ years over the world which has evolved into a satanic, totalitarian state. Is it any wonder that God compares this last human kingdom ruled by a dictator with the ruthless instincts of Satan to a "beast"?

The Antichrist's blasphemous deeds are performed with the intention of forcing the world into acknowledging him as "God" and worshipping him as such. Satan will use the Antichrist to try to establish his throne upon the earth in the very place where God dwelt above the mercy seat in the Jewish temple, and from where King Jesus will rule the earth in His Thousand-Year Kingdom.

I love the truth of the following quotation.

> "Ultimate power has been coveted by both angels and mankind, but the throne is occupied and there is no danger of a dethronement. God reigns without rival." [5] (Revelation 4; Psalm 93; Psalm 86:8-10)

Go to LESSON 22 CHART ONE. . .COMPARATIVE CHART OF THE BEAST at the end of this lesson. In the center column under **Revelation 13** fill in the blanks relevant to **2. v. 5** and **v. 6**

ADDING TO OUR COLLECTION OF CLUES

- A new element, seven heads which are seven Roman kings, appears as a vital component of the Beast, the World System of the Antichrist.
- The Antichrist/Beast is one of the seven heads (Roman kings) and is mortally wounded, healed and will live again after his death.
- The "*wounded head*", the Antichrist/Beast, becomes the supreme leader of the world. Satan gives his authority to this king.
- The Beast dominates the world in three areas: religion, government, and the world financial system.
- The False Prophet, a religious leader, forces earth people into bondage to the Antichrist and the World System of the Antichrist.
- Deception is the major tool used to carry out the schemes of both the System and the Person of the end-time evil empire.

A CHRONOLOGICAL DIAGRAM OF REVELATION 13

The following diagram will help us put into perspective the time of the reign of the Beast at the end of this Present Age.

CHRONOLOGICAL PERSPECTIVE

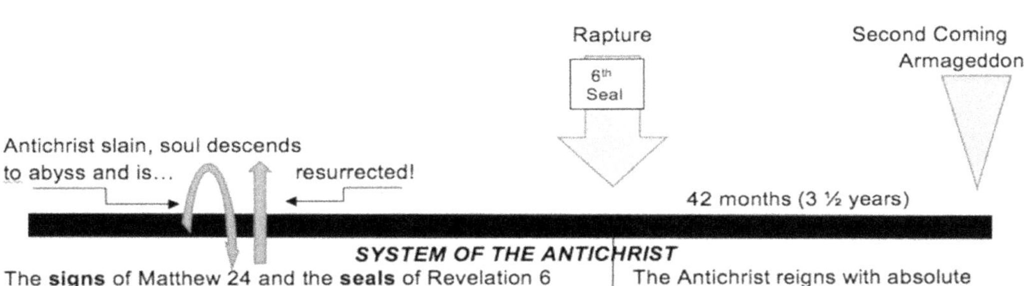

The **signs** of Matthew 24 and the **seals** of Revelation 6 *begin* with The World System of the Antichrist and *end* with the Rapture.

During The World *System* of the Antichrist and before the Rapture, the *Person* of the Antichrist/Beast will be killed and will come back to life. He then will rule over the World System of the Antichrist. The Beast is responsible for the persecution of Believers (Matthew 24) and martyrs of the 5th Seal. (Revelation 6:9-11)

The Antichrist reigns with absolute power for 42 months over the world which has evolved into a satanic, totalitarian state.

The Beast given full power and authority over the world after the Rapture takes place. Christian Jews are persecuted. The System and the Beast are destroyed at King Jesus' Second Coming at Armageddon. (Revelation 19)

EL SHADDAI—GOD THE ALL-BOUNTIFUL ONE

Genesis 17:1

LESSON 22 CHART ONE. . .COMPARATIVE CHART OF THE BEAST

Daniel 7	Revelation 13	Revalation 17
1. **v.7 ten** horns and **little** horn **v.20 ten** horns, the **other** horn **v.24 ten** horns are **ten** kings	**1.** **v.1** beast having ______ horns and ______ heads **v.3** ________ of his heads fatally wounded	
2. **v.8** little horn had a mouth that was **boasting arrogantly** **v.20** little horn. . .had a mouth that was **boasting arrogantly** **v.25** he will **speak out against the Most High**	**2.** **v.1** on his __________ a blasphemous name **v.5** given a ___________ speaking great things and blasphemies **v.6** he opened his __________ in blasphemy against God, to blaspheme His name, His dwelling, and those who dwell in heaven	
3. **v.21** horn was waging **war** against The saints and defeating them **v.25** He will **oppress** His saints, the saints will be handed over to him	**3.** **v.7** make ____________ with the saints and to overcome them	
4. **v.23** The fourth beast will devour **The whole earth**	**4.** **vs.8,12,14** _____________________ _____________________ are decieved and they worship him	
5. **vs. 25** for **time, times, and a half a time** (3½ years)	**5.** **v.5** __________ months (3½ years)	

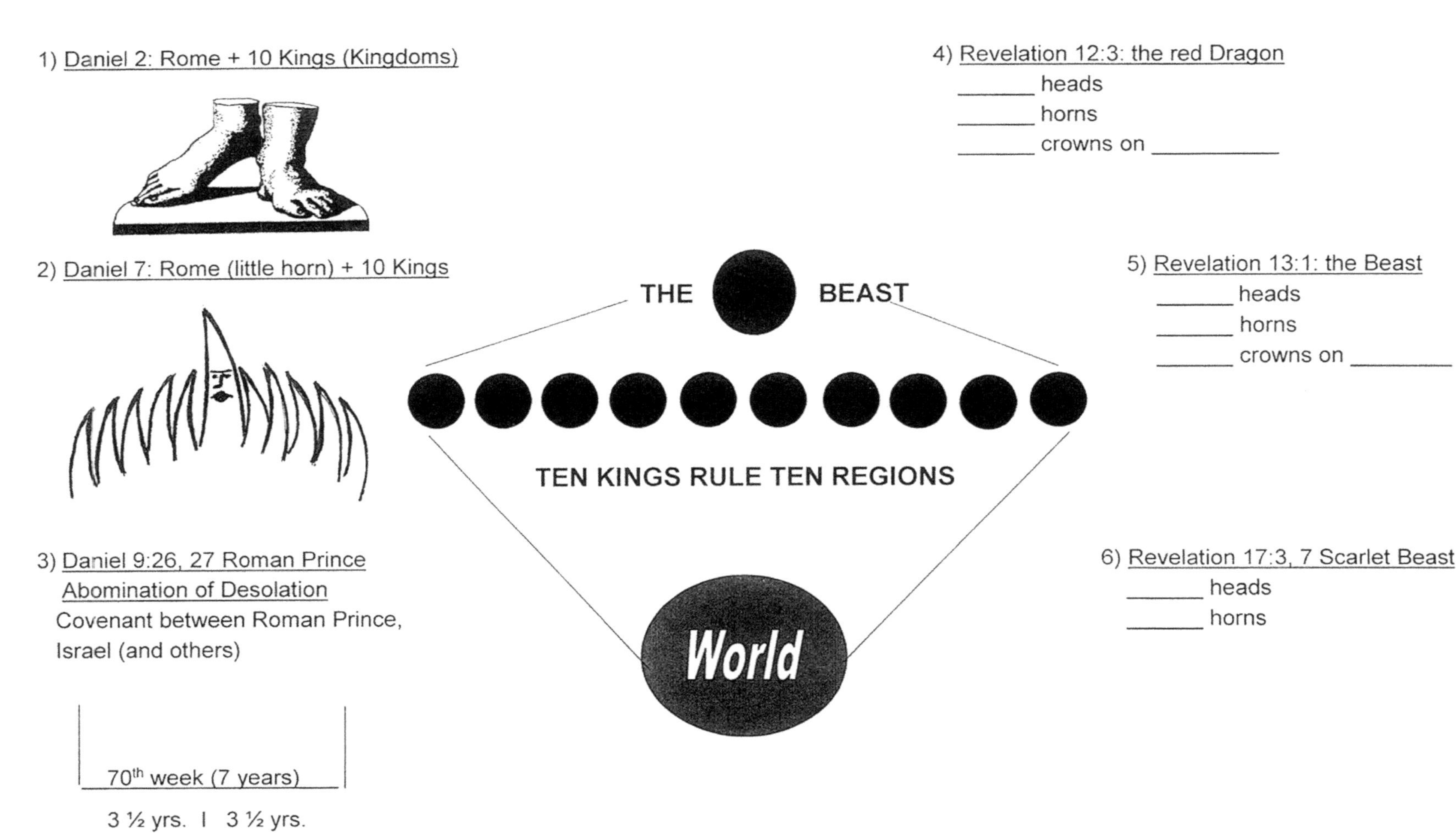
CHART TWO...SYSTEM OF THE ANTICHRIST—PARALLELS FROM DANIEL AND REVELATION
1) Daniel 2: Rome + 10 Kings (Kingdoms)
4) Revelation 12:3: the red Dragon
____ heads
____ horns
____ crowns on ____
2) Daniel 7: Rome (little horn) + 10 Kings
THE BEAST
5) Revelation 13:1: the Beast
____ heads
____ horns
____ crowns on ____
TEN KINGS RULE TEN REGIONS
3) Daniel 9:26, 27 Roman Prince
Abomination of Desolation
Covenant between Roman Prince, Israel (and others)
70th week (7 years)
3 ½ yrs. | 3 ½ yrs.
World
6) Revelation 17:3, 7 Scarlet Beast
____ heads
____ horns

LESSON 23

GOD—THE ANCIENT OF DAYS
Daniel 7:9

He alone sits on the fiery throne of the universe. "I fear God, and next to God I chiefly fear him who fears Him not." [1]

THE MYSTERY OF THE WORLD SYSTEM OF THE ANTICHRIST

THE MYSTERY OF THE HARLOT CITY

"Why are you so amazed? I will tell you the mystery of this woman and of the beast. . ."
Angel of the Seven Bowls (Revelation17:7)

Have you ever gone to an airport to pick up someone that you have never seen and have no clue as to what they look like? There are certain common-sense things to do in order to accomplish this. First, go to the right terminal and then to the correct concourse and gate. You can also communicate with the person beforehand to ask what clothing they will be wearing or to tell you something about themselves that will help to identify them.

We have discovered basic information from the book of Daniel to help us in our pursuit to understand the World System of the Antichrist. But how will we know the identity of the Antichrist? Does God give us enough information on this subject to enable us to be looking in the right direction as the time of the Antichrist's appearance draws near? Daniel chapters 2 and 7 have placed us in the terminal and Revelation 13 has given us directions to the right concourse. Revelation chapter 17 will lead us to the right gate by giving conclusive information to recognize the *Person* of the Antichrist. Perhaps you are beginning to realize that there will be no doubt in your mind about recognizing the Person when he comes into view.

Looking For Clues
Down through the centuries the tendency is to read present-day events into end-time prophecy. This is a natural tendency, but events should never be manipulated or forced to "fit" Bible prophecy like a size-ten foot crammed into a size-four shoe. If indeed the events of our day consistently reflect the end-time prophetic events announced and described in the Bible, then we must pay attention to the Word with renewed vigor and continue to evaluate the unfolding events.

Your observations are vital to developing a Bible-based conclusion regarding the identity of the Antichrist. The Holy Spirit will reveal meaning to those yielded to Him as open-minded seekers of truth. Keep in mind that we are looking for faithful-to-the-Scriptures consistency in our interpretation with no Scriptural contradictions. Let God's Word speak and it will lead you to truth. We are confidently going in the right direction which enables us to solve the mystery of the Scriptural identity of the Antichrist.

Solve [D]
"1. To find a solution to; answer; explain. 2. To work out a correct solution to (a problem)"… or mystery.

As you make your observations, keep in mind:
- Bible symbols represent things that are real and literal.
- The apostle John is looking at this vision from God's perspective.

- There are only two components that make up the end-time System of the Antichrist—Rome and Ten Kings (the iron and the clay.)

Read Revelation 17 and 18 in your own Bible before you begin your analysis.

REVELATION 17—THE ANTICHRIST

You will find in the following Scripture new information vital to your understanding of the World System of the Antichrist. **Underline** the new element that did not appear in the description of the Beast in Daniel 2 and 7 or Revelation 13. To which component does it belong, to Rome or to the Ten Kings? God gives many meaningful clues to the Mystery of the Beast in the following verses.

Make five observations.
Revelation 17:1-12, 15, 18 (NASB)

> [1] *And one of the seven angels who had the seven bowls came and spoke with me [John], saying, "Come here, I shall show you the judgment of the great harlot who sits on many waters,*
> [2] *with whom the kings of the earth committed acts of immorality, and those who dwell on the earth*
> *were made drunk with the wine of her immorality.*
> [3] *And he carried me away in the Spirit into a wilderness; and I saw a woman sitting on a scarlet beast, full of blasphemous names, having seven heads and ten horns.*
>
> [4] *And the woman was clothed in purple and scarlet, and adorned with gold and precious stones and pearls, having in her hand a gold cup full of abominations and of the unclean things of her immorality,*
> [5] *and upon her forehead a name was written, a mystery, "BABYLON THE GREAT, THE MOTHER OF HARLOTS AND OF THE ABOMINATIONS OF THE EARTH."*
> [6] *And I saw the woman drunk with the blood of the saints, and with the blood of the witnesses of Jesus. And when I saw her, I wondered greatly."*
>
> [7] *And the angel said to me, "Why do you wonder? I shall tell you the mystery of the woman and of the beast that carries her, which has the seven heads and the ten horns.*
> [8] *The beast that you saw was and is not, and about to come up out of the abyss and to go to destruction. And those who dwell on the earth will wonder, whose name has not been written in the book of life from the foundation of the world, when they see the beast, that he was and is not and will come.*
>
> [9] *Here is the mind which has wisdom. The seven heads are seven mountains [hills] on which the woman sits,* [10] *and they are seven kings. . .* [12] *And the ten horns which you saw are ten kings, who have not yet received a kingdom, but they receive authority as kings with the beast for one hour.*

> [15] *And he said to me, "The waters which you saw where the harlot sits, are peoples and multitudes and nations and tongues.*
>
> [18] *And the woman whom you saw is the great city, which reigns over the kings of the earth.*

Your Observations

1. ______________________________
2. ______________________________
3. ______________________________
4. ______________________________
5. ______________________________

Questions

The Scarlet Beast—The World System of the Antichrist
What phrase in verses 3, and 7 identifies this beast with the beast of Revelation 13. ________
____

This scarlet beast is clearly identified with the dragon, Satan, of Revelation 12:3 (NASB):

> *"And another sign appeared in heaven; and behold, a great* red *dragon having seven heads and ten horns, and on his heads were seven diadems."*

Daniel 2, and 7 and Revelation 13 and 17 are speaking of the same thing, the World System of the Antichrist and the Person of the Antichrist. Each chapter brings to light new information.

The seven heads represent Seven Roman Kings and the ten horns of the beast represent the Ten Kings of Ten Regions of the world as seen in Revelation 13.

For how long will the Ten Kings and the Beast receive authority according to verse 12? _______
To the world these kings will appear to be great, "but to God they reign but for one unimportant hour. They are associated with Antichrist and their day will be as brief as his." [2]

Jesus referred to this period, which coincides with the Wrath of God judgments, by saying: *"unless that time of calamity is shortened, not a single person will survive. But it will be shortened for the sake of God's chose ones."* (Matthew 24:22) The "one hour" which in reality will be 3 ½ years is a very short time for a powerful one world government to rule without any human opposition. King Jesus will break in upon the devastating rule of the World System of the Antichrist to destroy it completely. His Thousand-Year Kingdom will be established at that point in time.

What is the scarlet beast full of? (verse 3) ______________________________
"*Full of*" implies blasphemy in the fullest measure, and indicates a system of rule completely against God and Christian values and standards. The supreme leader of this system will use

blasphemous titles of attributes belonging only to God. No created being can legitimately claim them.

The Woman

In Revelation 17 what is the new element that has not been mentioned to this point? ________
What is the meaning of the symbol "*woman*" according to verse 18? ____________________
What does the symbol "*waters*" signify according to verse 15? ____________________
________________________________. In other words the whole ________________.
What do you think her position "*sits on many waters*" indicates? ____________________
____

Considering her location, "*sitting on* [on top of] *a scarlet beast,*" what does the woman's position indicate regarding her relationship to the beast? verses 3, 18 ____________________
____

To which component of the end-time System, Rome or Ten Kings, does the woman correspond?
____

It is very clear that the kingdom/beast of Daniel 2 and 7 in the Old Testament is one and the same with the beast of Revelation 13 and 17 in the New Testament. This prophecy was not fulfilled in Daniel's day nor in John's; it was to be fulfilled in the future, the last days.

Go to LESSON 23 CHART ONE. . .COMPARATIVE CHART OF THE BEAST at the end of this lesson. In column three under **Revelation 17** fill in the blanks relevant to: (**1. v.3, v. 7, v. 12**) and (**5. v. 12.**)

Go to CHART TWO. . .THE WORLD SYSTEM OF THE ANTICHRIST: PARALLELS FROM DANIEL AND REVELATION **at the end of Lesson 22** and fill in the blanks under**: 6) Revelation 17:3, 7 Scarlet Beast**.

The Woman/city in opposition to God

With whom did the woman/city commit acts of immorality? Verse 2 ____________________
Who did the woman/city make drunk with the wine of her immorality? verse 2 __________
____ This explains the end-time spiritual condition of the world. The word *immorality* in the Greek is *porneia* and means "to prostitute oneself" and figuratively speaking "to practice idolatry."

With what was the woman/city drunk? verse 6________________________________
____

What do you think the literal meaning of verse 6 is? ______________________________
____

The Great City

Now you are ready to discover the name of this "*great city.*" Read the following verses. God tells you that you will need a mind with wisdom. I think you will agree. You have been working throughout this book with symbols and their literal meanings, as a result, you have acquired some basic skills. To arrive at a credible interpretation, we will approach the wording with its natural, clear, and evident meaning.

Revelation 17:9-10 (NIV).

> [9] *"This calls for a mind with wisdom. The seven heads are seven hills on which the woman* [city] *sits.* [10] *They are also seven kings."*

Underline the two meanings above given to *"the seven heads."* We have learned from our study of Revelation 13 that the seven heads of the beast are Seven Roman Kings and is specified to be the case above in verse 10.

The Lord gives a second meaning to the symbol to help us to identify *the great city.* The woman, *the great city*, sits on ____________________________. Can you identify this city, a city that has been known for centuries as *"Urbs Septicollis"* the city of the seven hills? **Write** the name of this city. ________________________

I am sure that you discovered this city to be Rome and corresponds to the Roman component of the end-time System of the Antichrist.

The *seven hills* identify the city and the *seven kings* refer to the city's rulers who have been called ________________ for centuries. The seven heads, Seven Roman Kings, are the last kings to rule from this city.

The city *sits* on *"many* ___________________ (verse 1). It rules over all the peoples of the world, verse 15.

The city *sits "on* a ___________________________________ (verse 3). It rules over *"the kings of the earth,"* Satan's World System of the Antichrist verse 18.

The city *sits* on ______________________________________ (verse 9). It is the great city of Rome.

Purpose of this vision

What is the purpose of this vision according to verse 1? ____________________________

Go to LESSON 23 CHART ONE. . .COMPARATIVE CHART OF THE BEAST at the end of this lesson. In column three under **Revelation 17** fill in the blanks relevant to: (**2. v. 3**) and (**3. v. 6**) and (**4. v. 1**.)

Your answer to the question, "What is the meaning of the symbol "*woman*"?" should read: "*the great city.*" This city will reign over the kings of the earth. In other words, it will reign over the whole world. When we read chapter 17 we should always substitute the word *woman* with the word *city*. This city sitting on the beast also confirms that it has authority over the whole system of the Antichrist.

The blasphemous names located on the scarlet beast point out the religious aspect of the beast, as well as the city's singling out God's people for persecution and death.

THE CITY OF THE SEVEN HILLS

Revelation 17:9 (NIV)

"The seven heads are seven hills on which the woman [city] *sits."*

There is only one city in the world that meets the following biblical specifications.

- a *political* authority so powerful that it can reign over the Ten Kings of Ten Regions of the world Revelation 13:7.
- a *religious* authority that is able to achieve the worship of the whole world Revelation 13:4.
- a *financial* authority deeply involved in the world financial system Revelation 13:17.
- is located on seven hills

The "*great city*" is the Vatican City surrounded by the city of Rome, Italy. The Vatican City is so closely related to the city of Rome that their names are interchangeable because it was from there that the Roman church ruled for centuries. The present day Vatican City is located on Vatican Hill just across the Tiber River on the opposite side of the Seven Hills of Rome. Vatican City and St Peter's Basilica are built on *vaticanus mons* or *vaticanus collis. Vaticanus* in Latin means "prophecy" and *mons* means "mountain," *collis* means "hill"—*the mountain or hill of prophecy.* In ancient times before the Vatican was situated there, this hill was the location of fortunetellers and thus its name. Vatican City in Latin actually means *City of Prophecy.* I find that too remarkable to be a coincidence.

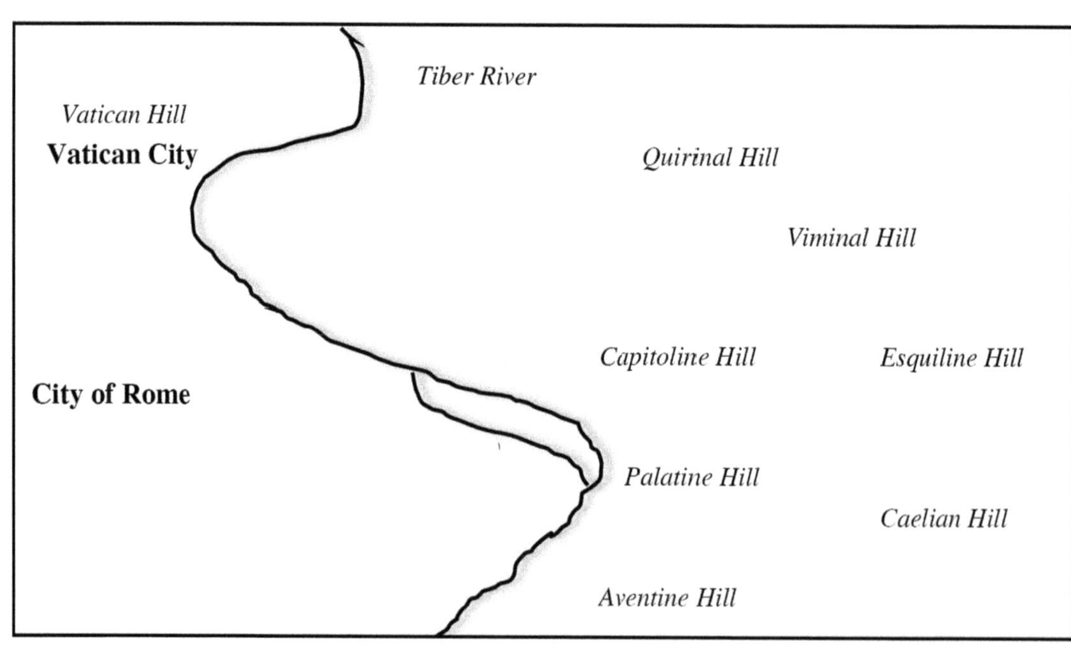

RELIGIOUS ROME FROM GOD'S POINT OF VIEW

God refers to this city as a harlot city. God's estimation and evaluation on anything is exceedingly valuable and highly esteemed. It is indispensable. In the case of the *harlot city*, God has placed in Scripture His specific view, warnings, and ultimate judgment of this religious system. No one can argue with God on this, or any other matter.

The appearance of this woman is one of grandeur, imperial splendor, and magnificence. She is clothed with purple and scarlet, veneered with gold and jewels. In her delusional pomp she says, "*Here I sit a queen on a throne; I am no woman who lacks a man and I shall never know sorrow.*" (Revelation 18:7 Phillips) She is a queen in her own eyes, but in Jesus' eyes, "*eyes like flames of fire,*" she is a prostitute. (Revelation 1:14; 19:12)

Revelation 17:1 (NASB)

> "*. . .the great harlot. . .*"

What is a harlot?

What does God communicate by using this term? Good question. The Hebrew word for *prostitute* is *zana* and "broadly refers to illicit or illegitimate sexual misconduct. . .is metaphorical and in most cases refers to those who follow after other gods instead of serving the Lord." [M] The harlot does not follow God and is used to illustrate idolatry.

Idolatry

The Greek word for *idolatry* is *eidololatria.* "Idolatry is not limited to the worship of false images, but it is placing anything or anyone before God as the object of allegiance and devotion." [M] To pray to or to give veneration to any created being or thing as supernatural (with powers to intervene in the course of natural laws) falls into the category of idolatry.

The Mother of Harlots

Harlots seduce and deceitfully draw individuals to themselves to form an illegitimate union. They steal for their own ends what legitimately belongs to another; they lead the victim to their ruin. We have studied in other lessons these very intentions on the part of the Antichrist. He desires to steal from God the worship and loyalty of His creatures. Rome's is a duplicitous system of person worship that ultimately leads to the abandonment of all relationship with God on His terms. Rome has not been spiritually true for centuries. Her spiritual unfaithfulness to God's written Word with each added unbiblical doctrine and dogma has cast an evil influence on mankind in the name of Christianity. "*Teaching as doctrines the precepts of men.*" (Mark 7:7 Philips) To be classified as *Babylon* is the worst designation she could possibly receive for this signifies corruption and outright rebellion against God.

Mother of harlots indicates the woman, the city, to be the source of all apostasy, all religious deviation. Her offspring is like herself; their allegiance and loyalty is not to God.

Jeremiah 3:3 (NKJV) "...you have had a harlot's forehead; you refuse to be ashamed."

THE HARLOT'S BLASPHEMOUS NAME

Revelation 17:5 (NASB)

> *"and upon her forehead a name was written, a mystery, BABYLON THE GREAT, THE MOTHER OF HARLOTS AND OF THE ABOMINATIONS OF THE EARTH."*

Something interesting here. Some Bible scholars believe that the harlot in Bible times had a trademark or a distinctive veil on her forehead. (Jeremiah 3:3; Genesis 38:15) "It was customary for Roman prostitutes to wear their names in the fillet [narrow ribbon] that encircled their brows." [3] Notice the harlot's title in verse 5 is on her *forehead.* The mark of the Beast imposed on earth people's foreheads or right hands will reveal that they too are spiritual adulterers and idolaters who worship Satan the dragon, the Beast and the image of the Beast. (Revelation 13:4, 12, 15)

Revelation 13:1 tells us there are blasphemous names on the seven heads of the beast. I will only mention a few of the pope's titles. Should any man bear these blasphemous names? *Vicar of Jesus Christ* (in the place of Jesus), *Supreme Pontiff* (high priest) *of the Universal Church, Most Holy Father, Our Most Holy Lord, Judge of the World, Your Holiness.*

But in 17:5 attention is focused on a specific name appearing on the forehead of the harlot. In canon law, the laws of the Roman Catholic Church, the pope is referred to as the "Roman Pontiff." His title *Highest Pontiff,* the ancient title *Pontifex Maximus* usually translated *Supreme Pontiff,* is especially significant in that the verse above refers to "Babylon the Great." In Lesson 20 this title was explained as follows:

> When Julius Caesar became emperor of Rome, he was the "Pontifex Maximus" or "Supreme Pontiff" (high priest) of the Etruscan religion that dated back to Nimrod of Genesis 10 and 11. From then on, the title and office of "Pontifex Maximus" belonged to the emperor of the Roman Empire and each succeeding emperor, thus, uniting the head of this ancient pagan religion with the head of the Roman Empire.

In A.D. 376 the Christian Emperor Gratianus refused to bear this priestly title as not "befitting" a Christian. Two years later Damasus I, bishop of Rome, took the title and position of *Supreme Pontiff,* (High Priest) of the Babylonian religion. This pagan title passed to the head of the Roman Church where it has remained ever since. It is this mystery title, the secret, which links the harlot city to *"Babylon the Great, the Mother of Harlots and of the Abominations of the Earth."* [4]

THE CUPS

The Gold Cup of Immorality

Revelation 17:4, 2 (NASB)

> [4] *"having in her hand a gold cup full of abominations and of the unclean things of her immorality. . ."*
>
> [2] *"with whom the kings of the earth committed acts of immorality, and those who dwell on the earth were made drunk with the wine of her immorality.*

She holds in her hand a gold drinking cup full of evil; earth dwellers are made drunk with her wine of abominable doctrines and immorality. Drunk is to be intoxicated, without reason or inhibitions. "Metaphorically, of the effect upon men of partaking of the abominations of the Babylonish system, Revelation 17:2" [V]

During this 3 ½ year period, earth dwellers will be intoxicated in a gradually deteriorating state of exhilaration due to unlicensed immoral acts to the point of stupefaction. This will cause them to be used as duped slaves to do the Antichrist's every bidding. (Romans 1:24-32) Can you imagine the depths of degradation mankind will reach in the last days?

This will be a world without the influence of God's people—the church. The salt is gone that would preserve the earth from total corruption and ruin. God's blessing on the world is gone. The light of the world has not been snuffed out by persecution, but rather, it has been removed at the Rapture. Evil wraps the world with the gloom of darkness. Will evil meet no resistance? Who will push back the darkness? Like the lighthouse beacon, the Christ-followers of Israel flash their faithful life-giving beam upon a vast, restless ocean of spiritual darkness; a pin point of light, but powerful nonetheless. Yet worst of all, the world will not know the restraining work of the Holy Spirit. (2 Thessalonians 2:7-8) The World System of the Antichrist creates an existence without God.

The Cup of Blood

Revelation 17:6 (Phillips)

> *"Then I noticed that the woman was drunk with the blood of the saints* [God's holy people] *and of the martyrs for Jesus."*

Revelation 14:12 "This means that God's holy people must endure persecution patiently, obeying his commands and maintaining their faith in Jesus."

Righteousness is exiled from the earth. God's people are not tolerated. The Greek meaning here is that the woman is "in a state of mental intoxication, through the shedding of men's blood profusely." [V] The filling of the cup began centuries ago with the blood of God's people and will be filled to the brim under the hand of the great oppressor, the Antichrist.

The Cup of God

Revelation 18:4-6, 8 (Phillips)

> 4 *"Then I heard another voice from Heaven, crying: 'Come out from her, O my people, lest you become accomplices in her* [the great city's] *sins and must share in her punishment. For her sins have mounted up to the sky, and God has remembered the tale of her wickedness. Pay her back in her own coin—yes, pay her back double for all that she has done! In the cup which she mixed for others mix her a drink of double strength! For the pride in which she flaunted herself give her torture and misery!* 8 *So in a single day her punishments shall strike her—death, sorrow, and famine, and she shall be burned in the fire. For mighty is the Lord God who judges her!"*

This judgment will actually be carried out in part by the Antichrist/Beast and the Ten Kings. (Revelation 17:16-17) They care nothing for the ancient Roman church. The Satan inspired Beast has his eyes fixed on Jerusalem where he will attempt to rule the world as God. Revelation 18 portrays this destruction of the harlot city.

Revelation 17:1 (RSV)

> *"Then one of the seven angels who had the seven bowls came and said to me, 'Come, I will show you the judgment of the great harlot who is seated upon many waters.'"*

This angel tells John that he is going to reveal to him the judgment that is coming which will begin with the destruction of the great city at the hands of the rulers of the world, and then at the hand of God.

Remarkable! Think about it. This particular angel delivered this vision to the apostle John in about year A.D. 95 He is one of the seven angels, who in the far off future from John's perspective, will be authorized by God to pour out the Trumpet/Bowl judgments on the world. This angel could very well be the seventh angel who brings about the actual judgment that he has announced. This last judgment, of a series of seven, utterly destroys what is left of the city of "Babylon," the harlot city—Rome.

Revelation 16:17-19

> [17] *"Then the seventh angel poured out his bowl into the air. And a mighty shout came from the throne in the temple, saying, "It is finished!* [18] *Then the thunder crashed and rolled and lightning flashed. And a great earthquake struck—the worst since people were placed on the earth.* [19] *The great city of Babylon* [Rome] *split into three sections, and the cities of many nations fell into heaps of rubble. So God remembered all of Babylon's* [Rome's] *sins, <u>and he made her drink the cup that was filled with the wine of his fierce wrath</u>. . ."*

THE SEVEN ROMAN KINGS

The beast of the following verses refers to the *Person* of the Antichrist, not to the <u>system</u> of the Antichrist. At first glance these verses seem to be unsolvable. However, if we continue to build on the knowledge that we have accumulated, we will be able to interpret these verses with their biblical meaning. The specifics of these verses at the actual time in which they will be fulfilled is another matter completely.

Revelation 17:9-11 appears to be an enigma, but is a very important prophecy which provides us with undeniable clues to identify the Antichrist.

Revelation 17:9-11 (NASB)

> [9] *"The seven <u>heads</u> are. . .*[10] *seven <u>kings;</u> five have fallen, one is, the other has not yet come; and when he comes, he must remain a little while.* [11] *And <u>the beast</u> which was and is not, is himself also an eighth, and is one of the seven, and he goes to destruction."*

Questions

What are the seven heads? ________________________________. How many have reigned and are now a thing of the past? ______________. *"One is"* (number six) indicates the ________________ tense, in other words, he is reigning at the time the vision takes place. What is the time stipulation for number seven? ______________________________ _______________. The Beast/Antichrist is number _________________ but is of the _________________. What will happen to him according to verse 11? ______________ _________________________________

The following is a diagram representing the kings. The eighth one is the Beast and destroyed by King Jesus at Armageddon. (Revelation 19:20) In the following diagram of the prophecy:

- **Draw a line** through the first five Roman kings of the past. **Write** "fallen" above these five numbers.
- **Circle** number 6 and **write** the word "is" above it.
- **Place** a question mark above number 7 representing *"he must remain a little while."*
- **Write** the word "Beast" above number 8.

1 2 3 4 5 6 7 8 ← destroyed by King Jesus

This diagram is the "bare bones" of this prophecy, visually restating it. One of these seven kings is the Antichrist. Because there are only *"seven heads,"* the eighth is one of the seven in some way. In the next lesson we will study an interpretation which will help us resolve the mystery.

Keep in mind, these are the last Roman kings to govern before King Jesus comes to set up His earthly Kingdom. Jesus dealings with the Antichrist and the False Prophet are still future. (Revelation 19:11-21) These things have not taken place in ancient history. Prophetic Scriptures, by telling us the things to come, serve to warn us and to enable us to recognize their fulfillment when they take place. This is precisely what God is doing here in chapter 17.

The Mystery Solved

We have arrived at the right terminal, concourse, and gate. We are looking in the right direction. We wait for the inevitable, preordained appearance of the Antichrist.

GOD—THE ANCIENT OF DAYS

Daniel 7:9

LESSON 23 CHART ONE. . . COMPARATIVE CHART OF THE BEAST

Daniel 7	Revelation 13	Revalation 17
1. **v.7 ten** horns and **little** horn **v.20 ten** horns, the **other** horn **v.24 ten** horns are **ten** kings	1. **v.1** beast having ten horns and seven heads **v.3 one** of his heads fatally wounded	1. **v.3** scarlet beast having ______ heads and ______ horns **v.7** beast has _______ heads and _____ horns **v.12** ______ horns. . .are _____ kings
2. **v.8** little horn had a mouth that was **boasting arrogantly** **v.20** little horn. . .had a mouth that was **boasting arrogantly** **v.25** he will **speak out against the Most High**	2. **v.1** on his head a blasphemous name **v.5** given a mouth speaking great things and blasphemies **v.6** he opened his mouth in blasphemy against God, to **blaspheme** His name, His dwelling, and those who dwell in heaven	2. **v.3** scarlet beast: ________________ ________________ ________________ against God were written all over it
3. **v.21** horn was waging **war** against The saints and defeating them **v.25** He will **oppress** His saints, the saints will be handed over to him	3. **v.7** make war with the saints and to overcome them	3. **v.6** drunk with the ____________ of the saints, and with the ___________ of the witnesses of Jesus
4. **v.23** The fourth beast will devour **The whole earth**	4. **vs.8,12,14 all who dwell on the earth** are decieved and they worship him	4. **v.1** seated on waters (v. 15) ___________ ________________ ________________
5. **vs. 25** for **time, times, and a half a time** (3½ years)	5. **v.5** forty-two months (3½ years)	5. **v. 12** for ______________ hour (brief time)

LESSON **24**

THE MYSTERY OF THE WORLD SYSTEM OF THE ANTICHRIST

JEHOVAH ELOHIM—THE ETERNAL UNCHANGING ONE
Malachi 3:6

"Change and decay in all around I see, O Thou Who changest not, abide with me." [1]

THE MYSTERY SOLVED

My Journey

Because it is so special and revealing concerning the great enigma of Revelation 17:9-11 this lesson must stand alone. I have watched this Scripture evolve over the years, and I would like to share with you on a personal basis what I see to be its probable fulfillment. That is why you will notice in this concluding lesson a more than usual personal commentary—my journey.

The Mystery:

Revelation 17:9-11 (NASB)

> [9] *"The seven heads are. . .*[10] *seven kings; five have fallen, one is, the other has not yet come; and when he comes, he must remain a little while.* [11] *And the beast which was and is not, is himself also an eighth, and is one of the seven, and he goes to destruction."*

It is important to stress that we are using interpretive principles that will hold us true to the Scriptures. Let us carry on where we left off in the last lesson and move from there to a remarkable discovery.

EXTRAORDINARY DEVELOPMENT!

THE CITY BECOMES A NATION

In order to know which will be the last seven Roman Kings of this Present Age, we would need to count backwards from Jesus' Second Coming. Sounds simple. . .except we do not know when King Jesus will appear at His Second Coming. One of the most extraordinary historical moments of the twentieth century took place when the headquarters of a religion became a nation. For that reason, we are going to explore a date that could possibly be the countdown date to the final Roman king. Let me tell you about it.

The Temporal Power of the Roman Church

The Roman Empire divided in the year 395 into the Western Roman Empire and the Eastern Roman Empire. The Western Roman Empire ended in the year 476 and out of its collapse arose the Papal Empire. Half the population of the world was Christian by the end of the First century. The title *pope* was assumed by the bishop of Rome around the year 500. He considered himself the single authority over the whole Christian church. Pope Leo III revived the Western Roman Empire by naming Charlemagne, King of the Franks, as emperor. With the Western Roman Empire coordinated with the Roman Catholic Church, the two together would have world-wide dominion. Popes and emperors worked hand in hand uniting the church and state.

This long-lasting union brought about years of unspeakable corruption to the leadership of the church. Unbiblical man-made doctrines and dogmas were added to the doctrines of the Bible.

Pepin, the father of Charlemagne, gave huge portions of central Italy to the pope called Papal States. The popes ruled this territory as kings, from the city of Rome, from 754 – 1870, more than one thousand years.

Empire:

1. A political unit, usually larger than a kingdom and often comprising a number of territories or nations, ruled by a single authority.

2. The territory included in such a unit. [D]

Papacy Looses Temporal Power
The Kingdom of Italy became a state in 1861 with the unification of the many regional states. In 1870 Rome was annexed to Italy to become the capital; as a result, the papacy was deprived of all its territories. With its temporal power abolished, the papacy was reduced to the Vatican, the Lateran palaces, and Castel Gandolfo on the outskirts of Rome.

Vatican City Becomes a Nation
From 1871 until 1929 the popes exiled themselves to the Vatican; self-imposed prisoners until their death. A final political agreement between the popes and the Italian government was not reached until 1929. The Lateran Treaty between Italy's dictator, Benito Mussolini, and Pope Pius XI recognized the independence and sovereignty of the Holy See and created the State of the Vatican City.

The pope was given a small section of Rome, 108.7 acres, around St. Peter's Basilica. It became "an independent state not legally within Italy at all." [2] Once again, religious Rome became a temporal power. The State of the Vatican City is recognized as a sovereign nation under international law.

State of the Vatican City
Can you imagine the headquarters of a religion becoming a nation? That is exactly what took place in 1929. The pope is Head of State as well as the head of the Roman Catholic Church. His title is "Sovereign of the State of the Vatican City" a city-state and nation. Take note that the apostle John made it known that the *harlot* that would rule the world "*is the great city.*" *City* is actually a part of this nation's name, State of the Vatican City! (Revelation 17:18) How precise is the Word of God!

The Roman Kingdom/Empire
In 1929, this Roman nation was born, a political, religious, and financial power (Vatican Bank). I believe this may well be the fulfillment of Daniel's prophecy regarding the Roman Kingdom. If that is the case, Daniel's prophecy was activated in 1929—the *Iron* Kingdom.

Who are the citizens of this strange nation? ________________________________ Yes, The Holy See is the central government of the Roman Catholic Church, and the pope reigns over the 1.2 billion Roman Catholics, *citizens* of his kingdom. The Vatican City will ultimately reign over the world, "*peoples and multitudes and nations and tongues.*" All people will become citizens of this kingdom. (Revelation 17:15; 13:7)

The Holy See has diplomatic relations with 175 nations. Papal ambassadors are called Apostolic Nuncios. The Holy See is a permanent observer of the United Nations. It is not a full member by choice. The United States maintained consular relations with the Papal States until 1870 when they were discontinued. The United States had personal envoys to the pope and periodic visits to the Holy See from 1939 until January 10, 1984 when full diplomatic relations were established by President Reagan. This act overturned an 1867 ban on funding a diplomatic mission to the Holy See.

Congress approves all ambassadors because all ambassadors, along with their staff, housing, etc., are funded with taxpayer money. For that reason, it was considered against the Constitution to recognize diplomatically an entity that was both a religion and a government. It was considered that "Roman Catholicism [in the United States] would have a special status accorded no other religion." [3]

Interesting. . .when the pope visits the United States, is the visit covered by taxpayer money as a Head of State or not covered because he is a religious leader?

A PREMISE IS BORN

In the Bible School in Colombia, South America, I had the privilege of teaching many subjects among which was Church History. As I taught events leading to the establishment of the Vatican City as a sovereign city-state nation it impressed me to be so unusual that it must have prophetic significance. I carefully considered 1929 as a possible date for the birth of the end-time Roman Kingdom as predicted in Daniel 2 and 7. Looking at it from different angles, I concluded that indeed the possibilities were great.

Premise [D]
"A proposition upon which an argument is based or from which a conclusion is drawn."

God's Word has declared a Roman Kingdom united with Ten Kings will rule the world in the end times. Daniel stated that this end-time kingdom would be a very different world empire. Daniel 7 declares this difference over and over again:

> *"It was different from any of the other beasts. . ."* (7:7) *"the one so different from the others. . ."* (7:19) *"which will be different from all the other kingdoms. . ."* (7:23 NASB) *"Then another king will arise, different from the other ten. . ."* (7:24)

God's Word always says what it means and means what it says. Although Revelation 17:9-11 is very puzzling, it has meaning and will take place just as stated.

The Premise Stated

From 1929 until the Second Coming of Christ, there will be *seven heads, kings* or popes, one will be the Beast. All popes before 1929 were religious leaders, since 1929 all popes are both *kings*, Heads of State and religious leaders. From 1929 forward every pope is the Head of State of the biblical end-time Roman Kingdom.

My Plan

- Keep a list of the popes beginning with the pope involved in the Lateran Treaty of 1929 which gave birth to the State of the Vatican City.

I began my list of popes (in Spanish) in the early 1970's. I still have the original paper which is around 45 years old.

- Apply Revelation 17:9-11 to this premise:

  [9] *"The seven heads are. . .*[10] *seven kings; five have fallen, one is, the other has not yet come; and when he comes, he must remain a little while.* [11] *And the beast which was and is not, is himself also an eighth, and is one of the seven, and he goes to destruction."*

My List

I was born six years after the Lateran Treaty of 1929. At the time I began my list Pope Paul VI was reigning. I wrote the four popes on my list; three had died, the fourth was the reigning pope at the time. Across the years, each new pope was added to the list.

ROME – 1929 ???

FIVE	1. Pope Pius XI	1922 – 1939
	2. Pope Pius XII	1939 – 1958
HAVE	3. Pope John XXIII	1958 – 1963
	4. Pope Paul VI	1963 – 1978
FALLEN	5. Pope John Paul I	1978 – 1978 *(33 days)*
	mortally wounded 1981	
ONE IS	6. Pope John Paul II	1978 – 2005
HE MUST REMAIN A LITTLE WHILE	7. Pope Benedict XVI *Resigned February 28, 2013*	2005 –_______
EIGHTH, IS OF THE SEVEN	8. Pope Francis	2013 –_______

The Historical Development as I Experienced It.

I was teaching this view in a prophecy class with some very sceptic students. In light of end-time developments taking place, the general feeling was a pope's reign lasts a long time, and, to the students, it would take forever to reach the last one. Time wise, this premise just didn't seem reasonable to them. A couple of weeks after finishing the class, the phone rang. "Katalina (name in Spanish), the pope died!" I wrote the date on my list—1978.

Pope John Paul I was elected, I wrote his name on blank number five. Thirty-three days later the phone rang, you guessed it. "Katalina, can you believe it, the pope died!" I wrote 1978 again by John Paul I. I also wrote "33 days" beside the date. *"Five have fallen."* Wow! I wrote the name of the *one is*, newly elected pope and the date 53 days later on blank number 6—Pope John Paul II.

John Paul II

On December 30, 1993 the Holy See and Israel finally signed an accord to establish relations between the Vatican and the State of Israel. This agreement was the Vatican's recognition of the Statehood of Israel, which had been established and recognized by most nations since 1948. Prophetically speaking, this was considered to be historic.

The report that really grabbed my attention came on May 13, 1981, an assassination attempt on John Paul II. He was shot three times, one in the abdomen, a *mortal wound,* in St Peter's square by a Turkish gunman. But, his wound was healed. I jotted down this information above his name. Then on May 12, 1982, the pope was wounded by a knife-wielding Spanish priest while visiting the shrine city of Fatima in Portugal.

The List Continues

In 2005, I recorded the date of the death of John Paull II. I wrote Benedict XVI's name and date on blank number seven by the Scripture *"he must remain a little while."*

Another subject I taught at the Bible School in Colombia was Hermeneutics, the laws and art of Bible interpretation. Hermeneutics stresses the importance of the study of the original languages of the Bible, Hebrew and Greek, in order to discover meaning. In the study of Revelation 17:9-11, I was drawn to the statement concerning the seventh king, "*he must remain a little while.*" I spent some time researching this qualifying phrase. The following is a result of this study.

THE SEVENTH KING

God expresses this prophecy in a peculiar way. The wording in the original Greek language in referring to the seventh Roman king is spoken in an intriguing manner. The following is a literal translation.

Revelation 17:10 (Young's Literal Translation)

> *"the other did not yet come* [future tense], *and when he may come, it behoveth him to remain a little time."*

The key word here is *behoove*, a word hardly used in modern times. The meaning of this word brings us to an amazing discovery. The following is a resume of the definition given by W.E. Vine. [V] The old spelling of the word *behoove* is used here.

Behove, Must

"Dei" is the Greek word for *behoved* meaning "it is necessary." An example, Luke 24:46 (KJV): *"Thus it is written, and thus it behoved Christ to suffer, and to rise from the dead the third day."* Behove here means [that it was necessary] "that the Christ should suffer." *Dei* expresses a logical necessity.

As you read the rest of this quotation from Vine's definition of the Greek word *dei* (behove) apply the definition first to Christ's death and resurrection recorded in Luke 24:46. You will gain a firm understanding of the word *behove* as well as enrich your understanding of the death and resurrection of Jesus. Second, apply this definition to the seventh Roman king to discover why God says that when he comes, *"it behoveth him to remain a little time.*"

"*Dei. . .*
- Of a necessity lying in the nature of the case.
- Of necessity brought about by circumstances.
- Of necessity as to what is required that something may be brought about.
- Of necessity arising from the determinate will and counsel [eternal decree] of God."

What does this signify?
The seventh Roman king, Benedict XVI, is voted into power, but he remains in his position as king for a short time because it seemed necessary to him to step aside or retire for motives related to the first three reasons of this definition. Unknown to him is the fourth reason for his withdrawal as king, God's "determinate will and counsel." God's sovereignty disposes what man proposes through the immutable foreordination of His will as recorded in the book of Revelation.

According to the Greek expression "*behoveth him*," the seventh Roman king withdraws himself to give place to the eighth Roman king who is identified as the Beast. God recognizes the Beast to be the eighth by succession. God also sees the eighth taking the place of the seventh when He states that the eighth is "*one of the seven*" heads/kings.

The eighth king, the Beast, comes to the vacated throne, apparently, while the seventh king is still living but not reigning.

This is the meaning of "*he must remain a little while.*"

Back To The List
Then came the announcement. Benedict XVI announced his resignation for February 28, 2013. "The papal announcement, delivered in Latin, stunned the church. Here was a Pope, in the ultimate exercise of free will, giving up his throne and his role as the Vicar of Christ." [4] This stunning resignation is highly unusual. I wrote below Benedict's name, "Resigned February 28, 2013."

Pope Francis took Benedict's place March 13, 2013. I wrote the name and date on the eighth blank. "*And the beast which was and is not, is himself also an eighth, and is one of the seven, and he goes to destruction.*"

There are no more blanks to fill.

Seven, Not Eight!
I hope that all through this study of the seven Roman kings, you have been saying, "Hey, hold on. There aren't eight heads, or eight kings! There are only seven heads in Revelation 12, 13 and 17! How is it that 17:11 says, '*And the beast which was and is not, is himself also an eighth. . .*?'"

Let me repeat. According to the Greek expression "*behoveth him*," the seventh Roman King withdraws himself to give place to the eighth Roman King who is identified as the Beast. God recognizes the Beast to be the eighth by succession. God also sees the eighth taking the place of the seventh when He states that the eighth is "*one of the seven*" heads/kings.

The following diagram illustrates this interpretation. **Write** "vacated" above "number 7," then **cross out** "number 7." **Write** "number 7" above "number 8." The eighth Roman king is both the eighth and the seventh.

1 2 3 4 5 6 7 8 ←**destroyed by King Jesus**

Revelation 17:8 (NASB) "The beast that you saw was and is not, and is about to come up out of the abyss and to go to destruction. And those who dwell on the earth will wonder, whose name has not been written in the book of life from the foundation of the world, when they see the beast that he was and is not and will come."

THE MYSTERY OF THE BEAST

THREE POSSIBILITIES OF FULFILLMENT

We are going to look at three interpretations of Revelation 7:9-11. Two interpretations are based on the date 1929 as the beginning date of the end-time Roman Kingdom. One interpretation is not based on 1929.

All three interpretations adhere to the fact that the Beast will die of a mortal wound and will come back to life from the abyss. Also all three interpretations are faithful to the established meaning of verses 10 and 11 that the eighth and the seventh kings are one and the same.

Revelation 17:9-11 (NASB)

> [9] *"The seven heads are. . .*[10] *seven kings; five have fallen, one is, the other has not yet come; and when he comes, he must [it behoveth him to] remain a little while.* [11] *And the beast which was and is not, is himself also an eighth, and is one of the seven, and he goes to destruction."*

INTERPRETATION ONE—NO DATE

This first interpretation does not consider the date 1929 as a basis for calculating the last seven Roman kings. It looks like this.

Five have fallen is 8th is the 7th

~~1 2 3 4 5~~ 6 7 8 ←**destroyed by King Jesus**

The Beast, the eighth king also the "*wounded head*," will replace the seventh king who vacates his throne. There is no way to determine beforehand when this will take place or to identify the last seven popes.

INTERPRETATION TWO—BASED ON YEAR 1929

This interpretation considers the date 1929, the establishing of the State of the Vatican City, as reasonable to determine the last seven Roman kings. It looks like this:

"KINGS" 1929

	1st Pius XI	1922 – 1939
Five	2nd Pius XII	1939 – 1958
have	3rd John XXIII	1958 – 1963
fallen	4th Paul VI	1963 – 1978
	5th John Paul I	1978 (lived as pope for only 33 days)
One is	6th John Paul II	1978 – 2005
	(mortally wounded but recovered from the wound in 1981)	
Short time	7th ~~Benedict XVI~~	~~2005 – 2013~~
	Francis	2013
The Beast Is of the seven	8. John Paul II	date unknown

According to this interpretation the sixth king who actually did receive a mortal wound in 1981, but was healed, died in 2005, and will rise from the abyss in (year unknown.) The emphasis on the sixth king, "*one is*," is very convincing.

INTERPRETATION THREE— BASED ON YEAR 1929

This interpretation considers 1929, the establishing of the State of the Vatican City, also as a credible date to determine the last seven Roman kings. It looks like this.

"KINGS" 1929

	1st Pius XI	1922 – 1939
Five	2nd Pius XII	1939 – 1958
have	3rd John XXIII	1958 – 1963
fallen	4th Paul VI	1963 – 1978
	5th John Paul I	1978 (lived as pope for only 33 days)
One is	6th John Paul II	1978 – 2005
Short time	7th ~~Benedict XVI~~	~~2005 – 2013~~ (vacated)
The Beast is of the seven	8th and 7th Francis 2013	

According to this interpretation, the eighth king, Pope Francis, takes his place on the empty throne left by Benedict's withdrawal, making Francis both the eighth and the seventh king. Francis will be killed and will rise to life again from the abyss to reign supreme over the world.

Look for the date 1929 on the extreme left of **Timeline One** (located at the end of Part One of this book.)

If the second or the third interpretation based on the 1929 date is correct, we do not have long to wait for our King to come. Even so come Lord Jesus.

> "What has puzzled us before seems less mysterious, and the crooked paths look straighter as we approach the end."
>
> Jean Paul Richter [5]

JEHOVAH ELOHIM—THE ETERNAL UNCHANGING ONE

Malachi 3:6

LESSON 25

THE BELIEVER—CROWN OF GLORY, ROYAL DIADEM

Isaiah 62:3 (NKJV)

"You shall also be a crown of glory in the hand of the LORD, and a royal diadem in the hand of your God."

THE HALL OF CROWNS

These are my last words to you, my fellow Believer. They are meant to impart courage and confidence and to embolden, hearten, and inspire you to continue in the right direction on your God-chosen pathway. Your path and mine may never cross again but rest assured we will meet on that Day.

The Pilgrim Way

But once I pass this way,
And then—no more.
But once—and then the Silent Door
Swings on its hinges,—
Opens. . .closes,—
And no more
I pass this way.
So while I may,
With all my might,
I will essay [attempt]
Sweet comfort and delight,
To all I meet upon the Pilgrim Way.
For no man travels twice
The Great Highway,
That climbs through Darkness up to
Light,—
Through Night
To Day. [1]

"Believe you have been sent from God as an arrow pulled from His own bow."

You have been purposefully shot like an arrow from God into this particular moment in time. You are living in the most unique of all moments in history—the end times—the last chapter of this Present Age. I trust the study of the prophetic events of your life that you are and will be living has revealed just how special you are to God and His eternal purposes. May your life be marked by an intentional endeavor to live fully for King Jesus. Enjoy this final lesson.

GOD'S TROPHY

I do not believe that we will ever fathom the depths of love and esteem that God has for His children. Isaiah 62:3-4 are God's words to the inhabitants of the New Jerusalem, the heavenly city of God, to His holy people the redeemed from all nations. Oh, how God delights in His people!

Isaiah 62:3-4 (NKJV)

> [3] *"You shall also be a crown of glory in the hand of the Lord, and a royal diadem in the hand of your God. . .[4] For the Lord delights in you."*

This is your description in your final and glorified state.

- God sees you as a "*crown of glory*" held in the palm of His hand. To God you represent a crown of honor, authority, and victory.
- God sees you as "*a royal diadem*" in His hand. To God you represent a king or queen, a majestic ruler.

God extends His hand and looks down upon you as a most valuable trophy of splendor and beauty—a crown, a diadem.

Because you are *in Christ* you will be exalted with Him. You will wear a crown of victory for all eternity. You are God's esteemed trophy.

THE EXALTATION OF KING JESUS

The Exaltation of Jesus on The Cross

Jesus' words recorded in John 8:28.

> *"When you have lifted up the Son of Man on the cross, then you will understand that I AM he."*

Jesus used the Greek word *hupsoo* which translates into English as "lifted up." *Hupsoo* means "to elevate" or "to exalt." In other words, Jesus was saying that men would attempt to destroy Him by nailing Him to a cross, but in the action of "lifting Him up," they would actually be exalting Him before all mankind—the exalted Savior. The thief hanging on a cross recognized Jesus as King of the kingdom of heaven. (Luke 23:42) The Roman centurion standing right in front of Jesus when He died exclaimed, "Truly this man was the Son of God!" (Mark 15:39) Millions since that time have looked to the Glory on the cross and by faith have confessed that "*Jesus is the Christ, the Son of the living God.*"

You lift up (exalt) Christ each time you speak of His work of salvation on the cross. You also exalt Jesus by your victorious life of holiness. By these actions you exalt Jesus in the eyes of the world. Now that's something to think about.

The Exaltation of Jesus at His Resurrection and Ascension

Seven steps in Jesus' Humiliation. Seven steps in Jesus' Exaltation.
Philippians 2:6-11

God	*1. "Though He* [Jesus] *was God,*
	2. he did not think of equality with God as something to cling to.
	3. Instead, he gave up his divine privileges,
God-Slave	*4. he took the humble position of a slave*
God-Man	*5. and was born as a human being. When he appeared in human form,*
	6. he humbled himself in obedience to God and
God-Savior	*7. died a criminal's death on a cross.*
	6. ***Therefore****, God elevated [huperypsoo] him*
God-Highly	*5. to the place of highest honor and*
Exalted	*4. gave him the name above all other names,*
	3. that at the name of Jesus every knee should bow, in heaven and on earth and under the earth,
	2. and every tongue confess that Jesus Christ is Lord,
	1. to the glory of God the Father."

Because of His life and death, God the Father *super-exalted* His beloved Son Jesus above all others to the very highest position. The Greek word *huperypsoo* in this case is "an intensified form" [M] of *hupsoo* meaning—"highly exalted!" Jesus sits highly exalted at the right hand of God. (Acts 2:33)

Revelation 19:12 "On his head are many diadems."

THE EXALTATION OF THE BELIEVER

The Exaltation of the Believer at His Resurrection and Ascension
1 Peter 5:6 (KJV)

> *"Humble yourselves therefore under the mighty hand of God, that he may exalt* [hupsoo] *you in due time."*

Humble yourself, as did Jesus your example, under God's sovereign power and authority as it personally applies to your life, and at the set time, "*due time*", you will be exalted. . . glorified. The Believer's exaltation or glorification begins with his resurrection from the dead and his ascension into heaven at the time of the "gathering together to Him," at the Rapture.

2 Thessalonians 2:1 (NKJV) "Now, brethren, concerning the coming of the Lord Jesus Christ and our gathering together to Him…"

The Greek word for *together* is *episunagoge* which means "a complete collection" [S] and in this case of *gathering together* it means "an assembling together at one place." [KW] This word conveys to us that at the time of the Rapture all glorified Believers will rise from every point of the compass and rally around King Jesus as He waits in the clouds in the air. This is the exaltation of the Believer. All God's children will be exalted together. You are a part of that glorious multitude!

All Believers will be "lifted up" (exalted) to heaven in a procession visible to all earth people.

The Exaltation of The Believer. . .Its Wondrous Meaning
Romans 8:30 (NASB)

> "*. . .and whom He* predestined [chose], *these He also* called; *and whom He called, these He also* justified; *and whom He justified, these He also* glorified."

Omniscient God knew all those He would choose. You were chosen, and you responded to His call. Consequently, God justified you by pardoning your sins and declaring you righteous, as if you had never sinned. Your justification is made possible through the work of Christ Jesus on the cross. God has also glorified you. Remember, God lives in timeless eternity, therefore, the act of your glorification is already assured.

"In the mind of God every believer shares complete identity with Christ from the cross to the throne. According to the Word, we are crucified with Him, buried with Him, raised with Him, exalted with Him, and enthroned with Him (Romans 6 and Ephesians 2)." [2]

Romans 3:23 Sinners "come short of or lack the glory of God, it means that they are not what God intended them to be. They lack His image and character." [KW]

The Greek word "to glorify" in this verse is *doxazo* and means to "give anyone esteem or honor by putting him into an honorable position. It means:

- to recognize, honor, praise
- to bring to honor, (to give importance)
- to make glorious, to glorify" [KW]

Think about it. Glorification is God's intention for each individual Believer. J.I. Packer sees glorification as a process beginning with our new birth.

> "Glorification (so called because it is a manifesting of God in our lives, 2 Corinthians 3:18) is the scriptural name for God's completion of what he began when he regenerated us, namely, our moral and spiritual reconstruction so as to be perfectly and permanently conformed to Christ. Glorification is a work of transforming power whereby God finally turns us into sinless creatures in deathless bodies." [3]

"His [Jesus] glory is ultimate; our glory is lesser and derived but is nevertheless glory."—"From Heavens View" [4]

The Exaltation of The Believer. . .His Rewards
We are going to exercise our God-given creative imagination to visualize the process of God's rewarding of His children. The reality will definitely far exceed the maximum stretching of our imagination.

The purpose of this type of pondering is to help make the exaltation of the Believer real to us. I want you to look at this great event as a student would look at the coming date of his graduation which is an event that will take place on a certain date at a specific time, and he will definitely be there to receive the honor due him!

You will receive your life rewards at the Judgment Seat of Christ. King Jesus will reveal to you, at that time, the status that He has chosen for you in His forever Kingdom.

Our creative imagination is now activated.

The reward process is remarkable. Accompanied by special angels, each individual is exalted and rewarded as he is led through multiple halls in the vastness of heaven. Each Hall has its own name that expresses the manifold facets of God's rewards. The multitude rejoices as much in seeing their companions receive the rewards due them as they do in receiving their own just reward. I will name just a few of the great Halls and then we will focus on the climactic Hall of Crowns. Remember, the Halls are imaginative thinking, the rewards are not.

- Hall of the Cup of Water: Rewards for all the compassionate deeds done for others. (Mark 9:41)
- Hall of the Blessed: Rewards for those who joyfully put God's Kingdom first in their lives. (Matthew 5:3-12)
- Hall of the Overcomer: Rewards for overcomers, those who overcame all adversity. (Revelation 2 and 3)
- Hall of the Book of Remembrance: A memorial of those who rightly fear God and honor His name, and in God's name they commune together around His Word to encourage and strengthen one another. (Malachi 3:16)
- Hall of the Secret Deeds: Rewards for secret acts of mercy, "closet" prayer, and fasting. (Matthew 6:4, 6)
- Hall of the Lover and Protector of God's Children: Rewards for those who provide for the needs of God's children, especially His ministers. (Matthew 10:40-42)
- Hall of the Enemy-Lover: Rewards for acts of benevolence toward their enemies. (Luke 6:27-36)
- Hall of Commandment-Keepers: Rewards for all who obey God's commandments. (Psalm 19:11)

THE HALL OF CROWNS

"Well done, my good and faithful servant," spoken by King Jesus as He places your crown upon your brow will be the most outstanding moment of all. Uncontainable joy! Like a broad-shouldered convert at the rescue mission said: 'I'm the happiest man in the room tonight. I couldn't be any happier unless I were larger." [5] You will definitely be the happiest person in the Hall of Crowns!

John 15:11 "I have told you these things so that you will be filled with my joy. Yes, your joy will overflow!"

The crown you will receive in this awesome Hall of Crowns will be a *stephanos*, a victor's crown—the highest honor bestowed on a Believer. Scores of God's faithful ones will receive more than one crown; some will receive them all.

What do we know about these crowns?

- They must be earned.
- They are of great value to the receiver.
- They have fathomless meaning to the Giver.
- They are awarded for specific achievement.
- The requirements to receive a crown are stipulated by the King.
- They reflect the priorities of God.

Some would question if these crowns will be literal. I believe King Jesus' *diadema*-crowns are literal and visible and our *stephanos*-crowns will be also. In the Eternal Age, we will live in a new creation where all things will have substance. The substance of our new existence may or may not be similar to what we experience in this Present Age, but it will be real nevertheless. For example, the clothing Jesus wore in His resurrection appearances was not of an earthly origin, nor was the clothing worn by angelic beings in their many appearances. With reference to the Five Victors Crowns, there is no biblical evidence, to my knowledge, that they are not of some tangible element. More than likely, the five crowns will differ in size, color, texture, and adornments. These crowns will distinguish the wearer throughout eternity.

An Exhortation

King Jesus earnestly admonishes the Believer today. "*I am coming soon. Hold on to what you have, so that no one will take away your crown.*" (Revelation 3:11)

> "The loss of a crown denotes the forfeiture of honor, splendor, and dignity. While a saint [Believer] cannot lose his soul, he can lose his reward. The crown that should have been his can remain without a wearer throughout eternity. What is it that robs a Christian of his crown—the lack of loyalty and steadfastness." [6]

Hebrews 10:35-39

> *"So do not throw away this confident trust in the Lord. Remember the great reward it brings you! Patient endurance is what you need now, so that you will continue to do God's will. Then you will receive all that he has promised.*
>
> *For in a little while, the Coming One will come and not delay. And my righteous ones will live by faith. But I will take no pleasure in anyone who turns away.*
>
> *But we are not like those who turn away from God to their own destruction. We are the faithful ones, whose souls will be saved."*

Death for the Unbeliever holds no ultimate prize to crown "success."

You finally arrive at the Hall of Crowns. You along with all your fellow Believers are adorned in regal robes of righteousness and stand in the majestic presence of King Jesus, high and lifted up. Awesome! Five golden tables are before Him. On each table contains a breathtakingly, beautiful crown. Which crown or crowns will King Jesus place upon your brow? Your name will be announced.

THE FIVE CROWNS

1. THE INCORRUPTIBLE CROWN (1 Corinthians 9:25-27)

For Victorious Living

You who have loved Jesus and a holy life will receive this crown. You put away all that would hinder a life that reflects the attributes of your Lord. You keep very short sin-accounts with God. "*Let* [my] *garments always be white*" is your watchword. (Ecclesiastes 9:8 NKJV) The love of the world cannot be found in you. The cross is ever before you, the world behind you. You live for eternity. Let me illustrate your life with the following story.

> "Some time ago, while turning the pages of a new book, I saw a heading that made me pause. "Face to Face With Christ," it read. My first impression was that it would be something about heaven and the bright life beyond these shadows. Instead, it was a singularly striking story out of the French Revolution.
>
> A lawless mob, so the story ran, had broken into the king's palace. Lusting wildly for loot and vengeance, they rushed down a long corridor and began stamping furiously into the room that stood at the end of it. Suddenly the looters grew quiet. The yelling and cursing ceased. More astonishing still, some of them knelt on the floor, while many more removed their hats. What had caused such a sudden hush to fall upon that howling mob? It was a painting of Jesus Christ which they had unexpectedly confronted, hanging there on the opposite wall of the room.
>
> Unfortunately the story does not end there. One of the leaders stepped forward, turned the picture of Christ toward the wall and shouted to the crowd to continue its plundering." [7]

You who stand in anticipation of receiving your crown from the King of kings do not live with the "picture turned toward the wall." You live in the presence of the Lord in the light (smile) of His countenance, and you walk in the Spirit as "*sons of light and sons of the day.*" (1 Thessalonians 5:5 NKJV)

O. Chambers "All God's people are ordinary people who have been made extraordinary by the purpose He has given them."

You quickly respond when your name is called. **King Jesus' smile follows you as you come forward and humbly kneel down before Him.** He holds your beautiful crown aloft and says, "This Incorruptible Crown will never tarnish. It is indestructible. It is eternal." He then places it on your brow, a perfect fit. Your eyes fill with tears as He speaks these glorious words to you, "You have lived a life *"worthy of the Lord, fully pleasing to Him. . .'"* (Colossians 1:10)

2. THE CROWN OF GLORY (1 Peter 5:1-4)

For Leaders in Ministry
Sacrifice of one kind or another walks every step of the way with you pastor, missionary, Bible teacher, evangelist, author, and Christian worker. For your very love of Jesus you joyfully take the Good News near and far, even to lands, cultures, and languages that are not your own. Like Peter, the reward of your love for Christ is the appointment as an under-shepherd to protect, guide, and feed your beloved flock great or small. (John 21:15-17) You faithfully uphold the Word of God; refusing to compromise or adapt its message to the pressures of ever changing values in society. You preach Jesus, not yourself. Your call and commission is dearer to you than life itself because it comes directly from God.

King Jesus holds His hand out to you, "Step forward faithful shepherd." The King places His hands on your shoulders. You see in His eyes that He knows every aspect of your life of

"The right way to live is to do the thing of the day on that day. This is all that God requires to be done. The affairs of one day at a time is as much as can be quietly committed to God in the daily exercise of faith. [8]

service to Him and to His people. He speaks, "Faithful shepherd, you readily responded to your high calling to teach My Word. You counted all worldly things as loss because of the surpassing worth of knowing Me and making Me known. Your greatness lies in your having looked beyond the burdensome task, the never-ending hours, the mountain heights of success and the valleys of failure, you saw the goal. Forgetting what lay behind, the bad and, yes, the good, you strained forward to what lay ahead. You pressed on, following the call summoning you to climb upward toward ultimate glory—to know Me, and to live in My presence forever. (Philippians 3:7-14) How well you have accomplished My will."

King Jesus reaches for a dazzling crown and says, "I place upon your head the Crown of Glory which will never lose its glow of glory." His eyes sparkle with joy and adds, "You will now share My glory with me forever and ever."

3. THE CROWN OF RIGHTEOUSNESS (2 Timothy 4:8)

For Faithful Service Carried Out in The Light of Jesus' Coming

You are the backbone, the bulwark of the church today, a dedicated Believer. You readily respond to and carry out any task God calls you to perform. Your life is dedicated to minister to the Body of Christ and to win lost souls to Jesus. You support the work of the church as a prayer warrior and financial supporter. You live with integrity and a burning love for Christ. You speak with knowledge of God's Word and not from your own opinions. You warn those who are slipping away from the truth or failing in holiness. You admonish Believers to take a stand against sin (to see it for what it really is.) You administer the Word of God to encourage the fainthearted who lack conviction. You lift up the discouraged and challenge them to press on. You are dismayed by those Believers who have *"left their first love." (Revelation 2:4)* You will not turn aside from the truth.

Jude 21 (NASB) "...keep yourselves in the love of God"

You have set your heart on the Coming of King Jesus. While others grow complacent and settle down in the world, you are spiritually awake and eagerly watch for His Coming in a confident, unwavering expectancy.

King Jesus turns directly toward you and says, "Great-Heart, you were one of My indispensable servants. Your eyes were so fixed on My coming glory that I could fully trust you to hold things together and keep My people walking in the faith. Many are here with us today because of your dependability and perseverance. You have been My right hand man/woman."

"I saw you those many times when you looked at a beautiful sunrise or sunset with a heart longing to see My Coming in the clouds of glory. You lifted your prayer to heaven, 'Maranatha! O Lord, come!' I whispered to you in the breeze, "Yes, I am coming soon!" The King adds, "Your wait is over. I have come."

"My beloved child, do you remember my words that were spoken to you: '*No eye has seen, no ear has heard, and no mind has imagined what God has prepared for those who love Him.'* (1 Corinthians 2:9) I will ultimately show you all these things, but I will begin with something that has been especially prepared for you—the Crown of Righteousness."

King Jesus slips on your head the priceless Crown of Righteousness. Amazing! The precious crown feels like it is a part of your head!

4. THE CROWN OF REJOICING (1 Thessalonians 2:19-20)

For the Soul-winner
You have a perfect sense of balance for the eternal: on the one hand souls in hell for all eternity and on the other hand souls in God's Kingdom for all eternity. You understand the work of the soul-winner, its limitations and what only God can do. Your sense of spiritual responsibility for those around you activates your intercessory prayer for their salvation. At God's promptings you give them God's message. Your mind-set is expressed so well in the words of Charles Spurgeon.

> "The saving of souls, if a man has once gained love to perishing sinners and his blessed Master, will be an all-absorbing passion to him. It will so carry him away, that he will almost forget himself in the saving of others. *If sinners will be damned, at least let them leap to hell over our bodies. And if they will perish, let them perish with our arms about their knees, imploring them to stay. If hell must be filled, at least let it be filled in the teeth of our exertions, and let no one go there unwarned and unprayed for.*" [9]

You understand perfectly why it is called the Crown of Rejoicing. What greater joy can there be than to bring a repentant soul to the foot of the cross; his eternal address has been assured forever!

Tenderly, King Jesus places your Crown of Rejoicing on your head and fills your heart with joy with these words, *"Those who are wise shall shine like the brightness of the firmament, and those who turn many to righteousness like the stars forever and ever.'* (Daniel 12:3 NKJV) You, my beloved, will shine like this crown—radiant in beauty—for all eternity."

5. THE CROWN OF LIFE (Revelation 2:10; James 1:12)

This crown will have significance according to the circumstance of the Believer.

For The Believer Who Is Faithful to Christ Until His Terminus—Death.
Through thick and thin you keep the faith. From the point of your new-birth until your last breath your life manifests an outstanding characteristic, faithfulness to Jesus.

For Those Who Persevere Under Trial
You suffer severe trials. . .a prolonged period of sickness, paralysis, you or an immediate loved one suffers a critical health condition, you undergo a life-changing turn of events, you suffer a very difficult living situation. You embrace Jesus' special promise to you: "*My grace is all you need. My power works best in weakness.*" (2 Corinthians 12:9) You believe it, you claim it, and you do not give up. You are made strong in faith and devotion to God through Jesus' Word and Presence. You stand faithful to Christ *no matter what*! Through eyes of faith you see the

glorious future. . . the crown. Your confidence in and your steadfast love for Jesus is your special witness of His grace to the world.

For Those Who Remain Faithful Even When Facing Death—The Martyrs
Misunderstood, afflicted, ridiculed, beaten, slandered, robbed of earthly goods, declared heretics, hardship, brunt of evil, pain, sickness, sorrow, grief. ". . .[you] *were tortured, refusing to turn from God in order to be set free.* [You] *placed* [your] *hope in a better life after the resurrection.* [You] *were jeered at, and* [your] *backs were cut open with whips.* [You] *were chained in prisons.* [You] *died by stoning,* [you] *were sawed in half, and* [you] *were killed with the sword.* [You] *went about wearing skins of sheep and goats, destitute and oppressed and mistreated.* [You] *were too good for this world, wandering over deserts and mountains, hiding in caves and holes in the ground."* (Hebrews 11:35-38) Burned at the stake, you ascended to heaven in chariots of fire.

You are God's faithful martyrs/witnesses who tenaciously hold on to God's promise: "*nothing can separate us from God's love. Neither death nor life, neither angels nor demons, neither our fears for today nor our worries about tomorrow—not even the powers of hell can separate us from God's love. No power in the sky above or in the earth below—indeed, nothing in all creation will ever be able to separate us from the love of God that is revealed in Christ Jesus our Lord."* (Romans 8:35-39)

King Jesus' eyes moisten. He beckons you forward. You approach His Majesty with utmost joy. He speaks, "Your suffering truly is nothing compared to the wondrous glory I am about to reveal to you." (Romans 8:18) The King steps towards you, reaches out, and enfolds you in His arms. Immediately, the vast multitude of the Redeemed, as a single body, drops to their knees, holy angels bow their heads. . . in tribute to you—faithful-until-death.

Prisms of light reflect from the Crown of Life as King Jesus rests it on your head. "I have cherished your loving devotion to Me as a living sacrifice. . .receive the crown of LIFE." Jesus enunciates each of His following words, "You will never, ever suffer or die again."

Joyfully He declares, "You endured for My sake, now you will reign with Me. (2 Timothy 2:12) Come with Me to My throne." With His arm around your shoulders you ascend to the Throne of God.

> "*That is why they stand in front of God's throne and serve him day and night in his temple. And he who sits on the throne will give them shelter. They will never again be hungry or thirsty; they will never be scorched by the heat of the sun. For the Lamb on the throne will be their Shepherd. He will lead them to springs of life-giving water.*
>
> *And God will wipe every tear from their eyes.*" (Revelation 7:15-17)

You are prepared and ready to reign forever with your God and King. Your beautiful, glorified body is clothed with righteousness, with fine linen, bright and pure. Your whole being radiates the glory shed upon you from your everlasting crown.

You are now what you were always meant to be.

Triumph crowns the brave and true. Can the Lord count on you?

THE BELIEVER—CROWN OF GLORY, ROYAL DIADEM

Isaiah 62:3 (NKJV)

APPENDIX A

A CHRONOLOGICAL ORDER OF THE BOOK OF REVELATION

DIVISION ONE
Chapters 1 through 6

1	2	3	4	5	6
Introduction Vision of Christ	Letters to the Seven Churches	Letters to the Seven Churches	The Heavenly Throne and Worship	The Lamb and the Book with Seven Seals	Six Seals (Rapture)

DIVISION TWO
Chapters 7 through 16

Chapters 7 and 14 are parallel (same topics) and should be read together. Chapters 8 and 15, and 9 and 16 are also parallel.

Chapter 10 is explanatory and reveals why the Trumpet/Bowl judgments are the same judgments. The Bowl Judgments are the repetition of the Trumpet Judgments. Observe where each judgment takes place, for example: earth, sea, rivers, etc. In chapter 10:11, God commands John to repeat the Trumpet Judgments as written in the little book.

7	8	9	10	11
144,000 Jews Sealed The Raptured White-Robed Multitude	Wrath of God 7th Seal Trumpet (1-4) Judgments	Wrath of God Trumpet (5-6) Judgments	The Angel and the Little Book (10:11)	Wrath of God Two Witnesses Trumpet 7 Announcement of 2nd Coming
14	**15**	**16**		
144,000 Jews Sealed The Rapture The Harvest	Wrath of God Intro. Bowl Jugdments	Wrath of God Bowl (1-7) Judgements		

I suggest you read the Scripture of Division Two in the following order:

7 with 14	144,000 Jews sealed, the Raptured and the Rapture Process
8:1 – 6 with 15:1 – 8	Introduction to Trumpet/Bowl Judgments
8:7 – 9:21 with 16:1 – 16	Trumpet/Bowl Judgments 1 through 6
11:1 – 14	Two Jewish Witnesses during Trumpet/Bowl Judgments
16:17 – 21 with 11:15 – 19	Seventh Trumpet/Bowl Judgment: Second Coming

Chapter 11:19 chronologically jumps to 19:11.

DIVISION THREE
Chapters 12, 13 and 17, 18

These chapters are parenthetical (explanatory) and give vital information about Satan, the Antichrist, the False Prophet, and Babylon/Rome. They should be read chronologically.

12	**13**	**17**	**18**
Satan the Enemy of God and God's people	System and Person of the Antichrist and the False Prophet	Harlot City System and Person of the Antichrist	Destruction of Babylon/Rome

DIVISION FOUR
Chapters 19 through 22

19	**20**	**21**	**22**
Marriage Supper Second Coming Armageddon	1,000 Year Reign of King Jesus Great White Throne Judgment	New Creation Eternal Age	New Creation Eternal Age

The Last Promise in the Bible 22:20. The Last Prayer in the Bible 22:20. The Last Benediction in the Bible 22:21. The Last Call to the Lost in the Bible 22:17.

APPENDIX B

DEFINITIONS OF THE EVENTS OF YOUR LIFE

EVENT 1: BIRTH

The beginning of your existence. Read Psalm 139:13-18.

EVENT 2: THE NEW BIRTH

To be born-again is to be born from above, from God, which means you experience a supernatural regeneration by God the Holy Spirit so that you are able to enter the Kingdom of God and adapt to its conditions. This takes place when you believe that Jesus took your sin upon Himself and died on the cross in your place, and thereby, repenting of your sin, you live for God's glory. Read John 1:12-13; 3:3

EVENT 3: THE WORLD SYSTEM OF THE ANTICHRIST

The end-time System which will govern the world. It is composed of the Antichrist, the supreme ruler, and Ten Rulers of Ten Regions of the world. This government is anti-God and extremely evil. It will be destroyed at King Jesus' Coming to establish His earthly kingdom. Read 2 Thessalonians 2:1-12; Daniel 2 and 7; Revelation 13 and 17)

The Great Tribulation

This is a prolonged period of God ordained, world-wide disasters that will occur during the World System of the Antichrist. The people of all nations of the world are affected. Faithful followers of Christ face added suffering due to great persecution during this time at the hand of the Antichrist because of his hatred of God and God's people. Read Matthew 24 and Revelation 6

EVENT 4: THE RAPTURE

When the last person has been born-again, whom God has chosen to be a part of His Kingdom, Jesus will appear in the clouds of the sky with all the dead in Christ. Jesus will then proceed to take His followers from earth to heaven. This will include both the living and the resurrected dead of all the ages. All Believers in immortal, glorified bodies will be with Jesus forever. Read 1 Thessalonians 4:13-18

The Salvation of Israel

The Salvation of Israel will take place when the Nation Israel will see Jesus and believe in Him as their Messiah/Savior at the time of the Rapture. This takes place 3 ½ years before the Second Coming of King Jesus. This is the Jews Event 3: The New Birth. Read Romans 11:25-27; Revelation 1:7; Matthew 24:30; Zechariah 12:10

EVENT 5: THE JUDGMENT SEAT OF CHRIST—BELIEVERS ONLY

This Event takes place in heaven after the Rapture. All Believers of all the ages will stand individually before King Jesus to give an account of themselves for all the things they have done in this life both good and bad. King Jesus will evaluate their life and give them their due rewards, or loss of rewards, according to how they fulfilled God's will for them. The Believer's status throughout the Eternal Age will be known at that time. Read 2 Corinthians 5:10 and Romans 14:10-12.

EVENT 6: THE MARRIAGE SUPPER OF THE LAMB—BELIEVERS ONLY

This is the perfect, final, and complete union of Christ with all His followers of all ages. It is a unifying starting point, like a new and perfect beginning into an eternity of glorious relationships in a God-directed forever existence. This Event will take place in heaven after the Judgment Seat of Christ. Read Revelation 19:5-9.

The Wrath of God

For the world. . .This is a series of seven catastrophic judgments known as the Trumpet/Bowl Judgments. This merited wrath will affect the entire world. This terrifying judgment from God will begin immediately after the Rapture and will last for a period of 3 ½ years until the Second Coming of King Jesus. Unbeliever, this is your Event 3. Read Revelation 8-9; 15-16; 11:15-19.

For Israel. . .The Jewish nation will receive Christ as their Savior at the Rapture but will not be translated to heaven. They will endure 3 ½ years of unparalleled persecution because of their refusal to worship the Antichrist. These faithful Christian Jews will be God's only witness in a dark and threatening world. Their deliverance comes when Christ appears at His Second Coming and Armageddon. This, my beloved Jewish brother, is your Event 4. Read Matthew 24:15-22; Zechariah 13:8-14:2; Revelation 7:1-8; 11

EVENT 7: THE SECOND COMING OF CHRIST

At the Second Coming, King Jesus will return from heaven to earth with His angels and all glorified Believers in a breathtakingly magnificent moment. King Jesus will stand supreme on the Mount of Olives in Israel and proceed to the temple of the Jews in Jerusalem where He will set up His Thousand-Year Reign. The Second Coming of Jesus will conclude the Wrath of God judgment. Armageddon takes place at this time.

Armageddon

Armageddon is the place in Israel where the evil hosts of Satan, the Antichrist, the False Prophet, and the Ten Kings and their armies will engage in battle with King Jesus at His Second Coming with His angels and glorified Believers. This Event is also called "*the great day of God Almighty*." The Antichrist, the False Prophet and all their followers will be consumed and destroyed with the breath of the Lord Jesus' mouth and the splendor of His Coming. Furthermore, Satan and his demons will be confined to the abyss for a thousand years. Unbeliever, this is your Event 4. Read Revelation 16:14, 16; 19:11-20:3; Zechariah 14:3-15; 2 Thessalonians 2:8

EVENT 8: KING JESUS' THOUSAND-YEAR REIGN ON THE EARTH

Jesus will return to earth as King of kings (the Second Coming) to reign over the surviving nations of the Wrath of God. King Jesus will reign in righteousness and peace from His earthly throne located in Jerusalem for a period of one thousand years. His rule will be a theocracy which means that God Himself, through His Son Jesus, is the Supreme Ruler. Believers will reign with King Jesus by carrying out His divine will.

King Jesus will govern directly in all human affairs. His will and laws will be absolute. The people living at this time will be:

- all of God's glorified people
- the unbelieving earth-people who were not present at the Battle of Armageddon.

At the beginning of Christ's reign, Satan and his demons will be imprisoned in the abyss, but will be released at the end of the thousand years. The vast number of offspring of the earth-people who will be born during the thousand years will follow Satan in the last rebellion against God which will quickly terminate in victory for Christ. Satan and his demons will be cast into the lake of fire where they will remain forever. Read Zechariah 14:9; Daniel 7:27; Revelation 20:7-10

THE GREAT WHITE THRONE JUDGMENT—UNBELIEVERS ONLY

God's final judgment takes place at the conclusion of Christ's Thousand-Year Reign—the end of Earth's history. Believers will be in attendance sitting on thrones.

All unbelieving dead from every age, nation, and language will be resurrected and will stand in their resurrected bodies before their Creator, Savior, and Judge. Each individual will be judged guilty based on the absence of his name written in the Lamb's (Jesus') Book of Life in which all the names of born-again, blood-bought Believers are recorded. Every Unbeliever will also receive retribution according to what he has done (thoughts and actions), and consequently, will be irrevocably committed to the lake of fire. . . forever. Unbeliever's Event 6. Read John 5:29; Revelation 20:11-15; 1 Corinthians 6:2-3

Those who are exempt from this judgment are those who have been chosen by God's grace through their faith in Jesus Christ as their personal Savior. Also, God's special application of Christ's redemptive work to infants who are beneath the age of discernment, and particular mentally impaired individuals who are unable to sin by choice. Read 2 Samuel 12:22-23 (infants); Isaiah 7:15-16 (small children); Deuteronomy 1:39 (small children); Jonah 4:11 (those who are unable to make moral choices.)

The Lake of Fire—The Second Death

The Lake of Fire—the Second Death, will be the place of conscious, never ending, punishment of extreme misery for all men born into sin. The second death means that the individual died physically and will be resurrected at the time of the Great White Throne Judgment. After his judgment, he will remain in a permanent state of *dying* as a sinner. Unbeliever's final Event 7. Read Matthew 25:41; Revelation 20:15

EVENT 9: NEW HEAVENS, NEW EARTH, NEW JERUSALEM

Your forever-home will be eternally glorious where literally everything will be new.

- You will be placed in a new environment of absolute beauty, a perfect, sinless environment—New Heavens and a New Earth. The old earth and heavens will be destroyed. Read 2 Peter 3:10-13; Isaiah 65:17

- You will enjoy new human relationships. Friendship, brotherhood, companionship, bonding, and oneness will take on a new depth of meaning. This will be a new social arrangement. Each glorified Believer will communicate kindness and goodness to His fellow brother. Nothing done in the Eternal Age will be outside the perimeters of love because God's love will be the very atmosphere that they will breathe and exhale. Read Revelation 21:4

- You will be you; however, you will be a new you. In every way, physically, emotionally, mentally, and spiritually, you will be perfect and liberated from all the bonds that kept your life from wholeness of joy, holiness, and usefulness. Read 1 John 3:2

- The New Jerusalem is a city, the present home of the souls and spirits of all the deceased redeemed, the holy angels, and most importantly, God. It is God's heaven. After Christ's Thousand-Year Reign on the earth, all the people of God in their glorified state will populate God's heaven. This heavenly city will descend to the new earth *"and the throne of God and of the Lamb shall be in it,"* and they will reign over God's eternal Kingdom. God's people will live both in the city, New Jerusalem, and in the new earth provided exclusively for them. Read Revelation 21 and 22

- A new relationship with God will consist of a flawless, face to face relationship with God the Father, God the Son, and God the Holy Spirit, which will bring unending delight to both the Godhead and you, His child. All other profound wonders of the Eternal Age pale in the light of this reality. Read Revelation 21 and 22; 1 Corinthians 2:9-10

END NOTES

Key to Hebrew and Greek words from Lexicons and Dictionaries. English words from Dictionary.

(D) William Morris, Editor, *The American Heritage Dictionary of the English Language*, American Heritage Publishing Co. Inc. and Houghton Mifflin Company, Boston/ New York/ Atlanta/ Geneva, Illinois/ Dallas/ Palo Alto, Copyright © 1969, 1970, 1971, 1973 by American Heritage Publishing Co., Inc.

(KW) Spiros Zodhiates, Th.D., Executive Editor, *Hebrew-Greek Key Word Study Bible*, AMG Publishers, Chattanooga, TN 37422, U.S.A., Copyright © 1984 and 1990 by AMG International, Inc.

(M) taken from *Mounce's Complete Expository Dictionary of Old & New Testament Words*, by William D. Mounce, General Editor, Copyright © 2006 by William D. Mounce. Used by permission of Zondervan. www.zondervan.com.

(S) James Strong, S.T.D., LL.D, *Strong's Exhaustive Concordance of the Bible with brief Dictionaries of the Hebrew and Greek Words of the Original with References to the English Words,* The Old-Time Gospel Hour, Lynchburg, Virginia, Dr. Jerry Falwell, Director.

(V) W.E. Vine, M.A. *An Expository Dictionary of New Testament Words* (Fleming H. Revell Company, Old Tappan, New Jersey,) 1966, no copy right.

INTRODUCTION

1. David J. Hesselgrave and Ronald P. Hesselgrave, *What in the World Has Gotten into the Church? Studies in the Book of Jude for Contemporary Christians* (Moody Press, Chicago, 1981) p. 14.

2. Charles Bridges, *Proverbs*. Copyright © 2001 by Watermark. Crossway Books, Wheaton, Illinois, Nottingham, England. p. 121.

LESSON 1

1. *Tell Me a Story: The Life-Shaping Power of Our Stories*, by Daniel Taylor, 2001 Bog Walk Press, 1605 Lake Johanna Blvd, St Paul, MN 55112 ISBN: 978-0970651105.

2. Dr. Ken Curtis, President of Gateway Films/Vision Video and Christian History Institute, *History of Christianity.*

3. Richard Paul Evans, *The Locket* (Simon and Schuster, 1998) preface page.

4. Kyle M. Yates Ph.D., D.D., LL.D., Litt.D. *Preaching From The Psalms* (Broadman Press, Nashville, Tennessee, 1948) p. 47. Copyright 1948 by Kyle M. Yates. Reprinted and used by permission.

5. Paul J. Achtemeier, General Editor *Harper's Bible Dictionary* (Harper & Row, Publishers, San Francisco, 1985) p. 8.

6. F.C. Jennings, *Studies in Isaiah* (Loizeaux Brothers, Neptune, New York) p. 180, 181. Used by permission of Wipf and Stock Publishers. www.wipfandstock.com.

LESSON 2

1. Steve Gallagher, *Intoxicated with Babylon*, Pure Life Ministries, 14 School St., Dry Ridge, KY 41035, Copyright © 1996 as *The Spirit of Antichrist* & 2001 as *Break Free from the Lusts of this World* by Steve Gallagher. p. 13 www.purelifeministries.org.

2. Lewis Sperry Chafer as quoted by Merrill F. Unger, *Unger's Bible Dictionary* (Moody Press, Chicago, 1966) p.195, 196.

3. Charles G. Finney, *Principles of Liberty* (Bethany House Publishers, Minneapolis, Minnesota 55438, 1983) p. 35.

LESSON 3A

1. *The World Book Encyclopedia, G vol. 8* (World Book-Childcraft International, Inc., A subsidiary of The Scott & Fetzer Company, Chicago, London, Sydney, Tokyo, Toronto, 1982) p. 346.

2. Gary H. Kah, *En Route to Global Occupation* (Huntington House Publishers, 1992) p. 42 www.garykah.org.

LESSON 3B

1. Leon Morris, *1 & 2 Thessalonians* (William B. Eerdmans Publishing Company, Grand Rapids, Michigan / Cambridge, U.K., 1984) p. 133 www.eerdmans.com.

2. Ibid., p.128.

3. Used by permission. *1&2 Thessalonians & Titus* by John MacArthur. p.71 Copyright © 2007 by John MacArthur (Thomas Nelson. Nashville, Tennessee) All rights reserved.

4. taken from *Battle For The Bible* by Harold Lindsell. pp. 25, 143. Copyright © 1976 by The Zondervan Corporation, Grand Rapids, Michigan. Used by permission of Zondervan. www.zondervan.com.

5. Used by permission. *The Believer's Study Bible* Editor, W.A. Criswell, Ph.D. p. 1887. Copyright © 1991 by the Criswell Center for Biblical Studies. Thomas Nelson. Nashville, Tennessee. All rights reserved.

6. taken from *The Expositor's Bible Commentary—Abridged Edition: New Testament, by* Kenneth L. Barker and John R. Kohlenberger III. p.1056. Copyright © 1994 by the Zondervan Corporation. Used by permission of Zondervan. www.zondervan.com.

7. Albert Barnes, *Notes on the New Testament* (Baker Book House, Grand Rapids, Michigan, Seventeenth Printing, August 1981) p. 80.

8. quoted in Lesson 1, Paul J. Achtemeier, General Editor *Harper's Bible Dictionary* (Harper & Row, Publishers, San Francisco, 1985) p. 8.

9. Bridges p. 109.

10. Taken from *Dawn's Light* by Terri Blackstock p. 9 Copyright © 2008 by Terri Blackstock Used by permission of Zondervan. www.zondervan.com.

11. Taken from *The Equipping Church Guidebook* by Sue Mallory & Brad Smith. p.36. Copyright © 2001 by Leadership Network, Inc. Used by permission of Zondervan.
www.zondervan.com.

12. © 1988 Warren W. Wiersbe. *Be Alert* is published by David C Cook. All rights reserved. p. 80.

LESSON 4A

1. Taken from *The Patmos Letters* p. 10 © Copyright 1969 by Fredk. A. Tatford, LITT. D. Published by Kregel Publications, Grand Rapids, MI. Used by permission of the publisher. All rights reserved.

2. Taken from *Life Application Bible Commentary: Revelation* by Bruce B. Barton, D.Min., Linda Chaffee Taylor, Neil Wilson, M.R.E., David R. Veerman, M.Div. p.60 Copyright © 2000 by The Livingston Corporation. Used by permission of Tyndale House Publishers, Inc. All rights reserved.

3. Taken from *Biblical Hermeneutics* by Milton S. Terry. p.186. All rights reserved. Used by permission of Zondervan. www.zondervan.com.

4. Lynn Hunt, Thomas R. Martin, Barbara H. Rosenwein, R. Po-Chia Hsia, and Bonnie G. Smith, *The Making of the West, People and Cultures, A Concise History, Volume II Since 1340* (Bedford/St. Martin's, Boston-New York, (2003) p. 866, 947.

5. This information is from: answers.yahoo.com.

6. William Barclay, *The Revelation of John Volume 2 (Chapters 6 to 22),* The Westminster Press, Philadelphia, 1976, p. 6 Used by permission of St. Andrew's Press, an imprint of Hymns Ancient & Modern Ltd.

7. (Internet) *2012 World Hunger and Poverty Facts and Statistics* (www.worldhunger.org).

LESSON 4B

1. Amy Carmichael, *Thou Givest. . .They Gather* (Christian Literature Crusade, 1958) p. 32.

2. Charles R. Erdman, *The General Epistles* (The Westminster Press, Philadelphia, 1919) p.81.

3. Milner quoted by Tryon Edwards, D.D., *The New Dictionary of Thoughts* (Standard Book Company, 1957) p.476.

4. Roger T. Forster and V. Paul Marston *God's Strategy in Human History* (Tyndale House Publishers, Inc., Wheaton, Illinois, 1973) p. 12.

5. Hesselgrave. pp. 85-86.

6. Taken from *The Expositor's Bible Commentary—Abridged Edition: New Testament, by* Kenneth L. Barker and John R. Kohlenberger III. p.110. Copyright © 1994 by the Zondervan Corporation, Used by permission of Zondervan. www.zondervan.com.

7. Taken from *Hearts of Iron Feet of Clay,* © 1979, 2005 by Gary Inrig. Used by permission of (Discovery House Publishers, Grand Rapids, MI 49501) All rights reserved. p.12, 13.

8. John MacArthur, Jr., *The MacArthur New Testament Commentary Matthew 24-28* (Moody Press/Chicago, 1989, p. 27.

9. Internet, First Published in the Church of England Newspaper, June 17, 2011.

10. Internet, Masterbuilders Trust (Voice of the Martyrs), March 25, 2010.

11. Copyright - RayStedman.org - *Authentic Christianity*, Revelation 12:1-17; Used with Permission.

LESSON 5A

1. Andrew Murray, *The Holiest of All* (Fleming H. Revell Company, Old Tappan, New Jersey) p. 405.

2. McCandlish Phillips, *The Bible The Super-Natural And The Jews, Horizon Books* (Camp Hill, Pennsylvania 1970) pp.320-321.

3. translated from: *El Pueblo Judio una Historia Ilustrada* (Keter Books Jerusalem, 1973) p. 18.

4. adapted from *El Pueblo Judio una Historia Ilustrada*, Keter Books Jerusalem, 1973, pp.18, 19 and William L. Langer, *An Encyclopedia of World History*, Houghton Mifflin Company Boston, The Riverside Press Cambridge, 1940 and 1948, pp. 199, 232, 282, 392.

5. *Eerdman's Handbook of Christianity* (Wm. B. Eerdman's Publishing Co., 225 Jefferson S.E., Grand Rapids, Michigan 49502, USA, 1977) p. 255 www.eerdmans.com.

6. Ibid., p. 321 www.eerdmans.com.

7. Taken from *"The One Year Christian History"* by E. Michael and Sharon Rusten. p.430. Copyright © by E. Michael and Sharon O. Rusten. Used by permission of Tyndale House Publishers, Inc. All rights reserved.

8. translated from: *El Pueblo Judio una Historia Ilustrada*, (Keter Books Jerusalem, 1973) p. 19.

9. *Eerdman's Handbook of Christianity* (Wm. B. Eerdman's Publishing Co., 225 Jefferson S.E., Grand Rapids, Michigan 49502, USA, 1977) p. 575, 576 www.eerdmans.com.

10. please go to Wikipedia through the words "Yad Vashem" to find some of the names and nationalities. If you click on the name, you will be able to read their story. Their heroism is beyond words. Most of this information has come from Wikipedia.

11. Nicholas de Lange, *Atlas of the Jewish World* (An Equinox Book published in North America by Facts on File, Inc., 460 Park Avenue South, New York, N.Y. 10016, 1984) p.71 Copyright © by Equinox (Oxford) Ltd 1984.

LESSON 5B

1. William Peterson, *The Christian Reader—October-November,* 1973, p.12.

2. Adapted from Home Page: Hebraic Heritage Ministries International (Hebraic Heritage Ministries International, P.O. Box 81, Strasburg, Ohio 44680).

3. Ibid.

4. This information is from multiple sources across the years, two contribuors are Louis H. Hauff, "*Israel en la Historia y la Profecia*" (Editorial Vida, Miami, Florida 33138, 1971). Nicholas de Lange, "*Atlas of the Jewish World*" (Facts on File Publications, New York, p. 74. Ian J. Bickerton and Carla L. Klausner),. *"A Concise History of the Arab-Israeli Conflict,"* (Prentice Hall, Upper Saddle River, New Jersey 07458, 2002).

5. The information concerning the Ethiopian Jews can be found on the internet by using "The Virtual Jewish World, Ethiopia."

6. translated from Louis H. Hauff, *Israel en la Historia y la Profecia* (Editorial Vida, Miami, Florida 33138, 1971) p. 38.

7. Charles L. Allen, *God's Psychiatry* (Spire Books, Fleming H. Revell Company, Old Tappan, New Jersey, 1953) p. 16.

8. *LOOK* (magazine), April 30, 1968, p. 31.

9. Peterson. p.11.

10. adapted from: Louis H. Hauff, *Israel en la Historia y la Profecia* (Editorial Vida, Miami, Florida 33138, 1971) p. 52.

11. Ibid., p. 52.

12. Used by permission. "*Nelson's New Illustrated Bible Dictionary"* Ronald F. Youngblood *General Editor*. p.655. Copyright © 1995, 1986 by Thomas Nelson. Nashville, Tennessee. All rights reserved.

13. LOOK (magazine), 8-8-67', p. 68.

14. *Time* (magazine), June 16, 1967 p. 23.

15. Ibid., p. 24.

16. Taken from: *The Coming Last Days' Temple* by J. Randall Price, Copyright © 1999 by World of the Bible Ministries, Published by (Harvest House Publishers, Eugene, Oregon 97402) p. 590 www.harvesthousepublishers.com Used by Permission.

LESSON 6A

1. Taken from "*Explore The Book*" by J. Sidlow Baxter. p.85. Copyright © by J. Sidlow Baxter. Used by permission of Zondervan. www.zondervan.com.

LESSON 6B

1. Taken from *The Expositor's Bible Commentary—Abridged Edition: Old Testament,* by Kenneth L. Barker and John R. Kohlenberger III. p.1515. Copyright © 1994 by the Zondervan Corporation. Used by permission of Zondervan. www.zondervan.com.

2. Ibid., p. 1515.

3. "The "so" (v.26) is apparently intended to correlate with "until" (v.25), thereby acquiring temporal force, such as "when that has happened." taken from *The Expositor's Bible Commentary—Abridged Edition: New Testament,* by Kenneth L. Barker and John R. Kohlenberger III. p.581. Copyright © 1994 by the Zondervan Corporation. Used by permission of Zondervan. www.zondervan.com.

4. F.F. Bruce, *Tyndale New Testament Commentaries Volume 6: Romans* (Inter-Varsity Press, USA, Inter-Varsity Press, England, 1985) p. 212.

5. (10a) Used by permission. *Vine's Topical Commentary Prophecy* by W.E. Vine with C.F. Hogg. p.110. Copyright © 2010 by W.E. Vine Copyright Ltd. Of Bath, England. Thomas Nelson. Nashville, Tennessee. All rights reserved.

LESSON 7A

1. Alexander Patterson *The Greater Life and Work of Christ* (Moody Press, Chicago) pp.201-202.

2. Taken from Concise Theology, a Guide to Historic Christian Beliefs by J.I. Packer. p. 127. Copyright © 1993 by Foundation for Reformation. Used by permission of Tyndale House Publishers, Inc. All rights reserved.

3. Taken from *The Expositor's Bible Commentary—Abridged Edition: New Testament* by Kenneth L. Barker and John R. Kohlenberger III. p.562. Copyright © 1994 by the Zondervan Corporation, Used by permission of Zondervan. www.zondervan.com.

4. Leon Morris, *The First Epistle to the Corinthians* (Wm. B. Eerdmans Publishing Company, Grand Rapids, Michigan, 1980) p. 233 © The Tyndale Press.

5. William Barclay, *The Gospel of John, Volume 2* (The Westminister Press, Philadelphia) p. 110 Used by permission of St Andrew's Press, an imprint of Hymns Ancient & Modern Ltd.

6. a study of the word *aman* (Hebrew) and *pisteuo, pistis, pistos* (Greek) from many sources.

7. Used by permission. *The Feasts of the Lord* by Kevin Howard and Marvin Rosenthal, 1997, (Thomas Nelson. Nashville, Tennessee) All rights reserved. p.15. ISBN 10:0-7852-7518-5 ISBN 13:978-0- 7852-7518-3.

8. Victor Buksbazen, *The Gospel in the Feasts of Israel* (The Friends of Israel Missionary and Relief Society, Inc., 1954) p. 24.

LESSON 7B

1. Harriet Beecher Stowe quoted by Tryon Edwards, D.D., *The New Dictionary of Thoughts*, (Standard Book Company, 1959) p. 396.

2. adapted and translated from Francisco Ordonez, *Historia del Cristianismo Evangelico en Colombia* (Tipografia Union, Medellin, Colombia) pp. 251-253.

LESSON 8A

1. Robert Ervin Hough, *The Christian After Death* (Moody Press, Chicago, 1947) p. 87.

2. William Barclay, *The New Daily Study Bible, The Revelation of John Vol. 2* (Westminster John Knox Press, Louisville, Kentucky, 2004) p. 228 Used by permission of St Andrew's Press, an imprint of Hymns Ancient & Modern Ltd.

3. Bruce Milne, *Know The Truth, A Handbook of Christian Belief* (InterVarsity Press, Downers Grove, Illinois 60515, 1982) p. 269.

4. Taken from *All the Divine Names and Titles in the Bible* by Herbert Lockyer. p.180. Copyright © 1975 by Herbert Lockyer. Used by permission of Zondervan. www.zondervan.com.

5. Randy Alcorn, *Deadline* (Multnomah Books, Sister, Oregon, 1994) p. 55 (Eternal Perspective Ministries www.epm.org).

6. Taken from *Respectable Sins* by Jerry Bridges. p. 54 Copyright © 2007. Used by permission of Tyndale House Publishers, Inc. All rights reserved.

7. (8a) Compiled and edited by Louis Gifford Parkhurst, Jr. *Principles of Liberty* (Bethany House Publishers, Minneapolis, Minnesota 55348, 1983) p.23.

8. Alcorn. p. 218-219.

9. Ibid., p. 219.

10. Copyright - Ray Stedman.org - *Authentic Christianity*, Ephesians 2:7-10; Used with permission.

11. The source of the story of Nahum Diaz is from my own memories and translated or adapted from the following: Roberto M. Searing D. and Gloria Alexandra Osuna A., *Pasando La Antorcha*, Impreso por (Editorial Buena Semilla, Carrera 31 No. 64ª – 34, Santafe de Bogota, Colombia, 1999 pp. 359, 379-383, 396. Francisco Ordonez, *Historia del Cristianismo Evangelico en Colombia*, p. 198. Jen Rohde, *The Secret of Nahum Diaz*, alife, Alliance Life, magazine of the Christian and Missionary Alliance, P O Box 35000, Colorado Springs, Colorado 80935-3500.

LESSON 8B

1. D. Edmond Hiebert, *Second Timothy* (Moody Press, Chicago, 1958) p. 75.

2. *How to Know God's Will* by Charles W. Shepson (Horizon House Publishers, Beaverlodge, Alberta, Canada, 1981) p. 104.

3. Ibid., p. 107.

4. Ibid., p. 107.

5. 4. Ron Hutchcraft, *Called to Greatness* (Moody Publishers, Chicago, 2004) p. 43.

6. John Phillips, *Exploring Romans* (Moody Monthly, Chicago, 1969) p. 101.

7. F.B. Meyer, *The Christ-Life for the Self-Life* (Moody Press, Chicago) p. 39.

8. Ibid., p. 39.

9. Taken from "*Romans, An Exposition of Chapter 6 The New Man*" by D.M. Lloyd-Jones. p.56. Copyright © 1972 by D.M. Lloyd-Jones. Used by permission of Zondervan. www.zondervan.com.

10. Meyer. p. 40.

11. Copyright - Ray Stedman.org - *Authentic Christianity*, Ephesians 2:7-10; Used with permission.

12. taken from *The Expositor's Bible Commentary—Abridged Edition: New Testament, by* Kenneth L. Barker and John R. Kohlenberger III. p.1195. Copyright © 1994 by the Zondervan Corporation. Used by permission of Zondervan. www.zondervan.com.

LESSON 9A

1. Edwards. p. 266.

2. Paul E. Billheimer, *Destined For The Throne* (Christian Literature Crusade, Fort Washington, Pennsylvania 19034, 1975) pp. 25-26 and #7 p.30.

3. Norman B. Harrison, *New Testament Living, The Inwardness of the Christian Life* (The Harrison Service, Inc., 3112 Hennepin Ave., Minneapolis 8, Minnesota, 1953) pp. 42-45

4. Editors: John F. Walvoord and Roy B. Zuck, *The Bible Knowledge Commentary, Old Testament* (David C Cook, 1983) p.1371.

5. William Barclay, *The Letters to the Galatians and Ephesians, Revised Edition* (The Westminster Press, Philadelphia, 1976) p. 116 Used by permission of St Andrew's Press, an imprint of Hymns Ancient & Modern Ltd.

6. Stanton W. Richardson, M.A., *Studies in Biblical Theology*, St. Paul Bible Institute St. Paul Minnesota, 1953, p. 109.

LESSON 9B

1. Bridges. p. 109.

2. William Barclay, *The Letters to the Galatians and Ephesians, Revised Edition* (The Westminster Press, Philadelphia, 1976) p. 116 Used by permission of St Andrew's Press, an imprint of Hymns Ancient & Modern Ltd.

3. A.W. Tozer, *The Tozer Pulpit, Volume One* (Christian Publications, 3825 Hartzdale Drive, Camp Hill, PA 17011, 1994) p. 121.

4. Augustus Hopkins Strong, D.D., LL D., *Systematic Theology, A Compendium Designed For The Use Of Theological Students*, Valley Forge, PA. (The Judson Press, Chicago, Los Angeles, 1907) p.963.

5. A.W. Tozer, *The Tozer Pulpit, Volume Two, The Presence of Christ: Meaning of the Communion* (Christian Publications, 3825 Hartzdale Drive, Camp Hill, PA 17011, 1994) p. 120, 121.

6. Merrill C. Tenney, Henry Jacobsen, Editor, *Bible Knowledge, The Revelation* (Christian Publications, Third and Reily Streets, Harrisburg, Penna., 1959) p. 610.

LESSON 10

1. Gleason L. Archer Jr., Paul D. Feinberg, Douglas J. Moo, Richard Reiter, *Three Views on the Rapture Pre-, Mid-, or Post-Tribulation,* Zondervan, 1984, 1996, p.84. Used by permission of Zondervan. www.zondervan.com.

2. Taken from "*All the Parables of the Bible*" by Herbert Lockyer. Copyright © 1963 by Herbert Lockyer. Used by permission of Zondervan. www.zondervan.com.

3. G.H. Lang, *The Parabolic Teaching of the Scripture* (Wm. B. Eerdmans Publishing Company, Grand Rapids, Michigan, 1955) p. 263 www.eerdmans.com.

4. Dr. David Jeremiah, *Angels the Host of Heaven*, Turning Point, published by (Walk Thru the Bible Ministries, Atlanta, Georgia, 1995 by Turning Point for God) p. 84.

5. Leon Morris, *The Book of Revelation* (William B. Eerdmans Publishing Company, Grand Rapids, Michigan / Cambridge, U.K., 1987) p.108 www.eerdmans.com.

6. Packer. p. 69.

7. Daniel 12:11. The 1,290 days of Daniel 12:11 are calculated backwards from the end of the seven years. Thus, the invasion of Israel by the Antichrist takes place approximately a month and a half after the Rapture, or 3 years 5 months from the start of the Seven Years Covenant made between the Antichrist and Israel.

LESSON 11

1. Mrs. Paul Friederichsen, *God's Way Made Easy* (Moody Press, Chicago, 1970) p.82.

2. Taken from *Psalms: Folk Songs of Faith,* ©2006 by Ray Stedman. Used by permission of Discovery House Publishers, Grand Rapids, MI 4950l. All rights reserved. p. 221.

3. Used by permission. "*The Believer's Study Bible*" Editor, W.A. Criswell, Ph.D. Copyright © 1991 by the Criswell Center for Biblical Studies. Thomas Nelson. Nashville, Tennessee. All rights reserved.

4. Mrs. George C. Needham, *Angels and Demons* (Moody Press, Chicago) p. 34.

5. Taken from "*Concise Theology, a Guide to Historic Christian Beliefs*" by J.I. Packer. p. 67. Copyright © 1993 by Foundation for Reformation. Used by permission of Tyndale House Publishers, Inc. All rights reserved.

6. Needham. p. 34.

7. Ibid., p. 41.

8. Ruth Paxson, *The Wealth, Walk and Warfare of the Christian* (Fleming H. Revell Company, New York, London and Edinburgh, 1939) p.182.

9. Robertson McQuilkin, *Understanding and Applying the Bible* (Moody Press, Chicago, 1992) p. 254-255.

10. Leon Morris, *The Book of Revelation* (William B. Eerdmans Publishing Company, Grand Rapids, Michigan / Cambridge, U.K., 1987) pp. 138, 139 www.eerdmans.com.

11. Terry. pp.411, 112.

12. Ibid. p. 416.

13. Baxter. p.344.

LESSON 12

1. Used by permission. "*Nelson's New Illustrated Bible Dictionary*" Ronald F. Youngblood *General Editor.* Copyright © 1995, 1986 by Thomas Nelson. Nashville, Tennessee. All rights reserved.

2. Paul J. Achtemeier, General Editor *Harper's Bible Dictionary* (Harper & Row, Publishers, San Francisco, 1985) p. 8.

3. Leon Morris, *The Book of Revelation* (William B. Eerdmans Publishing Company, Grand Rapids, Michigan / Cambridge, U.K., 1987) p.127 www.eerdmans.com.

4. *The Bethany Parallel Commentary on the New Testament* (Bethany House Publishers, Minneapolis, Minnesota 55438, 1983) p. 1461.

LESSON 13

1. Herbert F. Stevenson, *Titles of the Triune God* (Fleming H. Revell Company,1956) p. 168.

2. Used by permission. *Vine's Topical Commentary Prophecy* by W.E. Vine with C.F. Hogg. p.90. Copyright © 2010 by W.E. Vine Copyright Ltd. Of Bath, England. Thomas Nelson. Nashville, Tennessee. All rights reserved.

3. Henry Jacobsen, Editor, *Bible Knowledge, The Revelation* (Christian Publications, third and Reily Streets, Harrisburg, Penn., 1959) p. 552.

4. A.W. Tozer, *The Divine Conquest* (Christian Publications, Inc., Harrisburg, PA, 1950) p.104.

5. Leon Morris, *The Book of Revelation,* William B. Eerdmans Publishing Company, Grand Rapids, Michigan / Cambridge, U.K., 1987, p.123 www.eerdmans.com.

6. taken from *The Expositor's Bible Commentary—Abridged Edition: New Testament, by* Kenneth L. Barker and John R. Kohlenberger III. p.1173. Copyright © 1994 by the Zondervan Corporation. Used by permission of Zondervan. www.zondervan.com.

7. Edited by Charles F. Pfeiffer, *The Biblical World* (Baker Book House, Grand Rapids, Michigan, 1966) p.374.

8. Leon Morris, *The Book of Revelation* (William B. Eerdmans Publishing Company, Grand Rapids, Michigan / Cambridge, U.K., 1987) p.192 www.eerdmans.com.

9. This commentary is based on Isaiah 41:3.

George A.F. Knight, *Servant Theology A Commentary on the Book of Isaiah 40 – 55,* (The Handsel Press, Edinburgh, Wm. B. Eerdmans Publ. Co., Grand Rapids, 1984) p. 28.

Knight's commentary of Isaiah 41:3: "*'A path with his feet he does not tread'*, or in modern words, 'his feet (scarcely) touch the ground'. So fast does he advance that he goes like the wind." (see the Amplified Version) Knight sees this reading in reference to Cyrus. Garland sees Isaiah 41:3 as partial fulfillment in Cyrus, but a complete prophetic fulfillment in Jesus.

Note: Isaiah 41:2 speaks of "the Righteous Man [One] from the east." The King James Version of Isaiah 41:2 reads: "*Who raised up the righteous man* [one] *from the east, called him* [in righteousness] *to his foot, gave the nations before him, and made him rule over kings?. . ."* Author sees this entire chapter as referring to Cyrus as a type of Christ and is speaking of the Messiah, the Righteous Man [One].

Jamieson, Fausset, Brown in *The* Bethany *Parallel Commentary of the Old Testament*, (Bethany House Publishers, Minneapolis, Minnesota 55438, 1985) p. 1436:

"At the same time the full sense of *righteousness*, or *righteous*, and the whole passage, is realized only in the Messiah, Cyrus' antitype (Cyrus *knew not* God, ch. 45:4). He goes forth as the Universal Conqueror of the "nations," in righteousness making war (Ps. 2:8, 9; Rev. 19:11-15). . .Righteousness was always raised up from the East. Paradise was east of Eden. The cherubim were at the east of the garden. Abraham was called from the East. . ."

Albert Barnes in *Notes on the Old Testament Explanatory and Practical* (Baker Book House, Grand Rapids, Michigan 1956) p. 80:

"*The righteous* man *from the east.* Heb. *Tzedheq*—'Righteousness.' The LXX. render it literally,–Righteousness.' The Vulgate renders it, 'The just;' the Syriac as the LXX."

p. 81 "A second opinion is, that it refers directly and entirely to the Messiah. Many of the fathers, as Jerome, Cyril, Eusebius, Theodoret, Procopius, held this opinion." (Barnes, however, did not hold to that opinion).

10. William Barclay, *The New Daily Study Bible, The Revelation of John Vol. 1* (Westminster Press, Philadelphia, 1976) p. 35 Used by permission of St Andrew's Press, an imprint of Hymns Ancient & Modern Ltd.

11. Billheimer. p. 88.

12. Baxter. p.346.

LESSON 14

1. W.C. Stevens, *Revelation the Crown-Jewel of Biblical Prophecy* (Christian Publications, Inc., Harrisburg, PA, 1928) p. 180.

2. Leon Morris, *The Book of Revelation* (William B. Eerdmans Publishing Company, Grand Rapids, Michigan / Cambridge, U.K., 1987) p.144 www.eerdmans.com.

3. Taken from *The Expositor's Bible Commentary—Abridged Edition: Old Testament, by* Kenneth L. Barker and John R. Kohlenberger III. p.799. Copyright © 1994 by the Zondervan Corporation. Used by permission of Zondervan. www.zondervan.com.

4. Stevens. p. 183.

5. Ibid., p. 182.

6. Paul J. Achtemeier, General Editor *Harper's Bible Dictionary* (Harper & Row, Publishers, San Francisco, 1985) p. 8.

7. Leon Morris, *The Book of Revelation* (William B. Eerdmans Publishing Company, Grand Rapids, Michigan / Cambridge, U.K., 1987) p.147 www.eerdmans.com.

8. Robert E. Coleman, *A New Perspective on Revelation: Songs of Heaven* (Power Books, Fleming H. Revell Company, Old Tappan, New Jersey, 1980) p. 102, 103.

LESSON 15A

1. Taken from "*Revelation, The NIV Application Commentary*" by Craig S. Keener. p.459. Copyright © 2000 by Craig Keener. Used by permission of Zondervan. www.zondervan.com.

2. Norman B. Harrison, D.D., *The End, Re-Thinking the Revelation* (The Harrison Service, 3112 Hennepin Avenue, Minneapolis, Minnesota, 1941) p. 183.

3. William Barclay, *The Revelation of John Volume II,* (chapters 6 to 22) (Westminster John Knox Press, Louisville, Kentucky, 1976, 2004) p. 203 Used by permission of St Andrew's Press, an imprint of Hymns Ancient & Modern Ltd.

4. Kenneth L. Barker and John R. Kohlenberger III, *The Expositor's Bible Commentary, Abridged Edition, Old Testament*. p.1496. Copyright © 1994 by the Zondervan Corporation. Used by permission of Zondervan. www.zondervan.com.

5. Patterson. p. 339.

LESSON 15B

1. see Lesson 13 end note 15.

2. Harrison. p. 181.

3. Ibid., p. 181.

4. John MacArthur, Jr., *The MacArthur New Testament Commentary Philippians* (Moody Press/Chicago, 2001) p. 146.

5. Ibid. p. 149.

LESSON 16A

1. Stevens. p. 340.

2. From Lesson 1. Paul J. Achtemeier, General Editor *Harper's Bible Dictionary* (Harper & Row, Publishers, San Francisco, 1985) p. 8.

3. Taken from *The Expositor's Bible Commentary—Abridged Edition: New Testament, by* Kenneth L. Barker and John R. Kohlenberger III. p.654. Copyright © 1994 by the Zondervan Corporation. Used by permission of Zondervan. www.zondervan.com.

4. Taken from "*Revelation, The NIV Application Commentary*" by Craig S. Keener. p.467. Copyright © 2000 by Craig Keener. Used by permission of Zondervan. www.zondervan.com.

5. F.N. Peloubet, D.D., *The Teacher's Commentary on the Gospel According to St. Matthew* (Oxford University Press, American Branch, New York: 91 and 93 Fifth Avenue, London: Henry Frowde, 1901) p. 310.

6. © 1959 V Raymond Edman. *Bible Knowledge Matthew 16:13-28* is published by David C Cook. All rights reserved. p. 248.

7. From Lesson 5 the "Garden of the Righteous."

8. Leon Morris, *The Book of Revelation* (William B. Eerdmans Publishing Company, Grand Rapids, Michigan / Cambridge, U.K., 1987) pp. 240 www.eerdmans.com.

9. Taken from *Commentary on the Holy Scriptures Critical, Doctrinal and Homiletical–Galatians* by John Peter Lange, D.D. p.155. Used by permission of Zondervan. www.zondervan.com.

LESSON 16B

1. notes by Henry Blackaby, *Experiencing the Word Through the Gospels* (Holman Bible Publishers, Nashville, Tennessee, 1999) p.8.

2. Used by permission. *Nelson's New Illustrated Bible Dictionary,* Ronald F. Youngblood *General Editor.* p.1242. Copyright © 1995, 1986 by Thomas Nelson. Nashville, Tennessee. All Rights reserved.

3. Taken from "*The NIV Application Commentary: Hosea, Amos, Micah*" by Gary V. Smith. p.508 Copyright © 2001 by Gary V. Smith. Used by permission of Zondervan. www.zondervan.com.

4. Home Page: Hebraic Heritage Ministries International, (Hebraic Heritage Ministries International, P.O. Box 81, Strasburg, Ohio 44680).

5. Taken from "*The NIV Application Commentary: Hosea, Amos, Micah*" by Gary V. Smith. p.508. Copyright © 2001 by Gary V. Smith. Used by permission of Zondervan. www.zondervan.com.

6. Jennings. p. 149.

7. Taken from *Daniel and Revelation Riddles or Realities?* by A. Berkely, Mickelsen. p. 206-207 Copyright © 1984 by A. Berkely, Mickelsen. Used by permission of Thomas Nelson. www.thomasnelson.com. All rights reserved.

8. Ibid., p. 222.

9. Merrill F. Unger, *Unger's Bible Dictionary* (Moody Press, Chicago, 1957, 1961, 1966) p. 1092.

10. Taken from *Daniel and Revelation Riddles or Realities?* by A. Berkely, Mickelsen. p. 224 Copyright © 1984 by A. Berkely, Mickelsen. Used by permission of Thomas Nelson. www.thomasnelson.com. All rights reserved.

11. Alec Motyer, *The Message of Exodus, The Days of Our Pilgrimage* (InterVarsity Press, 2005) p. 199.

12. Jennings. p. 119.

LESSON 17A

1. T.W. Hunt and Melana Hunt Monroe, *From Heaven's View* (LifeWay Press, Nashville, Tennessee) 2002, p. 160.

2. Patterson. p. 355.

3. © 2010 Warren W. Wiersbe. *Be Victorious (Revelation)* is published by David C Cook. All rights reserved. p. 140.

4. John MacArthur, Jr., *The MacArthur New Testament Commentary Matthew 24-28* (Moody Press/Chicago, 1989) p. 119.

5. Ibid., p. 119.

6. Taken from *The End: A Complete Overview of Bible Prophecy and the End of Days* by Mark Hitchcock. p. 420. Copyright © 2012 by Mark Hitchcock. Used by permission of Tyndale House Publishers, Inc. All rights reserved.

7. Ibid., p. 420.

8. George Eldon Ladd, *A Theology of the New Testament* (William B. Erdmans Publishing Company, Grand Rapids, Michigan, 1974) p. 630-631 www.eerdmans.com.

9. Used by permission. *Vine's Topical Commentary Prophecy* by W.E. Vine with C.F. Hogg. p.72. Copyright © 2010 by W.E. Vine Copyright Ltd. Of Bath, England. Thomas Nelson. Nashville, Tennessee. All rights reserved.

10. V. Raymond Edman, *Storms and Starlight* (Van Kampen Press Inc., Wheaton, Illinois, 1951) p.59.

11. Matthew Henry, Jamieson/Fausette/Brown, Adam Clarke, *The Bethany Parallel Commentary on the Old Testament* (Bethany House Publishers, Minneapolis, Minnesota 55438) p.1373.

12. Jessie Penn-Lewis, *War On The Saints* (U.S.A. The Christian Literature Crusade, Fort Washington, Penna.) p. 7.

13. Ibid., Forward p. *vi.*

LESSON 17B

1. Leitch quoted in Augustus Hopkins Strong, D.D., LL D., *Systematic Theology* (The Judson Press, Valley Forge, PA., Chicago, Los Angeles, 1907) p. 1033.

2. Ladd. p. 563.

3. Robert H. Mounce, *The Book of Revelation* (William B. Eerdmans Publishing Company, 1977) p. 365 www.eerdmans.com.

4. McQuilkin. p.268.

5. Bridges. p.127.

6. Adapted from D. James Kennedy, *Evangelism Explosion* (Tyndale House Publishers, Inc., Wheaton, Illinois, Copyright © 1970, 1977, 1983, 1996) p. 42 (www.eeworks.org).

7. Bruce Wilkinson with David Kopp, *A Life God Rewards Bible Study* (Multnomah Books, 2002) www.multnomahbooks.com.

8. Packer. p. 262, 263.

LESSON 18A

1. Taken from *The Vision of His Glory* by Anne Graham Lotz. pp. 225-226. Copyright © 1997 by Anne Graham Lotz. Used by permission of Thomas Nelson. www.thomasnelson.com. All rights reserved.

2. John MacArthur, Jr., The MacArthur New Testament Commentary Philippians (Moody Press/Chicago, 2001) p. 260.

3. Warren W. Wiersbe, *Run With The Winners, A Study of the Champions of Hebrews 11* Living Studies, (Tyndale House Publishers, Inc., Wheaton, Illinois, 1985) p. 62.

4. William Barclay, *The Letters to the Galatians and Ephesians, Revised Edition* (The Westminster Press, Philadelphia, 1976) p. 116 Used by permission of St Andrew's Press, an imprint of Hymns Ancient & Modern Ltd.

5. Used by permission. *"1, 2, 3 John, Jude"* John MacArthur. p.16. by John MacArthur. Thomas Nelson. Nashville, Tennessee. All rights reserved.

6. Edwards. p. 128.

7. Dan Schaeffer, *A Better Country, Preparing for Heaven* (Discovery House Publishers, 2008) p. 118.

8. Hunt and Monroe, *From Heaven's View* (LifeWay Press, Nashville, Tennessee, 2002).

LESSON 18B

1. Ladd. p. 632.

2. Taken from *Hebrews"*by M.R. De Hann, M.D. p.149, 153. Copyright © 1959 by Zondervan Publishing House, Grand Rapids, Michigan. Used by permission of Zondervan. www.zondervan.com.

3. Taken from *Bible Doctrine* by Wayne Grudem. p.33. Copyright © 1999 by Wayne Grudem. Used by permission of Zondervan. www.zondervan.com.

4. Used by permission. *"Galatians, the Wondrous Grace of God"* John MacArthur. p.101. Copyright © 2007 by John F MacArthur Jr. Thomas Nelson. Nashville, Tennessee. All rights reserved.

5. Ibid., p.101.

6. Bridges. p.140.

7. Taken from *"The Epistle Of Paul To The Ephesians, An Introduction And Commentary"* by Francis Foulkes, M.A., B.D., M.Sc. p.53. Copyright © The Tyndale Press. Used by permission of Tyndale House Publishers, Inc. All rights reserved.

8. Kenneth S. Wuest, *First Peter In the Greek New Testament for the English Reader* (Wm. B. Eerdmans Publishing Company, Grand Rapids, Michigan, 1947) p. 56 www.eerdmans.com.

9. Hunt and Monroe. p. 147.

10. C.H. Spurgeon, *Spurgeon's Devotional Bible* (Baker Book House, Grand Rapids, Michigan) p.123.

LESSON 19

1. Francis A. Schaeffer, *How Should We Then Live?* (Fleming H. Revell Company, Old Tappan, New Jersey, 1976) p. 19.

INTRODUCTION—THE MYSTERY OF THE SYSTEM OF THE ANTICHRIST

1. Edwards. p. 433.

2. A. Berkeley Mickelsen, *Interpreting the Bible* (Wm. B. Eerdmans Publishing Company, Grand Rapids, Michigan, 1963) p. 292 www.eerdmans.com.

LESSON 20

1. *NewAgain, Re-Thinking The Bible For Outreach Today* (International Bible Society, 2001) p. 23.

2. Taken from *Daniel and Revelation Riddles or Realities?* by A. Berkely, Mickelsen. p. 86-87 Copyright © 1984 by A. Berkely, Mickelsen. Used by permission of Thomas Nelson. www.thomasnelson.com. All rights reserved.

3. Edwards. p. 46.

4. Taken from "*Daniel*: Bible Study Commentary" by Leon J. Wood. p.76. Copyright © 1975 by The Zondervan Corporation Grand Rapids, Michigan. Used by permission of Zondervan. www.zondervan.com.

5. Rusten. p. 324.

6. The Rev. Alexander Hislop, *The Two Babylons* (Loizeaux Brothers, Neptune, New Jersey, 1959) pp. 239-242.

7. Rusten. p. 325.

8. Taken from *Halley's Bible Handbook* by Henry H. Halley. Copyright © 1959 by Henry H. Halley. p.759. Copyright © 1962. Copyright © 1965. Used by permission of Zondervan. www.zondervan.com.

9. Ibid, p. 759.

10. Merrill F. Unger, *Unger's Bible Dictionary* (Moody Press, Chicago, Copyright 1957, 1961,1966) p.735.

11. Edward J. Young, Th.M., Ph.D., *The Prophecy of Daniel A Commentary* (Wm. B. Eerdmans Publishing Co., Grand Rapids, Michigan, 1977) p. 77 www.eerdmans.com.

LESSON 21

1. Taken from *All the Divine Names and Titles in the Bible* by Herbert Lockyer. p.11. Copyright © 1975 by Herbert Lockyer. Used by permission of Zondervan. www.zondervan.com.

2. Joyce G. Baldwin, B.A., B.D., *Daniel, An Introduction And Commentary* (Inter-Varsity Press, Leicester, England, Downers Grove, Illinois, U.S.A., 1978) p. 140.

3. Rusten. p. 324

4. Used by permission. *A History of the Christian Church* Lars P. Qualben. p.10, 17. Copyright © 1933 by Thomas Nelson. Nashville, Tennessee. All rights reserved.

5. R. Laird Harris, Editor, *Theological Wordbook of the Old Testament Volume 2* (Moody Press, Chicago, 1980) p. 950.

LESSON 22

1. George Eldon Ladd, *A Commentary On The Revelation Of John* (William B. Eerdmans Publishing Company, Grand Rapids, Michigan, 1972) p. 178 www.eerdmans.com.

2. Edward J. Young, *The Prophecy of Daniel, A Commentary* (Wm. B. Eerdmans Publishing Co., Grand Rapids, Michigan, 1949, 1977) p. 148 www.eerdmans.com.

3. Taken from *Revelation, The NIV Application Commentary* by Craig S. Keener. p. 347. Copyright © 2000 by Craig Keener. Used by permission of Zondervan. www.zondervan.com.

4. taken from *The Expositor's Bible Commentary—Abridged Edition: New Testament,* by Kenneth L. Barker and John R. Kohlenberger III. p.1193. Copyright © 1994 by the Zondervan Corporation. Used by permission of Zondervan. www.zondervan.com.

5. Used by permission. *The Woman's Study Bible,* Dorothy Kelley Patterson, General Editor; Rhonda Harrington Kelley, Managing Editor. p.854. Copyright © 1995 by Thomas Nelson. Nashville, Tennessee. All rights reserved.

LESSON 23

1. Edwards. p. 236.

2. Leon Morris, *The Book of Revelation,* William B. Eerdmans Publishing Company, Grand Rapids, Michigan / Cambridge, U.K., 1987, pp. 205 www.eerdmans.com.

3. taken from *The Expositor's Bible Commentary—Abridged Edition: New Testament,* by Kenneth L. Barker and John R. Kohlenberger III. p.1205. Copyright © 1994 by the Zondervan Corporation. Used by permission of Zondervan. www.zondervan.com.

4. You may wish to consult a true classic on this topic first written in 1858. *The Two Babylons* by Rev. Alexander Hislop (Loizeaux Brothers, Neptune, New Jersey, 1959)

LESSON 24

1. Taken from *All the Divine Names and Titles in the Bible* by Herbert Lockyer. p.19. Copyright © 1975 by Herbert Lockyer. Used by permission of Zondervan. www.zondervan.com.

2. R.R. Palmer and Joel Colton, *A History of the Modern World,* A Borzoi Book Published by Alfred A. Knopf, Inc., 1978, p. 594.

3. TIME magazine, December 26, 1983.

4. TIME Vol. 181, NO. 7 I 2013 p.20.

5. Jean Paul Richter, quoted by Tryon Edwards, D.D., *The New Dictionary of Thoughts* (Standard Book Company, 1957) p. 433.

LESSON 25

1. © 1956 V. Raymond Edman. *Sweeter Than Honey* is published by David C Cook. All rights reserved. p. 37.

2. Billheimer. p. 88.

3. Packer. p. 256.

4. Hunt and Monroe. p. 22.

5. Augustus Hopkins Strong, D.D., LL D., *Systematic Theology,* Valley Forge, Pa. (The Judson Press, Chicago, Los Angeles, 1907) p. 1031.

6. Taken from *All The Promises of the Bible* by Herbert Lockyer. p.600. Copyright © 1962 by Zondervan Publishing House, Grand Rapids, Michigan. Used by permission of Zondervan. www.zondervan.com.

7. Paul Stromberg Rees, *The Face of Our Lord* (Wm. B. Eerdmans Publishing Company, Grand Rapids, Michigan, 1951) p. 105-106 www.eerdmans.com.

8. Bridges. p. 163.

9. Ron Hutchcraft, *Called to Greatness* (Moody Publishers, Chicago, 2004) p. 37.

www.ingramcontent.com/pod-product-compliance
Ingram Content Group UK Ltd.
Pitfield, Milton Keynes, MK11 3LW, UK
UKHW052105240325
456661UK00010B/103

9 781595 558015